ADDICTION TREATMENT

A Strengths Perspective

KATHERINE VAN WORMER
University of Northern Iowa

DIANE RAE DAVIS
Eastern Washington University

AUSTRALIA • CANADA • MEXICO • SINGAPORE
SPAIN • UNITED KINGDOM • UNITED STATES

THOMSON

BROOKS/COLE

Executive Editor: Lisa Gebo
Assistant Editor: Alma Dea Michelena
Editorial Assistant: Sheila Walsh
Marketing Manager: Caroline Concilla
Marketing Assistant: Mary Ho
Advertising Project Manager: Tami Strang
Associate Production Project Manager: Stephanie Zunich
Print Buyer: Jessica Reed
Permissions Editor: Sue Ewing

Production Service: Gretchen Otto / G & S Typesetters
Text Designer: Jeanne Calabrese
Art Editor: Gretchen Otto / G & S Typesetters
Copy Editor: Elliot Simon
Illustrator: Glenda Hassinger / G & S Typesetters
Cover Designer: Andy Norris
Compositor: G & S Typesetters
Printer: Transcontinental Printing

For more information about our products, contact us at:
Thomson Learning Academic Resource Center
1-800-423-0563

For permission to use material from this text,
contact us by: **Phone:** 1-800-730-2214
Fax: 1-800-730-2215
Web: http://www.thomsonrights.com

Library of Congress Control Number: 2002102019

ISBN 0-534-59670-3

Brooks/Cole—Thomson Learning
511 Forest Lodge Road
Pacific Grove, CA 93950
USA

Asia
Thomson Learning
5 Shenton Way #01-01
UIC Building
Singapore 068808

Australia
Nelson Thomson Learning
102 Dodds Street
South Melbourne, Victoria 3205
Australia

Canada
Nelson Thomson Learning
1120 Birchmount Road
Toronto, Ontario M1K 5G4
Canada

Europe/Middle East/Africa
Thomson Learning
High Holborn House
50/51 Bedford Row
London WC1R 4LR
United Kingdom

Latin America
Thomson Learning
Seneca, 53
Colonia Polanco
11560 Mexico D.F.
Mexico

Spain
Paraninfo Thomson Learning
Calle/Magallanes, 25
28015 Madrid, Spain

CONTENTS

DEDICATION

To the frontline workers in the field of addiction, to the men and women for whom substance abuse treatment is not only a profession but a mission, who so often "have been there" themselves, persons who care so much that they may even burn out eventually, but who in the meantime will help save people from the demon that is addiction. We need to keep in mind that for every individual helped, one whole family is spared—from child abuse, violence, bankruptcy. Therefore, with gratitude to the professional helpers and AA/NA sponsors alike, I dedicate my contribution to this book to you.

And, in particular, to my son, Rupert van Wormer, MSW, a mental health case manager and harm reduction specialist who works with sheltered homeless drug addicts in Seattle (you can read about his work in chapter 8).

—Katherine van Wormer

To my family, who support me no matter what with their love—Zach, Andy, John, Jayne, Mike, and Donna, and to the men and women who are taking their lives back from addiction.

—Diane Rae Davis

There is nothing so practical as good theory.
—KURT LEWIN

PREFACE

Is cutting down on drinking and drug use a realistic option for alcoholics/addicts? Or is total abstinence the only path to recovery? The moderation versus abstinence controversy is easily the most hotly contested issue in substance abuse treatment today. Each position has its strengths, and each carries inherent risks. Addiction counselors who help clients merely moderate their destructive behavior run the risk of giving some of their clients false hopes and setting them up for failure. Proponents of immediate and total abstinence, on the other hand, can rest assured that they will drive away the majority of people who might otherwise come to them for help. Opponents on one side or the other of this controversy are discussing the issue both behind closed doors at the treatment center and openly on TV talk shows, in newspaper editorials, on social work and counseling list-serves. This debate—moderation versus abstinence—which has been a part of the European scene for decades, has now reached American shores. Unfortunately, the debate in the United States sometimes resembles a feud. How addiction treatment providers and their political allies resolve this dilemma will largely determine the shape of addiction treatment in the 21st century.

That it is no small matter is revealed, for example, in the case of Dr. Ales De Luca, the chief of an addiction treatment center in Manhattan who recently was forced to resign after he announced a plan to include a moderation management option for problem drinkers. "I was merely suggesting that you could engage people in a kinder, gentler manner," Dr. De Luca explained, "rather than telling them that they had to sign up for a goal achieving abstinence from the beginning" (Steinhaver, 2000, p. A26). Addiction treatment in the United States today is at a crossroads. Increasingly, the Twelve Step/total abstinence model and, more broadly, the disease concept are being subjected to public and professional scrutiny. This very questioning by commentators, and even the vociferous counter-response by representatives of mainstream organizations, is testimony to the fact that change is in the wind. Why not, as some commentators and even some substance abuse counselors are asking, be available to help people just cut down on their drinking and other drug use, protect themselves, even in small ways, from harm, and thereby enhance their motivation for change? Why not keep our treatment options open?

Granted there have been attacks on the one-size-fits-all approach from the beginning. What is new today is first that the attacks have been widely publicized, and second that much of the questioning of the orthodox position is coming from within the treatment field itself. Additionally, some viable alternative models are being used and being used successfully.

The favorable mass media coverage of moderation efforts, the volume of professional critiques of the disease model premises, the slew of harm reduction workshops—all are signals of impending change, of a paradigm shift of sorts. Central to this shift is the realization that so many people in desperate need of treatment—with binge drinking, compulsive cocaine use, and other high-risk behaviors—will never seek help under present circumstances and that many literally will die as a result.

Hence, this book: A new book for a new day. Consistent with the strengths approach, this is not a book to lambaste, denigrate, or ridicule contributions of pioneers who have charted the course in substance abuse treatment. Indeed, many thought-provoking and volatile critiques of the addiction-as-disease model have been written already. Much that needed to be said has been said. Now is the time to move forward, to reconcile differences and get on with the task of helping people in the throes of addiction. So, no, this is not a book to tear down methods that have a history of success, methods in the promotion of which both authors have been personally involved. In our fascination in determining which faction is correct and who owns the soul of chemical dependency treatment—the abstinence or individual responsibility folk—we lose sight of the whole picture.

Tearing down is simple. The primary task of *Addiction Treatment* is more complicated than that; the task is to shape a text grounded in a strengths or empowerment perspective, a theoretical framework that is inclusive and holistic. We hope to achieve this task by providing a digest of the theory, facts, and guidelines necessary for direct practice in a field whose practitioners and administrators have been traditionally resistant to change.

Sociologically speaking, the addictions field is one characterized by fierce loyalties and a devotion to principle not seen in any other comparable profession. Interventions flow logically from the basic premises. Two types of bias are common in the field of addictions. First is the tendency to see disease where there may be only bad habits or even emotionally dependent behavior. Second, there is the countertendency of these doctrinaire positions to see only bad habits—where there is great personal pain, illness, and suffering.

The addiction-as-disease bias, a carryover from the antiprofessionalism in the alcoholism treatment field of the 1980s, demands immediate and total abstinence from all mood-altering substances, with the usual exception of tobacco. And despite the fact that Twelve-Step groups operate on the principle that attendance is strictly voluntary and anonymous, this model requires regular attendance at meetings of an Alcoholics Anonymous or Narcotics Anonymous type of group. Bolstered at the societal level by government policies of zero tolerance for illegal drug use, this treatment approach, in its attention to structure and mandates, makes for a natural fit for work with criminal justice referrals. (To check out the tenets of the Twelve-Step movement, see Makela, 1996.)

At the other extreme is the school of thought bent on tearing down the basic precepts of the disease model. This "rational," highly critical orientation focuses on individual responsibility for ending the bad habits that have erroneously been labeled a disease. This approach is probably as blaming in its way as the predominant approach that it seeks to replace. Placing complete responsibility on individuals for their bad habits, this "rational" model expects people simply to control their excessive urges. As in the era before the disease model, emphasis is on willpower and self-control; this treatment approach (voiced most articulately by Fingarette, 1988, and Peele, 1999) is reflected in government and insurance policies that deny funding for therapy altogether. People, the reasoning goes, should be able to alter their bad habits on their own or at least with nominal intervention.

In truth, these seemingly polarized positions have rather more in common than their proponents would care to admit. Central to both approaches is a moralism and even, at times, a blaming that is characteristically American. This culturally based moralism will be explored from a historical standpoint in chapter 2.

In contrast to the extreme positions of these rival camps of "true believers," both of whom are apt to hold their views intransigently, passionately, against accusations from the other side, comes the harm reduction model. The *harm reduction model* is a grassroots movement that originated in Europe as a realistic response to serious public health problems, including the rapid spread of AIDS. A holistic approach, harm reduction is client centered and capable of absorbing elements from the disease model, depending upon client preferences as revealed through dialogue. Contrary to a popular misconception, this model does not preclude eventual abstinence for persons seeking help with substance misuse problems. We seek, in this book, to integrate rather than reject truths that, whether based on science or not, have been a godsend to so many. So instead of "tossing out the baby with the bath water," such as, for example, throwing out the Twelve Steps, we recognize Twelve-Step programs as a valuable contribution to individuals and society. Clearly, however, one size doesn't fit all. What this text will focus on is how to skillfully help people find the treatment they need to get well.

ORGANIZATION AND FRAMEWORK

In common with the disease model, this text puts an emphasis on biology as a key factor in understanding the nature of addiction. It is our belief that human behavior can only be understood in terms of its biological, psychological, social, and spiritual components. The biopsychosocial framework, accordingly, has been chosen as the organizing framework for this book. *Biologically,* we will be looking at recent developments in neurobiological and pharmaceutical research related to addictive behavior. From a *psychological* standpoint we will want to consider continuing treatment innovations and well-funded scientific research on treatment effectiveness. And *sociologically* we share the recognition that the individual addict does not live in a vacuum but is both shaped by and shaper of his or her social and political environment.

The organization of the book, in short, reflects the biopsychosocial roots of its subject, which is addiction. Divided into five parts, the first and last of which are introductory and conclusive, *Addiction Treatment* includes the three core sections that cover the biology, psychology, and social aspects of addiction, respectively. The spiritual dimension is included in the psychological and social sections.

STRENGTHS-BASED THERAPY

The terminology, ideology, and conceptual framework for this undertaking derive from the strengths perspective. This client-centered approach is compatible with the harm reduction model, in that the overriding purpose is to help the client reduce the harm to himself or herself or others. Harm reduction therapy allows for creativity in the design of treatment strategies. Total abstinence from dangerous drug use is certainly not discouraged, nor is total abstinence from alcoholic beverages by those with a genetic predisposition to get "hooked." But starting with "where the client is" rather than where we think the client should be—this is the basic principle underlying harm reduction. Placing faith in the client's ability to make choices is a related concept.

Our aim in writing this book is, above all, to be practical. The word *practical* is used here in the dual sense of being realistic and having relevance to direct practice. Of what use is theory, after all, without practical application? The focus on the strengths perspective in the treatment of addicts and alcoholics, accordingly, is not chosen because of some ideology of "looking at the bright side of things." Rather, it comes from the practical understanding that a focus on capabilities rather than defects fosters hope (where there is despair), options (where there is a perceived dead end), and increased self-efficacy (where there is a feeling of helplessness). Chapters 1, 3, and 10 will address the specifics of strengths-based therapy with addictive populations. Interventions will be directed at the individual, group, and community levels.

Social work and mental health counseling with clients suffering from alcoholism and other addictions must be performed within the constraints of political and economic realities. Economically, constraints on the form and length of treatment can be expected to continue under the dictates of managed care cost-saving restrictions. Largely because of the war on drugs, with the arrests and sentencing of so many drug users, much of treatment undoubtedly will continue to be provided under the auspices of departments of correction. In such a climate of oppression and mean-spiritedness, it is imperative that those of us who are in the helping professions work through political advocacy to improve treatment offerings for some of our most vulnerable citizens and their families.

BASIC ASSUMPTIONS

Congruent with the biopsychosocial, ecosystems configuration, the perspective being advanced in this book is that addiction, to be a viable concept, must be viewed interactionally. Each component of the system, in other words, is seen in constant and dynamic interaction with every other component; reality is rarely linear; cause and effect are intertwined. Related to addiction, the nature versus nurture controversy is resolved through an understanding that steers away from a dichotomized, "either/or" type of logic, as seen in the pointless is-it-nature-or-nurture arguments, for example. Our preference is for logic of the "both/and" variety. Consistent with this perspective, addiction is viewed as both a biological and a psychosocial phenomenon. There is, further, a spiritual dimension as well. The simplistic, adversarial view of human phenomena leaves us with only partial truths and fierce loyalties that hinder us in our understanding of complexity. To advance knowledge, we need to hear from a multiplicity of voices. That the nature of addiction is infinitely complex will be revealed in the pages of this book. Essential to the study of addiction is a theoretical approach that is eclectic; such an approach is inclusive and broadening, one might even say friendly rather than antagonistic toward diverse models.

To summarize, a major theoretical assumption of this book is that in our pursuit of knowledge concerning addiction and its treatment, our goal is to build upon the professional literature in the United States, Canada, and abroad and from old models and new models, whether psychodynamic or sociological, abstinence-based or experimental in nature.

Some other basic assumptions that underlie this presentation are:

- Addiction exists along a continuum; many people may be addicted to one substance or product; one person may be addicted to multiple substances or activities involving risk (in relationships).
- Much of the criticism concerning various models of addiction (such as the disease model and individual responsibility theory) is valid—these models do tend to be unidimensional and narrow—but, then, much of the criticism itself is unidimensional and narrow.
- There are hereditary tendencies toward addiction, but with work, these tendencies can usually be controlled.
- Better than forbidding adolescents from drinking is to have them learn moderate drinking from parents who drink moderately in the home.

- Whether or not alcoholism or addiction is regarded as a disease depends on the definition of disease; that addiction can be regarded as *like* a disease is a fact to which we can all agree.
- Involvement in mutual-help groups such as Alcoholics Anonymous can be invaluable in enhancing recovery and providing support to family members.
- When the focus is on promoting healthy lifestyles and on becoming motivated to change rather than on the substance misuse per se, many clients can be reached who would otherwise stay away.
- The war on drugs is politically and ethically misguided; issues of race, class, and gender define the parameters of this "war."
- Addiction counselors who are themselves recovering have some advantages over counselors who "have not been there"; however, this kind of personal involvement is no more essential in this field than in related fields such as health and mental health. A continuously self-reflective stance is necessary for both types of counselors to be effective.
- Addictive behaviors are highly destructive to the family as a system and to each family member within that system; treatment therefore needs to include strong family counseling components.
- Professional training in counseling skills and neurobiological and psychosocial knowledge is just as essential for work in this field as it is for comparable fields of practice.
- Specialized training in substance misuse and the various addictions should be a requirement for practitioners in this field; such training should take place outside the treatment center and be scientifically based.
- Treatment must be tailored to the needs of the individual seeking help and include family and community support for recovery.
- Treatment ideally should be offered in all systems across health and human services and juvenile justice systems, not only in specialized substance abuse treatment centers.
- Treatment effectiveness is most accurately measured in terms of the reduction of harmful health-related practices rather than by total abstinence from drinking and drug use.

Addiction Treatment: A Strengths Perspective is intended for use as a primary text in courses related to substance misuse or as a secondary text in courses, graduate or undergraduate, related to health, social work, mental health, offender rehabilitation, and family counseling. Suffused with case examples and summaries of the latest scientific research, this book is directed to many types of practitioners in the addictions or related fields—from those who work with addicts and their families on a day-to-day basis to those who rarely see an addict but who are in positions of supervision, management, and policymaking related to addiction issues. In the same way that hope is offered by counselors to even the most down-and-out addicts, we wish to offer hope (and appreciation) to the practitioners who dedicate their lives to work with those for whom other practitioners have little empathy or use. The hope that we would offer is ingrained in the strengths perspective itself. An approach that seeks resilience in clients and encourages workers to focus on possibilities rather than problems should go a long way toward preventing exhaustion and burnout in a field that is often characterized by both. The strengths perspective is not new to the chemical dependency field; in fact, as we argue in chapter 1, empowerment has been inadvertently used by caring counselors for years. What we are providing here is its formulation and, hopefully, reinforcement. In any case, working with addicts on the verge of self-destruction is a tough assignment. We constantly have to remember that the phoenix rose from a pyre of ashes, not a soft pillow, and that it's in those ashes that we find the embers of hope and change. That is what this book is about.

References

Fingarette, H. (1988). *Heavy drinking: The myth of alcoholism as a disease.* Los Angeles: University of California Press.

Makela, K. (1996). *Alcoholics anonymous as a mutual-help movement: A study in eight societies.* Madison: University of Wisconsin Press.

Peele, S. (1999). *Diseasing of America: How we allowed recovery zealots and the treatment industry to convince us we are out of control.* San Francisco: Jossey Bass.

Steinhaver, J. (2000, July 11). Chief of addiction center quits over policy. *New York Times*, A26.

A Word from Katherine van Wormer, MSSW, Ph.D., Professor of Social Work, University of Northern Iowa, Cedar Falls. Web site: uni.edu/vanworme/index.html

Being from an alcoholic background (my father) and an alcoholic city (New Orleans), I had no desire to do substance abuse counseling initially. But then in 1984, equipped with a brand new degree in social work, I ventured to Washington State in search of scenery and a job. After an inauspicious beginning in community home health and hospice, I found myself working at the community alcohol center in Longview, Washington. This treatment center was fairly laid back as far as substance abuse treatment centers go. Unlike at my previous job, the work was fun and highly creative, and the clients got progressively better instead of progressively worse. The two-year outpatient program brought palpable results that were gratifying to see.

In 1988 I found myself in another scenic part of the world, Norway. As part of a mini-migration of Americans to Norway and Sweden to bring the Minnesota Model or Twelve-Step-based treatment, I trained counselors in group skills and actually learned the rudiments of the American disease model from a fellow American. Although the inevitable personnel crises abounded in a program that was run by exclients with limited periods of sobriety, I again witnessed the miracles of recovery and experienced the joy of seeing lives on the mend. In my public relations capacity I spoke through translators to various community groups about alcoholism as a personal disease and as a family disease. Today I coordinate the substance abuse certificate for social work students at the University of Northern Iowa. Books I have written include *Alcoholism Treatment: A Social Work Perspective* (1995), and *Social Welfare: A World View* (1997), both with Wadsworth Publishing Company, and *Counseling Female Offenders and Victims* (2001, with Springer). I have coauthored *Social Work with Lesbians, Gays, and Bisexuals: A Strengths Perspective* (2000) and *Women and the Criminal Justice System* (2000), both published by Allyn and Bacon.

A Word from Diane Rae Davis, CSW, ACSW, Ph.D., Associate Professor of Social Work, Eastern Washington University, Cheney.

It seems that my entire life has been intertwined with one addiction or another. If you looked at my genogram, you would see addiction all over it, and the subsequent deaths, illnesses, and divorces that follow. You would also see pockets of recovery. My own recovery from alcoholism was a terrible struggle. It took three years to get clean and sober from the time I was absolutely convinced I was an alcoholic. When I finally did, I had no job, no husband, no home to live in, and a son in my care. Yet my middle-class background had protected me from many of the consequences that women who are addicted face: jail or prison, prostitution, bankruptcy, infectious disease, and so on.

During the years of my own recovery, I have witnessed hundreds of men and women recover from the most dire circumstances, and I have also witnessed the death or suicide of others who didn't make it. One effect of all this history may seem contradictory. On the one hand, I have a strong conviction "never to give up" on even the worst scenarios—I have seen way too many miracles to ever "close the case" on anyone. On the other hand, I have learned the hard way the futility of hanging on to my own agenda regarding someone else's recovery. People make changes on their own timing, doing the best they can, surviving how they can. Behaviors that look like "resistance" and " noncompliance" from the outside may have completely different meanings when viewed from the inside. I have learned about "letting go." And finally, I've learned that there are many paths to recovery and that "recovery" means different things to different people. It took a while for me to give up the idea that what saved *my* life is the path for everyone. Having given that up, I find I have increased my capacity to be helpful to others. I have a profound belief in the strengths perspective and the possibilities of change. Similarly, I support the harm reduction model because of its many paths to sobriety, including abstinence, and because it honors a person's dignity by offering choices over and over again, no matter what.

Professionally, I have stayed close to the addiction field in social work practice and academic teaching, publishing, and research. In 1992, I received my Ph.D. at the University of Texas at Austin under the mentorship of Dr. Diana DiNitto. I now teach a variety of courses at the School of Social Work and Human Services at Eastern Washington University, including "A Systems Approach to Substance Misuse" for MSW students. The publication of my article (with Golie Jensen) "Making Meaning of Alcoholics Anonymous" in *Social Work* (1998) allowed me to fulfill a personal mission to address the massive misunderstandings about mutual-help organizations among professional helpers. A newer version of this article is found in chapter 12.

My other areas of research and publications include women's addiction and recovery, rural substance abuse treatment, ropes course treatment, harm reduction, alternative "sobriety" schools, and methadone maintenance. Currently I am working on a project called "Women Who Have Taken Their Lives Back from Compulsive Gambling." This project involves an online research survey and qualitative interviews and can be found on the Web at sswhs.ewu.edu/gambling.

Note

We both share responsibility for this book as a whole, and each chapter is a collaborative effort by the both of us. However, the preface, chapters 1, 2, 4, 5, 6, 7, and 9, and the epilogue were the primary responsibility of Katherine van Wormer; chapters 3, 8, 10, 11, 12, and 13 were the primary responsibility of Diane Rae Davis.

Acknowledgments

The authors' appreciation goes to the following reviewers for their helpful critiques of the manuscript: Ted R. Watkins, Southwest Texas State University; Jim Arnett, University of Calgary; John Nickisson, Ferris State University; Gloria Wolfson, University College of the Fraser Valley; Edward Kruk, University of British Columbia; Gail Wallace, Texas Christian University; Christopher Faiver, John Carroll University; Allan Barsky, Florida Atlantic University; and Elizabeth Zelvin, www.LZcybershrink.com.

Special thanks is extended to Rose Hanrahan, who, as van Wormer's social work student assistant, handled the complexities of the computer and thus was a tremendous asset to this production. The authors would like to recognize Lisa Gebo, the publisher's executive editor, and Alma Dea Michelena, her assistant editor, who nurtured us through the process cheerfully and efficiently, and to thank Gretchen Otto at G&S Typesetters for her help and persistence. Additionally, Katherine van Wormer thanks the University of Northern Iowa for providing financial support in the form of a summer research grant.

INTRODUCTION

On the surface, our application of the strengths perspective to the field of addiction treatment marks a dramatic departure from the past. Our notion of reinforcing strengths in a self-directed program of harm reduction is seemingly a more extreme departure still. And yet the tone of this writing is intended to be conciliatory rather than adversarial; the focus is "building upon" rather than "tearing down."

Part 1 of this text, comprising chapters 1, 2, and 3, summarizes the current state of knowledge concerning the nature of addiction. A major task of the first chapter is definitional—to offer a conceptualization of addiction specific enough to be usable yet broad enough to encompass seemingly disparate behaviors such as compulsive overeating, compulsive gambling, excessive devotion to work, and out-of-control spending. Differentiating alcoholism from alcohol misuse is a related challenge. In these chapters, and throughout the book, attention is paid to the biological, psychological, and social aspects of addictive behavior.

The nature of addiction is complex. Its assessment and treatment represent such an inexact science that, in fact, numerous theories exist, each one convincing in its own right, each with a school of followers, and each explaining only a part of the whole. The questions in the field are few: What is addiction? Why are some people more addictive than others? How can addiction be controlled? Our perspectives—moralistic, scientific, and just plain oppositional—help shape our answers concerning the nature and treatment of addiction.

In order to learn where we are going, we need to look back to our cultural and historical roots. This is the purpose of chapter 2, to trace the roots of today's policies concerning drug use and society's attempts to control it. Central to this historical review are two basic themes. The first of these is technology, the second ideology. In Prohibition, as we will see, these themes converged. (Technologies such as alcohol distillation created a climate for change in public opinion about drinking.) Other forces, such as the Puritan legacy of the New England colonies, were involved as well. That a new temperance movement has emerged in the form of a war on drugs is a major argument of this chapter. That the drugs of choice that are most harshly punished and apt to be outlawed are those associated with poor minority groups is a second major argument. Moving from the realm of historical context to a meta-analysis of therapy designs, we examine strengths-based modalities (for example, the harm reduction model) in chapter 3.

These then—the nature of addiction and the history of its treatment—are among the issues tackled in these two introductory chapters. Our journey to exploring these dimensions begins with chapter 1, The Nature of Addiction.

The first task of this book, in short, is to explore the nature of addiction and its conceptualization. The second task, which is the subject of chapters 2 and 3, is to put today's conceptualizations in historical and theoretical context.

Many shall run to and fro, and knowledge
shall be increased —DANIEL 12:4

THE NATURE
OF ADDICTION

CHAPTER I

INTRODUCTION

"The suffering of a soul that can suffer greatly—that and only that, is tragedy." So said Edith Hamilton (1948, p. 131), the foremost authority on ancient Greek culture of her day. She was talking about Greek tragedy. The hero in classical Greek tragedy possesses a tragic flaw, *hubris,* that ultimately will be his or her undoing. Today, in real life as in drama, the source of personal tragedy is often some sort of compulsion or obsession. The "fatal attraction" may involve a person, a substance, or an activity.

Thus when we hear of the compulsive gambler who leads his or her family down the path of financial ruin, of the Internet whiz who, like the workaholic, sacrifices family life for an "affair" with cyberspace, of the drug addict who deals drugs or prostitutes herself to support her habit—we may find in us a sense of pity and awe, the essence of all great tragedy.

The effects of addiction are everywhere and nowhere, everywhere because they are in every family and workplace, nowhere because so much of the behavior is hidden from public view. Sometimes, as with Internet gambling or pill addiction, even family members are unaware of the problem until a major crisis ensues.

In contrast to the tales of classic literature, in real life there may be a way out of the pain, a way for the individual to get beyond the tragic flaw. The way out is called *recovery.* "I'm in recovery," says the proud member of AA (Alcoholics Anonymous). Similarly, the person who has gotten some personal counseling in reducing the harm announces that now his or her own life has gotten under control.

In our jails, hospitals, women's shelters, and child welfare departments, all the places where professional counselors and social workers are employed, the impact of substance misuse and addiction is a given. Where there is assault, incest, rape, child neglect, or attempted suicide,—more often than not some form of substance misuse is involved. The effects may be immediate—for example, the neglectful parent so strung out on methamphetamines (meth) that he or she has lost all sense of time, all sense of responsibility. The effect may be lifelong— for example, the woman who suffered sexual abuse by a male predator early in childhood and who has taken to using prescription drugs and alcohol for self-medication, to dull a pain the cause of which may or may not be remembered.

This chapter explores the nature of addiction. Each section of the chapter covers a different facet of drug and alcohol addiction—from definitional issues to an overview of the biological, psychological, and social aspects, to various treatment approaches and trends, to a look at the politics of addiction. Two concepts that form a theme of this book—the biopsychosocial model and the strengths perspective—are introduced in this chapter. Subsequent sections of this chapter will present an introduction to the art and science of addiction treatment and contemporary trends in treatment. (The intimate experience of substance misuse is shared by the addicts themselves, their children, and professionals in the field.)

WHAT IS ADDICTION?

Addiction is seen in the man in the detox unit of a hospital who is cringing from the pain of pancreatitis. He has no plans to quit drinking, his wife says. Addiction is evidenced in the two-pack-a-day smoker who coughs steadily from emphysema. Addiction is implicated in the actions of the trusted employee who was imprisoned for embezzlement; she needed more money to gamble.

The economic cost of addiction is incalculable. Certainly billions of dollars are involved. There is the health toll of alcohol and drug misuse, the astronomical expenditures in running the war on drugs and in incarcerating the over 1 million persons whose crime was related to alcohol or some other drug. Catering to people's addictions is big business and ranges from marketing tobacco to special populations, to setting up state lotteries, to organized crime.

So what is addiction? According to the *Dictionary of Word Origins* (Ayto, 1990), the roots of the word *addiction* are in the Latin past participle *addictus*, meaning "having given over or awarded to someone or being attached to a person or cause." The connotations were highly positive. Originally used as an adjective in English, its meaning has become increasingly negative over time.

In the substance misuse literature, addiction is variously defined as: "a brain disease" (Leshner, 1997, p. 46); a sin (Rosin, 2000); excessive behavior (Orford, 1985); a bad habit (Peele, 1995); a personal choice (Schaler, 1999); a spiritual deficiency (Morell, 1996). Or, simply put, addiction is an addiction.

For an official definition, we will first turn to the *DSM-IV-TR* (*Diagnostic and Statistical Manual of Mental Disorders, Text Revised*) (American Psychiatric Association [APA], 2000). Actually, the *DSM-IV-TR* avoids use of the term *addiction* in favor of the seemingly more scientific term *dependence*. The terms *addiction* and *substance dependence,* however, are more or less comparable. As defined by the APA, the diagnosis of substance dependence disorder requires the following: the presence of a maladaptive pattern of substance use, resulting in distress or clinically significant impairment and involving at least three of the following symptoms (all of which must occur within the same 12-month period):

- Tolerance
- Withdrawal problems
- Use of the substance longer than intended
- Unsuccessful attempts to control or reduce consumption
- Spending excessive amounts of time procuring, using the substance, or recovering from its effects
- Reduced involvement in important social, occupational, or recreational activities, and
- Continued use despite the presence of recurrent physical or psychological problems (APA, 2000, p. 197).

Typical substances named by the APA are alcohol, other drugs, and tobacco. A separate listing of similar criteria are provided for pathological gambling, even though it is found under Impulse Control Disorders, not Dependence. To receive a diagnosis of pathological gambler, a person must satisfy five of the following 10 criteria:

- Preoccupation with gambling
- Increased wagering in order to achieve the desired effect
- Restlessness or irritability when attempting to reduce or stop gambling
- Gambling as a way of escaping problems and reducing depression
- Gambling to recoup one's losses
- Lying to family members or to one's therapist about gambling
- Involvement in illegal activities to support gambling
- Jeopardizing or losing a significant relationship, job, or career or educational opportunity because of gambling
- Relying on others to provide money to relieve financial hardship caused by gambling
- Repeated unsuccessful efforts to curb or stop gambling. (APA, 2000, p. 674).

In the book *The Addiction Concept,* Walters (1999) notes that the criteria used by researchers for sexual addiction and eating disorders also involve the criterion clusters of progression, preoccupation, perceived loss of control, and negative long-term consequences. Walters strenuously objects to the use of such criteria and to the word *addiction* itself; he proposes an alternative concept—the lifestyle concept—that allows for an emphasis on personal choice. The "lifestyle concept," however, has problems of its own, chiefly in the direction of blaming. A focus on individual responsibility in the use of mood-altering substances plays into the punitive response so much in evidence regarding drug use in U.S. society. (We delve into this matter more in a later section, Treatment Trends.)

The responsibility argument is one that Gold, Johnson, and Stennie (1997) have little patience with. Eating disorders, as they indicate, are not due to a lack of self-control: The close similarity in dependence on drugs and on food, which is a powerful mood-altering substance, is borne out in scientific findings about brain reward systems and neurotransmitter aberrations, as, for example, among bulimics. Classification of eating disorders as an addiction, as these authors further argue, would help in our prevention educational efforts. Many of the addictive chronic disorders, such as compulsive overeating and pathological gambling, are characterized by loss of control, relapse, compulsiveness, and continuation despite negative consequences. Accordingly, as Gold et al. conclude, "As the well-known adage goes, if it looks like a duck, acts like a duck, it must be a duck" (p. 327). Before we progress any further into the maze of word usage, let us consider just how far into the depths of madness the addictive urge can lead us. Read Box 1.1, "A Social Work Major Working in a Casino," which takes us behind the scenes into a work environment that preys on the vulnerable ones—compulsive gamblers.

One unhelpful aspect of the *DSM* identified by Walters is its categorization of disease in terms of rigid dichotomies (e.g., substance dependence and substance misuse). Addiction, in fact, occurs along a continuum. Severe life-threatening dependence may be placed at one end, the misuse of substances somewhere in the center, and a use of substances without problems at the other end. Individuals or their behaviors can be placed along a continuum according to levels of misuse or addiction at various points in their lives. The *DSM-IV-TR*'s either/or categories fail to account for such dimensions of human behavior.

From a contemporary perspective, in marked contrast to the earlier view of alcohol dependence as a progressive and irreversible disease, most problem drinkers move in and out of periods of dependent drinking. From this perspective, as British social work educator Larry Harrison (1996) suggests, there are no rigid boundaries between normal and pathological populations or between common diagnostic categories. We need to keep in mind, of course, that persons who present themselves at specialist treatment agencies (often by court order, as is typical in the United States) are apt to have severe problems and represent the extreme end of the continuum.

We can take issue with the *DSM-IV-TR* for one other reason as well—the incompatibility of such labeling and diagnosis with the tenets of the strengths perspective. As the name would indicate, the *strengths perspective* is an approach geared to look for strengths rather than liabilities, not because they are more "true," but because it's more effective. Still, in the United States, mental health practitioners, rehabilitation counselors, and social workers in many fields utilize APA criteria for substance dependence as a means of justifying insurance reimbursement and vocational rehabilitation for their clients (Benshoff & Janikowski, 2000). The physical, psychological, and social aspects of dependence

BOX I.I	A SOCIAL WORK MAJOR WORKING IN A CASINO

BY JULIE TAYLOR

As gambling fever makes its way across the United States, we hear different views and opinions expressed in the media on what seems like a daily basis. Especially here in Iowa, where there is a constant controversy over issues such as the morality of gambling, how casinos affect the economy, the legality of gambling, and other pertinent issues. There are specials on television about addiction and how it has affected the Native American peoples, about the glamour and glitz of casinos, and about the money made and lost. I have talked with different customers about their winning or losing streaks. One night while I was working, there was a middle-aged man dressed in a very nice business suit playing a $5.00 slot machine. He kept putting in one hundred-dollar bill after another. I counted four times that he went to either the automatic teller machine (ATM) or the credit card machine. He was losing what I call a ton of money. He literally had sweat running down his head and had a look of sheer panic on his face. He looked up at me at one point and said, "I'm dead, I am just dead." I just stood there and with a look of sorry on my face said, "As much money as you've put in it, I can't believe it hasn't paid out yet." What I really wanted to say was, "Why don't you just go home before you lose more money!" I will never forget the look on that man's face. It was obvious to me that he had a serious gambling problem. I see it a lot at the casino.

One thing that you hear almost nothing about is what it is like to work at a casino. That's something I can tell you about. My husband Dave and I have worked at our local casino (Meskwaki Bingo, Casino, & Hotel) for just about two years, and I can tell you that there is certainly nothing glamorous about it. It is hard work not only from a physical point of view but more so from an emotional point of view.

Let's begin with the atmosphere in which we work. Customers, unless they are "regulars," don't really realize that they are being watched the entire time they are in there. There are literally hundreds of cameras rolling 24 hours a day from every angle. As the song goes, every move we make, every step we take, every single day, every single way, I'll be watching you. Why? It's not necessarily to watch the customers as it is to watch us employees! The assumption made by owners is that every employee is a thief. There is more truth in this than I like to imagine. The slightest mistake, the smallest unexplained movement, a sneeze, scratching your head, and touching another person can draw an instant call from "upstairs" surveillance and quite possibly a write-up, suspension, or being fired on the spot if they don't like what you did or how you did it. This atmosphere pervades every moment of your working life. To say the least, it is incredibly degrading. The joke in the employee break room is that the next thing we know, there will be cameras in the restrooms. Believe it or not, at one time there were microphones placed in the ceiling tiles in the break rooms so they could record what was being said by the employees. Swear, a true story.

Speaking of degrading, imagine what it is like to have customers screaming at you, swearing at you, doing everything short of physically attacking you because they are losing money (or, for that matter, winning money) or not getting the immediate service they feel is due them. One constant at the casino is they cannot keep enough people employed to service the enormous number of customers they deal with on a

continued

BOX I.I

A SOCIAL WORK MAJOR
WORKING IN A CASINO
(*continued*)

daily basis. The turnover rate of employees is phenomenal. In some departments, such as the pit (this is where the card games are played), we are 60 dealers short of being full staffed. The turnover rate is more than 70% per year. I love dealing cards to people. It is fun because I enjoy interacting with people and I know that isn't my lifetime career. I also attend college at the University of Northern Iowa full time.

Now let us move on to some things that people may not realize about casinos. For instance, when you see pictures in movies and on television of casinos, it appears that the customers are young, excited, partying people, when in reality, most customers are elderly folks living on social security and pensions. It is so sad to have an elderly woman crying to you about having lost her entire Social Security check and now having to go home and explain what happened to all the money that she had in the world. It tears your heart out and at the same time makes you realize why some people feel gambling should be illegal.

Another interesting thing about the casino life is that it is much like life in a bar. The customers are the same people day after day, night after night. Sometimes you wonder if they have any other life?! Their whole existence seems to be gambling. Like the bartender, we know their names, we learn their lives, we hear about their problems, their families, and their spouses. After a while I find myself offering advice just like a bartender does. (I also was a bartender for eight years.) However, because we are employees of the casino (and you never know who is listening), we have to say stupid things like, "That machine should hit anytime now," "Keep going, it has to pay off soon," or "At least you haven't lost as much as that person has." What you really want to say is, "Don't you people have homes you can go to?" or "Do you realize how many groceries you could have bought with the money you put in there?" I talked to a lady once who told me that she brought her rent money to try and win enough to pay her rent and light bill; she lost it all and left crying!

Something I learned about casinos: Until the last 20 years or so, casinos were the major way of laundering money for the mob and for drug dealers. This was accomplished simply by buying poker chips to gamble with, or placing cash in the casino's vault, or even exchanging $100 bills for smaller ones. This actually doesn't happen as much since the change in federal law requiring casinos to report all transactions over $1,200.00 to the IRS.

One more tidbit of information: Slot machines at casinos actually pay out 94 to 96%. That means that the casino actually only makes about 5 or 6% profit on slot machines. That doesn't seem like a lot does it? In fact, you might consider if you're a player that this means that if you play a machine long enough, the most you could lose would be 5 to 6% of the money you put into it. That would be true if the customer knew which machines were paying off and which ones weren't. Casinos take millions off of the 6% they take in on slot machines. Can you imagine the total money spent on them to get them to pay out? It boggles the mind.

In this politically correct decade, the most horrific politically correct term ever created is the one that the gambling industry has made into an everyday word: Gaming. There is no game here. You pay and you lose; that is the game.

Printed by permission of Julie Taylor.

as spelled out in this manual can be helpful, in fact, in assessment and communication among professionals and in giving testimony before the court.

So how does the diagnostic model differentiate dependence from abuse? The difference is found in the inclusion of three criteria—tolerance, withdrawal, and a pattern of compulsive use by which substance dependence is characterized. Substance abuse, in contrast, is defined in *DSM* terms of the absence of physical and psychological habituation to the substance. A problem semantically with the term *substance abuse* is that the substance is not being abused— the individual may be committing self-abuse, but the substance is merely being consumed or otherwise ingested; it is hard to abuse an inanimate object after all. The terms *substance use* and *substance misuse* are more accurate and even more sensible terms and are used in this text to refer more specifically to general and harmful drug use, respectively. The terms *substance abuse treatment* and *substance abuse counseling* will be used because of their familiarity rather than any descriptive accuracy.

For everyday social usage, Moncher, Schinke, and Holden (1992) prefer the flexibility of the word *addiction* in place of *DSM*'s substance dependence. The concept of addiction, they believe, is more compatible with the biopsychosocial model, which attends to the *subjective* compulsion to continue the behavior pattern. Freeman's (1992) definition of addiction is the one that will apply in this book:

> ADDICTION: A behavior pattern of compulsive substance abuse, relationships, or other . . . behaviors characterized by overinvolvement with the relationship or abuse as well as a tendency to relapse after completion of withdrawal (p. 252).

This concept of addiction is useful because of its emphasis on the *process* rather than on the substance itself. The word *pattern* utilized in this definition refers to symptomology and also to the fact that the addiction may be to a behavior (such as sex, work, experience) as well as to a substance (alcohol, food, tobacco). The terms *alcoholism* and *alcohol addiction* will be used synonymously in this book to signify continued alcohol use despite persistent physical or psychological problems.

Although the tendency is to equate addiction with loss of control, the extent to which the individual is truly beyond self-control cannot be proven but can only be inferred from external behavior. What's missing but needed, according to Howard Shaffer (1999) from the Harvard Medical School's Division on Addictions, is a "gold standard" independent of the behavior of the individual (in this case, gambling). In fact, such a standard may be around the corner, however. Shaffer himself cites encouraging recent brain research reflecting the impact that gambling has on the neurotransmitters in the brains of pathological gamblers. Research on biogenetic vulnerabilities in gamblers is showing promising results as well. Alan Leshner, director of the National Institute for Drug Abuse (NIDA), whose research is widely cited in chapter 4 of this text, declares that "addiction is, at its core, a consequence of fundamental changes in brain function" (p. 46). But, as he reminds us, addiction is not only a brain disease; the social and psychological pain can be overwhelming.

To understand the pain connected with addictive and compulsive behavior, one must first understand the *pleasure* side of these activities, their attractiveness. Books on treatment, whether written by scholars or by self-help members, focus almost exclusively on the harm of substance misuse, a harm inherent in the substances themselves. Yet, according to Volpicelli and Szalavitz (2000), it is crucial to learn why substances such as alcohol and licit or illicit drugs are useful as well as attractive, "that use itself is not always wrong or harmful, despite attempts by various factors to convince us otherwise." Alcohol, for example, when used in moderation, has many health-giving properties and, like the opiates, has been used for centuries for pain relief. Apart from nicotine, which is highly addictive, as Volpicelli and Szalavitz, further indicate, only a small percentage of drinkers, marijuana users, or heroin users exhibit the kind of problems that would define them as abusers or addicts.

Few areas of human life exist where individual differences are more pronounced than in regard to people's taste (or distaste) for mood-altering substances, including food. Some crave uppers, ranging from caffeine to methamphetamines; others would go to incredible lengths to get hold of downers, such as alcohol and Valium. Still others use such substances to enhance their sensual pleasures, but then only occasionally. Medical science is rapidly uncovering the clues to these individual differences, clues that go beyond pharmacology or even environmental circumstances into the realm of brain chemistry. But that is the topic of another chapter.

Of all the addictions, *alcoholism* is the most studied and the most common, next to nicotine addiction. In 1967, the American Medical Association (AMA) in 1968 offered the following definition, which is still widely used:

> ALCOHOLISM is an illness characterized by preoccupation with alcohol and loss of control over its consumption such as to lead usually to intoxication if drinking is begun; by chronicity; by progression; and by tendency toward relapse. It is typically associated with physical disability and impaired emotional, occupational, and/or social adjustments as a direct consequence of persistent and excessive use of alcohol. (AMA, 1968, p. 6)

The AMA definition identifies the three basic areas of ecological concern—the physical, the psychological, and the social. Thus it is the definition chosen for this text. The selection of the word *illness* to describe alcoholism provides a clear acknowledgment of alcoholism as a medical problem with widespread ramifications (social and moral). Illness is a nonjudgmental, non-victim-blaming term (van Wormer, 1995). The word *disease* originally was applied to alcoholism by Jellinek (1960), who said that alcoholism was *like* a disease. It was a short road from "like a disease," to "a disease," one with vast political and medical connotations. In the United States, in recent years a trend toward the "diseasing" of behavior not ordinarily considered pathological (for example, codependency) has been pronounced. Simultaneously, there has been a countertrend stressing individual responsibility for a range of addictive behaviors, now labeled "bad habit." This movement away from the disease models carries some risk of "throwing the baby out with the bath water," of turning the clock back on treatment availability. Disregarding the political aspects for the moment, let us draw upon the dictionary definition of disease.

DISEASE.
1. (Middle English) A pathological condition of a part, organ, or system of an organism resulting from various causes, such as infections, genetic defect.
2. A condition or tendency, as of society, regarded as abnormal or harmful.
3. Obsolete, lack of ease, trouble.

(*American Heritage Dictionary*, 2000, p. 517)

According to this, as in most dictionary definitions, alcoholism certainly qualifies, along with diabetes and certain heart conditions, to be considered a disease. In order to avoid the "ideological fervor" associated with the disease model, McNeece and DiNitto (1998, p. xv) have chosen an interesting resolution. Alcohol and drug dependence are viewed by these authors as an addiction but not a disease, except when discussing the consequences of alcoholism, such as, for example, pancreatitis. To denote the extensive pain and suffering wrought by the condition of alcoholism, we have chosen, as in the AMA definition, to favor use of the word *illness* over *disease*. Illness, to Conrad and Kern (1994), is the experience of being sick or diseased; it is a social psychological state caused by the disease. Thus, pathologists treat disease, whereas patients experience illness. The subjective level of illness, as previously suggested, makes this the term with more relevance to the helping professions' focus on the person-in-the-environment and on the interaction between the person and the world outside.

Germain's description of the ecology of serious illness applies to addiction even more than to other illnesses (1984, p. 64):

Serious illness represents perceived demands that may exceed perceived resources for handling them, and so is a source of stress. The stress of illness, in turn, may lead to stress in other realms of life, especially in family, work, and community roles, thereby interfering with recovery or with management of disability.

The concept of addiction as an illness of body, mind, and soul is part and parcel of the biopsychosocial understanding of this phenomenon. Through the initial act of drinking or drug ingestion, the body adapts remarkably, sometimes to the extent of permanent biochemical and psychological changes. As thought processes in the brain are altered, one's ability to adapt to stress may be weakened. Socially, the hard-drinking, drug-using life determines the company one keeps (and the company one loses); one's family members are affected in dramatic and devastating ways. The consequences of the substance misuse raise the stress levels; this, in combination with the physiological craving associated with heavy use, reinforces the urge to partake.

BIOPSYCHOSOCIAL MODEL

Social work and other counseling professions conceive of addiction holistically, with attention to biological, psychological, and social components in its causation and consequences. The pain and suffering of alcoholism and other addictions constitute the biopsychosocial reality. The *biology* of chemical use relates to the formidable hereditary components in the etiology of this illness and the physical problems that may arise with extended use. The *psychological* concept encompasses the thinking that leads to the drinking or injecting or snorting of the substance. These irrational or unhealthy thought processes may be associated with depression or anxiety, which, in turn, may encourage escape through drug use or other compulsive behaviors.

That the high has a psychological as well as a biological basis is revealed in this description from a male compulsive shopper (J. Anderson, 1994):

> It was like, it was almost like my heart was palpitating. . . . I couldn't wait to see what was there. It was such a sensation. In the store, the lights, the people; they were playing Christmas music. I was hyperventilating and my hands were beginning to sweat, and all of a sudden I was touching sweaters and the whole feel of it was beckoning to me. And if they had a SALE sign up, forget it; I was gone. You never know when you're going to need it.

The *social* component in addiction relates to *where* as opposed to *why*— where does the addictive activity take place and where is the impact felt? The peer group and family may be involved, respectively. One factor we should never lose sight of is social class. As Harrison and Luck (1996) remind us, the disadvantaged are more likely to suffer alcohol-related problems, even when drinking at the same level as more economically privileged groups, because they lack the material resources and often the social supports available to others.

Interactionism is a major component of the biopsychosocial model of addiction. In the language of systems theory, the basic principle of interactionism is that cause and effect are intertwined. In the language of ordinary conversation, we talk of a vicious cycle. The saying "What goes around comes around" is another way of saying the same thing.

Any member of an alcoholic family becomes aware of how pain and substance misuse feed into each other until the two become almost one and the same. As suffering induces the wish to escape unpleasant feelings through the use of chemicals, this indulgence in turn leads to pain at all four levels of the bio-psycho-social-spiritual model. The resultant pain exacerbates the urge to drown the feelings—physically, in the bottle.

A second major principle of interactionism concerns the overlap among the four aforementioned components. Body, mind, society, and spirituality—all are furiously intertwined in the cycle that is addiction. Cocaine may be used as an upper, for example, to dull the pain of organic or situational depression. The social costs of alternatively acting depressed and engaging in illicit drug use may be enormous.

Another form of interaction that figures in addiction is the interaction between stress and individual responses to that stress. Consider, for example, how persons under severe stress tend to use alcohol and/or tranquilizers to reduce their anxiety levels. According to a study by the National Center on Addiction and Substance Abuse (CASA) at Columbia University, substance abuse treatment admissions increased 10 to 12% nationally since the events of September 11 ("Terrorist Attacks," 2001). This phenomenon was reminiscent, according to the same article, of the heightened demand in Oklahoma following the Oklahoma City bombing.

Interactionism is seen most vividly in the dynamics of the family system. Much has been written about "the alcoholic family" (see chapter 9). The set of demands imposed upon the family members of an alcoholic or addict can be awesome, both emotionally and financially. Each family will have its own peculiar style of adaptation and coping, whether through blaming, denial, and/or overprotecting.

Because the family is a system, one member's malfunctioning throws the whole family's functioning out of whack. While the addict himself or herself remains to some extent "out of things," family members may take the tension out on each other. (See chapter 9 for a study in addict/alcoholic family dynamics.) In personal correspondence of September 8, 2000, a woman who identifies herself only as Sue shares a childhood memory:

> During the week, he was a Grandpa/"Poppy"/teacher/best friend. On the weekends, he was this stranger who stumbled home late at night long after the corner bar had closed. And, to mollify Grandma and me, he'd carefully carry two fish fry dinners home for us. But he never understood why greasy French fries at 3 a.m. never appealed to me.
>
> After school on Friday afternoon, he volunteered to drive me to a doctor's appointment. But he had started an early weekend and so had a bottle of brandy in the car. I guess no one in the family had seen it before he left the house. We never made it to the appointment. He totaled the car on a downtown bridge. I wound up in the hospital with four fractured limbs.
>
> My father threatened to kill him; my mother threatened to leave my father for threatening her father; my grandma threatened divorce. I was crying as if my heart would break, and Grandpa fell asleep in the hospital room visitors lounge, oblivious to the turmoil and heart-rending aftereffects of "a few early nips."

PREVALENCE OF SUBSTANCE MISUSE

Mental health professionals can expect that approximately 50% of their clients will have problems stemming from their own or a family member's alcoholism (Drake & Meuser, 1996).

Alcohol misuse figures widely also in marital counseling. Workers in child welfare observe firsthand the toll on the victims of neglect and abuse due to parental drinking problems. Correctional counselors encounter the effects of drug use and dependence as a constant in their treatment of offenders. An extensive study conducted by the National Center on Addiction and Substance Abuse at Columbia University (1998) found that 80% of people behind bars were involved with alcohol and other drugs at the time their crimes were committed. A Canadian study conducted in 26 communities across Canada revealed that more than half of the people arrested for criminal offenses were under the

BOX I.2

EXPERTISE IN ADDICTIONS
SAID CRUCIAL
*Seventy-one percent of social workers dealt
with substance abusers*
BY JOHN V. O'NEIL

The Practice Research Network (PRN) random survey of 2,000 regular NASW members showed a large involvement of members across many settings in diagnosing and treating substance abuse, but found that few members had in-depth education and training for the work.

A major objective of the Center for Substance Abuse Treatment (CSAT) in funding the survey was to discover the nature and extent of social work involvement with people who have substance use disorders.

The survey found that 71% of social workers had taken one or more actions in relation to clients with substance use disorders in the past year, a number called "astonishing" by Cathy King Pike, the member of NASW's PRN working group who prepared a report to CSAT on the survey.

In the past year, 43% of social workers performed screening for substance abuse; 26% diagnosed it; 19% treated primary substance abuse; 47% treated secondary substance abuse; 61% referred clients to substance abuse treatment; and 11% screened for compulsive gambling.

Social workers in organizational settings reported that 28.6% of clients had substance abuse as a primary or secondary diagnosis: 9% primary and 19.6% secondary. Those in private practice saw fewer people with substance abuse problems, 19.1%, with 5.9% primary and 13.2% secondary.

The survey found that NASW members in organizational settings treat more people with drug problems than do private practitioners. Of people with substance abuse diagnoses, 31.1% of those seen at organizations were treated for alcohol only, 19.8% for drugs only, and 49.1% for both. In contrast, private practitioners treated 45.5% for alcohol only, 15.7% for drugs only, and 38.7% for both.

Members in organizational settings spend more time on case management for substance abuse clients and less time on individual counseling than do members in private practice.

In organizational settings, members spend 22.1% of the time on screening clients for substance abuse; 25.9% on individual counseling; 13.8% on group/marriage/

---

influence of alcohol or illicit drugs or both when the crimes were committed (Garlick, 2000).

Social work practice with alcoholics takes place in a wide range of social work settings. Hospital social workers, for instance, encounter both the early- and late-stage effects of heavy drinking in patients. The estimate is that one hospital bed in four is occupied by a patient whose ailment is alcohol related. Alcohol misuse is the third leading cause of death, after heart disease and cancer.

A recent issue of the NASW (National Association of Social Workers) newsletter reports survey findings on the extent of member' professional involvement with clients with substance misuse problems. See Box 1.2 for the results.

family counseling; 15.3% on case management; 4.1% on advocacy; and 14.3% on administrative duties.

Private practitioners spend 18.9% of their time on screening/assessment; 47% on individual counseling; 15.3% on group/marriage/family counseling; 1.6% on advocacy; and 11.9% on documentation.

Those in private practice were asked what they typically do when clients present with substance abuse. Twenty-five percent said they had no clients with substance abuse problems. Others refer to self-help groups (44%); refer for substance abuse services but continue to treat for mental/emotional problems (39%); treat mental/emotional needs and substance abuse (35%); refer to a physician for medication assessment (34%); refer to formal substance abuse programs (30%); or refer to other independent practitioners (12%).

Four in five members (81%) reported some type of education and training in substance abuse disorders: 68% from workshops, seminars or other continuing education; 38% from formal coursework; 24% from clinical supervision in substance abuse; 16% from field placement; and 5% from volunteer work. Eighteen percent reported no substance abuse training.

Eighty-seven percent hold no certification in substance abuse, according to Pike's draft report for CSAT. Three percent have a certified alcohol and drug abuse counselor (CADAC) certification; 2% for a certified drug abuse counselor (CDAC) certification; and 3% hold a state certification or license in substance abuse.

It is not surprising that social workers see more substance abusing clients than some other helping professions, given the breadth of organizations and practice settings, said Pike's report. Yet two-thirds of social workers' training in substance abuse comes from workshops, seminars, and other continuing education.

This indicates the need for greater distribution among social work academic programs of courses in which substance abuse prevention and treatment are the sole focus and for more readily available certification programs, Pike's report asserted. Social work students need more information about the prevalence of substance abuse among their future clients to highlight the need for formal training in this area.

Because of the distribution of clients with substance abuse problems across the broad array of practice settings, training is needed regardless of whether students choose a practice concentration in substance abuse treatment. Funding and scholarships for certification programs in substance abuse would highlight the importance of this type of training and make certification more desirable to social work students, the report said.

Source: *NASW News*, Jan. 2001. Reprinted with permission of NASW (National Association of Social Workers).

THE GRIP OF ADDICTION

- "Mom Gets Probation: Girl Died at Poker Binge" (Smith, *Des Moines Register*, 1999, p. 3A)
- "Shopaholics Climb on the Wagon" (Lobet, *U.S. News and World Report*, 2000, p. 60)
- "They Call it Video Crack" (Novak, *Time*, 1998, p. 58)
- "Hooked on the Net" (Holliday, *Psychology Today*, 2000, p. 10)

- "Trapped in the Web" (Chang, *Psychology Today,* 1998, p. 66)
- "Ex-Smokers Get Stuck on Gum" (Barker, *USA Today,* 2000, p. 10D)
- "Toronto Inmates Would Rather Starve Than Quit: Plan for Smokeless Jail Draws Hunger-Strike Protests" (Brown, APBnews.com, 2000)
- "Is Sex an Addiction? Thousands Flock to AA-Like Treatment Sessions" (Nichols, *Maclean's,* 1998, p. 80)
- "Alcoholic Smokers Are Having Trouble Snuffing Out Both Habits, CDC Says" (Meyer, *Bowling Green Daily News,* 1997, p. 4C)

Such are the typical headlines in any regional and national newspaper on any given day. The concern with addiction is as universal as is the battle to control it. Some stories focus on individuals, with celebrities of course drawing the most attention. Numerous articles highlighted Robert Downey Jr.'s recent re-arrest. "If anyone ever had good reason to say no to drugs, it was surely Robert Downey, Jr." begins *Time* magazine's version (Lemonick, 2000, p. 97). This statement was in reference to the fact that this actor had recently completed treatment for cocaine and heroin use following an earlier arrest and had returned to a promising career, including a starring role in a Hollywood film with Julia Roberts, only to get caught possessing cocaine and speed shortly thereafter.

While the traditional psychologist might look to a pattern of self-destructiveness and the sociologist to professional stress, a multidimensional analysis would certainly take biological factors into account. Aided by powerful new diagnostic tools that can document changes in the brain as a result of drug use, researchers can now fathom the relentless craving that accompanies depletion of endorphins, or "feel-good" chemicals in the brain. The brain of the drug user is physically altered in ways that make resistance to further drug use very difficult (Leshner, 1997). More will be said about this in chapters 4 and 5.

Hereditary factors are involved in addiction as well. An anonymous male social work student shares this contradictory but revealing comment:

> Well, my Grandpa and brother are both alcoholics. Along with the rest of the family I drink, but not to that point. I believe I have a small alcohol/nicotine problem. Ever since I was 18, neither has been a big deal; now once I start drinking I really can't stop (Cedar Falls, Iowa, August 22, 2000).

An excellent portrayal of the grip of addiction and the harrowing process of recovery is given in the 2000 Hollywood movie *28 Days.* Gwen, the alcoholic who goes into inpatient treatment to avoid a jail term for a drunken driving episode lost her mother to alcoholism as a child. In treatment, Gwen injures her ankle climbing out of the window to retrieve some pills. "The definition of insanity," says her counselor, "is repeating the same behavior over and over and getting the same results."

Perhaps the most honest representation of an addict's surrender and recovery ever put on film is found in the 1988 movie *Clean and Sober,* starring Michael Keaton. A cocaine-addicted real estate executive in deep financial trouble, Keaton's character hides out in a rehab center. The transformation he undergoes is moving and informative at the same time.

And then there is *Traffic*. Addictive behavior is woven through every generation in this powerful 2001 film portrayal of a family and other persons caught up in the war on drugs. As the leading character, played by Michael Douglas, prepares to become the nation's new drug czar, his 16-year-old daughter sinks ever more deeply into the mire of drug addiction.

Marriages disrupted, kids getting into trouble, people committing illegal acts—the pattern is the same with nonsubstance addictions, sometimes called behavioral addictions, such as with chemical misuse. Compulsive shoppers, for example, have obsessive buying urges that lead them to have closets full of never-worn clothing and then go out the next day and buy some more. Medication seems to be helping reduce the strange cravings in many cases (J. Anderson, 1994).

Eating can present problems for persons who seem predisposed to addictive behavior. Here's how it was expressed in a speech by Wanda Haban (1999):

> I was a chronic dieter for 25 years. Today I'm eating healthy. To change habits is a forever process. My father is an alcoholic, so genetically or psychologically those traits are instilled in me. The first drink I had I had a blackout. So I knew there was a problem there. I had hangovers, so I didn't choose that drug as my choice. I chose food as my choice. Once I eat over a certain point, I can't stop.
>
> My ex-husband said, "Don't ever get fat." My dieting was starvation and bingeing, yo-yo dieting. I am still obsessed with dieting.

THE STRENGTHS PERSPECTIVE

Whereas the bio-psycho-social-spiritual model helps us gain understanding of the roots and intransigence of addiction, the strengths perspective is a model geared toward direct practice, which can shape our appreciation of particular treatment modalities (or aspects of these modalities) as well. Harm reduction alone is not enough; the client caught in the mire of addiction and personal pain needs help in developing a healthy outlook on life and even a dramatically altered lifestyle.

Given the horrendous grip of addiction for certain individuals, the self-defeating behavior, guilt feelings, busted relationships, it is clear that whatever treatment modality is used it would have to offer hope, a way out of the morass of the addiction cycle. Hope, guidance, and relationships are three key ingredients in successful recovery. Finding a spiritual connection can help tremendously as well.

Although most recovery does not stem from formal treatment, the incentive for sobriety can very well be an outgrowth of a treatment experience. And for the family of the alcoholic or addict, family counseling can be a godsend.

The strengths approach, as its name implies, builds on clients' strengths and resources. This is "a versatile practice approach, relying heavily on ingenuity and creativity, the courage and common sense of both clients and their social workers" (Saleebey, 2002a, p. 13). Traditionally, work in the substance abuse field has focused on *breaking* client resistance and denial (Rapp, 1998).

According to this more positive framework, however, client resistance and denial can be viewed as healthy, intelligent responses to a situation that might involve unwelcome court mandates and other intrusive practices.

THEMES IN RECOVERY

The strengths approach does not entail set rituals or dogma but involves certain basic principles that transcend treatment modality or style. Charles A. Rapp (1998) singles out six critical elements conducive to recovery. These are: identity as a competent human being; the need for personal control or choice; the need for hope; the need for purpose; the need for a sense of achievement; and the presence of at least one key person. While the experience of illness and recovery is unique to each person, these common themes emerge in the stories of recovery. Although Rapp's focus was on mental illness, these recovery themes pertain equally well to all biochemical disorders. In the following pages, we draw on firsthand narrative accounts to illustrate each of Rapp's recovery themes. The first critical element of recovery, which has important implications for treatment, occurs when the person moves from an all-consuming identification with the illness to a *position of managing the symptoms of the disorder*. The position is often expressed by persons who are successful in going from abusing alcohol to learning to drink moderately. As Rick Anderson (1997) states:

> My experience as an alcohol counselor and a former alcohol abuser fully supports the moderate drinking program approach. . . . Behavior management has worked best for most alcoholic abusers. We learn to be responsible, make decisions, obtain legitimate counseling, and, most important, empower ourselves. (p. 5)

Another substance abuse counselor and a strong AA proponent, Larry Heckert, similarly reveals the importance of separation of the illness and the self:

> Recovery comes through getting your priorities straight; you have to place yourself and your sobriety above everything else. Spirituality is important as well. (Personal correspondence of December 14, 2000)

Sometimes sobriety brings with it a change in personality. Susan Cheever (1999) offers this description of her father, John Cheever, the famous writer, upon his return from treatment:

> He went from being an alcoholic with a drug problem who smoked two packs of Marlboros a day to being a man so abstemious that his principal drugs were the sugar in desserts. . . .
>   Although he knew too well how easily he could slip, the change in him made it seem less likely than ever that he would. His self-pitying bombast was gone. There were apologies instead of accusations. He was a man who seemed involved with life again. (pp. 198–199)

The second theme concerns the need for personal control, *choice*. As we hear from a former methamphetamine addict, "four years clean and sober," whose family had earlier disowned her:

My mother took my daughter while I served the 36 days in jail. NA (Narcotics Anonymous) didn't work—all that "powerlessness" got to me. I still have a few beers—I'm cursed by my counselor for this. But by the grace of my mother and my daughter, I'm not going back. . . . Group therapy was really helpful for me. (Personal interview with Angie, September 2000)

Michael Beechem (1996), a social work professor who had tried AA to no avail, then after having been referred by the college administrator for treatment, shares the secret of his success:

I find myself actively engaged in the recovery process, aware of the insidious nature of alcoholism and how a small voice within me can threaten to coax me into indulging in "just one drink" to help during a stressful situation. (p. 48)

Choice is the hallmark of the harm reduction model, its task being to help clients find their own way, to carve out their own paths to sobriety. In Britain, this is the predominant model for treatment, one that is believed to be the most effective with young persons who express willingness to work on controlling their drinking and other drug use. The focus is on prevention, not cure. In his lecture before an audience of American social work students, Philip Guy (1994), of the University of Hull in England, described his counseling strategy. "I've never used total abstinence as a goal unless the client wishes," he said. "If I decide the goal, the client might as well go home. The key is choice."

The third theme, *hope,* is a quality emphasized throughout the literature on substance abuse counseling. Without hope, of course, there can be no effort, no working toward a meaningful goal. At the societal level, as Saleebey (2002b) informs us, the strengths-based counselor goal is forever searching the environment for forces that enhance human possibilities and resiliencies. "Rather than focusing on problems, your eye turns toward possibility. In the thickest of trauma, pain, and trouble, you can see blooms of hope and transformation" (2002a, pp. 1–23). Membership in AA offers hope to alcoholics through the fellowship of shared experience. Sayings such as "I can't do it alone, but together we can" reinforce the strength of mutual help.

A sense of *purpose* is the next critical ingredient in recovery. Many of van Wormer's clients expressed a sense of purpose or meaning, saying, in essence, "Now I know this all happened for a reason. So I could help people who are going through the same thing." The twelfth step of AA involves taking the message of what has been learned to others.

Spirituality is a cornerstone of the many self-help groups, a connection with a Higher Power that gives life meaning. Pat Coughlin, a substance abuse counselor from Marshalltown, Iowa, who once suffered from multiple drug addictions (including meth and cocaine), describes the change that came over his life following a bar fight. In inpatient treatment for the third time, Coughlin says:

I knew the game, knew it wouldn't work. I had a spiritual awakening. I got on my knees and prayed, and things began to change. I felt God was answering my prayers. Exactly what I prayed for came to be in the form of my six-months stay at the Recovery House. There I formed the habit of attending AA, the habit of praying and work with a personal sponsor. Then after 9 months sober, I started college. (Speech of November 28, 2000)

A *sense of achievement* is a healthy counterpart to the wrestling with feelings of grief and loss that accompany the early period of recovery. Common types of achievement listed by Rapp (1998) are helping others, personal success at work, and self-expression through hobbies and/or the arts. In reflecting on his life, Coughlin, the speaker in the preceding passage, described how his brother, so estranged from him in the past, now has turned to requesting help with his son who has started to drink. "To go from a drug-dealing nothing to being called to help with a drinking child—that is the miracle of AA, the power of The Program."

The final element in recovery delineated by Rapp is *the presence of at least one person*—a friend, professional helper, teacher, family member. This element parallels the focus on relationship in all client-centered therapies (see Carl Rogers [1931] for the classical formulation). Genuineness, empathy, and non-possessive warmth are the key components of the effective therapeutic relationship. Through warmth (and caring), many a tough-minded personal spokesman from AA or NA or GA (Gamblers Anonymous) has guided the seemingly most recalcitrant addict through the rough periods of early sobriety. Whatever the personal style of the helper, it is the sincerity and caring that are key. Witness this account from Tinia Holder, at the time of writing an inmate at the federal prison at Danbury, Connecticut. Here she comments on the help she received from a dedicated psychologist:

> They have yet to financially fund the Bridge Program for substance abuse treatment. Dr. Onorato is the sole staff who renders countless hours trying to assist with the plight of abused women. He always treats each of us as individuals. He is a kind soul. Without him, I firmly believe that I would have ended my own life. I have learned a great deal from the trauma program. Dr. Onorato, through his hours of counseling, has shown me that I am a strong, capable woman who is realizing that I don't have just arms and legs but that I am able to run and fight, give and take. I can reclaim all the pieces of myself that had been stolen by stronger, cruel people who did whatever they wanted. I have learned that I have not only a voice, but a strong voice that can shout the word NO! (Personal correspondence of July 7, 1998)

Central to all these stories of recovery is the theme of personal empowerment. Both harm reduction and mutual-help programs are based on a voluntary commitment to change. The greatest weakness of The Program—its dogmatism—is possibly also its greatest strength. The Program gives people who are highly vulnerable and clutching for support something concrete, something more faith based than scientific, to latch on to. One is hard put to fault the kind of personal support that so many recovering alcoholics and other drug addicts have derived from what is commonly referred to as The Program (see chapter 12 on mutual-help groups for an in-depth analysis).

For effective work with so-called dually diagnosed clients, those with both substance use and mental health problems, Amodeo (1997) recommends an approach that engages the client. Crisp (1999) differentiates chemical dependency theory, which takes "a hard-lined approach," from mental illness theory, which stresses client nurturance. The following passage describes the approach that she has found to be most effective for working with dually diagnosed clients:

> Much of the work I do with clients individually is based on a strengths perspective and motivational therapy techniques. Many clients have tried and failed many times in their sobriety and have little hope in their ability to recover from their addiction. I attempt to educate them about the process of relapse, help them identify individual strengths and resources that may be helpful in their recovery, confront them on their denial, and assist them in understanding elements of their substance abuse and their mental illness or depression. The most valuable thing I think I offer clients is a belief that if they are willing to do the work, they can recover. I let them know that they have the abilities to recover, but ultimately, they must complete the task themselves. (p. 174)

FINDING THE STRENGTHS
IN DIVERGENT MODELS

The strengths perspective is essentially an approach rather than a well-integrated therapy, or, as Perkins and Tice (1995, p. 452) describe it, "a collaboration of ideas and techniques" that tends to be applied solely at the client level. Because this is basically a focus, an outlook, there is no reason we cannot apply it to the macro level as well and look to the positives with an attitude of appreciation rather than devaluation.

In light of policy changes allowing increasing flexibility in the provision of treatment, the time is ripe for a comprehensive approach to the field of addiction treatment, an approach about acceptance of differences rather than one that takes sides among the various camps. As a highly adaptable and effective approach, the strengths perspective can serve to shape our conceptualization of client-centered policies, policies such as drug courts that favor treatment over punishment. This perspective also leads us to an appreciation for the high-quality work being done by men and women whose devotion to their multiply addicted clients is almost heroic, as well as to an appreciation for the many effective treatment strategies being used. Instead of asking the question "What is wrong with this or that approach?" a framework based on strengths seeks to find the strong points in diverse frameworks such as the Twelve-Step approach and the harm reduction alternative. For an unabashedly negative point of view, consider the title of Peele and Bufe's best-selling 2000 book, *Resisting 12-Step Coercion: How to Fight Forced Participation in AA, NA, or 12-Step Treatment.*

Granted, Peele and Bufe's attack is directed more to the courts for coercing individuals in trouble with the law into attending such groups and or Twelve-Step-based treatment programs than against the "once proudly voluntaristic religions' healing programs" (p. 14). Even nonaddictive drug users (of illegal drugs), as Peele and Bufe suggest, are being forced to say in treatment that they are "powerless" over the substance in question. This requirement is made in the belief that "according to drug war dogma there is no such thing as, for instance, moderate marijuana use" (p. 28).

These points are well taken; *Resisting 12-Step Coercion* is well documented and thought provoking. Missing in all its 200-plus pages, however, is any acknowledgment for a program that has clearly saved so many lives. We, the authors of the present text, have known firsthand of a number of seeming miracles of recovery from membership in a mutual-help group such as AA or from participation in a professionally run program such as the Minnesota Model. The Minnesota Model is defined by one of its founders in these terms:

> What we have done is successfully integrate the spiritual philosophy of Alcoholics Anonymous into the professional treatment program. And in doing this, something profound has happened. It seems that all we have done is to humanize our programs with the interpersonal mutuality found in most Alcoholics Anonymous relationships. (p. 29)

In this text we will refer to this model as the traditional disease model.

If anything, the critics of harm reduction are more vociferous than are the critics of the Minnesota Model. Let us consider what happened when the first program to be shown on a major U.S. television network to question the lack of alternatives to treatment in the United States was broadcast. "Drinking: Are You in Control?" aired in May 2000 on ABC's *20/20* to present alternatives to the Twelve-Step total abstinence approach. From the start, the reaction in the press and on the Internet was palpable. For example, here's how Bob Eck (personal correspondence of June 16, 2000) addressed subscribers to the NASW-ATOD section list-serve:

> To mislead thousands of actively using alcoholics and addicts that it is indeed possible for them to "control drink" or use again is cruel, and then to attempt to support that opinion by the use of some unknown, backyard research on some chimps is truly an attempt to put one over on all of us. It looks like it worked, because I am sure there are those out there who will latch onto any potentially good reason to return to using their drug of choice. Believe me folks, there is no such thing as controlled use for the chemically dependent. The chemically abusive? Possibly so, but be careful here also. Go to the DSM-IV for the definition of the difference. Every so often someone comes along with this theory and some people line up behind the pied piper. Not possible, folks.

In fact, studies reveal the effectiveness of both traditional disease-model-based treatment and motivational enhancement therapy, the therapy favored in harm reduction programs (see Project MATCH Research Group, 1997; Miller & Rollnick, 1991). Bob Eck does have a point, however. Moderate drinking is a possibility for some but not for all. How to tell who will be able to adopt this strategy—that is the difficulty.

EMPIRICAL RESEARCH

Treatment effectiveness can be measured by offering treatment to a large group of people and then evaluating their improvement in terms of reduced health care needs, dependency, lowered crime rates, success in employment, etc. When measured in this way, the cost effectiveness of substance abuse treatment pays for itself 10 times over.

In California, for example, a rigorously designed study of the effectiveness of alcohol abuse and other drug abuse treatment showed that the state received a $7 return for every dollar invested, the largest savings of which were from reductions in crime. Similar reports come from virtually every state (*Substance Abuse in Brief,* 1999). Sadly, according to the same report only 37% of all those needing substance abuse treatment receive it, mainly due to its high cost. Shortly before he left office, drug czar Barry McCaffrey (2000) declared that America is suffering from a significant treatment gap. "Approximately 5 million drug users needed immediate treatment in 1998, while only 2.1 million received it," he said (p. 2). What was the major factor in this treatment gap? Limited funding, McCaffrey said. Spending priorities, however, continue to be placed on cleaning up the wreckage of substance misuse, rather than on treatment and prevention. Thirteen percent of total state budgets, in fact, go to "shoveling up" the wreckage caused by substance use, according to a recent report from the Center on Addiction and Substance Abuse (Alter, 2001).

Similarly, a RAND corporation study determined that providing treatment to all addicts in the United States could save more than $150 billion in social costs over the next 15 years while requiring only $21 billion in treatment expenditures (Rydell and Everingham, 1994). An extensive body of federally funded research shows that, with treatment, primary drug (including alcohol) misuse decreases by nearly half. Other findings are that medical visits related to drug misuse shows a decline of more than 50%; criminal activity decreases by as much as 80%, and financial self-sufficiency (including employment and housing considerations) is engendered (SAMHSA, 1999).

For years researchers have argued over what scientific research says about the various treatments and their clinical recovery rates. Because virtually all U.S. programming relies on attendance at AA or NA as a supplement to treatment, solid studies comparing the disease model abstinence-based approach and alternative approaches have been few and far between.

Directed by the National Institute on Alcohol Abuse and Alcoholism, the multisite, eight-year-long comparison study, Project MATCH (1997), involved almost 2,000 patients in the largest trial of psychotherapies ever undertaken. The goal of this $28 million project was not to measure treatment effectiveness, but, rather, to study which types of treatments worked for which types of people.

The three treatment designs chosen for this extensive study were based on the principles of the three most popular treatment designs—conventional Twelve-Step-based treatment, cognitive strategies, and motivational enhancement therapy (MET). One uniqueness of the interventions offered under the umbrella of Project MATCH is that all treatment was one-on-one; no group therapy was provided. Attendance at AA meetings, which was stressed more by the therapists of the traditional disease model school, was the only group contact that clients received. Any conclusion concerning treatment outcomes, accordingly, needs to take into account that Project MATCH, in contrast to the usual treatment practice in North America, provided individually delivered counseling.

The first of three treatment philosophies employed in Project MATCH was the Twelve-Step facilitation design. Counselors using this design explained to their clients the basic principles of Alcoholics Anonymous. In short, alcoholism is a disease that is primary, progressive, chronic, and fatal if not arrested. Alcoholics need to acknowledge that they are powerless over alcohol and that only through turning to a power greater than themselves can they be restored to sanity. Recovering comes through regular attendance at mutual-help groups and through humility and surrender to a Higher Power.

Cognitively based treatment, as offered by the practitioners participating in Project MATCH, focused on relapse prevention. The underlying premise of this approach is the belief that people's cognitions, or the way they view the world, and their self-destructive behavior are intertwined. Social skills training and stress management are basic strategies used by cognitive therapists to help clients find ways of reducing stress alternative to the use of alcohol.

The third model selected by Project MATCH for scrutiny, MET, is the pragmatic approach most closely associated with the harm reduction model. MET is client centered; the therapist assesses the level of the client's motivation for change and never fights the client, but, rather, rolls with resistance. MET techniques are geared to help people find their own path to change; feedback is offered by reflecting back to the client what he or she seems to be saying about the need to reduce or eliminate self-destructive behaviors.

Although Project MATCH was designed to test the general assumption that matching could improve treatment outcomes, individuals were assigned randomly to three varieties of treatment so that researchers could determine which modality worked best for whom. The results showed that one year and three years after treatment, clients showed substantial improvement regardless of the modality used.

To the surprise of the research team, outcome evaluations showed that patient-treatment matching is not necessary for satisfactory results and that participants in the intensive Twelve-Step format did as well on follow-up as those in the cognitive-behavioral therapy and motivational enhancement designs. Treatments were provided over 8- and 9-week periods, with motivational therapy being offered only four times and the other two designs offering 12 sessions. All of the participants showed significant and sustained improvements in the increased percentage of days they remained abstinent and the decreased number of drinks per drinking day, the researchers said. However, they noted that outpatients who received the Twelve-Step facilitation program were more likely to remain completely abstinent in the year following treatment than outpatients who received the other treatments. Individuals high on religiosity and those who indicated they were seeking meaning in life generally did better with the Twelve-Step, disease model focus, while clients with high levels of psychopathology did not do better with this approach. Clients low in motivation did best ultimately with the design geared for their level of motivation.

In aftercare subjects, less successful outcomes were associated with male gender, psychiatric problems, and peer group support for drinking. Because there was no control group deprived of treatment, generalizations concerning the efficacy of treatment cannot be made, a fact that has brought this massive project in for considerable criticism (Bower, 1997). What this extensive and long-term study does show, however, is that all three individually delivered treatment approaches are relatively comparable in their results, that treatment that is not abstinence based (motivational enhancement) is as helpful in getting clients to reduce their alcohol consumption as the more intensive treatment designs. These findings provide support for the guiding principle of this book, which is to find what works in seemingly diverse treatment designs.

Keep in mind that Project MATCH was concerned with diagnosable alcohol-dependent individuals only. The treatment needs of persons with alcohol and other drug problems, most of whom never come to the attention of specialized treatment centers, are clearly different from the needs of chronic alcoholics and addicts coerced into treatment (Zweben & Rose, 1999). Such clients are often seen in general social service and counseling settings for issues such as marital conflict and employment problems. An overreliance on medical models for diagnostic criteria often misses these problem substance misusers. Certainly the conventional techniques of "breaking down denial" and forcing such individuals to abstain totally from drinking and drug using are counterproductive. When clients who enter treatment for personal problems seemingly unrelated to substance misuse are referred to a specialized chemical dependency treatment center, they often are lost to treatment altogether. A far more effective approach is to treat them for the issue at hand but to keep the channels of communication open.

We have described Project MATCH in detail not because it provides proof of treatment effectiveness—it does not, in the absence of a control group—but because it confirms the viability of diverse approaches. This finding that clients do well when treatment is steeped in Twelve-Step principles, cognitive skills training, or an approach geared for individual motivation for change validates the basic thesis of this book—the strengths inherent in each of the various standard treatment options.

Also worth noting is the manner in which treatment effectiveness was measured by Project MATCH researchers. No longer, in fact, is government-funded research using subjects' ability to obtain abstinence as the standard for recovery (as in the follow-up surveys asking "When did you have your last drink?"). Instead, the impact of treatment strategies is now being measured in terms of improvement in drinking and drug-taking habits. Retention in treatment itself is being used in some evaluations as an outcome measure of success. Harm reduction models, much more commonly used in Europe than in the United States, measure success simply by whether or not harm was reduced. For example, a

| BOX 1.3 | TREATMENT EFFECTIVENESS: DOES IMPROVEMENT COUNT? |

BY DIANE RAE DAVIS

I will never forget the day I first presented the results of Project MATCH to a group of first-year MSW students. I put the overheads up, showing graphs of the different treatment groups and the number of days of abstinence at 6 months and 15 months. As I was describing these results, trying to make it interesting by noting how few persons maintained 100% abstinence by the end of 15 months but how many had improved in number of days of abstinence, I noticed the visible agitation of a student near the back of the room. I knew she had come to the MSW program after several years of practice in the alcohol/drug treatment field, and I wondered what in the world could be upsetting her.

I finally asked her if she wanted to comment on anything. She blurted out that "improvement doesn't cut it" in treatment. The idea of presenting improvement as a "success" was totally foreign to her. In fact, she suspected the information as it was presented on the graphs might be some kind of attempt to erode the recognized standard of recovery, which is "abstinence." As she talked further, it became clear that her concern was for the clients who might hear the "improvement" message and take that as permission to relapse.

I am forever grateful to this student for launching a much deeper (than I had planned!) discussion on what "recovery" means and who has the power to decide the meaning. The class concluded, as we all know in our hearts, that there is no "right" answer to these two questions. The reality is that it depends on which group is valued and powerful enough to determine goals and outcomes. The MATCH outcomes were "value-free" on the surface, in that they just presented "the facts." However, by defining success as maintaining 80%–90% days of abstinence over the follow-up period, the study group of this very expensive and high-profile study in essence "legitimized" that improvement does count. At a later date, the student told me she was glad her "blinders had been taken off," although this was a painful experience. She felt more prepared to deal with the complexities and ambiguities of the treatment world that are too often presented as if all answers are known. Sometimes, my biggest job as a teacher is to instill doubt.

---

person who injects heroin might be reducing the harm of becoming HIV positive by using clean syringes. Rigid adherence to the traditional, total abstinence standard in the past is one reason that the myth of treatment effectiveness persists. See Box 1.3 for a classroom discussion that contrasts the all-or-nothing approach to measuring recovery in terms of a number of criteria related to a reduction in harmful pursuits.

In summary, the standard for "What is recovery?" is beginning to change in the United States, making room for broader definitions that include such variables as improvements and health, social, and legal status. A primary purpose of this text is to explore this wider vision and find even more ways to be helpful to individuals who want to reduce risks, improve their health, and/or stop practicing their addiction. As a starting point, let us explore the harm reduction model in greater depth.

HARM REDUCTION AND
THE STRENGTHS APPROACH

What is the harm reduction approach? To define *harm reduction,* we need to take into account the two aspects of the term that are often poorly differentiated in the literature—policy and practice. As *policy,* harm reduction is an outgrowth of the international public health movement, a philosophy that opposes the criminalization of drug use and views substance misuse as a public health rather than a criminal justice concern. The goal of the harm reduction movement is to reduce the harm to users and misusers and to the communities in which they live, including the harm caused by the criminalization of the substances (Jensen & Gerber, 1998). Punitive laws against drinking by young adults under age 21 and possession of or using certain substances are opposed as a new form of Prohibition. The war on drugs is seen as exacting a toll in terms of deaths generated by: use of contaminated, unregulated chemicals; the spread of hepatitis, tuberculosis, and AIDS through the sharing of dirty needles; and the social breakdown in America's inner cities; and political corruption elsewhere. In Europe, in fact, it was the AIDS epidemic of the 1980s that catapulted harm reduction policies into prominence in several countries. Drug use was medicalized and the behavior of drug use closely monitored at methadone and other clinics, where a safe drug supply was provided under medical supervision. Several U.S. cities, including Baltimore, have moved in the direction of such progressive policies.

At the *practitioner* level, harm reduction is an umbrella term for a set of practical strategies based on motivational interviewing and other strengths-based approaches to help people help themselves by moving from safer use, to managed use, to abstinence, if so desired. The labeling of clients, as is the custom in mental health circles ("He has an antisocial personality," "She is borderline") or in treatment circles ("He's an alcoholic," "She has an eating disorder"), is avoided; clients provide the definition of the situation as they see it. Clients who wish it are given advice on how to reduce the harm in drug use, such as, "Don't drink on an empty stomach," or "Always make sure to use a clean needle." Consistent with the strengths perspective, the counselor and client collaborate to consider a broad range of solutions to the client-defined problem; resources are gathered or located to meet the individual needs of the client. Above all, clients are viewed as amenable to change.

The harm reduction approach recognizes the importance of giving equal emphasis to each of the biopsychosocial factors in drug use. Together, in collaboration, the counselor and client consider a broad range of solutions to the consequences of drug misuse, abstinence being only one. Forcing the client to admit to addiction to a substance as a way of breaking through "denial," according to proponents of this approach, can lead to resistance and a battle of wills between worker and client. When the focus of the professional relationship, however, is on promoting healthy lifestyles and on reducing problems that the client defines as important rather than on the substance use per se, many clients can be reached who would otherwise stay away (Denning, 2000; Graham, Brett, & Bacon, 1994). Seeking help is rare among substance misusers until the problems are overwhelming, probably due to the stringent and off-putting requirements of traditional substance abuse treatment. All these arguments, pragmatic as opposed to dogmatic, have been introduced to America through international conferences and exchanges. Similarly, the Twelve-Step-based treatment program has made inroads in Europe, especially in private clinics, where its success with a certain type of client—extraverted, severely addicted, structure seeking—is reminiscent of the American experience (van Wormer, 1999). Common to all these treatments, especially in the United States is the recognition that problems with alcohol, other drugs, and compulsive behaviors such as gambling affect not only individuals, but whole families as well.

This more flexible, harm reduction approach would appear to be of more relevance to community-based treatment and prevention work than to counseling inmates sentenced for drug violations. Yet, as Donna Kerr (1998), writing in *Corrections Today*, indicates, these principles are being adapted to substance abuse treatment by the women's correctional system in Canada, a system that is rapidly moving from the old punishment paradigm into a paradigm of healing. Depending on their level of discomfort with their drug use and their desire to change, women are empowered to move forward. Inmates ready to leave the system with no parole restrictions can choose either an abstinence or a moderation goal. Each participant draws her own vision of what she wants in life. Community follow-up components of the program help the women deal with relationships, anxiety, and other challenges in the free world.

TREATMENT TRENDS

Even in the United States, a revolution of sorts is brewing in substance abuse treatment circles; a paradigm shift is clearly under way. Bolstered by extraordinary brain research showing the physiological basis in addiction, substance abuse treatment is moving slowly toward a more scientific, empirically based approach. Much of the impetus for change admittedly is economic. After expanding wildly in the 1980s, as explained in a popular magazine—*U.S. News & World Report*—residential Twelve-Step programs are falling on hard times; insurers and employers are seeking cheaper, less intensive alternatives (Shute, 1997). There is simultaneously a trend, for prevention purposes, to treat alcohol and drug users, people with only mild problems, problem drinkers, for example. Non-abstinence-based treatment programs, such as Moderation Management, that allow clients a set number of drinks are becoming increasingly popular (Shute). The demand for brief interventions is compatible with managed health care requirements in both commercial markets and public systems (Zweben & Rose, 1999). Clinicians must be innovative in treating the range of severity presented by persons with substance use problems, as Zweben and Rose suggest. The premium today is on flexibility and individualized treatment. We need to suit the treatment to the client, not force the client into a standardized world. In any period of paradigm change, however, there is always resistance.

This resistance was brought home recently to Ron Schauer (writing in private correspondence of November 8, 1998), who was called to return to the directorship of an agency in Washington State after a 15-year absence. He writes:

> My brief story back in the "field" was so surreal. People—a few talk about things that they see as cutting edge, which are things we thought, 15 years ago, were about to become commonplace: family treatment, etc., etc. But the old guard re-established control. Not unexpected in a reactionary, Puritan, and cost-cutting time. Two-year-degreed people come for much less.
>
> I was daily amazed at what my staff didn't know, think, or even see in the definition of treatment. All but three were *heavy* smokers; all had disastrous personal lives, just like in 1977, when I first began.
>
> Managed care itself is, in my view, something of an evil. Yet it has served to push CD treatment off center and demanded some innovation, even in the name of greater profits and competitiveness.

The fact that this poorly functioning treatment center has folded is perhaps a sign of the times. Its demise gives credence to the view that, as Washousky and Thomas (1996) thoughtfully put it, "With society's help, the field is reinventing itself to meet today's needs" (p. 30). The new addiction therapist, as they contend, must be prepared to meet the needs of polydrug-addicted clients, clients with mental health and addiction problems both, and persons referred from the criminal justice system.

Among the most significant developments in recent times are the twin movements to incarcerate and decarcerate. We are referring to the impact of America's war on drugs, a war that has been driven by moral and political rhetoric but that is clearly racist and classist in practice (see chapters 10 and 11). In any case, with 2 million people incarcerated in U.S. jails and prisons and most of them with chemical dependency problems and a large minority with severe mental disorders, the treatment needs are exhaustive. Although less than 13% of inmates needing addiction treatment receive it, according to the Center for Substance Abuse Treatment (1999), this still means a lot of substance abuse counselors are counseling inmates, often working through agency contracts.

As registered in a recent opinion poll, public opinion is changing. As an ABC News survey found, most Americans (69%) are in favor of treatment over jail for first- and second-time drug offenders ("Americans Support Drug Treatment Over Jail," 2001). Women, Democrats, and the better educated were the most favorable to treatment options for drug users.

A countertrend to the "lock 'em up" mentality is evidenced in the alternative-to-prison movement, which got under way in the 1990s, that is, the "drug court" movement, which created a large market for substance abuse counselors to work with offenders in the community. Drug courts began experimentally in Dade County, Florida, as an intensive, judicial-supervised, community-based treatment for felony drug defendants designed to reduce the increasing recidivism rates. *Restorative justice,* an exciting development with its roots in the rituals of indigenous populations and Canadian Mennonites, advocates non-adversarial forms of settling disputes and strives to restore individual law-breakers to the community rather than isolating them from it. Drug courts are an evolving approach consistent in underlying philosophy with the aims of restorative justice (see van Wormer, 2001).

According to a news account (Johnson, 1998), these new courts, which divert nonviolent drug offenders from the prison system into treatment, have proved that addicts can be returned to work, family, and ultimately the American mainstream. Today, there are just over 700 drug courts in 50 states. Knowing that jail time awaits them if they begin abusing drugs again can offer a strong incentive to change. The saving of approximately over $14,050 per year offers a strong incentive to the county to keep offenders out of jail as well. A review of this diversion program by the Justice Department indicates a 75% graduation rate. (To graduate one must remain drug free.) Estimates are that, long term, 20% will relapse. Over a nine-year period, 2,500 parents have regained custody of their children. In a systematic evaluation of the drug court operations across the state of Florida. Mayfield, Valentine, and McNeece (1998) applaud the programs as a feasible and more effective alternative to adversarial procedures to combat nationwide drug problems. Such programs offer extensive, long-term treatment at little cost to the offender; many opportunities exist for professionally trained counselors to find employment with such diversionary, community-based programs.

Graduates of a similar three-phase program in Delaware, extending from incarceration, where inmates live in a therapeutic community, to a 12-month work-release program and then to aftercare or parole, were found to be both drug free and arrest free at much higher rates than released prisoners in the control group (Hooper, 1997). Meanwhile in Iowa, over 90% of the defendants in drug court are methamphetamine users charged with nonviolent crimes. Although about half of the users have relapsed, corrections officials consider the program a success (Zeleny, 1997).

Just as new scientific discoveries are shaping knowledge about the biology of addiction, so political developments are changing the manner in which substance abuse treatment is being provided. Until recently in the United States, for example, non-abstinence treatment programs were virtually unheard of. Today, at many progressive treatment centers, never-before-questioned traditions are being turned around. Chain smoking, which was previously taken for granted in treatment circles, is now correctly regarded as an addiction not unlike any other. Clients are being counseled in moderate drinking and not terminated if they can't quit taking drugs altogether at once. Meanwhile, for the first time ever, television programs on the major networks discuss moderation treatment as a viable alternative to traditional treatments requiring immediate abstinence from all mood-altering substances (and activities). The recent reporting in the mainstream media and medical journals of the efficiency of a harm reduction philosophy is perhaps a harbinger of future advances.

Quietly, in September 2001, San Francisco became the first city in the nation to adopt harm reduction as its official policy. The new philosophy is apparent at the Department of Public Health's needle exchange sites, in a media campaign to teach any addicts how to reduce deaths from heroin overdose, and in the training of workers at dozens of agencies in harm reduction strategies (Torassa, 2001).

One significant change little noted in the literature or elsewhere is revealed in treatment effectiveness studies. Whereas formerly the standard for a successful treatment outcome was the length of time a former client abstained from the use of all psychoactive substances, today much more flexible and realistic measures of treatment success are being applied. Not surprisingly, these holistic measures of improvement in social and physical functioning are bringing much more positive results than measures recording a change from chronic binge drinking to drinking three glasses of wine a week as treatment failure. The use of an improvement standard in contemporary research is entirely consistent with the harm reduction approach and is bound to have an impact at the treatment delivery end.

To help bridge the gap between research and practice, the National Institute on Drug Abuse (NIDA) has called for grant applications to participate in clinical trials, using a variety of treatment methods, including pharmaceutical medications, methadone, maintenance, nutritional guidance, and other alternative approaches. With the ultimate goal of the National Drug Abuse Treatment Clinical Trials Network to have 30–40 regional sites around the United States, the results of this experimentation with new treatments should be far-reaching. Only in this way, in integrating practice with science, will the promising treatments that have been successfully applied in specialized clinical settings be adopted in the field. "The Clinical Trials Network," as Leshner (2000a) asserts, "will help us change the face of drug abuse treatment by enabling us to take what we learn in the lab and rapidly put it into practice across the country" (p. 1).

In any case, in light of new developments, there is no need to abandon the disease conception of addiction or of the Twelve-Step-based treatment strategies in favor of harm reduction. Clearly those who follow the "Program" and abstain from alcohol or drug use reduce the harm to themselves and their families. So the apparent dichotomy between the disease model and an alternative model geared toward public health is a false one. We may all have different allegiances, but in the end we all have the same allegiance to the pursuit of health. The basic thesis of this chapter and of this book, then, follows the principle of both/and, not either/or. The results of Project MATCH, the most extensive and expensive comparative research performed to date, confirm the viability of three internally consistent models of treatment—conventional the Twelve-Step-based approach (albeit without the group work), cognitively oriented therapy, and motivational enhancement strategies. This last is the preferred framework for treatment offered by harm reduction proponents. From the strengths perspective, we would be remiss not to extend our appreciation and gratitude to those pioneers in the field without whom there might be no profession known as substance abuse treatment today.

SUMMARY AND CONCLUSION

While the United States seemingly has unlimited resources for the imprisonment of drug users, managed care constraints and federal funding cutbacks have led to a shift from a clinical approach to a criminal justice approach, from a call for treatment to a call for punishment. At the start of the new century, however, two countertrends are evident. The first is the impetus under restorative justice initiatives for offenders to serve time in the community rather than behind bars; the second is continuous calls at the highest levels for more prevention and treatment dollars to be provided.

In state after state, studies on the cost effectiveness of drug treatment confirm tremendous savings to taxpayers and reduced crime rates. Increasingly, treatment is seen as a cost-effective alternative to incarceration. More and more, it is realized as well that prison is only a revolving door if inmates with addiction problems don't get the help they need before their release back into society. Protecting the health of the community as a whole requires protecting the health of drug users, and this requires providing adequate and diversified treatment for persons with substance abuse and dependency problems. A wide range of interventions is needed to meet the client where he or she is, at the client's individual moment of motivation.

Despite the economic constraints caused by managed care and federal cutbacks, this is an exciting time to be in the addiction treatment field. The horizons of this field have broadened considerably to include attention to a broad range of addictive problems (gambling, shopping, and sex addiction, for example) as well as the substance dependencies, such as alcoholism and cocaine addiction. As we move away from the doctrinaire views that have so stifled innovation and experimentation in this field in the past, the door has opened to greater professionalism by staff and more emphasis on client self-determination and empowerment. Meanwhile, advances in the scientific study of addiction as what Leshner (1997) terms a "brain disease" continue to enrich our knowledge of addiction in the causes and consequences.

Central to sound policy and treatment is an understanding of the nature of addiction, of addiction as a complex biological, psychological, and sociological phenomenon. Recent scientific discoveries, for example, information about unraveling the DNA code as a blueprint for behavior and availability of brain scan images that can show the extent of brain damage from drugs, have important implications for the addictions field. The connection between these discoveries and one's susceptibility to substance abuse are the subject of chapters 4 and 5.

Given the creation of an array of effective behavioral and pharmacological interventions, addiction treatment can now be as effective as treatment for the long-term, relapsing illnesses, such as diabetes and hypertension, with professional treatment that is tailored to the needs of particular clients (Leshner, 2000b). Promising developments in providing a gender-specific treatment curriculum for female alcoholics and addicts, such as that presented by Covington (1999), should do much to enhance treatment offerings for women. Overall, the movement away from having one and only one standardized treatment model to diverse, modified programs is the most encouraging development of all.

References

Alter, J. (2001, February 12). The war on addiction. *Newsweek, 36–39.*

American Heritage Dictionary of the English Language (4th ed.) (2000). Boston: Houghton-Mifflin.

American Medical Association (1968). *Manual on alcoholism of the American Medical Association.* Chicago, IL: AMA.

American Psychiatric Association (2000). *Diagnostic and statistical manual of mental disorders, text revised* (4th ed.). Washington, DC: American Psychiatric Association.

Americans support drug treatment over jail. (2001, June 6). ABC News report available online at www.atforum.com/siteroot/pages/news

Amodeo, M. (1997, October 5). Groups work with AIDS clients in early recovery. Presentation at annual NASW Conference: Baltimore, MD.

Anderson, J. (1994, July 15). Shop till you drop. *Chicago Tribune,* 1, 6.

Anderson, R. (1997, September 29). [Letter to the editor]. *U.S. News and World Report,* 5.

Ayto, J. (1990). *Dictionary of word origins.* New York: Little, Brown, and Company.

Barker, O. (2000, November 28). Ex-smokers get stuck on gum. *USA Today,* 10D.

Beechem, M. (1996, Spring). Chained open. *Reflections: Narratives of professional helping,* 2(2), 42–48.

Benshoff, J. J., & Janikowski, T. P. (2000). *The rehabilitation model of substance abuse counseling.* Belmont, CA: Wadsworth.

Bower, B. (1997). Alcoholics Anonymous. *Science News, 151,* 62–63.

Brown, B. (2000, May 24). Toronto inmates would rather starve than quit: Plan for smokeless jail draws hunger-strike protests. Available from APBNews.com

Center for Substance Abuse Treatment (1999, September). *Substance abuse in brief.* Available from www.samhsa.gov/csat/inbriefs/sept99.htm

Chang, M. (1998, March/April). Trapped in the Web. *Psychology Today,* 66–72.

Cheever, S. (1999). *Not found in a bottle: My life as a drinker.* Simon & Schuster.

Conrad, P., & Kern, R. (1994). The social production of disease and illness. In P. Conrad & R. Kern (Eds.), *Sociology of health and illness* (pp. 7–9). New York: St. Martin's Press.

Coughlin, P. (2000). Presentation given at the University of Northern Iowa, Cedar Falls, Iowa.

Covington, S. (1999). *Helping women recover: A program for treating substance abuse.* San Francisco: Jossey-Bass.

Crisp, C. (1999). Dual diagnosis: Substance abuse and mental health in an inpatient setting. In L. M. Grobman (Ed.), *Days in the lives of social workers* (2nd ed., pp. 171–176). Harrisburg, PA: White Hat Communications.

Denning, P. (2000). *Practicing harm reduction psychotherapy: An alternative approach to addictions.* New York: Guilford Press.

Drake, R. E., & Mueser, K. T. (1996). Alcohol-use disorders and severe mental illness. *Alcohol Health & Research World,* 20(2), 87–93.

Freeman, E. M. (1992). Glossary. In E. M. Freeman (Ed.), *The addition process: Effective social work approaches* (pp. 252–259). New York: Longman.

Garlick, R. (2000). *Action News, 10*(3). Canadian Center on Substance Abuse. Available at www.ccsa.ca/anv10n3e.htm

Germain, C. (1984). *Social work practices in health care: An ecological perspective.* New York: Free Press.

Gold, M. S., Johnson, C. R., & Stennie, K. (1997). Eating disorders. In J. H. Lowinson, P. Ruiz, R. Millman, & J. G. Langrod (Eds.), *Substance abuse: A comprehensive textbook* (pp. 319–337). Baltimore: Williams & Wilkins.

Graham, K., Brett, P., & Bacon, J. (1994, March 7–10). *A harm reduction approach to treating older adults: The clients speak.* Paper presented at the 5th International Conference on the Reduction of Drug-Related Harm, Toronto, Ontario, Canada.

Guy, P. (1994, September). *The British and German treatment models.* Guest lecture at the University of Northern Iowa, Cedar Falls, Iowa.

Haban, W. (1999, February 9). *Eating disorders.* Oral presentation given at the University of Northern Iowa, Cedar Falls, Iowa.

Hamilton, E. (1948). *The Greek way to Western civilization.* New York: Norton.

Harrison, L. (1996). Introduction. In L. Harrison (Ed.), *Alcohol problems in the community* (pp. 1–13). London: Routledge.

Harrison, L., & Luck, H. (1996). Drinking and homelessness in the U.K. In L. Harrison (Ed.), *Alcohol problems in the community* (pp. 115–140). London: Routledge.

Holliday, H. (2000, July/August). Hooked on the net. *Psychology Today,* 10.

Hooper, R. M. (1997, November/December). Attacking prison-based substance abuse. *Behavioral Health Management,* 28–29.

Jellinek, E. M. (1960). *The disease concept of alcoholism.* New Haven, CT: Yale Center for Alcoholic Studies.

Jensen, E. L., & Gerber, J. (1998). The social construction of drug problems: A historical overview. In E. L. Jensen & J. Gerber (Eds.), *The new war on drugs: Symbolic and criminal justice policy* (pp. 1–23). Cincinnati, OH: Anderson.

Johnson, K. (1998, May 15). Drug courts help addicts find way back. *USA Today,* 12A.

Kerr, D. (1998, December). Substance abuse among female offenders. *Corrections Today,* 114–119.

Lemonick, M. D. (2000, December 11). Downey's downfall. *Time,* 58–59.

Leshner, A. I. (1997, October 3). Addiction is a brain disease, and it matters. *Science, 278,* 45–47.

Leshner, A. I. (2000a). Cited in NIDA's clinical trials network launched. *National Drug Abuse Treatment Clinical Trials Network Report, 1*(1), 1–5.

Leshner, A. I. (2000b, June 17). Cited in M. Massey, Seeing drugs as a choice or as a brain anomaly. *New York Times,* A17.

Lobet, I. (2000, September 18). Shopaholics climb on the wagon. *U.S. News and World Report,* 60.

Mayfield, E. L., Valentine, P., & McNeece, C. A. (1998, March 5–8). *Evaluating drug courts: An alternative to incarceration.* Paper presented at the Council on Social Work Education Annual Program Meeting, Orlando, Fla.

McCaffrey, B. (2000). Cited in *Drug war facts,* p. 2. Available from www.drugwarfacts .org/treatmen.htm

McNeece, C. A., & DiNitto, D. (1998). *Chemical dependency: A system approach.* Boston: Allyn & Bacon.

Meyer, T. (1997, December 5). Alcoholic smokers are having trouble snuffing out both habits, CDC says. *Bowling Green Daily News,* 4C.

Miller, W. R., & Rollnick, S. (1991). *Motivational interviewing: Preparing people to change addictive behaviors.* New York: Guilford Press.

Moncher, M., Schinke, S., & Holden, G. (1992). Tobacco addiction: Correlates, prevention and treatment. In E. Freeman (Ed.), *The addiction process*. New York: Longman.

Morell, C. (1996). Radicalizing recovery: Addiction, spirituality, and politics. *Social Work, 41*(3), 306–312.

National Center on Addiction and Substance Abuse (CASA) (1998, January). *Behind bars: Substance abuse and America's prison population*. New York: Columbia University.

Nichols, M. (1998, February 9). Is sex an addiction? *Maclean's,* 80.

Novak, V. (1998, June 1). They call it video crack. *Time,* 58–59.

Orford, J. (1985). *Excessive appetites: A psychological view of addictions*. Chichester, England: Wiley.

Peele, S. (1995). *Diseasing of America: How we allowed recovery zealots and the treatment industry to convince us we are out of control*. San Francisco: Jossey-Bass.

Peele, S., & Bufe, C. (2000). *Resisting 12-step coercion: How to fight forced participation in AA, NA, or 12-step treatment*. Tucson, AZ: Sharp Press.

Perkins, K., & Tice, C. (1995). A strengths perspective in practice: Older people and mental health challenge. *Journal of Gerontological Social Work, 23*(3/4), 438–454.

Project MATCH Research Group (1997, January). Matching alcoholism treatment to client heterogeneity: Project MATCH post-treatment outcomes. *Journal of Studies on Alcohol, 58,* 7–28.

Rapp, C. A. (1998). *The strengths model: Case management with people suffering from severe and persistent mental illness*. New York: Oxford University Press.

Rogers, C. R. (1931). *Client-centered therapy*. Boston: Houghton-Mifflin.

Rosin, H. (2000, May 5). Bush puts faith in a social service rule. *Washington Post,* A1.

Rydell, C. P., & Everingham, S. S. (1994). Controlling cocaine: Supply versus demand programs. Santa Monica, CA: Drug Policy Research Center, RAND Corp.

Saleebey, D. (2002a). Introduction: Power to the people. In D. Saleebey (Ed.), *The strengths perspective in social work practice* (3rd ed., pp. 1–22). Boston: Allyn & Bacon.

Saleebey, D. (2002b). The strengths perspective: Possibilities and problems. In D. Saleebey (Ed.), *The strengths perspective in social work practice* (3rd ed., pp. 264–286). Boston: Allyn & Bacon.

SAMHSA (Substance Abuse and Mental Health Service Administration) (1999). Summary of outcomes in the National Treatment Improvement Evaluation Study, NEDS Fact Sheet 4, 1997. Rockville, MD: SAMHSA.

Schaler, J. (1999). *Addiction is a choice*. Chicago: Open Court.

Shaffer, H. J. (1999). Strange bedfellows: A critical new of pathological gambling and addiction. *Addiction, 94*(10), 1445–1448.

Shute, N. (1997, September 8). The drinking dilemma. *U.S. News & World Report,* 55–65.

Smith, B. (1999, July 21). Mom gets probation: Girl died at poker binge. *Des Moines Register,* 3A.

Substance abuse in brief (1999, August). Available from www.samhsa.gov/csat/inbriefs/aug99.htm

Terrorist attacks cause spike in treatment requests. (2001, December 6). Online at www.jointogether.org

Torassa, V. (2001, January 15). Changing method of treatment for drug addiction. *San Francisco Chronicle*. Available from www.cannabisnews.com/news/thread 8324.shtml

van Wormer, K. (1995). *Alcoholism treatment: A social work perspective.* Belmont, CA: Wadsworth.

van Wormer, K. (1999). Harm induction vs. harm reduction: Comparing American and British approaches to drug use. *Journal of Offender Rehabilitation, 29*(1/2), 35–48.

van Wormer, K. (2001). *Counseling female offenders and victims: A strengths-restorative approach.* New York: Springer.

Volpicelli, J., & Szalavitz, M. (2000). *Recovery options: The complete guide.* New York: Wiley.

Walters, G. D. (1999). *The addiction concept: Working hypothesis or self-fulfilling prophecy?* Boston: Allyn & Bacon.

Washousky, R., & Thomas, G. A. (1996). The changing face of addiction treatment. *Behavioral Health Management, 16*(2), 30–31.

Zeleny, J. (1997, October 19). Drug court: System's second chance. *Des Moines Register,* 1–2A.

Zweben, A., & Rose, S. (1999). Innovations in treating alcohol problems. In D. Biegel & A. Blum (Eds.), *Innovations in practice and service delivery across the life span* (pp. 197–246). New York: Oxford University Press.

What experiences and history teach is this—that people and governments never have learned anything from history. —HEGEL, 1832

HISTORICAL
PERSPECTIVES

CHAPTER 2

INTRODUCTION

What role do our drugs of choice play in society? In what ways has society tried to curb the use of drugs? Whether it's alcohol, nicotine, opium, or cocaine, our drugs of choice have been alternatively glorified and vilified. This chapter focuses on the history of America, Canada, and Europe's drug use and misuse, on economic and legal history, from the earliest days to the present time. The problems we see today are hardly new; they have existed in other forms and with other drugs throughout our history.

Before there was misuse, there was use—of all kinds of intoxicants, derived mostly from plants. There has been no civilization, as Zeldin (1994) suggests, in fact, whose citizens have not tried to escape from stress or tedium to alter their consciousness, with the help of alcohol, tobacco, tea, coffee, or plants of various sorts. The Aztecs, for example, had 400 gods of drink and drunkenness to help them escape into semiconscious bliss; the cacti and mushrooms they ate gave them hallucinations and courage for battle. Everyplace in the world where apples, grapes, and wheat grew there was a good chance humans discovered a use for them that went beyond mere satisfaction of hunger pangs. Since even animals of the various species have been known to seek out fermented berries, it seems obvious that the earliest humans would have done the same. The human uniqueness comes with the rituals surrounding the use of mood-altering substances, the planning entailed in their acquisition, and ultimately the social regulation pertaining thereto.

In this chapter, we will trace the use of how drugs, including alcohol, became defined and, over time, redefined. From evangelism to criminalization to medicalization, the road has been paved with many ill-fated attempts at social control. Starting with a look at the earliest civilizations, through the Middle Ages, to the modern world as represented by the United States and Europe (each taking divergent paths), we will study the policy aspect of drug manufacture and use. In our overview, we will see that at times, the technological advances—the ability to distill alcohol and produce smokable cocaine, for example—have exceeded our human capacity to absorb them.

Three themes will become apparent as we survey the history of substance use and addiction in a society that Denzin (1993) terms "the alcoholic society." The *ambivalence* accorded the role of intoxicants in society and the pleasure and pain associated with their use is one such theme. This theme is reflected in a combination of heavy alcohol or drug use coupled with strict social control policies.

The second major theme concerns the different reactions to the same drug over time, the health-inducing potion of one period of time banned as a dangerous substance (associated with dangerous people) some years later. The road from medicalization to criminalization, as we will see, is influenced less by the chemical properties of a drug than by considerations of race, class, and gender.

Third is the fact of the rising potency of drugs that has followed whenever they have been banned. Even as the sale of alcohol was outlawed in the 1920s, the consumption of spirits replaced the consumption of beer and wine. One striking parallel today is seen in the increasing purity and potency of cocaine and heroin, drugs in themselves easier to smuggle across borders than bulky marijuana.

EARLY USE AND MISUSE OF INTOXICANTS

Historical accounts from ancient Greece and Rome and other early civilizations describe the systematic doling out of alcoholic beverages to soldiers, along with food, weapons, and other military rations (Bower, 1994). Recent excavations provide evidence in the form of a yellowish residue preserved in a pottery jar of wine making by early settlers of northern Iran (Wilford, 1996). Archeologists date the pottery jar as having been produced over 7,000 years ago. Through chemical testing, archeological scientists were able to establish that a substance found only in large quantities of grapes was contained in the residue. Additionally, the residue contained a substance used in antiquity to keep wine from turning to vinegar. The significance is that now we know that wine was being made as early as 5000 B.C., which was about the time people were establishing their first permanent settlements, domesticating plants and animals. The fact that special wine gods were worshiped by ancient people is testimony to the special place that alcohol came to assume in early civilization. Ancient Romans had their god of drink, Bacchus, and the Greeks their Dionysus. As we know from papyri, Egyptian doctors included beer or wine in their prescriptions. In ancient Egypt, in fact, both beer and wine were deified and offered to the gods (Hanson, 1995).

In China, a variety of alcoholic beverages were used since prehistoric times and in all segments of society (Hanson, 1995). Evidence attests, as Hanson indicates, that alcohol played an important role in religious life and that the use of alcohol in moderation was the norm. In what is now Greece, wine making was commonplace. The ancient Greeks were known for the temperance of their culture, their avoidance of excess in all things, "teaching practical morality and forever emphasizing moderation" (Hamilton, 1940; p. 165). Traditional Roman values of temperance and simplicity, as Hanson indicates, resembled the Greek ways of being. Gradually, however, these values were replaced by practices related to degeneracy.

From the Old Testament of the Bible, we learn of drinking practices of the Hebrews. Abundant wine made from grapes was regarded as a blessing that could "gladden the heart of man" (Psalms 105:15, King James Version). That it also had the property to wreak some havoc is revealed in Genesis 9:20:

> And Noah began to be a husbandman, and he planted a vineyard: And he drank of the wine and was drunken; and he was uncovered within his tent.

Later we learn that the daughters of Lot got their father drunk in order to continue the family line (Genesis 19: 32–36). Although there is a lot of drinking mentioned in the Bible, both the Old and New Testaments condemn drunkenness. Indeed, the dangers inherent in strong drink have been known at least since biblical times. Proverbs 33: 29–30 provides a strong cautionary note:

> Who hath woe? Who hath sorrow? Who hath contentions? Who hath babbling? Who hath wounds without cause? Who hath redness of eyes? They that tarry long at the wine; they that go to seek mixed wine.

Whereas the large majority of the Hebrews rejoiced in wine and used it for medicinal and nutritional purposes, wine was relegated to a sacred and symbolic role. The New Testament depicts this common association.

While the Hebrews condoned drinking but not drunkenness, a different kind of religious control was adopted later in the seventh century by Islam. The Koran simply condemned wine altogether, and an effective prohibition against all alcoholic beverages prevailed. In the Far East, India, and China, alcohol consumption was secularized and widespread (Levin, 1995).

The long road from the sacred to the profane was shortened by a 10th century discovery of an Arabian physician (Kinney, 2000). The word *alcohol* itself is derived from the Arabic *al-kuhul* (Ayto, 1990). The discovery of distilled spirits, which made possible the manufacture of much stronger alcoholic concoctions, is an instance of the reach of technology exceeding its grasp. The devastation unleashed with this new development, however, did not occur suddenly but took place over centuries of use (Orford, 1985).

Originally, this distilled alcohol was not the drink we know today. It was used as a cosmetic to darken the eyelids and as a medicine. Use of distilled liquors gradually become common in Europe.

Self-indulgence in connection with food is demonstrated in the presence of the vomitorium in ancient Rome. The practices of feasting and drinking included vomiting so that people could keep repeating these processes. This was the forerunner of the binge/purge cycle known today as bulimia. Anorexia has its roots in holy fasting practices of the 13th century women whose self-denial provided them with praise and admiration. Some of the "holy anorexics" were canonized as saints for their troubles (Bell, 1987).

Like alcohol, the use of opium goes far back in time as well (Conrad & Schneider, 1992). Extracted from the white juice of certain species of poppy, opium is believed to have been used by the Sumerians, an ancient Middle Eastern people, to enhance their feelings of pleasure and by later civilizations for its medical properties.

Moving to the Americas, we find that while most of the pre-Columbian Native American peoples lacked knowledge of alcohol, several of the cultures of northern Mexico and the southwestern United States consumed wine and beer. Columbus found the Caribbean Indians drinking beer from fermented maize. Limited to communal fiestas, drunkenness was socially sanctioned and therefore not disruptive (van Wormer, 1995). The Spaniards introduced marijuana to the New World; the word *marijuana* comes from a Spanish word meaning "a substance causing intoxication" (Benshoff & Janikowski, 2000). Marijuana use, as Brecher (1972) claims, can be traced back to cultivation by the ancient Greeks, Persians, and Chinese.

Cocaine use as coca leaf chewing among South American indigenous peoples dates back centuries (Benshoff & Janikowski). The Spanish conquerors made the drug available to slaves to boost their stamina. This form of cocaine use was not culturally destructive, not associated with addiction, as Benshoff and Janikowski indicate.

The history of nicotine addiction goes back to the discovery of Columbus and his men of dried leaves in Central America. By the 1600s, tobacco was a permanent European commodity and used by all social classes (Goodman, 1993).

Later, in British America, however, the liquor-in-exchange-for-furs trade was to be culturally and economically devastating to a people who had no chance to develop a familiarity with its powers so as in the knowing, to resist them. The Catawba tribal leader's plea to the colonists to cease supplying spirits to his people is one of the Indian voices for restraint in Peter Mancall's (1997) *Deadly Medicine: Indians and Alcohol in Early America.*

THE EUROPEAN CONTEXT

In the *History of Intoxication,* Norwegian author, Bjorn Qviller (1996) argues that from Viking drinking guilds to wine-soaked symposia in ancient Greece, alcohol played a central role in the political life of western Europe. People drank together to knit friendships and make political allies. Not much is known about the role of alcohol in women's lives in ancient history. We do know from ancient records that women's misuse of alcohol was linked to its harmful effects on unborn children (Sandmaier, 1992).

In the days before purification, alcohol was often safer than water. Although Conrad and Schneider (1992) contend that opium held no special appeal for Europeans until the mid-1800s, Zeldin (1994) suggests that opium mixed with alcohol became the fashionable way to escape from pain and boredom from the 16th century. In any case, by 1854 opium was the most valued remedy of the day for everyday maladies such as indigestion. In reverse of today's war on international drug trafficking, the British began illegally smuggling opium into China in the early 18th century to exchange with Chinese traders for tea (Hamid, 1998). The opium was transported from India. Opium smoking became rampant among Chinese peasants. The Chinese were forced through a series of wars, known historically as the Opium Wars, which broke out in 1839, to keep their markets open to the opium trade (Abadinsky, 1996).

Sometimes technological advance exceeds a people's ability to handle it. So it was with the invention of the distillation process for making alcohol stronger. And so it was with the discovery by German scientists of how to isolate cocaine from the coca bush (Benshoff & Janikowski, 2000). Discovered in the 10th century by an Arabian physician, the process of distillation was widely used in the 15th century as a way of removing water from the fermented product, thereby increasing the concentration of alcohol (Levin, 1995). In 1575, a distillery was founded in Amsterdam, one that is still in operation today. From a concoction of grains, herbs, and juniper berries, *jenever*, or gin, was produced. The availability of cheap gin, combined with the population displacement caused by industrialization and associated with the growth of an urban proletariat, contributed to an epidemic of drunkenness (Levin, 1995). The devastation was so great, in fact, that a staggering infant mortality rate and child starvation rate combined to prevent a growth in population from 1700 to 1750. Public outrage at the drunken woman and neglectful mother may have reached its height, as Sandmaier (1992) indicates, during the infamous gin epidemics of London. Crimes of violence and immorality among all social classes, but most evident among the poor, gave the age a debaucherous character, preserved in political commentary and the early novel (van Wormer, 1995). Parliament, which earlier had actively promoted gin production to utilize surplus grain and to raise revenue, now passed legislation to discourage its use (Hanson, 1995). Gradually a change in attitudes, probably related to the industrial revolution and the need for a hard-working, sober workforce, coalesced to reduce the use of spirits considerably. The availability of higher-quality and more affordable beer was an additional factor in rum's decline.

COLONIAL AMERICA

We begin this section with a thought-provoking question, one commonly asked and best articulated by social work educator Ogden Rogers (in personal e-mail correspondence of June 2, 2000):

> Gathering people's thoughts on programs such as "Rational Recovery" or work by Stanton Peele on addictive behavior is met either by anger on one end of the

pole, or marginalization-almost-without-comment at the other. Whenever I encounter so much emotion about something I want to explore dispassionately, I ask myself "why?" Why is it that the subject of "use, abuse, and addiction" raises such passions? I suspect there must be deep values and/or fears enmeshed in the fabric of the issues. In an almost "X-files" sort of way, I'm impressed with how much of the conversation about drugs is focused in extreme ways. The "solutions" end up extreme as well: abstinence philosophy about many things; incarceration of huge masses.

For answer we must look back to the holy experiment known to the world as Puritanism, to that band of relatively humorless religious zealots who started things off in Massachusetts Bay. Like the very language that Americans speak, the present-day American value system is rooted in that New England experience. To Puritans who sought guidance for all daily activities in Scripture, the truth was perfectly clear: God had chosen an elite few to represent Him on earth (Erickson, 1966).

This is not to say, however, that sexual prudery or enforced abstinence from drink was a part of the Puritan scene. What these religious dissenters did was to set the tone for all that took place then and was to come later—the rigidity and punitiveness, but, above all, the moralism that was to become pervasive in American life.

The history of addiction in the United States begins but does not end, therefore, with alcohol (Walters, 1999). An article in the *Chicago Tribune* ("Documentary Looks at Drinking in America," 1999) puts the American experience with mood-altering substances into perspective:

> Most students of popular culture already are well aware that cocaine began insinuating itself into our society through the use of patent medicines and soft drinks; Bayer once marketed heroin alongside its aspirin products; and military service has turned more people into smokers than Humphrey Bogart, Lauren Bacall, and Joe Camel combined. What isn't well known, however, is how much booze was imbibed by our founding fathers . . . and mothers.

More beer than water was carried on the Mayflower. The Puritans saw alcohol as a blessing from God, as a good and healthy beverage (Peele, 1995; van Wormer, 1995). Colonial Americans of all ages drank daily; pregnant women and children, along with men, consumed a lot of beer. Punishments were reserved for drunkards who made nuisances of themselves. Still, the tavern was the center of much family, social, and economic activity.

When hard-drinking European trappers and hunters introduced alcohol to the native populations, the natives adopted the drug alcohol into their own cultural rituals. They drank not for conviviality but to alter their mood and achieve a different state of consciousness. The Indians assumed that alcoholic drinks served the same purpose as hallucinogenic plants and tobacco and treated them in the same way (Barr, 1999). To drink small quantities was considered pointless. Europeans, of course, took advantage of the Indian propensity to drink to the point of insensibility, as Barr reminds us, to cheat them out of their furs and other goods. Drunkenness for the Indians became a major social problem that has continued until the present day.

With the passage of time, liquor came to be valued by the early settlers for both its high alcohol content and its shipping advantages. The Puritans regarded rum as "God's good creature." Although an occasional drunk was placed in the stocks, the tavern was the center of social, economic, and political activity (Levin, 1995). As time passed, Jamaican rum seemed to have become the solution to the new nation's thirst.

As the colonists turned to distilling alcohol, they proved as adaptable as they had earlier in producing passable beer. Honey, corn, rye, berries, and apples were used in domestic production. A general lack of concern about alcoholism and its problems was one of the most significant features of the colonial era (Lender & Martin, 1982). Strong drink was thought to protect against disease and to be conducive to good health. Alcohol was used as a solvent antiseptic and, of course, as a painkiller. Since good drinking water was not always available, there was some substance to this argument. And as long as the social norms were followed, drinking excesses could be tolerated. Rum figured prominently in the economy of the new nation. For the sake of rum, made from the molasses that was imported in large quantities from Jamaica, New Englanders became the bankers of the slave trade that supplied the molasses needed to produce rum (Kinney, 2000). Rum was then, so the history books say, transported to Europe on the same ships that went to Africa to carry the slaves back to America. According to British journalist Andrew Barr (1999), however, the triangular trade notion is a myth; the New Englanders loved the rum they distilled from Jamaican molasses. They consumed it themselves and made large profits through exports. Their role in the slave trade, as Barr suggests, was limited.

On the home front, per capita consumption of copious amounts of alcohol was the norm among early European Americans, and alcohol was measured in barrels (Hamid, 1998). While severe restrictions were placed on drinking by slaves, laborers digging the Erie Canal were allotted a quart of whiskey a day. When Congress passed an excise tax on whiskey in 1791, farmers and distillers staged the notorious Whiskey Rebellion, which had to be crushed with federal troops.

From 1785 to 1835, however, attitudes concerning alcohol began to change dramatically. During this period, as Peele (1989/1995) argues, drinking became a disruptive force for many Americans. As farmers turned surplus grain into whiskey, the old pattern of communal drinking began to break down; new patterns of solitary and binge drinking developed. The availability of cheap spirits, alcohol misuse, and family breakdown were all intertwined. For a dramatic description of the kind of havoc that could be wreaked on a population by access to vast quantities of rum, consider what Robert Hughes (1987) had to say of an early convict settlement in Australia:

> The most sought-after commodity of all was rum, a word which stood for spirits of all kinds. . . . In this little community (of about 10,000) nearly all the men and most of the women were addicted to alcohol. In Australia, especially between 1790 and

1820, rum became an overriding social obsession. Families were wrecked by it, ambitions destroyed, an iron chain of dependency forged. (p. 290)

Dr. Benjamin Rush, Surgeon General during the American Revolution, had observed firsthand the devastation wrought by rum rations on soldiers. In his pamphlet recording his observations, Rush pinpointed the dangers of potent alcohol. Through such writings and his personal influence, Rush provided a scientific voice to the call for an end to the distillation and drinking of whiskey and other spirits. This call was echoed by concerned family members and members of the clergy, especially the descendants of Puritans, who aligned themselves with concerned citizens to condemn the wasteful behavior and debauchery that was characteristic of the day. The new focus was on saving the family (Metzger, 1988).

Two currents of thought, the temperance and medical approaches, were inextricably interwoven in the 19th century, as in recent times. At the time, these views—the one stressing evil and the other illness—appeared in opposition. While one stressed the supply side of the drug alcohol, the other focused on reducing the need for the drug. Unity came because of awareness of a major social problem and the urgent need to address it (van Wormer, 1995).

A point worth noting: The temperance movement was about moderation, as the word implies. It was about control of "spirits," the distilled beverages, not of beer and wine. Another point worth noting concerns African traditions. The Africans who were brought to America as slaves came primarily from West African cultures. These, as W. L. White (1998) indicates, had blended alcohol into economic, social, and religious customs since antiquity. Under the institution of slavery, slave masters came to promote excessive alcohol use on festive occasions such as Christmas and July 4th. The major problem for early African Americans, as White further states, was the risk they faced when white people were inebriated.

In the mid-1800s, alcohol consumption was cut in half, and from then on dependence on the bottle was a speciality of a minority (Zeldin, 1994). But then a craze developed for patent medicines with a high opiate content. Morphine, in fact, was heralded as a treatment for chronic drinking problems (Conrad & Schneider, 1992). Often prescribed to older white women of high socioeconomic class, morphine frequently resulted in iatrogenic, or medically induced, addiction.

The year 1900 marked a prohibition readers will find surprising—the prohibition of tobacco. It was illegal to sell cigarettes in 14 states, and selling a lottery ticket was a federal crime (Savage, 1999). By that year the modern tobacco industry was already under way. A ruthless businessman of North Carolina named James Buchanan Duke successfully made use of a cigarette-rolling machine that made mass production of cigarettes possible (McGinn, 1997). A free bag of cigarettes was presented to millions of male immigrants who stepped off the boat onto U.S. soil. Many became hooked then right from the start. The Supreme Court upheld Tennessee's prohibition in the belief that cigarettes were a noxious product and because of their deleterious effects among young people.

All the while, opium, morphine, and heroin were being sold over the counter. Chewing tobacco, similarly, was acceptable, presumably only for men.

Smoking of opium was associated with Chinese immigrant laborers; their foreign ways were feared and resented, as was their drug use (Musto, 1999). The invention of the hypodermic needle and the synthesis of heroin from morphine at the end of the 19th century exacerbated the problem as well (Joseph, 1995). Inevitably, there was a national outcry for legislation to curb what was seen as the moral degeneracy associated with drug use. The same xenophobia aroused by heavy drinking among the poor, Catholic, European immigrants was a factor in the outcry against narcotic use as well.

Warnings of addiction as a result of morphine use began to appear in medical textbooks around 1900. In 1909 the import of opium was banned. Opium itself then became increasingly scarce at the consumer level, and heroin, a far more potent substance, not smoked but injected, became the popular form of administration of this drug. By banning alcohol and drugs, as Gardner (2000a) informs us, governments actually pressed users toward the most dangerous method of taking it.

Meanwhile, the intolerance for the smoking of cigarettes began to dissolve, its popularity boosted tremendously with the free distribution of cigarettes to World War I troops in France (Fishbein & Pease, 1996). The United States, as Zeldin argues, was remarkable for the suddenness with which it moved from drug to drug, "from one escape to another" (p. 231). And when prohibition of alcohol spread throughout the country, cola drinks laced with cocaine, as Zeldin further indicates, stepped in as the savior. Cocaine, in fact, was considered the remedy for addiction to other substances. Coca-Cola contained cocaine until 1903 and, not surprisingly, was an extremely popular "pick-me-upper."

The culmination of the fear of addiction and the association of the use of narcotics with the lower classes and foreigners culminated in the Harrison Act, which became law in 1914. The Harrison Act severely restricted the amount of opioids or cocaine in any remedy sold without a prescription (Musto, 1998).

Following World War I, a sociologically interesting development took place: "America no longer spoke of the inordinate American demand for drugs but instead of the evil intentions of countries that supplied them" (Musto, pp. 59–60). This shift in attitude regarding drugs and foreign nations was to have an enormous impact on U.S. policy from then on.

Let's backtrack a moment to consider cocaine, a drug, the effects of which have been much more pronounced on society than the sedating opiates could ever be. Cocaine, which was particularly popular in literary and intellectual circles, was widely used for everything from sinus troubles to hysteria (Abadinsky, 1996). Cocaine began to get a bad name, however, because of its association with bizarre behavior, including violence. After the turn of the century, cocaine became identified with the urban underworld moreover, according to Abadinsky, and southern blacks. Fear of the effects of cocaine intensified until official regulation was inevitable.

Paradoxically, after restrictive laws such as the Harrison Act were passed, doctors became reluctant to prescribe drugs to addicts, and the street cost of heroin rose from $6.50 an ounce to almost $100 an ounce (Musto, 1999). The drug problem grew more prominent, accordingly, than it had ever done before. Public fear of dope peddlers grew with the increase in arrests. The same "perverse progression" seen with other drugs that were banned was seen with cocaine (Gardner, 2000a). Fairly benign forms of consuming cocaine gave way to much more dangerous practices through drug interdiction. Addicts, as Gardner further argues, bankrupted by the inflated cost of illegal drugs, sought out drugs that gave the most "bang for the buck" and proceeded to use those drugs in the most cost-efficient way.

Marijuana was associated with Mexican immigrants in the southwestern United States. *Marijuana* is the Mexican colloquial term for a plant that has been cultivated throughout the world for at least 5,000 years (Schlosser, 1994). When anti-immigrant sentiment grew in the early 20th century (associated with a wave of emigration to the American Southwest following the Mexican Revolution of 1910), rumors began to spread that Mexicans were distributing the "killer weed" to American schoolchildren (Schlosser). The drug was also associated with jazz musicians in New Orleans. Between 1914 and 1931, 29 states had outlawed marijuana. The Marijuana Tax Act of 1937 essentially criminalized the possession of marijuana throughout the United States.

Then as now, seeking to influence international policies in other nations, the United States organized international conferences on the "drug menace." In response to this pressure, Britain passed the Dangerous Drug Act, which, like the Harrison Act, was intended to limit legal distribution of addictive drugs. Unlike in the United States, however, the new law was interpreted in favor of physicians to give them final authority in providing drugs to addicts as a legitimate form of treatment (Conrad & Schneider, 1992).

PROHIBITION OF ALCOHOL

Just as technological advances relevant to the drugs heroin and cocaine had led to the creation of a product that seemed beyond the capability of human beings to control their use of it, so it was with alcohol. The distillation process mentioned earlier carried the seeds of destruction. The temperance women, for this reason following the teachings of Dr. Rush, targeted strong liquor as the source of the evils they saw around them—chronic drunkenness, violence, and family poverty.

The temperance woman represented the Victorian ideal of purity; she fought alcohol as a rude intrusion upon the family, a threat to the family's very survival. Yet as Sandmaier (1992) indicates, the temperance woman was in fact more radical than her image suggests. She fought against men's drunkenness and for the liberation of women from the tyranny of this form of indulgence. Eventually, this volunteer army of churchwomen led into another movement of renown, the women's suffrage movement. The two movements were interconnected, in that men feared women's moral fervor and independence and that they would restrict men's drinking. As it was, however, the *men* were to outlaw the sale of alcoholic beverages themselves; only shortly thereafter did the woman win the right to vote.

To understand how the women's suffrage movement and prohibition came together, let us examine the historical record in the nation's heartland. In Iowa, the legislature's plan to make Iowa the first state to give women the right to vote was destroyed by a confluence of volatile issues, chief among which was liquor. In tracing the history of the male resistance to women's suffrage, Fruhling (1996) cites the stated fear that if women were permitted to vote, they might use that political clout to close the saloons where men squandered their time and the family's money. Iowa's native thirst, as Fruhling further indicates, grew even larger with the tide of German and Irish immigrants that began arriving in the 1840s; the neighborhood saloon was a hallowed tradition.

"The modern drunk is a 100-fold worse than the ancient drunk." So said the most renowned preacher of his day, the Reverend T. DeWitt Talmage (1887, p. 599). His comment was in reference to the process of distillation. Talmage, like other Protestants, called for the politicians of his day to take a stand "in the battle between drunkenness and sobriety, God and the devil" (p. 604).

Once it got under way, the temperance movement, like any social movement, went to extremes. So what had begun as an effort to protect people from strong brew became to some extent an attack on the people themselves and on the sorts of people who were the most prone to heavy drinking—the thousands upon thousands of immigrants to the United States (Helzer & Canino, 1992). A tremendous amount of beer was consumed by the large numbers of German immigrants. The Irish immigrants also carried their drinking habits with them. Unlike the Germans, the Irish tolerated a pattern of regular intoxication. The anti-immigrant and anti-Catholic nativism combined to give the temperance movement a new and fierce momentum. Saloons, which were frequented by the working class and immigrants, were feared as threats to the middle-class home and as forums for labor union organizers (Helzer & Canino, 1992). The Anti-Saloon League grew out of these sentiments and became a strong lobbying group.

Ironically, as Americans become more industrialized and disciplined, saloon life became more civilized (Rivers, 1994). Food was now served and women began to accompany their menfolk to these establishments. Drunkenness became socially disapproved. The shift from a temperance, controlled-use philosophy to a total-abstinence model marked a shift in public perception of alcoholism as a moral failing to that of a socially proscribed behavior (Benshoff & Janikowski, 2000).

By the time World War I broke out, anti-German prejudice was overwhelming. The support of the corporate world, which had an interest in promoting sober worker habits and reducing spending on alcohol, was instrumental in the passage of the Eighteenth Amendment to the Constitution, establishing national prohibition in 1919 (to begin in 1920).

Of attempts throughout the world to control the use of alcohol, the most resounding failure was that of the United States from 1920 to 1933 (*Encyclopaedia Britannica*, 1993). The American experiment with prohibition—the "noble experiment"—gave drinking the allure of the forbidden and led to the burgeoning and glamorizing of crime, the growth of organized crime, the corruption of police and politicians, and the criminalizing of ordinary citizens.

As with the Harrison Act and its aftermath, previously legal activities became illegal at the stroke of a pen (Rivers, 1994). And while these substances—some drugs, including alcohol—were banned, the tides had reversed. The cigarette bans were lifted. Smoking was on the road to becoming a glamorous, all-American habit (Savage, 1999). Today, as Hamid (1998) suggests, Americans approve of alcohol and tobacco consumption, although these substances are no less potentially destructive than the ones they have outlawed.

Despite the restrictions on alcohol, people still drank, often consuming home-brewed alcohol that was legal, moonshine, or alcohol that was from questionable sources and likely to contain adulterants. During Prohibition, drinking patterns shifted from beer to more potent liquor, because the latter was easier to transport illegally (Benshoff & Janikowski, 2000). Marijuana became increasingly popular. During the 1920s, moreover, women began to drink openly. Their drinking, as Carter (1997) argues, accelerated because of the greater freedom women experienced following World War I, the right to vote, and the relaxed sexual mores of the day. Women who drank publicly, however, remained linked in the public eye to promiscuity and bad motherhood.

Prohibition proved counterproductive not only because it encouraged beer drinkers to convert to spirits (easier for bootleggers to transport) but also because it made drinking synonymous with drunkenness (Barr, 1999).

With the widespread disrespect for the law that developed during Prohibition's attempt to regulate what could not be regulated, the growth of organized crime became linked with police and political corruption. Although the overall quantity of alcohol consumed did go down during this time, and the rate of cirrhosis of the liver with it, the death rate from poisoned liquor was appallingly high (Thorton, 1992). Homicide rates in the large cities almost doubled.

Economic interests coupled with disillusionment combined to put an end to "the noble experiment." The Depression created a desperate need for more jobs and government revenue. Couldn't the reestablishment of the liquor industry help in this regard? In 1933, the Eighteenth Amendment was repealed.

Today, the legacy of Prohibition remains. Age-restrictive laws have been instituted. Young people are told, in fact, that for them there is no difference between drinking and taking drugs (Barr, 1999). In contrast to the United States, which passed the National Minimum Drinking Age Act in 1984, restricting drinking in public places to age 21, Canada has not raised their age, which remains at 18 or 19, depending on the province. In the South and on many Indian reservations, dry counties and townships still outlaw the sale of alcohol, while Sunday sales of alcohol are illegal in many places. The war against other drugs is still waged on legal fronts, sometimes by means of well-publicized semi-military-style operations.

The United States was not the only country to experience the ramifications of a temperance movement. After World War I began, support for prohibition increased in Canada. By 1918, every Canadian province except Quebec had adopted a prohibition law. Economic incentives were influential, however, in dimming Canadian enthusiasm for the restrictions. Great profits were to be made from sales to persons south of the border. The prohibition laws in Canada were therefore rescinded in most provinces.

Iceland, Norway, and Finland also outlawed the sale of alcohol for a period in the early 20th century. Today, Sweden, Finland, and Norway have high alcohol taxes by European standards and restrict sales to state-owned shops. Now that Sweden and Finland have joined the European Union, however, the days of state-sponsored temperance may be over. In Ireland, a strong religious-based temperance crusade resulted in large numbers taking a pledge of total abstinence (this pledge is the origin of the word *teetotaler*). Today almost 33% of the Irish are teetotalers (Clarity, 1995). A temperance movement in the 1920s in the Soviet Union was short lived, however; the answer to the serious vodka consumption problem was sought in the socialist way of life (S. White, 1996). Communism was incompatible with alcoholism, or so it was thought. Vodka, besides, had been a significant source of government revenue since the 16th century, a resource that was as significant as tax collection. For a brief period in 1985 under Gorbachev, directives against the use of alcohol at public banquets and receptions were issued, the sale of alcohol to persons under age 21 was forbidden, and public drunkenness was severely punished.

MARIJUANA CONTROL EFFORTS

During the 1920s and 1930s, most of the states with large Mexican populations enacted antimarijuana legislation. Because marijuana smoking was common among Mexican migrant workers and other marginalized groups, racism seemingly was the key factor in the passage of the restrictive legislation (Musto, 1998). Hysterical literature of the day portrayed the marijuana user as more or less deranged, as engaging in drug-induced acts of sadistic violence (Abadinsky, 1996). In 1937, influenced by media propaganda such as the 1936 motion picture *Reefer Madness* (a film that is a great source of amusement today), Congress passed the Marijuana Tax Act. A series of harsh antidrug laws carrying severe penalties were enacted in the 1950s.

Each of the postwar periods (following the world wars) was a time of fear and suspicion leading to scapegoating. So strict laws carrying mandatory sentences were passed at these times. Tolerance of addiction was then attacked, as Musto (1998) argues, as a weakness of ill-informed persons. Opposition to the harsh sentencing laws by the American Bar Association and the American Medical Association, however, remained strong. The pendulum of drug policy began to shift in peacetimes, accordingly, from a law enforcement model toward a treatment model (Abadinsky, 1996). Meanwhile, drug penalties had been reduced for all drugs, but especially for possession of marijuana, which had now become associated with middle-class youth. There was no longer a marijuana scare at this time.

MODERN WAR ON DRUGS

Presidential access to the media, in conjunction with the media's capacity to make or break a politician, is a dynamic not to be overlooked in setting the stage for a mobilization of public opinion. So even though drug use was on the decline in the 1980s, political leaders moved to place illegal drugs on the public agenda (Jernigan & Dorfman, 1996).

Controlling drug use was an attractive political issue for conservatives because it drew attention to individual deviance and immorality and away from questions of economic inequality and injustice (Jensen & Gerber, 1998). The drug scare was played up in the media with an orgy of news coverage to create an image of inner-city explosion centering on crack cocaine. Public opinion changed dramatically following the barrage of news "exposés." Actually, Richard Nixon was the first American president to declare what he metaphorically called a "War on Drugs," a strategy he devised to separate himself from Lyndon Johnson's liberal "War on Poverty." His metaphor grew into a reality as the Reagan, Bush, and Clinton administrations poured billions of dollars into a massive military operation to fight the enemy (drug suppliers) at home and on foreign soil. The political rhetoric connecting youth, violence, minorities, and crime has persisted in the minds of Americans for two decades, largely due to the crusading efforts of the New Right (Jensen & Gerber, 1998) (see chapter 13).

Like its predecessor, Prohibition, America's war on drugs is directed toward the poor, especially those associated with urban social disorder. Also as with the criminalization of alcohol, criminalization of these drugs represents a desperate attempt to curb the unstoppable. With 70% of the federal government's expenditure on the drug problem going to law enforcement agencies and just 30% for prevention and treatment (Mauer, 1995), the focus is clearly not on rehabilitation but on punishment. And like antidrug legislation in the past, much of the blame is aimed at foreign forces, namely, the drug suppliers. If the supply can be stopped, whether through use of weaponry or economic sanctioning, so the reasoning goes, illegal drug use on the streets can be curbed. Media accounts, as Jernigan and Dorfman (1996) document, play up the "us against foreigners" theme, the foreign governments generally being shown to lack commitment to work with the United States to eradicate the problem. One of the most disturbing aspects of the War on Drugs is the undeniable racism entailed in the discrepancy between the sentences mandated for possession of the cheaper variety of cocaine (crack) and for the more expensive variety (powdered cocaine).

As the War on Drugs has become a war on street crimes, a bonanza for drug enforcement enterprises has been created. Seizing drug-related assets has become more rewarding to police departments than the arrest itself. The profit side of property seizures is paralleled in the prison industry, now often privatized to meet the burgeoning demand for prison cells for persons convicted of drug offenses.

Relentless international pressure has been exerted on European as well as Latin American countries, much of it aimed at the United Nations World Health

Organization to conform to the image of drug use as a crime problem, not a health problem, and to reinforce drug control policies (Erickson & Butters, 1998). A special report in the Canadian *Ottawa Citizen* (Gardner, 2000b) provides details of the kind of economic pressure the United States has exerted on the Canadian, European, and Australian governments to pursue a global anti-drug military operation. European ideology, however, is geared toward a pragmatic, public health approach that is clearly at loggerheads with American moralism and inflexibility (see chapter 13 on public policy).

HISTORY OF ADDICTION TREATMENT

Our focus now turns from the control of drug use and sales to the treatment of individuals with substance misuse problems. Today, of the 13 million to 16 million people in need of treatment for addiction problems in any given year, only 3 million receive care (U.S. Department of Health and Human Services, 2000). Problems with alcohol account for almost half of all admissions, followed by opiates, cocaine, and marijuana (SAMHSA, 1998). Only 3% of pathological gamblers seek professional help.

Throughout most of the United States, as we have seen, religious institutions with a Protestant affiliation have viewed alcohol, gambling, and drug addiction as sinful or irresponsible behavior. Only after Philadelphia physician Benjamin Rush authored his influential pamphlet *An Inquiry into the Effects of Ardent Spirits on the Human Mind and Body* (1785) did a paradigm shift begin to emerge (Thombs, 1999). In his notion of alcohol, especially distilled alcohol, as highly addictive and the compulsion to drink as extremely powerful in some individuals, Rush anticipated much of the modern, post-Prohibition thinking about alcoholism and other addictions. Rush was also the first American medical practitioner to recommend medical treatment for chronic "inebriates."

When the attempt to control the supply side of alcohol that was Prohibition was revealed as a dismal failure, the emphasis was taken off the production of the beverage alcohol and on characteristics of the individual drinker (Thombs, 1999). During the second half of the 19th century, there was increased medical awareness of health problems associated with alcohol misuse, accompanied by a rapid growth in the number of institutions specializing in the treatment of addiction. Indeed, as William White (1998), author of the definitive study on addictions treatment history, *Slaying the Dragon: The History of Addiction Treatment and Recovery in America,* suggests, the notion of providing care for persons afflicted with alcoholic disorders goes back to ancient Egypt. And in America, mutual-aid societies were formed, often by groups of recovering alcoholics, some as early as 1750.

With the end of Prohibition in 1933, the population at large began to move toward the view that alcoholics were sick, not sinful (Barr, 1999; Robertson, 1998). The creation of Alcoholics Anonymous was instrumental in reducing some of the stigma associated with alcoholism and in offering a highly structured program for recovery. After the 21st Amendment to the Constitution was passed, a new approach to viewing the problem related to alcohol was needed. The remarkable contribution of two alcoholics, Bill W. (Bill Wilson) and Dr. Bob, was to join the new disease conception of alcoholism emerging out of academic research institutes and into a remarkable organizational network of supporters united by a set of simply formulated principles of sobriety, The Twelve Steps. Although Bill Wilson himself avoided referring to alcoholism as a disease to stay out of medical controversy, he did use terms such as malady, illness, and allergy to depict the condition of active alcoholism (Davis & Jansen, 1998). Both members of the Oxford Group Movement, an evangelical Protestant organization, Bill W. and Dr. Bob adopted the principles of the movement and, according to Peele and Bufe (2000), who cited Bill Wilson's writings, codified the central principles into the Twelve Steps. The notions of powerlessness, seeking divine guidance, confession making and restitution, and carrying the message to other persons were among the concepts borrowed. So influential was Bill Wilson, one of the two founders of Alcoholics Anonymous (AA), in fact, that recently, he was selected by *Time* magazine as one of the 100 most influential people of the 20th century, a trailblazer who helped shape the century. "From the rubble of a wasted life, he overcame alcoholism and cofounded the Twelve-Step program that has helped millions of others do the same"—or so the *Time* article on Bill W. begins (Cheever, 1999, p. 201). Today, as the article indicates, more than 2 million members in 150 countries hold meetings in church basements, school gyms, and hospital conference rooms. Although the original members of AA created the Twelve Steps as a guide for alcoholics, other self-help programs have borrowed them and adapted them to help people struggling with eating disorders, gambling addiction, cocaine and heroin addiction, and sexual compulsions, to name a few. Publication of the book *Alcoholics Anonymous* (affectionately known as "The Big Book") in 1939 marked a milestone in substance abuse treatment history. When an article on AA appeared in the *Saturday Evening Post* in 1941, the effect was stunning (W. L. White, 1998). Growth of AA groups skyrocketed from that point on. Narcotics Anonymous (NA) was officially launched in 1949. (See chapter 12 for more on mutual-help groups).

Not only was the AA influence felt at the level of self-help groups, but the reduction in stigmatization of alcoholics revolutionized professional treatment as well. Keep in mind that in the period before AA was founded, treatment for alcoholics was at a primitive level. The period is known today as the "snake pit" era of alcohol treatment (Knapp, 1997). "Inebriates," as they were called, when hospitalized, were usually locked up with the mentally ill and considered hopeless.

Today, the Twelve-Step influence is pronounced, although not dominant, in Europe. Disease-model programs designed along American lines generally are relegated to the private treatment sector and can be expensive. Ireland, perhaps because of its strong religious traditionalism, has embraced the Minnesota Model, which teaches the principle of powerlessness and the need to surrender oneself to a Higher Power, both principles derived from the Twelve Steps of recovery. Because of the compatibility between the precepts of this program and

Irish cultural norms, the Minnesota Model has come to exert a major influence on Irish services for problem drinkers (Butler, 1996). The nonhiring of social workers for these programs has resulted in the exclusion of approaches such as motivational interviewing and solution-focused therapy, which as Butler notes, are favored by Irish social workers. Norway, in contrast, a more secular country, officially has resisted incorporating treatment based on Twelve-Step principles in their social welfare system. And extensive media coverage of scandalous practices at one Minnesota-based treatment center did not help matters (see van Wormer, 1997). However, this model, as adapted for Norwegian consumption, thrives today in a small disease-model program in rural Norway, the only such program in that country that receives extensive county, as opposed to private, funding. Box 2.1 provides a rare look at this program.

Jellinek's Pioneering Study

In many ways, Jellinek's book *The Disease Concept of Alcoholism,* written in 1960, is more progressive and up to date than much of the writing from the past two decades, a lot of it paradoxically citing Jellinek on the disease model. E. M. Jellinek was a statistician who conducted systematic research on male AA members. His goal was to study alcoholism in its many varieties. Jellinek's worldwide travels for the World Health Organization helped provide him with an international perspective for research, a perspective that provided the basis for his typology of alcoholics.

The cultural patterns that differentiate one country from another, according to Jellinek, help account for the drinking patterns. Thus, the Italian contempt for alcohol intoxication is in contrast to the French tolerance for intoxication, accompanied by an insistence that everyone must drink. Furthermore, as Jellinek observed, the drinking patterns are to a large extent ascribable to the beverages that contain the alcohol—that is, wine or beer are associated with continual use and distilled spirits with "concentrated" consumption over short periods.

Using letters of the Greek alphabet, Jellinek singled out five "species of alcoholism" that he considered to be disease related:

- *Alpha alcoholism* represents an undisciplined use of alcoholic beverages. Drinking may relieve emotional disturbance, but relationship problems are caused thereby. There is no progression.
- *Beta alcoholism* involves heavy drinking, causing physical complications such as gastritis and cirrhosis of the liver, yet without physical or psychological dependence on alcohol.
- *Gamma alcoholism* is characterized by increased tissue tolerance, withdrawal symptoms when drinking is discontinued, and loss of control. A marked progression occurs, with interpersonal relations impaired to the highest degree. This variety predominates in Great Britain and northern Europe. Most AA members have experienced this kind of alcoholism.
- *Delta alcoholism* is similar to gamma alcoholism but without the loss of control over the amount consumed, only an inability to abstain for even one

	ALCOHOLISM TREATMENT
BOX 2.1	THRIVES IN NORWAY
	BY KATHERINE VAN WORMER, MSSW, PH.D.

Imagine a treatment center with little paperwork and no insurance reimbursement forms in a country where workers get paid leave as needed, even for family sessions. Literacy is 100%, and most alcoholism is still of the "pure" variety (except for pill misuse). This is the reality in Norway, an American substance abuse counselor's dream. It wasn't always this way, however.

The first time I went to Norway (I worked there from 1988 to 1990), I was hired to train alcoholism counselors about the basics of the Minnesota Model. My personal reasons for going had more to do with seeing the scenery and the desire to experience firsthand a truly benevolent social welfare state. This was just as well, given the way things turned out, because the treatment center was straight out of Schaef's *The Addictive Organization.* (To learn of the bizarre goings-on there, see van Wormer, 1997.)

In any case, I was back in Norway in the summer of 1997, less than 100 miles from where I had lived and worked before. Once again I found myself in the land of sculptured trolls and Vikings, snow-streaked mountaintops, log cabins, and pine-finished houses, purple wildflowers, perpetual summer light, and dark-green landscapes dotted with pale birch trees. And once again I was enjoying meals of moose meat with *tyttebaer* jam and baked salmon. But I wasn't here for the scenery or the meals. This time I was here for professional reasons.

In truth, I never expected to return to Norway, much less to an alcoholism treatment center where I would teach a workshop on the nature of addiction. But here I was in the company of two of the strongest personalities from my earlier work: Randi Isdahl, now the director of the clinic she founded, and Kirsten Male, a social worker and my personal translator. Isdahl, the director of *ValdresKlinikken* (Valdres Clinic), had been the assistant director and my supervisor previously at the other clinical position she had held with the fierce loyalty of the "true believer." But one day when the owner-director's antisocial behavior became apparent to her, she simply walked out.

Following a period of utter disillusionment and depression, Isdahl saw that her only chance to help fellow alcoholics as she had been helped would be through opening her own inpatient treatment center. Following a course of training in Sweden and at Hazelden in Minnesota, Isdahl assembled a group of talented people. Together they opened Valdres Clinic, a private, nonprofit, Twelve-Step inpatient program, the first treatment center of its kind in this part of Norway. Gradually, word spread about lives that were "turned around," and credibility with the local authorities followed. Male, my translator and political ally from previous days, had, like me, been fired for revealing the truth about client and staff abuse at the first treatment center.

Now happily working at a nearby social office (the equivalent of the Department of Health and Human Services in the United States), Male was a source of support and referral to the clinic. She and Isdahl, who had been on opposite sides of the earlier staff dispute, had become friends. Finding myself in Norway again, I marveled at the growing friendship and professional growth of these two extraordinary women, whose experience with life and addiction had instilled in them an almost religious calling to serve.

I expected the treatment center to be a small replica of Hazelden transplanted among fjords and cliffs. So I was not surprised that the basic program included group therapy, lectures, films, Alcoholics Anonymous meetings, and workbook assignments tied to the Twelve Steps of recovery. What did surprise me were certain innovations in treatment drawn not from Minnesota but from the East—from China and India.

Today, Valdres Clinic offers a comprehensive program built on the following elements:

- *From the West*—The concept of alcoholism as a disease—a personal and family disease—the treatment of which looks to extensive feeling work, communication emphasis, spirituality, and personal sharing.
- *From the East*—Detoxification of all clients, not through drugs but through acupuncture under medical supervision. This involves the application of needles to five points in the ear for 40 minutes a day in early treatment (ear points relate to the endorphins in the brain, liver, lungs, and kidneys); meditation with music; and a highly nutritious diet. [Isdahl brought these aspects of the program back from India, where she had visited an amazing treatment center for opium addicts on the upper floors of a New Delhi police station.]
- *From the welfare state*—The generous Norwegian social welfare system provides complete funding for five weeks of inpatient treatment, including an extensive family-week program. Aftercare is provided through the government-sponsored *Rusteam*, with its extensive network of clinics throughout the country. These state-run offices provide follow-up psychological work for trauma and mental disorders.

In the seven years I was away, Norway's alcoholism treatment program has improved, providing enhanced funding and greater options. Meanwhile, in the United States, treatment options are dictated more by reimbursement policies than by client need, and the extravagance of the War on Drugs charade ties up badly needed resources. In my return visit to Norway, I did not know how to explain what had happened to treatment in the United States in the past seven years. I didn't even try.

References

Stenius, K. (1991, Spring). The most successful treatment model in the world: Introduction of the Minnesota model in Nordic countries. *Contemporary Drug Problems, 18*, 151–179.

van Wormer, K. (1995). Whistleblowing against the company: A case of ethical violations at a Norwegian treatment center. *International Journal of Drug Abuse, 6*(1), 8–15.

van Wormer, K. (1997). Doing alcoholism treatment in Norway: A personal reminiscence. *Reflections, 3*(3), 67–71.

Source: NASW ATOD section: *Issues of Substance*, October, 1997, pp. 12–15. Reprinted by permission of NASW.

day. There are no distressing social problems over the quantity consumed, though health problems may result. This is the predominant pattern in France.

- *Epsilon alcoholism* is periodic alcoholism. In their periodic bouts, binge drinkers suffer a great deal of physical and emotional damage.

Of all the types of alcoholism, according to Jellinek, only the gamma and delta varieties can be considered addictions and/or diseases. Gorski (1998) includes the *epsilon* type, or binge drinking, in this category. Regardless, the significance in Jellinek's writings is his conception of varieties of alcohol problems, not of one monolithic drinking disorder. Unfortunately, his work has been immortalized in the form of the Jellinek curve. The curve, designed by Maxwell Glatt, depicted only one type of alcoholism, the gamma variety—primary, chronic, progressive, and, if untreated, fatal. Virtually every treatment center in the United States has adopted this formulation, often presented to their clients in the form of a lecture. The model of gradual progression into heavier and heavier drinking and to high tolerance as well as to physical, mental, and moral destruction applies to many but not to all, and not very well to polydrug or amphetamine misusers. *The Disease Concept of Alcoholism*, notes W. L. White (1998), remains one of the most frequently cited and least read books in the alcoholism field. This book, in fact, never said alcoholism was a disease: What Jellinek said was that alcoholism is *like* a disease.

"The problem that I had all along in the field of addiction," notes Gorski, "is that most people treating alcoholics never went back to this original source document, which very clearly presented an understanding of alcoholism and divided it into five subtypes" (p. 100). Gorski wisely warns his colleagues in the field against making one of two biased overgeneralizations—thinking everyone with a drinking problem has a progressive, fatal disease requiring treatment or, conversely, throwing out the disease model altogether and seeing only alcohol problems where there may be a devastating illness.

The Disease Concept of Alcoholism had a profound impact on the state of the art of addiction treatment. This work provided just the sort of data and analysis needed at the time to convince members of Congress and the medical community alike that alcoholics are not immoral but persons with a disease (or diseaselike condition) and that, once addicted, the problem drinker is no longer able to control his or her other drinking: These were the basic conclusions of Jellinek's work, conclusions that jelled nicely with the basic premises of AA and gave the rapidly growing organization a considerable boost.

The political implications of the disease concept should not be underestimated. The assumption that alcoholism is a pathology that lies within the individual and that the pathology can be measured and treated are basic to the medical or disease model. When the World Health Organization acknowledged alcoholism as a medical problem in 1951 and the American Medical Association declared alcoholism an illness in 1956 and a disease in 1966, the transformation to the medicalization of alcoholism was complete. The hospital now had replaced the church and legislators as the center of social control of a newly designated disease. Rather than punitive, the social response to alcoholism had become therapeutic. The new ideology provided a rationale for costly complex medical approaches and for an extensive treatment apparatus. It absolved alcoholics of responsibility for the etiology of the disease but gave them the responsibility to seek treatment. Moreover, the disease model appealed to moderate drinkers in its implication that only alcoholics are at risk. Finally, the American disease model was promoted by the alcohol beverage industry because it removed the blame from the alcohol and its sale and distribution (Barr, 2000).

In 1970, the Hughes Act was passed. This Act, which was named after its primary sponsor, Senator Harold Hughes, provided for major research funding by the federal government and emphasized improved services for alcoholics (McNeece & DiNitto, 1998). Known officially as the Comprehensive Alcoholism Prevention and Treatment Act, this statute created the National Institute on Alcohol Abuse and Alcoholism (NIAAA). The federal seed money spawned the growth of alcoholism treatment centers across the United States, a growth that, as W. L. White (1998) observes, was almost explosive in its intensity.

And how about treatment of other drug addictions? Public concern over drug use and dependency among returning Vietnam veterans and the whole baby boom generation led President Nixon to declare drug abuse "America's Public Enemy Number One" (cited by W. L. White, p. 266). The National Institute on Drug Abuse (NIDA) was established as a research institute, along with federally funded drug abuse treatment programs in what was to be the first national system of addictions treatment. Although alcoholism treatment centers and drug abuse treatment centers are no longer separate, NIAAA and NIDA continue as separate research entities, an artificial separation that is inconsistent with modern scientific research on the brain and the nature of addiction.

The Antitreatment Backlash

In his sweeping history of addiction treatment, *Slaying the Dragon,* William White provides the best account that we have come across in the literature of the ideological and cultural backlash against addiction treatment that took place in the 1980s and 1990s. In some ways the climate for the backlash was set under the Reagan era, when zero tolerance to drug users dominated the airwaves. In some ways too, the new ideology was promoted at the level of popular culture. A deluge of articles and books were published at this time, including Peele's (1989) *The Diseasing of America* and Fingarette's (1988) *Heavy Drinking: The Myth of Alcoholism as a Disease.* Although these writings said a lot that needed to be said concerning the multi-million-dollar substance abuse treatment industry and the oversimplified alcoholism-as-disease model that was its raison d'être, the impact of this intellectual denigration of mainstream treatment was profound. Book reviews were exclamatory and, at times, laudatory. From the back cover of *Heavy Drinking: The Myth of Alcoholism as a Disease,* we read, for example, "Herbert Fingarette is at the forefront of a social counterrevolution that could redefine how the United States views alcoholism (*Christian Science Monitor*)."

Such a counterrevolution is evident today in the growing number of court decisions upholding the denial of benefits on the grounds that alcoholism results, not from a disease, but from "willful misconduct" (W. L. White, p. 284). Moreover, in light of what the court saw as the religious aspect of AA and NA, court-mandated attendance at such meetings has been determined to be a violation of the First-Amendment requirement of separation of church and state. Uniformly, four higher courts have ruled on this matter (for details see Peele & Bufe, 2000). This is an issue within some U.S. prisons; substance abuse counselors, accordingly, are instructed, as in Iowa and New York State, to seek alternative treatment models. Significantly, Stephanie Covington's (1999) *Helping Women Recover,* espousing a program for use in the criminal justice system, is a multidimensional manual that is holistic in focus. The four modules of this program are devoted to work on self, relationships, sexuality, and spirituality. A holistic rather than traditional disease model is the underlying philosophy of this program.

The positive dimension of the rising skepticism over the dominant U.S. treatment model has been the opening of the door to alternative treatments. Unfortunately, the impact of the writings of scholars such as Fingarette and Peele seems to be associated with a trend to speak of "bad habits" instead of disease and even with a shift back toward blame and stigmatization of addicts and their substances of misuse. The available funding for treatment ironically is connected to the criminal justice system rather than to medically based services. Managed care treatment options, including generous reimbursement for inpatient and extended outpatient programs, have been severely curtailed (Gleick, 1996). Typically, managed care companies accept as providers only traditional mental health professionals (Vandivort-Warren, 1996).

The impact has been positive for the professionalization of the substance abuse field but negative in terms of the bureaucratic restraints. In a country (alone among industrialized nations) without nationalized health care, comprehensive insurance coverage for alcoholism and other drug addiction treatment needs to be mandated for all insurance and public welfare policies. To exchange the disease model for a punitive focus on individual responsibility may be less a step forward than two steps back.

A *Washington Post* article by Rosin (2000) illustrates the point. Church-based drug treatment centers with little accountability to the state have sprung up in Texas under then-Governor Bush's experiment in social welfare reform. "Drug addiction is NOT a disease. It's a sin." So says the sign over the door of one of the new treatment centers. All the major counseling professions, including the American Counseling Association, the American Psychological Association, and the National Association of Alcoholism and Drug Abuse Counselors, have gone on record to oppose public funding of faith-based substance abuse treatment. This approach is hardly the one secular critics such as Fingarette and Peele had in mind. What they share is a focus that is not disease based and not therapeutic.

The Introduction of Harm Reduction

The history of substance abuse treatment is still being written. During the 1980s, a grassroots movement called *harm reduction* emerged in the Netherlands and northern England; it emerged somewhat later in Australia (Inciardi & Harrison, 2000; MacCoun, 1998). The spread of AIDS at this time was seen as a bigger threat than illegal drugs and the prospect of a plague of deaths as more compelling than addiction. The focus therefore is pragmatic: In order to save lives, help drug users modify their behavior. Thus, in the interests of public health, interventions such as needle exchanges—the exchange of dirty needles for clean ones—methadone maintenance, and treatment instead of incarceration are applied.

Remember that in Britain, the medical profession had almost unlimited freedom to prescribe morphine and heroin to addicts. This policy persisted into the 1960s (Abadinsky, 1996). A significant increase in the number of heroin users and a scandal caused by a few doctors who diverted heroin onto a black market brought inevitable restrictions. Today, only specially licensed doctors can provide heroin or cocaine to verified addicts.

In the United States, over 100 needle exchange programs have been set up in urban areas. For political reasons, however, federal funding has been denied. Whereas the British approach is to provide carefully monitored doses of heroin to heroin addicts (in heroin maintenance programs), the substitution of the synthetic drug methadone for heroin is the only legal recourse.

With regard to alcohol use, harm reduction focuses on such preventive measures as designated driver programs and moderate versus binge drinking. One of the most significant developments in substance abuse treatments is the growing popularity of motivational enhancement therapy, an approach introduced by American psychologist William Miller and his associates to European audiences (see Miller, 1996, and chapter 3 in this text). Immediately popular in Europe, where harsh confrontation of addicts was never popular, this client-centered approach is one of that is increasingly favored by insurance companies because of its cost effectiveness.

When the Hazelden Treatment Center opened in Minnesota in 1949, drug and alcohol sanitaria were popularly conceived as snake pits run by quacks (Karlen, 1995). The medical profession, like the general public, had little faith that alcoholics, once hooked, could recover. As developed at Willmar State Hospital and later at Hazelden, the Minnesota Model took a multidisciplinary approach (W. L. White, 1998). From psychology, therapy was borrowed, from the clergy (usually Lutherans), spirituality, and from the mutual-help group of Alcoholics Anonymous, group-based treatment and the Twelve Steps. The integration of recovering, nonprofessionally trained counselors as a legitimate component of the alcoholism treatment team was the key innovation of this model. In the early days there was harsh confrontation in group settings; today, the regime is a pale replica of some of the antics that went on before. Gender-specific programs are offered for men and women. The sexes, in fact, are kept completely separate at all times to prevent what Norwegian Minnesota Model counselors call "abstinence romance." So much treatment takes place in the state today that Minnesota sometimes is facetiously called "the land of 10,000 treatment centers." In fact, thousands of former clients of this and the dozens of other similar treatment centers in Minnesota, many of whom come from cities on the East and West Coasts, have stayed on in nearby Minneapolis for the group support that is provided there.

In the late 1970s, when Betty Ford went public with her alcoholism, 28 inpatient days of treatment was the norm. Insurance coverage was readily available, and mass media accounts of celebrities in recovery following treatment were positive. The cumulative effect of two decades of public education on alcoholism, coupled with growing concerns about a youthful polydrug epidemic, bore legislative fruit (W. L. White, 1998). By the early 1970s, more than 30 separate agencies and departments of the federal government were involved in some aspect of substance abuse treatment. A new trend was the integration of drug treatment and alcoholism treatment, fields that had been totally separate previously. The thinking had been that these addictions were unrelated. Sometimes as a result, as White indicates, residential drug abuse treatment centers focused entirely on drinking, which left alcoholic clients open to switch to other sedatives, such as prescription medications. Awareness of the reality of cross-addiction and, later, of facts about brain chemistry of addiction-prone people encouraged a merging of the two specializations, alcoholism treatment and drug abuse treatment. In the growing use of terms such as *addiction, substance abuse,* and *chemical dependency,* the professional literature reflected this merger. During the 1970s and 1980s, a parallel big business emerged, the substance abuse treatment industry. Many faltering hospitals' finances were jacked up by filling an extensive number of hospital beds with recovering alcoholics. Beginning in the 1990s, third-party payers balked; many in need of treatment were now denied it. Sadly, the building of prisons to house persons in trouble because of their substance misuse seems to have become the current ideological focus.

SUMMARY AND CONCLUSION

Professional addictions treatment arrived on the scene late. Long before there was professional treatment, there was the enjoyment of a variety of mood-altering substances. Whether deriving their pleasure from fermented fruit, coca leaves, or poppy flowers, people have always and will always seek refuge through the means available to them. In this chapter, we have seen how the drug of choice during one era was the substance most vile in the next. The way a particular drug was regarded depended on the circumstances of its use, on the political climate, but especially on what sorts of people were associated with its use (for example, war heroes, "down-and-outs," genteel ladies.). The decision pertaining to which drug or drugs to outlaw clearly had little to do with public health considerations.

In the days before water purification, alcohol was often safer than water. Although the Puritans who set up their theocracy in early America set the climate for a kind of moralism that would long outlast its religious bearings, they and their earliest descendants consumed vast quantities of beer and cider. There were few problems associated with this drinking; drunkenness was frowned upon, punished through public ridicule, and for the most part avoided.

The switch from wine to beer to more potent liquor was associated with public drunkenness and violent behavior. In Britain, the infant mortality rate soared; on American shores, male-drinking cults disrupted family life. Thus the stage was set for a temperance movement, with international consequences. Since excessive drinking in America came to be associated with newly arrived immigrant groups, a politically charged call for abstinence was in order.

Throughout this chapter, we have seen the pendulum swing from prohibition of one substance to prohibition of another. Zero tolerance of certain drugs has culminated in a War on Drugs of vast proportions: A military crusade in drug-supplying countries is matched on the home front by the incarceration of over 1 million people for drug-related crimes. Meanwhile, the sale of illegal drugs has become an underground enterprise of unbelievable proportions. Not only are individual and family economies affected, but also the economies of entire nations.

Economics, too, has played a role in the sale and distribution of legal drugs. On the North American continent, as this brief historical review shows, products with addictive properties assumed great economic importance. Tobacco was a commodity that, as the early settlers realized, could sustain the economic life of a colony, both in terms of exports and in the money raised from taxes. The sale and consumption of alcohol, likewise, played a major role in American economic history. Economics determined the manner in which alcohol was consumed, whether as wine from cultivated vines or in the form of distilled spirits, such as rum, which could be produced cheaply from molasses and transported cheaply as well. During Prohibition the price of liquor shot up, and many working-class people could no longer afford to drink. For those who could afford to buy it, distilled alcohol became much preferred over beer. Liquor was easier to conceal, and people who were now breaking the law anyway were inclined to go all out, gulping down drink after drink with the abandonment that often accompanies lawbreaking.

Besides the obvious harms caused by Prohibition, including the personal and political corruption, the economic incentive to get people back to work following the Great Depression was a key factor in the legalization of alcohol. Once the distilleries and breweries were humming again, tax revenues were pouring in, and people's drinking habits could be to some extent controlled. The quality of the alcohol sold could be controlled as well. Gambling, similarly, has gone from the underground economy to being a big money maker for the states and Indian reservations. Some form of legalized gambling is available in all but three states in the United States (Utah, Hawaii, and Tennessee), and in Oregon it's the second-highest source of revenue for the state budget.

Economic interests and ideology came together as the disease model began to gain currency in the public mind. While temperance leaders had blamed both the drinker and the drug itself for drug-related problems, AA proponents later shifted the focus to *individual* susceptibilities. This shift in focus away from placing the blame on the drug alcohol was of course highly acceptable to the liquor industry. Ideologically, the strong punitive slant evidenced in the United States today has its roots in the moralism of an earlier time. The story of substance abuse treatment in this and other countries is a story of the wrestling between the forces of moralism and diseases, forces that philosophically are often hard to separate.

Starting in the 1950s, as we have seen, the treatment for alcoholism took a progressive turn in its conceptualization of addiction as a disease rather than a sin. What we now sometimes call the Minnesota Model adopted many of the precepts of Alcoholics Anonymous. Harsh confrontation of alcoholics "in denial" has given way in recent years to a more client-friendly approach. Today, Alcoholics Anonymous, Narcotics Anonymous, and family member self-help groups have brought help and guidance to millions across the world. As the addictions field has matured, it has moved away from the dogmatic authoritarianism of the early days to the use of motivational strategies geared to clients' individual needs. Still, much disagreement and confusion remain about the nature of addiction; this confusion spurs acrimonious debates about public drug control policy. Issues that need to be resolved in the future relevant to addictions treatment are inequities in the sentencing laws, the War on Drugs, which has become a war on poor people of color, the need for a return to judicial discretion (as opposed to mandatory minimum sentencing of drug users), and more treatment/prevention options for people with chemical dependency problems.

References

Abadinsky, H. (1996). *Drug abuse: An introduction* (3rd ed.). Belmont, CA: Wadsworth.

Ayto, J. (1990). *Dictionary of word origins.* New York: Arcade.

Barr, A. (1999). *Drink: A social history of America.* New York: Carroll & Graf.

Bell, R. (1987). *Holy anorexia.* Chicago: University of Chicago Press.

Benshoff, J., & Janikowski, T. (2000). *Rehabilitation model of substance abuse counseling.* Belmont, CA: Wadsworth.

Bower, B. (1994). Ancient site taps into soldiers' brew. *Science News, 146,* 390.

Brecher, E. M. (1972). *Licit and illegal drugs.* Boston: Little, Brown.

Butler, S. (1996). Substance misuse and the social work ethos. *Journal of Substance Misuse, 1*(3), 149–154.

Carter, C. S. (1997). Ladies don't: A historical perspective on attitudes toward alcoholic women. *Affilia, 12*(4), 471–485.

Cheever, S. (1999, June 14). Bill W.: The healer. *Time,* 201–204.

Clarity, J. F. (1995, January 17). In Irish pubs, sober talk of a new road hazard. *New York Times,* A6.

Conrad, P., & Schneider, J. (1992). Opiate addiction. In P. Conrad and J. Schneider (Eds.), *Deviance and medicalization: From badness to sickness* (pp. 110–144). Philadelphia: Temple University Press.

Covington, S. (1999). *Helping women recover: A program for treating substance abuse, special criminal justice edition.* San Francisco: Jossey-Bass.

Davis, D. R., and Jansen, G. G. (1998). Making meaning of Alcoholics Anonymous for social workers: Myths, metaphors, and realities. *Social Work, 43*(2), 169–183.

Denzin, N. (1993). *The alcohol society: Addiction and recovery of the self.* Somerset, NJ: Transaction.

Documentary looks at drinking in America (1999, September 13). *Waterloo-Cedar Falls Courier,* C8.

Encyclopaedia Britannica (1993). Alcohol and drug consumption. Chicago: Encyclopaedia Britannica.

Erickson, K. (1966). *Wayward puritans: A study in the sociology of deviance.* New York: Wiley.

Erickson, P., & Butters, J. (1998). The emerging harm reduction movement: The de-escalation of the war on drugs? In E. L. Jensen and J. Gerber (Eds.), *The new war on drugs: Symbolic politics and criminal justice policy* (pp. 177–196). Cincinnati: Anderson.

Fingarette, H. (1988). *Heavy drinking: The myth of alcoholism as a disease.* Berkeley: University of California Press.

Fishbein, D. H., & Pease, S. E. (1996). *The dynamics of drug abuse.* Boston: Allyn & Bacon.

Fruhling, L. (1996, September 29). Allow women to vote? Ha! *Des Moines Register,* IA, IOA.

Gardner, D. (2000a, September 12). Do our drug laws harm us more than help? *Ottawa Citizen.* Available from www.ottawacitizen.com/columnists/gardner/000911/4122508.html

Gardner, D. (2000b, September 5). Why the war on drugs has failed. *Ottawa Citizen.* Available from www.ottawacitizen.com/columnists/gardner/00905/4090140.html

Gleick, E. (1996, February 5). Rehab centers run dry. *Time,* 44–55.

Goodman, J. (1993). *Tobacco in history: The cultures of dependence.* New York: Routledge.

Gorski, T. T. (1998). Alcoholism should be treated as a disease. In S. Barber (Ed.), *Alcohol: Opposing viewpoints* (pp. 98–104). San Diego: Greenhaven Press.

Hamid, A. (1998). *Drugs in America: Sociology , economics, and politics.* Gaithersburg, MD: Aspen.

Hamilton, E. (1940). *The Greek way to Western civilization.* New York: Norton.

Hanson, D. J. (1995). *Preventing alcohol abuse: Alcohol, culture, and control.* Westport, CT: Praeger.

Helzer, J., & Canino, G. (1992). *Alcohol in North America, Europe, and Asia.* New York: Oxford University Press.

Hughes, R. (1987). *The fatal shore: The epic of Australia's founding.* New York: Knopf.

Inciardi, J. A., & Harrison, L. D. (2000). Introduction: The concept of harm reduction. In J. A. Inciardi and L. Harrison (Eds.), *Harm reduction* (pp. vii–xviii). Thousand Oaks, CA: Sage.

Jellinek, E. M. (1960). *The disease concept of alcoholism.* New Haven, CT: Yale Center for Alcoholic Studies.

Jensen, E. L., & Gerber, J. (1998). The social construction of drug problems: A historical overview. In E. L. Jensen & J. Gerber (Eds.), *The new war on drugs: Symbolic politics and criminal justice policy* (pp. 1–23). Cincinnati: Anderson.

Jernigan, D., & Dorfman, L. (1996). Visualizing America's drug problem: An ethnographic content analysis of illegal drug stories on the nightly news. *Contemporary Drug Problems, 23,* 169–195.

Joseph, H. (1995). *Medical methadone maintenance: The further concealment of a stigmatized condition* (dissertation). New York: City University of New York.

Karlen, N. (1995, May 28). Greetings from Minnesota. *New York Times Magazine, 32–35.*

Kinney, J. (2000). Alcohol. In J. Kinney (Ed.), *Loosing the grip: A handbook of alcohol information* (pp. 2–40). Boston: McGraw-Hill.

Knapp, C. (1997). *Drinking: A love story.* New York: Delta.

Lender, M., & Martin, J. (1982). *Drinking in America: A history.* New York: Free Press.

Levin, J. D. (1995). *Alcoholism: A bio-psycho-social approach.* Washington, DC: Taylor & Francis.

MacCoun, R. J. (1998, November). Toward a psychology of harm reduction. *American Psychologist, 53*(11), 1199–1208.

Mancall, P. (1997). *Deadly medicine: Indians and alcohol in early America.* Ithaca, NY: Cornell University Press.

Mauer, M. (1995). Sentencing of criminal offenders. In *Encyclopedia of Social Work* (19th Ed., pp. 2123–2129). Washington, DC: NASW Press.

McGinn, A. P. (1997, July/August). The nicotine control. *World Watch, 18–27.*

McNeece, C. A., & DiNitto, D. M. (1998). *Chemical dependence: A systems approach.* Boston: Allyn & Bacon.

Metzger, L. (1988). *From denial to recovery.* San Francisco: Jossey-Bass.

Miller, W. (1996). Motivational interviewing: Research, practice, and puzzles. *Addictive Behaviors, 21*(6), 835–842.

Musto, D. (1998). The American experience with stimulants and opiates. In *Perspectives in crime and justice: 1997–1998 lecture series* (pp. 51–78). Washington, DC: U.S. Department of Justice.

Musto, D. (1999). *The American disease. Origins of narcotic control* (3rd ed.). New York: Oxford University Press.

Orford, J. (1985). *Excessive appetites: A psychological view of addictions.* Chichester, England: Wiley.

Peele, S. (1989/1995). *The Diseasing of America.* Lexington, MA: Lexington Books.

Peele, S., & Bufe, C. (2000). *Resisting 12-step coercion.* Tucson, AZ: Sharp Press.

Qviller, B. (1996). *Rusens historie (History of Intoxication).* Oslo: Det Norske Samlaget.

Rivers, P. C. (1994). *Alcohol and human behavior: Theory, research, and practice.* Englewood Cliffs, NJ: Prentice Hall.

Robertson, N. (1988). *Getting better: Inside Alcoholics Anonymous.* New York: Fawcett.

Rosin, H. (2000, May 5). Bush puts faith in a social service role. *Washington Post, A1.*

Rush, B. (1785/1943). An inquiry into the efforts of ardent spirits upon the human body and mind. Reprinted in *Quarterly Journal of Studies on Alcohol, 4.* Entire issue.

SAMHSA (Substance Abuse and Mental Health Service Administration). (1998). *Highlights.* Online at wwwdasis.samhsa.gov/teds98/highlights_m.htm

Sandmaier, M. (1992). *The invisible alcoholics: Women and alcohol* (2nd ed.). Bradenton, FL: Human Services Institution.

Savage, D. G. (1999, December 27). U.S. law has come full circle on personal vices in the last century. *Los Angeles Times, 24A.*

Schlosser, E. (1994, August). Reefer madness. *The Atlantic Monthly, 274*(2), 45–59.

Talmage, T. D. (1887). *Live coals.* Chicago: Fairbanks and Palmer.

Thombs, D. (1999). *Introduction to addictive behaviors* (2nd ed.). New York: Guilford Press.

Thorton, M. (1992, March). Prohibition's failure: Lessons for today. *USA Today* magazine, 70–73.

U.S. Department of Health and Human Services (2000). Changing the conversation: Improving substance abuse treatment. Available at www.samhsa.gov

Vandivort-Warren, R. (1996). Surviving in a managed care market. *Issues of substance, 1*(3), 1, 3.

van Wormer, K. (1995). *Alcoholism treatment: A social work perspective.* Belmont, CA: Wadsworth.

van Wormer, K. (1997). Doing alcoholism treatment in Norway: A personal reminiscence. *Reflection: Narratives of professional helping, 3*(3), 37–71.

Walters, G. D. (1999). *The addiction concept: Working hypothesis or self-fulfilling prophesy?* Boston: Allyn & Bacon.

White, S. (1996). *Russia goes dry: Alcohol, state and society.* Cambridge, England: Cambridge University Press.

White, W. L. (1998). *Slaying the dragon: The history of addiction treatment and recovery in America.* Bloomington, IL: Chestnut Health Systems.

Wilford, J. N. (1996, June 6). In the annals of winemaking, 5000 B.C. was quite a year. *New York Times,* B11.

Zeldin, T. (1994). *An intimate history of humanity.* New York: HarperCollins.

We help the soul's beauty come to the surface. We polish it
until it gleams. —RABBI ABRAHAM J. TWERSKY, M.D. (2001)

3 CHAPTER STRENGTHS-BASED HELPING STRATEGIES

THE ROSE

By Andrea Davis

The queen shouts profanities as I lay her jeweled head and losing face
  upon the green felt table.
My bleeding ulcer twists and turns, flaring up with the extra acid
  from adrenaline.
I bear to admit I have lost everything I thought I won.
My back is bent, hunching me forward,
The weight is huge, larger than my being.
I am kneeling on all fours.
Crying that I might never get up.
Maybe I'll just fold beneath the weight, and let it suffocate me.

I live a life the hue of coal, dark, solid, and cold.
And I am trying to press the precious stone out of it.
Looking for something to fill the void.
Searching for the beauty within me.
Hoping for the knowledge that I am loved.
In self-defeat, self-loathing, self-destruction, I am still loved.
Life calls me on.
Today, tomorrow, forever I hope.
And in that hope I feel free.
For the gleam that speckles the inside of my dark cocoon with prisms
  of light
Shows me, I am not just the darkness, my secret life.
I am beauty.

Printed with the permission of Andrea Davis.

INTRODUCTION

Practitioners of strengths-based helping strategies fiercely adhere to the hope offered in the preceding poem by Andrea Davis that "I am not just the darkness, my secret life. / I am beauty." Strengths-based practitioners believe that no matter how dismal the circumstances, people have possibilities, resiliencies, and capacities for change and even transformation. They look for and try to nurture the "gleam" that is often hidden by misery, protective strategies, and the failure to achieve goals set by others.

Diane Rae Davis once heard a highly regarded professor in social work state emphatically that ("for your own good") you just have to "write off" anyone who has been in treatment over five times. An alternative, strengths-based understanding is that addiction is a chronic, relapsing condition that may require extended interventions not even possible in a single episode and that there is evidence that more times in treatment is related to less use (Hser, Grella, Chou, & Anglin, 1998). "Don't give up until the miracle happens" is an AA saying that applies to clinicians as well as clients. This does not mean that you as a counselor must doggedly chase down a client and try to force your agenda for change! It does mean that you continue to focus on strengths rather than liabilities, not because they are more "true" but because it's a more effective way of helping a client find the hope, motivation, and self-efficacy necessary for making changes.

The strengths perspective in social work practice and other helping professions continues to develop conceptually. Strengths-based practice, as eloquently defined by Saleebey (2002), is a dramatic departure from conventional practice, as "a versatile practice approach, relying heavily on ingenuity and creativity. . . . Rather than focusing on problems, your eye turns toward possibility" (p. 1). Saleebey offers a "lexicon of strengths" that also serves as a statement of principles. Key concepts in the strengths lexicon are: empowerment of individuals and communities; membership, or belongingness; resilience, healing, and wholeness; dialogue, and collaboration; and suspension of disbelief in what the client says.

Choice is the hallmark of a strengths-based intervention. In the substance misuse arena, this means: choice about the goals of the helping relationship (harm reduction, including abstinence); informed choice about a variety of treatment contexts (same gender, group, individual, day treatment, outpatient, inpatient, mutual-help groups); and informed choice about treatment methods (cognitive-behavioral, Twelve-Step approach, solution-focused, motivational interviewing, types of nicotine replacement therapy, etc.). The emphasis on choice of treatment, of course, implies that a variety of community resources *are* available to help people alleviate their troubles with substance misuse and that these treatment choices are affordable. Granted, these kinds of choices are an ideal, not a reality, in the United States, but we advocate finding ways to weave a variety of options into existing programs to the fullest extent possible.

People who use illicit drugs or are dependent on alcohol, gambling, purging, etc. are typically marginalized in their choices about what they need or want to change and how best to accomplish it. This stance is based on the belief that such people are not capable of making a good choice and must be manipulated or coerced into doing the right thing for themselves and concerned others. Granted, it is tempting to play God, particularly with people who may have wreaked havoc on themselves and others. However, in a strength-based approach, one concedes that it simply doesn't work. A Canadian research group has discounted claims about the effectiveness of mandated treatment as non-empirical and replete with methodological problems in a review of 850 articles on the topic (Wild, 1999). Inevitably, people seem to find a way to use and misuse alcohol and drugs, gamble, smoke, etc., even in prison and in treatment centers, if that is their goal.

By honoring choice and providing options, a strengths-based practitioner respects the right of the individual to manage his or her own destiny and to take responsibility for his or her own actions. In the field of social work, this is called the value of "self-determination," the belief that people have a right to arrange their lives in accordance with their own preferences (National Association of Social Workers, 1996). However, the right of clients to pursue their own goals regarding their addiction, take risks or reduce harms, make mistakes, and even harm themselves in the process is not uniformly endorsed by social workers or other clinicians. Many professional social workers justify or simply "go along" with legal and agency interference to these rights because of the "risk clause," i.e., "social workers may limit clients' right to self-determination when in the social workers' professional judgment, clients' actions or potential actions pose a serious, foreseeable, and imminent risk to themselves or others" (NASW, Standard 1.02).

Chronic alcohol and drug addiction, however, is not in the same crisis category as imminent suicide. It is what the ethicist Reamer (1998, p. 29) refers to as one of "the more subtle forms of self-harming behavior that pose difficult ethical dilemmas for social workers." He says many practitioners have "instincts to protect vulnerable people from engaging in self-destructive behavior." It is this very instinct, based on good intentions, that may be a barrier for social workers and other practitioners to honor self-determination with persons who are misusing substances or addicted.

In strengths-based interventions, we try to keep in mind that alcohol, drug use, and addiction are risky behaviors that have been occurring since ancient times. These behaviors are usually tolerated and "self-determined" in the middle and upper classes. However, if you are economically poor or a member of an oppressed minority group and live in the United States, these same behaviors can make you extremely vulnerable to incarceration, losing custody of your own children, and having limited options for reducing the harm of your addiction. Harm reduction and strengths-based practices would extend the right of choice and self-determination to all economic and racial/ethnic groups.

The third basic tenet of strengths-based approaches is to pay attention to the readiness of the clients and/or client systems to make changes in the arena they have chosen. No longer are people assumed to be eager for the counselor to tell them what to do and labeled resistant if they are not eagerly compliant! Instead, change is seen as a process on a continuum that moves from a position of unwillingness to even consider making the change to acting on behaviors

TABLE 3.1 | COMPARATIVE APPROACHES TO ADDICTION

Traditional Counseling Approach	Strengths-Based Therapy
Biological	Biological
Looks to the individual for specific causes of disease	Stress on multiple, interactive levels of influence
Dichotomizes reality, for example, alcoholic vs. nonalcoholic	Addiction-like behaviors seen as existing along a continuum
Psychological	Psychological
Problem focused	Strengths focused, looks to possibilities
Labels such as alcoholic, codependent used	Tries to avoid use of negative labels
Assesses problems and losses	Assesses and builds on strengths
Client seen as typically resistant, in denial	Client seen as active participant in a collaborative, health-seeking effort
Client motivation unimportant	Intervention geared to level of client motivation to change
Focus to prevent slip or relapse	Focus to maintain moderation or abstinence as client wishes
Expulsion from treatment for relapse	Client self-determination stressed; meet the client where he or she is
Confrontation used to elicit change, break denial	Roll with the resistance; redefine resistance as a challenge
One size fits all	Individualized treatment; client choice is stressed
Social	Social
Identity as member of self-help group encouraged	Holistic approach
Identifies pathologies from upbringing in chemically dependent home	Seeks strengths in upbringing
Looks for codependency in family members	Family perceived as potential resource

that will maintain the change. Relapse is regarded no longer as a personal failure but rather as an integral part of the change process.

According to Velicer (1996), the vast majority of the population for any addictive behavior are in the first two stages of change: *precontemplation* (haven't even thought about making a change) and *contemplation* (thought about it, but ambivalent). Yet almost no interventions have been systematically developed and implemented for this group in the United States. See Table 3.1

for a theoretical comparison of the basic premises of traditional approach (primarily a medical model) with a strengths-based orientation.

In this chapter we describe four strengths-based approaches. What these approaches have in common is that they honor the principle of client self-determination, attend to the client's stage of readiness, and focus on the resources and capabilities the client and client's family may use to further their goals. The four approaches are: the practices of harm reduction; motivational interviewing; solution-focused interventions; and narrative therapy. Although some of these practices are well entrenched outside the United States, within the United States they are typically practiced outside the addiction field or on a limited basis within the addiction field.

The last section of the chapter describes the traditional system of treatment care usually available in the United States—detoxification, treatment, and aftercare—and suggests ways to incorporate strength-based approaches. We invite you to consider the evidence available about the effectiveness of these approaches with substance misusers and others struggling with addictive processes and compare it to the effectiveness of the disease model approach as it is widely practiced in addiction treatment in the United States. In particular, we hope that you will examine the assumption of self-determination in these strength-based practices and decide how that matches your own values and beliefs regarding professional helping processes.

HARM REDUCTION

All programs that deal with people who are misusing substances or are addicted, including abstinence-only programs, share the goal of reducing harm caused by the addiction. Specific harm reduction strategies, which we will describe in this section, refer to those practices that aim at reducing drug-related harm without requiring abstinence from the drug itself (Riley et al., 1999). Based on a public health model of primary, secondary, and tertiary prevention, harm reduction (at the tertiary level) attempts to alleviate the social, legal, and medical problems associated with unmanaged addiction and, in so doing, to limit the harms, such as infectious diseases like HIV, hepatitis, and tuberculosis, violence, criminal activity, and early death, without necessarily attempting to "cure" the addiction (Nadelmann, McNeely, & Drucker, 1997). Abstinence may be an ideal outcome for many addicted persons, but harm reduction advocates point out we are not 100% effective in convincing people to become abstinent. Project MATCH Research Group (1997), for example, found that only 19% of the outpatient subjects maintained complete abstinence throughout the 12-month follow-up period, however, there was substantial positive improvement. This same group abstained on average more than 80% of the days posttreatment, compared with slightly more than 20% pretreatment. From a harm reduction standpoint, abstinence is viewed as *only one of several means* of improving.

Because of all the myths surrounding harm reduction practices, it may be helpful to start with what harm reduction is not. It is not:

- A conspiracy to seduce alcoholics or addicts into thinking they can use alcohol or drugs moderately, thus prolonging their agony. (Rather, the extent of a person's drug/alcohol use per se is not the focus of harm reduction—use is secondary to the risk of harms *consequent* to use.)
- A potent excuse for an alcoholic, compulsive gambler, or drug addict to continue to use alcohol or drugs or gamble. (Rather, for a person who is in the throes of addiction, the principles of harm reduction are no more potent than "today it is raining" as a reason to use alcohol, drugs, gamble, etc.)
- A foolish, dangerous model designed by academics or people who don't know anything about addiction or don't care about the consequences of not getting people to abstain from their addiction. (Harm reduction practices evolved from the demands of injection drug users for strategies to prevent the spread of HIV.)
- A misguided approach that makes it easier for addicts to keep on being addicted by furnishing shelter, food, clean needles, methadone, even heroin to people who are addicted. (Most harm reduction programs attend first to the most pressing needs of an individual as a step in the direction of less risky use or, if appropriate, abstinence.)

Harm reduction practices can be understood by looking at how one might treat a person with diabetes. Harm reduction practitioners would not wait until the person was in a diabetic coma and brought into the hospital for treatment. Rather, they would try to educate health providers and other likely contacts about diabetic symptoms so people who are in harm's way can be alerted and given informed choices about different ways to proceed and the cost/benefits of such actions. Resources would be available to assist the persons in finding the right path for them, whether a different diet or insulin shots. Families and the community at large would be educated about the typical harms of the disease, such as the emotional roller coaster that can result when the problem is ignored. People with diabetes would be encouraged to reduce the various harms of going untreated, and resources would be made available to assist them. Their choices would be respected (even if we don't agree with them), and we would expect them to take responsibility for their choices. Sound familiar? This is the way it actually works in the public health system. The harm reduction model simply applies this approach to addiction.

Reducing Barriers

Harm reduction practitioners reduce barriers that make it less likely that people who are misusing alcohol/drugs or addicted will get help. Typical barriers present in many treatment programs today include program locations inaccessible to or remote from the community they are trying to target, professional staff who may be perceived as knowing little about street culture or survival rules, waiting lists for intake and treatment, financial costs, and a requirement that abstinence be the goal of treatment. Since it is estimated that only one out of six persons who are injecting drug users (IDUs) are in treatment at any given time, less than 10% of substance abusers receive professional treatment for alcohol or drug problems (Narrow, Regier, Rae, Manderscheid, & Locke, 1993), and only 3% of pathological gamblers seek professional help (National Research Council, 1999), reducing barriers is critical.

By far the most controversial aspect of harm reduction strategies in the United States is promoting "low-threshold" access to services by not requiring abstinence as a precondition for receiving treatment. Marlatt (1998) says abstinence-based treatments raise a "high-threshold" barrier that does not distinguish between lighter and heavier use and degrees of harm. In addition, it promotes stigmatizing individuals who use or misuse alcohol and drugs as either "criminal/immoral addicts or victims of an incurable genetic or biological disease" (p. 55). Neither one of these options would be seen as user friendly or likely to appeal to people who first of all want help in reducing the problems associated with their addiction. Harm reduction services are offered with the fewest possible restrictions, requirements, or goal expectations and the smallest possible amount of paperwork in order to appeal to the widest group.

Recruiting members of the targeted group to do community-based street outreach is a common approach to reduce barriers. For example, the Indigenous Leader Outreach Model (ILOM) used in Denver, Colorado, to reduce the spread of HIV hires and trains recovering drug users. They do this because "they have insider access to the drug-using community, they know the rules governing the social systems of the streets, and they are able to develop trusting relationships with the target population of active drug users" (Booth, Kwiatkowski, Iguchi, Pinto, & John, 1998, p. 117). Several projects and programs use active injection drug users as outreach workers—there is growing documentation that this is effective in helping street addicts control, reduce, or stop their use of drugs (see the special issue of *Journal of Drug Issues* 25(3), 1995, on "Drug Users as Risk Reduction Agents"). In the introduction to the special issue, Broadhead (1995, p. 505) notes that injection drug users have been helpful in "preparing and distributing bleach kits, recruiting users who need help, helping outreach workers learn about new drug scenes and copping areas, and vouching for outreach workers that need to be established."

Outreach often involves providing drug education materials telling the user how to reduce the risks associated with using drugs as well as building a relationship and providing referrals for treatment and support services. Examples of pamphlets available in English and Spanish on the Internet from the Harm Reduction Coalition include: "Taking Care of Your Veins: Rotate Your Spot!" and "Avoiding Arteries and Nerves When You Want a Vein" (http://www .harmreduction.org).

Increasing accessibility to harm reduction aids is accomplished in a variety of creative ways, some of which may surprise the American reader. For example, in Amsterdam, police stations provide clean syringes on an exchange basis; automated syringe exchange machines are accessible 24 hours a day in many European and Australian cities; in several provinces in Canada, pharmacists are actively involved in syringe exchange programs; in the United Kingdom, Europe, and Australia, methadone is available from general practitioners as well as clinics, and some even distribute through "methadone buses" (Riley et al., 1999). Activities more common in the United States include mobile vans or street workers delivering services to parts of the community where injection drug users live or "hang out." Even in the United States there are creative ways of improving access, such as a needle exchange program aimed at younger users in Portland, Oregon, located in a trendy café, and an outreach site in Boulder, Colorado, near a gymnasium to target steroid injectors (Peterson, Dimeff, Tapert, Stern, & Gorman, 1998).

A goal of harm reduction practitioners in the United States is to make methadone treatment and needle exchange programs more accessible. Although the United States has institutionalized methadone maintenance programs since the 1960s, the distribution of methadone is confined to specialized clinics, usually in larger cities, subject to strict federal and state regulations that require exacting compliance from clients. Needle exchange programs in the United States continue to be unfunded by federal dollars and legally harassed in many localities, despite abundant research on the positive results of these programs. Approximately 10% of IV drug users in the United States have access to needle exchange programs, and 45% of these programs operate illegally (Nadelmann, McNeely, & Drucker, 1997). Unfortunately those that are legal operate under the same type of strict guidelines that make the methadone maintenance programs user unfriendly.

Other strategies that have demonstrated effectiveness in reducing barriers include "rapid intake" (Dennis, Ingram, Burks, & Rachal, 1994), where people who want to enter treatment are no longer delayed; and lowered financial barriers, such as passing out free coupons for treatment. In a New Jersey study where coupons for free methadone treatment were passed out in the IDU community, 59% redeemed treatment coupons. Nearly half of these people had never been in treatment; 58% tested HIV positive (Bux, Iguchi, Lidz, Baxter, & Platt, 1993). In a random assignment study in Denver that included free treatment compared to paying for treatment, 52% of the injecting drug users assigned to free treatment entered treatment, compared to 32% for those who had to pay (Booth et al., 1998). In spite of this evidence, lowering financial barriers is not endorsed by professionals who believe that clients "have to pay" in order to receive positive benefits from programs.

Looking for larger system interventions that would be helpful in reducing the barriers for women to get help with gambling problems, the "Queen of Hearts" Australian project (Brown & Coventry, 1997) elicited suggestions from women gamblers. Their ideas include (1) timely access to other supporting services, such as mental health and especially financial counseling; (2) access to female counselors because of the need to disclose problems such as physical, sexual, and emotional abuse; and (3) easily accessible services in downtown areas as well as rural environments where services are collocated with other supportive services to lessen stigmatization and promote referrals.

Other examples of harm reduction strategies that improve access are: selling nicotine replacement therapies over the counter instead of requiring a prescription, making clean syringes and methadone available in prisons, supplying free bleach kits for cleaning injecting equipment to prevent hepatitis, providing testing for street drugs at "rave" dances, developing "tolerance zones" or "injection rooms" where drug users can get clean equipment, condoms, medical advice, and attention and even take drugs in a safe environment, and launching various Web sites to keep consumers informed, such as the "ravesafe" organization that started in South Africa in 1993 (http://www.ravesafe.org.za). Although many of these practices are controversial in the United States and Canada, the overall purpose of improving access to a treatment system that is not yet user friendly (some say built for providers to punish consumers) has to be respected.

Choosing to Reduce Harm: Who Chooses?

Diane Riley and her colleagues (1999), of the Canadian Centre on Substance Abuse National Working Group on Policy, raise some thought-provoking questions: What drug-related "harms" should be given priority? Is preventing HIV infection more important than eliminating dependence? Abstinence-only proponents tend to view dependence as top priority; many harm reduction proponents do not. Success in harm reduction terms is "any reduction in drug-related harm" (Denning, 2000, p. 37). Another critical question is who decides. In abstinence-based treatment, professionals decide the priorities to be addressed, starting with abstinence. In the harm reduction approach, the person/consumer/client decides the priorities to be addressed, i.e., what harms are to be addressed and in what order.

Recognizing the importance of choice in finding one's own path, Patt Denning (2000, p. 25) states that "people have the right to make their own decisions in life. . . . The fact that they may make treatment choices and life choices that conflict with my professional or personal beliefs does not relieve me of my responsibility to offer them what help I can." Denning is a therapist who lives in San Francisco, where, since September 2000, official city policy has required that all substance abuse and HIV/AIDS treatment providers address how they will provide harm reduction treatment options and that they develop harm reduction guidelines. As a consultant and trainer to many treatment providers, Denning (2000) acknowledges that harm reduction strategies may focus on what the user might see as more pressing problems than drug or alcohol use, such as housing, repairing broken relationships or support systems, jobs, social skills training, and psychiatric symptoms. The goals within the professional helping relationship are based on the rights of individuals to make their own choices. Consequently, cultural, racial, and ethnic differences that may influence goals are not problematic but are looked on as resources and potential supports.

In Denver, a program developed to reduce the harm of HIV transmission uses a hierarchy of behavioral options called "The Indigenous Leader Outreach Model" to describe the choices available to injecting drug users (Booth, Kwiatkowski, Iguchi, Pinto, & John, 1998, p. 117):

- Quit using drugs.
- If you can't or won't stop using drugs, then stop injecting.

- If you can't or won't stop injecting, then don't share needles or syringes and other works.
- If you can't or won't stop sharing, then disinfect your needles and syringes with bleach between sharing partners.

Although reducing the probability of HIV transmission is a common goal among most treatment providers, other "harms" that are the focus of harm reduction strategies include the risks of procuring illegal drugs, such as legal consequences, incarceration, and the loss of custody of children. Larger system "harms" may include the alarming growth of prisons, the marginalizing of certain groups, such as "crack moms," and the large amount of national resources devoted to interdiction instead of treatment (see chapter 13 on Public Policy). The definition of "harms" also varies, depending on the type of problem and the co-occurrence of other problems, such as mental disorders, gambling, homelessness, and domestic violence.

For a homeless woman with a history of substance misuse who finds a place to live through a social agency, the most immediate "harm" of using alcohol or drugs may be the risk of homelessness. Kate Fewel, MSW, works in a downtown women's drop-in center in Spokane, Washington, and case-manages four homeless women (with histories of alcohol/drug misuse and/or domestic violence) in their own apartments through a neighborhood-housing program. She notes the difference between the women she works with, who are required to maintain abstinence not only from drugs or alcohol but also from abusive relationships, and an alternative model in her same community that practices harm reduction. In her housing model, abstinence is required in order to encourage the women to focus on the issues that led to their homelessness. However,

> the stress level is higher because they are more immediately accountable (but not over the long run) and they are at risk of losing housing if they break the rules or get caught. In the harm reduction setting, the women may experience relapse, but not at the risk of losing their housing. Because housing is the safety net, their relapses are actually informing them and helping them solidify their foundations of recovery. For example, a woman in my program drank. I had to kick her out. However, I was able to get her in the other program (harm reduction), and even though she continued to relapse a couple of times, in the long run she was able to go to outpatient treatment, resume participation in recovery meetings, and all the things that can't happen when you are homeless. (Personal interview with Davis, March 21, 2001)

Women who gamble experience their own particular "harms." The Queen of Hearts Australian project (Brown & Coventry, 1997) found that women who were experiencing problems with gambling also experienced stigmatization, loneliness, oppressive role requirements as women with few opportunities to socialize without the company of men, and serious financial and emotional turmoil. Suggestions from the women gamblers for reducing harm on a larger system level include: (1) involvement of all the groups associated with gambling (including women gamblers, financial institutions, gaming operators, and government) to work on solutions, instead of leaving it up to the "victims" to cope; (2) establishing alternative recreations for women in neighborhoods; (3) decreasing the accessibility of gaming venues, removing them from shopping centers, strip malls, clubs, and hotels throughout the state; and (4) timely access to other supporting services, such as mental health and especially financial counseling.

Many of the harm reduction strategies used with tobacco addiction are initiated by people on their own, without professional help or intervention. It is estimated that "self-change" or "natural recovery" occurs with 80% to 90% of all those who stop smoking altogether (U.S. Department of Health and Human Services, 1988). In a review of harm reduction strategies with nicotine, Baer and Murch (1998) describe several interventions that may help reduce tobacco use. These include further restrictions on the accessibility of tobacco through increased taxation and limits on advertising, offering "controlled smoking" clinics, changing the product by reducing tars and nicotine, and nicotine replacement treatments, such as nicotine gum, "patches," nasal sprays, inhalers, and lozenges. The authors note that these strategies deserve more research attention, particularly around the question of how harm reduction strategies can be integrated with smoking cessation programs.

Harm reduction strategies for alcohol misuse are based on the premise that alcohol use ranges across a continuum, starting with no consequences for use and ending with devastating consequences for use, with lots of states in between. Harm reductionists emphasize the research evidence that alcohol problems are more likely to be intermittent or discontinuous, are subject to "natural recovery" without formal intervention, just like quitting smoking, and can continue at a stable level for years at a time (Sobell, Ellingstad, & Sobell, 2000; Vaillant, 1996; Larimer et al., 1998). These conclusions are difficult to swallow for professionals who have been trained to see a "progressive, fatal, disease state" that never gets better once you have it. As Larimer and her colleagues (p. 75) point out, "the occurrence of even a single case of controlled drinking by an alcoholic challenges the very definition of alcoholism as a disease." Controversy over the research on this subject has been going on for 30 years since Davies (1962) found seven "normal" drinkers among a treated group of 93 male alcoholics in the United Kingdom. Other research that consistently replicates the finding that moderation drinking is an outcome of treatment for some alcohol-dependent clients (both in moderation treatments and abstinence treatments) has been vilified and even called "fraudulent" by people who adhere to the disease model. The review of the research by Larimer and her colleagues (pp. 81–84) led them to conclude:

1. A majority of people with drinking problems self-recover with no formal treatment.
2. Over time, rates of abstinence (compared to controlled drinking) tend to increase.
3. A choice of goals tends to result in greater treatment retention and the recruitment of a broader range of problem drinkers.
4. When given a choice, people tend to choose the goal that is most appropriate for the severity of their problems.

Harm reduction strategies for alcohol misuse and dependence primarily involve offering more choice about outcome goals (moderation training as well as abstinence training), brief interventions that focus on advice and increasing motivation to change, and brief assessments that give people the opportunity to assess harm without prescriptions for a particular treatment.

An example of strategies for reducing the harm of heavy drinking in college students at the University of Washington is the recent Lifestyles Project. In this program, a thorough assessment was offered all incoming freshmen, and 25% were identified as at risk for drinking-related problems. These students were randomly assigned to the experimental group that received motivational interviewing (see the next section on Motivational Interviewing) with feedback about drinking patterns and risks, or to a control group that received only a more detailed assessment. Students in the motivational interviewing group were encouraged to evaluate their risk status and think about the possibility of behavior change. Resources were offered, but the goals about change were left to each student. Feedback reports were also sent to the students at the 6- and 12-month follow-up sessions. Results indicate that the experimental group reported significantly less drinking, consuming less on each drinking occasion, and a lower peak quantity over time (Larimer et al., 1998).

Attending to Readiness to Change

All of the harm reduction strategies just described are based on a common assumption: People are ultimately capable of making an informed choice in their own best interest. The choices they make depend on their readiness to change, i.e., what stage of change they are in. The stages-of-change model, sometimes referred to as the *transtheoretical model* because it relies on several theories of social psychology, was first proposed by Prochaska and DiClemente (1986). It has since been applied and adopted in many addiction treatment and other helping settings around the world.

The stages-of-change model is a circular process that includes five stages in the process of behavior change. A sixth stage, precontemplation, lies outside the wheel, because the person in this stage sees no need to change or has no intention of changing behavior at this time. The "precontemplator" may be defensive or angry when confronted or even questioned about alcohol or drug problems. Once there is a glimmer in the minds of the client that a problem does exist, the person enters the circle and proceeds through each stage several times before finally achieving stable change. The stages are: (1) *precontemplation* (characterized by defensiveness about substance use), (2) *contemplation* (where the person is aware that a problem exists but is ambivalent about making a change or has anxiety about what change will mean), (3) *preparation* (where the person intends to make a change in the near future or has unsuccessfully taken action in the past year), (4) *action* (where the person takes action to change his or her behavior or environment to overcome a problem behavior, such as becoming abstinent or cutting down on drug use), (5) *maintenance* (where the person consolidates gains and works to prevent relapse), and

(6) *relapse* (which may occur repeatedly and is considered a normal, inevitable part of the behavior change process (Miller & Rollnick, 1991).

Most treatment programs and mutual-help organizations such as Alcoholics Anonymous are designed to help people who are in the action stage of change; that is, they already have a "desire to stop drinking" and are ready to take action. Regrettably, a number of studies indicate that most people start at the precontemplation or contemplation stage of change. Consequently, counselors need to know how to work with unmotivated clients who may have been forced into treatment by their families or the legal system.

Many professional counselors also assume that the person is in the action stage of change or *should be in the action stage,* given all the obvious (to the counselor or family) reasons for changing behaviors. When clients are in the precontemplative or contemplative stage, they have been labeled "unmotivated," "resistant," or "in denial." Instead of the counselor's jumping to this conclusion, Miller and Rollnick (1991) propose that these problems occur when a counselor is using strategies that don't match up with a client's current stage of readiness to change. They designed the process of "motivational interviewing" (see the next section) to provide a more productive fit between counselor behavior and client reality.

Harm reduction practices are designed to help people move through the stages of change at their own pace. Instead of a dualistic framework of either recovery or relapse, harm reduction practice offers a wider path that encompasses and honors all of the stages in the change process. The application of this model to families may require some modification, for everyone may not be in the same stage at the same time. Barbara Aranda-Naranjo, who works at the South Texas AIDS Center for Infants and Their Families in San Antonio, recommends that the stages-of-change model be explained to families in a way they can understand, as part of their right to be informed of the tools and models that practitioners use to meet their needs (Fitzgerald, Aranda-Naranjo, & Denenberg, 1996). In her clinic, the model is translated into Spanish to increase the understanding of these processes.

MOTIVATIONAL INTERVIEWING

Twenty years ago it would have been difficult to persuade me that a brief intervention of this kind could have such a potent and lasting impact on behavior. (Miller, 1996, p. 840)

The development of motivational interviewing (MI) is credited to the relentless, spirited questioning by student interns in Norway of William R. Miller as he demonstrated how he would work with clients in various settings (Miller, 1996). This kind of questioning ("Why have you taken this approach rather than another?") required Miller to "make explicit the approach I had learned from my clients" (p. 835). The result was a beginning conceptual model, published in 1983 (Miller, 1983), that was followed by years of testing and refinements and that culminated in the text *Motivational Interviewing: Preparing*

People to Change Addictive Behavior (Miller & Rollnick, 1991). Since then, MI has been adapted to create motivational enhancement therapy (MET) in Project MATCH (1997), the multisite collaborative trial of three treatments for alcoholism (see chapter 1). It has also been applied in a wide variety of settings, including child welfare (Hohman, 1998), medical practice (Kushner, Levinson, & Miller, 1998; Compton, Monahan, & Simmons-Cody, 1999; Botelho & Novak, 1993), low-income, urban, community-based organizations (Carey et al., 2000), and a number of different problem areas, such as bulimia (Treasure, Katzman, Schmidt, Troop, Todd, & deSilva, 1999), domestic violence (Easton, Swan, & Sinha, 2000), HIV risk behavior (Carey et al., 2000), and smoking (Rollnick, Butler, & Stott, 1997).

In the MI framework, as we have seen in previous illustrations, a person who is exhibiting addictive behaviors is viewed as having a diminished capacity for self-control over time, but this capacity is believed to be retrievable. Miller (1998, p. 2) notes that even extreme disease-model proponents and programs still rely on the client's "volitional abstinence" to interrupt the destructive behavior. However, in MI terms, retrieving the capacity for self-control is much more than will power, or "just saying no." Motivation to change the addictive pattern comes from a combination of complex factors that includes learning, conditioning, emotion, social influences, and biology. The way out of the cycle of addictive behavior for MI proponents involves an internal accounting of suffering and negative consequences associated with the addiction and enough hope that this behavior can change.

Therefore, the goal of motivational interviewing is not to get clients to admit they have a problem or for the counselor to provide solutions to the problem. Rather, it is for the counselor to provide a mirror for the clients to "look back upon themselves" and see the costs and find within themselves the means to change it. Miller (1998, p. 6) says this kind of empathic merger with the clients' perspective and lending them a mirror to see themselves differently is "essentially a form of loving."

Motivational interviewing is defined as a "directive, client-centered counseling style for eliciting behavior change by helping clients to explore and resolve ambivalence" (Rollnick & Miller, 1995). It is directive in terms of the process and techniques of resolving client ambivalence, not directive about the outcome of the counseling. It is client centered because all the benefits and consequences of making a change are elicited from the client. Motivational interviewing assumes that the *state* of motivation may fluctuate from one time or situation to another (Miller & Rollnick, 1991). Therefore, this "state" can be influenced. By providing a safe, nonconfrontational environment, eliciting hope, helping clients clarify their ambivalence about making a change, counselors can be helpful in "tipping the scales" in favor of readiness to make a positive change.

Motivational interviewing utilizes specific strategies to enhance motivation. The strategies are not new, but how they are used (to increase motivation, not to get answers) is new. For example, MI counselors pay a great deal of attention to eliciting the person's current level of motivation, or stage of change, instead of assuming that the person is ready to jump into action behavior. Scaling questions can be used to do this, such as the following (Rollnick & Miller, 1997, p. 195):

1. If, on a scale of 1 to 10, 1 is not at all motivated to give up smoking and 10 is 100% motivated to give it up, what number would you give yourself at the moment?
2. If you were to decide to give up smoking now, how confident are you that you would succeed? If, on a scale of 1 to 10, 1 means that you are not at all confident and 10 means that you are 100% confident you could give it up and remain a nonsmoker, what number would you give yourself now?

These questions can help identify a person's stage of change, and the answers can also be used to build motivation or confidence by encouraging the client to identify arguments for change. This is done by asking specific follow-up questions:

1. Why did the person score as he or she did rather than a lower number, for example, "Why did you give yourself a 4 rather than a 1?" The client will then respond with some positive reasons for being motivated or confident, such as "I know it's bad for my lungs to keep on smoking" or "I think I've finally had enough."
2. What would have to happen for the person to move up the scale to more motivation or confidence? For example, "What does it take for your motivation (or confidence) to move one step higher from a 5 to a 6?" The client will then respond with strategies that will increase his or her motivation or confidence, such as "I think I need to get tested for my actual lung damage so far."

These types of questions illustrate how MI techniques can help the client with his or her primary task, that is, to identify and mobilize the client's own values and goals for behavior changes. The principal obstacle in the way of change is seen as ambivalence, and it is the client's other major task to articulate and resolve that ambivalence.

TECHNIQUES FOR ENHANCING MOTIVATION

Motivational interviewing practitioners rely on the following general principles (Miller & Rollnick, 1991) to enhance a person's motivation to change:

1. *Express empathy.* The MI style is warm, respectful, and accepting. Irrational ideas and ambivalence about change are accepted as a normal part of human experience. The client is seen as "stuck," not pathological.
2. *Develop discrepancy.* Create and amplify the discrepancy between present behavior and important personal goals. Reflective listening and focused feedback can help to highlight discrepancies using the client's own words. For example, "On the one hand you say it's important to you to get out of debt, but every time you gamble you lose hundreds of dollars. Tell me about this."

3. *Avoid argumentation.* In contrast to other, more traditional approaches that evolved from the Minnesota Model, MI practitioners do not try to persuade, confront, or argue to clients that they are in deep trouble and would be much better off giving up their addiction. "Breaking through denial" is seen as a tactic that is not just useless but that actually can increase the likelihood of resistance and decrease the likelihood of change (Rollnick & Miller, 1995).

4. *Roll with resistance.* Compliance from the client is not a goal. Resistance can be redirected by the simple statement "It's really up to you." Reluctance and ambivalence are understood to be a natural stage of the change process (contemplation stage). New perspectives are invited, but not imposed. For example, "What you do with this information is entirely up to you."

5. *Support self-efficacy.* If people have no hope for change, then regardless of how serious they believe the problem, they will not make an effort to change. The counselor can support people's confidence that they can change by removing the false idea that the counselor will change them, by showing them the success of others, and by inviting them to choose from alternative approaches to what they've already tried. A series of relapses or treatment "failures" can be reframed as "getting closer to their goal."

Elaboration on these techniques, as well as a review of some of the verbal traps that counselors may fall into when a client is in the precontemplation or contemplation stage of change, can be found on the motivational interviewing Web site at http://www.motivationalinterview.org.

GROUP MODELS

A group therapy manual based on motivational interviewing has been developed by Ingersoll and Wagner (1997) for use in Virginia's public sector, for polysubstance-dependent clients. Although this has not yet been empirically validated, it does offer three types of MI group formats: the single-session, four-session, and eight-session formats.

The eight-session format begins with an introduction of the purposes of the motivational group, and then moves to an explanation of the stages of change, an exploration of the group members' ambivalence about substance use, assistance in developing hope, potential changes, and discrepancies, an exploration of change success stories, and the development of a concrete plan for change. The authors recommend that in exploring ambivalence about substance use, employing the terms "good things" and "less good things" is helpful, because it avoids developing resistance by beginning with the "good things." This also remind us that we can't assume that a "less good thing" is a concern for the group member, even if it is a concern for you. More information on the content and formats for the different group models can be found on the MI Web site at www.motivationalinterview.org/clinical/satoegroup.html.

Research on Effectiveness

Evaluation studies of MI consistently indicate its effectiveness in reducing alcohol and other drug abuse (Project MATCH, 1997; Saunders, Wilkinson, & Phillips, 1995; Carey et al., 2000; Miller, 1996). Wilk, Jensen, & Havighurst (1997) conducted a meta-analysis of brief interventions of less than 60 minutes with heavy drinkers and found that those who received the intervention were about twice as likely to successfully reduce their alcohol use, compared to heavy drinkers who did not receive the brief intervention. Another meta-analysis of 32 controlled studies of brief intervention for problem drinkers (Bien, Miller, & Tonigan, 1993) found that persons who received the brief intervention reduced their drinking and were abstinent at a rate comparable to more extensive treatment.

Project MATCH (1997) compared motivational enhancement therapy (4 sessions) to cognitive-behavioral coping skills therapy (12 sessions) and Twelve-Step facilitation (12 sessions). The focus of MET was to employ motivational interviewing strategies (as described earlier) in order to produce internal motivation for change, not to guide the client through particular steps to recovery. The results indicated little difference in outcomes by type of treatment, but overall improvements in drinking outcomes were achieved by all. In aftercare, 35% of the subjects reported continued complete abstinence throughout the 12 follow-up months; 65% slipped or relapsed during that period. For the outpatient subjects, 19% maintained complete abstinence throughout the follow-up, 46% had a heavy-drinking period, and the rest "slipped." Outpatient clients low in motivation ultimately did better in MET than in the other types. The complete therapy manual for MET procedures can be obtained for no charge from NIAAA, Project MATCH Monograph Series (Miller, Zweben, DiClemente, & Rychtarik, 1995).

SOLUTION-FOCUSED THERAPY AND NARRATIVE THERAPY: "THIRD WAVE" APPROACHES

Solution-Focused Therapy

Although there are some differences between solution-focused therapy and narrative therapy, for the purposes of this chapter we will consider them together as two strengths-based therapeutic approaches that have recently been applied to the problems of addiction. O'Hanlon (1994) coined the term "Third Wave" to apply to narrative therapy, and "Pre–Third Wave" to apply to solution-focused therapy, as a way of signaling that these approaches take a new direction, away from the pathology-focused "First Wave," dominated by psychodynamic theory, and the problem-focused "Second Wave" of the 1950s, characterized by behavioral therapy, cognitive approaches, and family therapy. Another way of looking at this is that in the "First Wave" approach the problem/pathology/addiction is located within the individual, in the "Second Wave" approach the problem is located in small, interactive systems, and in the "Third Wave" approach the person is never the problem—the problem is the problem. In addiction, a "Third Wave" practitioner would not see the person as an "alcoholic" or an "addict," but would work hard to help the person get "unstuck" from his or her label in order to mobilize the person's energy and confidence to find a new life path, provided that is the direction the person wants to go. Both approaches are based on postmodern philosophy that people make meaning and that meaning is not made for us.

The origins of solution-focused therapy are found in the work of Milton Erickson (1954), who strongly believed (1) that solving the problem was more important than finding and elaborating on the root "cause" of the problem and (2) that clients had the ability within themselves and/or their social system to bring about change. The development of the solution-focused brief therapy approach began in 1978, when Insoo Kim Berg and Steve deShazer borrowed money and put up their house for collateral to open a small Brief Therapy office in Milwaukee (see Berg, Background Information, on the Brief Therapy Web site at www.brief-therapy.org). Since then, what has been called a "different paradigm" is practiced in many different settings all over the world.

This approach treats problem gambling, substance misuse or dependence, and eating disorders using the same assumptions and techniques practiced with any other need or problem that a client may bring to the therapeutic environment. Like the feminists and narrative therapists, solution-focused practitioners would not see the particular addiction as a "unitary disease" that affected everyone alike, but rather would assist the person to define his or her own conception of the problem and goals for change. In a national sample of 284 alcoholism counselors (members of the National Association of Alcoholism and Drug Abuse Counselors), Osborn (1997) found that 79% of the counselors endorsed solution-focused principles, such as identifying and using client strengths and abilities, client–counselor collaboration throughout the course of treatment, highlighting and promoting already occurring non–problem behavior, meeting the client's goal(s), and constructing solutions rather than resolving client problems. However, the counselors identified belief in different conceptual frameworks: 54% agreed or strongly agreed with a psychosocial concept of alcoholism (social learning theory—alcohol dependence is understood as a continuum) and 45% agreed or strongly agreed with the tenets of a disease concept of alcoholism. These results suggest that a strong adherence to the disease concept by alcoholism counselors may not be as prevalent as some have reported and that, even when it is the dominant framework for some clinicians, it is not incompatible with practicing solution-focused treatment.

Specific techniques to find out what is important to the client might involve the "miracle question," asking for exceptions to the problem, scaling questions, and coping questions. Strengths and past successes in dealing with problems of living would be highlighted instead of deficits or "pathology." The person would be seen more as a valuable resource to form goals and find solutions than as an impaired person with poor judgment. The client's immediate goal would be accepted as a good goal, whether or not it involved quitting the addiction (Berg & Miller, 1992).

A classic example of solution-focused therapy applied to addiction is the story of "Mr. Glue-Head" (Berg & Miller, 1992, p. 15). The subject is a young man who was ordered to treatment again because of his arrest for "sniffing glue" and public intoxication. He had a long history of arrests and treatment episodes, but nothing had changed. Using a solution-focused approach that emphasized cooperation with the client, the therapist asked what he wanted to accomplish with this referral.

Elmer made it very clear that discontinuing glue sniffing was not what he wanted. He only wanted to stop getting arrested. The therapist then wondered whether sniffing glue on the back porch might be an acceptable alternative to getting high on the front porch—a place, the therapist pointed out, where the police could see him easily. He readily agreed to try out the idea as "an experiment" and to return in a week to report his findings.

When "Elmer" returned the following week, he reported that the police never even bothered to check the back porch, even though they had driven by his home on several occasions. The only time the police had stopped was late one afternoon as he sat relaxing on the front porch, "enjoying the sunset" without the help of sniffing glue. After this experience, Elmer began sitting out on the front porch straight just for the fun of it! The result, of course, was that he did not get arrested again or referred for any more treatment. Once the arrests and referrals had stopped, Elmer began to curtail his use of inhalants on his own.

The case example of "Mr. Glue Head" illustrates several main tenets of the solution-focused approach. The therapist avoided issues that had always been considered problems by the therapist and others but that were not identified as problems by Elmer. Instead, the focus was shifted to a problem that Elmer identified, "not getting arrested." By following Elmer's lead, the therapist avoided perpetuating the past nonsolutions and worked with Elmer on "doing something different."

Solution-focused therapy is based on the assumption that the future can be created and negotiated, regardless of the problem. The future "is not a slave of the past events in a person's life; therefore, in spite of past traumatic events, a person can negotiate and implement many useful steps that are likely to lead him/her to a more satisfying life" (Berg, 2001, p. 4). The resources, skills, and knowledge to take such steps can be uncovered through the use of several techniques.

The miracle question is a technique that is particularly helpful in supporting hope that things can be different in spite of many past attempts and failures to change. This question leads the client directly into imagining, describing, creating, and embellishing on a day in the future without the burden of the particular problem that led or required the client to seek help. The question is (Berg & Miller, 1992, p. 13), "Suppose that one night, while you are asleep, there is a miracle and the problem that brought you into therapy is solved. However, because you are asleep, you don't know that the miracle has already happened. When you wake up in the morning, what will be different that will tell you that this miracle has taken place? What else?"

Through persistent questioning about what the person would be doing different on this new, problem-free day, who would notice the difference, and what effect this would have on the person, a rich picture emerges that can provide momentum for a person to start making changes. Since the "different behaviors" are already specified in the imagined future (such as "I would get up in the morning feeling good, no hangover," "I would sit down and eat breakfast with my son," "I would be humming as I got him dressed for school," etc.), it's a natural progression to find out what small step the person could take in reality to reach a little bit of the "miracle picture."

For example, one of the goals of a young anorexic woman in a case described by O'Halloran (1999) was to "get taller." After learning from the dietician that her low intake of calcium was likely to impact bone growth, she began to add previously rejected foods such as cheese, yogurt, and milk back into her diet very slowly. She was able to do this because the food became "medicine," not food with calories.

Scaling questions are used in a variety of ways to help the client assess the client's level of hope, determination, confidence, and sadness, how much change has occurred, etc., similar to the motivational interviewing scales described earlier. For example, "On a scale of 1 to 10, where 10 stands for the worst upset you have ever felt, how upset are you today? What would it take for you to move up by 1 point? When you move up by 1 point, what would your husband (friend, cat, coworker) notice that would tell him that you are doing a little bit better?"

Coping questions can be used to bring out the survival strategies of people who have been managing somehow in spite of their addictions. This is very helpful in building hope and self-efficacy, two key ingredients for change. For example, "You've been through a lot in the last month with your gambling. How in the world have you coped with so much while still holding down a job?" "What else have you managed to do in spite of your addiction?"

Both solution-focused and narrative therapies have an unintended consequence of helping counselors feel less burned out, more optimistic, and less likely to be "captured by our clients' despair" (O'Hanlon, 1994). Besides focusing on strengths, these models recognize that if you try to sell something like abstinence to people who aren't ready or don't want it, then the counselor will be frustrated most of the time (Ross, 1997). For example, a Pregnancy Outreach Program in Prince George, British Columbia, developed solution-focused strategies for promoting tobacco reduction with disadvantaged, high-risk prenatal clients (Browne, Shultis, & Thio-Watts, 1999). As clients increased in confidence and self-efficacy scores, the counselors also experienced an increased sense of efficacy in their work. They were able to apply this approach to other areas of concern to the clients, such as diet, alcohol use, and relationship problems. The authors saw this as a way of "fostering tolerance and respect for clients' values, capabilities, circumstances, and culture" and particularly relevant to women from disadvantaged groups, who often receive discriminatory treatment from mainstream culture (p. 173).

Narrative Therapy

Narrative therapy, like solution-focused therapy, is also premised on the innate strengths and resources people possess. However, narrative therapy pays even more attention to the patterns of meaning as reflected in life histories and as experienced within a particular culture. Narrative therapy was developed principally by the work of Michael White and David Epston of Australia, who in turn were inspired by anthropologist and psychologist Gregory Bateson's ideas about the "news of difference" and influenced by French historian Michel Foucault's ideas on the damaging effects of normalizing practices that undermine people's efforts to lead a life of their own making. The word *narrative* refers to the "emphasis that is placed upon the stories of people's lives and the differences that can be made through particular tellings and retellings of these stories" (Dulwich Centre, 2001).

Narrative therapy is perhaps best recognized by the practice of "externalization," that is, linguistically separating the problem from the personal identity of the client. An "alcoholic" becomes a "person oppressed by the Alcohol Bully," or "Booze." An "addict" is a "person ground down by Meth" who works to "stand up to Cravings." "Crappy Attitude" may be working to rule a woman's life and keep her from the path to recovery. The name of the problem is decided in collaboration with the client or family, and has the effect of liberating the affected person from the label in order to strategize how to deal with "it."

Narrative therapy tends to follow a sequence that requires intense listening and persistence (O'Hanlon, 1994). After externalizing and naming the problem, the next task is to track the problem's effect on the client's life and the tactics the problem uses to "influence, trick, or recruit" the person. For example, "How long has Anorexia been lying to you?" is a common question that can open up the whole area of distorted perceptions around weight without requiring the person to defend herself. She can then use that defensive energy to fight the problem.

Narrative therapy also uses "exception" questions, like solution-focused therapy but with a different emphasis. Instead of asking "Tell me about a period when you haven't been getting drunk," a narrative therapist might ask, "So what's the longest time you've stood up to Mighty Meth?" Again, the purpose is to increase hope that change is indeed possible. At this point, the narrative therapist will become intensely interested in uncovering the evidence of past competence and using these stories as evidence that the person is strong, even if the individual hasn't incorporated this view of self in the present. According to O'Hanlon (1994, p. 26), this is where "the person's identity and life story begin to get rewritten. . . . This is the *narrative* part."

After developing this "new life story," the person is encouraged to speculate on what future developments may emerge from this reframed life and on the effects this may have on others. For example, "As you continue to stand up to Crappy Attitude, what will be different about your future?" Narrative therapists, cognizant of the social context in which problems develop, will use letters, family members, and other people who have been successful in "standing up to the problem" as witnesses to reinforce this new life path. For example, narrative therapist Steve Madigan (1994, p. 27) reports on the letter-writing campaign of the "antianorexic/antibulimia group he was facilitating in an inpatient treatment center in Vancouver, B.C. In response to a call for help from a woman in a remote area, the group decided to initiate a monthly exchange of letters with the woman, "in which group members described their experiences with anorexia and bulimia and offered strategies on how to resist everything from anorexic guilt and women's magazines to the debilitating effects of medication—what the group calls 'psychiatric' drugs."

Using a narrative approach with people experiencing alcohol and drug problems might require giving up the medical metaphors that are so common in this field (diagnosis, assessment, treatment, recovery). Although recognizing that the medical approach has been effective for many people, narrative therapists would argue that "one size doesn't fit all" and that a useful idea is not a universal truth (Winslade & Smith, 1997). Narrative therapy offers the possibility of transforming an object of medical-psychological practice to a person who is a responsible subject through and exploration of the following issues (Winslade & Smith, 1997, p. 160):

- The many conflicting messages about alcohol that circulate in various communities
- The implication of discourses about race, gender, and class in the construction and maintenance of "alcohol problems"
- The effects of the normalization of alcohol and the effects on the people of the definitions of "normal" patterns of alcohol use
- The impact of commonly held notions, such as "alcoholic," on the counseling process itself
- The opening up of space for descriptions of self that are not subsumed by the description that "alcohol trouble" brings
- The opening up of space for the development of lifestyles that are preferred over an "alcohol lifestyle"

Narrative Therapy in Group Settings

Not surprisingly, narrative therapy has a different approach to working with groups than a traditional skills (facilitator/didactic) approach, because of the premise that participants are expert with knowledge, skills, and resources in their own lived experience. The work of the group consists of removing the "problem-dominated personal and cultural stories that describe the individuals as inadequate in some way . . . and allowing space for preferred alternative stories" (Silvester, 1997, p. 234). The Anti-anorexia/bulemic League in Vancouver, B.C., offers an example of how a group of young women help each other act to bolster their non–problem identity and externalize the problem. As a group, they publicly denounce "proanorexic/probulimic" activities against women's bodies by writing letters to magazines, newspapers, and company presidents, printing stickers with the slogan "Starvation kills your appetite for Life" and "YOU are not just a body," placing them over proanorexic billboard advertising and at diet centers, and holding accountable the professional systems that marginalize women with "eating disorders" (Madigan, 1995).

Research on the Effectiveness of "Third Wave" Approaches

Both "Third Wave" approaches lack rigorous controlled studies to support any superiority in their effectiveness. It is not surprising that narrative therapy, given its postmodern philosophy that "objective reality" is a matter of interpretation, has not produced empirical methods of evaluation or empirical findings on effectiveness. True to the narrative vision, stories are used primarily as anecdotal evidence that this is a viable therapeutic approach. In addition, research on the outcome of psychotherapy has produced no major findings other than that, with a few exceptions (such as cognitive-behavioral interventions with panic and phobic disorders), there are no significant differences among the different types of therapies and that therapy is better than no therapy (Stalker, Levene, & Coady, 1999).

Research studies on the effectiveness of solution-focused therapy are also scarce. On the one hand, Gingerich and Eisengart (2000) cite 15 controlled outcome studies on solution-focused brief therapy that provide preliminary support for the efficacy of this approach, but they caution that more study is needed. On the other hand, Coady, Stalker, and Levene (2000) find these same studies problematic, and they conclude that there is no empirical evidence of the superiority of solution-focused therapy. Even Insoo Kim Berg and Peter de-Jong (1996, p. 388), two major developers of this approach, state that "the effectiveness of solution-focused therapy remains to be demonstrated using controlled experimental designs."

TRADITIONAL TREATMENT
AND STRENGTHS-BASED APPROACHES

The treatment system for persons with an alcohol or drug misuse problem is commonly conceptualized as: (1) detoxification, (2) intensive treatment, (3) residential programs, (4) outpatient services, and (5) aftercare services. Although this continuum of care is not available in many rural areas of the United States, it is usually possible to piece together all of these elements by utilizing programs from other states or metropolitan areas.

The primary purpose of detoxification services is to help the client medically stabilize and reduce or endure withdrawal symptoms that could be fatal without intervention. Commonly referred to as "detox centers," these centers may either stand alone in community-based programs or be attached to a hospital-based treatment program. Staff includes physicians and nurses for medical supervision and a variety of professional helpers to attend to other immediate needs and encourage the client to continue utilizing help. Clients in community-based detox centers are often referred by police, probation/parole officers, and mental health practitioners and are frequently from poverty or homeless situations; many are dually diagnosed. Although detox programs consistently provide safe withdrawal environments, their effectiveness in reducing drug or alcohol use is minimal (McNeece & DiNitto, 1998). According to the National Institutes of Drug Abuse, "Detoxification is not designed to address the psychological, social, and behavioral problems associated with addiction and therefore does not typically produce lasting behavioral changes necessary for recovery" (National Institute of Drug Abuse, 1999, p. 2).

A strengths-based approach to detoxification services may see this as an opportunity to introduce the client to choices about how to take care of immediate needs such as housing, financial assistance, and job related services. As discussed in chapter 8 on Substance Misuse with a Coexisting Disorder or Disability, basic areas of inquiry that are consistent with harm reduction and motivation enhancement practices include finding out what stage of change the person is in, how much insight the person has about the harms and benefits of the use of alcohol/drugs, and what personal strengths and resources (past exceptions to the present troubles, important persons or family that care about the person, survival strategies, and capacities for development) might be helpful (Denning, 2000; Drake & Meuser, 2000).

In an ideal world, treatment would be a seamless process connected to detox services and aftercare. In the real world, there is usually a long waiting list for treatment programs that are often located in states or metropolitan areas far from the day-to-day lives of the clients, and aftercare services may be pasted together in the local community with whatever resources exist. Many treatment programs currently involve some combination of intensive inpatient services for up to a week, intensive outpatient services or all-day sessions for another week or two, and regular outpatient services several times a week that gradually evolve into "aftercare" appointments once a month. Research has demonstrated that there are few differences in the long-term outcomes of inpatient and outpatient care (Finney, Hahn, & Moos, 1996); however, inpatient treatment is still recommended for persons who live under conditions unfavorable to recovery, such as few financial resources, risky environments, or co-occurring disorders (National Institute on Alcohol Abuse and Alcoholism, 2000).

Residential services include halfway houses (originally designed to serve alcoholics), therapeutic communities (originally designed to serve drug addicts), and missions. These programs provide a safe environment where people practice living sober with one foot in the community. The best outcomes are associated with longer stays, although there is no research evidence indicating how long that should be (McNeece & DiNitto, 1998).

Outpatient treatment is primarily group counseling with adjunct individual sessions, offered several times a week for a period of 8–12 weeks. Content may include topics similar to those with inpatient treatment, such as information on the effects of alcohol and drugs, an increasing emphasis on relapse prevention, and, in the United States, an introduction to Twelve-Step programs. Given the lack of specificity about treatment modalities and a lack of research, it is difficult to evaluate the effectiveness of group treatment compared to individual treatment or to recommend one modality over another. No single approach has been found clearly superior in the treatment of alcoholism (NIAAA, 2000).

Aftercare is the final formal link between professional help and the client's recovery process, and it usually involves monthly meetings with the service provider. This phase may also involve attendance at a Twelve-Step group or other support system, such as religious counseling, and/or adjunctive services to help with other problems the client may be experiencing in early recovery. More intensive case management services may be provided to persons with coexisting mental disorders, as discussed in chapter 8. Aftercare programs may also be the mechanism for monitoring progress for mandatory court requirements.

Many strengths-based approaches are already incorporated into the existing treatment system, especially offering support and encouragement to people who may be particularly hopeless about their abilities, tolerating relapses, and turning them into learning opportunities, encouraging family and extended family support, and incorporating the clients' needs into formal treatment goals. Further steps in the direction of strengths-based practice would include a serious assessment of the stage of change the client is in when entering treatment and an effort to gear treatment strategies to the needs of that stage, offering an array of change options that include abstinence but are not limited to abstinence, and honoring the ability of the person to make choices that will eventually benefit him or her.

SUMMARY AND CONCLUSION

In this chapter we have described four strengths-based approaches that honor the principle of client self-determination, focus on the resources, capabilities, and possibilities that the client/client system may be able to use to further client goals, and pay attention to the client's stage of readiness. The practices of harm reduction are well entrenched in addiction treatment outside the United States, but a growing number of practitioners in the United States and Canada are finding reasons to creatively incorporate harm reduction methods in a variety of settings. Motivational interviewing techniques, with the focus on readiness to change and resolving ambivalence, have become well-accepted practices in many areas of addiction treatment. The "Third Wave," postmodern therapies of solution-focused brief interventions and narrative therapy are just beginning to be acknowledged as viable alternative conceptualizations that differ from the "problem-saturated" approach of the medical model. Both therapies offer new ways of connecting to a person experiencing problems and help us appreciate the diverse ways people develop meaning and find new life paths within their cultural, racial, and ethnic influences.

References

Alcoholism and Drug Abuse Weekly (2001, January 29). Do mainstream treatment, harm reduction mix? San Francisco says yes. Manisses Communications Group, pp. 1–3.

Baer, J. S., & Murch, H. B. (1998). Harm reduction, nicotine, and smoking. In G. A. Marlatt (Ed.), *Harm reduction: Pragmatic strategies for managing high-risk behaviors* (pp. 122–144). New York: Guilford Press.

Berg, I. (2001). What is unique about solution-focused brief therapy? Online at www.brief-therapy.org/student.htm

Berg, I., & deJong, P. (1996). Solution-building conversations: Co-constructing a sense of competence with clients. *Families in Society, 77*, 376–397.

Berg, I., & Miller, S. (1992). *Working with the problem drinker: A solution-focused approach*. New York: Norton.

Bien, T., Miller, W., & Tonigan, J. (1993). Brief interventions for alcohol problems: A review. *Addiction, 88*(3), 315–336.

Booth, R. E., Kwiatkowski, C., Iguchi, M. Y., Pinto, F., & John, D. (1998). Facilitating treatment entry among out-of-treatment injection drug users. *Public Health Reports, 113*(1), 116–128.

Botelho, R., & Novak, S. (1993). Dealing with substance misuse, abuse, and dependency. *Primary Care, 20*(1), 51–71.

Broadhead, R. (1995). Introduction. Special issue of *Journal of Drug Issues, 25*(3), 505.

Brown, S., & Coventry, L. (1997). *Queen of Hearts*. Financial & Consumer Rights Council, Victoria, Australia. Online at www.home.vicnet.au/~fcrc/research/queen/part1.htm

Browne, A., Shultis, J., & Thio-Watts, M. (1999). Solution-focused approaches to tobacco reduction with disadvantaged prenatal clients. *Journal of Community Health Nursing, 16*(3), 165–177.

Bux, D. A., Iguchi, M. Y., Lidz, V., Baxter, R. C., & Platt, J. J. (1993). Participation in a coupon distribution program for free methadone detoxification. *Hospital Community Psychiatry, 44*, 1066–1072.

Carey, M., Braaten, L., Maisto, S., Gleason, J., Forsyth, A., Durant, L., & Jaworski, B. (2000). Using information, motivational enhancement, and skills training to reduce the risk of HIV infection for low-income urban women: A second randomized clinical trial. *Health Psychology, 19*(1), 3–11.

Coady, N., Stalker, C., & Levene, J. (2000). A closer examination of the empirical support for claims about the effectiveness of solution-focused brief therapy: Stalker et al. respond to Gingerich. *Families in Society, 81*(2), 223–227.

Compton, P., Monahan, G., & Simmons-Cody, H. (1999). Motivational interviewing: An effective brief intervention for alcohol and drug abuse patients. *The Nurse Practitioner, 24*(11), 27–47.

Davies, D. (1962). Normal drinking in recovered alcoholics. *Quarterly Journal of Studies on Alcohol, 23*, 94–104.

Denning, P. (2000). *Practicing harm reduction psychotherapy*. New York: Guilford Press.

Dennis, M. L., Ingram, P. W., Burks, M. E., & Rachal, J. V. (1994). Effectiveness of streamlined admissions to methadone treatment: A simplified time series analysis. *Journal of Psychoactive Drugs, 26*, 207–216.

Drake, R., & Meuser, K. (2000). Psychosocial approaches to dual diagnosis. *Schizophrenia Bulletin, 26*(1), 105–118.

Dulwich Centre (2001). What is narrative therapy? Online at www.dulwichcentre.com .au/questions.html

Easton, C., Swan, S., & Sinha, R. (2000). Motivation to change substance use among offenders of domestic violence. *Journal of Substance Abuse Treatment, 19,* 1–5.

Erikson, M. (1954). Special techniques of brief hypnotherapy. *Journal of Clinical and Experimental Hypnosis, 2,* 109–129.

Finney, J., Hahn, A., & Moos, R. (1996). The effectiveness of inpatient and outpatient treatment for alcohol abuse: The need to focus on mediators and moderators of setting effects. *Addiction, 91*(12), 1117–1796.

Fitzgerald, B., Aranda-Naranjo, B., & Denenberg, R. (1996). Applying the transtheoretical and harm reduction models. *Journal of the Association of Nurses in AIDS Care, 7*(1), 33–40.

Gingerich, W., & Eisengart, S. (2000). Solution-focused brief therapy: A review of the outcome research. *Family Process, 39*(4), 477–499.

Hohman, M. (1998). Motivational interviewing: An intervention tool for child welfare case workers working with substance-abusing parents. *Child Welfare, 127*(3), 275–289.

Hser, Y., Grella, C., Chou, C., & Anglin, M. (1998). Relationships between drug treatment careers and outcomes: Findings from the National Drug Abuse Treatment Outcome Study. *Evaluation Review, 22*(4), 496–519.

Ingersoll, K., & Wagner, C. (1997). Motivational enhancement groups for the Virginia Substance Abuse Treatment Outcomes Evaluation (SATOE) Model: Theoretical background and clinical guidelines. Richmond, VA: Virginia Addiction Technology Transfer Center.

Kushner, P., Levinson, W., & Miller, W. (1998, September 15). Motivational interviewing: What, when, and why. *Patient Care,* 55–70.

Larimer, M. E., Marlatt, G. A., Baer, J. S., Quigley, L. A., Blume, A. W., & Hawkins, E. H. (1998). Harm reduction for alcohol problems: Expanding access to and acceptability of prevention and treatment services. In G. A. Marlatt (Ed.), *Harm reduction: Pragmatic strategies for managing high-risk behaviors* (pp. 69–121). New York: Guilford Press.

Madigan, S. (1994, November/December). Body politics. *Networker,* 27.

Madigan, S. (1995). *The politics of identity: Tales from the anti-anorexia/bulimia league.* Paper presented at the Narrative therapy conference, Vancouver, B.C.

Marlatt, G. A. (1998). *Harm reduction: Pragmatic strategies for managing high-risk behaviors.* New York: Guilford Press.

McNeece, C., & DiNitto, D. (1998). *Chemical dependency: A systems approach.* Boston: Allyn & Bacon.

Miller, W. (1983). Motivational interviewing with problem drinkers. *Behavioral Psychotherapy, 11,* 147–172.

Miller, W. (1996). Motivational interviewing: Research, practice, and puzzles. *Addictive Behaviors, 21*(6), 835–842.

Miller, W. (1998). Toward a motivational definition and understanding of addiction. *Motivational Interviewing Newsletter for Trainers, 5*(3), 2–6. Internet address: www.motivationalinterview.org/clinical/motmodel.html

Miller, W., & Rollnick, S. (1991). *Motivational interviewing.* New York: Guilford Press.

Miller, W., Zweben, A., DiClemente, C., & Rychtarik, R. (1995). Motivational enhancement therapy manual: A clinical research guide for therapists treating individuals with alcohol abuse and dependence. National Institute on Alcohol Abuse and Alcoholism, Project MATCH Monograph Series, Vol. 2, NIH Publication No. 94-3723, Rockville, MD.

Nadelmann, E., McNeely, J., & Drucker, E. (1997). International perspectives. In J. Lowinson, P. Ruiz, R. Millman, & J. Langrod (Eds.), *Substance abuse: A comprehensive textbook* (3rd ed., pp. 22–39). Baltimore: Williams & Wilkins.

Narrow, W. E., Regier, D. A., Rae, D. S., Manderscheid, R. W., & Locke, B. Z. (1993). Use of services by persons with mental and addictive disorders: Findings from the National Institute of Mental Health epidemiologic catchment area program. *Archives of General Psychiatry, 50,* 95–107.

National Association of Social Workers (1996). *Code of ethics.* Silver Spring, MD: Author.

National Institute of Drug Abuse (1999). *Principles of drug addiction treatment: A research-based guide.* NIH Publication No. 00-4180. Available at www.nida.nih.gov/PODAT/PODATindex.html

National Institute on Alcohol Abuse and Alcoholism (NIAAA) (2000). *10th special report to the U.S. Congress on alcohol and health.* Rockville, MD: U.S. Department of Health and Human Services.

National Research Council (1999, April 1). *Pathological Gambling: A Critical Review.* Online at www.ngisc.gov/reports/fullrpt.html

O'Halloran, M. (1999). Family involvement in the treatment of anorexia nervosa: A solution-focused approach. *Family Journal, 7*(4), 384–389.

O'Hanlon, B. (1994, November/December). The third wave. *Networker,* 19–26.

Osborn, C. (1997). Does disease matter? Incorporating solution-focused brief therapy in alcoholism treatment. *Journal of Alcohol and Drug Education, 43*(1), 18–30.

Peterson, P. L., Dimeff, L. A., Tapert, S. F., Stern, M., & Gorman, M. (1998). Harm reduction and HIV/AIDS prevention. In G. A. Marlatt (Ed.), *Harm reduction: Pragmatic strategies for managing high-risk behaviors* (pp. 218–296). New York: Guilford Press.

Prochaska, J., & DiClemente, C. (1986). The transtheoretical approach. In J. C. Norcross (Ed.), *Handbook of eclectic psychotherapy* (pp. 163–200). New York: Brunner/Mazel.

Project MATCH Research Group (1997). Matching alcoholism treatments to client heterogeneity: Project MATCH posttreatment drinking outcomes. *Journal of Studies on Alcohol, 58,* 7–29.

Reamer, F. (1998). *Ethical standards in social work: A critical review of the NASW Code of Ethics.* Washington, DC: NASW Press.

Riley, D., Sawka, E., Conley, P., Hewitt, D., Mitic, W., Poulin, C., Room, R., Single, E., & Topp, J. (1999). *Substance Use and Misuse, 34*(1), 9–24.

Rollnick, S., & Miller, W. (1995). What is motivational interviewing? *Behavioral and Cognitive Psychotherapy, 23,* 325–334.

Rollnick, S., Butler, C., & Stott, N. (1997). *Patient Education and Counseling, 31,* 191–203.

Ross, G. (1997). Preventing burnout with solution-focused assessments. *EAP Digest, 17*(2), 26–27.

Saleebey, D. (2002). Introduction: Power in the people. In D. Saleebey (Ed.), *The strengths perspective in social work practice* (3rd ed., pp. 1–22). Boston: Allyn & Bacon.

Saunders, B., Wilkinson, C., & Phillips, M. (1995). The impact of a brief motivational intervention with opiate users attending a methadone program. *Addiction, 90,* 415–424.

Silvester, G. (1997). Appreciating indigenous knowledge in groups. In G. Monk, J. Winslade, K. Crocket, & D. Epston (Eds.), *Narrative therapy in practice: The archaeology of hope* (pp. 233–251). San Francisco: Jossey-Bass.

Sobell, L. C., Ellingstad, T. P., & Sobell, M. B. (2000). Natural recovery from alcohol and drug problems: Methodological review of the research with suggestions for future directions. *Addiction, 95,* 749–764.

Stalker, C., Levene, J., Coady, N. (1999). Solution-focused brief therapy—One model fits all? *Families in Society, 80*(5), 468–477.

Treasure, J., Katzman, M., Schmidt, U., Troop, N., Todd, G., & deSilva, P. (1999). Engagement and outcome in the treatment of bulimia nervosa: First phase of a sequential design comparing motivation enhancement therapy and cognitive behavioral therapy. *Behavior Research and Therapy, 37,* 405–418.

Twersky, A. J. (2001, March 2). Good deed feels better than fix. *Spokesman Review* (Spokane, WA), D8.

U.S. Department of Health and Human Services (1988). The health consequences of smoking: Nicotine addiction, a report of the Surgeon General. Washington, DC: U.S. Government Printing Office.

Vaillant, G. (1996). A long-term follow-up of male alcohol abuse. *Archives of General Psychiatry, 53,* 243–249.

Velicer, W. F. (1996). Introduction to special issue. *Addictive Behaviors, 21*(6), 681–682.

Wild, T. C. (1999). Compulsory substance-user treatment and harm reduction: A critical analysis. *Substance Use and Misuse, 34*(1), 83–102.

Wilk, A., Jensen, N., & Havighurst, T. (1997). Meta-analysis of randomized control trials addressing brief interventions in heavy alcohol drinkers. *Journal of General Internal Medicine, 12*(5), 274–283.

Winslade, J., & Smith, L. (1997). Countering alcoholic narratives. In G. Monk, J. Winslade, K. Crocket, & D. Epston (Eds.), *Narrative therapy in practice: The archaeology of hope* (pp. 158–192). San Francisco: Jossey-Bass.

THE BIOLOGY
OF ADDICTION

PART

Despite lip service to the biopsychosocial model of human behavior, substance abuse counselors often overlook the *bio* piece of the equation. Yet knowledge of the biology of addiction is crucial for an understanding of the hold that certain chemicals or behaviors have on people, the cravings that grip them, and the health problems associated with substance misuse. An awareness of the genetic features in addiction is also important. Thanks to advances in technology, namely, the development of positron emission tomography (PET) and functional magnetic resonance imaging (fMRI), scientists can capture chemical images of the brain at work; they can also observe not only structures but also actual functions or processes of the living brain. The ability to observe directly the effects of neurological damage caused by long-term substance abuse is a significant accomplishment in itself; being able to demonstrate the impact of craving itself on the pleasure circuits of the brain is even more remarkable. Due to neuroimaging technology, accordingly, things can be known today that in previous decades could only be guessed at or only inferred from behavior. To see, as we can today, a slide of the serotonin-depleted brain is to see, in a very real sense, the face, the insanity, of addiction. In providing this glimpse into the inner workings of the mind, modern technology is truly revolutionary. Chapter 4 tackles this awesome task.

Why is it that one person can drink and use drugs moderately over a lifetime while another person gets "hooked" after a short period of time? Why does the alcoholic tend to smoke and have a high tolerance for many of the depressant drugs? The answers are not simple—otherwise this section of the book would be a good deal shorter.

The two chapters that comprise the biology section are concerned with the physiological and pharmaceutical aspects of drug misuse and dependence and with related interventions. Chapter 4 provides an overview of the addictive properties of various drugs, the metabolization process, and the effect of chronic use on the major organs of the body. Major emphasis is placed on the most complex organ of the body—the brain. We will see, through a review of the latest research from neuroscience and with the help of diagnosis how addicting drugs work *in* the brain and *on* the brain. We conclude Part 2 with a chapter unique to this book, a presentation of biologically based interventions, the subject of chapter 5. Aversion treatment, the use of prescription medications, and cognitive treatment strategies directed toward that biological side of addiction are among the topics discussed. More specifically, chapter 5 focuses on interventions that relate directly or indirectly to biology, to interventions introduced very early in treatment, while the individual is apt to still be toxic. Included under the rubric of biologically based interventions are aversion therapy, pharmaceutical remedies, assessment, and early-stage, highly structural group work. The most intriguing part of this chapter is the description of experiments in altering brain chemistry through behavior therapy.

SUBSTANCE MISUSE, DEPENDENCE, AND THE BODY

CHAPTER 4

INTRODUCTION

If you down a scotch and soda, take a drag of a cigarette, or snort cocaine, trillions of potent molecules surge through your bloodstream and into your brain. Try injecting a drug such as heroin or meth directly into the veins and you get a rush within 30 seconds. Whatever the chosen method of ingestion—swallowing, inhaling, or injecting—psychoactive drugs are absorbed into the bloodstream and carried to the central nervous system. Unlike many other drugs, such as penicillin, these kinds of drugs pass the blood–brain barrier, causing the release of neurotransmitters (feel-good chemicals) in the brain (Abadinsky, 1996). Eventually drugs are detoxified by metabolic processes or eliminated from the body as waste material (Jung, 2001).

The result of experimentation with drugs ranges from benign to seriously destructive. The purpose of this chapter is to show what happens to mind and body after drugs enter the system, facts concerning the chemical properties of the various drugs—depressants, stimulants, hallucinogens, and cannabis. Highlights include a discussion of addiction as registered in the brain, including pathways to addiction, and the organic consequences. Finally, the physiological effects of drugs on the brain, heart, liver, and reproductive system, including the developing fetus, will be described.

PROPERTIES OF ALCOHOL AND OTHER DRUGS

A *drug* is any substance, natural or artificial, other than food, that by its chemical nature alters structure or function in the living organism (Benshoff & Janikowski, 2000). Psychoactive drugs are mood altering and used for purposes of recreation or self-medication. Such drugs can be categorized in various ways, but the usual division is into depressants (or downers), stimulants (or uppers), and hallucinogens. These substances all affect the central nervous system and therefore alter the user's mood and even sensory perceptions in some cases. The major drugs of misuse, whether uppers or downers, mimic the structure of neurotransmitters, the chemicals in the brain that give us pleasure.

Depressants

This category of drugs includes alcohol, barbiturates, tranquilizers, and narcotics. Narcotics may be natural (opium derivatives, such as morphine and codeine), semisynthetic, such as heroin, or synthetic, such as morphine and Demerol (Abadinsky, 1996). These drugs depress the central nervous system, reduce anxiety at low dosages, and can induce anesthesia and death at high dosages.

Alcohol   "Cunning, baffling, powerful!" These are the descriptive words used for alcohol in an oft-cited passage from the "Big Book" (Wilson, 1939/1976, pp. 58-59). Alcohol is a chemical and a drug; the kind that people drink is ethyl alcohol, or ethanol (C_2H_5OH), popularly abbreviated as ETOH. Ethyl alcohol is a colorless, flammable, volatile liquid with a burning taste (Royce & Scratchley, 1996).

Alcohol is widely used as a solvent in industry, where it is denatured by adding a toxin to make it unpalatable (Benshoff & Janikowski, 2000). The kind of alcohol we drink is produced by the fermentation of substances, such as fruit, containing sugar, by enzymes that are produced by a microorganism, yeast (Levin, 1995). Through the process of distillation, the solution containing the alcohol is heated and the vapors are collected and condensed into liquid form again. This process, as we saw in chapter 2, increases its potency considerably.

In whatever form of alcohol is consumed, when taken to excess, different levels of intoxications are likely to be observed with different individuals and at different time points. Early in the drinking period, as the *DSM-IV-TR* (American Psychiatric Association, 2000) indicates, when blood alcohol levels are rising, symptoms often include talkativeness, a sensation of well-being, and a bright, expansive mood. Later, when blood alcohol levels are falling, the individual is likely to become depressed, less rational, and withdrawn. At the highest level a nontolerant individual is likely to become sleepy.

Individual differences in brain chemistry may explain the observation that excessive alcohol intake consistently may promote aggression in some persons but not in others (National Institute on Alcohol Abuse and Alcoholism [NIAAA], 1997). Van Wormer (1995) cites Father Martin (1972) from his

FIGURE 4.1

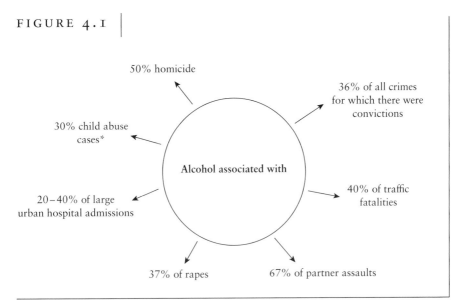

50% homicide

36% of all crimes
for which there were
convictions

30% child abuse
cases*

Alcohol associated with

40% of traffic
fatalities

20–40% of large
urban hospital admissions

37% of rapes   67% of partner assaults

*As reported by NIAAA (2001) Strategic Plan 2001–2005. Available at *www .niaaa.nih.gov/about/stratext.htm*. All other percentages reported in U.S. Department of Health and Human Services (2000).

charismatic lecture-film *Chalk Talk*, who semihumorously depicts four categories of drunks. Each category can represent a progressive stage in the course of an evening, or each can represent the drug-induced behavior of a particular individual. The types are:

- The *jocose* drunk, who is a barrel of laughs
- The *amorose* drunk, who can't keep his hands to himself
- The *bellicose* drunk, "the new man with the new teeth"
- The *lachrymose*, or crying, drunk, full of self-pity

To these we have a few additions of our own:

- The *somnos*, or sleepy, drunk
- The *clamorose*, or loud, drunk
- The *scientose*, or "know-it-all," drunk

The toll that alcohol takes on U.S. society can be seen most graphically in Figure 4.1. Domestic violence, child abuse, rape, and other crimes (including, of course, driving while intoxicated), serious illness, and accidents requiring hospitalization—all are linked to alcohol misuse (only some to alcoholism). The large majority of drunken drivers in fatal car crashes, for example, are casual or social drinkers rather than chronic alcoholics (Judson, 1998).

In Australia, similarly, the toll of alcohol misuse has received considerable attention. The National Alcohol Action Plan 2000–2003, prepared by the Intergovernmental Committee on Drugs, reveals a picture of extensive destruction of human life due to alcohol misuse, with over 10 deaths a day related to alcohol consumption. Over one-third of men and women are consuming alcohol at harmful levels, according to this report ("Alcohol in Australia," 2000).

A recent study in Sweden indicates that, similarly, 29% of all "unnatural deaths" in Sweden during a five-year period were found to be associated with alcohol (Sjogren, Erikson, & Ahlm, 2000). By *unnatural deaths* is meant non-disease-related deaths, such as accidents, suicides, falls, traffic injuries, and homicides. The concern of many Swedes, according to this article, is that when their very high taxes on alcohol are lowered as required to adapt to those of the rest of the European Union by 2004, major changes in consumption and alcohol-related deaths will result.

As McNeece and DiNitto (1998) argue, almost nothing good can be said about the effects of alcohol on the human body. True, there are substantial health risks linked to alcohol, as we will see presently when we consider the damage to the various organs of the body through long-term alcohol misuse. Researchers, however, have long reported the health benefits of moderate drinking, namely, in preventing coronary heart disease and stroke. Because they are less prone to coronary artery disease—the leading killer of men and women in the United States—moderate drinkers tend to live longer than abstainers (Peele, 1999; U.S. Department of Health and Human Services, 2000). (*Moderate* drinking is defined as up to two drinks per day for men and one for women.) The healthful effect of moderate drinking is also evident in preventing colds and protecting the stomach from tainted or unsanitary food (Shapiro, 1996). Because of the fear by American public health officials, however, that word of the documented benefits of alcohol would encourage alcohol misuse, public proclamations, according to Peele, tend to stress only the negative aspects of alcohol consumption. To such negative aspects we now turn our attention.

One property of alcohol not usually listed under properties is its addictiveness. The mechanisms that promote addiction occur primarily in the brain and relate to the effect of the chemical on the brain over time. Although researchers are only at the threshold of uncovering the mysteries of addiction, it is known that about 7 to 10% of drinkers develop dependency. As Harold Kalant, a former researcher of the Toronto Center for Addiction and Mental Health, speculates, drugs like cocaine and heroin are more addictive than alcohol; about 30% of users becoming addicted to these (Gardner, 2000). Only one drug causes addiction among a majority of its users—nicotine, as Kalant indicates.

Tolerance, Withdrawal, and Blackouts   Most heavy drinkers are proud of their high tolerance for alcohol, that they can drink their friends "under the table." Some people have a high tolerance by nature; others develop their ability to handle large quantities of alcohol as the nervous system accommodates to its effects and the liver gets more efficient at metabolizing alcohol. Alcoholics, therefore, because of their behavioral tolerance, may drive fairly well, even though legally intoxicated. *Behavioral tolerance* refers to the process of learning to adapt one's behavior to the presence of the drug. Chronic alcoholics may be only moderately drunk at the blood alcohol level of .4, a level at which a normal drinker might be comatose. Many individuals, similarly, smoke a pack of cigarettes a day, a feat that would be highly unlikely for novice smokers, who haven't yet developed that tolerance.

Low sensitivity to modest amounts of alcohol—as indicated by good performance on a test of coordination and balance—shows a strong link to future alcoholism among the sons of both alcoholic and nonalcoholic fathers, according to a longitudinal study by Schuckit, reported in *Science News* (Bower, 1994). At age 30, 10 years after the tolerance measures were taken, alcoholism afflicted 43% of those who showed the least response to alcohol, compared to only 11% of those deemed most sensitive to alcohol.

Tolerance levels are subject to alteration following a period of abstinence. Practitioners in Seattle, Washington, working from a harm reduction model, go to great pains to warn their clients immediately on their release from jail, "Don't take your usual level of drugs. Your body won't be able to handle it." Clients have died or nearly died in the past as they rush from jail to take their usual drug dose. (Information obtained in personal communication with Rupert van Wormer on May 12, 2001.)

Tolerance reversal is the phenomenon associated with aging in which the drinker loses his or her ability to handle alcohol. The liver is no longer efficient, and the experienced drinker now gets drunk on the first drink.

Cross-tolerance occurs as the tolerance developed for one drug generalizes to another drug in the same pharmaceutical class. Barbiturates, general anesthetics, and alcohol are all sedative-hypnotic drugs, so tolerance for one is tolerance for all (van Wormer, 1995).

Withdrawal is defined by the *DSM-IV-TR* (APA, 2000) as "a maladaptive behavioral change, with physiological and cognitive concomitants" of a reduction of intake following prolonged use of a substance. When the depressant effects of a sedative drug such as alcohol are removed, there is a rebound effect, and the central nervous system becomes hyperactive. This is because if the drug causes one effect, the body adapts, and removal of the drug brings the opposite reaction. (For example, opioids may produce constipation, whereas withdrawal produces diarrhea.) Sleeping problems related to alcohol withdrawal may be horrendous. For stimulants such as cocaine and crack, the visible withdrawal reaction is relatively mild (APA, 2000). Depression following the discontinued use of stimulants is common, however, as the person's body crashes from the artificially induced high. The craving for more of the drug can be relentless during this period. There are no withdrawal symptoms with LSD, however.

Withdrawal symptoms usually start within 24 hours and can last up to several days. The typical medical treatment for alcohol withdrawal involves the use of another drug for the same class. The use of newer drugs, such as clonidine, beta-adrenergic blockers, and naltrexone, have been employed successfully (Jung, 2001). In Spain, Israel, and Mexico, doctors are using massive injections of naltrexone to speed drug addicts dependent on opioid drugs through the harrowing process of withdrawal. Instead of shaking, sweating, and retching for 10 days, the patients are placed under heavy sedation for a rapid detox (Cowley, 1995).

Black coffee and other favorite remedies do nothing to speed up the brain's recovery from a night or weekend of indulgence. Caffeine plus alcohol creates a wide-awake drunk; reaction time is still impaired. Even the next day after a binge, functions involving coordination and concentration are seriously altered. The most common and least debilitating of the postintoxication withdrawal syndromes is the *hangover*. The hangover simply has to be lived through; the condition is unpleasant but not dangerous. People who don't get hangovers after a hard night of drinking should realize this lack of aftereffects could signal addiction. Advice to prevent a hangover is to drink on a full stomach, avoid darker drinks, such as a brandy, red wine, tequila, and whiskey, which have a higher content of congeners (toxic byproducts of alcohol fermentation), and drink lots of liquids, such as water (Lee, 2001). Better yet, drink moderately in the first place.

Withdrawal from alcohol addiction consists of such symptoms as tremor of the hands, tongue, or eyelids; nausea or vomiting; anxiety, depressed mood or irritability; illusions, headache, insomnia. Seizures may occur. The patients who have gotten into serious trouble with alcohol may be found in the detoxified wards of most local hospitals. Of those who develop withdrawal symptoms, fewer than 10% will develop severe symptoms such as tremors (APA, 2000). Seizures are experienced by up to 15% of alcoholics during withdrawal. Structural brain imaging shows brain shrinkage in the frontal lobes of persons who have had seizures (NIAAA, 2000b). The "DTs," or delirium tremens, which are rare but life threatening, involve visual and auditory hallucinations. The "DTs" can be avoided by coming off the alcohol gradually or by using a medication such as Valium or Librium.

Different drugs bring different withdrawal symptoms. Withdrawal from heroin or other opiates causes diarrhea, chills, fever, and a runny nose (Benshoff & Janikowski, 2000). Caffeine withdrawal produces frontal headaches, as many coffee drinkers know. Valium withdrawal produces seizures. These may occur two or more weeks after cessation of drug use. Since alcoholics are sometimes pill users too, a big problem in Norway, clients in inpatient treatment commonly have seizures long after their bodies are clear of the alcohol.

The most powerful portrayal of the throes of withdrawal is given in the classic movie *The Lost Weekend,* produced by Billy Wilder in 1945. Starring Ray Milland and Jane Wyman, this movie marked a milestone in viewing alcoholism as a progressive and chronic disease. The long, lonely weekend contains one unforgettable scene as the hero, locked in a mental ward, suffers extremely gross hallucinations.

Blackouts are perhaps the most intriguing phenomenon associated with alcohol use and the one about which the least is known neurologically. *Blackout* is a term used by both alcoholics and health researchers to describe the total inability to recall events that occurred while the person was drunk, even though the person appeared normal at the time. There is no lapse of consciousness with a blackout. The inability to store knowledge in long-term memory is attributed to a high blood alcohol level, usually over .30 blood alcohol concentration (BAC) (Sweeney, 1990). As more alcohol is consumed, larger sections of the brain are turned off, preventing cells from firing and new memories from being laid down ("Unlocking the Secrets," 1997). When blackouts are studied experimentally, they are found to be neither selective nor predictable; nor can they be anticipated by observed behavior. To have a blackout, the person must have considerable tolerance; hence, having blackouts is probably a good indicator of alcoholism. The exact neurological process of this loss of memory is not fully understood.

Get a group of recovering alcoholics together, and the casualness with which they discuss blackout episodes can be daunting. Often, the blackout is a source of amusement, if not amazement. Women may tell of waking up in bed in a strange place with a strange man; men may speak of having to search endlessly for a "lost" car. One man proposed marriage; this led to an altercation later. Friends later said these people seemed to be acting normally. A typical difficulty encountered by the alcoholic is hiding liquor and then searching high and low for it later, to no avail. Another memorable scene in *The Lost Weekend* graphically depicts the alcoholic hero's utter joy on leaning far back in a chair and spotting his coveted bottle directly overhead in the ceiling lamp.

When experiencing a blackout, it is said, one can remember something for perhaps 15 minutes, long enough to drive a car to a destination. One can think and plan. But nothing is stored in the memory; there is no way to retrieve the memory once lost. This is in contradistinction to repression, in which the memory is buried in the unconscious. The following story provided by Lisa L. (2001) is typical:

> The blackout, as explained to me by an RN, is a chemical amnesia. It won't ever come back. There is stuff I did that I had no awareness of later. Many times I'd wake up and wouldn't know how I got home. Sometimes my car was there and sometimes not; "Where did I leave that damn car?" No matter how much I tried, I couldn't get that memory back.

Legally, the implications of a blackout are significant. Hang around any courtroom and you will commonly hear the accused say, "I don't remember, I don't remember." In one case that van Wormer attended, the prosecutor told the jury, "Isn't that convenient? He killed his wife and he says he doesn't remember." In fact, even the defense attorney (who thought her client had repressed the memory) did not realize the defendant, who had consumed a case of beer, had experienced a blackout. Being in a blackout does not exonerate a person from responsibility for crime—the person was thoroughly conscious at the time and probably knew right from wrong—but it does relate to the truthfulness of a witness with a blocked memory.

Because of the memory problem, a major risk in criminal investigation is that the accused will have been "turned in" by the actual culprit for a crime that the accused did not commit. Then, on the assumption of guilt, the accused will sign a confession. Mark Twain (1876) presented a fictional rendition of this happenstance in *Tom Sawyer*. Fortunately, Tom Sawyer and Huckleberry Finn, who were witnesses, were able to save the falsely accused man shortly before he was to be hanged.

In real life, Joe Giarratano was placed on Virginia's death row after confessing to a murder committed by a right-handed person. Giarratano is left-handed. He was also in an alcohol- and drug-induced blackout at the time the crimes were committed. Because of questions raised in the case, Giarratano's sentence was commuted to life in prison (McCarthy, 2000). A team of supporters continues to work for his release.

In a rare TV news special, "Blackout Binge," Connie Chung (1999) of *20/20* explored the connection among college students between binge drinking and blackouts. The program began with a description of a fiery car wreck in which five church elders were killed by a drunken man driving the wrong way on a New Jersey State parkway. His BAC had been twice the legal limit when the crash occurred. The driver, Kevin Price, is now serving a 21-year prison term for reckless manslaughter. Today he does volunteer work in prison to teach the dangers of drinking and driving. "Kevin Price," as stated in the broadcast, "now believes his behavior can be explained, at least in part, by a little-understood phenomenon known as alcoholic blackout." The night of the crash he had had 10 beers in less than two hours playing a drinking game called Quarters with college friends.

To show how a person having a blackout can appear completely normal to others, the *20/20* broadcast treated viewers to a videotape of a wedding and a soundtrack of the bridesmaid confirming that because of the effects of alcohol, she had no memory of the wedding at all. Two experts interviewed for the program provided the following facts: Youths are the most likely age group to experience a blackout; 10 to 20% of college-age people have had them; and, finally, a blackout is even stronger when combined with Valium, sleeping pills, or muscle relaxants.

Opiates and Opioids   *Opiates* are naturally occurring chemicals derived from the opium poppy. *Opioids* are similar synthetic drugs. Opiates or opioids are narcotics used by physicians to supplement endorphins in the brain in preventing the release of pain neurotransmitters (Benshoff & Janikowski, 2000).

Because opium is not easily absorbed in the digestive tract, oral ingestion produces little effect (Jung, 2001). Opiate users, therefore, inject, smoke, or snort the substance for maximum effect. Some mix heroin and cocaine and shoot it; this extremely dangerous practice is called "speedballing" (APA, 2000). The even more dangerous combination of heroin and crack is popularly known as "chasing the dragon."

Heroin is cheaper and purer than in the past and is therefore more accessible to young people, who can now smoke or snort it. Opiates produce a powerful rush accompanied by feelings of contentment. The rush results because these drugs bind into endorphin receptor sites located in the pleasure centers of the brain. Although used for physical pain, as Levin (1995) suggests, their appeal is in alleviating psychological pain. Morphine, an extract of opium, is a powerful pain reliever and antidiarrhetic agent. Morphine blocks pain signals administered to the spinal cord, effectively blocking pain signals at the spine, a practice that is revolutionizing surgery (Gorman, 1997). Heroin is a synthetic derivative of morphine, originally developed to treat opium and morphine addiction. All the opioids are prescription drugs. Demerol is a relatively strong analgesic that has become the drug of choice among addicted medical personnel (Benshoff & Janikowski, 2000).

Morphine and heroin are rapidly metabolized by the liver and excreted by the kidneys, and they disappear from the body in four to five hours (Levin). Tolerance is incredibly strong for this drug, with users continually chasing that first high. Withdrawal is painful but not dangerous as compared to alcohol withdrawal, as Levin (1995) suggests. The horrible agony of heroin withdrawal was presented to us in the wrenching bedroom scene in the British film *Trainspotting*, based on Welsh's (1996) novel of the same title.

Heroin overdose takes place due to a reaction to impurities present in this street drug. In Britain, where heroin may be prescribed directly under the close supervision of a registered physician, there are no such dangers accompanying its use. Probably the best-known opioid to treat addicts, methadone, is used in Britain, as in the United States, to block withdrawal symptoms and reduce cravings. Addictive and euphoric for nonaddicts, its euphoric effects are much less than those of heroin (Benshoff & Janikowski, 2000). The effect of orally administered methadone lasts up to 72 hours. Heroin and methadone maintenance treatment are provided in Britain, the United States, and many other countries to reduce contraction of the AIDS virus, to reduce the patient's temptation to engage in crime to support the habit, and to monitor other drug use. The forms of treatment are a major component in the harm reduction philosophy geared to helping the addict live a stable and normal life.

OxyContin, a morphine-like substance, was introduced as a painkiller for terminally ill cancer patients. The advantage of this drug is that it is time released and effective over a long period (Cohen, 2001). Unfortunately, this drug is in big demand in the underground drug market. Illegal drug prescriptions and pharmacy robberies have escalated. Numerous deaths from overdoses have been reported in Kentucky and Ohio. Drug users crush the tiny white tablets to remove the time-release coating then snort or boil them to inject the drug to get their high. As new restrictions are being placed on the way this drug is prescribed, it is the cancer patients, unfortunately, who will suffer.

Inhalants   Used almost exclusively by children and teens, inhalants are a group of volatile chemicals or chemicals that easily evaporate and can be inhaled, often directly from their container. These gaseous substances, which were never intended for human consumption, are primarily nervous system depressants (McNeece & DiNitto, 1998). Most of the inhalants ingested today are common household products found in the kitchen or in the garbage—aerosols, paint, gasoline, airplane glue, and lighter fluid. Users sniff, or "huff," these substances, sometimes by putting their heads in a paper bag to inhale the vapors. The intoxication produced by most inhalants is comparable to that produced by alcohol and includes a light headache. At high levels, permanent damage can be done to the central and peripheral nervous systems (APA, 2000). An overdose can lead to coma. Proclaiming the dangers of inhalant use, former head of the Office of National Drug Control Policy, General Barry McCaffrey, with funding from the Johnson Institute, produced a free-of-charge video warning parents and teachers of the dangers of "huffing" and "sniffing." In the video, parents mourn the death of their young son; another youth describes his recovery following substance abuse treatment. Because of the association of this drug with children, many teens sent to group therapy for substance misuse are reluctant to disclose inhalants as their drug of choice. According to Iowa substance abuse counselor Denise Mead (1999), many youths referred for inhalant use claimed to have problems with marijuana instead.

Stimulants

Substances in this category stimulate the central nervous system, increasing alertness and relieving fatigue. Stimulants range from the mild, such as caffeine and nicotine, to the more powerful cocaine and methamphetamines. Stimulants may be sniffed, smoked, injected, or swallowed. Physiological reactions to stimulants include increased pulse and blood pressure rates, dilated pupils, insomnia, and loss of appetite. Usage may be chronic or episodic with binges punctuated by brief drug-free periods. As with alcohol misuse, aggressive or violent behavior is associated with amphetamine dependence (APA, 2000). As tolerance develops, substantial escalation of the dose is common.

Cocaine   Processed from the coca leaf, cocaine is a white powder that is usually snorted. It may also be dissolved in water and injected or smoked as freebase cocaine or crack. Freebasing involves the addition of some dangerously combustible chemicals, which can explode (Gardner, 2000). Today, instead of freebasing, some users convert cocaine into crack (named for the cracking sound heard when the mixture is smoked), which involves cooking cocaine in a mixture of water, ammonia, and baking soda (Stevens-Smith & Smith, 1998). Whereas snorted cocaine takes several minutes to reach the brain, the cooked crack delivers the same effect in seconds. Developed in the mid-1980s, crack is more concentrated than other forms of cocaine because the water base is boiled out through the heating process. The product is a crystal, or rock (Jung, 2001). Two percent of Americans surveyed used cocaine in 1996, while 0.6% used crack (APA, 2000). A laboratory study of cocaine's effect on the brain reported in the *Journal of the American Medical Association* ("Medical News," 1998) revealed that the maximal drug effect occurred in women in about 5 minutes on average and in men in 8 minutes. Physiological risks for women from cocaine use should therefore be greater than for men at the same consumption levels. Cocaine's behavioral effects do not differ much with the means by which this drug is delivered, but the effect is much more immediate when it is smoked or injected than when snorted. Feelings of sexual arousal often accompany cocaine use, probably because of an increase in blood flow to the genitals (Stevens-

Smith & Smith). Cocaine is associated with violence; today crack use is down and heroin use is up in the inner city. Some researchers attribute the decreased homicide rate to this switch (Butterfield, 1997).

Cocaine is rapidly metabolized by the brain from the bloodstream and then travels back to the blood. The drug can be found in the urine up to eight hours after ingestion. The high lasts only about 15 to 20 minutes (Fishbein & Pease, 1996). PET scanners show that cocaine works by blocking dopamine transporter sites, preventing the reuptake of dopamine. Short-acting drugs such as cocaine wear off quickly, leaving an unpleasant crash in the wake. The addictive nature of cocaine is revealed in rat studies; addicted rats will continue to press a lever administering cocaine, to the neglect of food and water. Eventually they die of seizures or dehydration (Fishbein & Pease). Because it is easy to develop a tolerance for cocaine, the frequency and dosage must be increased to maintain the same effect. In cocaine addicts, dopamine levels are quickly depleted, leading to severe depression, aggressive behavior, anxiety, and intense craving. Damage to the heart is another major consequence of regular cocaine use. Acting directly on the heart muscle, cocaine causes the heart to beat inefficiently. The most common causes of death from cocaine are heart attacks, strokes, and respiratory failure (Stevens-Smith & Smith, 1998).

Scientists have found that cocaine misuse coupled with the use of alcohol leads to poorer performance on tests of learning and memory than does the ingestion of either cocaine or alcohol alone. The negative effects on thinking persist for at least a month after the substance use, according to a NIDA (2000a) news release. The mixture of cocaine and alcohol is probably the most lethal of any two-drug combinations known.

Amphetamines and Methamphetamines   Unlike cocaine, amphetamines are synthetic drugs, yet many of the physiological effects are the same. Amphetamines in nonhyperactive people increase their adrenaline level and suppress the appetite. Hence they are widely used as diet pills. Tolerance develops quickly, however, so the dosage has to be increased. Ritalin is an example of an amphetamine; it is a prescription drug used to treat hyperactivity. This drug helps children and adults focus their attention more strongly. Although generally considered relatively harmless, recent research with gene expression in an animal model suggests that it has the potential for causing long-term changes in brain cell structure and function ("Ritalin May Cause," 2001).

Methamphetamines ("meth" or "crank") are usually available in powdered ("crystal meth") form and can be snorted, injected, or smoked to produce a two- to four-hour high (Abadinsky, 1996). This drug is hardly new—Nazi troops used methamphetamines to stay awake during World War II battles, and it was later associated with Hell's Angels motorcycle gangs (Stewart & Sitaramiah, 1997). Today a far more potent formula using common chemicals has been developed; this drug is cheap to make and can be manufactured easily in local laboratories because the ingredients are readily available. The active ingredient is either ephedrine or pseudoephedrine, both of which are found in over-the-counter cold medicines ("High in the Heartland," 1999). In meth labs, products such as drain cleaners are used to transform the substance into a powder that can be ingested. Compared to cocaine, meth has a much longer duration—up to 12 hours—although the rush is not as strong when the drug is snorted. Users stay awake for days, often weeks at a time. Paranoia, aggression, and a breakdown in the immune system often occur with regular use of this drug (Fishbein & Pease, 1996). Because of its energizing properties and relative low cost, meth is highly popular among blue-collar workers in the Midwest, many of whom have more than one job. Its manufacture is extremely hazardous because of the toxic fumes and possible explosions during the cooking process (Willmsen, 1997).

Use of methamphetamines is linked to several serious medical complications, such as heart damage, stroke, and psychosis. Long-term neurological damage can result. For recovery, physical withdrawal is not the problem, but, rather, anhedonia. Anhedonia is an inability to experience pleasure at the normal joys of life. Five percent of former users will have permanent delusional disorders with paranoia (flashbacks) (Salemy, 1998).

Nicotine   Nicotine, a highly toxic central nervous system stimulant, comes from the dried tobacco plant, which is native to North America. Native Americans have known about tobacco for centuries; documented use by the Mayan culture goes back over 2,000 years (Benshoff & Janikowski, 2000). Dependence on nicotine resembles that of the other drugs discussed in this chapter, in that it produces compulsive patterns of use, craving, tolerance, and physical dependence. Tobacco smoke contains many toxic compounds, including the highly addictive nicotine, tar, and carbon monoxide. Alone or in combination, these compounds are responsible for most smoking-related diseases (Stevens-Smith & Smith, 1998). Although far less serious than lung or heart disease, premature wrinkling of the skin has long been known to be associated with smoking. New researchers are learning how smoking causes wrinkling by reducing the skin's elasticity. In a study conducted by London dermatologists, scientists discovered that a gene implicated in wrinkles caused by sunbathing is also highly active in smokers ("Wrinkles Are Traced," 2001).

Cigarette and cigar smoking, pipe smoking, and tobacco chewing are the favorite methods of tobacco use. (The nicotine patch is a modern means of helping wean smokers from their habit.) After inhalation, it takes about seven seconds for nicotine to reach the brain. One of the effects is to elevate blood and brain levels of serotonin, producing a calming effect. Uniquely, this drug can stimulate or relax the user depending on his or her emotional state and expectations (Dunn, 2000). A major feature of cigarette smoking is its ability to help the smoker lose weight via the release of specific neurotransmitters and the chronic stimulation that increases metabolism (APA, 2000).

Among the facts known about tobacco use from the extensive research on this product and on smokers is that: between 80 and 95% of alcoholics smoke cigarettes; approximately 70% of alcoholics are heavy smokers (over a pack a day); smokers are 10 times more likely to develop alcoholism than nonsmokers

(NIAAA, 1998). The reason for the co-occurrence of alcoholism and smoking is not entirely clear but may relate to the generalized tendency for addictive people to be highly susceptible to dependency on whichever drugs are readily available to them. Compounding this innate tendency is another factor—cross-tolerance. Drawing on animal studies, the NIAAA suggests that alcohol's sedating effects may mitigate the aversive effects of nicotine—increased heart rate, etc.—while, conversely, nicotine gives a charge to drinkers who may be in the slump. This cross-tolerance is further revealed in the fact that to achieve the required effect, smoking alcoholics may require higher doses of nicotine in their nicotine patches than nonalcoholics (NIAAA, 1998). Nicotine patches, incidentally, do not cause the health problems of smoking, problems related to the smoking itself and to the harmful ingredients that cause lung cancer and respiratory problems (Price, 2000). Taken together, alcohol and tobacco greatly increase one's risk of getting cardiovascular and lung diseases, along with other forms of cancer. The risk involved in both smoking and drinking, according to the NIAAA report, is much higher than the sum of the risks for use of each drug individually. Changes in the liver, coupled with the breakdown of the immune system caused by long-term alcohol misuse, create a heightened susceptibility to the toxic chemicals released in the burning cigarette. A related fact is that nicotine dependence is very common among individuals with mental disorders such as schizophrenia; 55 to 90% of individuals with mental disorders smoke (APA, 2000).

A recent report used by Philip Morris in a lobbying effort to influence politicians in the Czech Republic who had complained that the tobacco industry was saddling the country with huge health care expenses ("Philip Morris' Spin," 2001) refuted those claims by showing that, inasmuch as smokers die sooner than nonsmokers by over five years, smokers saved the government millions of dollars from reduced costs in health care, pensions and housing for the elderly. Not surprisingly, a storm of protest emerged from these findings, not only in the Czech Republic but also throughout the world.

Due to its addictive powers, prevention works far better than treatment in curbing nicotine use. No one who smokes, of course, sets out to get addicted. One wonders how many actors, when forced to smoke in the movies, get turned on to nicotine. Malachy McCourt (2000), in his autobiographical *Singing My Him Song*, describes his romance with cigarettes:

> Of the bad habits available, I missed very few. I drank too much, ate too much, philandered too much. I had managed, though, to somehow remain a nonsmoker, a state I remedied at about that time. I really disliked the damn things, but in the course of the commercial (for TV and for Lark cigarettes), I got hooked. I got paid around $300 for the day's work and proceeded to spend thousands of dollars to maintain my new habit, not to mention my damaged health and yellowed teeth and the hundreds of little burn holes I put in various garments (my own and others') over the years. (pp. 33–34)

Quitting smoking, as everyone knows, is immensely difficult; although 80% of smokers desire to quit, only 45% of smokers eventually can do so

BOX 4.1	TO DIE FOR A CIGARETTE
	BY TAMMY PEARSON

I have quit smoking. Finally. As an adult, I'd think, "I'm not hooked, I can quit any time." Until the day I said, "I need help." I'm a responsible person; everything else I did was in moderation. Everybody smoked. In elevators, in hospitals as employees, the grocery stores. In those days you just stomped it out in the floor. Those were the days when you'd ride in the car with smoking parents, the windows up, the car going 80 m.p.h. and no seatbelts.

Once I witnessed an outstanding example of a man exhibiting the helplessness of a nicotine addiction. I was living in Washington State and was shopping with my mother. We had just come outside to the parking lot when a man drove past, very aggressive in his hurry. When he got to his selected parking space he quickly lit a cigarette, and began an extreme act of deliberate and desperate smoking. We stayed to observe this whole ordeal. The car windows were up and he was dragging on this cigarette so hard and long that I almost expected him to just rumple it up and stuff it in his mouth, eating it. He smoked it down to where it was burning his fingers, then lit another off of the end. Now, I have also chain-smoked, but when this guy finished the first butt he cracked his car window just barely enough to stuff the butt out. He didn't even want the smoke to escape the car. My Mom and I watched the rest of this in disbelief; both of us agreed to never let the other get "that bad" and we went on our way. . . .

I remember when the doctor told me I was pregnant. "Now you're going to quit smoking," he said. I made it one-half hour. My son's father's smoke made me sick. I did everything to stop—threw the car ashtray out of the car. Once I went on crutches to the 7-11 at 2 A.M.! I had to have a cigarette. I busted out the stitches in my foot, undoing the recent surgery.

My parents had smoked for years. My Dad had a cardiac arrest. He woke up from

---

(APA, 2000). Withdrawal effects take place within hours of the last cigarette; one's craving subsides in three to four weeks.

See Box 4.1, "To Die for a Cigarette," for Tammy Pearson's account of nicotine addiction, an account as gripping as that of any alcoholic or heroin addict.

Chewing Tobacco   Even more devastating in its effects on the body is chewing tobacco, or "snuff." When tobacco is chewed, the nicotine is absorbed into the bloodstream and travels to the brain. We hear from a former snuff user and recovering alcoholic in this passage:

When I was 18 years old (I refuse to tell how long ago) I saw an advertisement for Skoal chewing tobacco. It featured an ad with Walt Garrison, who was a football star with the Dallas Cowboys and in rodeos. It featured the phrase "Just a pinch between the cheek and gums." If you sent in the ad you got a free can of tobacco. I thought it looked cool, so I did. We males are attracted to the use of spit tobacco at an early age (I was floored by the average age of 9) because we think it makes us look macho. I thought I was grown up and had a mystique about me when I first a coma in a hospital where no smoking was allowed. He woke up totally disoriented. We moved him to the V.A. hospital so he could get a cigarette. He calmed down immediately and came back to himself. There I saw all those veterans—one man had smoked in the navy; he was smoking through his trachea. Later I became Dad's caregiver. Dad had a bubble on his lung that could burst at any time. I would rub his back so he could breathe and it was horrible. 1988 was the last time I performed CPR on him. Mom and I were still smoking all this time.

In Washington State there was an ad on TV—people were throwing dirt on a grave. "Eventually everybody stops smoking," the ad said. Mom developed respiratory problems; she was on oxygen 24 hours a day. She had to go on Prednisone, a drug that causes your bones to break. I got a job at the National Jewish Medical Center in Denver, where she became a patient. I learned so much. Some of my friends there were world-famous scientists. To try to save my mother they even brought in drugs from foreign countries. Mom was deeply loved by everyone. But no one could save her. She suffered so much. I eventually became her primary caregiver. In April of 2000 we lost her to lung cancer.

For myself, I tried patches. I thought I needed a patch over my mouth! Oh God, that's me. Nobody was more addicted than me.

How did I quit? I didn't quit watching my son get sick from secondhand smoke, my mother dying, all the shameful things I did—smelling like smoke, going around feeling dirty like a salamander. I wished someone would just lock me up!

No, there was never a good time to quit. I worked at the number-one respiratory hospital in the world but I was going to have my cigarette! By now I had scar tissue on my lungs; my lungs were so shot. There never was a good time to quit, certainly not when I was happy; quitting would ruin my whole day. Finally, a bad day came. I was so miserable that any more pain wouldn't matter—"kick me while I'm down." Now is a good time. "I'll use this as a marker," I thought. And I did, and I died a thousand deaths but I did it.

Source: Speech given at the University of Northern Iowa, Cedar Falls, February 13, 2001. Printed with permission of Tammy Pearson.

used. I was hooked for the next 17 years of my life. I burnt my lower lip from chewing, so I switched to my upper lip. I finally said, "Enough is enough!" and quit cold-turkey 26 months ago. But as I thought about it I had a huge urge to chew again that I did not act on. I have so many friends who use chewing tobacco that started when they were kids years ago, I can imagine the oral cancer epidemic that is forthcoming in the near future. What kids don't realize and tobacco companies don't tell you is that the nicotine is absorbed into the bloodstream very quickly through the lip and has a very short trip to begin its effects on the brain. (Larry Cranston, private correspondence with van Wormer, 2000)

Hallucinogens

Hallucinogenic plants have been used for centuries as medicines, to cause an altered sense of reality, and for spiritual or religious purposes. *Psychedelic* is a term employed by users of hallucinogenic chemicals. Such substances occur in the natural world and can be produced synthetically. These drugs overwhelm the central nervous system and produce such desired outcomes as "out-of-body" experiences, sensory illusions, strange tactile sensations, an altered sense of time, and hallucinations (Abadinsky, 1996).

LSD and PCP   Perhaps the best-known example of a hallucinogen is LSD (lysergic acid diethylamide). This synthetic drug achieved great popularity during the late 1960s and 1970s as youths sought a different level of reality and consciousness and the collective bonding experiences of "taking a trip." Taken orally, this drug is odorless, colorless, and tasteless, often squirted onto a small sugar cube. (A unique property of LSD is that it can be absorbed directly through the skin.) Effects take place approximately one hour after use and can last up to eight hours. Heavy users sometimes experience flashbacks, even years after use; the effect is an involuntary return to the drugged state. A key danger in the use of LSD is the drug-induced psychosis that can lead users to think they could, for example, fly out the window or walk on water. Such illusions led to many well-publicized deaths in the late 1960s. "Bad trips" were also commonly reported as the drugged state turned nightmarish for some individuals. The long-term effects of LSD use are not known; this drug is not addictive, but tolerance does develop (APA, 2000).

Phencyclidine (PCP, "angel dust"), another synthetic drug, became a street drug in the 1970s because of its ability to produce trancelike states (Jung, 2001). Developed as an anesthetic for humans, it was later used for a while as an animal tranquilizer. It was associated with drug-induced psychosis and violence. PCP can be swallowed, smoked, snorted, or injected for a high that peaks after 30 minutes and can last for four to six hours (Stevens-Smith & Smith, 1998).

Peyote and Mescaline   The peyote cactus is native to Mexico and the south-western United States. This psychoactive plant, dried to form a hard button, may be chewed directly or ingested in powder form (Fishbein & Pease, 1996). American Indians have ritualistically harvested and eaten these plants in ceremonial fashion without ill effects, according to Hill (1990).

Mescaline, another psychedelic drug, occurs naturally in mushrooms. Less potent than LSD, it was a popular drug in the 1960s.

Ecstasy, Rohypnol, and GHB   Developed by a German pharmaceutical firm as an appetite suppressor, MDMA, or Ecstasy, which was rediscovered in the 1980s, is sometimes known as a designer drug. While consumption of drugs like cocaine and marijuana among American teens has stabilized, Ecstasy's popularity has increased exponentially (Klam, 2001). Churned out from underground factories run by international crime syndicates, Ecstasy can produce both stimulant and psychedelic effects (NIDA, 1999). Chemically, MDMA is similar to amphetamines and to the hallucinogen mescaline. MDMA releases the brain chemical serotonin, elevating mood and acting as a short-term antidepressant. In low doses, Ecstasy produces no hallucinogens but, instead, heightens one's sensory experiences and awareness of self. Popular among troops in the military and with youths at "raves" and dance clubs, this drug, in its stimulant effect, enables users to dance for extended periods; it may also lead to dehydration, hypertension, and heart or kidney failure (NIDA, 1999). Long-term brain damage has been reported as well.

Klam (2001, p. 40), a journalist with personal experiences with Ecstasy, describes the visceral effect of this drug as follows:

> The what-ifs, the self-doubts, are knocked flat, and instead a hunger for human connection and a desire to empathize firmly take hold. No other drug produces this kind of feeling. It's also a whopper of an antidepressant. Whereas Prozac-type SSRI antidepressants keep your brain from emptying reservoirs of serotonin too quickly, Ecstasy floods your brain with the stuff. You feel restored, energized.

Although users consistently describe that initial high as one of life's greatest experiences, due no doubt to chemical changes in the brain, replicating that original high is close to impossible, as Klam (2001) informs us. Many of the problems associated with this drug stem from the fact that dangerous chemicals are sometimes added. According to information distributed by the harm reduction network DanceSafe (2000), much of what is sold as Ecstasy on the black market actually contains other drugs, such as PMA, speed, and PCP. Youths who consume Ecstasy tablets are advised to have the tablets chemically tested for foreign substances by DanceSafe representatives. Users are also advised to drink large quantities of water. The deaths associated with Ecstasy use, according to DanceSafe, usually occur as a result of the heat stroke connected with dehydration. Mixing Ecstasy with alcohol or other drugs increases the risk of adverse reactions.

No club drug is benign, as the NIDA bulletin notes. Chronic misuse of MDMA appears to produce long-term damage to serotonin-containing neurons in the brain. Damage is most likely associated with depression, sleep abnormalities, and memory disturbances. Despite the damaging aspects, a government-approved study in Spain is using Ecstasy to treat rape victims for which no other treatment has worked (Klam, 2001). This treatment is promoted because of the ability of MDMA to reduce the fear response to stimuli and because of anecdotal reports of success in reducing the impact of past trauma.

Rohypnol, better known as the "date rape drug" or "roofies," is a sedative manufactured in Europe as a sleeping pill. Although a sedative chemically very similar to Valium, it is included here as a newer drug and a partying drug. Rohypnol is cheap, which makes it popular on college campuses and in gay and lesbian bars. Much of the roofies used in the United States are obtained by prescription in Mexico. Although this drug is reportedly used by date rapists, usually dropped surreptitiously into a woman's drink, women are also known to use this drug purposely for its intoxicating effects. Roofies are often used to moderate the effects of a cocaine binge or to enhance the effects of alcohol or heroin. This drug causes amnesia of events that happened while under the drug's influence. Blackouts can last up to 24 hours (Center for Substance Abuse Prevention, 2000).

GHB (gamma-hydroxy-butyrate) is a substance currently circulating within the dance music scene as an alternative to Ecstasy or speed. An odorless, colorless, and nearly tasteless liquid, GHB is misused for bodybuilding effects and, in cities, is associated, like Rohypnol, with sexual assaults.

Cannabis (Marijuana)   Although cannabis at high doses possesses some of the properties of hallucinogens and at low doses some of the properties of depressants, the *DSM-IV-TR* (APA, 2000) recommends a separate category for this drug due to its unique behavioral effects. The plant *Cannabis sativa* (Latin for "cultivated hemp") grows wild throughout much of the tropical and temperate zones of the world (Abadinsky, 1996). *Cannabis sativa,* grown by George Washington to make rope, is the hemp plant and has varying potency depending on the type of plant grown and on the climate and soil (Brick & Erikson, 1998). Known variously as Indian hemp, reefer, marijuana, pot, or grass, cannabis can be smoked in pipes or in a cigarette called a joint, eaten (as in brownies), or drunk. As the older generation tells the younger generation, the potency of marijuana has drastically increased in the United States. This has occurred, in part, as California growers have been successful in cultivating an unpollinated plant known as *sinsemilla* (Stevens-Smith & Smith, 1998). Hashish is the resin obtained from the flowering tops of the female plant; it is considerably more potent than marijuana (Levin, 1995). Tetrahydrocannabinol (THC), the psychoactive ingredient in marijuana, has been found, in large amounts, in imported products as well.

After marijuana is smoked, the THC is absorbed by the lungs; the longer the smoke is held in the lungs, the higher the dose (Benshoff & Janikowski, 2000). Smoking marijuana provides a more immediate high than eating food laced with marijuana. The effect is a state of relaxation, well-being, much gaiety, and laughter. Because THC lowers blood glucose levels, pot smokers often develop voracious appetites. Recent findings confirm that marijuana activates the very receptors in the brain that are involved in the increase of appetite (Evans, 2001). This attribute has a medicinal value in the treatment of cancer and AIDS patients; and marijuana is legally available in some places for this purpose. Regrettably, the U.S. Supreme Court has ruled unanimously that even for ill patients, there is no exception to the federal law classifying the drug as illegal (Lane, 2001).

THC is fat soluble and is readily stored in the body's fat cells and organs; its presence can be detected for long periods. No physical tolerance or withdrawal has been clearly documented with marijuana use; the long-term effects on the brain are not well known; and overdose is not fatal (Benshoff & Janikowski, 2000). Levin (1995, p. 27) is more negative: "Chronic pot use results in apathy, social withdrawal, and impairment of goal-directed behavior. Impairment of short-term memory also results from chronic use." Lung cancer, as Levin further indicates, has been found to result from heavy marijuana smoking, which leaves a residue in the lungs.

To compare the various commonly used drugs in terms of their modes of administration and addictive qualities, see Table 4.1.

TABLE 4.1 | DRUGS OF MISUSE

Drug	Dependence Physical/Psychological	How used	Duration (hours)
Narcotics			
Opium	High/High	Oral, smoked	3–6
Morphine	High/High	Oral, smoked, injected	3–6
Codeine	Mod./Moderate	Oral, injected	3–6
Heroin	High/High	Smoked, injected, sniffed	3–6
Depressants			
Barbiturates	High/Moderate	Oral	1–16
Methaqualone	High/High	Oral	4–8
Tranquilizers	High/High	Oral	4–8
Ethyl alcohol	Possible/Possible	Oral	1–4
Stimulants			
Cocaine	Possible/High	Sniffed, smoked, injected	1–2
Amphetamines	Possible/High	Oral, injected	2–4
Methamphetamine	Possible/High	Oral, injected	2–4
Hallucinogens			
PCP, angel dust, loveboat	Unknown/High	Smoked, oral	Injected, up to days
LSD, acid, green/red dragon	None/Unknown	Oral	8–12
Mescaline, peyote	None/Unknown	Oral, injected	8–12
Designer drugs* Ecstasy—PCE	Unknown/Unknown	Oral, injected, smoked	Variable
Cannabis			
Marijuana, pot, grass	Unknown/Moderate	Smoked, oral	2–4
Hashish	Unknown/Moderate	Smoked, oral	2–4

*"Designer drugs," made to imitate certain illegal drugs, are often many times stronger than drugs they imitate.

Source: Adapted from "Drugs of Abuse." The National Clearinghouse for Alcohol and Drug Information. Available from SAMHSA at www.health.org/govpubs/rpo926/

METABOLISM

Metabolism is the sum total of the chemical processes and energy exchanges that take place within an organism (Levin, 1995). Metabolic processes, in which complex substances, including food, are broken down into smaller ones for elimination from the body as waste, take place in every cell and tissue of the human body. But the liver is the major organ that metabolizes larger amounts of alcohol and other drugs. When ingested, alcohol passes from the stomach into the small intestine, where it is rapidly absorbed into the bloodstream due to the small size of its molecules. The body reacts to drugs as though they were toxins and attempts to eliminate the drugs by metabolizing and neutralizing them (Benshoff & Janikowski, 2000). If a drug is water soluble, like alcohol, it will mix freely with the blood plasma and travel throughout the entire body, including the brain (Dunn, 2000). A minute amount of alcohol escapes metabolism and is excreted unchanged in the breath and urine (Gordis, 1997). Because alcohol is distributed so quickly and thoroughly, it affects the central nervous system. No digestion is required; alcohol is simply absorbed by the stomach and 80% by the small intestine. The absorption of alcohol from the stomach is very quick, especially when there is little food in the stomach and when the alcohol is at relatively high concentration. Absorbed alcohol is rapidly carried throughout the body in the blood until an equilibrium is reached such that blood at all points in the system as well as the breath and urine contains approximately the same concentration. Consumed with carbonated beverages, alcohol will have an increased intoxicating effect.

Once alcohol enters the bloodstream, it is transported to every cell in the body. Alcohol is diffused in the body in proportion to the water content of the various tissues and organs. Alcohol's small molecule and its solubility in water make it readily transportable across cell membranes, with the effect of harm to many different organs (Levin, 1995).

Since this metabolic activity in the liver takes place at a fixed rate, only part of the alcohol being pumped through the liver is metabolized at a time, while the rest continues to circulate (Royce & Scratchley, 1996). Alcohol is metabolized by enzymes, which are body chemicals that break down other chemicals. In the liver, an enzyme called alcohol dehydrogenose (ADH) mediates the conversion of alcohol to acetaldehyde (Gordis, 1997). The formation of this poison is the first step in the process. The chain of events is as follows:

alcohol > acetaldehyde > acetic acid > carbon dioxide and water

The breakdown of alcohol that occurs in the stomach differs significantly in men and women. In chronic male alcoholics and in all women the amount of alcohol metabolized by ADH is lower than in nonalcoholic men. This action takes place in the stomach; more pure alcohol is delivered, therefore, into the bloodstream of women and of chronic alcoholics than of men (Braun, 1996). Women get drunk faster than men not because they are smaller or have different body fat composition, as Braun asserts, but because alcohol-destroying enzymes in the stomach work better in men. Gordis (1999), however, argues that women have a higher concentration of alcohol in the blood than men after drinking equivalent amounts of alcohol because they have less body water than men. More research on how women metabolize alcohol is needed to clear up confusion on this point. Women will have higher blood alcohol levels than men, given equal consumption of alcohol.

The toxicity of acetaldehyde is not usually a problem. However, there is a prescription drug, Antabuse (disulfiram), that stops the breakdown of acetaldehyde by blocking ADH. The usefulness of this medication is in preventing drinking. Once Antabuse is ingested, drinking produces a severe physical reaction: nausea, flushing, and shortness of breath. Even if alcohol is placed on the skin, such as with perfume, a strong reaction will occur. Although consumption of alcohol is dangerous to most alcoholics who have ingested Antabuse, some chronic alcoholics will "brag" that they can drink freely with no negative consequences. There is as yet no substantiation of these claims, however, in the literature. For many individuals, Antabuse has a high risk of serious side effects, usually due to a reaction to another medication (Benshoff & Janikowski, 2000).

The flushing response of some Asians and a minority of Caucasians to drinking is thought to derive from a low ADH level, which insulates them from ingesting an excess of alcoholic beverages.

Healthy people metabolize alcohol at a fairly consistent rate, usually eliminating on average 0.25 to 0.5 ounces of alcohol per hour. One-half ounce of pure alcohol can be found in a 12-ounce can of beer, a 6-ounce glass of wine, or a 1-ounce shot of whiskey. The same alcohol is found in beer, wine, and spirits distilled from wine or beer. Most U.S. beer contains between 4 and 5% alcohol; European beer is stronger. Natural wines contain between 8 and 12% alcohol. Fortified wines have had alcohol or brandy added for a higher alcohol content. Spirits, including vodka, gin, whiskeys, and rum, usually contain between 40 and 50% alcohol. The word *proof* in the United States refers to twice the percentage of alcohol: 100-proof liquor is 50% ethanol. In Canada and Britain, 100-proof liquor is 57% ethanol. Beverage alcohol consists of ethanol, various byproducts of fermentation known as congeners, flavoring, coloring, and water. See Figure 4.2 to learn the amount of alcohol in various drinks.

One's blood alcohol concentration (BAC) is of special interest because of the laws regarding drinking and driving. A BAC of .1% is a ratio of 1 part alcohol to 1,000 parts blood. Most states in the United States use a .08 BAC cutoff point, reinforced by a law passed by Congress in 2000 withholding millions of dollars in federal highway money from states that do not adopt the lower standard by 2004. In Scandinavia the legal limit ranges from .02 to .05, in Canada it's .08, in Britain .08, in Japan .05. Although in Russia drivers may have no alcohol whatsoever in their bloodstream and police administer roadside tests, arresting officers are highly subject to bribery (Grier, 1997). In Bulgaria and El Salvador, however, driving under the influence can bring the death penalty.

Because of the known dangers of drinking and driving, an effective means of measurement of one's blood alcohol level is essential. The most effective is a blood test. However, the drawing of blood is an invasive and expensive

FIGURE 4.2

In normal measure, the drinks shown contain roughly the same amount of pure alcohol. You can think of each one as a *standard drink*.

What's a standard drink?
1 standard drink =

1 can of ordinary beer or ale, 12 oz

A single shot of spirits, 1.5 oz

A glass of wine, 6 oz

A small glass of sherry, 4 oz

A small glass of liqueur or aperitif, 4 oz

Source: U.S. Department of Health and Human Services (1999). *Brief Interventions and Brief Therapies for Substance Abuse,* TIP Series 34. Rockville, MD: Substance Abuse and Mental Health Services Administration.

procedure and therefore cannot be required. Urine alcohol testing indicates the presence of alcohol in a person's system but not the current condition ("Breath-Scan," 2000). After 1½ to 2 hours the alcohol shows up in the urine, so this is a measure of the drinker's condition from several hours before. A dehydrated person, moreover, will have a higher BAC than one with a normal level of fluid in his or her system. This information is crucial in contested driving-while-intoxicated (DWI) cases. The breathalyzer is the next-most-accurate measure.

Most people are quite intoxicated at .15% and comatose at .4%. Individual differences, however, are striking, with high-tolerance alcoholics functioning well up to levels of .3% when others would appear visibly drunk. When alcohol levels are between .5 and 1%, the breathing center in the brain or the action of the heart may be anesthetized. If vomiting does not prevent intoxication at this level, death will swiftly follow. Since marijuana prevents nausea and inhibits the vomiting response, the combination of alcohol and marijuana can be lethal.

For a better understanding of what drugs do to the body, let us look more closely at the metabolization process. Alcohol, as we have seen, is metabolized more slowly than it is absorbed. Thirty to forty-five minutes after the consumption of one standard drink, the BAC peaks. After a night of hard drinking, therefore, the person may find himself or herself still legally intoxicated when driving to work the next morning. At two drinks per hour, a 160-pound man would have a BAC of .047% at the end of the first hour. If he had two cans of beer each hour for six hours, his BAC would be .191%.

Because it is technically a food and because it enters the body by being swallowed, alcohol can be readily metabolized. Other drugs, such as Valium and amphetamines, tend to be swallowed as well. Swallowing drugs, as Jung (2001) indicates, is a relatively slow form of delivery, so the effects are not felt for a few minutes to an hour. Other methods of drug delivery are more direct, such as inhalation, as in the case of cocaine snorting, tobacco snuff, or glue sniffing. These drugs, like those that are injected, reach the brain quickly and so have a rapid intoxicating effect.

Valium, unlike alcohol, is transformed by the liver's enzymes into various compounds that have greater, rather than lesser, effects on the user (Benshoff & Janikowski, 2000). Whereas Valium is only very gradually eliminated from the body, amphetamines are completely eliminated about two days after the last use. Their peak effect occurs about two to three hours after use. Caffeine is absorbed into the body in about a half-hour, with the maximum impact occurring about two hours later. About 90% of this drug is metabolized or absorbed and about 10% excreted through the urine (Benshoff & Janikowski). Unlike alcohol, which is detectable in the blood and urine, cocaine, due to its rapid metabolism, cannot be so readily detected (Jung, 2001).

Fascinating in its implications, recent research by Chen, Parnell, and West (2001) shows that in laboratory rats, nicotine lowers one's BAC. As a result, more alcohol was consumed to achieve the desired effect. Implications for humans who drink and smoke are that, due to their high tolerance, they will be inclined to consume large quantities of alcohol. Consequently, long-term damage to the body organs associated with long-term alcohol misuse are likely. For pregnant women who drink and smoke, damage to the fetus can be expected to be serious for the same reason.

Cannabis, or marijuana, which is fat soluble but not water soluble, is metabolized by the liver and distributed throughout the body much more slowly than alcohol. Cannabis enters readily through cell membranes and is retained in the body for long periods of time (Jung, 2001). Drugs that are fat soluble leave long-lasting traces due to their slow release from fat stores (Price, 2000). For this reason, many persons on parole have been returned to prison for drug use even though tested one month after ingesting marijuana.

Drugs tend to be used not singly but in combination. Many of the deaths caused by drug-taking occurs because the impact of drugs in combination is far greater than the potency of each drug singly or added together. The chemical reaction of two drugs together often has a multiplying or synergistic effect. Among the elderly drinking can be especially dangerous because of the interactions of alcohol with medications they are apt to be taking (U.S. Department of Health and Human Services, 2000). The prevalence of polydrug use is often overlooked in research and surveys. The combination of alcohol and tobacco is commonplace, as is the use of illicit drugs and alcohol. Sometimes the user combines drugs to maximize the effect, sometimes to subdue it. For the latter purpose, alcohol is frequently drunk in conjunction with cocaine and amphetamines (Jung, 2001). Valium may be used as well to counter the overstimulating effect of cocaine. This combination apparently was what TV and film actor Robert Downey Jr. was after when he had his much-publicized relapse (four small bags of cocaine and 16 Valium pills were found in his hotel room). He later tested positive for both drugs (France & Horn, 2001). A large proportion of deaths due to heroin overdoses are actually the result of taking alcohol and heroin together (Gardner, 2000). The most dangerous practice is the combining of two sedatives, such as alcohol and Valium. Many deaths have occurred as well from the liver damage due to the combination of alcohol and Tylenol (U.S. Department of Health and Human Services, 2000). Alcohol impairs the liver's ability to clear toxins from the blood and can easily lead to an overdose. The combination of cold and flu remedies plus Tylenol can lead to liver failure as well. The surprising fact about this popular over-the-counter drug, according to an article in *Time* (Smith, 2001), is how unaware the public is of its dangers.

From NIDA's *Infofax* (2000) we learn that in 1999 in more than 74% of known drug-related deaths, more than one drug was involved. Heroin was the drug most frequently involved in accidental deaths, followed by cocaine.

Price (2000) describes drug interactions as occurring from the byproducts formed by two dangerous drugs in combination. Alcohol and cocaine in combination, for example, may be especially toxic to the heart and liver. Moreover, alcohol is metabolized by enzymes in the liver. If another drug requires the same enzymes, the removal of both is slowed, with possibly dire consequences.

THE BRAIN AND ADDICTION

If we can unravel the secrets of the brain, we can understand the forces that drive humans into paths of destructiveness, their cravings, passions, and dreams. Today we may not know all the answers, but for the first time neuroscientists have captured images of the brain of addicts in the throes of craving a drug. And it is this craving that is the root of addiction itself, the craving that sends people back into the dungeon—the gambling den, the bar, the crack house—again and again.

The actions of alcohol and cocaine that cause intoxication, initiate and maintain excessive drug-using behavior, and drive the relentless craving during abstinence occur primarily in the brain. Some basic understanding of the effects of drugs like alcohol and cocaine on the mechanisms underlying brain function is essential to develop and improve addiction prevention and treatment strategies. New research on the brain and behavior is forthcoming all the time; such research helps clarify the mysteries of addiction. Two aspects of brain research are crucial for our understanding of addiction: First is the adaptation factor—how the brain adapts to and compensates for the abnormal signals generated by the drug. The second aspect, one we know far less about, concerns uniqueness in the brains of potentially addicted persons. Before coming to the innate differences in the way the brains of addicts respond to drugs, the genetic component, let us summarize what scientists know about the workings of the brain itself with regard to addiction.

The Brain

The brain and the spinal cord together make up the central nervous system. The brain and spinal cord are hollow structures filled with cerebral-spinal fluid (Levin, 1995). Alcohol, as a drug affecting the central nervous system, belongs in a class with the barbiturates, minor tranquilizers, and general anesthetics—all depressants. Whereas at low levels of alcohol ingestion an excitement phase may set in, including emotional expression uninhibited and erratic, later a gradual dullness and stupor may occur. The effect of the alcohol on motor activity is seen in slurred speech, unsteady gait, and clumsiness. Functioning at the higher level—thinking and remembering and making judgments—is tangibly impaired by alcohol. Before considering some of the grave neurological consequences of long-term alcohol and other drug misuse, we will consider how alcohol affects the brain at the cellular and biochemical levels, levels that directly affect the emotions.

Each nerve cell of the brain is separated from its neighbor by a narrow gap called a *synapse*. Nerve cells communicate with one another via chemical messengers called *neurotransmitters;* most commonly, however, drugs disrupt neurotransmitter functions because they happen to resemble the chemical structure of the brain's own neurotransmitters (Lambert, 2000). Neurotransmitters underlie every thought and emotion as well as memory and learning (Nash, 1997). A good half dozen out of some 50 are known to play a role in addiction. See Figure 4.3 for an illustration of the neuron cell membrane.

Cocaine, like alcohol, brings about marked changes in brain chemistry. According to the Harvard Medical School (1993), accumulated evidence indicates that cocaine's chief biological activity is in preventing the reuptake (reabsorption) of the neurochemical transmitter dopamine. Drug-addicted laboratory rats will ignore food and sex and tolerate electric shocks for the opportunity to ingest cocaine. A depletion of dopamine following cocaine use probably accounts for cocaine binges, tolerance, craving, and the obsessive behavior of cocaine users. And, as researchers and the general public are increasingly aware, nicotine behaves remarkably like cocaine, causing a surge of dopamine in addicts' brains. Dopamine is the "feel good" neurotransmitter; too little dopamine is implicated in the tremors of Parkinson's disease, while too much causes the bizarre thoughts of schizophrenia. This drug-generated surge in dopamine is what triggers a drug user's high (Nash, 1997).

Serotonin is another neurotransmitter highly influenced by alcohol and other drug use. Serotonin is involved in sleep and sensory experiences. Serotonin has received a great deal of attention from researchers and the popular press. Decreased levels of this neurotransmitter have been linked to behaviors associated with intoxicated states, depression, anxiety, poor impulse control, and aggressiveness and with suicidal behavior.

FIGURE 4.3 | NEURON CELL MEMBRANE

Structural features of a presynaptic and postsynaptic neuron: This schematic drawing depicts the major components of neuronal structure, including the cell body, nucleus, dendritic trees, and synaptic connections.

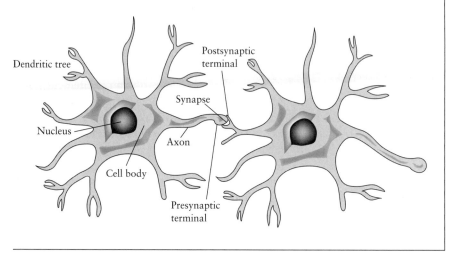

Source: U.S. Department of Health and Human Services (1997). *Ninth Special Report to the U.S. Congress: Alcohol and Health*. Rockville, MD: National Institute on Alcohol Abuse and Alcoholism, p. 66.

As Figure 4.4 shows, cocaine blocks the reuptake of certain chemicals by neurons in the brain. It is these nerve cells that release the neurotransmitters. Recent studies with genetically altered mice suggest that cocaine's effect may involve not only dopamine but possibly dopamine and serotonin in combination (Stocker, 1999). Further research is needed to reveal the exact effect of the multiple neurotransmitters.

The discovery through brain imaging and genetics of the role that serotonin plays in addiction and also in mental disorders, in conjunction with simultaneous discoveries of drugs that reduce drug cravings in rats and monkeys, has opened up a whole world of medical possibilities. We now know now that nicotine, for example, sends a rush to the brain's "pleasure center," where cocaine and amphetamines do their work (McFarling, 1998). Continued smoking, like other drug use, actually changes the brain. People with brain receptor types more prone to addiction could be helped with intensive prevention efforts. One antidepressant, Zyban, was recently approved as an aid in stopping smoking. For addictive types, breaking the smoking habit is reportedly as difficult as ending heroin addiction. Preliminary reports from Europe document that a drug used to treat epilepsy (gamma-vinyl—GABA) appears to curb cocaine craving in rats and monkeys ("New York: Anti-addiction Drug," 1998). This drug could prove to be a powerful weapon against numerous addictions, including cocaine and nicotine, according to the report.

FIGURE 4.4 | COCAINE IN THE BRAIN

In the normal communication process, dopamine is released by a neuron into the synapse, where it can bind with dopamine receptors on neighboring neurons. Normally dopamine is then recycled back into the transmitting neuron by a specialized protein called the dopamine transporter. If cocaine is present, it attaches to the dopamine transporter and blocks the normal recycling process, resulting in a build-up of dopamine in the synapse that contributes to the pleasurable effects of cocaine.

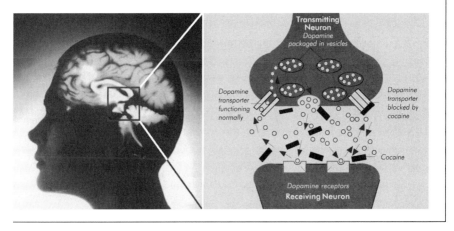

Source: *NIDA Research Report—Cocaine Abuse and Addiction*. Available from http://165.112.78.61/ResearchReports/Cocaine/cocaine3.html

Alcohol, as Sharon Begley (2001) suggests, opens the neurotransmitter floodgates. Dopamine, serotonin (governing our sense of well-being), and GABA (which, when released, regulates anxiety and has a soporific effect) are all involved in producing a high.

Through the use of sophisticated technology such as functional magnetic resonance imaging (MRI), scientists can observe the dynamic changes that occur in the brain as an individual takes a drug. Researchers, as Leshner (1999), the director of NIDA, explains, are now recording the brain changes that occur as a person experiences the rush, or high, and, later, the craving for cocaine. They can even identify parts of the brain, the pleasure circuits, that become active when a cocaine addict sees stimuli such as drug paraphernalia that trigger the craving for the drug. The memories of drug use are so enduring and so powerful that even seeing a bare arm beneath a rolled-up sleeve reawakens the cue-induced craving (Begley, 2001). The situation is similar to Pavlov's dog salivating when it heard the bell ring, a bell associated with food. Relapse occurs, as every AA member knows, from visiting the old haunts from drinking days ("Slips occur in slippery places"). Now there is scientific proof for this folk wisdom about the importance of avoiding people, places, and things associated with past drug use. See Figure 4.5 for a diagram showing the reward pathway in the brain.

FIGURE 4.5 | THE REWARD PATHWAY

One pathway important to understanding the effects of drugs on the brain is the reward pathway, which consists of several parts of the brain highlighted in this diagram: the ventral tegmental area (VTA), the nucleus accumbens, and the prefrontal cortex. When the brain is activated by a rewarding stimulus (e.g., food, water, sex), information travels from the VTA to the nucleus accumbens and then up to the prefrontal cortex.

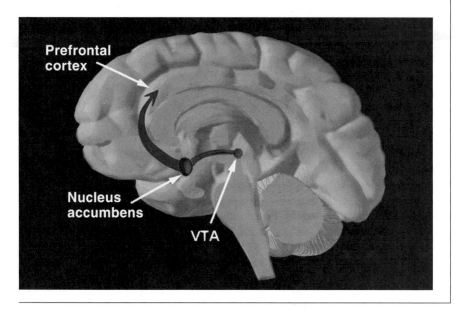

Source: The National Institute on Drug Abuse. Available online at
http://165.112.78.61/Teaching/largegifs/slide-9.gif

Relapse might also reflect the brain changes described by Leshner (1998). Recall that to produce a high, a drug such as cocaine keeps the transporters of dopamine from clearing the synapse of dopamine following the release (U.S. Department of Health and Human Services, 2000). Cocaine, for example, blocks the removal of dopamine from the synapse, resulting in an accumulation of dopamine and feelings of euphoria. As Begley (2001) explains, "When all the seats on this so-called transporter molecule are occupied by cocaine, there is no room for dopamine, which therefore hangs around and keeps the pleasure circuit firing" (p. 42). This firing releases dopamine into the synapse. The neurotransmitter in turn must attach itself to receptors on the next cell to fire some more (Myslinski, 1999). Repeated activation enhances the high. Repeated activation also leads to cell adaptation over time. Drugs, therefore, don't have the same effect as they did before (tolerance). With the same dosage, the drug user can't achieve that original high; his or her brain has changed.

Addiction is a brain disease, as Leshner (1998) suggests. Even though the initial drug taking is a voluntary act, Leshner explains, once neurochemical changes have occurred with prolonged use, the compulsion to return to drug taking or drinking is no longer voluntary. "An addict's brain is different from a nonaddict's brain and the addicted individual must be dealt with as if he or she is in a different brain state" (p. 5).

As some researchers indicate, however, the notion of brain injury is more accurate than the notion of brain disease in describing the course of events involving changes in the brain due to substance misuse. It can be argued, as does Thombs (1999), that the brain of the addict is not so much diseased as injured by exposure to self-administered toxins. As with other injuries, healing can occur when the source of the injury has been eliminated.

The discovery that different parts of the human brain are activated during cocaine *rush* versus cocaine *craving* may be useful in the development of medications for reducing the craving that makes relapse almost a matter of course (Stocker, 1998). Particular regions of the brain can be associated with levels of feeling because cocaine-addicted volunteers can now, with the new technology, rate their rush experiences and their cravings associated with cues. Cues trigger this memory, cues such as the smell of marijuana or cigarette smoke, pictures of drugs such as meth or cocaine. The fact that memory sites are involved in connection with the cues is consistent with drug users' reports of strong feelings associated with drug use, with their intense response to what researchers term their "feeling memories."

The craving that can preoccupy an addict's mind and very being involves the irresistible urge to get another rush. The memory of past euphoria, coupled with dopamine deficit related to long-term use, means the addict seeks out drugs in order not to feel low (Nash, 1997). Due to neuronal damage caused by extensive drug use, the individual can no longer feel pleasure normally. Traditionally it was thought that the reason addicts continue to drink and use was to ward off withdrawal symptoms. As Derrington (2000) indicates, however, study of various drugs of addiction reveals this is not the case. Cocaine produces no physical withdrawal symptoms yet is recognizably more addictive than heroin. The drive to return to drug use therefore must be associated with memory as well as with the changes in brain chemistry. Psychoactive drugs are said to hijack the brain, or at least the part of the brain that could overcome the intense craving or avoid continued drug misuse ("Memory Linked to Relapse," 2000).

How about craving for alcohol? Viewing pictures of alcoholic beverages does activate specific areas of the brain, according to recent research from the Medical University of South Carolina ("Images of Alcohol," 2001). The significant finding in this research is that heightened brain activity shows up in problem drinkers only and not in moderate drinkers. This result speaks to biological differences between persons inclined toward addiction and those not so inclined.

Researchers can diminish the euphoric effects of alcohol and other drugs in addicts by giving them drugs that increase the availability of serotonin ("Unlocking the Secrets," 1997). Such medications reduce craving, since the addiction is to the rush, the euphoria, not to the substance itself. Later in this chapter and in chapter 5, we will see how medications such as Ondansetron, which acts on serotonin, can help some alcoholics in recovery by reducing their craving for drugs. Following a year or two of recovery, the brain, as far as we know, replenishes itself (Thombs, 1999). Perhaps this is why long-term treatment has been found more successful than the short-term variety. Those who remain in treatment for at least a year, notes Alter (2001), are more than twice as likely as short-termers to remain clean.

What do the brain studies show about male/female differences in neurological damage caused by drug use? Only in recent years have brain studies devoted attention to alcohol-related brain damage in alcoholic women. Results of brain imaging studies show that thinking and memory abilities are markedly affected in female alcoholics, as compared to females without drinking problems (Center for Substance Abuse Treatment, 2001). This research confirms earlier speculation that women alcoholics perform as poorly on memory and special tasks as male alcoholics, even when they haven't been drinking as long as the men.

Research on cocaine's effects on male and female brains, on the other hand, seems to indicate that women have the advantage. Recent human brain studies show that women cocaine users are less likely than men to exhibit abnormalities of blood flow in the brain's frontal lobes (NIDA, 2000b). These findings suggest a gender-related mechanism that may protect women from some of the damage cocaine inflicts on the brain, according to the report.

Although science is uncovering so many mysteries of the neurobiology of addiction, one question left unanswered is why some people are so highly susceptible to the effects of addictive substances while so many others can just "take it or leave it." These differences in people probably, at least in part, have something to do with genetic makeup.

The Role of Genes

A widely publicized study of over 20,000 people in mental hospitals, nursing homes, and prisons found that 53% of those who used chemical substances had a mental disorder such as schizophrenia, anxiety, or major depression (Holloway, 1991). These findings suggest an underlying biological vulnerability for a number of disabilities. The usual search for whether the mental disorder or the addiction came first may thus be futile. Similarly, specific vulnerability may not be to alcohol misuse, but, rather, to problems with a number of substances. A brain susceptibility to addiction itself may prevail.

Although the *DSM-IV* dichotomizes substance dependence and substance abuse for purposes of classification, the most recent genetics research indicates that the tendency toward addiction, like varieties of mental illness, exists along a continuum (Begley, 1998). A gene that relates to risk taking and impulsiveness, for example, is found to vary along a continuum from healthy behavior to high risk taking to extremes, with heroin addicts having the gene for extreme novelty-seeking behavior. The new research gives scientific support to long-standing claims that alcoholism and other addictions are intergenerational.

That there appears to be a genetic tendency for alcoholics and drug addicts to be likely to use an array of different mood-altering substances is revealed in the following description provided by an anonymous wife of an alcoholic:

> At most AA meetings candy, cakes, doughnuts, etc. will be available in large quantities. This appears to be the norm; the addict gives up one substance, but the psychological attribute that allowed addiction to one also carries over to other substances.
>
> My father-in-law, when trying to stop drinking, would become obsessed with ice cream and frozen yogurt. He lived in the country, but would travel to town at least three times a day to eat his ice cream, shakes, sundaes.
>
> My husband has been in recovery for 10 years. His father, grandmother, grandfather, mother, uncles, aunts, all are alcoholics.

Why does alcoholism seem to run in families? Is alcohol behavior learned or inherited? The search for genetic links began in earnest in the early 1970s with adoption studies in Scandinavia. The aim of these studies was to separate out environmental from hereditary determinants. Goodwin (1976) sought an answer by interviewing 133 Danish men who'd been adopted as small children and raised by nonalcoholics. Health records were used to substantiate the interviews. The findings are striking: The biological sons of alcoholics were four times as likely to have alcohol problems as the children of nonalcoholics. That result, according to an article in *Time* magazine (Desmond, 1987), helped put to rest the popular assumption that alcoholics take up drinking simply because they learned it at home or turned to it because of abuse suffered at the hands of an alcoholic parent.

Cloninger et al.'s research in Sweden (1989) helped clarify the role of environment as well as heredity in the development of alcoholism. In the early 1980s, Cloninger joined a team of Swedish researchers and began gathering extensive data on a large group of adopted-away sons of alcoholics. Sweden was chosen, as Denmark before, because of the availability of thorough government records on every citizen.

In Cloninger et al.'s (1989) study of 259 male adoptees with alcoholic biological fathers (out of a total of 862 male adoptees), it was found that a somewhat larger proportion of the adoptees with alcoholic fathers were registered with Swedish authorities for alcohol-related problems than were adoptees with nonalcoholic fathers. Alcohol misuse in the adoptive parents, however, was not a determinant of alcohol misuse in the sons. The adopted men were subdivided according to their frequency and severity of registered misuse. Herein lies the major significance of the study—it determined that there is more than one kind of alcoholism.

Cloninger's first group of alcoholics, the Type 1 alcoholics, about 75% of the total, developed the illness gradually over time. It was also known as "milieu-limited alcoholism" because of the environmental influence; low socioeconomic status of the adoptive father seemed to be the key influence. Type 1 alcoholics have personality traits that make them susceptible to anxiety. In response to the antianxiety effects of alcohol, they rapidly become drug-tolerant and dependent and have difficulty terminating drinking binges once they have started. The individual prone to this type of alcoholism avoids situations involving harm or risk and seeks approval from others. Guilt feelings are associated with the drinking and with its consequences.

The Type 2 alcoholic, on the other hand, is a risk taker. Type 2 is also called "male-limited alcoholism" because of the male dominance in this category. Personality traits that distinguish this type of drinker are: early and sudden development of alcoholism, hyperactivity, traits of the antisocial personality, and a history of fights while drinking. Type 2 alcoholism is highly hereditary, passing from father to son, and associated with low levels of serotonin and dopamine in the brain. Cloninger recognizes that Types 1 and 2 are not completely discrete categories and that there is much overlap between categories.

Brain scans do reveal striking differences among nonviolent alcoholics of the Type 1 variety and among alcoholics with a history of violence (Immen, 1995). A research team in Finland discovered that Type 2 people have a higher-than-normal number of receptors in the brain and that the substance is absorbed almost immediately, for an intense but short-lived rush. Type 1 individuals, in contrast, get to enjoy the substance for a longer period.

A school counselor from Oshkosh, Wisconsin (in personal correspondence with van Wormer of November 8, 1999), describes the characteristics of two of her family members:

> Oh my goodness, the Type 1 characteristics personify my father completely. He is prone to severe anxiety and turns to alcohol due to its antianxiety effects. He has never, to my knowledge, attempted to stop drinking. Rather, he turns to alcohol whenever trouble arises. For instance, recently we had to call the ambulance because my mother collapsed. While I turned to prayer, I saw him reach for the bottle, his whole hand shaking. We were both very upset over the situation; however, we turned to different sources for comfort. Further, he avoids situations involving any harm or risk and is very conscious of what others think of him. He is the type of father who doesn't like it when his children do an activity together, such as go on vacation, because his "eggs are all in one basket." He doesn't hunt and has many fears of succumbing to harm. I have not noticed any guilt feelings, but we don't have heart-to-heart conversations, either!
>
> Although I did not know it at the time, my ex-husband was definitely a Type 2 alcoholic. He started drinking at an early age and developed a high tolerance for alcohol. He could be described as hyperactive. He had difficulty sitting still and flitted from one activity to another. He definitely had an antisocial personality, and frequently got into fights while drinking. His pattern was quite predictable; however, I didn't even recognize it as alcoholism at the time. He would get dressed up to go out for the evening. This would consist of visiting several bars. He would never just have a couple of drinks. He always drank rapidly and heavily until he achieved intoxication. He would start to act silly and sometimes speak loudly, and would frequently end up fighting with someone. He had a quick temper to begin with, and drinking made it much more worse.

Similarly, from a prison inmate (in personal correspondence with van Wormer in July 1997) we learn:

> I don't like to diagnose myself, but under Cloninger's theory I would say that I do tend to fit this category of Type 2 traits. I have taken risks all my life, e.g., drunk

driving, stealing liquor, confrontation with police, indiscreet relationships. I have been hyperactive in my early years. I definitely have to some degree today an anti-social personality: I tend to want to be by myself; I don't like having long conversations with anyone. And I have been in many physical confrontations over the years; in fact, that is why I am in prison now. Also, I believe that I have a low level of serotonin. That is why I believe that I have suffered from depression and suicidal thoughts in the past. After a few years of sobriety, I have just started to come out of the depression and now have a heart to learn about what the heck is wrong with me. The one thing that scares me about Cloninger's study is the fact it can be passed down from father to son. I have two adult sons, and as far as I know neither one of them drinks (their mother never drank). I hope it stays that way.

Further scientific validation for the Type 1/Type 2 theory in experimentation with a multiauthored study led by Bankole Johnson, M.D., on effects of the medication Ondansetron. Ondansetron, which appears to work by acting on serotonin, was found, in a highly empirical, randomized study, to have little or no effect on the Type 1, or late-onset, variety of alcoholic. It was effective in reducing consumption in patients of the early-onset variety, however. These results led the researchers to conclude that Ondansetron may ameliorate an inherited abnormality in that alcoholic subtype (National Institutes of Health, 2000). Personal e-mail correspondence with Bankole Johnson of September 13, 2000, confirms that this drug was effective with the small sample of Type 2 females as well.

Elsewhere ("Alcoholism a Product of Genetics," 1987) a correlation is drawn between pain sensitivity and Type 2 alcoholism. According to this study, researchers have shown that all alcoholics perceive stimuli strongly, as do children of alcoholics. Drinking may be one way to adapt to the sensitivity.

Electroencephalographic (EEG) tests of sober alcoholics reveal excessive high-frequency brain waves. Researchers have found that male children of alcoholics also have lower voltage of EEG activity, overall, as do Native Americans, indicating a possible susceptibility to alcoholism (Schuckit, 2000). However, not all EEG studies are in agreement on these findings. A more recent report using modern technology confirmed this finding of brain chemistry differences in children of alcoholics, differences in natural opioid activity in the brain. Because of the inadequacy in this area of the brain in many children of alcoholics, they may have difficulty handling stress, according to the report ("Children of Alcoholics," 1999).

Rodent studies provide evidence for genetic factors in alcoholism. As described in the *Tenth Special Report to the U.S. Congress: Alcohol and Health* (U.S. Department of Health and Human Services, 2000), scientists have bred strains of rats with different levels of susceptibility to alcohol effects. Through selective breeding, one strain voluntarily works to acquire large amounts of alcohol. Alcoholic rats get excited when mildly intoxicated; the nonalcoholic strains of rats do not. EEG patterns may vary also. When the drug fluoxetine (Prozac), which raises serotonin levels, is administered to alcoholic rats, alcohol consumption is reduced accordingly.

Twin studies, brain wave studies, and animal studies are other areas of research linking genetics and alcoholism. Studies on twin males suggest that, in men, a strong craving for sweets is linked to a tendency to alcoholism, according to new research from the University of North Carolina. This finding, although on a small sample of 19 sets of twins who were not alcoholic but who had alcohol problems may be significant in leading to a screening test for youths at high risk ("Study Links Cravings," 2000).

Studies of identical twins indicate a likelihood that if one identical twin is alcoholic, the other is likely to be alcoholic also (Begleiter & Porjesz, 1988). Research shows that between 40 and 60% of alcoholism vulnerability has a genetic basis and that when one in a pair of identical twins is alcoholic (or a smoker), the likelihood that the other twin has the same problem is between 40 and 60% (NIAAA, 2000a). Adoption studies reveal a risk in children of alcoholics who were adopted at birth by other parents that is three to four times the risk for other children (APA 2000). Finding the genes that are involved in addiction vulnerability is thus a high priority for scientific research. In both animal experiments and research on humans, low sensitivity to alcohol-induced sedation is associated with higher alcohol consumption levels, as the NIAAA report indicates. By identifying the proteins these genes encode and the mechanisms that determine the animal's response to alcohol, scientists can pursue the development of pharmaceuticals that short-circuit these genetically defined processes (U.S. Department of Health and Human Services, 2000).

Genetic differences in personality factors may indirectly render some individuals more vulnerable than others to drug dependence. People who compulsively seek novelty, the adventure seekers, also tend to experiment with drugs more than persons who are cautious by nature and prefer routine. The same dopamine system, in fact, is apparently activated both by drugs and by risk-taking adventures such as parachute-jumping (Begley, 2001).

It has long been known that introverts, subject to a strong reaction to stimuli and concomitant anxiety, are inclined to get sleepy under the influence of alcohol, while extraverts are inclined to feel more stimulated and ready for action. Variously called introverted, shy, or harm avoidant, individuals who react strongly to stress are prime candidates for misuse of alcohol and tranquilizing drugs. Monkey research offers some evidence that future drinking may be predicted by response to stress during infancy. Genetic factors showed that some monkeys separated from their mothers at birth had high cortical concentration in their blood. In adulthood, these more sensitive monkeys drank more alcohol than did other monkeys that had endured the same degree of stress (NIAAA, 2000c). Relevant revelations from a study on children from alcoholic families, presumably highly stressful situations, show that many exhibit extreme play inhibition (Bower, 1999). Together, both studies confirm the nature/nurture dyad.

Now researchers are finding that mice lacking an enzyme (PKCe) are far less likely to consume alcohol than those with this enzyme ("Enzyme Linked," 2000). Mice lacking PKCe react strongly to a limited amount of alcohol and to tranquilizers (benzodiazepines) as well; the absence of this enzyme enhances the effect of alcohol and other depressants on a molecule receptor involved in the transmission of feelings of relaxation and sedation. According to one of the researchers, this study supports the emerging concept that increased sensitivity to intoxication lessens the likelihood that a person will become an alcoholic. If these results are confirmed in humans, they may provide a means to help identify high-risk youth for targeted intervention programs (NIAAA, 2000a).

Genetic differences in people can also inhibit the risk of addiction. Many Asians, for example, suffer rapid metabolism of alcohol to the poison acetaldehyde. This leads to greater buildup of this toxic product in the bloodstream, producing flushing and palpitations (U.S. Department of Health and Human Services, 2000). Marc Schuckit (2000) includes Israelis and the Maori peoples of New Zealand along with Asians as groups that experience negative reactions to alcohol consumption. All three groups have a lower rate of alcoholism than other ethnic populations, at least in part because of this genetic anomaly.

Another "defective" gene sometimes found in humans prevents nicotine addiction. Men with this genetic mutation are unlikely to become addicted to cigarettes and are likely to be able to quit smoking easily, according to recent research (NIDA, 2000c).

Differences in brain chemistry may predispose some people to become users of stimulants as well. In this case, those with lower levels of dopamine D2 receptors in their brains are more inclined than others to like the effect of stimulants (NIDA, 1999). Research on dopamine receptor genes in smokers, reported in *Science News*, reveals a strong link between a deficiency in this area and severe problems in quitting the habit (Seppa, 1998). Because nicotine is a stimulant and alcohol a depressant, and in light of findings based on twin studies showing a strong correlation between smoking and alcoholism in twins, recent speculation is that smoking may increase the risk of alcoholism by reducing sensitivity to alcohol ("Why Do Some People?" 2000). Although the gateway theory that one drug leads to another has been largely discounted, these research findings give some credence to the notion that the effect of smoking may well increase the tolerance for drinking, and tolerance, as we know, is associated with alcohol dependence. For persons wishing to curb their drinking consumption, smoking cessation might be the place to start.

In his book on attention deficit disorder (ADD), Gabor Maté (1999) comments on the high rate of smoking among what he calls the ADD population. It is easy to understand, he says, the appeal addictive substances have for the ADD brain. Nicotine improves mental efficiency, for example. Typically, the ADD person, often hyperactive, is driven—to work excessively, to spend money, also excessively, and to engage in risk-taking such as experimentation with drugs. The self-medication factor is pronounced as well in drug use by the person with ADD, treating themselves "for a condition they are not even aware of having, as Maté suggests.

In conclusion, there is no one genetic marker by which scientists or physicians could determine who will become alcohol dependent. As with other genetic disorders, as Schuckit (2000) cautions, it is likely that a variety of genetic characteristics, in combination with key environmental factors, contribute to the risk of addiction.

MEDICAL CONSEQUENCES OF SUBSTANCE MISUSE

Alcohol misuse costs the United States a staggering $185 billion a year, more than all illegal drugs combined; these costs were attributed to lost productivity, health care expenditures, motor vehicle crashes, etc.; 100,000 will die this year from alcohol-related causes (Kalb, 2000).

Because alcohol is water soluble, the body absorbs alcohol directly into the bloodstream. Alcohol's molecules easily travel across the blood–brain barrier, affecting brain functioning almost immediately. It can even cross the placental barrier, affecting fetal development in a way that no other drug can do. Over the years, medical scientists have documented the effects of alcohol on the body's organs and its role on the development of a variety of psychological problems, including brain structure and functioning, liver cirrhosis, cardiovascular diseases, and fetal alcohol syndrome ("Health Risks," 2000). In this section, we will therefore focus more on alcohol than other drugs; our starting point is the most complicated organ in the body—the brain.

Brain Impairment

Alcohol contributes to brain damage both directly and indirectly. Levin (1995) provides a threefold classification of damage to the nervous system through alcohol misuse: (1) damage in the form of a shrinking of the brain from the toxic effects of the alcohol itself; (2) poisoning of brain cells by toxins circulating in the blood as a result of the failure of a diseased liver to metabolize them; and (3) damage to the nervous system because of nutritional deficits associated with alcoholism. Wernicke's syndrome and Korsakoff's psychosis are thought to derive from a lack of thiamine, or vitamin B1. Some researchers, however, believe the effect of alcohol per se is partially involved (Levin, 1995).

Wernicke's syndrome is characterized by paralysis of normal eye movements, mental confusion, and problems with walking and balance. This syndrome, according to Osher (2000), affects one part of the brain—the midbrain and third and fourth ventricles. Korsakoff's psychosis results from damage to areas of the brain important to memory function. Wernicke's syndrome is often associated with *peripheral neuropathy,* or damage to the peripheral nerves. Numbness in one's lower legs is the consequence. If the numbness does not disappear with vitamin therapy, this is an indication that the damage to the nervous system is permanent and irreversible.

Korsakoff's psychosis, sometimes called Wernicke–Korsakoff's syndrome and popularly known as "wet brain," is the long-term results of brain damage over time. Patients with this disease experience much confusion and severe short-term memory deficits. They may not retain information. *Confabulation* is a unique characteristic that involves fantasizing to fill in the gaps of memory. Although the "tall tales" seem to be ridiculous fabrications or downright lies, there appears to be no "method in this madness" other than an inability to distinguish fact from fiction. Although individuals with this affliction can become paranoid on occasion, generally they have a carefree unconcern about the pres-

FIGURE 4.6 | REDUCED BRAIN MASS IN ALCOHOLICS

Axial magnetic resonance images from a healthy 57-year-old man (right) and a 57-year-old man with a history of heavy alcohol consumption (left).

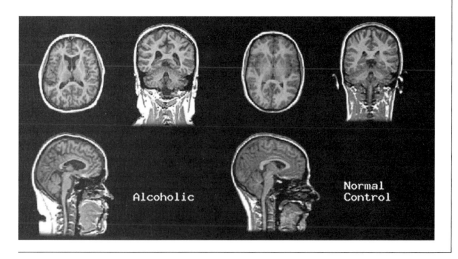

Source: U.S. Department of Health and Human Services, 2000, Special Report to the U.S. Congress on Alcohol and Health. Rockville, MD: NIAAA, p. 135. Images courtesy of Dr. Adolf Pfefferbaum.

ent or future. See Figure 4.6 for photographs of cross sections of the brain, one of which is severely damaged by alcohol misuse.

Oliver Sachs (1985), neurologist and author of *Awakenings* and *The Man Who Mistook His Wife for a Hat,* provides rich case histories of persons with neurological disorders. In the second of these books, portraits of two individuals with Korsakoff's psychosis are given. Mr. Thompson, an exgrocer with severe Korsakoff's, was institutionalized for his memory problems. As Sachs describes the working of Mr. Thompson's mind, "Deprived of continuity, of a quiet, continuous, inner narrative, he is driven to a sort of irrational frenzy—hence his ceaseless tales, his confabulations, his mythomania" (p. 111). Lack of feelings is a key characteristic of this condition. This man had become desouled, according to Sachs. Typically such patients fail to realize the tragedy of the situation or the distress of their loved ones in dealing with them. (van Wormer's father suffered from Korsakoff's psychosis for the last two decades or so of his life.)

Use of the popular drug Ecstasy also may cause long-term impairment. Brain scans of heavy Ecstasy users provide evidence of neuron damage associated with an inability to use serotonin (Leshner, 1999). Similarly, after heavy methamphetamine use, the impact is seen in memory and motor coordination ("Studies Say," 2001). Studies using brain CAT scans of the brains of heavy marijuana users have produced conflicting results; more research is needed in this area (Brick & Erickson, 1998).

Liver Damage

Because the liver metabolizes alcohol ahead of anything else, the toll to the body through alcohol misuse is enormous (van Wormer, 1995). Chronic exposure to alcohol may result in liver damage, with some individuals being more highly susceptible than others. The first manifestation of alcohol-related liver problems is the development of a fatty liver. Although the symptoms are not obvious, this condition can easily be detected through blood tests (Doweiko, 2002).

About one in three heavy drinkers eventually develops scars in the liver associated with cirrhosis—a disease in which liver cells are destroyed and the organ no longer is able to process nutrients in food. *Alcoholic hepatitis* (not the same as general hepatitis, which has a different etiology) can be considered the second stage of alcoholic liver disease. This highly dangerous condition is characterized by liver swelling, jaundice, and fever. Many persons with liver disease take on a yellow skin color; the color comes from excessive amounts of bile that circulate in the bloodstream. With abstinence, this condition can be reversed. If the condition is not reversed, *cirrhosis* of the liver can occur. About 10% of all people who have been diagnosed as alcoholics develop cirrhosis (Benshoff & Janikowski, 2000). With the progression of this disease, all of the liver's functions are compromised, including, first and foremost, the immune system.

As more and more tissue of the liver is damaged over time, the liver is no longer able to effectively remove toxins from the blood. Blood pressure builds up within the vessels, and increasing pressure is put on the heart (Doweiko, 2002). Alcoholics who smoke more than one pack of cigarettes per day have three times the risk of cirrhosis as nonsmoking alcoholics (NIAAA, 1997). The scarred liver, unable to handle the usual blood flow, moreover, causes the body to seek alternative routes to the heart. A tremendous pressure builds up in alternative vessels. When bulging veins emerge on the surface of the esophagus, the potentially fatal condition called *esophageal varices* occurs. Spidery veins may appear on the face and chest; hemorrhoids may develop. The patient may die from hemorrhaging. Edema, which is fluid accumulation in other parts of the body, is another serious consequence of cirrhosis. Large amounts of fluid can collect until the abdomen is shockingly distended.

Treatment of alcoholic cirrhosis consists of total abstinence from alcohol and careful attention to diet. For terminally ill patients, a liver transplant provides the only possibility of survival. A summary of empirical research results with liver transplantation for alcoholics reveals a survival rate equal to that of nonalcoholics who get liver transplants (NIAAA, 1993). Scientific policy evaluation, in this case, went against popular opposition to providing replacement for alcoholics who had destroyed their livers through drinking.

Because chronic heavy drinking is the primary cause of cirrhosis, the World Health Organization presents annual mortality rates by country for death due to cirrhosis. The rates provide researchers with the most reliable estimates we have of a nation's alcoholism rates. Interestingly, as a study of these rates will show, high alcohol consumption in a population does not always mean a high rate of disease. The reason is illustrated by the case of Wisconsin, where consumption may be spread fairly evenly across the population (Wisconsin ranks as number 1 in overall consumption and 43rd in cirrhosis deaths) ("Cirrhosis Mortality," 1999).

Alcoholics, especially those with liver disease, suffer a host of infections. Since alcohol interferes with the function of white blood cells, heavy drinkers are highly susceptible to colds and pneumonia. Skin diseases such as psoriasis may cover the entire body. Alcoholics also are inclined toward malnutrition, itself related to liver dysfunction. Malnutrition in alcoholics is related to poor food intake and poor metabolism of the food taken in. Additionally, digestive abnormalities and chronic diarrhea contribute to the overall susceptibility to disease. Poor nutrition, in itself, influences all aspects of immunity (Mendenhall, 1992).

The pancreas is another trouble spot for heavy users of alcohol. A major organ of the body, the pancreas secretes digestive enzymes and insulin, which converts blood sugar. Diabetes may result from the cell damage. *Acute pancreatitis,* often caused by alcohol-induced inflammation, is an extremely painful and dangerous condition.

The Heart

Although moderate drinking reportedly has a positive effect on the heart, heavy drinking over long periods will likely have the opposite effect. Chronic alcohol use results in the suppression of normal red blood cell formation and can harm the cardiovascular system. Such heavy drinking can also cause the heart to become enlarged and lose some of its ability to contract ("Medical Consequences," 2000). Damage to heart muscle tissue is a common occurrence over long periods of time.

Nicotine is incontrovertibly implicated in the genesis of cardiovascular disease (Jung, 2001). Nicotine is both water and fat soluble and thus accumulates throughout the organs of the body. The effect on the smoker's heart rate is immediate (Doweiko, 2002). While the heart rate is increased, the peripheral blood flow in the body is reduced, due to constriction of the blood vessels. The blood pressure rises and the heart has to work harder. Over 400,000 persons per year die due to tobacco use; the majority of these deaths are from heart disease and stroke, not lung cancer (Fishbein & Pease, 1996). Because of the propensity to continue to smoke during recovery from alcoholism, the leading cause of death for recovering alcoholics is tobacco-related illness (Varner, 1992).

Cocaine is the drug most closely associated in the public mind with heart problems and heart attacks. Cocaine-related deaths may occur on the first use of cocaine, although rarely, and are often a result of cardiac arrest or seizures followed by respiratory arrest. Researchers at the State University of New York at Buffalo now calculate that roughly one-fourth of nonfatal heart attacks among people aged 18 to 45 result from use of the drug ("Cocaine Link," 2001). More common is a disturbance in heart rhythm, detected as an irregular heartbeat. The risk comes not in occasional use of small amounts but after tolerance has developed and increased dosage leads to toxicity (Benshoff & Janikowski, 2000). The deaths that do result are commonly due to the synergistic effect of cocaine and alcohol in combination (NIDA, 2001).

The Genitourinary Tract

In both sexes, problems with urination may result from excessive alcohol use. Indirect interference in the filtration process and the elimination of the waste produced by the kidney seems to be the problem. When *kidney failure* follows, according to Osher (2000), the trouble is not in the kidneys themselves, but in a circulating toxic factor resulting from the associated liver disease.

Effects on the *reproductive system* are widely known to accompany heavy alcohol use. The *Ninth Special Report to the U.S. Congress: Alcohol and Health* (U.S. Department of Health and Human Services, 1997) reviews the most advanced clinical and endocrine studies in the literature. The few clinical studies of alcoholic women suggest ovulation and menstrual difficulties are caused by alcohol-induced hormonal imbalance. In men, impotence, low testosterone levels, low sperm count, and testicular atrophy are widely reported. Breast enlargement has been observed in alcoholic men, as has an absence of body hair accompanied by a lower rate of baldness.

Inasmuch as intoxication lowers inhibitions and caution may be "thrown to the wind," the risks of both AIDS contraction and unwanted pregnancy multiply. Perhaps the most tragic consequences of substance use in one generation are seen in the birth defects of the next generation. *Fetal alcohol syndrome* (FAS) is now recognized as the leading known cause of mental retardation. Medical reports confirm that the fetus takes in alcohol from the mother's blood. Whereas classical fetal alcohol syndrome may be readily identified by physical characteristics in the child—smaller upper lip, flat nose, and small head—milder defects, classified as *fetal alcohol effects* (FAE), are properly diagnosed only rarely. See Figures 4.7 and 4.8 to observe the discriminating features characteristic of children with FAS.

Although the percentage of hard-drinking mothers who have spontaneous abortions or babies with FAS is not known, it is known that habitual or even occasional drinking by an expectant mother can endanger the health of her fetus. The effect on neurological development is the greatest in the first three months of pregnancy. By the time a fertile woman confirms her pregnancy, the damage may already be done.

A large dose of alcohol given to a pregnant mouse experimentally produces severe abnormalities in the developing fetus. The eye damage, stunted brain, and facial deformities that result are reminiscent of human babies with FAS (Steinmetz, 1992).

The role of intoxication on male sperm and its impact on the conceived child has only recently been studied. Sperm susceptibility to environmental damage, such as pesticides, of course has been known for years; recent studies link male smoking to the birth of underweight infants. Rodent experiments reveal learn-

FIGURE 4.7 | FETAL ALCOHOL SYNDROME

Facial features characteristic of fetal alcohol syndrome (FAS).

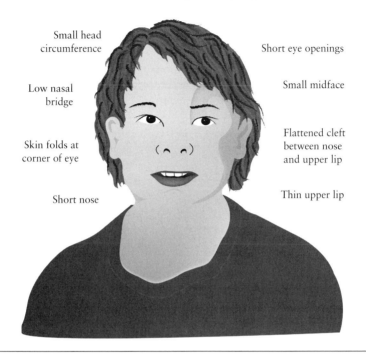

Small head
circumference

Low nasal
bridge

Skin folds at
corner of eye

Short nose

Short eye openings

Small midface

Flattened cleft
between nose
and upper lip

Thin upper lip

Source: *Alcohol Health and Research World,* 1991, volume 15, no. 3, p. 245.
Rockville, MD: NIAAA. Illustration by James Sottile, Jr.

ing difficulties in offspring of morphine-exposed fathers. Data on cocaine's ability to bind to sperm ("Cocaine May Piggyback," 1991) indicate the need for further studies on the long-unrecognized impact of male intoxication on development of the fetus. In a review of studies on the impact of alcohol consumption in male rats on their offspring, the U.S. Department of Health and Human Services (1997) concluded that damaged sperm may indeed have an impact on the development of the unborn child.

Longitudinal studies indicate that FAS and FAE exist on a continuum of cognitive-behavioral defects. School-age children born of heavily drinking mothers are found to be highly distractible in their learning operations. Hyperactivity, subnormal intelligence, and mood problems are found to persist over time. Long-term treatment for high-risk pregnant women is one of the greatest unmet needs of alcoholism prevention efforts today. Help for adults who suffer the effects of FAS is hard to come by also.

Diagnosis of FAS and FAE has always been difficult. Through magnetic resonance imaging (MRI), we can now compare brain structures in normal adolescents with those exposed in utero to the effects of maternal heavy drinking.

FIGURE 4.8

EVOLVING FACIAL MORPHOLOGY OF FAS PATIENTS, FROM CHILDHOOD THROUGH ADOLESCENCE

These changes can make it difficult to diagnose FAS in postpubescent patients.

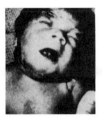   

The first patient to be given the diagnosis of FAS at birth as a newborn and at ages 5, 10, and 14 years. He has been growth deficient and microcephalic throughout his life. As he has aged, his nose has shown considerable relative growth, resulting in a high, wide nasal bridge. His philtrum has remained smooth.

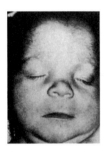 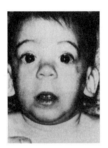  

Adolescent girl whose condition was diagnosed as FAS at birth, with later intellectual functioning in the borderline range, as a newborn, at 9 months, and at 5 and 14 years of age. Although her facial features are gradually maturing, she still has small palpebral fissures, a relatively long, smooth philtrum, and a narrow upper lip.

Woman whose condition was diagnosed as FAS at 4 years of age; she now has an IQ of 85 to 90. Photographs show her at 9, 13, and 19 years. Her early FAS manifestations have evolved into a fairly normal facial phenotype by adult life. At 19, her head circumference was below the 1st percentile, her height was below the 5th percentile, and her weight was around the 10th percentile.

Source: *Alcohol Health and Research World,* 1994, vol. 18, no. 1, p.77.

Imaging studies have demonstrated structural abnormalities in some brain regions but not in others. While such research is in its infancy, what we do know is that prenatal alcohol exposure can cause specific irreversible damage and that such brain damage may be present even in the absence of identifiable facial characteristics. Although too expensive for regular use, this technology offers much promise for the future detection of fetal alcohol syndrome in children and adults and clarification of which areas are most affected.

What is the effect of cocaine use on unborn children? Are "crack babies" the hopeless cases that earlier media reports made them out to be? In fact, as experts inform us, alcohol and nicotine pose greater dangers to unborn babies than does crack cocaine ("Tobacco, Alcohol," 1998). Fortunately, infants exposed to crack often outgrow their health problems, especially when placed in a nurturing environment. The same is not true for alcohol-exposed babies, however. Tobacco use by pregnant women, according to this report, is highly associated with sudden infant deaths and respiratory problems in babies. Oddly, recent research on mother–child pairs seems to indicate that among adolescent girls whose mothers smoked, drug use is common. Boys whose mothers smoked had a high rate of conduct disorder (Varisco, 2000).

Opiates, like alcohol, cross the placental barrier in pregnant women; babies born to heroin addicts thus have withdrawal symptoms, and some die as a result (Benshoff & Janikowski, 2000). In the Midwest, an increasing number of methamphetamine-addicted babies are being delivered in area hospitals. Because meth is a drug more long-lasting in its effects than cocaine, experts fear the impact of prenatal exposure could be more long-lasting (Lippert, 2000).

SUMMARY AND CONCLUSION

For direct practice with alcoholics and other addicts, the helping professional requires advanced knowledge of the physiology of chemical addiction, including the basic characteristics and organic effects of each of the popular sedative and stimulant drugs. To work with clients, a biological understanding of the nature of addiction, and especially of the kind of relentless craving, that accompanies drug use is essential. (Recovering professionals have an experiential knowledge of such urges that puts them on the same wavelength as their clients; all counselors and educators can benefit, however, from an awareness of the brain changes that make addiction what it is. Brain imaging has brought about unprecedented breakthroughs in our knowledge. Virtually all psychoactive drugs, as we now know, affect a single pathway deep within the brain and activate the limbic reward system in various ways. The new techniques that enable researchers to view these workings within the limbic system also make it possible to observe changes in the brain caused by prolonged use of harmful chemicals. Previously those alterations could only be inferred. Scientists can now experience addiction secondhand as an image on a screen; in so doing they have hit upon some elements in human nature that defy logic; in a real sense they have brought us face to face with some of our most primitive drives, those pleasure-seeking drives that may or may not spell addiction.

We are all creatures of biology and of our genes. If we succumb to getting hooked to toxic substances, the physiological damage can be severe—to the brain, liver, heart, unborn child. In focusing on the *bio* portion of the biopsychosocial model of addiction, this chapter has described the most commonly used drugs of choice. Divided into four basic categories—depressants, stimulants, hallucinogens, and cannabis—the drugs of choice were discussed in terms of their chemical properties and metabolism. Then we proceeded to move into more uncharted territory in addressing the imponderables: Is addiction a brain disease? How are the brains of addicts different from those of nonaddicts? Why is it that some individuals are more susceptible to becoming hooked on psychoactive substances than others?

The genetic factor was revealed in research on mice bred to prefer alcohol to water and in studies of children of alcoholics, many of whom displayed a high tolerance for alcohol, a tolerance that paradoxically is correlated with the later development of alcoholism. Research over the past decade has begun to confirm not only why addiction runs in families but also the damage that psychoactive substances do to the body, most interestingly to the brain. The addicted brain, as we now realize, is significantly different from the normally functioning brain. Through long-term drug misuse, the depletion of the brain's natural opiates creates a condition ripe for the kind of relentless craving that is known to all "who have been there." Compounding the problem of molecular alterations in the brain (experienced as a general malaise) is the fact that each time a neurotransmitter such as dopamine floods a synapse through the introduction of a powerful drug like crack or meth into the body, circuits that trigger pleasure are indelibly imprinted in the brain. So when the smells, sights, and sounds associated with the memory are experienced, these feeling memories are aroused as well. So palpable, in fact, are these feeling memories that researchers can now compare the brain of the addict in a state of craving (elicited by these behavior feelings) with the brain of the addict in a stationary state.

Solutions, to be true solutions, must be directed at the source of the problem. First, the rather tired motto "Learn to say no" should be replaced with the advice "Learn to stay away." Seek out a health-supportive environment in which to heal. Second, recognize that replacing unhealthy cognitions with healthy ones can help repair much of the brain damage done by heavy drug use. One of the most promising messages coming out of current research is that biochemical abnormalities associated with drug misuse can be reversed through cognitive work. Finally, consider checking out one of the new medications that have been developed to target the dopamine and serotonin receptors in reducing the equivalent of hunger or thirst for the drug. We will explore both pharmaceutical and cognitive interventions in chapter 5.

References

Abadinsky, H. (1996). *Drug abuse: An introduction* (3rd ed.). Chicago: Nelson-Hall.
Alcohol in Australia: Issues and strategies (2000). National Alcohol Action Plan 2000–
    2003. Available online at www.drinkingchoices.com

Alcoholism a product of genetics, the environment, and drinking. (1987). *Substance Abuse Report, 18*(22), 1–4.

Alter, J. (2001, February 12). The war on addiction. *Newsweek,* 36–39.

American Psychiatric Association (APA) (2000). *Diagnostic and statistical manual of mental disorders, text revision* (4th ed.). Washington, DC: Author.

Begleiter, M., & Porjesz, B. (1988). Potential biological markers in individuals at high risk for developing alcoholism. *Alcoholism, 12,* 488–493.

Begley, S. (2001, February 12). How it all starts in your brain. *Newsweek,* 40–43.

Begley, S. (1998, January 26). Is everybody crazy? *Newsweek,* 50–55.

Benshoff, J. J., & Janikowski, T. P. (2000). *The rehabilitation model of substance abuse counseling.* Belmont, CA: Wadsworth.

Bower, B. (1994). Alcoholism exposes its "insensitive" side. *Science News, 145,* 118.

Bower, B. (1999, April 10). Social fears may raise alcoholism risk. *Science News, 155,* 230.

Braun, S. (1996). *Buzz: The science and lore of alcohol and caffeine.* New York: Oxford University Press.

BreathScan (2000). Alcohol testing—BreathScan. Available online at www.breathscan.com/alcohol.htm

Brick, J., & Erickson, C. (1998). *The pharmacology of abuse and dependence.* New York: Haworth.

Butterfield, F. (1997, October 27). Drugs in homicide rate linked to crack's decline. *New York Times,* A10.

Center for Substance Abuse Prevention (2000, August 4). Prevention works. Available online at www.health.org/govpubs/prevalert/v3i26.htm

Center for Substance Abuse Treatment, SAMHSA (2001, March). Addiction science: Specifying alcohol-related brain damage in young women. Available online at www.nattc.org/asme/01-3March.html

Chen, W.-J., Parnell, S., & West, J. R. (2001). Nicotine decreases blood alcohol concentration in neonatal rats. *Alcoholism: Clinical and Experimental Research, 25,* 1072–1077.

Children of alcoholics at risk of addiction. (1999, April 1). Available online at www.jointogether.org

Chung, C. (1999, October 18). Blackout binge. ABC *20/20* television broadcast.

Cirrhosis mortality low in Wisconsin, drinking high. (1999, February 4). *Waterloo Courier,* C9.

Cloninger, C. R., Sigvardsson, S., Gilligan, S., van Knorring, A., Reich, T., & Bohman, M. (1989). Genetic heterogeneity and the classification of alcoholism. *Advances in Alcohol and Substance Abuse, 7,* 3–16.

Cocaine link to heart attack bolstered. (2001, January 13). *Science News 159,* 24.

Cocaine may piggyback on sperm into egg. (1991). *Science News, 140,* 246.

Cohen, G. (2001, February 12). The "poor man's heroin." *U.S. News and World Report,* 27.

Cowley, G. (1995, January 30). A new assault on addiction. *Newsweek,* 51.

DanceSafe (2000). Promoting health and safety within the rave and nightclub community. Available online at www.dancesafe.org

Derrington, A. (2000, April 29). Drugs that flip your switches: Toe to toe. *Financial Times,* 2.

Desmond, E. (1987, November). Out in the open: Changing attitudes and new research give fresh hope to alcoholics. *Time,* 42–49.

Doweiko, H. E. (2002). *Concepts of chemical dependency* (5th ed.). Pacific Grove, CA: Brooks/Cole.

Dunn, P. (2000). Dynamics of drug use and abuse. In A. Abbott (Ed.), *Alcohol, tobacco, and other drugs: Challenging myths, assessing theories, individualizing interventions* (pp. 74–110). Washington, DC: NASW Press.

Enzyme linked to alcohol craving. (2000, June 16). *Substance Abuse News.* Available online at www.jointogether.org

Evans, M. (2001, April 12). Marijuana-like substances are found to trigger appetite. *Des Moines Register*, 7A.

Fishbein, D., & Pease, S. (1996). *The dynamics of drug abuse.* Boston: Allyn & Bacon.

France, D., & Horn, J. (2001, February 12). Robert Downey Jr. takes one day at a time. *Newsweek*, 52–54.

Gardner, D. (2000, September 11). Do our drug laws harm us more than they help? *Ottawa Citizen Online.* Available online at www.ottawacitizen.com/columnists/gardner/000911/4122508.html

Goodwin, D. (1976). *Is alcoholism hereditary?* New York: Oxford University Press.

Gordis, E. (1997). Alcohol metabolism. *Alcohol Alert*, 35 (371), 1–6.

Gordis, E. (1999). Are women more vulnerable to alcohol's effects? *Alcohol Alert*, 46, 1–4.

Gorman, C. (1997, April 28). The case for morphine. *Time*, 64–65.

Grier, P. (1997, September 3). Drunk driving draws global wrath. *Christian Science Monitor*, 1, 18.

Harvard Medical School. (1993). Update on Cocaine. Part II. *Howard Medical Health Letter*, 10(3), 1–8.

Health risks and benefits of alcohol consumption. (2000). *Alcohol Research and Health*, 24(1), 5–11.

High in the heartland. (1999, February 6). *The Economist*, 29.

Hill, T. (1990). Peyotism and the control of heavy drinking: The Nebraska Winnebago in the early 1900s. *Human organization* 49, 255–265.

Holloway, M. (1991, March). Treatment for addiction. *Scientific American*, 95–103.

Images of alcohol stimulate craving in alcoholics. (2001, April 17). Available online at www.jointogether.org

Immen, W. (1995, June 30). Drugs may help overcome alcohol problems, study finds. *Globe and Mail*, A4.

Johnson, H. C. (1999). *Psyche, synapse, and substance: The role of neurobiology in emotions, behavior, thinking, and addiction for nonscientists.* Greenfield, MA: Deerfield Valley.

Judson, D. (1998, December 29). Study points to casual drinkers as biggest danger. *USA Today*, 1A.

Jung, J. (2001). *Psychology of alcohol and other drugs: A research perspective.* Thousand Oaks, CA: Sage.

Kalb, C. (2000, February 12). Alcoholism: Can this pill stop you from hitting the bottle? *Newsweek*, 48–54.

Klam, M. (2001, January 21). Experiencing Ecstasy. *New York Times Magazine*, 38–43, 64–73.

L., Lisa. (2001, January 25). Alcoholism—my personal story. Class presentation, University of Northern Iowa, Cedar Falls.

Lambert, C. (2000, March/April). Deep cravings: New research on the brain and behavior clarifies the mysteries of addiction. *Harvard Magazine*, 60–68.

Lane, C. (2001, May 15). Court rules against "medical marijuana." *Washington Post*, A1.

Lee, D. (2001, January 1). About that hangover. (Louisville) *Courier-Journal*, 1E.

Leshner, A. I. (1998, October). Addiction is a brain disease—and it matters. *National Institute of Justice Journal, 2–6.*

Leshner, A. I. (1999). We can conquer drug addiction. *The Futurist, 33*(9), 22–30.

Levin, J. D. (1995). *Introduction to alcoholism counseling: A bio-psycho-social approach.* Washington, DC: Taylor & Francis.

Lippert, J. (2000, June 23). Meth infants called the new "crack babies." *Des Moines Register.* Available online at www.apbnews.com/newscenter/breakingnews/2000

Martin, Fr. J. (1972). *Chalk talk on alcohol,* revised. Video. Aberdeen, MD: Kelly Productions.

Maté, G. (1999). *Scattered: How attention deficit disorder originates and what you can do about it.* New York: Plume.

McCarthy, C. (2000, July 23). Life sentences, no time off for innocence. *The Sun* (Baltimore), 1A.

McCourt, M. (2000). *Singing my him song.* New York: HarperCollins.

McFarling, V. L. (1998, August 4). New nicotine therapy targets brain. *Lexington (KY) Herald-Leader,* A1, 5.

McNeece, C. A., & DiNitto, D. M. (1998). *Chemical dependency: A systems approach.* Boston: Allyn & Bacon.

Mead, D. (1999, April 8). Guest lecture on youth and drugs. University of Northern Iowa, Cedar Falls.

Medical consequences of alcohol abuse. (2000). *Alcohol, Research and Health, 24*(1), 27–31.

Medical news & perspectives. (1998, July 8). *Journal of the American Medical Association 280,* (2), 122.

Memory linked to relapse. (2000, June 27). Available online at www.jointogether.org

Mendenhall, C. (1992). Immunity, Malnutrition and Alcohol. *Alcohol Health and Research World, 16*(1): 23–28.

Myslinski, N. R. (1999). Addiction and the brain. In H. T. Wilson (Ed.), *Drugs, society and behavior* (6th ed., pp. 64–69). Guilford, CT: McGraw-Hill.

Nash, M. (1997, May 5). Addicted. *Time,* 69–76.

National Institute on Alcohol Abuse and Alcoholism. (1993, April). *Alcohol Alert,* 1–3.

National Institute on Alcohol Abuse and Alcoholism. (1997, October). Alcohol violence, and aggression. *Alcohol Alert,* 1–6.

National Institute on Alcohol Abuse and Alcoholism. (1998, January). Alcohol and tobacco. *Alcohol Alert, 39,* 1–5.

National Institute on Alcohol Abuse and Alcoholism. (2000a, July). From genes to geography: The cutting edge of alcoholism research. *Alcohol Alert, 47,* 1–4.

National Institute on Alcohol Abuse and Alcoholism. (2000b, April). Imaging and Alcoholism: A window on the brain. *Alcohol Alert, 47,* 1–6.

National Institute on Alcohol Abuse and Alcoholism. (2000c, May 22). Stress hormone linked to increased alcohol consumption in animal model. *NIH News Advisory,* 1–2.

National Institute on Drug Abuse. (1999). Community drug alert bulletin. Bethesda, MD: National Institutes of Health.

National Institute on Drug Abuse. (2000a, June 26). Cocaine and alcohol combined. NIDA news release. Available online at 165.112.78.61/MedAdv/00/NR6-26.html

National Institute on Drug Abuse. (2000b). Gender differences in drug abuse risks and treatment. *NIDA Notes, 15*(4), 1–2.

National Institute on Drug Abuse. (2000c). Update on nicotine addiction and tobacco research. *NIDA Notes, 15*(5), 1–2.

National Institute on Drug Abuse (NIDA). (2001). *Cocaine abuse and addiction.* Bethesda, MD: National Institutes of Health.

National Institutes of Health. (2000, August 22). *NIH News Advisory.* Available online at silk.nih.gov/silk/niaaa1/releases/potential.htm

New York: Anti-addiction drug to be tested in fall. (1998, August 6). *Lexington (KY) Herald Leader,* A3.

NIDA Infofax (2000). Hospital visits. Available online at 165.112.78.61/Infofax/HosptialVisits.html

Osher, F. C. (2000). Medical complications. In J. Kinney (Ed.), *Loosening the grip: A handbook of alcohol information* (6th ed., pp. 66–129). Boston: McGraw-Hill.

Peele, S. (1999, October). Bottle battle. *Reason, 31*(5), 52–55.

Philip Morris' spin on dying draws fire. (2001, August 9). *Waterloo-Cedar Falls Courier,* A6.

Price, T. (2000). Alcohol and the body. In J. Kinney (Ed.), *Loosening the grip* (6th ed., pp. 41–65). Boston: McGraw-Hill.

Ritalin may cause brain change in children. (2001, November 12). *Washington Post,* A8.

Royce, J., & Scratchley, D. (1996). *Alcoholism and other drug problems.* New York: Free Press.

Sachs, O. (1985). *The man who mistook his wife for a hat and other clinical tales.* New York: Harper and Row.

Salemy, S. (1998, November 8). A drug that steals souls. *Des Moines Register,* A1.

Schuckit, M. A. (2000). Genetics of the risk for alcoholism. *American Journal on Addictions 9,* 103–112.

Science and technology: Sins of the fathers. (1991, February 23). *Economist,* 87.

Seppa, N. (1998, March 7). Exploring a genetic link to smoking. *Science News 153,* 148.

Shapiro, L. (1996, January 22). To your health? *Newsweek,* 52–54.

Sjogren, H., Erikson, A., & Ahlm, K. (2000). Role of alcohol in unnatural deaths: A story of all deaths in Sweden. *Alcoholism: Clinical & experimental research, 24*(7), 1050–1056.

Smith, I. K. (2001, April 9). The Tylenol scare. *Time,* 81.

Steinmetz, G. (1992). Fetal alcohol syndrome. *National Geographic, 181*(2):36–39.

Stevens-Smith, P., & Smith, R. L. (1998). *Substance abuse counseling: Theory and practice.* Upper Saddle River, NJ: Prentice Hall.

Stewart, P., & Sitaramiah, G. (1997, November 13). America's heartland grapples with rise of dangerous drug. *The Christian Science Monitor,* 1, 18.

Stocker, S. (1998). Cocaine activates different brain regimes for rush versus craving. *NIDA Notes, 13*(5), 1–4.

Stocker, S. (1999). Cocaine's pleasurable effects may involve multiple chemical sites. *NIDA Notes, 14*(2), 1–5.

Studies say meth damages brain. (2001, March 2). Available online at www.jointogether.org

Study links cravings for sweets, alcohol. (2000, November 8). *USA Today,* Life section, 2.

Substance Abuse and Mental Health Services Administration. (2000). Highlights from the treatment episode data set. Available from www.dasis.samhsa.gov/teds98/highlights_m.htm

Sweeney, D. (1990). Alcoholic blackouts: Legal implications. *Journal of Substance Abuse Treatment, 7,* 155–159.

Thombs, D. L. (1999). *Introduction to addictive behavior,* (2nd ed.). New York: Guilford Press.

Tobacco, alcohol more harmful than cocaine during pregnancy. (1998, November 17). Available online at www.jointogether.org

Twain, M. (1876). *Adventures of Tom Sawyer.* New York: Harper.

Unlocking the secrets of alcohol's killer grip. (1997, August 27). *Waterloo — Cedar Falls Courier,* D2.

U.S. Department of Health and Human Services. (1997). *Ninth special report to the U.S. Congress: Alcohol and health.* Washington, DC: Government Printing Office.

U.S. Department of Health and Human Services. (2000). *Tenth special report to the U.S. Congress: Alcohol and health.* Washington, DC: Government Printing Office.

van Wormer, K. (1995). *Alcoholism treatment: A social work perspective.* Belmont, CA: Wadsworth.

Varisco, R. (2000). Drug abuse and conduct disorder linked to maternal smoking during pregnancy. *NIDA Notes, 15*(6), 1–2.

Varner, S. (1992, October). Preventing relapse from going up in smoke. *Professional Counselor,* 31–32.

Welsh, I. (1996). *Trainspotting.* Scranton, PA: Norton.

Why do some people drink too much? (2000). *Alcohol Research and Health, 24*(1), 17–26.

Willmsen, C. (1997, April 6). Cranking it out. *Waterloo Courier,* 1A, 4A.

Wilson, B. (1939/1976). *Alcoholics anonymous.* New York: Alcoholics Anonymous World Services.

Wrinkles are traced to tobacco. (2001, March 23). *Des Moines Register,* 4A.

Drugs to get us off drugs? Just imagine—
a generation of Americans trading in martinis
for meds! —CAROLINE KNAPP (1999, P. 19)

5 CHAPTER INTERVENTIONS RELATED TO BIOLOGY

INTRODUCTION

In chapter 4, we saw how, through prolonged drug exposure, ongoing damage to the brain creates a situation of high drug tolerance and relentless craving. A major emphasis of neurobiological research today is on finding ways to restore normal brain functioning, to treat what Leshner (1997) argues is a brain disease. Just as individuals with schizophrenia require medical treatments to normalize their behavior, so we need to contemplate similar treatment for persons whose brain states have been altered artificially through drugs. Far from being a threat to traditional therapy, medical interventions should help clients shape up sooner and, accordingly, be more amenable to treatment.

In this chapter, again, we will focus on the first segment of the biopsychosocial whole, on biologically based strategies that are being applied to reduce the relentless cravings that make relapse all but inevitable. Although the psychological and social components of the illness must be attended to, as long as the "brain is screaming for booze," as Knapp (1996) puts it, "no number of revelations about underlying causes is going to counter that call" (p. 129).

In recent years, the development of medications to treat substance dependence has ushered in a new era of treatment and attitudes toward treatment. Until 1995 when Naltrexone obtained government approval, the only medical treatment approved for alcoholism in the United States was Antabuse (or Disulfiram). Antabuse simply kept people from drinking, in the knowledge that when combined with alcohol, this drug would provoke intense vomiting ("Research Refines Alcoholism," 2000). The bulk of the early research in the field of substance abuse treatment focused on reducing withdrawal pain and risk. Today, pharmacological researchers are conducting clinical trials with medications, singly and in combination, designed to help alcoholics and addicts manage drug cravings and avoid a return to alcohol and often drug misuse. The search is on for new and more effective medications appropriate for populations not previously included in clinical trials—adolescents, women, and older adults with various addictions and mental disorders. One of the most promising recent research developments related to the biology of the brain comes ironically from the cognitive school. According to this research, which is still preliminary, behavioral therapies geared toward helping individuals who have problems stemming from low levels of serotonin or dopamine available in the brain can actually alter these levels of the brain's natural opiates through deliberate changes in thought processes.

This chapter takes a look at interventions related to both pharmaceutical and cognitive/behavioral approaches. We will start, in fact, with a description of a medical treatment, highly controversial, that is founded on the principles of behavioral-conditional theory—aversion therapy. Other approaches chosen for highlighting in this chapter are methadone maintenance and other harm reduction interventions with a strong medical component, such as needle exchange and DanceSafe programming. Alternative therapies such as nutritional and herbal remedies, yoga, and acupuncture are briefly described as well. Because most of the items on assessment scales relate to the physiological dimension of alcohol and other drug use—the ingesting of the substance, how much, how often, and effects on the body such as vomiting and sleeping problems, we include them in this chapter on interventions related to biology. A discussion of group interventions for clients in a very early stage of recovery concludes this chapter. The link among these seemingly diverse interventions is that they are all directed toward the biological side of addiction. For example, the group techniques chosen are those with special relevance to helping clients in the throes of early-stage recovery, when much of their thinking is still drug-affected.

BEHAVIORAL THERAPIES
Chemical Aversion Treatment

Based on Pavlov's classical conditioning in the form of noxious drugs that produce nausea when paired with alcohol is the controversial treatment intervention known as aversion treatment (Burman, 2001). After four sessions of intense vomiting, patients begin to gag at the mere sight of alcohol. This form of treatment became familiar to van Wormer while she was working in Washington State counseling graduates of that program. Schick Shadel (1997), described on its Web site as a hospital "staffed by caring, compassionate physicians, nurses, and counselors" (p. 1), is a licensed medical faculty that qualifies for insurance reimbursement by the major insurance companies. The Web site includes the smiling faces of exclients and current staff.

The oldest behavioral conditioning approach to alcoholism, aversion therapy was popular before the advent of AA. In fact, as Nan Robertson (1988, p. 184) informs us, Bill Wilson, before he cofounded AA, was treated unsuccessfully in a "purge and puke" program. This type of therapy is based on Skinner's operant conditioning principles: If drinking alcohol leads to rewarding consequences it is likely to continue; if it leads to punishment it is likely to be discontinued. For effective results, the punishment must be closely connected to the act. The hangover the day after or bankruptcy a year later is too far removed from the stimulus to yield to aversion therapy.

Treatment relies on nausea-inducing drugs (apomorphine, or Emetine) given in conjunction with alcohol. When this is repeated over time, the alcohol itself, ideally, will elicit nausea. Throughout California more than 50 unlicensed alcohol and drug treatment centers specialize in aversion therapy. A police investigation is being held at clinics where patients reportedly died after being forced to drink rubbing alcohol ("Alcohol Aversion Therapy," 1998).

The Shadel Hospital in Seattle, however, is a reputable treatment facility, purportedly with high success rates. Serious precautions are taken at Schick Shadel to screen clients with health problems that could put them at risk from painful procedures. For clients with heart conditions or high blood pressure or for bulimic patients (with their damaged vomiting reflexes), shock treatments are substituted for the Emetine. Pregnant women are excluded altogether from these treatments.

Infliction of pain, nausea, sickness, and electric shock in order to condition aversion to alcohol in the patient raises serious ethical concerns (Akers, 1992). Reports in the late 1970s of high death rates among elderly clients caused several of these types of treatment centers to close their doors. Box 5.1 provides a rare glimpse inside the doors of Schick Shadel. The interviewee, who was referred to van Wormer's former student by a friend, "tells it as it is." Facts revealed in this testimony were corroborated by a second interview with the director of this treatment center. A special note: It is the pairing of the alcohol with the emetic that causes the nausea, in order to create the desired association of the experience of vomiting with the drinking.

Covert Sensitization

Another variety of aversion therapy, one that, according to Burman (2001), has been shown to be effective, involves instructing clients to imagine physical discomfort in association with drinking. Imagining the sensation of throwing up while drinking can bring positive results. Covert sensation and imagining are easy for clients to learn and apply when they think they might be using again; it can be tailored for individual use (Stevens-Smith & Smith, 1998). Besides, as Peele (1995) comments, this form of behavioral therapy is much more palatable than chemical or electric shock treatments.

BOX 5.1	INTERVIEW WITH A FORMER PATIENT OF SCHICK SHADEL
	CONDUCTED BY JAMIE PAIGE

Q: Well, let's take a few minutes for you to drive me through the actual aversion therapy. This is going in, talking about what all they did in the treatment room.

A: All right. Well, you start out by getting plenty of fluids in you. You can't have anything to eat but you can drink as much water . . . and they recommend it and they stress it because you're going to be throwing up! You go into the treatment center and get a shot of Emetine. Then they give you two glasses of salt water.

Q: Oh! How can you drink that?!

A: Well, you just gag it down! In fact when I went through the treatment the first time, around a year ago, I couldn't go to the ocean because of salt water.

Q: At this point do you just have a nurse? I am wondering who helps you clean up or for anything really?

A: No. You're in a room where you are puking right into a bowl! It's kind of like a hair salon bowl, you know . . . a metal bowl, it's in the Duffy Room. We call it the Duffy Room because that's what they call those, duffies. (*Authors' note: Duffy refers to Duffy's Tavern from a 1940s radio show.*) When you're done, then you kind of have the chills. So you have a blanket and she takes you back to your room. She'll soak a washcloth in beer or alcohol, and once you go back in your room and you're in your room, you have to be quiet. You can read any alcohol literature you want or listen to tapes. You are in your room I think for, like, two and a half hours. You have to smell the vomit. You have a vomit bucket and you continue throwing up. They monitor that. They look in on you every 20 minutes or so and check that out. Then they'll put a bottle of whatever is nauseous and you are throwing up for probably an hour. Then the last hour and a half you're just kind of nauseous but you are starting to feel better. I got diarrhea really bad with it. So they have to give you pills for that.

Q: I understand on alternate days you are given sodium Pentothal, truth serum.

A: Oh yes, definitely. I went back when I got sober 10 years ago, I went back every three months to have my sodium Pentothal treatment.

Q: What is the point of this treatment, to make you talk?

A: Yes, but if it goes too fast you go to sleep right away. Once I went to sleep so fast that I didn't think I got the therapy portion of it. That was what I was there for. I wanted therapy.

Q: Is this treatment covered by insurance?

A: Yes, and Schick Shadel was really good to me because they knew I had gone through 10 years ago and they remembered me. They gave me $5,000 off the $10,000 bill.

Q: Have you ever had another kind of treatment?

A: Oh yes, I had outpatient treatment and it helped me because it was so intense. It was five hours a day for both weeks. They are totally AA—Twelve Step. They

continued

<table>
<tr><td>BOX 5.1</td><td>INTERVIEW WITH A FORMER
PATIENT OF SCHICK SHADEL
(*Continued*)</td></tr>
</table>

hound you . . . I mean I got into several fights with my counselor. Then I realized later that she was doing what she was supposed to—trying to get that anger out. I never had any of that at Schick.

Q: Didn't it make you nervous when you went to Schick, knowing how painful it would be?

A: No, I think it boils down to how much you want help. Most alcoholics don't know anything about a Twelve-Step program and so they go to Schick. Lots of people just associate this place with the puking . . . but now for cocaine and marijuana addiction, it's aversion therapy with electric shock! They hook up electrodes to you and every time . . . you get shocked.

Note: The interview ended on a friendly note. I thanked Kim, the former client for her honesty.

Interview conducted June 3, 1997.

Because of the intense craving associated with cocaine use, a key factor in relapse, aversion therapies were used by an inpatient unit with a sample of 70 crack cocaine–abusing veterans (Bordnick, 1996). Results showed a complete reduction in craving following eight sessions. Both chemical aversion treatment (inducing vomiting with Emetine hydrochloride) and use of covert sensitization were effective in reducing craving by session 8. Chemical aversion treatment, however, achieved remarkable results and, as Bordnick argues, offers a highly efficacious method for eliminating craving.

Chemical aversion therapy, in fact (the tastelessness and cruelty of this procedure notwithstanding), consistently has been shown to be of high effectiveness for alcoholism treatment (Peele, 1995).

CHANGING BRAIN CHEMISTRY

The bad news about heavy intoxicants, as we learned in chapter 4, is the neurological brain injury that can result. The good news, as Fulton Crews (2001), director of the Center for Alcohol Studies at the University of North Carolina, assures us is that some of the brain degeneration can be reversed through therapy. Clinical studies, as Crews indicates, suggest that exercising the brain likely brings about regrowth in the frontal cortex. Improvement in this part of the brain enhances one's chances of recovery. Additionally, thiamine therapy seems to increase treatment effects (depletion of this vitamin is thought to be implicated in brain dysfunction associated with alcoholism).

Dowling (1998) likewise believes that psychological counseling can actually alter brain chemistry, possibly restoring more normal functioning. And how is this done? Jeffrey Schwartz (1997), the author of *Brain Lock,* describes an experiment in which clients suffering from obsessive-compulsive disorder were guided to substitute healthy for unhealthy thoughts every time an obsessive urge came over them. After 10 weeks of behavioral instruction, neuroimaging revealed observable changes in brain chemistry in the part of the brain thought to be affected by this disorder.

Further support is lent to the notion that brain structure and function can be altered by cognitions in studies of the impact of trauma on the brain. Particular hormones secreted in times of severe stress can alter neurochemistry sufficiently to effect long-term changes in neurons and brain systems. PET scans of eight children reared in Romanian orphanages until their adoption showed such abnormalities, as Harriette Johnson (1999) indicates.

The technological revolution in neurological research is providing documentation for theories that previously were based only on behavioral observation. Although more has been learned in the past few years than in the several decades before, we are just on the brink of understanding addiction and the roots of addiction in the brain.

PHARMACEUTICAL INTERVENTIONS

If drug dependency is considered less a matter of will than of brain chemistry, then the development of medications to prevent the lows or block the highs is inevitable. The growing awareness of serotonin's central role in mood and compulsive behavior has been paralleled by a boom in the introduction of drugs that target serotonin levels (Lemonick, 1997). Serotonin reuptake inhibitors, such as Prozac, Zoloft, and Paxil, are prescribed to treat a wide range of disorders, such as binge drinking and eating, obsessive-compulsive disorder, as well as autism, panic attacks, schizophrenia, and uncontrolled aggression. While health care providers, in this time of tight fiscal constraints, are in search of effective but brief interventions, pharmaceutical companies have a strong economic stake in producing and marketing products to meet the growing medical demand.

Biochemical problems call for biochemical solutions. The findings from brain research have laid the groundwork for a series of clinical trials of various prescriptions to be funded by the two major research funding organizations—NIAAA and NIDA. Even many of the leading treatment centers, such as Hazelden in Minnesota, are conducting research on the effectiveness of medications that act on the brain as an aid in recovery.

The concept of taking a pill to curb excessive appetite is hardly new. Still, resistance to the use of any mood-altering substances such as Prozac persists in substance abuse treatment circles (Challender, 1999). Recovering addicts quoted in a recent *Newsweek* article, for example, assert that there are no shortcuts to staying sober (Kalb, 2001).

But maybe there are. Already, as we will see, medications that target the brain are being prescribed—for alcoholics, smokers, cocaine and methamphetamine users, persons with eating disorders, compulsive shoppers, and pathological gamblers. For alcoholism, the bold drugs for pharmaceutical results have been especially promising.

Alcoholism

Several types of medications are being used to help alcoholics avoid relapse. The first type are the antidepressants of the newer variety, drugs such as Zoloft and Prozac, which have been prescribed over the last decade to alleviate depression in alcoholics. People who are depressed, as all counselors know, lose their incentive to stay sober. Keeping their spirits up, especially early in treatment, is vital.

Naltrexone, the drug approved by the Federal Drug Administration in 1995 to reduce craving in heroin addicts, is in a separate class from addictive drugs such as Valium and Librium. Naltrexone and the even more promising drug Acamprosate (widely used in Europe) work by blocking alcohol–brain interactions that produce a high. In studies with rats on Naltrexone that were later given alcohol, the medication was shown to decrease the amount of alcohol-induced dopamine (U.S. Department of Health and Human Services, 2000). Naltrexone is an abstinence-enhancing drug. Basically, the fun is removed from the drinking, so patients taking these drugs lose their desire to partake. Remember the brain studies that showed how visual cues associated with drugs of choice produced conditioned responses in the brain? Well, Naltrexone has been shown to block the chemical changes in the brain elicited by the environmental cues (smell of alcohol, sight of foaming beer, etc.) ("Research Refines Alcoholism," 2000). Usually taken several times a week in pill form, Naltrexone is now available in a dosage form good for 30 days or more (Office of National Drug Control Policy, 2001). Patients found to derive the most benefits from these drugs are those with poor cognitive skills coupled with an intense urge to keep drinking. Of 300 patients at a facility for homeless persons treated with this drug, 80% were found to be abstinent at the end of six months ("Clinical Concepts," 2000). Other studies show more modest but consistently positive benefits; long-term prospects with this drug are excellent as well (U.S. Department of Health and Human Services, 2000).

Acamprosate, which works on the glutamate system of the brain, the part responsible for arousal and attention, is currently being tested in clinical trials in the United States for safety. Its effectiveness has been demonstrated in empirically sophisticated comparison studies in Europe in trials involving more than 3,000 alcoholic subjects who were undergoing traditional treatment ("New Advances," 2000). Unlike Naltrexone, this drug is not metabolized in the liver and therefore is effective for patients with liver dysfunction. Because Naltrexone and Acamprosate both work on different neurotransmitters, research is currently under way to study the advantage of using these two drugs in combination (U.S. Department of Health and Human Services, 2000).

Some of the most exciting and significant research findings were published in the *Journal of the American Medical Association* by Johnson and eight associates concerning experiments with Ondansetron, a medication currently prescribed to curb nausea in chemotherapy patients ("Ondansetron Effective," 2000). Among alcoholics in the study, this drug increased abstinence by 40% and cut down consumption by 39%, compared with those given a placebo. The study found Ondansetron to have few side effects and that it can be given to alcoholics who are still drinking, precluding the need for detoxification. Oddly, Ondansetron significantly reduced alcohol use among patients with biological or early-onset, not late-onset, alcoholism. This drug appears to block serotonin receptors in the brain, thus decreasing the craving for alcohol. Interestingly, as we saw in chapter 4, only men and women who had developed alcoholism early—by age 25—benefited from the drug, presumably because there was something abnormal about their brain chemistry in the first place. It is often said that seriously addicted alcoholics can never learn to drink moderately. Indeed, without the help of a medication that apparently normalizes their brain, they probably cannot handle alcohol—the alcohol handles them. Other drugs, such as Prozac, had failed to help such clients, although, as Kranzler (2000) indicates in his commentary on this report, a selective serotonin reuptake inhibitor (for example, Prozac) might be used in patients with low-severity, late-onset alcoholism. As it turns out, though, according to a recent *Alcohol Alert* newsletter ("New Advances," 2000), the antidepressant Zoloft (but not Prozac) appears to reduce drinking in late-onset, but not early-onset, alcoholics. As this report indicates, a great deal more research is needed to match the appropriate medications to different client types. One direction for future clinical trials involves the mixing of two prescribed medications, such as Ondansetron and Naltrexone. The implications of the discovery of the differing effects of medication on different types of alcoholism are dramatic, not only for the future treatment of addiction but for what it says about the biological basis of alcohol dependence in general. Successful medication trials such as the Ondansetron study, targeting subtypes of alcoholics, mark the dawn of a new day in the alcoholism field.

Nicotine Treatment

Nicotine takes a terrible toll on American health, greater than does any other drug; over 400,000 people die per year from smoking-related causes. For women, tobacco-related illness is now the deadliest malignancy in women (Rubin, 2001). The fact that women continue to smoke in large numbers is attributed to tobacco advertising, which long has linked smoking with values that women care about—independence, sophistication, sex appeal, and, above all, slimness (Healton, 2001). Yet, as the title of an article by Bavley (1999) tells us, "Kicking the Habit [Is] a Tough Row to Hoe for Hard-Core Smokers" (p. A8). In fact, the urge to light up a cigarette is practically irresistible for the 50 million or so who are still puffing. Those who would or could quit more easily have already done so (Whereas in 1965 52% of men and 34% of women smoked, in 2000 those percentages had changed to 26% of men and 22% of women, according to Rubin, 2001). In recent years, nicotine chewing gum, skin patches, inhalers, nasal sprays, and antidepressant medications such as Zyban have helped to quell cravings for tobacco's addictive ingredient. Smoking-cessation classes that draw on mild aversion exercises are also popular.

Because continued smoking, like drinking, changes the brain, quitting brings about depression and irritability (McFarling, 1998). Of the 50 million smokers, at least 20 million try to quit each year, but fewer than 6% succeed. Treating nicotine addiction as the medical problem is essential if any headway is to be made in helping people break their life-threatening habit.

For smokers motivated to quit, there are several medications on the market. Of these, Zyban (the brand name for bupropion) is the most prominent. The effectiveness of this antidepressant was discovered by accident when a doctor noticed that many depressed patients on bupropion gave up smoking (Bavley, 1999).

A yearlong study of pack-a-day smokers who wanted to stop found that of 615 smokers, 23% of the group that got the highest level of the medications had quit one year later, compared to 12% of the central group ("Antidepressants Help Smokers," 1997). One of the most significant and surprising findings of the study was that while on Zyban, subjects gained only a few pounds, compared to quitters who stopped cold turkey. After six months, however, all those who quit smoking gained on average almost 12 pounds.

An insurance agent who quit with the help of Zyban explains what the craving is like without the drug: "You get virtually uncontrollable urges. You're going to go nuts if you don't have a cigarette. Even with the (nicotine) patch, you get these tremendous cravings" ("Antidepressant Proves Beneficial," 1998, p. A8). Zyban is designed for limited use, to help smokers get past those first weeks or months of intense craving. Zyban can be used along with the nicotine patch for maximum effect.

Naltrexone, commonly used to reduce addictive behavior in alcoholics and heroin addicts, also helps with smoking cessation, even in moderate smokers, according to the results of an empirical study reported in *Journal Watch Psychiatry* (Roy-Byrne, 1999). Unlike Zyban, Naltrexone blocks the reward circuits in the brain. Although Naltrexone users did not fully abstain in a related study of 22 smokers, they did significantly cut down (Ritter, 1997). Moreover, compared to those using a placebo, those who used Naltrexone did not suffer weight gain.

Experiments are currently under way with Methoxsalen, a drug that mimics the gene that some people have that blocks the body's ability to break down nicotine and makes a little nicotine go a long way (Zickler, 2000). Turning chain-smokers into moderate smokers carries significant health benefits and can make quitting ultimately easier.

Nicotine maintenance products, such as gum, skin patches, and nasal sprays, help smokers wean themselves from cigarettes. Nicotine elevates mood and sharpens concentration, a fact that explains why people with a history of depression, attention deficit disorder, or schizophrenia are likely to smoke and to get seriously hooked (Schultz, 2000). Although nicotine gum is intended to be used only for several months, researchers are finding that in a small minority of exsmokers, nicotine gum is chewed for years and years, as the only way they can stop themselves from inhaling nicotine ("Downside of Nicotine Gum," 2000).

NIDA-supported research has played a major role in providing crucial insights into the neurobiological aspects of nicotine addiction; these understandings, in turn, have paved the way for the pharmaceutical advances in treatment. Treating nicotine addiction as a medical problem helps remove the stigma attached to a person's difficulty in giving up smoking. In short, a medical understanding takes some of the blame off smokers and places it on the tobacco companies. This recognition of the similarity of nicotine addiction to other forms of chronic addiction, moreover, has brought about a major shift in thinking for the chemical dependency treatment field. The shift has evolved from clients smoking with staff in their therapy sessions, to smoking only in special areas, to having their smoking addiction treated as a drug dependency like any other.

Although inpatient treatment has been available for some time for alcoholics and other addicts with severe problems, chronic smokers, whose habits may be just as life threatening, have been denied this privilege. According to a study at the Mayo Clinic ("Checking Smokers into Treatment," 2001), hospitalizing smokers who cannot quit via traditional methods significantly increases the chances of turning an addicted smoker into a long-term exsmoker. Health insurers would do well to provide coverage for this intensive but cost-effective form of treatment.

For alcoholic smokers, better to quit both addictions at once, according to new research on rats done at the Indiana University School of Medicine ("Nicotine Increases Alcohol Craving," 2000). Both nicotine and alcohol lead to release of dopamine; repeated smoking is thought to enhance the pleasurable effects of alcohol. Just as some addiction treatment centers are pushing clients to stop smoking and drinking simultaneously, guidelines for stopping smoking should emphasize curbing alcohol intake as well, if this research is confirmed in continuing experiments.

Antidotes for Cocaine and Methamphetamine

A vaccine for cocaine and meth? At least five drug companies and several university scientists are testing "vaccines" for these hard-to-treat stimulant addictions, according to an article in *Utne* (Ready, 2000). This variety of drugs, like vaccines, programs the body to produce immune-system proteins called antibodies. Some of these treatments keep the psychoactive drugs from reaching the brain, while others break these toxins up into harmless chemical bits. A NIDA-funded project has already had some success in inoculating rats and monkeys. In human tests, a group of recovering cocaine addicts reported good results with no serious side effects; the antibodies were still in their bodies a year later.

Another pharmaceutical strategy to medical treatment for cocaine addiction is to develop a drug that blocks production of dopamine produced in conjunction with cocaine use. Gamma vinyl-GABA, or GVG, a drug used for years in Europe and Canada to treat epilepsy, has shown its effectiveness in brain scans of baboons (Manning, 1998). When placed in the equivalent of a crack house for rats, cocaine-addicted rats did not seek out cocaine when given GVG.

Another approach involves the use of a natural hallucinogen, Ibogaine, a drug illegal in the United States but used in experiments in the Caribbean, the Netherlands, and Panama (Cowley, 2001). Patients take it just once; supposedly it masks withdrawal symptoms for opiate addicts and creates a new perspective on life for all drug users.

Methadone Maintenance

For the nation's 1 million heroin addicts, the primary remedy is methadone (Leinwand, 2000). In reality, however, as former drug czar General McCaffrey (1999) argues, only about one in eight heroin addicts participate in methadone programs. Long waiting lists are common; in Seattle, for example, drug users may wait one year for treatment. While methadone therapy helps keep addicts off the streets and reduces the crime rate significantly, its use is scarce in the United States, due to political resistance. Congress consistently has refused to fund methadone therapy programs in the belief that use of methadone substitutes one addiction for another. Physicians, moreover, have been severely restricted in their authority to dispense this medication.

Methadone maintenance (and, in Britain, heroin maintenance) is the preferred treatment for heroin addicts in Europe, where it has been used with some success, especially in reducing the number of AIDS cases. Methadone works by occupying the opiate receptors of the brain that are involved in heroin craving. Given orally, and requiring daily visits to a clinic, methadone gives users a mild high that does not interfere with their ability to work or function. Because tolerance to this drug remains steady, patients can be maintained indefinitely on a fixed amount. Because methadone reduces the harm (risk of heroin overdose, criminal activity to support the habit, contracting AIDS through use of dirty needles), methadone therapy is a mainstay of harm reduction treatment. Still, methadone maintenance is not panacea. Only about half of heroin patients who attend methadone maintenance clinics are able to stay off heroin ("Heroin Addiction's Genetic Component," 2000).

Although methadone maintenance is considered an overall success in its lifesaving and crime-reducing aspects, many heroin addicts seem resistant to methadone treatment. Researchers in one study, as reported on the Join Together Web site ("Heroin Addiction's Genetic Component," 2000), discovered that the addicts who failed the program were likely to have a genetic variation making them highly addictive and less amenable than other addicts to standardized forms of treatment. Interestingly, this gene—DRD2—has been implicated in more virulent forms of alcoholism, smoking, and compulsive eating as well.

Another reason for treatment failure no doubt relates to the failure of many methadone maintenance treatment programs to prescribe adequate daily doses of methadone. Persons unresponsive to treatment in an experimental study in Switzerland, for example, all did well when levels of the drug were raised well above the usual 100-mg level ("MMT & Beyond," 2001). Over the years, street heroin has gotten purer in quality and lower in price. Consequently, there is greater need for higher doses of methadone today than is currently considered adequate by previously held standards.

Rachel Baldino (2000), writing in *Welcome to Methadonia,* provides a candid account of working (until she burned out) at a methadone clinic. This book chronicles the authoritarian rules, humiliating urinalysis tests (to see if clients were taking other drugs), and the emotional wear and tear of working with heroin addicts around the clock. Here are her recommendations: Counselors should not be required to play a disciplinary role, such as monitoring urinalysis results; counselors should not have more than a few heroin addicts at a time in their caseload; treatment should be decentralized so that clients can be treated at various doctors' offices, to avoid the drug-ridden atmosphere of the clinics; and, finally, methadone should be replaced with longer-acting LAAM.

Released by the Food and Drug Administration in 1993, LAAM, is chemically similar to methadone, but needs to be taken only once every three days. Take-home doses are not allowed because of the risk of diversion (for illicit sale). According to a former methadone clinic social worker, Christine Atkinson (in a personal interview of April 3, 2001), clients prefer methadone to LAAM. They get shaky with LAAM they say; it isn't strong enough to do the trick. Another revelation that emerged in this interview is the considerable resistance of criminal justice personnel to having their clients on methadone. "They have to be told it is legally approved," according to Atkinson. With recent reports coming in from Europe of cardiac rhythmic disorders associated with LAAM, physicians are being advised to switch their patients to methadone (Addiction Treatment Forum, 2001).

Less controversial are the antiopiate medications, such as buprenorphine and Naltrexone, discussed earlier. Waismann terms this preferred form of treatment "opioid receptor management" (2000, p. 32). In contrast to methadone, which, as he argues, only masks the problem, neurological regulation can be achieved through the use of medications allowing the patient to get through withdrawal while unconscious. An article in *Newsweek* (Cowley, 1995) discusses the procedure called "quick detox" as regularly performed in Spain and Israel and for Americans in Mexico, but at high cost. Injected with large doses of Naltrexone, the patient writhes unconsciously for hours until the withdrawal process is complete.

At Waismann's clinic in California, patients, upon discharge, are prescribed a regimen of Naltrexone, a non-mood-altering medication that successfully reduces the craving for opiates. Such treatment also can be applied in the care of "heroin babies" to replace the long, painful, and damaging current approaches of getting addicted infants through withdrawal. Opiate addiction, as Waismann further argues, should be viewed as a disorder of the central nervous system that can be reversed with appropriate medical treatment.

New laws have been introduced to allow physicians who take qualifying training classes to prescribe antiopiate medications from their offices ("Buprenorphine Legislation," 2000). The new drug buprenorphine acts like extra-mild methadone at low doses (Cowley, 2001). But unlike methadone, it diminishes the high even when taken as an overdose. This drug, which can be prescribed directly by doctors once federal approval is granted and which can be taken in lozenge form, should significantly increase the number of heroin addicts receiving treatment.

Naltrel, a time-released, injectable version of Naltrexone, is designed to last 30 days and, it is hoped, will increase the number of addicts seeking treatment. The promise of nonaddictive treatment drugs such as Naltrel has fueled the effort to shift treatment from clinics to doctors' offices (Leinwand, 2000). One serious drawback with these types of drugs, however, is the low motivation of addicts to use them. After all, these antagonist drugs block the pleasure of drug taking, something many addicts may have no interest in doing. To keep addicts off the streets, they need to have a choice, therefore, of whether they would like to be treated with an addiction substitute such as LAAM or methadone or to be rendered immune to the drug's euphoric properties with a blocker medication such as Naltrexone.

Medication for Eating Disorders

Why do compulsive eaters feel such intense cravings for chocolates and other sweets (or potato chips)? It may be that they have some of the same abnormal brain chemistry seen in drug addicts (Boyce, 2001).

Eating is a survival behavior that must be pleasurable to sustain the species. The same primitive reward system in the brain is central to the development of both excessive eating and chemical addiction. The high rate of comorbidity between eating and other disorders, as discussed in chapter 7, bears out the interconnectedness in these addictive/compulsive tendencies.

Chemical addiction and eating disorders share many common clinical features. The commonalties, as Gold, Johnson, and Stennie (1997) suggest, are not limited to behavioral observations but involve an array of neurotransmitter abnormalities. Dopamine is involved in both. Thus it stands to reason that teasing out dopamine's effects could lead to new drugs for the millions of Americans who are obese (Boyce, 2001). What is not known at this point is whether a deficit in receptors in the brain cells of obese people is a cause or a result of the overweight. Future studies should make the connection clear.

Those eating disorders that are characterized by compulsive binge eating and purge behaviors (bulimia) are highly correlated with alcohol and other drug misuse (Halmi, 1998). Whereas bulimics suffer more from depression, anorexics suffer more from anxiety. Because of the extreme rigidity and ritualism found in anorexics, a disturbance in serotonin functioning is probably responsible, as Halmi theorizes.

Luvox, a drug similar to Prozac, has been found to produce significantly better outcomes in binge-eating outpatients than those given a placebo (Figgitt & McClellan, 2000). Although this drug is considered an antidepressant, it is effective in persons with or without depression. Study results summarized by McGilley and Pryor (1998) indicate that cognitive therapy focusing on challenging rigid thought patterns and healthy expression of feelings in combination with medication is more effective than the use of medication alone.

Help for Behavioral Addictions

Very little is written in the literature about the use of prescription medication for the behavioral addictions, such as compulsive gambling and shopping. Given the interrelatedness of these addictions and drug addictions, however, it stands to reason that similar medication would work for both varieties of compulsions—drug-seeking or money-related behavior.

Dr. Donald Black and his colleagues at the University of Iowa Medical School have had success in prescribing Luvox to compulsive shoppers. The medication, according to preliminary findings, makes it possible for sufferers to walk through a store and spend what they intended. Interestingly, as the research on 55 compulsive buyers showed, close relatives of these subjects suffered disproportionately more from depression and drug use than did persons in the comparison sample (Black, Repertinger, Gaffney, & Gabel, 1998).

For compulsive gamblers and also kleptomaniacs (persons who compulsively steal), Naltrexone is being used experimentally to curb their destructive behavior. The focus at the University of Minnesota Medical School is on using drugs to block the receptors in the brain that register the pleasurable high (Chin, 2000). Other techniques used to help kleptomaniacs are antidepression drugs, shock treatments, and therapy in which the patient is instructed to hold his or her breath or think of vomiting when experiencing the urge to steal. As one expert stated in the article, "Stealing may be a symptom of some conditions, such as an eating disorder or bipolar disorder. Treat these conditions, and the stealing goes away" (p. 7A). Alternatively, all these disorders can be seen as different manifestations of a disturbance in brain chemistry; treatment directed at the root cause of the disturbance should relieve the various symptoms. (See chapter 7.)

HOLISTIC APPROACHES

Other remedies directed toward the physical side of drug use are more natural, holistic approaches. These include various herbal remedies, acupuncture, massage, hypnosis, and biofeedback.

A quick look at the popular literature on herbal remedies reveals that one day's wonder drug is the next day's despair. Until scientific testing is conducted, the truth is hard to ascertain. For example, an article in *USA Today* (Sternberg, 1997) describes a Vietnamese concoction, Heantos, containing a mixture of 13 herbs that reportedly makes drug cravings disappear. Used for opium addicts in Vietnam, the drug is consumed for four days in half-quart doses. The United Nations Development Program is funding a scientific study into its effectiveness. A later report, however, states that after two patients died, the Vietnamese Health Ministry shut down the inventor's clinic ("Vietnamese Addiction Treatment Derailed," 1997). A Norwegian article from the *Aftenposten* ("Testing av Urtemedisin pa Narkomane," 1999), however, and other European sources express a serious interest in the possibilities of this drug.

Ibogaine, mentioned earlier as a treatment for heroin withdrawal, is a drug derived from a West African shrub. "Tales of Ibogaine's effectiveness are legion among addicts, but data are in short supply," according to an article in *U.S. News & World Report* (Koerner, 1999). Troubled by reports of seizures in monkeys and dogs under its influence or out of fear because of its hallucinogenic properties, Congress has made this drug illegal in the United States ("Release of Anti-Addiction Drug Stalled," 2000). Although over 100 academic papers have been written on Ibogaine, what is missing, according to a report from the Associated Press ("Attacking Addiction," 2000), are comprehensive studies to convince government authorities that the drug is safe. In the Netherlands, the drug is readily available to suppress withdrawal symptoms and reduce drug cravings. Experiments continue today on the Caribbean Island of St. Kitts, where Ibogaine reportedly has been highly effective not only in blocking withdrawal from opiates but also in counteracting the "crash" from stimulants like cocaine.

Saint John's Wort, considered nature's own Prozac, is widely prescribed in Germany for depression and sleeping problems (Miller, 1997). The German emphasis is on the natural healing powers of the body, so their preference is for herbal and homeopathic remedies (Payer, 1996). Prozac is rarely prescribed there. American health food stores are now carrying this herb as well as the kava root, which has mildly calming properties, according to Miller.

Kava assumes a social importance in many Pacific Island societies similar to that of wine in southern Europe: a sacred drug, a social drink, and a cash crop (Lebot, Merlin, & Lindstrom, 1992). As used by the aboriginal people of Australia, however, as Lebot et al. indicate, this drug from the kava plant species is dangerous in the way that "alien poisons" often are to people who have no history with the drug. Heavy kava drinkers in Australia appear to be substituting kava for alcohol; it is destroying their health in the same way that alcohol has done; the medically harmful effects have been pronounced.

The goal of holistic therapies is to restore the body to its naturally healthy state. Holistic philosophy, as Apostolides (1996) suggests, overlaps with the harm reduction approach to addiction in its focus on treating the entire person, often with psychotherapy as well as medical remedies. In the major U.S. cities, a number of harm reduction centers now offer programs that include acupuncture, massage therapy, yoga, and substance misuse counseling.

Acupuncture consists of stimulating certain points on or near the surface of the body by insertion of needles. Practiced in China for more than 5,000 years, its use in the treatment of narcotic addiction goes back only several decades (Smith et al., 1997). In a clinical trial of 82 dually addicted participants (cocaine and some other drug), individuals in a methadone program were assigned to a control group—needles inserted in the wrong parts of the ear—or a group with correct ear placement or a relaxation group. Over half of the acupuncture patients later tested free of cocaine, compared to 23.5% of the control acupuncture group and 9.1% of the relaxation group ("Study Finds Acupuncture," 2000). Other studies indicate a reduction in craving for alcohol and heroin (Smith et al., 1997).

Acupuncture appears especially valuable during early-stage treatment. According to Smith et al. (1997), acupuncture patients report more calmness and reduced cravings for cocaine even after the first treatment. For methamphetamine use, similarly, studies show a high rate in early treatment when acupuncture is used. Even extremely antisocial people benefit from this treatment (Smith et al., 1997).

Massage therapy has achieved impressive results in tests on people dealing with anorexia, bulimia, smoking, and other addictions (Apostolides, 1996). The neurological response to body contact and to the loosening of tight muscles releases tension and helps clients "reconnect physically and center themselves emotionally" (p. 37). Similarly, yoga helps people get in tune with their physical processes, including muscular exertion—holding certain positions—and breathing. Simple exercise is effective in reducing tension and in elevating mood because, with continuous activity, the body produces endorphins the natural way (Dorsman, 1996).

Heavy drinking and other drug misuse can cause hypoglycemia, or low blood sugar, as well; the craving for sugar by alcoholics is a consequence. Vitamin C sometimes is used by nutrition therapists to modify the withdrawal symptoms of detoxification (Apostolides, 1996). To replenish the body's nutrients that have been depleted through chemical misuse and faulty diets, accordingly, is an important component of recovery. Drinking large quantities of alcohol, for example, depletes the body of thiamine and other vitamins (Volpicelli & Szalavitz, 2000). Nutrients such as niacin, amino acids, and magnesium are given to alleviate problems caused by low levels of glucose in the brain. In early recovery, sleeping in a nondrugged state can present major problems. Drinking a glass of milk or one of the herbal teas, such as "Sleepy Bear," can be immensely helpful. Melatonin is an over-the-counter drug that induces a natural sleep and has few side effects.

Hypnosis is another remedy that helps people gain control over their urges to use, in this case through the use of suggestion. While in a trance, patients may be told to view their drug of choice with distaste (Fishbein & Pease, 1996). From a more positive stance, people can rehearse coping with urges to use until they develop the capacity to do so while in a non-trancelike state. Like hypnosis, biofeedback and acupuncture are administered by persons with specialized training. The aim of biofeedback is brainwave training to reduce stress. And also like hypnosis, biofeedback, also called brainwave training, is a "mind over matter" phenomenon in which the individual, through training, learns to attain a deep level of relaxation for the purpose of helping in the maintenance of sobriety. Levin (1995) describes the way this method works: Electroencephalograph (EEG) measures of anxiety levels are obtained so that the individual can monitor his or her response in conjunction with the feedback. After pretraining, individuals receive alpha-theta brainwave training. While in the alpha, or deeply relaxed, state, the substance user might be instructed in refusing drinks or drugs. Although this method has shown some success, there are two basic drawbacks noted by Levin: The equipment is expensive, and there are unexpected effects, such as the return of repressed traumatic memories that may lead to emotional distress.

ASSESSMENT OF ALCOHOL AND OTHER DRUG USE

Since assessment usually precedes treatment, this process to determine the level and effect of drug and alcohol use comes early, while the mind is often still clouded with the effect of drug taking and alcohol use. The cessation of accustomed drug use leads to all kinds of physiological responses as well. In the end, however, as we will see in later chapters, however difficult is the road to physical recovery, the psychological aspects are even more profound.

For assessment of substance use problems, cultural awareness is a must. Among Native Americans, for example, peyote use is considered a ritualized experience, not a destructive practice associated with loss of control. In mountain areas of Colombia, similarly, chewing of the coca plant (a key ingredient in cocaine) is associated with good health and protection against the stresses of the high altitude. Questions on assessment forms concerning hallucinations need to take into account Native American practices in some tribes where participants go to great lengths to induce hallucinations for spiritual purposes.

Alcohol screening questionnaires, invariably designed for male populations, need to be sensitive to female physiological and psychological drinking experiences. A review of alcohol screening questionnaires in the *Journal of the American Medical Association* (Bradley, Boyd-Wickizer, Powell, & Burman, 1998) examined screening devices for effectiveness in detecting alcohol dependency in white women and black women. Since women suffer adverse consequences at lower levels of drinking and experience fewer economic and employment consequences perhaps than men, yet are more stigmatized by heavy drinking, questionnaires validated for male populations may fail to measure alcoholism in women. The computer search of questionnaire evaluations conducted by Bradley et al. revealed that CAGE and TWEAK were the optimal tests for identification of alcohol dependence in women. (See Table 5.1) However, effectiveness varied by ethnicity. For black obstetric patients and for white women, questionnaires that asked about tolerance for alcohol, for example, TWEAK, were more sensitive. For use with mixed populations, therefore, the researchers recommend TWEAK. The advantage of these questionnaires is that they are so brief that they can easily be carried around in the counselor's head.

A lengthier instrument for assessing adverse consequences of alcohol misuse is offered by the National Institute of Alcohol Abuse and Alcoholism (NIH Publication No. 95-3911). This 50-item instrument, the Inventory of Drug Use Consequences, is presented in a manual of the much publicized Project Match Monograph Series, Vol. 4 (Project MATCH Research Group, 1997). It is in the public domain and therefore can be reproduced without permission or expense. (To order, call 1-800-729-6686.)

TABLE 5.1	CAGE AND TWEAK TESTS FOR ALCOHOL DEPENDENCE

C	Have you ever felt you ought to Cut down on your drinking?
A	Have people Annoyed you by criticizing your drinking?
G	Have you felt bad or Guilty about your drinking?
E	Have you ever had a drink in the morning (Eye opener) to steady your nerves or get rid of a hangover?

Scoring: 1 point for each "yes" response; sum all points; total, 0–4 points. An answer of "yes" to two of these items is considered problematic.

T	Tolerance: How many drinks can you hold ("hold" version: 6 or more drinks indicates tolerance), or how many drinks does it take before you begin to feel the first effect of the alcohol? ("high" version: 3 or more indicates tolerance)
W	Worried: Have close friends or relatives worried or complained about your drinking in the past year?
E	Eye openers: Do you sometimes take a drink in the morning when your first get up?
A	Amnesia: Has a friend or family member ever told you about things you said or did while you were drinking that you could not remember?
K	Kut down: Do you sometimes feel the need to cut down on your drinking?

The World Health Organization of the United Nations has delineated seven Major Life Areas for determining whether or not a substance misuse problem exists. Consistent with harm reduction, the word *harm* is used throughout their report. The Major Life Areas, which have been chosen because of their universal qualities for cross-national research are: physical health; family and relationships; leisure; emotional health; finances; the law; and social life/employment.

GROUP WORK FOR EARLY-PHASE TREATMENT

Substance abuse counselors need to shape their interventions to match the biological readiness of the client to participate. A brain damaged by alcohol and other drugs can take in only so much. A client with six months of physical recovery and six months of practice in social skills and motivational work is clearly in better shape to work on deep emotional issues than a man or woman sober for only 10 days. Long-term outpatient programs using a stages-of-change model are desirable, especially for polyaddicted clients, whose bodies require long periods of time to get clean of any substance.

For simplicity, we will describe a treatment modality designed for a group of clients all presumed to be at the initial stage of recovery. In reality, most actual working groups contain clients at various stages of recovery, with those with longer periods of sobriety and group participation ideally serving as models for newcomers. Drawing upon the stages-of-change model proposed by Prochaska, DiClemente, and Norcross (1992), we are providing guidelines for work at the very first stages of thinking about change, stages termed "precontemplation" and "contemplation." What we have added to this model is an allowance for the kind of thinking impairment related to brain dysfunction that is character-istic of a history of substance misuse. An awareness of the brain's regenerative powers is an important consideration as well. This focus on healing parallels the strengths perspective's emphasis on the human potential for growth and re-covery and the belief that it is never too soon to start the process of tapping into people's inner resources.

Treatment strategies, in short, cannot exceed the mind's ability to absorb them. Interventions, therefore, must correspond to the client's biological state of recovery. Immediately following detoxification, for example, the stress is on the biological aspect of recovery, on clinical interventions geared to healing the mind and body. This, the first period of treatment, ideally lasts for several months. Psychologically based therapy (as described in chapter 7) is only effec-tive at a later stage, when the mind is free of chemicals and alternative ways of dealing with stress have been mastered. In the phase approach, the progression is from supportive, highly structured individual sessions or groups, to work in the later period on deeper, more psychologically disturbing issues with long-term ramifications (e.g., career planning, relationships). The following guide-lines are geared toward group facilitation; with a few modifications, however, they can serve to inform individual therapy as well.

Group Process in Early-Stage Treatment

Will clients be required to abstain totally from use of all mood-altering (non-prescription) medications, or will they be able to attend group sessions while they make up their minds what to do about their drug intake? In reality, the choice very rarely is in the hands of the group facilitator or even always of the agency. In the United States, clients are often under court-ordered sanctions. Total abstinence generally is required for the duration of treatment. The focus during the first part of treatment is on the *biological* side of alcoholism and re-covery. The question "How do you feel?" is apt to be answered at this time in terms of how the members slept last night, what they are eating, and what kind of mood they are in. Today, one day at a time, keeping things simple, learning how to reduce stress—these are the guiding principles of an early-recovery group. Typically, an individual in early recovery is very literal and concrete in his or her thinking and may have great difficulty in handling ambiguity (Wallen, 1993). As Patt Denning (2000) indicates, heavy alcohol intake or excessive use of tranquilizers is associated with diminished abstract reasoning ability; para-noid thinking may be evident in long-term stimulant users.

The basic function of initial treatment is to provide basic education on the addictive process and to impart a sense of hope—hope that the alcoholic can somehow overcome and prevail against this addiction that has created so much havoc. Group structure is tight; the group leader lectures, uses diagrams, and generally fulfills the information-giving function of early treatment. Information must be provided on particulars of the total program and of the legal requirements, if any. Finally, general, not terribly complicated information concerning the physical illness of addiction is given. Slides of the "brain on drugs" can be immensely helpful in eliciting self-understanding and preparing clients for the down feelings that accompany the early period of sobriety. As a supplement to lecture material, educational films are often shown. Such films teach the effects of substance misuse on the mind, the body, and relationships. Because of the newness of the material, it is often advisable to show each film more than once and to repeat important points periodically.

In the early phase of treatment, the primary focus of intervention is to establish a favorable client–therapist relationship as a springboard for building trust and motivation (Barber, 1994). Once trust is established, the group facilitator is in a position to give advice and, better yet, in a skillful drawing out of helpful comments from group members, to reinforce their insights, which are often quite astute. Group feedback is far more powerful than individual feedback. Group members who may not be ready to assess their own behavior realistically often do quite well in assessing others' behaviors accurately. In van Wormer's women's therapy group in Washington State, for example, group members, many of whom were involved in destructive, often battering relationships, were quick to realize when another woman was being exploited by her boyfriend.

The group norms that develop early can "make or break" the evolving alcoholism therapy group. The leader's role in developing therapeutic group norms is essential. The norms desired are those that promote sharing in the group, sobriety, and individual change efforts. Norms *not* desired are those that sanction complaining about the courts, the police, or the program or those that reinforce externalization and fatalism.

As clients begin to trust the leader and the group, they will begin to self-disclose. As they take more and more risks and get supportive feedback, they come to trust the group more. In working with male alcoholics on gender-based issues, the group leader might first model the desired behavior and then encourage sharing. This process assists members in realizing that they are not alone in their anxieties and inhibitions.

Getting Started

The group leader can help members set their own rules; then he or she can help the group enforce these rules. First the leader lists the agency rules, such as:

- No smoking or drinking pop in the group
- No admission of intoxicated members into the group

Then group members are asked to suggest rules they would like to set for their group. Invariably the following suggestions are made and approved:

- What is said in the group stays in the group
- No put-downs or attacks on individuals
- No interruptions when someone is speaking; don't all talk at once
- No name-calling; no shouting

When the leader must remind the group that rules *they* have set are being violated, group members are often relieved to have this form of external protection. They make the rules, and they can rely on the leader to help enforce them.

What is the addiction counselor's role in promoting appropriate group norms? The trained leader makes use of effective group interventions at key points in the group process. Early in the group's life, skillful intervention serves as a model for group members, who are thereby being groomed to assume responsibility for this function at some later stage of the group process. Significantly, well-timed interventions help to keep members working on their goals and to give everyone a sense of security and structure.

Skills of Group Work

Experts in the field recommend a highly structured approach in the initial sessions (Vannicelli, 1982; Yalom, 1974). Group leaders have to contend with denial, defensiveness, and ingenious avoidance tactics (avoidance of emotionally painful areas). Under the circumstances, leaders have to closely monitor the discussion and continually be prepared to shift the focus back to the therapeutic goals. A helpful strategy in lengthy group sessions is to vary group size. Many individuals who are uncommunicative in large groups will work well in dyads, triads, and groups of four or five. To maintain a sense of unity in the large group, the small groups may choose a spokesperson to report on what they accomplished in their discussion (van Wormer, 1995).

A useful way to begin the process in individual or small-group sessions has been proposed by Denning (2000). The therapist divides a sheet of black paper into two halves. The top half is entitled "Change my drinking/drug use" and the bottom half, "Continue the way I am now." On the left side under each heading is the space to list the pros, and on the right side, to list the cons. The purpose of the exercise is to promote decision making and help motivate clients in the direction of change. Hopefully, the negative side of drug use will emerge in a compelling fashion through this activity.

When Intervention Is Called For

The group counselor can expect to "step in" with an appropriate question or comment when:

1. A group member monopolizes the group and other members either seem uncomfortable or too comfortable with this role (common in groups of involuntary clients).

2. A group member focuses on external events (court, parents, spouse, loss) in ascribing blame and fails to take any personal responsibility.
3. A group member falls into the widely recognized "all-or-nothing" thinking fallacy. Typically heard "all-or-nothing" statements are these: "There are two types of people—the weak and the strong"; "If you don't get an A in a course, why bother?"; 'If you can't be the best they why bother at all?"
4. The recovering member expresses an abnormally high degree of guilt or self-blame over the drug abuse and its consequences.
5. Members fail to confront someone or to indicate their concern for one who is "setting him- or herself up" for personal tragedy.
6. Group members are sidetracked and turn the session into a "gripe session."
7. A member fails to see any *positive* thread in his or her attempt to grow and needs appropriate reinforcement for the small steps taken.
8. A client arrives at a group intoxicated or expresses views conducive to harmful behavior.
9. The mood of the group is too heavy and should be lightened. Or conversely, the mood is too light and thoughts should be moved in a more serious direction.
10. Effective individual and group maneuvers are observed; these should be positively reinforced as a model to all participants.
11. When group members make eye contact with the leader but not with each other. Say, "Tell the group, don't tell me."

Group Exercises

Group exercises during the beginning of treatment focus on getting acquainted, building trust among members who will be sharing parts of their lives with each other, and setting the stage for deeper, more intensive work to follow.

1. Communication
   Purposes: To get acquainted; to explore levels of communication.
   Clients divide into groups of four. They are told to communicate for the first three minutes at a superficial level: talk about the weather, food, clothes. The second three minutes, they will talk of a recent event—a movie or sports. The third three minutes, they express opinions on controversial topics. The next three minutes they will fill out cards that say:
   I feel scared when _____
   I feel happy when _____
   I feel jealous when _____
   I feel rejected when _____
   Clients take turns filling in with their responses. The fifth period of time is focused on "the peak experience." Each member describes a peak moment of time of great revelations in his or her life.
   While the interaction is taking place, the leader rotates visits among the various groups. He or she announces the end of each period of time and beckons members to move on to the next level. Following the last exchange, the groups rejoin each other. The leader may engage the participants in discussion

by introducing such questions as: *At which level did you feel the least, the most comfortable? Did you learn something meaningful about each other? What surprised you about this exercise? At which level do you usually communicate throughout the day?* Discussion ensues.

2. Use of Cards

Purposes: To get acquainted; to learn to feel safe; to begin to learn to express feelings in the group.

Group members fill out cards on which questions or statements are written. Some sample statements and questions are:

Say something positive about yourself!

My favorite childhood memory is _____

Something I value highly is _____

Name a famous alcoholic/addict and tell this person's story: _____

_____

If I could have three wishes, I would wish _____

My advice to a young person is _____

My understanding of alcoholism is _____

3. Positive Feedback

Purpose: To boost self-esteem.

Sometimes a group member who is relating well to others puts himself or herself down. Group members are asked to say positive things about the member. The person records the messages. In later sessions, the person is asked to repeat these positive comments. This exercise helps provide substance for improved "self-talk" and to replace negative thoughts with positive ones.

We have considered basic elements of the group during the early stages, not only in the group treatment process but also in the addict's sobriety. In many ways the early period of therapy is the most difficult—individual resistance is at a maximum; relapse is common; and defensiveness is a characteristic. Principles of motivational interviewing come into play in the group setting as in the individual setting. The individuals are not pushed into decision making but encouraged through compassionate listening to move in a health-seeking direction. As the group leader models this client-centered approach, the members follow. Then two major aims of the first months of treatment are accomplished: group bonding is developed, and the group members function as a supportive, working group.

SUMMARY AND CONCLUSION

Understanding addiction as largely a biologically based phenomenon may help explain an individual's difficulty in achieving and maintaining abstinence without appropriate treatment. The tendency to relapse is now (thanks to neurological imaging of the brain) known to be as much a biological as a psychological phenomenon. The use of medications to quell the biological urges to relapse is today revolutionizing the field of addiction treatment. The shibboleths of the profession are changing; this includes absolutes such as "Abstain from all mood-altering substances." The pharmaceutical advances should hasten clients' progress in treatment indirectly through improving their mental states. Since one of the leading causes of relapse is depression, medications that help replenish the brain of the natural opiates (for example, Prozac) are an effective adjunct to relapse prevention. Naltrexone, a drug in a different category from the serotonin-boosting medications, functions by blocking cravings for substances like alcohol and heroin. Since alcoholics and addicts seem to have an underlying vulnerability for a number of compulsive behaviors, including compulsive gambling and eating disorders, medication geared toward normalizing brain functioning should reap benefits in these related areas as well.

The pharmaceutical treatment of addictive behaviors is in its infancy. The next few years should see remarkable progress in this area as new and more effective therapies are developed. As is always the case with new technologies, there is a cultural lag between discovery and treatment. This lag is reflected in public policies, policies predicated on threats of punishment to the neglect of sound biomedical and psychological research. A second major development of note is the realization that cognitive therapies can help reverse irregularities in the brain as well. Such cognitively based therapy can be provided in individual or group settings. Moreover, behavioral strategies that can be learned in a group can help people during that crucial early stage of recovery to cope with their drug cravings and to avoid drug-related cues. (Such high-risk situations, in all probability, are due to euphoric memories that were imprinted in the mind, memories that readily can trigger a return to drug-using behavior.)

This chapter focused on therapies aimed at work with clients during their period of maximum craving for chemical relief and vulnerability for relapse. Guidelines were provided for group treatment that uses a phase approach, where interventions are matched to the biological and psychological stages of recovery. Focusing on the mechanics of setting up a nonthreatening therapeutic experience, we provided a framework that is adaptable for use in a variety of settings and with a variety of philosophical approaches. Having completed Part 2 of this book—the study of the biology of addiction—we proceed to a look at the equally compelling psychological aspects.

References

Addiction Treatment Forum. (2001). *LAAM sales suspended in the EU*. Available online from www.atforum.com/siteroot/pages/news

Akers, R. (1992). *Drugs, Alcohol, and Society*. Belmont, CA: Wadsworth.

Alcohol aversion therapy clinics expand in California. (1998, June 16). Available from www.jointogether.org

Antidepressant proves beneficial in helping smokers kick the habit. (1998, January 21). *Waterloo-Cedar Falls Courier*, A8.

Antidepressants help smokers to quit. (1997, November 15). *Science News, 152*.

Apostolides, M. (1996, September/October). How to quit the holistic way. *Psychology Today*, 35–43, 68–70.

Attacking addiction. (2000, January 4). *Waterloo-Cedar Falls Courier,* A4. From the Associated Press.

Baldino, R. (2000). *Welcome to methadonia: A social worker's candid account of life in a methadone clinic.* Harrisburg, PA: White Hat Communications.

Barber, J. G. (1994). *Social work with addictions.* New York: New York University Press.

Bavley, A. (1999, May 2). Kicking the habit a tough row to how for hard-core smokers. *Waterloo-Cedar Falls Courier,* A8.

Black, D. W., Repertinger, S., Gaffney, G., & Gabel, J. (1998, July). *American Journal of Psychiatry 155*(7), 960–964.

Bordnick, P. S. (1996). Evaluating the relative effectiveness of three aversion therapies designed to reduce craving among male cocaine abusers. *Dissertation Abstracts 56*(10-A), 4145.

Boyce, N. (2001, February 12). The debt to pleasure. *U.S. News & World Report, 59.*

Bradley, K. A., Boyd-Wickizer, J., Powell, S. H., & Burman, M. L. (1998, July 8). Alcohol screening questionnaires in women: A critical review. *Journal of the American Medical Association 280*(2), 166–171.

Buprenorphine legislation hailed as treatment breakthrough. (2000, October 20). Available from www.jointogether.org

Burman, S. (2001). Strategies for intervention with individuals. In A. Abbott (Ed.), *Alcohol, tobacco, & other drugs: Challenging myths, assessing theories, individualizing interventions* (pp. 204–246). Washington, DC: NASW Press.

Challender, M. (1999, April 18). They thirst for sobriety. *Des Moines Register,* 1E, 2E.

Checking smokers into treatment. (2001, April 6). Available at www.jointogether.org

Chin, R. (2000, December 10). Drug may suppress impulse to steal in kleptomaniacs. *Des Moines Register,* 7A.

Clinical concepts—naltrexone in action against alcoholism. (2000, winter). *Addiction Treatment Forum.* Available from www.atforum.com/pages/current_pastissues/winter2000.html

Cowley, G. (1995, January 30). A new assault on addiction. *Newsweek, 51.*

Cowley, G. (2001, February 12). New ways to stay clean. *Newsweek, 45–47.*

Crews, F. T. (2001, March). Cited in: How sensitive is your brain to alcohol-induced damage? *Addiction Science.* Available on www.nattc.org/asme/01-3March.html

Denning, P. (2000). *Practicing harm reduction psychotherapy: An alternative approach to addictions.* New York: Guilford Press.

Dorsman, J. (1996, January). Improving alcoholism treatment: An overview. *Behavioral Health Management, 16*(1), 26–29.

Dowling, J. E. (1998). *Creating mind: How the brain works.* New York: Norton.

Downside of nicotine gum examined. (2000, November 30). Available from www.jointogether.org

Figgitt, D. P., & McClellan, K. J. (2000). *Drugs, 60*(4), 925–954.

Fishbein, D. H., & Pease, S. E. (1996). *The dynamics of drug abuse.* Boston: Allyn & Bacon.

Gold, M. S., Johnson, C. R., & Stennie, K. (1997). Eating disorders. In J. H. Lowinson, P. Ruiz, R. Mulliman, & J. G. Langrod (Eds.), *Substance abuse: A comprehensive textbook* (pp. 319–337). Baltimore: Williams & Wilkins.

Halmi, K. A. (1998). A 24-year-old woman with anorexia nervosa. *Journal of the American Medical Association, 279*(24), 1992–1999.

Healton, C. (2001, March 26). Smoking clouds women's futures. *USA Today,* 19A.

Heroin addiction's genetic component. (2000, September 26). Available from www .jointogether.org

Johnson, H. C. (1999). *Psyche, synapse, & substance: The role of neurobiology in emotions, behavior, thinking, & addiction for nonscientists*. Greenfield, MA: Deerfield Valley.

Kalb, C. (2001, February 21). Alcoholism: Can this pill stop you from hitting the bottle? *Newsweek*, 48–54.

Knapp, C. (1996). *Drinking: A love story*. New York: Delta.

Knapp, C. (1999, May 9). The glass half empty. *New York Times Magazine*, 19–20.

Koerner, B. (1999, December 6). For heroin addicts, a bizarre remedy. *U.S. News & World Report*, 82.

Kranzler, H. R. (2000, August 23/30). Medications for alcohol dependence—new vistas. *Journal of the American Medical Association 284*(8), 1016–1017.

Lebot, V., Merlin, M., & Lindstrom, L. (1992). *Kava: The Pacific drug*. New Haven: Yale University Press.

Leinwand, D. (2000, May 31). New drugs, younger addicts fuel push to shift treatment from methadone clinics. *USA Today*, 1A.

Lemonick, M. (1997, September 29). The mood molecule. *Time*, 76–82.

Leshner, A. I. (1997, October 3). Addiction is a brain disease and it matters. *Science*, 45–47.

Levin, D. L. (1995). Introduction to alcoholism counseling: A bio-psycho-social approach. New York: Taylor and Davis.

Manning, A. (1998, August 5). Drug could mute effects of cocaine. *USA Today*, 1A.

McCaffrey, B. R. (1999, January 25). Heroin access spurs need for methadone. *USA Today*, 13A.

McFarling, V. L. (1998, August 4). New nicotine therapy targets the brain. *Lexington Herald-Leader*, A1, A5.

McGilley, B., & Pryor, T. (1998). Assessment and treatment of bulimia nervosa. *American Family Physician 57*(11), 2743–2751.

Miller, S. (1997, May 3). A national mood booster. *Newsweek*, 74.

MMT & beyond—redefining "adequate" methadone dose. (2001, winter). *Addiction Treatment Forum*. Available online at www.atforum.com

New advances in alcoholism treatment. (2000, October). *Alcohol Alert*, 1–4.

Nicotine increases alcohol craving. (2000, February 2). Available from alcoholism .about.com/library/weekly/a

Office of National Drug Control Policy. (2001). *National Drug Control Strategy: Annual Report*. Washington, DC: U.S. Government Printing Office.

Ondansetron effective for treating early-onset alcoholism. (2000, November 17). Available at www.jointogether.org

Payer, L. (1996). *Medicine and culture*. New York: Holt.

Peele, S. (1995). *Diseasing of America*. San Francisco: Jossey-Bass.

Prochaska, J. D., DiClemente, C. C., & Norcross, J. C. (1992). In search of how people change: Applications to addictive behaviors. *American Psychologist 47*, 1102–1114.

Project MATCH Research Group. (1997). Matching alcoholism treatments to client heterogeneity. *Journal of Studies on Alcohol 58*, 7–27.

Ready, T. (2000, November/December). High immunity. *Utne*, 20.

Research refines alcoholism treatment options. (2000). *Alcohol Research and Health 24*(1), 53–61.

Ritter, M. (1997, May 21). One last puff: Drug used to treat alcoholism may help smokers quit. *Daily News* (Bowling Green, KY), B1.

Robertson, N. (1988). *Getting better: Inside Alcoholics Anonymous.* New York: William Morrow.

Roy-Byrne, P. (1999). Naltrexone for smoking cessation? *Journal Watch Psychiatry, 5*(3), 27.

Rubin, R. (2001, March 28). Women total 40% of smoking deaths. *Des Moines Register,* 1A.

Schick Shadel Web site. (1997). Schick Shadel hospital's effective treatment program. Available from www.schick-shadel.com/treatment.html

Schultz, S. (2000, May 29). Would-be quitters get help winning against nicotine. *U.S. News & World Report,* 58–60.

Schwartz, J. (1997). *Brain lock: Free yourself from obsessive compulsion behavior.* New York: HarperCollins.

Smith, M. O., Brewington, V., Culliton, P., Ng, L., Hsiang-lai, W., & Lowinson, J. H. (1997). Acupuncture. In J. H. Lowinson, P. Ruiz, & R. Millman (Eds.), *Substance abuse: A comprehensive textbook* (pp. 484–492). New Haven: Yale University Press.

Sternberg, S. (1997, June 24). Herbs may ease addiction. *USA Today,* D1.

Stevens-Smith, P., & Smith, R. L. (1998). *Substance abuse counseling: Theory and practice.* Upper Saddle River, NJ: Prentice Hall.

Study finds acupuncture shows promise for treating cocaine addiction. (2000, August 13). *NIDA News Release,* 1–2.

Testing av urtemedisin pa narkomane (Testing herbal medicine for drug addicts). (1999, April 5). *Aftenposten,* 1.

U.S. Department of Health and Human Services. (2000). *10th special report to the U.S. Congress on alcohol and health.* Washington, DC: U.S. Government Printing Office.

Vannicelli, M. (1982). *Removing the roadblocks: Group psychotherapy with substance abusers and their family members.* New York: Guilford Press.

van Wormer, K. (1995). *Alcoholism treatment: A social work perspective.* Belmont, CA: Wadsworth.

Vietnamese addiction treatment derailed. (1997, May, 12). Available from www.jointogether.org

Volpicelli, J., & Szalavitz, M. (2000). *Recovery options: The complete guide.* New York: Wiley.

Waismann, A. (2000, September). Hope beyond heroin. *USA Today* (magazine), 32–33.

Wallen, J. (1993). *Addiction in human development: Developmental perspectives on addiction and recovery.* New York: Haworth.

Yalom, I. (1974). Group therapy and alcoholism. In F. Seixas, R. Cadoret, & S. Eggleston (Eds.), *The person with alcoholism* (pp. 85–103). New York: New York Academy of Sciences.

Zickler, P. (2000). NIDA-funded researchers identify compound that inhibits nicotine metabolism, decreases urge to smoke. *NIDA Notes 15*(5), 1–3.

THE PSYCHOLOGY
OF ADDICTION

The three chapters that make up this part of the book take us into the heart of therapy itself, therapy that gets at the thinking side of addiction and concomitantly at the feelings that emerge during the working stage of substance abuse treatment.

Chapter 6, Addiction Across the Life Span, was placed in the psychological section because it draws on the developmental stages of life and relates the role of drugs to these life stages. For this discussion we draw on the work of ego psychologist Erik Erikson and family development theorist Jacqueline Wallen.

Chapter 7, Eating Disorders and Gambling, Shopping, and Other Addictions, is at the intersection of biology and psychology; biological aspects of the various disorders are discussed—for example, in the etiology of anorexia—while a cognitive focus is adapted from psychology as the intervention of choice.

Mental disorders, the subject of chapter 8, also links biology with psychology. We have included mental disorders in this book on addictions because of the frequent overlap between these dual disorders. Harm reduction therapists and other substance abuse counselors need to be alert to psychological problems, especially those of a serious nature, that can interfere with treatment and recovery. In the past, clients who had a continuation of substance misuse and mental health problems were often treated for one diagnosis to the neglect of the other. Alternatively, persons with dual and multiple diagnoses were shuttled back and forth between systems of care. Today, mental health agencies are apt to have substance abuse specialists on the staff, while chemical dependency treatment centers are anxiously recruiting counselors with expertise in mental illness. There is no easy way to assess the relative impact of drug misuse on mental conditions. Another major difficulty is the drug interaction between psychotropic medication and the so-called recreational drugs. Chapter 8 delves into this complex area of so-called dual-diagnosis treatment; the central argument of this chapter is the call for integrated treatment of persons suffering from several disorders simultaneously instead of shuffling clients back and forth between specialists for mental and addiction problems.

All the world's a stage,
And all the men and women merely players:
They have their exits and their entrances;
And one man in his time plays many parts,
His acts being seven ages.
—WILLIAM SHAKESPEARE, *AS YOU LIKE IT,* I (139)

ADDICTION ACROSS THE LIFE SPAN

CHAPTER 6

INTRODUCTION

Since most of this textbook is concerned with middle adulthood, because most adults in treatment are in this age category, this chapter has as its focus people at either end of the life span—teens and young adults at one end and the elderly at the other. Because society and the media are much more concerned with the habits and destructive behavior of the young than of the old, the literature is extremely lopsided on this subject. Policies to curb substance misuse, similarly, focus almost entirely on social control of the young. Since the beginning of time, the older generation has been preoccupied with ways to control the sexual and other pleasure-driven appetites of the young.

THE STAGES OF GROWTH AND DEVELOPMENT

The behavioral problems associated with alcohol and other drugs emerge, in most people, during late adolescence and early adulthood (Rose, 1998). Identifying and understanding the course of those problems, accordingly, requires a developmental perspective. Many of the risk factors, as Rose indicates, can already be spotted in early childhood by children's parents, teachers, and counselors, even as early as preschool.

Erik Erikson (1963) proposed a theory of psychosocial development consisting of eight stages. His model, like other models of growth and development across the life span, focused on how an individual's personality interacts with biological and social systems to affect behavior. From birth to old age, in this conceptualization, life consists of a chronological series of age-related developmental stages and tasks that need to be completed. For the practitioner, knowledge of psychological milestones normally negotiated, such as during adolescence and young adulthood, is important for the overall assessment of behavior and functioning (Zastrow & Kirst-Ashman, 2001).

In Erikson's terminology, at each critical juncture of life an individual must resolve a crisis relevant to that developmental stage before moving to the next one. Often, as Jacqueline Wallen (1993), the author of *Addiction in Human Development*, contends, behaviors that seem "symptomatic" are in fact coping strategies that enable the individual to survive hardships in childhood.

Three stages that concern us in this chapter are Stage 5: Identity vs. role diffusion (12–17 years), Stage 6: Intimacy vs. isolation (young adulthood), and Stage 8: Ego integrity vs. despair (older adulthood). As substance abuse counselors are aware, when life crises are resolved through consistent use of chemicals, the resolution of crises is put on hold and the level of maturity does not match the chronological age. In conjunction with the damage done to the drug-exposed brain, the individual addict/alcoholic experiences regression rather than progression.

A formal intervention, according to Wallen, is a technique for persuading an alcoholic or addict to accept treatment. In this process, family members and friends express their concern and caring for an individual in need of help. Following developmental theory, as Wallen indicates, interventions with older persons must proceed differently than interventions with youths. In particular, they must be conducted much more slowly. Awareness of the special needs of older adults and of the difficulty for them of making changes is important for the therapist. Sensitivity to age-stage differences in recovery will also enhance the treatment effort.

The transition between childhood and adulthood is associated with a variety of challenges as youths struggle to acquire the behavioral skills necessary for later, independent living (Spear, 2000). Certain features of the adolescent brain may in fact predispose a youngster to behave in ways that place him or her at particular risk for trying alcohol or other drugs. Many teenagers engage in foolish, high-risk behavior that seems incongruous with their values or level of intelligence. Now new findings from pediatric neuroscience offer a viable explanation: The prefrontal cortex of the brain does not reach full maturity until after age 20 ("Teenagers' Brains," 2000). This part of the brain is linked to judgment, novelty seeking, and self-awareness. Most teens probably lack the skills to resist peer pressure for this reason. Evidence of brain immaturity during the teen years comes from MRI scans of the adolescent brain. As demonstrated in nonhuman primate research, changes in brain cell chemicals that make one more susceptible to emotional responses occur during the adolescent period (Spear, 2000). When hormone changes, peer pressure, and the need for autonomy are added to the equation, the end result can be quite volatile.

TEENAGE DRINKING AND USING

Identity vs. Role Diffusion

During adolescence the childhood imitation of adult roles ("playing house," for example) is replaced by experimentation and struggle for a meaningful identity. The risk during this period, every parent's nightmare, is that the adolescent will experiment with drugs and drunkenness and hang around with antisocial peers. The individual who is able to resolve the demands of this period will have a sense of who he or she is and toward which adult roles to aspire (Wallen, 1993).

Identity comes as we internalize others' responses to our person and come to see ourselves as others see us. During the turbulence of adolescence, when the growing child pursues his or her identity independent of parents, peer group influence is at its strongest. According to a national survey by the Substance Abuse and Mental Health Services Administration (SAMHSA) (2001), peer drug use and peer attitude are two of the strongest predictors of marijuana use. The odds of youths aged 12 to 17 using marijuana were found to be 39 times higher for those whose close friends used marijuana than for those who did not. At the same time, when the peer group held strong antidrug attitudes, drug use by the youths was uncommon. Parental attitudes were also influential, but less so than peer group attitudes. Use of tobacco and alcohol were other risk factors for marijuana use.

Extent of Drug Use

Providing an international perspective on alcohol and other drug use, the World Health Organization conducted classroom surveys of teenagers in the United States and Europe, from the United Kingdom to the Ukraine (Associated Press, 2001). The study found that 41% of U.S. teens questioned said they had tried marijuana, 16% had used amphetamines, and 10% had used LSD, compared with 16% of the European youth who had used marijuana and 6% who had tried another illicit drug. A separate study of drug use, conducted by the European Union (EU), indicates that British teenagers are the heaviest users in Europe. Use of cannibis, glue sniffing, and Ecstasy and amphetamine use are higher in Britain than anywhere else in the EU, according to the report ("Forty Percent of Teenagers," 2000). With regard to alcohol and tobacco, the situation was reversed. Whereas 26% of U.S. youths had smoked in the month of the study, 37% of Europe's youth had done so. Sixteen percent of American teens had used alcohol at least 40 times, compared to 24% of European youth.

In American surveys, alcohol is the drug of choice, as always, for American teens aged 12 to 17. In fact, teen illicit drug use, with 9% of youths reporting such use in the month of the survey, is at its lowest level in six years, but the rate for young adults (18 to 24 years old) continues to climb. More than 18% of that age group reports using these kinds of drugs. Data are from the Annual National Household Survey (2000) conducted by the U.S. Department of Health and Human Services. In a separate survey of teens in grades 7–12, the Partnership for a Drug-Free America found that teens are increasingly using more dangerous drugs, such as Ecstasy (tried by 10%), and inhalants (tried by 13%) (Leinwand, 2000).

Melissa Hoekstra, a school counselor (in private correspondence with van Wormer on April 5, 2000), describes her experience as a 16-year-old exchange student in Argentina:

> It was a wonderful experience, and one thing I learned was the United States is going about handling the alcohol situation the wrong way.
>
> In Argentina there was no drinking age. We did not have milk for supper; we had wine or beer. I believe that the norm in Argentina is to drink to be social, not to get drunk. I believe that there should be no drinking age law and that, instead, we should emphasize teaching moderation.

Cigarette use, according to the Annual National Household Survey, was 15.9% in the 12- to 17-year age group. Nineteen percent of these youth reported that they drank at least once in the past month, with 52% drinking from time to time. Regarding binge drinking (or the drinking of five or more drinks on one occasion), 10.9% of youths engaged in this activity in the past month. Five of the ten states in the top tier for binge alcohol use were in the Midwest and four were in the West.

The rates of current illicit drug use for major racial/ethnic groups were 6.6% for whites, 6.8% for Hispanics, and 7.7% for African Americans. The rate was highest among the American Indian/Alaska Native population (10.6%) and among persons reporting multiple race (11.2%). Asian Americans had the lowest rate, 3.2%. In school surveys, African Americans reported the lowest rates of drinking and getting drunk, and Hispanic rates were lower than those of whites in the higher grades. This discrepency between the household and school surveys reflects the fact that African and Latino Americans have significantly higher dropout rates than whites (O'Malley, Johnston, & Bachman, 1998). Although more males than females reported drinking, the difference was only by a small margin. The gender difference was greater for those who had been drunk in the past month.

The National Council on Alcoholism and Drug Dependence (2000) indicates that 80% of U.S. high school seniors have used alcohol, 62% have smoked, 49% have used marijuana, and 9% have used cocaine. Thirty-two percent of twelfth graders have been drunk during the last month. The total cost of alcohol use by youth—including traffic crashes, violent crime, burns, drowning, suicide attempts, fetal alcohol syndrome, and treatment—is more than $58 billion per year. (Similarly, for Canada, 43% of 15-year-olds said that they had been "really drunk" at least twice in their lives, according to a Health Canada survey ["Canadian Teens," 1999]). Children and adolescents who begin drinking before age 15 are four times more likely to develop alcoholism than those who begin at age 21. Similarly, those who begin smoking before age 13 are more likely than later smokers and nonsmokers to have problems with alcohol and other drugs. People who developed their addiction problems at an early age are more likely than others to have psychiatric problems as well (C. Martin & Winters, 1998).

Other intriguing facts revealed by the National Council on Alcoholism and Drug Development:

- 40% of college students have binged on alcohol during the past two weeks.
- 31.9% of youth under 18 in juvenile institutions were under the influence of alcohol at the time of the arrest.
- 30% of children in grades four through six report that they have received a lot of pressure from their classmates to drink beer; 31% to try marijuana, and 34% to try cigarettes.
- A survey of high school students found that 18% of females and 39% of males say it is acceptable for a boy to force sex if the girl is stoned or drunk.

Data from reports such as these reveal a strong relationship between emotional state, risks to health and life, and alcohol use. Furthermore, teens who misuse alcohol at a young age are at high risk for further drinking problems, other substance abuse, depression, and personality disorders as they get older ("Teens Who Abuse Alcohol," 2001).

What are the implications of using alcohol and cigarettes together? This question was probed by researchers at Buffalo's Research Institute on Addictions ("Alcohol, Cigarette Use," 2001). Analysis revealed a synergistic effect in a combination of drinking and smoking that increased one's likelihood for illicit drug use. In each survey examined in the study, about one-third of regular teen drinkers smoked, and almost all current smokers also drank alcohol.

While media attention focuses on drugs such as Ecstacy, and the government spends billions on the controversial war on drugs, little attention is directed toward misuse of the teen drug of choice—alcohol. During the 1980s, the drinking age was raised to 21. Fewer kids drank after that, but those who do drink today consume huge amounts at one time (Rivera, 2000). "The booze business is big business," according to a TV new special on *Rivera Live*. Based on alcohol consumption statistics, youths under 21 consume $10 billion worth of alcohol; advertisers beam the message that it's cool to drink. Anheuser Busch, the largest beer company in America, spends $30 million a year on advertising. Because this and other beer and liquor companies are the most aggressive and well-funded lobbies in Washington, D.C., the government's political focus has been on the kind of drugs that can't be legally marketed. According to commentators on *Rivera Live*, money was put into antidrug ads— a $1 billion White House advertising compaign to educate children about drugs. Proposals to include alcohol in these ads, with announcements such as "2.6 million teenagers don't know a person can die from an alcohol overdose," limits on primetime alcohol ads, and higher taxes on alcohol, all died in Congress. Earlier, according to Anna Quindlen (2001), when members of Congress tried to pass legislation that would make alcohol part of the purview of the nation's drug czar, the measure failed.

Another problem that has been pushed to the background because of governmental (in this case, the states') vested interest is gambling. Legalized gambling is now a source of revenue that is deeply embedded in state politics. Children are exposed to gambling on the Internet, while many (as revealed in surveys) have played video poker, slot machines, and the lottery (Schouten, 2000). More alarming to researchers is new evidence showing that children get addicted to gambling at a much higher rate than adults; perhaps this is related to the immaturity of the brain at the younger age. Studies show that 4 to 8% of teens in the United States and Canada show signs of serious gambling problems. Kids who gamble often steal money from family members, shoplift, and consider suicide. This is the first generation of children to be saturated with gambling possibilities (Schouten, 2000).

Big money is, of course, involved in cigarette sales. Given the fact that 80% of adult smokers in the United States began lighting up before age 18, tobacco companies have a vested interest in maintaining the smoking rate of youth (Lavelle, 2000). In the wake of the unprecedented tobacco industry settlement with the states, tobacco companies are now targeting young adults, who can legally smoke. But, as Lavelle argues, this ploy merely enhances the appeal of cigarettes by introducing flavored varieties and financing prevention programs while simply telling kids they're too young to smoke, which is unlikely to curb their desire to smoke. Meanwhile, smoking figures prominently in Hollywood productions.

A clever, roundabout way to get youths to quit smoking is to involve them in strenuous exercise programs. According to an article in the *Washington Post* health section (Krucoff, 1999), a study of male runners showed that 70% of those who smoked quit subsequently. Almost half of the women in an exercise group quit smoking as well.

Psychological Risk Factors

Rose (1998) presents an overview of longitudinal studies conducted in several countries to ascertain whether behavioral assessments made by teachers and classmates could distinguish which children were likely to abuse alcohol by middle or late adolescence. Findings from Sweden were that evaluations done at ages 10 and 27 showed that high novelty seeking and low harm avoidance (daredevil behavior) predicted early-onset alcoholism. Similar results were obtained in Canadian and Danish research studies. Data from Finland differentiated the pathway to alcoholism in males and females. Aggression at age 8 predicted alcoholism 18 to 20 years later in males. For females, children who cried easily when teased or who were anxious and shy were most apt to develop problems later. For both sexes poor school success was a predictor of later drinking problems.

In his assessment of twin studies in Europe and North America, Rose (2000) concluded that although hereditary factors are important, the age of initiation, which is environmentally determined, is equally influential in the development of alcoholism. Such influences are family drinking patterns, the availability of alcohol, and peer group habits. Although further research is needed, it seems reasonable to assume, as Rose suggests, that children at elevated risk for alcoholism may decrease that risk by remaining abstinent throughout adolescence.

Parents are primary role models for their children; their drinking and drug-using behavior are positively associated with adolescent patterns of substance use ("Youth Drinking," 1997). A survey of nearly 600 teens in drug treatment in New York, Texas, Florida, and California indicated that 20% had shared illicit drugs with their parents—usually marijuana (Leinwand, 2000). On the positive side, parental support and communication about proper and improper drinking behaviors are correlated with fewer problems among adolescents.

The teen–father relationship has been found, in a survey of 2,000 youths and 1,000 parents undertaken by the Center on Addiction and Substance Abuse (Associated Press, 1999), to be crucial in affecting youth substance abuse. Teenagers who don't get along with their fathers are more likely to smoke, drink, and use other drugs than those raised by single mothers. Moreover, teens who reported their fathers have more than two drinks a day have a high risk of substance abuse themselves.

Child abuse and other traumas are serious risk factors for later-adolescence and adulthood drinking. According to a groundbreaking report from the Center on Addiction and Substance Abuse (CASA) based on a survey of 915 child welfare professionals across the United States, alcohol and other drug abuse was found to be a factor in seven out of ten cases of child abuse or neglect (Reid, Macchetto, & Foster, 1999). Tragically, according to this report, most parents who need treatment don't receive it, and much of the treatment is not appropriate for these, predominately female, parents.

Adolescents in treatment for alcohol problems report higher rates of physical abuse, violent victimization, witnessing violence, and other traumas, compared with controls ("Youth Drinking," 1997). In a Canadian study based on a population health survey of 10,000 respondents, it was found that children who are spanked and slapped are twice as likely to develop alcohol and other drug abuse problems as children who were never so treated ("Spanking," 1999).

Regarding trauma among adults in treatment, the literature consistently reports a strong link between childhood abuse and the later development of alcoholism (Clark, Lesnick, & Hegedus, 1997). Girls who are sexually abused are three times more likely to develop drinking problems later than are girls not so abused, according to a national study conducted by Wilsnack (reported by Elias, 1998). The interpersonal interviews in the study revealed that those molested as children have more than double the depression rate of other women. Abuse is the single strongest predictor of alcohol dependency in girls, even stronger than a family history of alcoholism, as the conductor of this research noted. A study of 597 female adolescents in inpatient substance abuse treatment found that 35% reported a history of sexual victimization (Edwall, Hoffmann, & Harrison, 1989). In a sample of 938 adolescents in residential therapeutic communities, Hawke, Jainchill, and DeLeon (2000) found prevalence rates of sexual abuse were 64% for girls and 24% of boys. The sexual abuse was correlated with earlier onset of alcohol and illicit drug use. Interestingly, boys who were sexually abused were more likely to be diagnosed with conduct disorder, dysthymia (mild depression), and ADHD, while girls were likely to be diagnosed with posttraumatic stress disorder and major depression.

Clark et al. (1997) conducted a comparative study of 183 adolescents with alcohol abuse and dependence diagnoses and a control group of 73 adolescents recruited from the community. Trauma history was assessed in interviews. As predicted, adolescents with drinking problems were six times more likely to have a physical abuse history and 18 times more likely to have a sexual abuse history than were the controls. Sexual abuse was more common in females and violent victimization in males. We cannot conclude the relationship is necessarily causal, because other variables, such as parental substance use, may figure in. Yet in order to identify youths at risk for substance abuse, we need to help them deal with life events that may be of a traumatic nature.

How do we explain the early sexual abuse/later alcoholism link? The explanation given by Hawke et al. (2000)—the self-medication hypothesis—is the one provided throughout the literature: The drug use functions to ameliorate feelings of depression and poor self-esteem that accompany childhood abuse. Based on her work with alcoholic women in the United States and Norway, van Wormer (1995) provided a somewhat more complicated explanation of the sexual trauma/alcoholism link:

> What is the meaning of all this? If childhood sexual abuse can be considered a factor in the later development of alcoholism, there must be some intervening variable resulting from the abuse and leading to the drinking later in life. My hunch is that the combination of a general sense of shame and self-disgust prevails but that specific events (and feelings associated with them) may be repressed to make survival possible. The child survives, but the adult may appear emotionally stunted; there is little resilience for ordinary life crisis. There is no "talking things out" or "laughing it off." The discovery of alcohol, often in the teenager years, may seem to offer relief.
>
> A client I once had (I'll call her Mary) seemed as cold as ice. Her mother, also in treatment as a result of a court-ordered referral, told me that Mary had once been a sweet and affectionate little girl. But at age 11, "when her father started messing with her," she began to change. When Mary initially told about her father's activities, her mother did not believe her. For years Mary was thought to be a liar. Then one day the mother discovered the truth. By then, the daughter, overwhelmed by the original feelings, plus the anger at her mother and, perhaps, at her own helplessness, had built up her own wall of defenses. Now a mother herself, Mary was verbally abusive and suspicious. Although Mary learned to control her drinking as a practical matter (her mother did not), she never learned to trust or to love. Unable to love herself, she could not reach out to others. Her extremely low self-esteem is characteristic of both alcoholic women and incest survivors; perhaps this connection occurs because of the overlap between these two categories. (pp. 169–170)

This theory linking early trauma and a later inability to cope with psychological stress is entirely consistent with recent neurological evidence of brain chemistry changes that result from early trauma. Because of these changes, the former victim's stress response is weakened; this fact sets the stage for future psychological problems, especially under conditions of repeated stress (Sternberg, 2000).

The mechanisms responsible for the relationship between childhood trauma and adolescent alcohol use disorders are relatively unexplored, according to the authors. Probable explanations are the use of alcohol for emotional pain relief, dulling bad feelings about the self, and anxiety related to the abuse through heavy alcohol consumption. We know from animal studies that stress and alcohol consumption levels are highly correlated (Spear, 2000). Presumably, the physiological response to stress—increased heart and pulse rates, for example—is being subdued through self-medication with alcohol.

As Albert Ellis said long ago, it is not the event itself but our perception of the event that is important (1965). There is evidence, in fact, that sensitivity (defined as an exaggerated response to stimuli, which is perceived as stress) is an inborn trait (Aron, 1996) and that it is correlated with alcoholism (see chapter 4). In any case, researchers have postulated that the presumed increase in anxiety and stress during adolescence contributes to the frequent initiation into drug use observed at this time. Experiments have shown that juvenile mice exhibit a greater overall hormonal response to stress than both younger and older animals (Spear, 2000). Compared to mature rodents, those of adolescent age exhibit a heightened response to alcohol and to other drugs as well. Spear (2000) cites research findings that the adolescent's perception of the events as being stressful was a more important predictor of alcoholism than the absolute number of such events. The need for further research into the effects of stress on the development of alcohol problems in humans is clearly indicated.

The link between trauma and stress is further confirmed in a remarkable study on child abuse presented in the *Journal of the American Medical Association*, as reported by Sternberg (2000). It is touted as the first human study to find persistent changes in stress reactivity in adult survivors of early trauma. A comparative study of 49 healthy women revealed detectable biochemical abnormalities in those who had been severely abused in childhood. In a laboratory situation women survivors were four times more likely than other women to develop excessive stress responses to mild stimuli. Those who were abused and now have anxiety disorder or depression are six times more likely than other women to suffer an abnormal stress response.

Psychiatric Disorders

Boys with attention deficit hyperactivity disorder (ADHD) have been found to have significantly higher rates of substance misuse than boys without ADHD ("Youth Drinking," 1997). Studies of adult cocaine abusers have found that many of them had had undiagnosed ADHD as children (Stocker, 2000). NIDA-supported researchers have been trying to explain the connection between ADHD and later substance abuse. In a Massachusetts study, 56 boys with ADHD who were medically treated with stimulants, 19 untreated boys with ADHD, and 137 boys without ADHD were studied over four years. Findings as reported by Stocker were that only 25% of children treated for ADHD,

18% of boys without ADHD, and 75% of the unmedicated ADHD boys had started to show drug and alcohol problems. This research has important implications for treatment of children with this attention deficit disorder.

Other psychiatric disorders, such as anxiety and depression, are highly correlated with substance misuse among youths. Depression tends to be higher in girls than in boys ("Alcohol Use Among Girls," 1999). Suicidal behavior is highly correlated with alcohol misuse as well ("Youth Drinking," 1997).

Special Risks for Girls

More girls are being arrested and jailed for drug abuse, assault, and loitering than ever before, according to a study by the American Bar Association ("Girls Being Arrested," 2001). One reason for the increase in arrests is an expansion of the definition of domestic violence to include assaults by girls of their parents. A lack of services aimed at helping troubled girls is another reason cited in the report for the fact that girls are the fastest-growing segment of the juvenile justice population.

Girls who have been sexually assaulted (as indicated earlier), physically abused, or neglected are twice as likely to be arrested as juveniles and twice as likely to be arrested for violent crimes as girls who were not similarly victimized (Widom, 2000). Victimization may lead girls into delinquency indirectly through their alcohol and other drug involvement or through causing them to run away from home. As runaways, girls may engage in panhandling, petty theft, prostitution, and drug use. Early intervention in the lives of victimized children is crucial to protect them from a path of self-destructiveness.

Here are some of the facts revealed in a special report from the National Clearinghouse for Alcohol and Drug Information ("Alcohol Use Among Girls," 1999):

- Adolescent girls who are heavy drinkers (drunk five or more drinks in a row on at least five different days in the past month) are more likely than boys to say that they drink to escape problems or because of frustration or anger.
- Friends have a big influence on teenagers overall, but girls are particularly susceptible to peer pressure when it comes to drinking. Adolescent girls are more likely than boys to drink to fit in with their friends, while boys drink largely for other reasons and then join a group that also drinks.
- Girls often are introduced to alcohol by their boyfriends, who may be older and more likely to drink.
- Early-onset drinking is a major risk factor for developing alcohol abuse or dependence.
- Teenage girls who are heavy drinkers are five times more likely to engage in sexual intercourse and a third less likely to use condoms, which can result in pregnancy and in the contraction of sexually transmitted diseases, including HIV/AIDS. Women make up the fastest-growing segment of the population infected with HIV in the United States, and adolescents and young women are at particularly high risk.

- Alcohol is involved in up to two-thirds of all sexual assaults and date rapes among adolescents and college students.
- Among 8th grade girls who drink heavily, 37% report attempting suicide—compared to 11% who do not drink.
- Daughters of alcoholics are at increased risk for alcoholism. They are also more likely to marry men who are alcoholics. (pp. 1, 2)

Media-generated weight obsession is a major problem among girls of European American ethnicity. Not only does this obsessiveness lead to major problems with eating, such as anorexia and bulimia (as discussed in chapter 7), but many whites are resorting to another high-risk behavior—cigarette smoking—for the purpose of weight control. Teenage girls who diet frequently also seem more likely to smoke. In one study, over a third of the smoking initiation by girls was attributable to dieting ("Smoking, Dieting Linked," 2001). The statistics on cigarette smoking reveal that females smoke ("National Estimates," 1999). For black females, however, only 6.9% report past-month use of cigarettes.

So striking are the racial differences in female smoking that several years ago the Centers for Disease Control and Prevention commissioned a study that involved talking with 1,000 adolescents in 150 focus groups ("Black Teens," 1996). Findings were that some white women equated smoking with empowerment and sexual equality; white girls appeared to buy into advertising images of smokers as attractive and competent.

Special Risks for Boys

The biggest threat to life and health for adolescent boys is alcohol-related accidents. Surveys show that males 12 to 20 years old are more likely than their female peers to report binge drinking (22.3% compared to 16%) ("National Estimates," 1999). Such heavy drinking in males is highly associated with car crashes, sexual assaults, and other violence (Dizon, 2000).

The male counterpart to anorexia in females is muscle dysmorphia, a newly identified psychiatric disorder. According to medical investigations of 54 male bodybuilders in the United States and England, the typical sufferer is a man so preoccupied with his body that he might spend all day in the gym or weigh himself throughout the day (E. Smith, 1997). Although studies are filling the psychiatric literature, the *DSM-IV-TR* (APA), 2000) discusses body dysmorphic disorder only briefly and in a gender-neutral manner. (This is in sharp contrast to their extensive treatment of anorexia.)

The extent to which obsessive bodybuilding is a major problem for young males is revealed in the popularity of anabolic steroids, manmade substances related to male sex hormones. "Anabolic" refers to muscle building. These drugs are available only by prescription to treat conditions related to testosterone deficiencies. According to a nationwide survey, 2.7% of all male high school seniors reported using steroids or having used them at one time (U.S. Department of Health and Human Services, 2000). Pressure from coaches, parents, and peers to gain muscle weight and strength are attributed as factors in enticing athletes and weightlifters to take this drug. Also revealed in the survey were the following facts:

- More than two-thirds of the heavy users began steroid use before age 16.
- About 44% said they shot or ingested several types of steroids at the same time.
- And 38% used injectable steroid packages—putting themselves at risk for contracting a disease such as AIDS.

Here are the words of a former steroid user (from a personal interview with van Wormer of February 20, 2001):

> Any bodybuilder would be on steroids. Ventura (governor of Minnesota) in his wrestling days took that. . . . The drugs are transported to this university from a big guy who brings them in from Mexico. . . . I was lifting weights and hit a plateau. I'm goal oriented. Some guys said, "You should get on the juice. One time won't hurt; the results are great. I take an injectable steroid from Mexico."
>
> I'm 6 feet tall, had a 48-inch coat size. Taking eight shots once a week, after two months I took a 56-inch coat size. I had to buy all new clothes. I never was comfortable. I could feel my kidneys hurt; my blood pressure rose; I couldn't breathe. A lot of my friends stacked—took a lot all in a row. I was really in a bad mood for two months straight. The drug is not physically addictive but psychologically addictive. Here we were sticking needles in each others' butts. You have to switch cheeks and it hurts. All the things I thought wouldn't happen to me did happen: balding (see, my hair never grew back), weight gain, water retention, sleeping problems. I blew a disc in my back from the weight. My chin got big. Before I was a happy-go-lucky guy. But steroids change you; you get aggressive and people back off. On juice you start to like that. I remember a guy who hit a kid who hit on his girlfriend. He left him lying unconscious in the snow.

Health hazards of misusing anabolic steroids include risk for heart attacks and strokes, liver problems if taken orally, and undesirable body changes, such as breast development and shrinking testicles, stunted growth, and acne (U.S. Department of Health and Human Services, 2000). During withdrawal, antidepressants may be required to alleviate depression. That steroids may be physically addictive is indicated by experiments that show for the first time that rats will self-administer drinks laced with testosterone ("Rats Get Hooked," 1999). Like other addictive drugs, testosterone and its synthetic counterparts may activate pleasure pathways in the brain, according to the scientists who conducted this study.

Binge-Drinking in Young Adults

Talk of "underage" drinking laws swept across the United States after President Bush's college-student daughters, "the Bush daughters," as they are now known, received citations. One was cited for using a false identification card, the other for possession of alcohol (Kenworthy, 2001). Because of laws restricting public drinking in the United States to persons over age 21, a debate of sorts about the laws has ensued. In any case, they are not obeyed. "Party till you puke" is a sign occasionally posted in University of Northern Iowa dorms to announce a pending raucous event. On this Midwestern campus, one's 21st birthday is celebrated by being taken by friends from bar to bar for unlimited free drinks. This initiation into adulthood has led to hospital trips for some individuals with low tolerance.

"Binge Drinking and Teetotaling Spread at U.S. Colleges" is the title of an article that reveals the growing divide between youth who drink to the point of intoxication and those who abstain from all alcoholic beverages (Clayton, 2000). The Harvard School of Public Health conducted a widely cited survey of 14,000 students nationwide. In 1999, one in five students said they abstained entirely, a large increase from earlier years. At the same time, the percentage of students who reported binge drinking grew from 19.8% to 22.7% (Clayton). Also revealed in the study: In fraternity and sorority houses, 80% are binge drinkers. Among male athletes, 61% reported binge drinking in the previous two weeks. Awareness of student alcohol-related deaths, vandalism, and sexual assault have contributed to a certain revulsion against drinking excesses that have been widely publicized. Many fraternities are working hard to clean up their reputation for uninhibited revelry.

The conservative British magazine *The Economist* describes the American fraternity scene as follows:

> Although it is illegal in America to serve alcohol to people under 21 (an absurdly high age limit by European standards), teenagers get booze with ease in fraternity houses. And this is not a matter of a few cocktails before dinner. American students—all the more defiant, perhaps, for being deprived of it for so long—prefer determined binge drinking on Friday and Saturday nights. A 1995 Harvard study suggested that half of American students are binge drinkers. In an attempt to improve matters, some fraternities have followed the sororities in banning alcohol. ("Raise a Fond Last Glass," 1997, p. 37)

In the 1980s, in an overzealous attempt to curtail drunken driving by youth, the U.S. government imposed (through funding directives) a nationwide minimum drinking age of 21. Thus we had Prohibition on the basis of age. Harsh total abstinence campaigns were conducted on college campuses, with some unintended negative consequences. Michael Clay Smith, a professor of criminal justice, argues for a repeal of such laws (M. Smith & Smith, 1999). Legal adulthood occurs at age 18 in the United States—this is the first point. Other arguments are: The drinking age of 21 has driven students to partying underground, and away from faculty supervision; students are getting police records for sharing alcohol with underage friends; it has soured relations between students and police. Finally, the policy of Prohibition is leading to binge drinking and probably other drug use, just as it did in the 1920s.

In recognition of these facts and in light of high-profile cases in the media of campus rioting and students dying of overdoses, a number of U.S. colleges are changing their approach to on-campus drinking ("Beer Companies," 2000).

Replacing messages of "Don't drink" are messages of moderation. In fact, Anheuser-Busch, a leading beer brewing company has committed hundreds of thousands of dollars to six colleges for social norms campaigns. An example of such a message—displayed on T-shirts and posters—is: "'A' students average no more than three drinks when they party, while 'C' students average five."

Another new strategy is to notify parents when their underage children get into trouble because of their drinking. A more controversial measure, one affecting recovering drug addicts, is Congress's decision to deny financial aid to college students who have been convicted of drug offenses. Students from underprivileged and minority backgrounds are expected to be hit especially hard by this law ("Attack on Campus Drug Use," 2000).

Colleges have been slower to restrict enticing beer ads from campus newspapers and "happy hour" traditions at bars (two drinks for the price of one). Restrictions of this sort would be consistent with harm reduction. A first-time study released by the White House Office of National Drug Control Policy portrays the degree of alcohol, tobacco, and illicit drug use in popular movies and music (Weber, 1999). Findings reveal that 98% of movies and 27% of the songs studied depicted substance use. The entertainment media clearly have an enormous input on young people, who are inundated with these messages favorable to substance use.

Brief Alcohol Screening and Intervention for College Students: A Harm Reduction Approach, by Dimeff, Baer, Kivlahan, and Marlatt (1999), is an instructive manual designed to assist colleges in helping students reduce their alcohol consumption and decrease the behavioral and health risks associated with heavy drinking. Useful reproducible handouts and assessment forms are included in this book. At the University of Washington's Addictive Behaviors Research Center, from the same research group that produced the book, brief interventions were provided for college students identified as high-risk drinkers from high school. In comparison with a control group of other high-risk drinkers, students who received the services reduced their drinking four times as much as those who did not ("Intervention Helps," 1999).

Other countries, such as New Zealand and England, have looked toward harm reduction strategies. The New Zealand parliament voted to lower the drinking age from 20 to 18 because the old law was not enforceable ("New Zealand," 1999). A school in England—Warminster School—acquired a license to open a bar on campus to control the drinking of young people. Open only on Friday and Saturday nights, the bar caters to students age 17 and over. A staff member is always present, and the amount of alcohol supplied is restricted (Prestage, 1996).

Long-term studies concerning alcohol and other drug use offer encouraging news. Most individuals mature out of the kind of wild drinking days of early adulthood. Bachman's (1997) analysis of data gathered annually on more than 33,000 young adults reveals how they change over time. Drinking is heaviest among singles and the divorced. College students who live in dorms or share apartments have the highest binge rates. Yet they typically have settled down to moderate drinking a few years later. The one exception to the trend toward moderation, as Bachman points out, concerns cigarettes. The majority of men and women who smoked a half a pack or more daily in high school are still smoking by age 32. Because of the well-recognized addictiveness of nicotine, prevention efforts are far more effective than treatment long after the addiction has set in.

PREVENTION OF SUBSTANCE MISUSE IN TEENS

Harm reduction principles apply at various levels, ranging from community-based educational programs to individual guidance. Some methods of reducing harm are indirect—for example, reducing the size of schools and classes to create a more personal learning environment. Unlike law enforcement strategies that focus on reducing the supply side of drugs, harm reduction strategies are geared to reducing the demand for drugs in the first place. This form of prevention, sometimes termed *primary* prevention, includes interventions to reduce primary risk factors, such as child abuse, as well as early-prevention education and treatment programs. The aims of all these efforts are to help children get through adolescence relatively unscathed and to prevent experimentation with substances whose use carries the potential for personal destructiveness down the road. Many of the developmental changes that are necessary prerequisites for healthy adulthood increase an adolescent's risk of smoking, drinking heavily, or using drugs (Botvin & Botvin, 1997). Due to adolescents' unique developmental issues, differences in priorities, and susceptibility to peer influence, they must be approached differently than adults.

The public health approach to preventing harm is multidimensional and ideally operates across systems. Knowledge of the developmental progression of substance use is important for the focus and timing of preventive interventions (Botvin & Botvin, 1997). Knowledge of the typical pathways that lead to the reckless use of substances is also instrumental in alleviating or treating underlying psychological problems that can increase the risks for harmful experimentation. Prevention of early-childhood abuse and trauma is key to prevention of the development of the kind of substance misuse that relates to affect—use of chemicals to counteract low feelings resulting from early-childhood trauma. Social policy initiatives must include a coordination of services to protect children from the earliest age onward. Parenting courses, periodic public health nurse visits to all homes where there are babies, a well-funded child welfare system to ensure the safety of children as the first priority—these are among the initiatives sorely needed. In the United Kingdom, the Labour government has introduced new strategies based on a coordination of efforts across national and local bodies, including education, health, and prevention services to reduce the demand for drugs (Howard, 1998). The message to the British "drug tsar," according to this report, is that treatment is a cornerstone to reducing demand; harm reduction gets the seal of approval.

For our purposes, primary prevention efforts can be divided into seven general strategies:

- Child protection aimed at the cycle of violence and substance misuse
- School-based prevention programs directed toward social influences prompting youths to smoke
- Information dissemination approaches focusing on the immediate consequences of smoking (bad health, breathing problems)
- Mass media campaigns showing the negative side of alcohol, tobacco, and other drug misuse
- Social resistance and personal competence skills approaches (e.g., anxiety management skills, assertiveness training)
- Campaigns to reduce or eliminate TV beer ads, student newspaper local bar and national beer ads
- Advocacy for the hiring of more school counselors and social workers to work with high-risk students (bullies, victims, children who suffer from mental disorders, children of alcoholics/addicts)

An underlying assumption of this prevention model is that an all-out effort should be made to keep youths from ever starting to smoke; this effort should be bolstered by community and media support. Because many families can enjoy moderate drinking while condemning intoxication and because cultural traditions come into play here, our second major assumption is this: Moderate drinking and abstinence should be presented by health education classes as equally acceptable choices. Since practically all youths will at least sample alcohol, a focus on safe and unsafe practices associated with its use is the only practical course to take. Expecting youngsters not to drink until they reach 21 and then suddenly to become responsible drinkers is unrealistic (Boroson, 1993). Information based on ideology rather than fact, furthermore, will be given little credibility by teens. The whole strategy of demonizing alcohol for youth and reserving its pleasures for adults over a certain age merely increases its attractiveness.

In personal correspondence (of March 5, 2000) a behavior disorders teacher from rural Iowa draws a link between the words "prohibit" and "defiance":

> When another person tells me what to do and leaves no room for alternative or choice, I become offended. The same applies to our youth and consumption. Choices provide my students with a sense of integrity and responsibility for their actions. When I present my behaviorally challenged students with alternatives, defiant behavior decreases. Part of the reason we have such a high rate of illegal consumption during adolescence is because no choice is allowed. If we taught our youth to drink moderately and allowed them to think for themselves, defiant behavior would decrease. Currently, the right to consume is celebrated on an individual's 21st birthday. Is this the positive alternative we want to provide our youth for the abstinent use of alcohol: a drunken celebration? Why not teach our youth to drink moderately, if at all? After all, our society seems to welcome moderate consumption in the social arena. In my behavior disorder classroom I am constantly providing choices of socially appropriate behavior. Isn't the moderate consumption

of alcohol socially appropriate? If not, then maybe we as adults are living a double standard! It's my belief that the Prohibition movement has caused us to become negligent in imparting healthy social values. Our youth deserve better!

Given the high rates of pregnancy, sexually transmitted diseases, growing rates of HIV infection, and risk of lethal overdose among teens, especially marginalized teens, harm reduction holds the maximum potential of protection (de Miranda, 1999). Leshner (1999) describes two paths to drug use. The first path involves the group of kids who are seeking novelty or excitement, who are striving to be "cool." These kids are most likely to be responsive to prevention education about the harmful effects of drugs on their bodies. The second path to substance use involves dynamics of another sort. Using drugs to escape emotional pain, youths in this category are bent on self-medication. Their problem is getting through today; messages about long-term damage are apt to have little impact, therefore. Fear-arousing messages, paradoxically, are apt to attract the risk takers among them. Leshner recommends professional help for these youth. Unfortunately, however, only one in five of all adolescents in need of treatment services actually receives treatment (U.S. Department of Health and Human Services, 2001).

One very helpful resource relevant to prevention and available in most communities free of charge is the self-help group for children of alcoholics, Al-Ateen, the children's equivalent of Al-Anon, which addresses the needs of families and friends of alcoholics. Supervised by an adult, often a recovering adult, Al-Ateen is a support group where the children of alcoholics can learn that they are not alone and not at fault. The attention given to expressing one's feelings can do much to stem the intergenerational cycle of addiction.

Research on prevention effectiveness surveyed by Botvin and Botvin (1997) points to social life skills training, either alone or in combination with other approaches, as having the most effective impact on substance use behavior. These approaches, as Botvin and Botvin indicate, utilize well-tested behavioral intervention techniques; they also provide preparation for dealing with strong feelings without resorting to the use of alcohol and other drugs. The coping mechanisms acquired here should be invaluable in later life as well.

The war on drugs is exacting a double toll on children, first in taking their parents away and subjecting them to the tragedy of premature separation. Second, the stigma of having a parent incarcerated weighs heavily upon a growing child. Half of the 1.5 million kids with a parent in jail or prison, in fact, will commit a crime before they turn 18 (Drummond, 2000).

Youths who get into trouble with drugs and who are sent to juvenile facilities have high rate of recidivism (Noble & Reed, 2000). Yet more and more youths are being dealt with harshly in juvenile court for minor crimes and tried as adults for major crimes. The drug court movement—an innovative and carefully orchestrated development—provides mandatory alcohol and drug treatment and a continuum of community services to ensure compliance with its two-year program. Education, vocational experiences, and life skills training are provided. Results from the over 300 programs nationwide indicate that drug courts have been highly effective in saving taxpayers money ("Study Shows," 1998). Addiction treatment costs between $2,000 and $3,000 per person, compared to $25,000 to incarcerate someone. Today there are treatment strategies, moreover, such as those geared to a person's maturity level or, in other words, to his or her readiness to address the substance use problem.

Motivational Enhancement Strategies

Ideally suited for work with troubled and rebellious substance misusers, the harm reduction model meets the youth where the youth is and is disarmingly nonthreatening. There is no moralizing tone here, no forcing teens to sit in a circle and label themselves as alcoholics or addicts. A certain amount of ambivalence is expected, deemed healthy, in fact. In every stage of the stages-of-change model, originally formulated by Prochaska and DiClemente (1992)—precontemplation through maintenance or relapse—resolving ambivalence is a central theme of focus. Helping people make decisions that will benefit their lives is the overriding good of motivational enhancement therapy. See Table 6.1 for typical client statements at each stage of the stages-of-change continuum.

Through a close therapeutic relationship, the counselor can help a person develop a commitment to change. The way motivational theory goes is this: If the therapist can get the client to do something, *anything,* to get better, this client will have a chance at success. This is a basic principle of social psychology. Such tasks that William Miller (1998) pinpoints as predictors of recovery are: going to AA meetings, coming to sessions, completing homework assignments, taking medication (even if a placebo pill). The question, according to Miller, then becomes, How can I help my clients do something to take action on their own behalf? A related principle of social psychology is that in defending a position aloud, as in a debate, we become committed to it. One would predict, according to motivational enhancement theory, that if the therapist elicits defensive statements from the client, the client would become more committed to the status quo and less willing to change. For this reason, explains Miller, confrontational approaches have a poor track record. Research has shown that people are more likely to grow and change in a positive direction on their own than if they get caught up in a battle of wills. In their seven-part professional training videotape series, W. R. Miller and Rollnick (1998) provide guidance in the art and science of motivational enhancement. In this series, the don'ts are as revealing as the do's. According to this therapy team, the don'ts, or traps for therapists to avoid, are:

- A premature focus, such as on one's addictive behavior
- The confrontational/denial round between therapist and client
- The labeling trap—forcing the individual to accept a label such as alcoholic or addict
- The blaming trap, a fallacy that is especially pronounced in couples counseling

TABLE 6.1 | STAGE-SPECIFIC MOTIVATIONAL STATEMENTS

Stage of Change	Adolescent Comments
Precontemplation	My parents can't tell me what to do; I still use and I don't see the harm in it—do you?
Contemplation	I'm on top of the world when I'm high, but then when I come down, I'm really down. It was better before I got started on these things.
Preparation	I'm feeling good about setting a date to quit, but who knows?
Action	Staying clean may be healthy, but it sure makes for a dull life. Maybe I'll check out one of these groups.
Maintenance	It's been a few months; I'm not there yet but I'm hanging out with some new friends.

- The question/answer habit, which is characterized by asking several questions in a row and reliance on closed yes-or-no responses, which exchange paves the way for the expert trap
- The expert trap, whereby the client is put down (the opposite of a collaborative exchange of information)

These precautions relate exceptionally well to work with teens, as does the motivational theorists' handling of client resistance. As he states in the videotape on motivational enhancement, Miller is uncomfortable with the concept of *resistance;* his preference is to think of clients as simply cautious in trusting the therapist. To establish this trust and enable the client to elicit the desired self-motivated or insightful statements, such as "I think I do have a problem," the skilled therapist relies on open and multifaceted questions, reflective listening, and purposeful summarizing of the client's story. Key to this process is the reframing of the client's story in the direction of decision making. A format such as "I sense that you are saying, on the one hand, that smoking means a lot to you and, on the other hand, that you are beginning to have some health concerns about the damage that the smoking is causing you or may cause you in the future" provides helpful feedback to the reluctant client by reflecting back to him or her what is heard.

Following the formulation set forth by W. R. Miller and Rollnick (1991) and Wallen (1993), major tasks for the adolescent's counselor at each stage of decision making directly parallel the client's state of mind. At the *precontemplation* stage goals are to establish rapport, to ask rather than to tell, and to build trust. Eliciting the young person's definition of the situation, the counselor reinforces discrepancies between the client's and others' perceptions of the problem. During the *contemplation* stage, while helping to tip the decision toward reduced drug/alcohol use, the counselor emphasizes the client's freedom of choice. "No one can make this decision for you" is a typical way to phrase this sentiment. Information is presented in a neutral, "take-it-or-leave-it" manner. Typical questions are: "What do you get out of drinking?" "What is the down side?" and (to elicit strengths) "What makes your sister believe in your ability to do this?" At the *preparation* for change and *action* stages, questions like "What do you think will work for you?" will help guide the youth forward without pushing him or her too far too fast. When there is resistance, as there inevitably will be with young substance misusers, Miller and Rollnick advise rolling with the resistance instead of fighting it. Use of reflective summarizing statements is helpful, for example, "Let's see if I've got this right. You have a concern that I'm trying to get you to give up smoking and drinking all at once. We do seem to be moving along too fast. Why don't we look at some things people have done in this situation, some of the options you might want to consider?" Central to this whole treatment strategy is the belief that clients are amenable to change and that timing is crucial in persuading clients to take the steps that will free them from harm.

GENDER-SPECIFIC PROGRAMMING FOR GIRLS

Equality does not mean sameness; recognition of male/female developmental differences is important in shaping approaches that will tap into the interests and strengths of each gender. As Belknap and Holsinger (1997) inform us, programs for boys are more successful when they offer ways to advance within a structured environment, while programs for girls do better when they focus on relationships and assertiveness within relationships. Special attention to girls' unique biology and body image concerns are essential as well, for these are major female concerns. In view of the recognition of girls' special needs, so often ignored in male-oriented treatment programs, the *Juvenile Female Offenders* report (Office of Juvenile Justice and Delinquency Prevention, 1998) recommends the establishment of girls' group treatment homes. Such homes would provide gender-specific programming focused on healthy relationships, a female-centered school curriculum, caring mentors to provide encouragement in setting realistic educational goals, and special services for pregnant and parenting young women. Individual and group counseling for survivors of sexual abuse trauma would be provided as well; these matters cannot be properly addressed in mixed settings or in gender-neutral programs.

Rudolph Alexander (2000) describes a pilot treatment program at the Santa Monica Hospital Medical Center developed for girls who have been sexually abused. After engaging in friendly warm-up exercises, the girls played the "Hat Game," in which they all get to answer a question pulled out of a hat, with the questions relating to how they feel their bodies have changed since they were molested and whether they would say to a girl who had been molested that they thought it was her fault. The girls later wrote their own questions: "Have you felt like killing yourself?" "Have you ever felt real crazy?" were examples (p. 208).

In Waterloo, Iowa, group homes that were once coed now specialize in the care of teenage girls, many of whom are already mothers. A system of nurturant foster care has been established in Waterloo, Iowa, in conjunction with Quakerdale, the only youth residential facility in Iowa that accepts pregnant teens. "Patterning with families . . . restoring hope" is the theme of this program that places pregnant teens in trouble with the law in the residential facility. Following their release date, teens have the option of moving into foster care with their babies (Hemenway-Forbes, 2001). Central to all these program innovations is the theme of personal empowerment. In the program that is empowering, the client is aided to build a positive self-identity and find strength in her own voice and pride in her cultural heritage.

The learning of life skills and the importance of family can flow naturally and spontaneously through involvement in mutual-aid or support groups focused on a common, all-absorbing task. From a strengths perspective, the hallmark of the effective group leader is enthusiasm and unshakable confidence in the young women's latent talents and abilities. The leader or social worker's role, as Gutiérrez and Suarez (1999) state, should be that of consultant and facilitator, rather than instructor, so as not to reinforce the sense of powerlessness that these victimized and addicted girls need to overcome. Small groups, according to these authors, have special relevance for empowerment practice with Latinas, because it is in keeping with the Latinos' history of working with one another to provide mutual aid. African American culture is similarly oriented more toward family and community systems than toward individual achievement.

The importance of such group work for all the participants is that gaining competency in one area—writing poetry, drawing, parenting—can lead to skills in performing adult roles valued by society. The socially empowering group, even within the confines of the stark juvenile justice setting, can be individually transformative, the more so among women who have been removed from and punished by society, estranged from loved ones, and forced into lockstep with institutional demands. The actively working, fun-loving group can thus represent a strange and powerful anomaly, given where it is and the personal history of its members. Such a group can serve as a bridge to the cultural and social milieu of the larger society (Wilson & Anderson, 1997). And above all, reintegration of the juvenile offender into society is the one thing the present correctional apparatus is the most tragically, shamefully, ill prepared to do. The negative labeling and punitive response to girls in trouble with the law puts them at more risk of further drug misuse in the future, often by way of self-destructive relationships. We concur with Carol Lee Pepi's (1997) call for a paradigm shift from society's current retributive justice response to the healing model of gender-based restorative justice. In restorative justice, the focus is on restoring individual family networks: Healing, not punishment, is emphasized (see van Wormer, 2001).

ADDICTION PROBLEMS AMONG THE ELDERLY

Moving to the other end of the spectrum, we come to the final stage of life. The challenge at this stage, according to Erik Erikson (1963), is to achieve ego integrity rather than despair. Ego integrity is defined as the ultimate form of identity integration; people who attain this attribute, suggests Erikson, enjoy a sense of peace and pride in their contribution and accomplishments. Others fail to cope satisfactorily, however; retirement, widowhood, and the accumulation of losses can lead to loneliness and depression.

Persons aged 65 and older constitute about 13% of the U.S. population; they are the fastest-growing age cohort. Few realize the true extent of substance abuse by the elderly, since the elderly are more likely to drink and use drugs (prescription medication) at home than in public. Alcohol-related consequences of heavy drinking, moreover, are often confused by health professionals and family members with medical or psychiatric conditions among the aged. In any case, the diagnosis and treatment of alcohol problems are likely to become increasingly important as this segment of the population grows (NIAAA, 1998).

In contrast to young alcohol abusers, the elderly drink smaller amounts at one time, use drugs prescribed by doctors (licit as opposed to illicit drugs), experience a hidden alcohol problem, and drink in connection with a number of late-life stresses, including bereavement from the loss of family and friends and loss of occupational roles through retirement. Unlike young adults, who seek out drugs for recreational use, the elderly may be seeking a therapeutic effect, such as relief from pain (Schonfeld, 1993).

Surveys of various age groups in the community suggest that the elderly consume less alcohol and have fewer alcohol-related problems than younger persons (NIAAA, 1998). As might be expected, this segment of the population consumes 20 to 25% of all prescription medications (Benshoff & Janikowski, 2000). Of great concern to health and mental health professionals is the large number of elderly using a variety of prescription medications without proper physician supervision. Prescription drug misuse is estimated to affect as many as 17% of older adults (U.S. Department of Health and Human Services, 1998). Addiction to the benzodiazepines, such as Valium and Xanax, is quite common in this age group.

In contrast to studies of the general population, surveys conducted in health care settings have found a substantial prevalence of alcoholism—6 to 11% of those admitted to hospitals, 20% in psychiatric wards, and 14% in emergency rooms (NIAAA, 1998). The prevalence of problem drinking in nursing homes is high as well, but this finding may reflect a trend toward using nursing homes for short-term alcoholism rehabilitation stays.

Investigators have distinguished two types of elderly alcoholics—the early onset and the late onset. The early-onset alcoholics are those who began to have drinking problems early in life and have carried them into old age. Persons who have been drinking heavily their whole lives are more apt than others to be dually or multiply diagnosed and to have a family history of alcoholism (Gambert, 1997). Early-onset alcoholics are more likely to be men; late-onset are more likely to be women (U.S. Department of Health and Human Services, 1998). Approximately two-thirds of the elderly alcoholics are of the early-onset variety (Lawson, 1989). In an empirically based comparative study, Schonfeld and Dupree (1991) matched 23 early-onset alcoholic abusers admitted for treatment with 23 late-onset abusers in treatment. Early-onset subjects were likely to have changed residence, to have been intoxicated more often, and to have experienced more severe levels of depression and anxiety. A large group of early-onset but now abstinent male alcoholics reside in nursing homes and suffer from Korsakoff's syndrome and other alcohol-related neurological problems (Benshoff & Janikowski, 2000). For both groups, depression, loneliness, and lack of social support were the most frequently reported antecedent to readmission drinking behavior. In contrast to the long-term drinkers, late-onset subjects were more likely to remain in treatment.

In van Wormer's experience, the late-onset group had close family ties; initially, these clients were overcome with the stigma of the alcoholism diagnosis: After a life of sobriety, a tainted self-image in old age (such as following a DWI arrest) was an unexpected blow. For these well-motivated but sensitive clients, an empathic therapeutic environment is essential.

One reason for a finding of a lower rate of alcoholism among the general population of older adults undoubtedly is related to the high mortality rate among heavy alcohol consumers and smokers. Also reflected in the statistics is the fact that a disproportionate number of the elderly are women. And elderly women, due to sex role expectations from their youth, are apt to drink little if at all (Benshoff & Janikowski, 2000). If they do drink to any great extent, they are careful to keep this fact hidden.

In spite of the increased recognition in recent years that elderly alcoholism is a growing problem, many researchers believe that the numbers are grossly underestimated. Few of the older alcoholics are getting the help they need. Reasons contributing to their neglect as singled out by Beechem (1997) are:

- The elderly tend to avoid substance abuse services.
- They rarely are rarely referred from court services for drug-induced criminal activity.
- The problem of misdiagnosis mentioned previously exists.
- Friends and relatives can be indulgent or neglectful.
- Established criteria for classifying alcohol problems among the aged are inadequate or irrelevant.
- So much of their time is spent alone.

Biological Considerations

One reason drinking inventories are inadequate as diagnostic tools for people over a certain age is that their bodies metabolize alcohol differently. Any psychoactive drug, in fact, is likely to have a more pronounced effect in an elderly person than in someone younger. A decline in body fluid and an increase in the proportion of body fat makes for a decreased volume of distribution for alcohol. The impact on the central nervous system is more pronounced, therefore (Gambert, 1997). In later years, the high tolerance that younger alcoholics so seem to enjoy gives way, and tolerance reversal is characteristic. As Father Martin phrased it in his memorable videotape *Chalk Talk on Alcohol* (1972), "You get drunk quicker and it ain't worth it." (Virtually all the standard drinking inventories include high tolerance as a criterion of alcohol dependence.)

The inability to handle alcohol with advancing age is related also to slowed rates of metabolism and excretion and the fact that elderly persons are apt to have other drugs in their system already, drugs that exacerbate the effect of alcohol, often with serious consequences. Alcohol use among the elderly is most often a case of polydrug (not single-drug), use with all the problems that may ensue from this eventuality.

Compared to younger persons, elderly drinkers are more prone to addiction due to their more frequent use of medications, especially of depressants, blood pressure medication, and painkillers, and due as well to the high prevalence of depression and anxiety disorders in this age group (Gambert, 1997). Death due to the synergistic effect of drug interactions is higher among the elderly than among any other group, including adolescents (Beechem, 2002).

Other medical complications associated with long-term alcohol misuse include:

- Problems in the gastrointestinal system—ulcers, pancreatitis, cirrhosis of the liver
- Hip fractures related to decrease in bone density and falls while intoxicated
- Injuries in car crashes
- Alcohol–medication interactions that decrease the effectiveness of prescription medications
- A likelihood of suicide associated with depressive disorders
- Brain damage in the cerebellum affecting balance and in the frontal lobes affecting functioning
- The incidence of pneumonia, pulmonary disease, heart disease, and lung cancer is extremely high here, since the majority of elderly alcoholics smoke

Social Risk Factors

Aging in our society is equated with obsolescence and physical decay—witness all the magazine and TV ads highlighting products to disguise the aging process. In a future-oriented society, those with a claim on the past may find themselves considered passe. Stresses in old age are related to the accumulation of losses—loss of family members and friends, loss of meaningful activities (including work), of identity as a teacher, truck driver, construction worker, etc., and loss of health. In Erik Erikson's terms, in the absence of integrity there is despair.

Psychological factors related to loss and unresolved grief contribute to drug and alcohol problems among the elderly. The isolation and withdrawal associated with substance misuse reduce one's inclination to socialize and lead an active life. Family members may avoid or reject heavy-drinking individuals out of embarrassment and/or accumulated anger over previous episodes. In the belief that the elderly are unlikely to change, relatives rarely bring them in or commit them to treatment. They often come to treatment because of arrests for drinking and driving. Once in treatment, their recovery prospects, especially for late-onset drinkers, are very good (Benshoff & Janikowski, 2000).

ASSESSMENT

Health care providers are advised to include questions about drinking and smoking habits on their health inventory forms, and most of them do. Very brief interventions at the doctor's office—advice to quit or cut down—have proven effective. Advice to older patients should include warnings about medical conditions, such as high blood pressure and ulcers, that can be worsened by drinking, and the risks of taking over-the-counter and prescription drugs in combination with alcohol (NIAAA, 1998).

When clients appear at a treatment center, a thorough assessment of their drinking and drug-using habits is undertaken. As mentioned previously, the standard forms, like the diagnosis from the *DSM-IV-TR*, contain several items that are inappropriate for clients of advanced age (for example, items concerning tolerance and legal and occupational consequences of substance misuse).

Two well-known alcohol screening devices that have been validated for use with older adults are CAGE and the Geriatric MAST (NIAAA, 1998). CAGE consists of four simple questions (see chapter 5). The MAST-G (Michigan Alcoholism Screening Test—Geriatric Version) consists of 24 questions with special relevance to the elderly. Samples are: "Does having a drink help you sleep?" "Did you find your drinking increased after someone close to you died?" "When you feel lonely, does having a drink help?" (NIAAA, p. 55)

Treatment Interventions

Whether to treat older patients in age-segregated settings or with the regular substance abuse treatment population is an unanswered question in the research literature. Kathleen Farkas (1997) convincingly makes the case for senior programs. Based on her experience, Farkas has found that older adults bond with each other, because, like the young, they share similar problems. In mixed groups, the issues of the young may be horrifying to elderly clients; prostitution among heroin addicts is one such example; use of strong language is another. In age-specific programs, which are slower paced and use treatment techniques adapted for older clients, such clients feel more comfortable and will remain in treatment longer. Many treatment centers do not have the luxury of separate programming. Van Wormer (1995), in any case, found that many clients thoroughly enjoyed the mix of ages in her therapy groups: Older clients seemed to benefit from giving advice and sharing their stories with younger group members. Also, they seemed to like getting personally involved in hearing of the intrigues and relationship crises of others in the group. Other sources, such as the Treatment Improvement Protocol of the U.S. Department of Health and Human Services (1998), agree that age-specific settings are preferable where feasible. Treatment works best, according to this report, when the issues dealt with are congruent with the life stage of the client. One drawback was the general lack of patience toward those occasional group members who were hard of hearing. Their chiding of participants to speak up had a dampening effect on group interaction.

The panelists who prepared the *Substance Abuse Among Older Adults* treatment improvement protocol (U.S. Department of Health and Human Services, 1998, p. xxi) recommend incorporating six features into treatment of older alcohol misusers:

- Age-specific group treatment that is supportive and nonconfrontational and aims to build or rebuild the patient's self-esteem
- A focus on coping with depression, loneliness, and loss (e.g., death of a spouse, retirement)
- A focus on rebuilding the client's social support network
- A pace and content of treatment appropriate for the older person
- Staff members who are interested and experienced in working with older adults
- Linkages with medical services, services for the aging, and institutional settings for referral into and out of treatment, as well as case management

Additional tips provided by this government source are: to provide a clear statement of the goal and purpose of each session; to make use of simultaneous visual and audible presentation of material, enlarged print, nonglaring light, reduction of background noise; to keep group sessions short (55 minutes maximum); and to begin each session with a review of previous material.

In her work with elderly females, van Wormer found them remarkably receptive to treatment, grateful for the opportunity to come to group, and, as often as not, seeing the crisis that brought them through the treatment doors as a blessing. When two elderly graduates of the program requested diplomas to put on their walls, the receptionist obligingly rushed out to have some made up. (Such a request had never been made before.) In working with older women, one can expect that feelings of guilt and shame about drinking will emerge. Cohen (2000) recommends approaching an older woman about her drinking in an atmosphere of privacy and respect for her personal history, and understanding the stigma that the words "alcoholism" and "alcoholic" might hold for her. Terms like "drinking" and "drinking problems" can be used instead. A focus on health and a healthy lifestyle is usually well received.

One exemplary program described by Graham and Brett (1994) utilized a harm reduction approach to treating older adults with substance dependence problems. Funded by a grant from the city of Ottawa, the project, Lifestyle Enrichment for Senior Adults, was designed to reach senior apartment residents suspected of having problems with alcohol and psychoactive medication. Participants learned of the project through news stories, via hospital referrals, or from friends. This client-centered program was conducted in the tradition of Carl Rogers, a tradition high on empathy and warmth and low on confrontation. Unique to this program was the acceptance given to persons who had little or no desire to quit drinking or drug using, persons who would have been excluded from conventional, abstinence-based programs. By focusing on the harm associated with substance use rather than solely on the use itself, both counselor and client could consider a broad range of solutions (such as delaying drinking until the evening). In order to reduce the stigma of slips and relapses, the focal point was on personal issues rather than substance use. For example, a person who had begun using drugs or alcohol following the death of a spouse might, in developing a rapport with the counselor or group, find solace through dealing with repressed feelings related to unresolved grief and/or in joining a local bereavement support group.

In their in-depth interviews with participants and graduates of the Enrichment for Senior Adults Program, Graham and Brett found the clients' dependence problems to be of two varieties. Either they were related to a mental disorder and were longstanding in nature or, more often, the addiction problems had evolved out of loneliness and isolation. Program participants improved their health-seeking behaviors considerably as a result of the treatment interventions and personal attention received. Social events were an active and popular component of this program; group meetings served as aftercare insurance against relapse.

Although based on a small sample, Graham and Brett's findings are consistent with research demonstrating that in working with older people with alcohol or drug problems, a nonconfrontational approach achieves considerable objective success (U.S. Department of Health and Human Services, 1998). As recorded in their interviews, clients gave evidence that they understood the health goal of the program and were actively working toward minimizing drinking as a part of this goal. Personal empowerment came from a focus on client successes rather than failures. "Perhaps it's time for the addictions field to adopt a less dogmatic and more pragmatic approach to addressing alcohol and drug abuse," as the authors thoughtfully concluded (p. 19).

Many elderly problem drinkers in harm reduction and conventional programs decide abstinence is the best course for them. Some of the most active members of Alcoholics Anonymous are retired individuals who derive great personal satisfaction in helping newly sober younger alcoholics. AA's use of storytelling is attractive to older people, who often have spellbinding stories from years past. Most cities have meetings specifically for older AA members. Attendees often derive great satisfaction from the camaraderie and interactive ritualism of such mutual-support groups.

Beechem (2002, in chapter 8) delineates common pitfalls for the counselor who provides substance abuse treatment to an elderly clientele: (1) *ageism* and stereotyping of which the counselor may be unaware (use of derogatory off-the-cuff remarks such as "This dates me" sends a message that old is bad); (2) *countertransference*, the unconscious process in which elderly persons trig-

ger feelings in the helper about his or her parents and grandparents that interfere with therapy; (3) *avoidance and denial* of the addiction problems in assessing elderly clients; and (4) *expressing sympathy* rather than empathy, which
compounds the clients' self-pity and helplessness.

Contemporary barriers to health care stemming from managed health care
restrictions and federal and state cutbacks take a heavy toll among elderly alcoholics in need of treatment. Whereas Medicare, the health care provision for
the elderly, traditionally covered 12 days of inpatient alcohol treatment, many
states, under pressure from managed care companies, are eliminating this coverage. In view of the large number of physical and cognitive problems among
polydrug-using older adults, including lengthy withdrawals, coverage of at least
12 days of inpatient treatment is an extremely important option (U.S. Department of Health and Human Services, 1998).

PREVENTION OF RELAPSE

Relapse, or a "lapse" as it is commonly called by harm reduction model proponents, does not mean, in AA parlance, "one drink, one drunk." Nor does it
refer to a failed drug test that shows one is "dirty" if one smokes a single marijuana cigarette over a month's time. A relapse is not a one-time slip or setback
but, rather, a process. A client's return to harmful use can be interpreted as a
temporary lapse in the path to changing addictive behavior. At the thinking
level, relapse is seen as leading back from the action stage to the contemplation
or precontemplation level (Daisy, Thomas, & Worley, 1998). By helping clients
appreciate that changing addictive behavior is a learning process, lapses can be
reframed as valuable learning opportunities rather than indications of personal
failure (Weingardt & Marlatt, 1999). This reframing is crucial to keep the
lapses from leading to a full relapse. Once a client is overwhelmed with guilt and
conflict, his or her sense of failure can easily become a self-fulfilling prophecy.
Specific strategies to prevent a lapse from turning into a full-blown relapse, offered by Weingardt and Marlatt (1999), are:

- Stop, look, and listen. Clients can be taught in advance that a lapse is a
  warning signal that they are in danger and need to retire to a quiet place to
  review these strategies as summarized on their reminder card.
- Stay calm; avoid feelings of guilt and self-blame; a lapse is a mistake, not a
  failure.
- Renew your commitment; think back over the reasons you decided to
  change in the first place.
- Review the situation leading up to the lapse.
- Make an immediate plan for recovery, such as getting rid of the pills or alcohol or leaving the high-risk situation.
- Draw on your support network for help.

Broadly speaking, interventions for relapse management can be thought of
as efforts to minimize the harm associated with a return to unhealthy practices
following a period of abstinence or controlled use.

The return to addictive patterns following treatment, as Marlatt and Gordon (1985) maintain, is born out of negative emotions, such as anger, anxiety, depression, and boredom. While "triggers" such as peer pressure and work-related problems are common among younger alcoholics, the elderly alcoholic is more apt to be influenced by late-life situations (Beechem, in press). Depression, loneliness, and unresolved loss-grief issues are negative emotions that may be associated with the use of a chemical to dull the senses, if not to get high. In extreme cases, such low feelings combined with drug use can be a precursor to suicide.

Beechem offers a cognitively based three-stage approach to relapse prevention geared toward high-risk situations for the elderly. In Stage One, high-risk situations are spelled out. Although a standardized checklist of typical risks may be provided, the client's personal list is derived through collaboration and discussion. Typical risks that may be listed are: watching old family movies; returning home from a family reunion or funeral; suffering sleep loss; harping on one's regrets in life ("if only I had . . . "); hanging around bars.

In Stage Two, clients are helped to monitor the antecedents of drinking urges. Together with the counselor a plan for continuous self-monitoring of negative thoughts and deeds is drawn up. Evolving from homework assignments is a clear sense of the client's strengths, support systems, and capabilities. Through prompting, as the elderly client reviews his or her life crises and blessings, the counselor can help the client appreciate his or her coping style, strengths, and purpose in life (professional and/or personal triumphs). Stage Three stresses the self-management and self-efficacy that are keys to sober living.

Central to this three-stage approach of high-risk prevention is the notion that clients are consumers and that their concerns and needs are paramount. Forcing them to conform their thinking to standard belief systems that have worked for some (for example, to have to say, "My sobriety comes first") is less effective than helping an individual to elicit his or her own insights. Many clients have a spiritual life, or did at one time. Helping the client tap into his or her spirituality can provide a source of strength and comfort. Other persons with substance misuse problems might be of a more secular bent; a group such as Rational Recovery or Women for Sobriety might suit their particular needs. In Patt Denning's words, "We as workers have the responsibility of developing a needs hierarchy for the people under our care that is based on *their* assessment of their needs more often than *our* assessment of their needs" (1997, p. 15).

Loss and Grief

Burial of their loved ones is a constant fact of life for persons who survive into old age; loss and grief are therefore inevitable at this stage of life. Most people grieve and go on. Unresolved grief and depression, however, sometimes is associated with excessive drinking and pill use.

As alcoholics share their life histories in treatment, the link between grief and loss and other feelings such as guilt and anger become apparent. In long-term alcoholics, an early loss that was deeply troubling and even traumatizing may have played a role in the later use of chemicals as a form of relief. Guilt feelings connected to the early childhood loss would now be compounded by the addictive behavior.

In elderly widows and widowers, too, many of whom never had a drinking problem, unhealthy guilt feelings may arise in connection with a dying family member. Three types of guilt typically found in family members of the terminally ill are survivor guilt, a sense of helplessness, and ambivalence guilt. Interestingly, these same unhealthy responses are often seen in the families of alcoholics, torn as they are by feelings of helplessness and responsibility (van Wormer, 1995).

Survivor guilt occurs when one person is spared death or a calamity while another or others are not. The one who is spared may go into a depression marked by obsessive thoughts. The "Why me?" syndrome of the victim has its counterpart in the "Why not me?" reaction of the survivor. The survivor, such as the person who lived through Hiroshima or a plane crash, may feel a need to justify his or her own survival. Underneath, there may be a feeling of unworthiness.

Parents who have lost children, children who have lost parents, and surviving spouses and partners—all can experience their own version of survivor guilt. For parents who survive their children, their failure to carry out the most fundamental task of protection arouses a special, overwhelming despair. Sometimes the very elderly have outlived a middle-aged son or daughter.

When a family member is terminally ill, the partner or spouse invariably will feel a sense of personal failure, for the caretaker is unable to do what ought to be done—namely, to heal the one who is suffering and make the pain go away. This is the second type of guilt—guilt due to *helplessness*. The dying person's dependence on drugs for relief may further contribute to the survivor's sense of helplessness and frustration, especially when the drugs fail to bring the relief desired. Futile attempts to get the dying patient to eat can also be problematic.

Ambivalence guilt is present as the caregiver begins to resent this role. Loss of a partially loved spouse is sometimes more difficult than loss of a beloved spouse. As one elderly woman in this situation once said to van Wormer, "Sometimes I wish this whole thing would end. Do you think I'm terrible?"

Persons who work with elderly clients with addiction problems would do well to explore the dynamics of grieving and the relationship between negative feelings and the use of substances to quell them. Therapy groups for older clients can delve into bereavement issues as they arise. In helping group members understand the emotional impact of death and dying and to accept any alien feelings for what they are—an integral part of the grieving process—the practitioner can help them cope better.

A poem, such as the following, written by William Faulkner for his epitaph, can be read and shared with the group:

> If there be grief, then let it be but rain,
> And this but silver grief for grieving's sake
> If these green woods be dreaming here to wake

Within my heart, if I should rouse again.
But I shall sleep, for where is any death
While in these blue hills slumbrous overhead
I'm rooted like a tree? Though I be dead,
This earth that holds me fast will find me breath.

(Cited by Wilde & Borsten, 1978, p. 75)

The ability to come to terms with loss and grief, and thereby to transcend them, is a major factor in the alcoholic's successful recovery.

SPIRITUAL HEALING

Many early psychologists, Jung and Maslow being the most renowned among them, have written of the essence of experience that goes beyond the "natural" realm into a higher level of consciousness (Wallen, 1993). Today, however, spirituality is a resource that is often overlooked in the literature, and especially in the literature on empowerment practice and harm reduction. And yet, if they seek to draw on the strengths of clients and of their community, how can practitioners disregard a force that traditionally has offered marginalized people the greatest support of all?

"In a crisis or occasion of grief and loss, there is often a shaking of the foundation of one's sense of meaning," suggests social work professor, Edward Canda (interview by D. W. Miller, 2001), "who one is, what life is about, and what reality is about. We cannot escape these questions." Thanks to lobbying by Canda and others, religion was added by the Council on Social Work Education in 1994 to key characteristics of diversity and, more recently, spiritual development as a central aspect of human behavior. The American Psychological Association, however, according to Wallen, has not given official acknowledgement to an explicit focus on spiritual development. "Spirituality is a force that needs to be understood, enhanced, and utilized because it is quintessentially starting where the client is" (Ortiz & Smith, 1999, p. 318).

Attention not only to the biopsychosocial but also to the spiritual dimension has special relevance to the field of substance abuse treatment because of the strong spirituality component of AA. The Twelfth Step (which begins, "Having had a spiritual awakening as the result of these steps . . . ") sums up this focus, which entails a move away from a self-centered view of the world to one that places the individual in relation to a larger universe. Spirituality is of special relevance to addictions treatment not only because of the AA stress but also in its own right. The heavy load of guilt feelings that recovering people often carry explains the desire that many persons in recovery have for reconciliation and renewal, even forgiveness. Some who once derived great satisfaction from membership in a religious organization may seek a return to that type of involvement. Elderly clients in treatment for alcohol or other drug problems very often have spiritual needs related to their stage of life, perhaps to their growing familiarity with the prospect of death. In the face of despair associated with earthly losses, spirituality can bolster one's courage in taking risks to pursue personal change and maybe get involved in a formal association or a reading group.

If we conceptualize recovery as a kind of journey, we can see it as a path leading from isolation to meaning, as the achievement, in the final analysis, of serenity and of spiritual health. Grief work can help people who want to pursue it to move beyond self-blame into a realm of higher consciousness. Recovery itself can be conceptualized as a grieving process. Letting go and grieving, as Maria Carroll (1999) suggests, is integral to the human and spiritual journey.

Citing two research studies, Royce (1989) noted that an overwhelming majority of alcoholism treatment clients complained that their spiritual needs were not met in standard treatment programs. Spirituality is a word used even less by most harm reduction enthusiasts. Patt Denning (2000), in fact, states in the introduction to her book on practicing harm reduction psychotherapy that her increasing resistance to Twelve-Step-based interventions, "particularly the emphasis on powerlessness and spirituality," led her to seek out an alternative model (p. xvi).

Maria Carroll (1987, 1999) conceptualizes the spiritual journey in terms of breaking the bonds to earthly attachments and achieving a mastery of oneself through strengthened virtues. For the recovering alcoholic, one earthly attachment is to the substance alcohol. Only when the bond to their addiction is broken can alcoholics move to higher things and embark on "a journey home." To Carroll, the journey home entails constructing a personal reality, becoming disillusioned with this reality, letting the ego-self disintegrate, surrendering, reframing the old reality, and then allowing a new reality to develop as the transformed state. Through *surrendering* to the reality of the present, the recovering alcoholic moves through a spiritual awakening process toward wholeness and a larger humanity. Drawing on her exploratory and in-depth research on spirituality and recovering alcoholics, Carroll (1993) suggests that the Twelve Steps can offer a guide toward increasing self-knowledge, giving to others, and reaching a higher state of consciousness. Other ways of achieving spiritual well-being and belongingness include religious faith and a sense of harmony with nature and the universe.

Writers on spirituality contributed to the alcoholism literature in their conceptualization of alcoholism as a spiritual illness, a condition seen as resulting from a spiritual void in one's life, from a search for a connectedness. As Royce (1989) suggests, alcoholics may be unconsciously seeking to fulfill their spiritual needs with alcohol. This is an important issue in need of further research.

For the alcoholic, merely being well does not provide enough protection to withstand future temptations of alcohol and/or some other addiction. Mantell (1983) believes that in order to ensure sobriety, alcoholics must achieve a level that is "weller than well." Spiritual well-being is considered by Cowley (1993) to be the epitome of health. It may come from a sense of unity with the cosmos, from a personal closeness to God or to nature. The experience of wholeness and integration are not dependent on religious belief or affiliation. Fulfillment of the spiritual dimension is important in providing a sense of meaning in life.

Studies on addiction recovery indicate that approaches to heightened spiritual awareness markedly increase a sense of purpose in life (O'Connell, 1999). A growing body of research indicates, moreover, as O'Connell reports, that spiritual practices such as prayer, contemplation, yoga, and Zen and transcendental meditation have a measurable effect on physiological processes in the brain. The fact that spiritual contemplation can be registered in terms of brain activity (actually inactivity in one region of the brain) gives the experience a neuroscientific reality. Recent advances in neuroscience help explain why some people experience ineffable, transcendent events to be as real as their normal range of sensory impressions (Begley, 2001). O'Connell's recommendation is that the client's attitude toward and sense of spirituality be routinely assessed in the recovery process. There is a growing recognition among providers of culturally specific programs such as those for African Americans and North American Native populations that spiritual beliefs offer a great resource. Clients from other ethnic groups, as well, can benefit from tapping into this often-overlooked resource, a resource with special meaning to persons who have reached the time of life when they are inclined to review the past, looking back over the years and reflecting on the turning points. Wrestling with issues of mortality and immortality, people in late adulthood are prone to ponder the meaning of their lives and of life itself.

In the words of theologian Karen Armstrong (1993), "Human beings cannot endure emptiness and desolation; they will fill the vacuum by creating a new focus of meaning" (p. 399). Without imposing their own religious and spiritual beliefs on their clients, professionals in this field should help clients in their search for spiritual truth. All clients should have access to spiritual literature and the possibility of consultation with a spiritual mentor.

SUMMARY AND CONCLUSION

The first and the last, the new and the old—this chapter has focused on the major psychological growth tasks and pitfalls confronting youths and the elderly. Although problems with drinking and drug use occur across the life span, we have chosen to focus on these two stages of life because of the special vulnerabilities accruing to these transitional stages. If we were following the lives of particular clients in treatment for one of the substance use disorders, we could see that unresolved crises and bad habits from the earlier period of life have come to a head at a later stage. Adolescent addicts require intensive treatment stays because of attitude, whereas the elderly require a lengthy recovery period because of biology. While the young have little or no sense of their mortality, the old may be too much absorbed with this same issue.

Two prevalent myths in society are that the young will not listen and the old will not learn. According to this logic, there would be little point in treatment for either of these groups. In fact, cost effectiveness research reveals just the opposite: Prevention and treatment at each level of maturity can be highly effective when geared toward the special concerns of the clients in that age group. Each stage of life carries its own reward for sobriety and its own treatment needs. As a basic principle of effective leadership and counseling states: Lead a person only as far as he or she is likely to follow. The focus is set by the client, not the counselor, and so is the rhythm of therapy.

References

Alcohol, cigarette use by adolescents. (2001, February 16). Available online at www .jointogether.org

Alcohol use among girls. (1999). The National Clearinghouse for Alcohol and Drug Information. Available online at www.health.org/govpubs/RP0993/index.htm

Alexander, R. (2000). *Counseling, treatment, and intervention methods with juvenile and adult offenders.* Belmont, CA: Wadsworth.

American Psychiatric Association (APA). (2000). *Diagnostic and statistical manual of mental disorders* (text revision). Washington, DC: Author.

Annual national household survey. (2000). U.S. Department of Health and Human Services. Available from www.samhsa.gov

Armstrong, K. (1993). *A history of God: The 4,000-year quest of Judaism, Christianity, and Islam.* New York: Ballantine Books.

Aron, E. (1996). *The highly sensitive person: How to thrive when the world overwhelms you.* New York: Broadway Books.

Associated Press. (1999, August 29). Teen–father relationship called substance abuse key. *Waterloo–Cedar Falls Courier,* A1.

Associated Press. (2001, February 22). U.S. teens use drugs more than Europeans. *Des Moines Register,* 6A.

Attack on campus drug use ends up teaching kids to lie. (2000, June 13). *USA Today,* 16A.

Bachman, J. G. (1997). *Smoking, drinking, and drug use in young adulthood: The impact of new freedoms and new responsibilities.* Nahwah, NJ: Lawrence Erlbaum Assocs.

Beechem, M. (1997). Beechem risk inventory for late-onset alcoholism. *Journal of Drug Education* 27(4), 397–410.

Beechem, M. (2002). *Elderly alcoholism: Intervention strategies.* Springfield, IL: Charles C. Thomas.

Beer companies back college alcohol policy changes. (2000, November 3). Available at www.jointogether.org

Begley, S. (2001, May 7). Religion and the brain. *Newsweek,* 52–57.

Belknap, J., & Holsinger, K. (1997). Understanding incarcerated girls: The results of a focus. *Prison Journal* 77(4), 381–405.

Benshoff, J. J., & Janikowski, T. P. (2000). *The rehabilitation model of substance abuse counseling.* Belmont, CA: Wadsworth.

Black teens more likely than whites to reject cigarettes. (1996, November 22). *Waterloo–Cedar Falls Courier,* A11.

Boroson, W. (1993, August 8). Drinking age: Abstinence vs. moderation. *The Record,* 17–20.

Botvin, G., & Botvin, E. (1997). School-based programs. In J. H. Lowinson, P. Ruiz, R. Mulliman, & J. G. Langrod (Eds.), *Substance abuse: A comprehensive textbook* (pp. 764–775). Baltimore: Williams & Wilkins.

Canadian teens say chill out about drinking. (1999, November 5). Available at www
.jointogether.org

Carroll, M. M. (1987). Alcoholism as an attachment and a gift on a spiritual journey. *Journal of Consciousness and Change, 10*(2), 45–48.

Carroll, M. M. (1993). *Spiritual growth of recovering alcoholic adult children of alcoholics.* Unpublished doctoral dissertation, University of Maryland, Baltimore.

Carroll, M. M. (1999). Spirituality and alcoholism: Self-actualization and faith stage. *Journal of Ministry in Addiction & Recovery, 6*(1), 67–84.

Clark, D. B., Lesnick, L., & Hegedus, A. M. (1997). Traumas and other adverse life events in adolescents with alcohol abuse and dependence. *Journal of the American Academy of Child and Adolescent Psychiatry, 36*(12), 1744–1752.

Clayton, M. (2000, March 15). Binge drinking and teetotaling spread at U.S. colleges. *Christian Science Monitor,* 2.

Cohen, M. (2000). *Counseling addicted women: A practical guide.* Thousand Oaks, CA: Sage.

Cowley, A. D. (1993). Transpersonal social work: A theory for the 1990s. *Social Work 38,* 527–534.

Daisy, F., Thomas, L. R., & Worley, C. (1998). Alcohol use and harm reduction within the Native community. In G. A. Marlatt (Ed.), *Harm reduction: Pragmatic strategies for managing high-risk behaviors* (pp. 327–350). New York: Guilford Press.

de Miranda, J. (1999, June 7). Harm reduction holds potential to reach marginalized youth. *Alcoholism & Drug Abuse Weekly 11*(23), 5.

Denning, P. (1997, spring). Clinical psychology and substance use management. *Harm Reduction Communications, 4,* 13–15.

Denning, P. (2000). *Practicing harm reduction psychotherapy.* New York: Guilford Press.

Dimeff, L. A., Baer, J. S., Kivlahan, D. R., & Marlatt, G. A. (1999). *Brief alcohol screening and intervention for college students: A harm reduction approach.* New York: Guilford Press.

Dizon, N. Z. (2000, June 4). *College drinking arrests up.* Associated Press. Available online at file:///C/TEMP/$WPM2B64.hmt

Drummond, T. (2000, November 6). Mothers in prison. *Time,* 105–107.

Edwall, G. E., Hoffmann, N. G., & Harrison, P. A. (1989). Psychological correlates of sexual abuse in adolescent girls in chemical dependency treatment. *Adolescence, 24,* 279–288.

Elias, M. (1998, January 5). Study links sexual abuse, alcoholism among women. *USA Today,* 1A.

Ellis, A. (1965). Commentary in *Three approaches to psychotherapy.* Montreal, Canada: Peerless Film Processing.

Erikson, E. (1963). *Children and society.* New York: Norton.

Farkas, K. J. (1997, October 7). *Substance abuse and elderly people issues for clinical social work practice.* Paper presented at the National Association for Social Workers conference. Baltimore, MD.

Forty percent of teenagers have tried cannabis. (2000, November 22). Available online at uk.news.yahoo.com/991122/29/bjcf.html

Gambert, S. R. (1997). The elderly. In J. H. Lowinson, P. Ruiz, K. Mulliman, and J. G. Langrod (Eds.), *Substance abuse: A comprehensive textbook* (pp. 764–775). Baltimore: Williams & Wilkins.

Girls being arrested at record rate. (2001, May 2). Available online at www.join together.org

Graham, K., & Brett, P. J. (1994, March 7–10). *A harm reduction approach to treating older adults. The clients speak.* Paper presented at the 5th International Conference on the Reduction of Drug-Related Harm. Toronto, Ontario.

Gutiérrez , L., & Suarez, Z. (1999). Empowerment with Latinas. In L. A. Gutiérrez & E. A. Lewis (Eds.), *Empowerment of women of color* (pp. 167–186). New York: Columbia University Press.

Hawke, J. M., Jainchill, N., & DeLeon, G. (2000). The prevalence of sexual abuse and its impact on the onset of drug use among adolescents in therapeutic community drug treatment. *Journal of Child & Adolescent Substance Abuse* 9(3), 35–49.

Hemenway-Forbes, M. (2001, April 30). Comfort in love. *Waterloo–Cedar Falls Courier,* B4.

Howard, R. (1998, October 8–14). Labor in power. *Community Care,* 17–29.

Intervention helps college-age drinkers. (1999, April 12). Available online at www .jointogether.org

Kenworthy, T. (2001, June 1). Bush daughters cited in Texas. *USA Today,* 3A.

Krucoff, C. (1999, March 23). Smoke and mirrors. *Washington Post,* 20.

Lavelle, M. (2000, February 7). Teen tobacco wars. *U.S. News & World Report,* 14–16.

Lawson, A. (1989). Substance abuse problems of the elderly: Considerations for treatment and prevention. In G. Lawson & A. Lawson (Eds.), *Alcoholism and substance abuse in special populations* (pp. 11–34). Rockville, MD: Aspen.

Leinwand, D. (2000, August 24). 20% say they used drugs with mom or dad. *USA Today,* 1A, 2A.

Leshner, A. I. (1999). Science-based views of drug addiction and its treatment. *Journal of the American Medical Association, 282*(14), 1314–1316.

Mantell, M. (1983). Student and employee assistance programs: A model for secondary prevention. *Labor-Management Alcoholism Journal, 12,* 113–124.

Marlatt, G. A., & Gordon, J. R. (Eds.). (1985). *Relapse prevention: Maintenance strategies in the treatment of addictive behaviors.* New York: Guilford Press.

Martin, C. S., & Winters, K. C. (1998). Diagnosis and assessment of alcohol use disorders among adolescents. *Alcohol Health and Research World, 22*(2), 95–105.

Martin, Fr. J. (1972). *Chalk talk on alcohol,* revised. Video. Aberdeen, MD: Kelly Productions.

Miller, D. W. (2001, May 18). Programs in social work embrace the teaching of spirituality. *Chronicle of Higher Education,* 36.

Miller, W. (1998). Enhancing motivation for change. In W. Miller & N. Heather (Eds.), *Treating addictive behaviors* (2nd ed., pp. 121–132). New York: Plenum Press.

Miller, W. R., & Rollnick, S. (1991). *Motivational interviewing: Preparing people to change addictive behavior.* New York: Guilford Press.

Miller, W. R., & Rollnick, S. (1998). *Motivational interviewing: Professional training videotape series.* Directed by Theresa Moyers. University of New Mexico: Albuquerque.

National Council on Alcoholism and Drug Dependence. (2000). *Youth, alcohol and other drugs.* Available online at www.ncadd.org/facts/youthalc.html

National estimates of substance use. (1999). Available online at www.samhsa.gov/oas/ NHSDA/1999/Chapter2.htm

New Zealand lowers drinking age. (1999, July 29). Available online at www.join together.org

NIAAA (1998, April). Alcohol and aging. *Alcohol Alert,* 1–4.

Noble, M. C., & Reed, C. (2000, January). Kentucky drug courts. *Bench & Bar, 64*(1), 6–10.

O'Connell, D. F. (1999, December 13). Spirituality's importance in recovery cannot be denied. *Alcoholism & Drug Abuse Weekly, 11*(47), 5.

Office of Juvenile Justice and Delinquency Prevention. (1998). *Juvenile Female Offenders.* Washington, DC: Office of Justice Programs.

O'Malley, P. M., Johnston, L. D., & Bachman, J. G. (1998). Alcohol use among adolescents. *Alcohol, Health & Research World, 22*(2), 85–93.

Ortiz, L., & Smith, G. (1999). The role of spirituality in empowerment practice. In W. Shena & L. M. Wells (Eds.), *Empowerment practice in social work: Developing richer conceptual foundations* (pp. 307–319). Toronto: Canadian Scholars Press.

Pepi, C. L. (1997). Children without childhoods: A feminist intervention strategy. *Women & Therapy, 20*(4), 85–101.

Prestage, M. (1996). Sensible drinks all around. *Time Educational Supplement, 4155,* A14.

Prochaska, J., & DiClemente, C. (1992). In search of how people change: Applications to addictive behaviors. *America Psychologist, 47,* 1102–1114.

Quindlen, A. (2001). The drug that pretends it isn't. In H. T. Wilson (Ed.), *Drugs, society, and behavior* (pp. 79–80). Guilford, CT: McGraw-Hill/Dushkin.

Raise a fond last glass to Dionysus. (1997, October 4). *The Economist,* 36–37.

Rats get hooked on testosterone. (1999, November 13). *Science News 156,* 319.

Reid, J., Macchetto, P., & Foster, S. (1999). *No safe haven: Children of substance-abusing parents.* Available online at www.casacolumbia.org/publications1456

Rivera, G. (2000, July 14). *Smashed: Kids and alcohol.* MSBC TV. Transcript available at www.msnbc.com/news/421198.asp

Rose, R. (1998). A developmental behavior-genetic perspective on alcoholism risk. *Alcohol Health & Research World, 22*(2), 131–143.

Royce, J. E. (1989). *Alcohol problems and alcoholism: A comprehensive survey* (Rev. ed.). New York: Free Press.

Schonfeld, L. (1993). Research findings on a hidden population. *The Counselor,* 20–26.

Schonfeld, L., & Dupree, L. (1991). Antecedents of drinking for early- and late-onset elderly alcohol abusers. *Journal of Studies on Alcohol, 52,* 587–592.

Schouten, F. (2000, March 12). Gambling takes toll on teens. *Des Moines Register,* AA.

Smith, E. (1997, November 24). Bodybuilders fret "flip side" of anorexia. *USA Today,* 1A.

Smith, M. C., & Smith, M. (1999, March 12). Treat students as adults: Set the drinking age at 18, not 21. *Chronicle of Higher Education,* B8.

Smoking, dieting linked among teen girls. (2001, March 2). Available online at www.jointogether.org

Spanking linked to substance abuse. (1999, October 7). Available online at www.join together.org

Spear, L. (2000). Modeling adolescent development and alcohol use in animals. *Alcohol Research & Health, 24*(2), 115–123.

Sternberg, S. (2000, August 2). Abuse can damage girls' brain chemistry. *USA Today,* 10D.

Stocker, S. (2000). Medications reduce incidence of substance abuse among ADHD patients. *NIDA Notes, 14*(4), 1–4.

Study shows drug courts reduce substance abuse, crime. (1998, November 11). Available online at www.jointogether.org

Substance Abuse and Mental Health Services Administration (SAMHSA). (2001, March 7). Key influences on youth drug use identified. *SAMHSA New Release,* 1–2.

Teenagers' brains not fully developed. (2000, September 25). *Waterloo–Cedar Falls Courier*, A8.

Teens who abuse alcohol face lifelong problems. (2001, January 3). Available online at www.jointogether.org

U.S. Department of Health and Human Services. (1998). *Substance abuse among older adults.* Treatment protocol series 26. Rockville, MD: U.S. Government Printing Office.

U.S. Department of Health and Human Services. (2000). *Anabolic steroid abuse. Research Report* (pp. 1–8). Washington, DC: National Institutes of Health.

U.S. Department of Health and Human Services. (2001). *National drug control strategy: 2001 annual report.* Washington, DC: Office of the National Drug Control Policy.

van Wormer, K. (1995). *Alcoholism treatment: A social work perspective.* Belmont, CA: Wadsworth.

van Wormer, K. (2001). *Counseling female victims and offenders: A strengths restorative approach.* New York: Springer.

Wallen, J. (1993). *Addiction in human development: Developmental perspective on addiction and recovery.* New York: Haworth.

Weber, M. (1999, April 28). *New study first to quantify illicit drug and substance use in movies and music popular among youth. Press release from SAMHSA.* Available online at www.whitehousedrugpolicy.gov/news/press/042899.html

Weingardt, K. R., & Marlatt, G. A. (1999). Sustaining change: Helping those who are still using. In W. R. Miller & N. Heather (Eds.), *Treating addictive behaviors* (2nd ed., pp. 337–351). New York: Plenum Press.

Widom, C. S. (2000). Childhood victimization and the derailment of girls and women to the criminal justice system. In *Research on Women and Girls in the Justice System* (pp. 27–36). Washington, DC: U.S. Department of Justice.

Wilde, M., & Borsten, O. (1978). *A loving gentleman.* New York: Simon & Schuster.

Wilson, M. K., & Anderson, S. C. (1997). Empowering female offenders: Removing barriers to community-based practice. *Affilia: Journal of Women and Social Work,* 12(3), 342–359.

Youth drinking: Risk factors and consequences. (1997, July). *Alcohol Alert 37,* 1–4.

Zastrow, C., & Kirst-Ashman, K. (2001). *Understanding human behavior and the social environment.* Belmont, CA: Wadsworth.

All addictions are anesthetics. They separate us from the distress in our consciousness. —GABOR MATÉ (1999, P. 297)

No hay mal de por bien no venga. (There is nothing so bad that good cannot come of it.) —POPULAR MEXICAN *DICHO* (SAYING), SUGGESTED BY VIRGINIA RONDERO IN PERSONAL CORRESPONDENCE WITH VAN WORMER.

EATING DISORDERS AND GAMBLING, SHOPPING, AND OTHER BEHAVIORAL ADDICTIONS

CHAPTER 7

INTRODUCTION

The addictions we are talking about in this chapter, rarely covered in books on substance misuse, are not your ordinary addictions, and only one involves a substance—food. What these addictions have in common is that they all involve everyday legal activities: eating, shopping, sexual activity, gambling, and "surfing" the Internet. What these behavioral or pleasure-related addictions have in common with the substance dependencies is that they are compulsive and obsessive and involve euphoria that is not induced artificially by a drug. Like all addictions, the ones we discuss in this chapter have strong biological, psychological, and social components.

For helping professionals working in the substance abuse treatment field, an understanding of these other addictive behaviors that are commonly found in clients receiving treatment for another disorder is essential. For example, an alcoholic may suffer from bulimia; the meth addict may be a pathological gambler. In recovery from drug misuse, the client may become a workaholic or, worse, a shopping addict.

"I get addicted to everything I touch." How often this comment is heard in substance abuse treatment circles! Yet the dynamics of this phenomenon, the tendency of some individuals to take everything to extremes, have not been properly understood or even acknowledged by scientists until now. Today, there is mounting evidence that all addiction—chemical or otherwise—arises from the same neurobiological processes, processes located deep inside the brain and not in the cerebral cortex, which is the rational, thinking part of the brain. Recent research shows, for example, that compulsive gambling may hijack the reward and pleasure pathways of the brain in the same way that psychoactive drugs do (National Research Council, 1999).

In his book on attention deficit disorder, *Scattered*, Galon Maté (1999) puts it best:

> Less obvious (than alcoholic lurches) but no less physiological are the effects on the brain of self-stimulating behaviors. The gambler and the sexaholic, the compulsive shopper, and the man or woman who insists on skiing uncharted glaciers are all looking for the same hit of dopamine and endorphins that the ingestion of substances gives the drug addict. Whatever gets you through the night. (p. 298)

Some individuals, because of genetic predisposition or trauma early in life, are especially vulnerable neurologically to the disorganizing effects of substance misuse. They have what Watkins, Lewellen, and Barrett (2001) term "fragile brain chemistry" (p. 3); they are inclined to get "hooked." The source of the addiction may be a mood-altering substance or a love relationship or a thrilling pastime, such as betting on horses, or all three. Based on our theory of vulnerability, we would predict that medication for any one of these "maladies" should alleviate the other problems as well. This, in fact, is the case. Drugs that reduce the craving to drink, for example, might make an individual more "laid back" in other areas as well. Turning from the biological to the psychological aspects of addiction, we find that whether the addiction is to a substance such as heroin or to a behavior such as gambling, the pattern is more or less the same. Psychologically, this pattern entails all the mind games that the addict engages in to continue the mad pursuit (such as for inappropriate sex or betting on cards). Socially—the impact on family, peers, and colleagues—the consequences are relatively comparable as well. Could anyone argue that the parents of an anorexic child don't suffer as much as the parents of a child using drugs?

In this chapter we consider both the commonalities and uniquenesses of numerous varieties of addiction—eating disorders, gambling addiction, shopping addiction, sex addiction, as well as Internet addiction, the newest "kid on the block."

Consistent with the psychology-of-addiction focus of this section of the book—Part 3—our concern is with cognition. The fundamentals of cognitive therapy, including the thinking/feeling work and the use of positive self-talk that are described in the final portion of this chapter, are principles as relevant to working with alcoholics and drug addicts as with individuals out of control with eating, gambling, or sex. The cognitive interventions presented in this chapter are not viewed as a separate treatment modality, but rather as strategies that transcend all the basic modalities. All therapy and counseling is about helping people take control of their lives, learning how to cope, learning how to survive. All therapy is psychological in this sense. Here what we do is single it out and define the tools therapists need to help clients modify, and thereby moderate, unhealthy thought patterns (e.g., "I'm going to fast for a week"; "I'm going to gamble for big stakes to get back what I lost."). Management of anger and stress, reframing of one's definition of self, and the therapeutic use of humor are among the other topics covered. In contrast to much of the cognitive work engaged in by counselors today, especially in working with offenders and addicts, our approach is consistent with the strengths/empowerment perspective.

EATING DISORDERS

"Eating Disorders Start in Brain" (2001)—so states the headline in *USA Today*. Although researchers have known for several years that a person's chances of developing an eating disorder depend partly on genetics, this is the first time, according to the article, that an anorexia-related gene has been identified. Twice as many subjects in the European study had a variant form of a gene that stimulates appetite as did subjects without anorexia. There are many other genes as well involved in this compulsive behavior.

Anorexia nervosa is characterized by a refusal to maintain a minimally normal body weight, even to the extent of self-starvation. One of the most perplexing aspects of anorexia is that its victims continue to think they are fat, despite the ribs and bones showing through. Bulimia, in contrast, is characterized by repeated episodes of binge eating followed by vomiting, abusing laxatives or diuretics, taking enemas, or exercising obsessively in order to get rid of the food or burn the calories (National Institutes of Mental Health [NIMH], 1997). Some anorexics binge and then purge to maintain their low weight. Family, friends, and physicians have difficulty detecting bulimia in someone they know because the person's body weight may be normal. Dentists may detect telltale tooth enamel damage in vomiters.

As with anorexia, bulimia typically begins in adolescence. More than 90% of cases of these two eating disorders occur in females. The lifetime prevalence of anorexia among girls and women is 0.5% and that for bulimia approximately 1 to 3% (American Psychiatric Association [APA], 2000). A surprise finding with regard to bulimia in men is that when it does exist, its medical consequences are severe and its occurrence is related to low levels of the male hormone testosterone ("Anorexia," 2000).

Anorexia Nervosa

The *DSM-IV-TR* (APA, 2000) includes in its diagnostic criteria for anorexia that weight loss be less than 85% of normal body weight; intense fear of weight gain; and amenorrhea in young women (the absence of at least three consecutive menstrual cycles). Many of the physical signs and symptoms are attributable to starvation—cold intolerance, lethargy, constipation, and the appearance of lanugo, or fine body hair. Mortality from anorexia is over 10%, with death most commonly resulting from starvation, suicide, or electrolyte imbalance.

People with eating disorders share certain personality traits: low self-esteem, clinical depression (which often runs in their families), and an inability to handle stress (NIMH, 1997). Perfectionism is pronounced among anorexics, as is a likelihood of athletic involvement (especially gymnastics and ballet). The following description found in *Dancing on My Grave,* by prominent ballerina Gelsey Kirkland (1986), is typical:

> I sat in bed at night and thumbed through fashion magazines, memorizing faces and figures. This began as a game I played to beat insomnia. I wanted to be a gorgeous someone, anyone other than who I was. I clung irrationally to the idea that my body had been the cause of all my problems. I prayed for a perfect body. Please, God, make me into the doll that everyone wants me to be. I stared at pictures of models and imagined that I might wake up in the morning as one of them. I wanted to free myself from the weight of artistic choice. . . . Starvation and poisoning (from cocaine) were not excesses, but measures taken to stay within the norm, both professionally and aesthetically. (pp. 205–309)

Similarly, Angie Huisman (in personal correspondence with van Wormer of October 1997) shares her earlier struggle with an eating disorder, a struggle that led to her hospitalization and treatment:

> I knew that I was not healthy. I stopped having my period, was tired all the time, and became very easily agitated. Despite all of this, I kept up my rituals without hesitation. I weighed myself at least three times a day, praying that I had lost at least a pound. If I didn't, I would do anything to get the weight off. By that time, I was too weak to do almost anything, so I did as many sit-ups or jumping jacks as I could until I literally passed out. Then one day I got on the scale and it said 89 pounds. I stared at myself in the mirror and broke down. I was so weak and tired, but still I wanted to lose more weight.

Note the theme of compulsive ritualism in this description. The connection between anorexia and obsessive-compulsive disorder (OCD) is more than coincidental; it is real. Before reviewing the research findings on this connection, let us examine the psychiatric criteria provided by the APA (2000). Under the heading OCD, obsessions and compulsions are defined separately; the person with OCD may have one or the other or both of these. *Obsessions* are defined as recurrent and persistent thoughts or impulses that are experienced as intrusive and that cause marked anxiety or distress. *Compulsions* are the repetitive behaviors (compulsive handwashing, checking, etc.) often associated in the public mind with OCD. These rituals may be associated unrealistically with some dreaded event. Scientists, according to the NIMH (1997), have found biochemical similarities between people with eating disorders and OCD. The similarities relate to abnormal serotonin levels. NIMH researchers have found that many patients with bulimia have OCD as severe as patients actually diagnosed with OCD. A genetic trait is likely a key factor in the development of eating disorders, according to recent psychiatric research at the University of Iowa (Segall, 2001). Interestingly, OCD, like anorexia, often begins in adolescence (Schwartz, 1996).

As explained by Jeffrey Schwartz (1996), OCD can be considered "brain lock" because "four key structures of the brain become locked together—messages from the front part of the brain get stuck there" (p. xv). This leads to maddening repetition of unwanted thoughts. The form of the process—the relentless intrusiveness—is universal in persons with OCD, but the content varies with individual and culture.

The fact that these disorders occur primarily in cultures or subcultures that value thinness and present media images of "Barbie doll"-shaped bodies attests to the fact that there is a cultural aspect to this disorder as well. The usual explanation is that mothers, concerned about their own weight, transmit the cultural prescription to their daughters. Writing in the journal *Pediatrics,* Davison and Birch (2001), however, reported that girls who were constantly dieting said it was their father's opinion that was goading them on. For men, homosexuality is a risk factor, owing to a stress on slimness in the gay community. Lesbians, on the other hand, rarely have this disorder (Andersen, 1999).

Bulimia Nervosa

Unlike anorexics, bulimics may have a history of weight gain or come from a family in which overweight is a problem. In terms of personality, bulimics usually are extraverted, have voracious appetites, and experience episodes of binge eating (Dove, 1995).

In her fascinating book *Wasted: A Memoir of Anorexia and Bulimia,* Hornbacher (1998), who herself suffered from both problems, differentiates bulimia from anorexia:

> Bulimia, of course, gives in to the temptations of the flesh, while anorexia is anointed, is a complete removal of the bearer from the material realm. Bulimia hearkens back to the hedonistic Roman days of pleasure and feast, anorexia to the medieval age of bodily mortification and voluntary famine. (p. 153)

A key characteristic of bulimia is its common association with alcohol and other drug misuse; estimates of their co-occurrence range from 30% to 70%, according to a recent report in the *Journal of the American Medical Association* (Vastag, 2001). Eating disorders, similarly, are very common among cocaine addicts and alcoholics in substance abuse treatment (Gold, Johnson, & Stennie, 1997). Whether it's cutting a line of cocaine or a slab of cake, the symptomology of eating disorders and substance misuse is the same. Both health-threatening disorders are long term, chronically relapsing, and life threatening.

Women with bulimia are three times more likely to have been sexually abused as children than women who do not suffer from this disorder, according to data from an Ontario Health Survey ("Many Bulimic Women," 1995). Thirty-five percent of women with severe bulimia reported childhood sexual abuse; many were also likely to have lived in foster homes, often because of the alcoholism of their parents, according to this survey. Perhaps because compulsive eating stimulates a rise in the levels of mood enhancers in the brain, food can serve as a drug to curb the feelings of shame, self-disgust, and depression that often accompany compulsive eating problems. This may explain, as Wooley (1994) notes, why sexual abuse is more predictive of bulimic than of anorexic symptoms and related to severity of symptoms.

And how about those individuals who binge eat but don't throw up? Compulsive overeating, in the absence of bulimia, is a grave health risk, because persons with this disorder sometimes put on hundreds of pounds. Yet compulsive overeating, sadly, is an area of scant research in the United States and is included in the *DSM-IV-TR* only under the category "criteria sets and axes provided for further study." Nor has NIDA conducted the research that is needed on compulsive eating and drug dependence as entwined illnesses, according to the director of NIDA, as cited by Vastag (2001). And substance abuse treatment centers do not routinely screen for eating disorders.

From the British medical journal *Lancet* ("Scientists Find Link," 2001) comes a groundbreaking study on the neurological characteristics of morbidly obese people. A lack of dopamine receptors in the brains of morbidly obese people has been documented through the use of PET scans. The greater the weight of the person, the lower his or her level of receptors. More research is needed, however, to see if the excess weight affects brain chemistry. Research is planned on persons before and after stomach-stapling surgery to rule out the possibility of any confounding variables (Vastag, 2001).

A related study, this one focusing on male twins, found that a strong craving for sweets may be linked with a tendency toward alcoholism and that the cause may be genetic ("Twins," 2000). As reported by the subjects in the study, cravings were worse when they were nervous or depressed. If verified in future studies, a test could be devised to screen youngsters with a predisposition to alcoholism.

Treatment Interventions

A combination of pharmaceutical and cognitive interventions is the preferred treatment for disordered eating. Selective serotonin-enhancing antidepressants have been found to be helpful for bulimia (Vastag, 2001). Ondansetron, a drug normally given to cancer patients to prevent nausea and vomiting, also works for bulimics. (Ondansetron has also been found effective with alcoholism of the highly hereditary variety.) In a study comparing 14 bulimic patients given Ondansetron with 12 others given a placebo, the patients on the real drug showed a marked decline in the number of bingeing-and-vomiting episodes. This drug not only helped bulimics know when to stop eating, it also acted to make more serotonin available in the brain.

In severe cases of anorexia, where clients have lost 25% of their expected body weight, inpatient treatment is necessary. The sole focus in the initial period is weight restoration. Once weight is restored to a level that is no longer life threatening, much of the depression lifts and thinking becomes more rational.

According to Vastag (2001), no drugs have been shown to ameliorate anorexia. It stands to reason, however, because of the close connection between OCD and anorexia, that the same drug would be effective for both. Halmi (1998) recommends medical management as a useful adjunct to cognitive behavioral treatment of anorexia. Kramer (1993), who has studied the "disorders of pleasure," recommends Prozac in the management of eating disorders, especially anorexia. Anorexia, unlike the addictions, is not about getting high or dulling the senses. Anorexia has more in common with compulsive, ritualistic behavior based on delusion; it is related more to avoidance of pain than to pleasure.

A related disorder, equally compulsive and irrational, is self-mutilation, or cutting. Adolescent girls slice themselves not to die, but seemingly out of their own inner turmoil. Many have been abused, often sexually (Kalb, 1998). The cutting impulse can be quelled by the drug Naltrexone and training in stress management techniques.

The favored treatment for eating disorders is multimodal intervention; this includes, in addition to medication to reduce the obsessiveness, education on the basics of good nutrition, consciousness raising concerning media images, and intensive psychotherapy in cases of a history of early childhood sexual abuse.

Research indicates the efficacy of various types of group work with eating-disordered individuals (Krahn, 1991; Kuba & Hanchey, 1991). The effectiveness of group treatment for women troubled with eating problems stems from the tremendous sharing and support that derive from a positive collective experience. Women's relationships become more open through the process of mutual decision making and feedback. Women can develop a sense of self in relation to others in a group setting. When a woman begins to build trust and empathy with others, she also may begin to look at herself differently, to "loosen up" (Kuba & Hanchey, 1991; van Wormer & Askew, 1997).

The primary challenge in eating disorders treatment compared to other substance abuse treatment is that, because food, unlike alcohol and cocaine, is required for life, treatment protocols that involve a commitment to abstinence (successful with alcohol and cocaine) do not apply. Moderation must be learned by those with eating problems. As many cigarette smokers are aware, it is often easier to give up a substance altogether than to practice moderation. A second factor affecting recovery evaluation and outcomes is the difficulty in defining or detecting a relapse of abnormal eating patterns. The binge/purge cycle, in fact, can go on for years undetected by family members as well as practitioners. Third, as every adolescent girl or woman knows, society rewards slimness far more than it rewards moderation.

Cognitive-behavioral therapy is the treatment of choice in addressing the complex interplay of irrational thoughts that plague persons with eating disorders. The focus here is on the beliefs that power the distorted thoughts and the behavior based on those thoughts. Women's pursuit of the cultural stereotype of feminine beauty is characterized by thoughts such as "If I am fat then I am ugly, and if I am ugly, I am unlovable," and "Since I have eaten three cookies, I might as well eat the whole box." These self-defeating thoughts and the resultant actions serve to sabotage women's lives and perpetuate the eating disorder (Ellis, McInerney, DiGiuseppe, & Yeager, 1989).

According to Vandereycken (1990), the skilled cognitive-behavioral therapist will selectively address issues of weight phobia, distorted perceptions of the body, fear of loss of control over eating and weight, and negative perceptions of self. Cognitive-behavioral treatment is generally focused on the present, serving to identify the immediate behavioral consequences of irrational beliefs.

Affective (feeling) work is critical in the treatment of persons with eating disorders. Inability to cope with early painful experiences such as rape, incest, an alcoholic family, and transitions from childhood to adolescence or from adolescence to adulthood are common underlying dynamics.

Because these persons may lack experience in identifying and expressing a broad range of feelings, counseling sessions initially may be oriented toward examination of affective states, with counselors modeling appropriate affect for given situations and practicing healthy modes of expression (van Wormer & Askew, 1997).

Family therapy, particularly for the adolescent girl, is an important first step in educating the family as a whole to the apparently strange behaviors of eating-disordered individuals. Parents need to be encouraged to set clear boundaries about appropriate behaviors, such as insisting on some financial contribution to the household grocery bill from a daughter who regularly binges on "family" food. Family members also need a forum in which they can express the feelings of frustration, confusion, and mistrust that accompany life with an eating-disordered person, as well as a place to begin to explore the familial issues that encourage the dysfunctional eating.

For clients who are overweight, strict dieting is discouraged because, in many people, food deprivation sets the stage for a starvation/binge eating cycle. Besides, counting calories reinforces food and eating obsessiveness. Used alone or with other treatments, cognitive-behavioral therapy results in significant reductions in behavior associated with disordered eating (McGilley & Pryor, 1998). Such therapy principally addresses irrational thought patterns, such as distorted body image, low self-esteem, perfectionism, and preoccupation with the body and with gaining weight.

A cognitive-based, "love-them-back-to-health" approach was taken by Peggy Claude-Pierre (1997), author of *The Secret Language of Eating Disorders*. Claude-Pierre became a celebrity following extensive television coverage of her work in saving the lives of starving anorexics. Little attention was paid to early childhood experiences; the focus was on the "here and now." The girls at her center (since closed down by the British Columbia health authorities after allegations of forced-feeding were made) did attend workshops to learn practical strategies to survive. They kept journals with two columns per page, one for recording the self-talking voice of anorexia or bulimia, the other for the voice that argued against the negative thoughts. Although the television broadcasts focused on miracle cures, this form of treatment in the absence of medical supervision is highly controversial.

Nevertheless, training by reputable professionals in the control of rigid thought patterns, including the identification and handling of feelings and assertiveness, can have lifelong benefits. The insights and tools acquired for dealing with an eating disorder can empower a person to overcome any number of challenges and obstacles in day-to-day life.

In an interview with van Wormer on February 7, 1997, Nicole, age 20, described her battle overcoming bulimia:

I weighed 160 pounds in college, got into exercising so I could wear cute shorts. It was normal dieting at the beginning; I got my weight down to 120. The social pressures were enormous, so many compliments, "What are you doing to look so good?" I ate it up. . . . In reality, I was a mess, addicted to laxatives, surviving on apples and graham crackers. After taking 10 laxatives, I landed in the hospital and from there into counseling. Social workers and a dietician worked with me and my family.

In family counseling we explored family secrets; we were a "perfect" family. Rules were set for us—not talking about food. I learned about underlying factors in my behavior—my feelings, the "voice in my head."

Later I joined a support group. An educator showed us magazine clippings and explained how distorted our images are. We made lists: Ten things to do, instead of bingeing. My list said: "Go for a walk, call a friend, sister, pray." I deal with my problem every single day.

Gradually, most adolescents with eating disorders mature out of it; nobody knows why. Perhaps it's related to the maturity of the brain, the stabilizing of hormones. Still, there is no cure for this disorder. As Hornbacher (1998) describes her state of recovery in her memoir, aptly entitled *Wasted,* "It is not a sudden leap from sick to well. It is a slow, strange meander from sick to mostly well" (p. 284).

Because similar problems in men—obsession over the way their bodies look—have been largely ignored, male-oriented treatments are scarce. While some men with eating disorders have a kind of fat phobia and become emaciated, it is the impetus to have a muscular build that creates for men, according to one newspaper headline, "The 'Flip Side' of Anorexia" (Smith, 1997). Bodybuilders seeking physical perfection may become preoccupied with weightlifting, watch every ounce of food they eat, gorge on protein, weigh themselves throughout the day, and devote hours per day to lifting weights. *Muscle dysmorphia* is the psychiatric term for this disorder. Sufferers commonly take steroids (see chapter 6). The good news according to the article is that antidepressants can control this behavior. The bad news is that only a few will seek help.

Overeaters Anonymous (OA) is the self-help group for individuals who seek group support for a variety of eating problems. The beauty of OA is that it is ubiquitous in the United States, is free, can be attended as needed, and is open to all who desire to stop eating compulsively. Founded in 1960 by three people in southern California and patterned after AA, OA now has approximately 9,000 meeting groups in over 50 countries throughout the world (Overeaters Anonymous, 1996).

A semihumorous encounter with OA is given by Malachy McCourt (2000). Refusing to deal with his alcoholism problem McCourt decided to do something about his weight problem. After getting poor results, he tried a number of diets, among them the protein diet and the grapefruit diet. Weight Watchers costs money, so he decided to go to OA:

I sat with a group made up almost entirely of women, of every age, and heard horrendous stories of anorexia, bulimia, starvation, bingeing, and other stuff I never knew went on in this prosperous society. . . . People talked about "stuffing down feelings with food."

(Following a month of meetings, McCourt came to the realization that his problem was alcohol.) So I stopped drinking, just like that—suddenly, precipitately, and perhaps foolishly, but being a man of extremes, it seemed the right thing to do. (pp. 175–176)

COMPULSIVE GAMBLING

Because some form of gambling has become legal in every state except three (Utah, Hawaii, and Tennessee) and casino or casino-style gambling is available in 21 states, gambling has become much more socially acceptable and accessible for both women and men (Davis, 2002; National Research Council, 1999). Consequently, many men and women suffering the consequences of excessive gambling are surfacing and asking for help. The economic cost of gambling— treatment for addiction, domestic violence, job loss—is estimated by a government-appointed commission at $5 billion a year (Cohen, 1999). In general, pathological gambling (the lay term for which is "compulsive" gambling) is defined by the National Research Council (1999, Ch. 2, p. 4) as a "mental disorder characterized by a continuous or periodic loss of control over gambling, a preoccupation with gambling, and with obtaining money with which to gamble, irrational thinking, and a continuation of the behavior despite adverse consequences." A clinical diagnosis is reached when a person meets five or more of the Diagnostic and Statistical Manual-IV criteria (APA, 2000). Among the criteria are a preoccupation with gambling, a need to gamble with increasing amounts of money, making repeated efforts to quit, gambling from stress, lying to conceal activities, and borrowing money to pay debts (see chapter 1). Pathological gambling is listed under "impulse control disorders not otherwise classified" along with kleptomania and pyromania. Yet the symptoms of this addiction, as certified gambling counselor Patricia Sweeting (2000) indicates, are interwoven with those of all mood-altering substance disorders. The loss of control, the family disintegration, increased tolerance—the features, tragedies, of one addiction are the features, tragedies of the other. In its power to captivate and hook the player, video poker is said to be the "crack cocaine of gambling." A more blunt description, based on clinical evidence, would be that "pathological gamblers engage in destructive behaviors: they commit crimes, they run up large debts, they damage relationships with family and friends, and they kill themselves" (National Research Council, 1999, p. Exec. 2).

"Problem gambling" is a category generally used in research studies to indicate that the person has developed some family, work, or financial problems because of gambling but hasn't met at least five of the *DSM-IV* criteria. It is also applied to adolescents, regardless of their scores on various assessment instruments, because of a reluctance to label them "pathological" while in the midst of fluctuating/experimental behavior patterns. Many times the general term "problem gamblers" is used inclusively to indicate both pathological and problem gamblers (Pavalko, 1999).

How big is the problem? The National Gambling Impact Study Commission (1999) estimates that there were 125 million American adults who gambled during 1998. Most experienced no negative consequences; approximately 7.5 million were either problem or pathological gamblers. The National Research Council's (1999) estimates that between 3 and 7% of those who gambled in the past year reported some symptoms of problem or pathological gambling. Prevalence breakdowns by race are rare; however, a 1993 study for the North Dakota Department of Human Services found that 14.5% of Native Americans in the sample were probable pathological gamblers, compared to 3.5% in the general population (Volberg, 1993). A look at the prevalence studies of the upcoming generation, the first generation brought up with sanctioned gaming, indicates that adolescents are at particular risk of developing problems with gambling. The National Research Council's (1999) survey of the research literature revealed estimates of the "past year" rate of adolescent problem and pathological gambling combined range from 11.3% to 27.7%, with a median of 20%.

Perhaps even more than with other addicts, gambling strikes at families, places of employment, and friends (Davis, 2002). As compulsive gamblers begin to lose and to lose big, forever chasing that original high of an early win, they sell or pawn possessions, plead for loans from all around them, and steal the rest—embezzlement is a big problem among addicted gamblers (Beaucar, 1999). Writing about the wives of compulsive gamblers, LairRobinson (1997) reports that they are not only constantly harassed by bill collectors but very often physically abused by their husbands. These wives have a high rate of suicide attempts as well. Children of such gamblers have double the rate of suicide attempts as their peers; they are also more likely then their peers to develop a gambling problem themselves.

Gender Differences

Epidemiological surveys consistently report that men are much more likely to be pathological or problem gamblers than are women. Approximately one-third of pathological gamblers are female. In treatment programs, females are underrepresented; they are only 2 to 4% of the population of GA (APA, 2000).

Most of the state problem gambling helplines, however, report that the percentage of women seeking help with gambling problems has been increasing. As early as 1993, an Alberta, Canada, study concluded that women are the gender group now most likely to experience gambling problems. In New Jersey, calls about women have doubled since 1990. In Texas, calls about women problem gamblers have increased from 34% in 1992 to 40% in 1999 (Texas Council on Problem and Compulsive Gambling, 2000).

In contrast to women, who are inclined to gamble as an escape mechanism, even to the point of feeling "hypnotized" or in a "trance" (personal communication to Davis, September 2000), men are more likely to be characterized as "action" gamblers; that is, gambling for men began early in life, has been a long-term problem of 10 to 30 years, focuses on "skill" games, such as poker, horses, and sports, and provides "action" as well as escape (Arizona Problem Gambling Council, 2000). Another motivation for women to gamble compulsively may be the social stereotypes and economic limitations that are still imposed on many of them. Female gamblers coming into treatment after "losing it all" on slot machines had taken up gambling as an escape from very unhappy lives (Beaucar, 1999). Many of these women are elderly. In a pioneering study of women in Gamblers Anonymous, Lesieur (1987) found that two major reasons for escape in over half of the 50 women interviewed were "escape from memories of parental upbringing and escape from troubled husbands and loneliness" (p. 234). Similarly, preliminary results from an online survey of women in recovery from compulsive gambling (Davis, 2000) reveal that many women reported getting started with gambling as a way of dealing with the death or loss of a significant family member, such as the death of a parent.

Co-Occurrence of Other Problems

According to the National Research Council (1999), substance use disorders (non-gender-specific) are associated with both progression to problem gambling and subsequent pathological gambling. Lifetime substance use disorders among pathological gamblers range from 25% to 63%. In a general population study in St. Louis, problem gamblers were three times more likely to meet criteria for depression, schizophrenia, alcoholism, and antisocial personality disorder than nongamblers. According to the National Council on Problem Gambling, the suicide rate for pathological gamblers is higher than for any other addictive disorder (National Gambling Impact Study Commission, 1999). At a minimum, shame, guilt, and remorse are constant companions, making it even more difficult for a woman problem gambler to seek help (see Davis, 2002).

Treatment Provisions

Because most health insurers and managed care providers do not reimburse for pathological gambling treatment, and because persons with gambling problems are in no position to "self-pay," the treatment provisions are sparse. State helplines are now operating in only 35 of the 47 states that have some form of legalized gambling. About half of these states support some type of treatment with public funding, but the level of funding is miniscule compared to the amount of income the states receive from gambling enterprises. For example, in Minnesota in 1997, treatment allocations for gambling comprised 0.5% of the state's income from gambling; in New York in 1998, treatment allocations were 0.1% of the state's income from gambling (National Research Council, 1999). Given this current state of affairs, it is even more important that helping professionals become knowledgeable about compulsive gambling and be willing to address gambling problems that may exist within the client population they are serving.

The addiction/disease model is the conceptual basis for using treatment methods established in substance abuse treatment centers and slightly modifying them for pathological gamblers. Since many of the *DSM* criteria are indicative of physiological dependence, treatment professionals are relying on the strategies of other addictive disorders, including the prescription for abstinence. Treatment centers for persons with gambling problems commonly refer the clients to the Twelve-Step group of Gamblers Anonymous (GA) for additional help. Out of the GA Twenty Questions (based on the *DSM* criteria), most compulsive gamblers will answer yes to at least seven (Gamblers Anonymous, 1999). As is customary in Twelve-Step groups, the final "diagnosis" is left up to the person to decide for himself or herself. The criteria for membership is not a diagnosis, but "a desire to stop gambling." When a person has reached that point, abstinence from all gambling is deemed a necessary goal. The GA program acknowledges Alcoholics Anonymous (AA) as a guide and foundation, and utilizes the same Twelve Steps of recovery and the same organizational principles. The only requirement for membership is "a desire to stop gambling" (Gamblers Anonymous, 2000, p. 2). GA is run entirely by recovering compulsive gamblers, who volunteer their time to be sponsors, chair meetings, arrange for meeting places, secure GA literature, and respond to requests for help day and night. GA meetings can be found by calling the state problem gambling helpline, looking in the yellow pages of the phone book for a local contact number, or accessing the Gamblers Anonymous International Service Office online site at http://gamblersanonymous.org/. For family members, Gam-Anon can be extremely helpful; information and listings are available at this same site.

Even the brains of normal people register increased blood flow to the same region of the brain affected by cocaine use, according to a widely publicized study from Massachusetts General Hospital (Wen, 2001). What differentiates these normal euphoric states from those in compulsive gamblers is probably a matter of intensity or the contrast between this high and the person's normal state of mind. Experiments with medications such as serotonin-reuptake inhibitors to treat compulsive gamblers are currently under way (Blanco, Ibanez, Saiz-Ruiz, Blanco-Jerez, & Nunes, 2000). The addiction/disease model is bolstered by recent research indicating that dopamine and serotonin brain functions are altered in pathological gamblers (APA, 2000). Another promising area of research is the use of Naltrexone, an opioid antagonist that has been used to block the excitement of addictive drugs such as alcohol, cocaine, and heroin. Naltrexone may help mitigate the frequent and intense cravings experienced by compulsive gamblers; new controlled trials of this drug are proceeding (National Research Council, 1999). Drugs such as lithium, used to treat concurrent bipolar disorder, have also been found to decrease compulsive gambling. See Box 7.1 for the portrait of a compulsive gambler, the tale of a highly respected African American youth worker who ended up getting "hooked."

BOX 7.1	REFLECTIONS OF A MALE COMPULSIVE GAMBLER

Gambling is a source of entertainment for many people in the world today. With the increase in casino outlets, as well as the influx of offshore gambling available through the Internet, Americans can bet on practically anything imaginable. For many of these people gambling does not present a serious problem (to borrow a phrase from the Iowa lottery advertisements). However, for a small percentage statistically, gambling can become a serious addiction. I, myself, fall into this category. For nearly five years I was addicted to sports betting. Although I have not related this story to anyone previous to now, I hope that it will shed some light on the subject of compulsive gambling.

In Omaha, I worked with behaviorally impaired adolescent boys. In this field, the support staff is dominated by males who usually have a background that includes, at some level, participation in competitive sports. Such men are supposedly more equipped to deal with the rough nature of the clients involved. It was in this environment that I was first introduced to the world of sports gambling. The circumstances were that a colleague would pick up a bookie sheet (a form containing a list of all of the available games that could be bet on during a particular day) and bring it to work. Initially I only looked at college and professional football games that were played on the weekends. This, however, did not produce the winning I imagined. My gambling eventually became daily, if not twice daily. I went from betting on weekend games to daily gambling on basketball, baseball, and hockey contests and as this happened over the period of five years, I lost thousands and thousands of dollars and numerous other possessions. Before it was over, I nearly lost my family.

In the beginning my wife had participated in the "fun" of gambling. The very occasional wins were encouraging and euphoric. As I began to delve deeper into the gambling, however, she bored of the losses and began to see less pleasure in the hobby. In fact, she encouraged me to get out of the practice. But by then the compulsion for me was too great.

As I began to spend a large portion of my salary on gambling, this created a strain on the marriage. My wife is a certified teacher and makes a considerable amount of money working with students who are emotionally and behaviorally impaired in a private educational setting. In one year, according to our tax returns, we earned nearly $50,000, and yet we had to file bankruptcy not once, but twice! The bank account just could not keep up with the mounting losses.

My ambition in life became the same as other compulsive gamblers, to get my money back. I was always going to win big. Be persistent—that's the thought pattern of a compulsive gambler.

Located in the heart of the black neighborhood, these bookie joints are packed with people; one would be hard pressed to find a larger crowd at any of the local churches in the area. There is a distinct culture among the gamblers who socialize while discussing the odds. What's the hot pick of the day? Who's guaranteed to lose? and so forth. There isn't a Caucasian in sight. If one does appear, there is hushed silence until the stranger is identified as a regular or knowing someone present. The staff of about six or seven (two who remain behind a counter while the others mingle in the crowd) write tickets and collect the money. In the particular neighborhood I frequented, there is no credit issued when you place a bet. The fee is paid up front; this eliminates the need for henchmen to go collecting on outstanding bets. After placing the bet, my favorite thing to do would be to watch the game.

For the casual gambler, the win or loss would put an end to the matter for the day. However for the compulsive gambler, this is just the beginning. As soon as the outcome was determined—win or lose—I would be racing out of the door to place my afternoon bet. If I lost, I was going to get it back. If I won, I was going to make more money to make up for past losses. It was an endless cycle. The excitement of the game was my driving force. Often after losing in the afternoon games on the weekend, I would rush off to the bookie joint with the intention of betting on the night games. If the place was closed, I would be extremely upset that I had arrived late. Dejected, I would return home to consider my losses and to plot for the next day's picks. It was very difficult to suppress my emotional roller-coaster from my wife and children. My mood swings were apparent. As things began to collapse around me I sought help from the local Gamblers Anonymous group. After a short period of sobriety though, I returned to gambling. Gambling had simply become a part of my life that I couldn't avoid. It was entrenched in my social contacts and easily accessible, making it very difficult for me to stop. For me, a geographical relocation was the answer.

Living in Omaha had become increasingly difficult. The embarrassment that accompanies the life of a compulsive gambler, although at times nonexistent to the gambler, is always apparent to their family. Evictions, repossessions, cut-off utilities, collection agencies, and the daily concern of paying the bills are real to the family. My wife was advocating for a "new life," one she believed could exist without gambling. She was also at a point in her career that she needed a change, and she began to explore graduate programs. I, myself, had not completed a bachelor's degree, earning only 40 credits in my many attempts at college, and I began to contemplate seriously a return to school.

It is frequently said in Alcoholics Anonymous that a geographical relocation is not a cure. As one adolescent treatment counselor once said, "A drunk in South Dakota can as easily be a drunk in Iowa." This is probably true for all addictions. However, in my case, the geographical relocation was my answer for a cure. I have not gambled in four years, have completed my BA in History, and am one semester away from my MA in sports psychology. My relationship with my wife has improved dramatically, and I now have time to spend with my kids. I can watch sports without feeling the need to bet on who will win—with the exception of an occasional $1 bet with my 11-year-old son.

Personal story presented to van Wormer on July 27, 2000, for use in this book. The author, due to the nature of his work, wishes to remain anonymous.

Motivational and Cognitive Therapy

It is important to remember that with gambling, the main source of information about the behavior is self-report from the gamblers themselves. There is no urine drug screen or even the typical patterns of withdrawal symptoms that might confirm recent use or severity of the problem. Many sources in the literature focus on the gambler's "uncanny ability to deceive relatives and clinicians, at least in the short run" (Blanco et al., 2000, p. 401). In the alcohol/drug field as practiced in the addiction/medical model in the United States, this behavior is commonly interpreted as "resistance and denial." Gathering collateral information from friends, spouses, partners, and relatives is recommended in order to confront the person with his or her behavior and "break down" the denial. The therapist in this framework is allied with the forces (legal, familial, societal) that aim to stop the person from further gambling and further damage.

A perspective based on strengths, in contrast, is less concerned with breaking down defenses, which are coping mechanisms, after all, and more concerned with building trust. Motivational interviewing is especially relevant to work with clients such as compulsive gamblers who, typically, are plagued with guilt feelings, having thrown so much of their and others' earnings away. If they do not feel backed into a corner by a confrontational therapist, they likely will welcome the opportunity to "open up." To the extent that there is "resistance," a motivational-interviewing model or a solution-focused therapy model interprets this as a natural product of a confrontational environment (Miller & Rollnick, 1991; Berg & Miller, 1992). Interviewing strategies that would engage the person in formulating his or her own goals for change and be congruent with the client's process of change are preferred. The strengths-oriented therapist is allied with the client in working on goals, even if these goals don't initially include giving up gambling (Berg & Miller, 1992).

Work in the Cognitive Area

"I'm wondering how gambling activities or the gambling of someone in your family may play into what we've been discussing. Could I ask you a few questions?" This is one of the exploratory-type questions that might be asked in a typical counseling session. Drawing on principles from a solution-focused rather than problem-focused approach, the therapist would assist the client in defining his or her own conception of the problem and goals for change. Specific techniques to find out what is important to the client might involve asking for exceptions to the problem and about how he or she coped with earlier difficulties in life. Strengths and past successes in dealing with problems of living would be highlighted, instead of deficits or "pathology." The strengths-based therapist will strive to reinforce the client in the direction of positive thinking ("I think I can") while helping the client to eliminate counterproductive and superstitious beliefs. Here are the words of one gambler, for example:

The lady on the other side of me swears, and I glance at her machine just in time to see that she'd "missed" the white 7's by one. "They look like they're ready to come," I say. "Just teasing me," she replies. (Anonymous contribution, GA Web site, 2000)

This excerpt illustrates two cognitive distortions common among compulsive gamblers—giving the slot machine human qualities, and misunderstanding the nature of randomness. The cognitive model is based on the premises that thoughts influence emotions and behaviors and that distorted/maladaptive thoughts can be brought to awareness and changed, resulting in behavior change. Especially relevant to gambling, cognitive therapies emphasize the development of irrational cognitive schemas in response to early and repeated wins. These include illusions of control, biased thinking, the attribution of human qualities to gambling devices, and erroneous beliefs about the nature of randomness (Turner, 2000; Blaszczynski, 2000).

The most common errors include a false belief concerning the phenomenon of randomness and the extent to which outcomes could be predicted ("I've put so much money into this machine, it's bound to hit!") and the personification of the gambling machines or dice (giving them human qualities, as in "Come on baby!"). Gender comparisons in one small study ($n = 20$) revealed that women were more likely than men to personify the slot machines (Delfabbro & Winefield, 2000). Other common distortions include (1) "the illusion of control," such as believing that conditions such as the choice of a dealer or a certain table, choosing a favorite slot machine, and walking into a casino through a certain entrance will enhance success; (2) "flexible attributions," such as transforming losses into "near wins," predicting a loss after it has happened by identifying "fluke" events that contribute to the loss; (3) the "availability bias," where a person judges an event's probability based on the sounds of winning around him or memories of highly publicized winners; and (4) the "fixation on absolute frequency," where the gambler measures the absolute frequency of wins (they win a lot because they gamble a lot), not the relative frequency (they lose more than they win) (Griffiths, 1994).

The role of the therapist in cognitive therapy is to help the clients identify the irrational thoughts that influence them to continue to gamble, bring those thoughts to conscious awareness, monitor them, and replace them with rational and more adaptive thoughts (Davis, 2002).

Here are several questions that have been found to aid professional counselors in identifying gambling problems once clients are willing to proceed ("Screening," 2000):

1. Have you ever borrowed money in order to gamble or cover lost money?
2. Have you ever thought you might have a gambling problem or been told that you might?
3. Have you ever been untruthful about the extent of your gambling or hidden it from others?
4. Have you ever tried to stop or cut back on how much or how often you gamble?

Answering "yes" to any one of these questions suggests a problem and indicates that further exploration would be useful.

Here are several practical suggestions that may help the individual with gambling problems to avoid further problems:

1. Carry the minimum amount of money needed for that day.
2. Turn personal checks/credit cards over to the care of someone else.
3. Require an additional signature to withdraw money from a bank.
4. Voluntarily request a "ban" from frequented casinos, card rooms.
5. Avoid the company of other gamblers.
6. Avoid going to places where gambling is allowed.

As noted by Blanco et al. (2000), "After more than 10,000 years of the existence of the disorder, the field of pathological gambling research and treatment is still in its infancy" (p. 406). The bulk of the research has been done on male, not female, problem gamblers. Nevertheless, women with gambling problems (sometimes reported in the news in cases of embezzlement) are becoming more visible to the general public, and research studies have begun to focus on women and report gender differences that should be of interest to practitioners.

SHOPPING ADDICTION

Shopping addiction and spending addiction derive from the same urge to get something for nothing, to drive a hard bargain, the "urge to splurge." They are both examples of impulsive buying. The consequences in unpaid bills and wrecked families are the same as well. The problem isn't the shopping, of course, it's the buying of merchandise that one doesn't need or even later want, buying for a momentary euphoria or high.

Compulsive shopping is a disorder of impulse control. It is not about materialism or attachment to what consumers buy, but rather a lack of control over buying itself. The following self-description from "an exercise freak" and compulsive dieter is typical:

> I also have this disorder in relation to shopping for clothes through mail-order catalogs. I have had it for a good 10 years but it probably started before that. I spend a lot of time every day thinking about, listing, planning for clothes that will go together if I order them and the costs involved and the time spent ordering, looking at the items over and over, etc. I have so many clothes now; I could probably go over a year and never wear the same thing twice. My common sense tells me that I have all I will ever need. My will to say no and not give in doesn't always work. I went eight months last year without buying a thing. Then after my mom died I got depressed and gave in and started buying all over again. This is kind of like the alcoholic who can be sober for a period of time and something happens in their life to drive them to drink again or becomes the excuse they use to drink again. It is the same for me as a shopaholic—I even worked with a company to figure out payments for the credit cards I have with mail-order companies to get them all paid off in two years. I was able to stick to the schedule for a while but am flounder-

ing again. I finally reached a point where I closed accounts as I paid each one off, and I wrote the mail preference service to have my name taken off mail-order lists. I hope I can be successful, but this is how I see obsessive-compulsive disorder. I have it. Thank God I don't drink, because with my family history I would probably be the all-or-nothing type. (In personal correspondence with van Wormer of January 1999)

An assessment done at the University of Iowa on people with obsessive buying urges found that the typical troubled shopper was a 31-year-old female who had overspent for 13 years and was awash in clothing, shoes, and compact discs (Anderson, 1994). Most of those studied had multiple credit cards; many had bounced checks and fought with their spouse over money.

Mental health professionals say compulsive shoppers feel euphoric as they buy and spend. The druglike high following a purchase can lead to kleptomania, particularly if the money has run out (O'Leary, 2000). The index of the *DSM-IV-TR* does not list shopping dependence or any other listing for shopping. It does list *kleptomania*, defined as the stealing of items not needed, an act associated with a buildup of tension beforehand and gratification or relief afterward. Kleptomania, according to this source (APA, 2000) "may be associated with compulsive buying" (p. 667). This is not the usual form of shoplifting and characteristic of only around 5%. Shopping addiction, or compulsive buying, isn't the usual form of shopping either

Luvox is the drug prescribed by Dr. Donald Black, Professor of Psychiatry at the University of Iowa, who initially reported success in turning compulsive buyers into people who can pass through a store without making a purchase while buying only what they need. Later, when a placebo pill was used, success was also reported. Black attributes the success to the behavioral therapy that accompanied the medicine that was given (Frankenfield, 1999). More research is currently under way. Some credence is given to the neurobiological aspect of this disorder, in that its victims have been found to have more than one psychiatric disorder, while their close relatives are likely to suffer from depression and a drug use disorder (Black, Repertinger, Gaffney, & Gabel, 1998).

In an interesting development, a woman facing up to 18 months in prison for the theft of $250,000 from her employer to finance her shopping addiction was sentenced to probation. The federal judge ruled that the defendant suffered from diminished mental capacity due to her shopping addiction (O'Connor, 2001).

Debtors Anonymous (DA) groups are springing up all over the United States (Lobet, 2000). DA members, like those in AA, first admit they have a problem and then try to fight it by devising a budget they can live with and a realistic repayment plan. According to the DA Web site, "Today numerous DA members come to us from court programs and counseling services, some arrive voluntarily; others do not. . . . Our primary purpose is to stay solvent" ("Information for Professionals," undated).

Related to compulsive buying is hoarding, or the refusal to throw anything away. Typically, hoarders have basements and rooms in their houses that look like flea markets or garbage dumps. This bizarre compulsion that makes it almost impossible for its sufferers to move around in their living space is thought to be a form of OCD (Messina, 1999; Schwartz, 1996).

LOST IN CYBERSPACE

The media today are full of accounts of a new, technology-generated disorder variously called "computer addiction," "pathological Internet use," or "online obsession." There is even a special Web site for people who fear they are "caught in the Net": Netaddiction.com. According to that Web site and the book *Caught in the Net* (Young, 1998), typical warning signs are: preoccupation with the Internet; using increasing amounts of time online; failed attempts to control this compulsion; jeopardized relationships; lying behavior; and escape from problems. How do these heavy Internet users spend their time? Clinical research conducted by the psychologists associated with this Web site reveals that these users spend their time mainly in chat rooms (a practice that often leads to "cyberaffairs") and playing multiuser dungeon games. The cure offered on this Web site? Online therapy at their "Virtual Clinic"!

According to recent surveys, approximately 6% of Web users develop serious problems with their pastime (Yang, 2000). Online activity is a fairly acceptable way of shifting consciousness: Some users enter a fantasy world where they "bare their souls" to strangers; often they use fictitious names. Among employers, a real concern is that workers are using their office computers to enter chat rooms and pornography sites and to trade stocks (Hershey, 1999). Internet activity at the workplace is increasingly being monitored, often with embarrassing results.

Here are some harm reduction strategies for people whose Internet use is not out of control (Potera, 1998): Set a kitchen timer and force yourself to log off when it rings; visit only sites needed for work or for information, and don't detour; and cut back mailing list memberships.

Drawing on William Miller's motivational enhancement therapy (MET), Maressa Orzack (1999), a psychologist and coordinator of Computer Addiction Services, provides four sessions for compulsive Internet users. Sessions take place over a three-month period. The MET methods are summarized by the acronym FRAMES (p. 8):

- *Feedback:* The therapist assesses the computer use of patients in great detail and reaffirms their acknowledgment of the need for help.
- *Responsibility:* Patients are told that they are responsible for changing their behavior.
- *Advice:* Patient and therapist together work out the goals, which include learning how to recognize the difference between healthy and addictive computer use.
- *Menu:* A schedule is devised by which the patient monitors computer use and the associated thoughts and feelings.
- *Empathy:* The efforts of patients are constantly reaffirmed, and they are not scolded for slips or failures.

- *Self-efficacy:* Patients learn to use the computer mainly for work, with the help of feedback through telephone contacts with the therapist. In the last session, therapist and patient review progress, renew motivation, and re-affirm the patient's commitment to change.

SEX ADDICTION

When former President Bill Clinton was battling against allegations of multiple sexual transgressions, there was speculation that he might be the victim of sex addiction (Nichols, 1998). Among the arguments put forward were that Clinton was prone to lying; he had an insatiable need to be loved; he grew up in an alcoholic and violent household; he learned to use sex as an escape; and he would risk all for reckless sexual intrigues (Levin, 1998). There is no consensus, however, that there is such a disorder at all; sexual addiction is not recognized by the American Medical Association or its Canadian counterpart, not even as an impulse disorder. Most clinicians, however, agree there is such a thing as pathological sexuality. But questions remain about how this condition should be classified, whether as an impulse-control disorder or as an addictive behavior (Goodman, 1997). The empirical data that could provide a basis for most statements about this subject are not yet available.

In the minds of members of Sex Addicts Anonymous, there is no doubt, however, that having "out of bounds" sex is an addiction. Sex addicts in this group may request to have sponsors help them monitor their behavior. Sobriety is defined as remaining "in the bounds." There are thousands of adherents to this self-help movement (10,000 members of Boston-based Sex and Love Addicts Anonymous alone), and 10 or more agencies in the United States and Canada offering treatment programs (Nichols, 1998). Therapists and other experts say the problem usually has its origins in childhood, often in homes plagued by addiction, violence, and sexual abuse of the child. High-risk behavior typically progresses into riskier behavior. The addictive act, once it has begun, invariably fuels the problem with guilt, shame, lowered self-esteem, and isolation (Hyatt, 1997). These feelings, in turn, can lead to a seeking after a dangerous sexual situation, the thrill of which produces an intense adrenaline rush (Parker, 1998). Who the partner is makes little difference. Treatment consists of psychotherapy, group counseling, prescription medication in some cases, and referral to a self-help group.

COGNITIVE THERAPY AND
THE STRENGTHS PERSPECTIVE

Distortions in thinking are common in all addictions, but they play a special role in the addictions discussed in this chapter. Compulsive gamblers, as we saw earlier, suffer from denial, superstitions, overconfidence when the rush is on, and/or an unrealistic sense of power or fate. Anorexics have the delusion that they are fat in conjunction with a phobia about being fat. Sex addicts and compulsive spenders keep having lapses in judgment. Common to all these addictions is the tendency toward extreme and immoderate behavior.

As far as the biological side of addiction is concerned, medication may provide a boost and be immensely helpful during the first stages of sobriety. And as for the social aspects, one's social world certainly plays a role in sustaining (or controlling) high-risk behavior. But in the final analysis, the psychological component is primary. The client, in conjuring up his or her inner resources, can channel biological impulses of a destructive sort into productive directions while controlling the social environment through selection of friends and activities conducive to health.

Although cognitive-behavioral therapy (CBT) can be considered a specialized modality, such as the CBT strategies used in Project MATCH, a formulation that taught specific social skills and stress management techniques (Project MATCH Research Group, 1997), the *cognitive approach*, as the term is used here, is much broader. The focus of clients' thought patterns is characteristic of all the treatment modalities except for aversion treatment, in fact. The success of AA, OA, GA, etc. is due, in part, to the help they provide people in clearing up their "stinking thinking," in replacing thoughts conducive to harmful, addictive behavior with healthy, calming slogans, such as "one day at a time" or, as the Norwegians say, "Hurry slowly."

The method known as "rational recovery" (RR) is built almost exclusively on cognitive work. As Jack Trimpey (in personal correspondence of November 30, 2000) describes it, "Rational recovery is purely a program of planned, permanent abstinence." Trimpey, an alcoholic who disliked AA, originally based RR on rational-emotive behavior therapy but then developed an online course for self-development. RR, therefore, no longer holds meetings but offers a for-profit crash course on its Web site (Volpicelli & Szalavitz, 2000).

Motivational enhancement therapy (MET) is a strategy designed to mobilize the patient's own motivation and resources for change. MET can be differentiated from other cognitive strategies in that its techniques are derived from principles of social psychology about getting people to change their behavior. Argumentation and confrontation are avoided in favor of a focus on "building up" rather than "tearing down." MET is both cognitively based and client centered at once. In contrast to MET, rational-emotive therapy (RET), formulated by Albert Ellis, is adversarial in tone. (The guidebook *Rational-Emotive Therapy with Alcoholics and Substance Abusers* [Ellis et al., 1989] contains an excellent chapter on unhealthy relationships, however.) Instead of "rolling with resistance," the strategy is more authoritative; the therapist, in the role of educator, teaches the client what is wrong with his or her thinking. Much more negative are the cognitive principles presented by Yochelson and Samenow (1976) and Samenow (1984). Unfortunately, these theories and techniques, which are geared toward criminal thinking and manipulations, are commonly used in correctional addictions programming. In such programming, offenders are required to focus on their wrongdoings, with the goal of instilling self-disgust and a desire to reform their errant ways (see van Wormer, 2001).

Collaboration and choice are hallmarks of MET. Cognitive therapy, as Volpicelli and Szalavitz (2000) indicate, is often used in conjunction with motivational enhancement to help people unlearn what their addictive lifestyle has taught them. As with RET, the focus is on thoughts (cognitions) and the addictive behaviors associated with them. The MET therapist's style here is demonstrably different from the RET therapist's style, however. Instead of telling the client what is wrong, the MET therapist gets the client to achieve this insight and tell the therapist what is wrong (in continuing to gamble, for example). Then therapist and client together will collaborate to identify, assess, and plan for situations that may be problematic (Stevens-Smith & Smith, 1998). These situations include negative emotional states, interpersonal conflict and stress, and social pressures. Having a balanced lifestyle and avoiding excess is emphasized throughout.

How to Elicit Strengths

Self-defeating thoughts are intertwined with low feelings, a sense of fatalism. The leading cause of relapse is depression of this sort: "Who cares? I might as well go back to what I was doing before."

The starting point for behavior change is a collaborative analysis of the thinking/feeling realm. Developed by Aaron Beck in the 1970s, cognitive therapy is based on the theory that the way a person thinks determines how he or she feels and behaves (see Beck, 1991). Underlying most of the problems for which people seek counseling—depression, addiction, anger, violence—is an intensity of feeling or emotional pain. The challenge for the worker is to help the client separate the feelings from the thoughts and the thoughts from the actions as a first step toward alleviating the pain. The cognitive approach, so often used to break addicts' defenses, such as denial, can be much more effectively directed toward promoting motivation while at the same time building a sense of self-worth and awareness of inner strengths and capabilities.

McQuaide and Ehrenreich (1997) have devised a very useful, 38-item strengths questionnaire that the client can fill out together with the counselor. The complete questionnaire is provided in their article (p. 209), "Assessing Client Strengths." Among the agree/disagree items in this clinical instrument are the following: I am a creative person; I have an accurate view of my strengths and weaknesses; I think about my mistakes and learn from them; I have techniques I use to calm myself down when I'm upset. A wealth of invaluable information is contained in this thoughtful and positive questionnaire.

Sheafor, Horejsi, and Horejsi (1997) have drawn up sample questions to help clients identify their strengths. Among these are: Can you tell me about times when you successfully handled problems similar to those you now face? Where did you find the courage and energy to deal with those problems? How have you managed to cope up to this point? What kept you going? Despite your current problems, what parts of your life are going fairly well? What do other people like about you? What strengths or advantages do others see in your approach to life? What would you not change about yourself, your situation, and your life? (p. 325)

When counselors think from a strengths-based perspective, such questions as these will emerge naturally. Building on client strengths, as Sheafor, Horejsi, and Horejsi (2000) indicate, may require looking at a client's problems from a different angle.

The strengths assessment process itself, as Rapp (1998) suggests, is often experienced by clients as a unique experience for them, because they are not used to thinking of their talents and dreams. This exercise is highly motivating as the client recalls past successes long forgotten. Helping clients see the well part of themselves, as Rapp indicates, is a way to reinforce their wellness.

Miller and Rollnick (1991) recommend pretreatment testing such as addictions inventories, not only for screening purposes but as a foundation for motivational counseling. Test results can be very helpful in mobilizing the client toward commitment for change. Results can be presented with a prefatory comment, as the authors recommend (p. 98), that underlines the freedom of choice: "I don't know what you will make of this result but . . . " Any scare tactic tone is avoided. Finding the positive in test results gives a boost to an approach centered on uncovering client strengths. A cautionary reminder: The role of "expert" should be underplayed; the client and helper *collaborate* on figuring things out (Saleebey, 2002). Clients are usually the experts on their own situation; *they* are the ones who have been there, after all.

Self-Talk and Positive Reframing

Through the learning of positive "self-talk" and cognitive restructuring, clients can be actively helped to replace unhealthy thought processes with healthy and productive ones. In leading a client to awareness of his or her own resources and the possibility of utilizing them, the strengths perspective joins the cognitive approach. Self-defeating patterns of behavior, we need to remember, are often associated with criminality as well as addictive behavior. The legal and social problems that result in turn compound the original negativism and even fatalism. One way out of this maze of destruction is through collaboration work with a therapist to help eliminate illogical and/or self-defeating thought patterns. Positive self-talk is taught by the counselor's juxtaposition of the client's defeatist cognition—"I might as well quit"—with more encouraging pronouncements—"I can do it; I've done it before!" The client can be trained to say "Stop!" when the old words appear and then to very deliberately substitute new formulations for them. Often the client may have been previously unaware of the destructive nature of the thoughts that were going through his or her head as well as of their emotionally draining power. The underlying premise of this approach is the belief that people's cognitions, or the way they view the world, and their motivation to improve their life circumstances are intertwined. Sometimes, as in the case of a younger woman suffering from bulimia, the self-destructive behavior and low self-esteem are rooted in the past, an outgrowth of early sexual trauma. This abuse often does not end in childhood, but continues as a damaging feature of adult experiences as well. Theorists writing about motivational interviewing and cognitive therapy nevertheless focus only on "the here and now." The Twelve-Step Program, similarly, and even the emphasis on sharing your "experience, strength, and hope," presents a largely a present-oriented focus. That you can't change the past, that what happened in the past is just an excuse for bad behavior—these are the themes of most modern-day approaches, a reaction against the dwelling on the past of an earlier day.

The cognitive approach can be reformulated, however, to incorporate the past, to help women and men come to terms with their lives, to see themselves as survivors rather than victims of their childhood. "Start where the client is"— this is the cliché in social work. If the client's problems (and low self-esteem) are rooted in the past, this is the place to begin. The unconscious mind knows neither past nor present; sometimes, in order to go forward, you have to trace your steps backward and find out where you took a wrong turn. The cognitive techniques of restructuring our view of the past are essential to self-acceptance. The cognitive framework is ideally suited for this task.

The repetitive nature of information provided to clients in the early stage of recovery serves to reinforce learning and memory. New members of Twelve-Step groups are continually restructuring self-defeating beliefs through slogans such as "Easy does it" and "Let go and let God." When the thinking gets a little frantic or the "old tapes" start playing again, the universally known Serenity Prayer may be said: "God grant me the serenity to accept the things I cannot change, the courage to change the things I can, and the wisdom to know the difference."

Feeling Work

Treatment centers often have clients list their losses in connection with their addictive behaviors. Sometimes they have to add up the costs in dollars as well. Such exercises, however, only reinforce the negative, feelings of loss, compounded now with public shame as these "consequences" are shared in group. Compulsive gamblers and spenders have problems enough with self-flagellation; there is no need to accentuate these kinds of thoughts. Better would be to provide information concerning how slot machine owners bilk their customers or how marketers of products seduce unwitting buyers. Information concerning the brain and addiction can help the client overwhelmed with the consequences of his of her behavior make sense of things. Being with others in a supportive group can bring home the awareness that good people can make foolish choices.

Anger Management   Male gamblers who have "lost it all" may be consumed with anger; they may displace this anger on their family members. Their female counterparts may be unaware of the anger, which has become internalized, and be overcome with depression or guilt. Among addicts in recovery, anger may cause problems both in its suppression and its manifestation (such as periodic explosions of rage). Sometimes anger at one object (for example, the judicial system) is displaced onto another (the counselor or correctional officer).

Knowledge of feelings and the thought processes connected with these feelings ("I hate my mother," "I hate myself") will help clients work toward change.

Sheafor, Horejsi, and Horejsi (1997, p. 474) describe four guidelines for helping clients get in touch with their feelings. These can be summarized as follows:

1. Identify what you are feeling and thinking right now.
2. Listen to your self-talk. Look for extremes in thinking—avoid the use of words such as *never, can't, always,* and *everybody.*
3. Examine objective reality. Once the facts are identified, relax, take a deep breath, and repeat them *out loud* three times. (For example, "I used drugs to escape from problems. I now have learned solid coping skills and I have been clean for two years. My children are proud of me. My life is not ruined.")
4. Note how your feelings change.

Sometimes anger that surfaces is a cover for another, deeper emotion, such as a feeling of betrayal or even insecurity. An intriguing question to ask the perpetually angry client is "If you weren't feeling anger, what would you be feeling?" The answer may be a revelation to the client as well as to the therapist.

Some women who have difficulty labeling or expressing anger become compulsive house-cleaners, energizing themselves in the endless war on dust and dirt. Such individuals need coaching to help them learn to absorb the angry feeling without fear and to mobilize that energy in a positive direction. Assertiveness training can help people get their needs met. Persons who have difficulty containing their anger should work on the deescalating techniques of anger management.

Anger management training teaches the origins of anger, what triggers extreme anger and why, and that there is nothing wrong with having stormy feelings. Learning to express anger verbally, calmly, for example, to say, "When you do . . . I feel insulted (or rejected, or annoyed)," instead of lashing out physically or with cursing, is the kind of training that can be offered in groups. Group members enhance their self-esteem as they take more responsibility for themselves and learn to channel the energy that goes into outbursts of anger into more productive and rewarding directions.

One anger management program with a lot of promise is described by Talan (1998) in *Psychology Today.* The article cites research performed at the UCLA Neuropsychiatric Institute on the link between hostility and brain chemistry. Hostile people might have deficits on the right side of the cerebrum and an inability to control negative emotions or to be unaware of physiological changes that occur when they are angry. Teaching people to be more self-aware of bodily cues, such as a racing heart, the program at the Institute helps them to protect themselves from chronic anger.

Venting anger inappropriately not only might get the client in trouble but also might actually increase his or her level of hostility. This is what psychology research has always shown, in fact. Repression is bad, but unhealthy release of anger (such as beating the dog) is bad as well ("Blowing off Steam," 1999). See Table 7.1 for healthy ways to deal with anger.

Stress Management   The perpetual nervousness that plagues many individuals can be readily reduced through cognitive therapy techniques. Worrying, anxiety-provoking self-talk ("My kids will hate me; my parents will never forgive me")

TABLE 7.1 | DEALING WITH ANGER

Goal	Means of Achievement
Learn to control angry outbursts	Use "time-outs"
Reduce feelings of anger	Find healthy outlets for feelings of anger—exercise
Lessen periods of angry thoughts	Use healthy self-talk to replace angry thoughts
End violent angry outbursts	Learn to verbalize the reasons for anger; join an anger management group
When appropriate, feel the anger	Explore the socialization history of your anger suppression; assertiveness training

can be replaced with new ways of thinking ("I'll do my best to explain things; they'll be happy to see how much healthier I am now that I'm sober").

Some commonly set therapeutic goals pertaining to fear and anxiety are learning to handle fears, managing to face fears calmly, identifying what one is truly afraid of, and being emotionally prepared for likely outcomes. Imagining the worst possible thing that can happen is often helpful. For clients who have phobias, or irrational fears, the origins of the phobias should be traced. Behavioral treatment provides for exposure to the feared source (e.g., a snake) in slow steps until the panic response is extinguished.

Through cutting down on the use of stimulants, such as coffee and tea, physical anxiety can be reduced greatly. A drink of warm milk at any time can produce a quieting effect. When adrenaline is high, brisk exercise aids in using up the excess energy and enhancing relaxation. The usefulness of physical exercise as a treatment intervention was verified recently in an empirically conducted study utilizing a control group (Palmer, Vacc, & Epstein, 1998). Results indicated significantly reduced levels of both anxiety and depression by virtue of the physical training provided.

Perfectionism is almost always a part of the compulsiveness found in pathological dieting; it also may play into the relentless drive to strike it rich through gambling or day trading on the Internet. The perfectionism itself is not a side effect of these disorders but a personality trait that puts people at risk for these problems and for substance misuse as well ("Persistent Perfectionists," 1996).

All-or-Nothing Thinking   An all-or-nothing mode of thinking causes people to get trapped in their destructive behavior. "I can't quit until I win the jackpot" is typical of this line of thought. An anonymous graduate student describes this phenomenon "to a tee":

> People who are all-or-nothing thinkers need to be the best at things or they are not worth trying. An example of a situation involving several all-or-nothing thinkers

could be found within a casino. I have gone with people to the casino who had the attitude that they were either going to win big or lose all of their money. An interesting thing about one such person is, even if he gets $100 ahead in the casino, he still does not stop. This does not seem to be big enough of a win for these people, who end up staying until they lose all that they had just won.

Some people with weight disorders also have all-or-nothing thinking. They may feel that if they cannot have the perfect figure, then why even try to diet or exercise.

Examples of illogical beliefs, in a checklist that can be used very effectively in group sessions, may include the following (van Wormer, 1995):

- All-or-nothing thinking.
- Jumping to negative conclusions.
- Overgeneralizing about others.
- Making mountains out of molehills.
- Putting down members of your own group (such as other women).
- Self-blaming.
- "I can't live without" a certain person.
- I must be perfect.
- Everyone must like me.
- If things do not go according to plan, it is a catastrophe.
- I never forgive or forget a wrong.
- People are either all good or all bad.
- Victims of crime have themselves to blame.

Sometimes, the simple act of realizing that one's present thinking is irrational brings about a major improvement in this area. In talking to a counselor who is nonjudgmental and enthusiastic about analyzing thought processes we all share, clients will begin to question and challenge many of their long-held assumptions and find they can change the way they feel (depressed, anxious, guilty) by being more accepting of themselves and of others.

Use of Humor   One of the best ways to conquer the kind of catastrophizing and fatalistic thinking that leads to dangerous forms of escape (from indulgence in addictive behavior to suicide) is through the use of humor. Humor provides perspective on the human condition and on one's personality quirks in a healthy way. In many treatment centers, unfortunately, clowning and laughing are pathologized and off-limits. The episode in the movie *28 Days* effectively captures this tradition. After Gwen, the young woman sentenced to 28-day rehab, cracks a joke, a counselor asks her, "Do you always use humor to deflect things when you're uncomfortable?"

In recognition of the contribution it makes to group bonding and enjoyment, the typical AA meeting uses humor quite a bit. Here are a few examples collected by van Wormer over the years:

- A man attending an AA meeting said he was like Dr. Jekyll and Mr. Hyde when drunk. "Too bad you sobered up the wrong one," a member called out.

- A good Irish joke is "Last week I drank only twice, once for three days, once for four."
- There is even a group for paranoid people. It's called Paranoids Anonymous—PA. The only problem is if you call the number in the phonebook, they won't tell you where they are.

Exercises for Feeling Work in the Group

Consistent with the principles of strengths-based MET as described in this chapter are the following exercises. Such exercises can be used to provide structure for a therapy group. The focus of these activities is on allowing deep feelings to arise spontaneously in a warm, supportive group setting.

1. Art Therapy

Purpose: To reveal feelings that may not be expressed. May bring out perfectionism as a secondary function. Have clients draw their world during the time before they came to treatment, during treatment, and after treatment. Clients are told they can draw stick-people—no need for talent. This exercise, seriously undertaken, gives an indication of future hopes and fears. Those who, because of lack of confidence or anxiety, resist this exercise can have someone else draw what they describe in words.

2. Turning Points

Purpose: To promote critical thinking about one's life and reinforce change from a life of crime. Have participants as a homework assignment write about or prepare to tell about a turning point in their lives. At the next session, they will share their revelations.

3. Faces

Purpose: to elicit discussion of feelings. Use a sheet of faces with diverse expressions on them. Simple cartoon faces, including duck faces, are effective. This exercise works with nonreaders and equally well with men and women. The following instructions are given: "Choose the face that shows how you feel today and also one that shows how you felt earlier in the week. Each of you will share your selection with the group."

4. Grief and Loss

Purpose: To reveal underlying feelings of grief and guilt over loss. On a sheet of paper have clients:

    a.   Identify a significant loss. (This can be a person, a job, or some other loss.)

    b.   Describe the support you have received for the loss and what you have learned from this experience.

5. Quiz Cards

Purpose: To share in the group; to elicit a wide range of responses. This exercise is a continuation of the card game described in an earlier group exercise. These questions call for deeper-level responses.

Examples:

When I think of my mother _____

When I remember my father _____

Eating, spending money, cocaine, heroin, etc. was for me _____
Sobriety is _____
As a child, I was lucky I had _____
Love is _____
I feel proud of myself for _____

6. Dream analysis

Purpose: To help clients get in touch with a part of themselves they may have little awareness of. Give an ongoing homework assignment for participants to record their dreams on paper immediately after they have them. Then have those who can remember them share their dreams in the group as members look for meanings. Themes to look for are fears, anxieties, anger, forgiveness, attempts to communicate with loved ones, sobriety issues, and return of repressed memories. This often-untapped resource of recalling dream content can speak to group members, often in unexpected ways. Dream content can provide counselor and group members with clues about the individual's readiness to make changes. (Native Americans are often very skilled at remembering and learning from their dreams.)

7. Assertiveness

Purpose: Clients in treatment, when asked to set a goal for themselves, often say they would like to be more assertive or to work on assertiveness. Assertiveness training is geared toward persons who come across as aggressive when they do not intend to do so and persons who need to learn to speak up for themselves so as to get their interests met. Assertive behavior involves expressing preferences without undue anxiety in a manner that will be well received by others. Alternatives to aggressive reactions include calming self-talk, making polite requests, and reframing situations so that they do not overwhelm the individual (Gambrill, 1997).

SUMMARY AND CONCLUSION

In vulnerable individuals, influences by the mass media and corporate marketing create situations ripe for problems, problems with overeating or self-starvation, buying products never used or needed, games turned into nightmares. In this chapter, as in others, we looked at the biological, psychological, and social factors related to the addictions in question—eating disorders and gambling, shopping, sex, and Internet addiction, among others. Research using new brain imaging techniques indicates that gambling may share the same addictive process and have similar effects as those produced by psychoactive drugs. New medications are currently being developed to target the dopamine and serotonin levels in the brain, hopefully to quell the addictive urges thereby.

We chose this chapter as one to present a focus that is psychologically based—the theory and therapy of cognitions. Cognitively based therapy has been found to be very effective in helping people cope with their problems and stresses and, somewhat remarkably, if the reports from studies on obsessive-compulsive disorder are accurate, to promote recovery of the brain as well. Although usually geared toward thinking/feeling patterns related to the disorder

at hand, cognitive therapy is also suitable for helping clients deal with past issues. From the vantage point of today, clients can begin to view themselves as
survivors rather than as victims of their lives. From a strengths perspective, a
counselor can help clients reframe their life stories to identify strengths and survival skills that were all but taken for granted until then. In so doing, they might
let go of some of the anger they have felt for family members as well.

Speaking of stories, in this chapter we have heard from a self-starved ballerina; a bulimic student whose desperate practices landed her in the hospital;
an overweight Irishman who gave OA and later AA a try; and a youth counselor who unwittingly got in "over his head" with compulsive betting. What
these narrators all had in common, apart from their addictive behavior, was
that they eventually got the help they needed for a new start in life. Some of the
techniques they might have learned in treatment were presented here—stress
management, anger management, and ways to deal with powerful feelings and
somehow get beyond them. In the next chapter, we will see how many of these
same interventions can be adapted to serve the needs of clients who are dually
diagnosed, in other words, who are mentally ill and have serious substance misuse problems as well.

References

American Psychiatric Association (APA). (2000). *Diagnostic and statistical manual of
mental disorders* (text revision). Washington, DC: Author.

Andersen, A. E. (1999). Gender-related aspects of eating disorders: A guide to practice.
Journal of Gender-Specific Medicine 2(1), 47–54.

Anderson, J. (1994, July 15). Shop till you drop. *Chicago Tribune,* 15.

Anorexia, bulimia, found more dangerous in men. (2000, June 7). *Chicago Tribune,*
evening update, 7.

Arizona Problem Gambling Council. (2000). Available online at www.azccg.org

Beaucar, K. O. (1999, October). When games turn into nightmares. *NASW News,* 3.

Beck, A. (1991). Cognitive therapy: A 30-year retrospective. *American Psychologist*
46(4), 368–375.

Berg, I., & Miller, S. (1992). *Working with the problem drinker: A solution-focused approach.* New York: Norton.

Black, D. W., Repertinger, S., Gaffney, G. R., & Gabel, J. (1998). Family history and
psychiatric comorbidity in persons with compulsive buying. *American Journal of
Psychiatry 155,* 960–963.

Blanco, C., Ibanez, A., Saiz-Ruiz, J., Blanco-Jerez, C., & Nunes, E. (2000). Epidemiology, pathophysiology and treatment of pathological gambling. *CNS Drugs, 13*(6),
397–407.

Blaszczynski, A. (2000, March). Pathways to pathological gambling: Identifying typolo-
gies. *E-Gambling: The Electronic Journal of Gambling Issues,* 1. Online address:
www.camh.net/egambling/issue1/feature

Blowing off steam may not be such a good idea, a new study suggests. (1999, March 26).
Waterloo–Cedar Falls Courier, C5.

Claude-Pierre, P. (1997). *The secret language of eating disorders.* New York: Times
Books.

Cohen, W. (1999, June 14). Don't bet on gambling reform anytime soon. *U.S. News &
World Report,* 26.

Davis, D. (2000). *Women who are taking their lives back from compulsive gambling.* Online survey at sswhs.ewu.edu/gambling

Davis, D. (2002). Queen of diamonds: Women and compulsive gambling. In S. L. Straussner & S. Brown (Eds.), *The handbook of women's addictions treatment: Theory and practice.* New York: Jossey Bass.

Davison, K. K., & Birch, L. L. (2001). Weight status, parent reaction, and self-concept in five-year-old girls. *Pediatrics 107*(1), 46–53.

Delfabbro, P., & Winefield, A. (2000). Predictors of irrational thinking in regular slot machine gamblers. *Journal of Psychology, 134*(2), 117–128.

Dove, J. (1995). *Facts about anorexia.* U.S. Department of Health and Human Services. Available online at mentalhelp.net/factsfam/anorexia.htm

Eating disorders start in brain. (2001, April 9). *USA Today,* 4D.

Ellis, A., McInerney, J. F., DiGiuseppe, R., & Yeager, R. J. (1989). *Rational-emotive therapy with alcoholics and substance abusers.* New York: Pergamon Press.

Frankenfield, G. (1999, December 21). Could popping a pill help those who shop 'til they drop? *Lycos Health.* Available online at www.WebMD.lycos.com

Gamblers Anonymous (GA). (1999). *Sharing recovery through Gamblers Anonymous.* Los Angeles: Author.

Gamblers Anonymous (GA). (2000). *Gamblers Anonymous: A New Beginning* (4th ed.). Los Angeles: Author.

Gambrill, E. (1997). *Social work practice: A critical thinker's guide.* New York: Oxford University Press.

Gold, M. S., Johnson, C. R., & Stennie, K. (1997). Eating disorders. In J. H. Lowinson, P. Ruiz, R. B. Millman, & J. G. Langrod (Eds.), *Substance abuse: A comprehensive textbook* (pp. 319–330). Baltimore: Williams & Wilkins.

Goodman, A. (1997). Sexual addiction. In J. H. Lowinson, P. Ruiz, R. B. Millman, & J. G. Langrod (Eds.), *Substance abuse: A comprehensive textbook* (3rd ed)., pp. 340–354. Baltimore: Williams & Wilkins.

Griffiths, M. (1994). The role of cognitive bias and skill in fruit machine gambling. *British Journal of Psychology, 85,* 351–369.

Halmi, K. A. (1998). A 24-year-old woman with anorexia nervosa. *Journal of the American Medical Association 279*(24), 1992–1999.

Hershey, R. D. (1999, May 21). Workers ignore jobs to trade stocks on Net. *Lexington Herald-Leader,* A11.

Hornbacher, M. (1998). *Wasted: A memoir of anorexia and bulimia.* New York: Harper Flamingo.

Hyatt, R. (1997, November). *USA Today* (magazine), 66–68.

Information for professionals. (undated). Debtors anonymous to work with you. Available online at www.debtorsanonymous.org/professional.html

Kalb, C. (1998, November 9). An armful of agony. *Newsweek,* 82.

Kirkland, G. (1986). *Dancing on my grave.* New York: Jove Books.

Krahn, D. D. (1991). The relationship of eating disorders and substance abuse. *Journal of Substance Abuse, 3,* 239–253.

Kramer, P. D. (1993). *Listening to Prozac.* New York: Viking.

Kuba, S. A., & Hanchey, S. G. (1991). Reclaiming women's bodies: A feminist perspective on eating disorders. In N. VandenBergh (Ed.), *Feminist perspectives on addiction* (125–138). New York: Springer.

LairRobinson, R. (1997). Men and gambling. In S. L. Straussner & E. Zelvin (Eds.), *Gender and addictions: Men and women in treatment* (pp. 471–492). Northvale, NJ: Jason Aronson.

Lesieur, H. (1987). The female pathological gambler. In W. R. Eadington (Ed.), *Gambling research: Proceedings of the Seventh International Conference on Gambling and Risk Taking* (pp. 230–258). Bureau of Business and Economic Research, University of Nevada, Reno.

Levin, J. D. (1998). *The Clinton syndrome: The president and the self-destructive nature of sexual addiction.* New York: Random House.

Lobet, I. (2000, September 18). Shopaholics climb on the wagon. *U.S. News & World Report,* 60.

Many bulimic women were abused as kids, study says. (1995, July 10). *Toronto Globe and Mail,* 6.

Maté, G. (1999). *Scattered: How attention deficit disorder originates and what you can do about it.* New York: Plume.

McCourt, M. (2000). *Singing my him song.* New York: HarperCollins.

McGilley, B. M., & Pryor, T. L. (1998). Assessment and treatment of bulimia nervosa. *American Family Physician 57*(11), 2743–2751.

McQuaide, S., & Ehrenreich, J. H. (1997, March/April). Assessing client strengths. *Families in Society,* 201–212.

Messina, G. (1999, December 23). *Hoarding to excess.* Available online at www .abcnews.go.com/onair/2020

Miller, W. R., & Rollnick, S. (1991). *Motivating interviewing: Preparing people to change addictive behavior.* New York: Guilford Press.

National Gambling Impact Study Commission. (1999, June 18). *Report of the Commission.* Washington, DC: Government Printing Office. Online at www.ngisc.gov/reports/fullrpt.html

National Institute of Mental Health (NIMH). (1997). *Eating disorders.* Available online at www.nimh.nih.gov/publicat/eatdis.htm

National Research Council. (1999, April 1). *Report of the Commission: Pathological gambling: A critical review.* Available online at www.ngisc.gov/reports/fullrpt.html

Nichols, M. (1998, February 9). Is sex an addiction? *Maclean's,* 80.

O'Connor, M. (2001, May 24). Judge buys shopaholic defense in embezzling. Available online at www.chicagotribune.com

O'Leary, S. (2000, November 23). *Shopping addiction: Out-of-control spending can ruin lives and families.* Available online at healthsurfing.com/health/2000/11/23/?p=1

Orzack, M. H. (1999, January). Computer addiction: Is it real or virtual? *The Harvard Mental Health Letter 15*(7), 1–8.

Overeaters Anonymous. (1996). *What Is OA?* Available online at www.oaeastbay.org/What.html

Palmer, J., Vacc, N., & Epstein, J. (1998). Adult inpatient alcoholics: Physical exercise as a treatment intervention. *Journal of Studies on Alcohol, 49,* 418–421.

Parker, M. (1998, April 8). Addiction to sex. *Waterloo–Cedar Falls Courier,* C5.

Pavalko, R. M. (1999). Problem gambling. *National Forum, 79*(4), pp. 28–34.

Persistent perfectionists. (1996, May/June). *Psychology Today, 29*(3), 11.

Potera, C. (1998, March/April). Trapped in the Web. *Psychology Today,* 66–72.

Project MATCH Research Group. (1997). Matching alcoholism treatments to client heterogeneity: Project MATCH posttreatment drinking outcomes. *Journal of Studies on Alcohol 58,* 7–29.

Rapp, C. A. (1998). *The strengths model: Case management with people suffering from severe and persistent mental illness.* New York: Oxford University Press.

Saleebey, D. (2002). Introduction: Power in the people. In D. Saleebey (Ed.), *The strengths perspective in social work practice* (4th ed.). Boston: Allyn & Bacon.

Samenow, S. E. (1984). *Inside the criminal mind.* New York: Times Books.

Schwartz, J. M. (1996). *Brain lock: Free yourself from obsessive-compulsive behaviors.* New York: Regan Books.

Scientists find link between dopamine and obesity. (2001). News Release. Available online at www.bnl.fov/bnlweb/pubaf/pr/bnlpr020101.htm

Screening for pathological gambling. (2000, June). *Beyond the Odds.* Online at www.miph.org/bto/jun00/screen.html

Segall, R. (2001, March/April). Never too skinny. *Psychology Today,* 22.

Sheafor, B., Horejsi, C., & Horejsi, G. (1997). *Techniques and guidelines for social work practice.* Boston: Allyn & Bacon.

Smith, E. (1997, November 24). Bodybuilders' fret "flip side" of anorexia. *USA Today,* 1A.

Stevens-Smith, P., & Smith, R. L. (1998). *Substance abuse counseling: Theory and practice.* Upper Saddle River, NJ: Prentice Hall.

Sweeting, P. (2000, July). The invisible addiction. *Issues of Substance, 4,* 10, 11.

Talan, J. (1998, July/August). Cardiac consciousness-raising. *Psychology Today,* 25–35.

Texas Council on Problem and Compulsive Gambling. (2000, July 7). E-update on problem gambling new. *Women and Problem Gambling, 1*(23), 1–3.

Turner, N. (2000, August). Randomness, does it matter? *E-Gambling: Electronic Journal of Gambling Issues, 2.* Centre for Addiction and Mental Health. Online at www.camh.net/gambling/issue2/research

Twins share alcohol preferences. (2000, November 13). Available online at www.join-together.org

Vandereycken, W. (1990). The addiction model in eating disorders. *International Journal of Eating Disorders 9*(1), 95–101.

van Wormer, K. (1995). *Alcoholism treatment: A social work perspective.* Belmont, CA: Wadsworth.

van Wormer, K. (2001). *Counseling female offenders and victims: A strengths-restorative approach.* New York: Springer.

van Wormer, K., & Askew, E. (1997). Substance-abusing women and eating disorders. In S. L. Straussner & E. Zelvin (Eds.), *Gender and addictions: Men and women in treatment* (pp. 243–262). Northvale, NJ: Aronson.

Vastag, B. (2001). What's the connection? No easy answers for people with eating disorders and drug abuse. *Journal of the American Medical Association, 285*(8), 1006–1008.

Volberg, R. (1993, April 23). *Gambling and problem gambling among Native Americans in North Dakota.* Report to the North Dakota Department of Human Services, Division of Mental Health.

Volpicelli, J., & Szalavitz, M. (2000). *Recovery options: The complete guide.* New York: Wiley.

Watkins, T., Lewellen, A., & Barrett, M. C. (2001). *Dual diagnosis: An integrated approach to treatment.* Thousand Oaks, CA: Sage.

Wen, P. (2001, May 24). An addictive thrill. *Boston Globe,* A1, A21.

Wooley, S. C. (1994). Sexual abuse and eating disorders: The concealed debate. In P. Fallon, M. A. Katzman, & S. C. Wooley (Eds.), *Feminist perspectives on eating disorders* (pp. 171–211). New York: Guilford.

Yang, D. J. (2000, January 17). Craving your next Web fix. *U.S. News & World Report,* 41.

Yochelson, S., & Samenow, S. (1976). *The criminal personality* (Vol. 1). New York: Jason Aronson.

Young, K. S. (1998). Caught in the Net: How to recognize the signs of Internet addiction. New York: Wiley.

I was much too far out all my life
And not waving but drowning.
—STEVIE SMITH (SMITH, 1983, P. 303)

SUBSTANCE MISUSE WITH A COEXISTING DISORDER OR DISABILITY

CHAPTER 8

INTRODUCTION

Mental illness is terrifying when it spirals out of control. Repeated alcohol or drug misuse often brings misery, regret, and dire consequences. When the two are combined, the result can be a double whammy of troubles for the person experiencing it. This applies to a person who also has a developmental, physical, or cognitive disability or any other major challenge to living life and uses alcohol and drugs in a way that hurts the individual. One such person is Eddie, mentally ill with an alcohol or other drug (AOD) disorder, who was interviewed for the Washington, D.C., Dual Diagnosis Project (Quimby, 1995, p. 266): "All I do is smoke and do drugs. I be drinking and drugging. I hope someone can help me. My family don't help me at all. They don't want to help me when I got problems. And I bother them for help."

Getting help when you have multiple needs, like Eddie, has not been easy. Professional treatment providers and educators in the mental health, disability, and substance misuse field have acted as if a person could be divided up into just one area of trouble at a time. Competition around traditionally separate national and state funding streams, turf battles over which disorder is "primary," different attitudes toward treatment methods, and educational deficits for professionals in each field have contributed to this unhelpful stance. In the recent past (and even today), a person who is diagnosed both bipolar and alcoholic and still drinking could be refused treatment at a mental health facility because she wasn't abstinent and at the same time refused treatment at a substance abuse treatment center because of her mental health

247

symptoms or unless she gave up her antidepressant medication. As one treatment provider put it, "All of us treat dually diagnosed patients, but few of us provide dual diagnosis treatment" (Shulman, 1995, p. 33).

Similarly, persons with physical disabilities or cognitive impairments have generally not been served well by existing treatment and support systems. For example, professionals and families in these fields have tended to overlook substance misuse problems; treatment facilities and self-help groups are not accessible for those with mobility problems; written and other visual materials are designed for people who see and don't have brain trauma or learning needs; and interpreters for the deaf are seldom employed.

Overwhelming evidence documented that the "hardening of the categories" between mental health, disabilities, and substance abuse was not working. Most research studies indicated that parallel or sequential treatment approaches for dual disorders had annual rates of stable remission of less than 5%. Traditional approaches protected program boundaries but were "invariably doomed to failure"(Meuser, Drake, & Noordsy, 1998, p. 131). Something had to give— and did. Reforms began developing in the mid-1980s, catalyzed by 13 federally funded demonstration projects across the country in 1987. The implications from these projects, other pilot programs, and recent research findings have stimulated substantial and dramatic changes in traditional treatment practices. In addition, concurrent developments of the consumer and advocacy movement in the mental health field and the independent living movement in the disability field have supported the direction of these changes. Some people refer to this as a movement toward a "nonpunitive helping stance."

One of the major ideological conflicts around which problem was "primary" receded from view when it became possible to treat clients simultaneously with an "integrated" approach for all their needs. The introduction of harm reduction techniques and motivational interviewing has been helpful in engaging people who were alienated by traditional assessment and treatment strategies. Abstinence is now considered a more realistic long-term goal for many, instead of being a rigid requirement for receiving treatment. Categories variously named *dual diagnosis, coexisting disorders, persons with mental illness and chemical abuse or addiction* (MICAA, indicating an Axis I mental disorder), or *persons with chemical abuse and mental illness* (CAMI, indicating an Axis II personality disorder) were created to help organize new treatment approaches. Funding streams for research and pilot programs are now available. New approaches that emphasize self-determination, client strengths, and harm reduction have shown promising results.

This chapter will present the new body of knowledge that has been developed in the last 15 years to address the needs of persons with coexisting problems. For purposes of clarity, the chapter is divided into three sections: The first section presents a brief summary of the prevalence, characteristics, and typical concerns that a person with multiple problems may present. Then, following a description of the basic mental disorders, we discuss treatment practices for persons who have substance misuse and mental health problems. Next we address working with persons who have substance misuse and developmental, cognitive, or physical disabilities. Throughout this chapter we discuss treatment approaches and programs that show promising results and provide practical tips for working with several types of coexisting disorders.

SUBSTANCE MISUSE AND MENTAL DISORDERS

Prevalence and Characteristics

Prevalence rates depend on what is included in the "mental disorders" category. The definition is far from simple. On the one hand, based on brain imaging and finding new genes, some researchers are speculating that we are all mentally ill to some degree ("Is Everybody Crazy?" 1998). If this is true, all persons with substance misuse would be in the category of dual diagnosis. At least some clinicians in the substance abuse treatment field would agree that it is rare to uncover a normal, well-adjusted average person hiding under a serious addiction, because the substance misuse in and of itself takes a heavy psychological and emotional toll (Denning, 2000).

On the other hand, people with severe mental illness seem to have a heightened sensitivity to the effects of alcohol or psychoactive drugs. Just a small amount can be their undoing, precipitating hospitalization or other major living problems. Very few persons who are severely mentally ill (less than 5%, according to Drake & Wallach, 1993) can even drink alcohol or use drugs at a moderate level without consequences. Consequently, most of these people (about 50%) choose abstinence, and those who do use are unlikely to sustain heavy use (Drake & Meuser, 2000). In the case of severe mental illness, any use at all may be considered enough to put a person in the category of "coexisting disorder."

For persons clinically diagnosed with a severe mental illness, coexisting substance misuse is at least more common than not, especially if they are young, male, single, less educated, and have a history of substance misuse or conduct disorder or if they are homeless, in jail, or present to an emergency room (Drake & Meuser, 2000). For example, the Epidemiologic Catchment Area study reports a lifetime substance misuse in the general population of 17%, compared with 48% for persons with schizophrenia, 56% for persons with bipolar disorder, and 22% for persons with lifetime mental disorders (Regier et al., 1990). The National Comorbidity Survey found that 51% of persons with a lifetime addictive disorder also have a lifetime mental disorder (Kessler, Nelson, & McGonagle, 1996). About 45% of the people who smoke cigarettes have a diagnosable mental illness ("Mentally Ill," 2000).

Alcohol, cannabis, and cocaine, in that order, are the most commonly used substances by persons with severe mental illness (Lehman, Myers, Dixon, & Johnson, 1996; Mowbray, Ribisl, Solomon, Luke, & Kewson, 1997). In a recent sample of 497 persons diagnosed with either schizophrenia or schizoaffective disorder, 79% had an alcohol use disorder, 46% a cocaine use disorder, 32% a marijuana use disorder, and 8% an opiate use disorder (Ziedonis &

Trudeau, 1997). Persons with coexisting disorders appear to use alcohol and other drugs for the same reasons persons without coexisting disorders use substances, i.e., loneliness, anxiety, boredom, and insomnia (Meuser, Drake, & Wallach, 1998). This finding, from an extensive review of the research, contradicts the popular notion that persons with mental illness use alcohol and other substances to "self-medicate" their symptoms or the side effects of their medication.

Persons who are dually diagnosed with substance misuse and mental disorders can expect more vulnerability than just plain substance misusers, in a variety of ways. They are more likely to experience frequent hospitalizations, relapse, depression and suicide, severe housing and financial problems, homelessness, high rates of sexually transmitted diseases, violence, incarceration, and legal problems. At the same time, they are less likely to comply with their medication regimen (Drake & Meuser, 2000), and medication may be less effective (for example, nicotine decreases the potency of standard antipsychotic medication; Goff, Henderson, & Amico, 1992).

The problems of mental illness and substance misuse are particularly severe among poor, urban individuals. A homeless, dually diagnosed woman interviewed in the Washington, D.C., Dual Diagnosis Project describes her situation as follows: "Sometimes I do think I'm going to get murdered. I was raped and stuck up before. . . . I was just spending money on drugs. . . . People—friends, relatives and mental health staff—just did me in. They did enough torture to put a butcher knife to me and throw me off the bridge" (Quimby, 1995, p. 266).

All too frequently, these extremely vulnerable persons are still shuttled back and forth between the mental health system and the alcohol/drug system and receive neither sequential nor parallel treatment, or they are excluded altogether from one or the other system because of their coexisting disorder.

THE PERILS OF DIFFERENTIAL DIAGNOSIS

In the best of all worlds, clinicians and treatment providers would be able to determine with some certainty whether the specific mental illness is independent of or is dependent on the substance abuse, and they could plan treatment accordingly (see Case Study 3). For example, anxiety symptoms (worry, apprehensive expectations, tension, sweating, hyperarousal, insomnia, irritability, poor concentration) are the most common psychiatric symptoms manifested in substance misusers (Center for Substance Abuse Treatment [CSAT], 1994, p. 51). However, most of these anxiety symptoms are gone within a few days or weeks of abstinence, in which case little or no treatment is required. If mild to debilitating anxiety continues long after abstinence, it makes sense to assess the person for a coexisting anxiety disorder that may require specific medication and treatment intervention.

Unfortunately, many real-world problems interfere with this neat and tidy diagnostic regime. For example, numerous studies have found that the majority of mentally ill persons do not start out ready and motivated for abstinence-based treatment (Mercer-McFadden, Drake, Brown, & Fox, 1997); consequently a period of abstinence to tease out whether the anxiety is dependent on the substance use or is independent of the substance abuse frequently does not occur right away, and sometimes it never occurs. Taking a detailed history from the person to determine the presence of a mental illness prior to substance misuse may not be an option if the person is confused, depressed, or agitated in some way. Some people start drinking or using drugs at an age earlier than when mental illnesses become apparent. Persons who are homeless are unlikely to have reliable family members available to elaborate on their history. Careful attention to prior inpatient and outpatient records is a good strategy, but is only viable when those records can be found and made available in a timely manner.

Other problems in diagnosis occur because AOD use can cause symptoms that mimic almost every psychiatric problem, especially during acute intoxication or withdrawal. For example, acute intoxication from a stimulant type of drug can cause highly agitated states or paranoid psychosis. A person withdrawing from stimulants may become seriously depressed, with suicidal thoughts. A further complication is that AOD use can help hide some psychiatric symptoms and disorders.

Sometimes the historical division between treatment systems contributes to an underdiagnosing of coexisting disorders. For years, psychiatric symptoms were overlooked, unrecognized, or misunderstood as "acting-out behavior" in substance abuse treatment. Similarly, mental health staff explained away substance use or misuse as "self-medication" or as normal behavior. If a mental health or substance abuse problem was diagnosed, it frequently resulted in the ejection of the person from the system.

Because of the problems in making an accurate differential diagnosis in the short run, Denning (2000, p. 167) advocates working without a diagnosis or with a partial diagnosis "with a general spirit of courage and risk taking on the part of clinicians." She cites the wasted time in arguing about a correct diagnosis, the need for constant reassessment, and the growing knowledge base in pharmacology and treatment strategies as good reasons to carry on working with a person even though a differential diagnosis may not be readily apparent. Assessment in this framework really becomes part of ongoing treatment. Specific strategies will be discussed later in the section on Integrated (Seamless) Treatment Practices.

Prescribing psychiatric medication can be another challenge connected to diagnosis, especially if the medications are psychoactive or potentially addictive. Addiction treatment staff historically avoided the use of any medication. This made sense given the number of patients they saw addicted to prescription drugs and the large number of primary care physicians that were prescribing antianxiety medications, many of which (such as the benzodiazepines) were psychoactive and could be addictive. However, this prohibition has changed as treatment providers have become trained in the appropriate use of non-addicting psychiatric medications and come to understand that withholding psychiatric medication can increase relapse. For more information on medications commonly prescribed in mental health treatment and the effects these drugs may have on the recovery process of an individual who is also misusing alcohol or drugs, see the Center for Substance Abuse Treatment publication *Treatment Improvement Protocol (TIP)*, Series 9 (available at www.samhsa .gov/centers/clearinghouse/clearinghouses.html). Medication strategies are still in the process of being developed in this complex area; some of these will be discussed in a later section on new treatment practices.

DISORDERS AND DISABILITIES THAT COMMONLY COEXIST WITH SUBSTANCE MISUSE

This section describes mental disorders that coexist with substance misuse in many cases. The diagnostic labels are from the *DSM-IV-TR* (American Psychiatric Association [APA], 2000) and are provided as a means of communicating with other mental health professionals trained to use these categories.

Anxiety

Anxiety symptoms are experienced by everyone at some time in their lives— cold, clammy hands, tremulous voice, the shakes, panic, shortness of breath, increased heart rate, restlessness, or the almost relentless urge to move about. Anxiety is a normal response to danger. However, in persons with AOD disorders, anxiety and mood disorders are the most common psychiatric symptoms encountered. In recovery, anxiety can be the result of acute or prolonged abstinence syndromes, especially from alcohol, sedative depressant drugs, opiates, and long-term cocaine use. Anxiety is sometimes a direct result of ingesting psychoactive drugs, such as stimulants, marijuana, and hallucinogenic drugs. Most anxiety symptoms related to AOD misuse clear within 2 to 4 weeks. Anxiety is frequently combined with depression, and the combination puts the person at high suicide risk. When symptoms persist after 30 days of abstinence, the person should be should be assessed for an independent coexisting anxiety disorder that might interfere with recovery.

Pathological (Compulsive) Gambling

Prevalence rates for pathological gamblers are higher in populations in treatment for AOD disorders than in the general population, with estimates for pathological gambling at around 10 to 15%, with another 10% reporting problem gambling (Blume, 1997). According to the National Research Council (1999), substance use disorders are associated with both progression to problem gambling and subsequent pathological gambling. Not surprisingly, persons who are compulsive gamblers have a much higher chance of having coexisting substance use disorders over their lifetime, with estimates ranging from 25% to 63%. In a general population study in St. Louis, problem gamblers were three times more likely to meet criteria for depression, schizophrenia, alcoholism, and antisocial personality disorder than nongamblers.

Attempted suicide and suicide may be real threats. Various studies indicate that up to 75% of compulsive gamblers in treatment populations suffer from depression; 61% report suicidal ideation, and over 22% have made actual suicide attempts (Blaszczynski, 1995). According to the National Council on Problem Gambling, the suicide rate for pathological gamblers is higher than for any other addictive disorder (National Gambling Impact Study Commission, 1999). A short, user-friendly screen for gambling problems and, if positive, a suicide assessment are highly recommended (Davis, 2002).

Eating Disorders

This category covers binge eating, anorexia, and bulimia. There is a high co-occurrence of eating disorders and AOD addiction (up to 37%) (Gold, Johnson, & Stennie, 1997). Treatment centers report eating binges and starvation as relapse triggers. Food is also a powerful mood-altering substance on its own, and is sometimes used (by bingeing or starving) to enhance the euphoric effect of drugs (see chapter 7).

Mood Disorders

Mood disorders, which include major depression, dysthymia, mania, hypomania, bipolar disorders, and cyclothymia, are basically abnormal (pathological) highs and lows in mood. Since all psychoactive substances affect mood, it is not surprising that mood disorders, along with anxiety, are the most common psychiatric diagnoses for persons with an AOD disorder. Among persons with a coexisting AOD disorder, women, Native Americans, patients with HIV, patients on methadone, and the elderly are all at higher risk for depression. Manic symptoms can be induced by a variety of substances, such as stimulants, steroids, hallucinogens, and can also occur during withdrawal from alcohol. Depressive symptoms can result from acute or chronic drug use and can also be triggered by withdrawal. It is critical to assess whether the person is at imminent risk for suicide or a danger to themselves or others. Symptoms that persist after 30 days of abstinence or 30 days after acute intoxication should be assessed for an independent coexisting mood disorder that might mildly to severely interfere with the recovery process.

Personality Disorders

Personality disorders—such as borderline, dependent, antisocial, or narcissistic personality and passive-aggressive and obsessive-compulsive disorders—are described as rigid, maladaptive patterns of deeply ingrained behaviors and thoughts that cause great distress to the person as well as present challenges to the treatment counselor. Unfortunately, the diagnosis of a personality disorder has too often been the result of cultural, ethnic, or personal bias; for example, women are most often diagnosed with dependent, histrionic, or borderline personality disorders; men are most often diagnosed with antisocial personality disorders. Many persons with AOD disorders do not meet the criteria for antisocial personality once they become abstinent; the "antisocial" behaviors were part of their strategy for maintaining addiction. The CSAT (1994) says that it is helpful to conceptualize personality disorder behaviors as "survivor behaviors" because they have helped the person survive serious difficulties. Suicidal behavior or threats of other self-harm must be taken seriously and attended to promptly. Counseling strategies for personality disorders often involve working with (not against) the person to reach his or her own stated goals (provided they are legal) in small, concrete, measurable steps.

Psychotic Disorders

Persons who suffer from psychotic disorders (such as schizophrenia and schizo-affective and delusional disorders) typically experience periods when they cannot distinguish between information from the outside world and information from the inner world of the mind. This may cause problems in concentration or in their ability to relate to or tolerate others or paranoia. Drug and alcohol use and misuse are likely to occur. For example, the Epidemiologic Catchment Area study reports a lifetime substance misuse in the general population of 17%, compared with 48% for persons with schizophrenia. As noted earlier, treatment of persons with coexisting disorders requires a highly supportive, long-term commitment and integration of both substance abuse and mental health treatment strategies.

INTEGRATED (SEAMLESS) TREATMENT PRACTICES

A recent study from the Substance Abuse and Mental Health Services Administration (SAMHSA) (2001) provides a breakdown on treatment provisions in three states for individuals treated for mental health and substance misuse problems. Eleven percent of persons treated (in the data pool of clients treated for substance misuse and/or mental disorders) were diagnosed as having dual disorders. About half of these were treated under both the mental health and substance abuse agencies, with the remainder provided services almost exclusively under the mental health agency. The purpose of the study was to determine how to coordinate services in order to use resources to serve more individuals. Were services more completely integrated, the likelihood is that far larger numbers of individuals would receive diagnoses for dual and multiple problems.

One of the most important system changes for a person needing help with coexisting disorders is the development of the integrated treatment program. Integrated treatment (in contrast to sequential or parallel treatment) provides simultaneous treatment for the mental illness and the substance use disorder. The person no longer has to travel to two different locations to receive and try to reconcile two different messages. Although this may sound like mere common sense from today's vantage point, it required (and still requires in many parts of the country) massive system changes in order to become a treatment option.

Although this section focuses on integrated treatment programs, traditional treatment (parallel and sequential) programs can benefit from these as complementary to their programs. Many traditional treatment programs have already become less confrontational and more collaborative, and the mental health "consumer" movement has underscored the rights of the individual patient (Minkoff, 1996; Evans & Sullivan, 1990).

At the crux of integrated treatment is the designation of one clinician (supported by a treatment team that may include professionals such as physicians, probation officers, AOD and mental health specialists, self-help sponsors, and housing specialists) to provide a seamless and individualized menu of interventions for a specific person over a long period of time. This shift alone requires providers to:

- Acknowledge that their profession doesn't have all the answers.
- Find a home for the integrated program (outpatient mental health programs, separate hospital units, community agencies).
- Change admission criteria to include persons with dual diagnoses; implement serious cross-training of professional staff.
- Change the target population of the agency.
- Sort out funding streams, state regulations, and legal requirements.
- Create new procedures for confidentiality, data collection, and reimbursement.
- Participate with other providers in developing long-term structural mechanisms (coordinating bodies, letters of agreement, etc.) and planning that will improve the delivery of seamless services to persons with a dual diagnosis (see CSAT, 1994).

Is it worth it? As the result of integrated treatment practices, stable remission rates have gone up from 5% per year under the traditional system to 10 to 20% per year (Meuser, Drake, & Noordsy, 1998). Although this may still seem very low, it comes close to the same rate as persons with only substance use disorders. There are also other positive improvements that are associated with integrated treatment, such as more and better housing, decreased victimization, more satisfaction with life, decreased shame, open expression, increased socialization, learning, and insight (Drake, Yovetich, Bebout, Harris, & McHugo, 1997; Meuser, Drake, & Noordsy, 1998; Sciacca & Thompson, 1996).

Research findings and clinical experience with integrated treatment models suggest a new repertoire of treatment practices that providers and staff members may find challenging to their traditional stance. Not only is integration the responsibility of the clinician, not the client, but there are several core components of most integrated treatment programs that are different from historical treatment procedures (Meuser, Drake, & Noordsy, 1998; Mercer-McFadden et al., 1997; Drake & Meuser, 2000).

There are some new screening and assessment practices. Knowledge that between 25 and 35% of persons with a severe mental illness have had a substance use disorder during the past 6 months is good reason to screen for this problem. Unfortunately, screening for substance misuse still does not occur routinely in the mental health field, especially with woman who present with severe mental illness (Breakey, Calabrese, Rosenblatt, & Crum, 1998). In addition, many traditional screens are confusing, too long, or irrelevant with persons with severe mental illness. However, recent evaluations of traditional screenings for persons with mental disorders have given some guidance to their use, and a new instrument has been created specifically to detect substance misuse in this population.

The 18-item screen called the Dartmouth Assessment of Lifestyle Instrument (DALI) has recently been constructed, taking items that fit for persons with mental illness from several traditional instruments (Rosenberg et al., 1998). Initial findings suggest that the DALI functioned significantly better than traditional instruments such as the TWEAK, T-ACE, MAST, and CAGE for detecting alcohol, cannabis, and cocaine use (which are the most common substances used among persons with severe mental illness). It is short and easy to use and can be obtained easily (and free) directly from the authors at the New Hampshire-Dartmouth Psychiatric Research Center Web site (www.dartmouth .edu/dms/psychrc/).

The Alcohol Use Disorders Identification Test (AUDIT) has been tested in Australia for use with people diagnosed with schizophrenia, and was found to have high sensitivity (87%) and specificity (90%) in detecting diagnosed alcohol disorders (Dawe, Seinen, & Kavanagh, 1999). The AUDIT is also readily available (Saunders, Aasland, Babor, De La Fuente, & Grant, 1993) and short (10 questions), can be self-administered, and requires only a seventh-grade reading level, and the questions do not refer to symptoms that could be confused with symptoms of schizophrenia. Another recent investigation found that the CAGE (see chapter 5) had reasonably high sensitivity (76%) for detecting lifetime prevalence of alcohol use disorder in persons with serious mental illness (Breakey et al., 1998). Either of these instruments will help mental health clinicians identify the possibility of a coexisting disorder.

If the obvious problem is substance misuse, it may be necessary to screen for a mental disorder. A brief mental status exam and the history of psychiatric medications/treatment can be helpful in screening for coexisting disorders. However, this can occur only when the person has been detoxified from the substances he or she was using. Safety is the first concern if the patients appear in a toxic or dangerous withdrawal state or if their behavior is suicidal, violent, impulsive, or psychotic. In this case, a rapid response will be required, such as inpatient detoxification or a trip to the nearest emergency room.

Deeper assessment begins after a positive screen and continues throughout the professional relationship. A goal of integrated treatment is that the person him- or herself become adept at assessing changes in mood, the effects of changing circumstances or relationships, and the interactive effects of alcohol or drugs on their mental health status and well-being. The integrative model provides for one primary clinician or case manager to work consistently with the individual. This provides many opportunities for both client and clinician to observe how the person's life is developing. A helpful stance to practice is that of a "curious anthropologist" delving into details and finding meanings that matter to the client.

The goal over time is an ongoing multidisciplinary assessment that includes the client's perspective. If other disciplines are represented on the team, their specialty areas would be also included. Basic areas of inquiry that are consistent with harm reduction and motivation enhancement practices (Denning, 2000; Drake & Meuser, 2000) include finding out what stage of change the person is in, how much insight the person has about the harms and benefits of her or his use of alcohol/drugs, and what the personal strengths and resources are (past exceptions to the present troubles, important persons or family that care about the person, survival strategies, and capacities for development) that may be helpful.

In addition to finding out the details about the person's use of alcohol and drugs (such as type, frequency, amount, patterns, expectancies related to use, positive and negative results), it is just as important to find out the details of any prescribed psychiatric medications, both past and present, and the person's particular patterns in taking the medication. This can lead to a discussion of any other attempts the person has made to help him- or herself or alleviate symptoms, such as professional treatment, self-help group participation, and religious or cultural practices. What helped and what didn't?

Eventually, it will be important to elicit personal goals in the area of use of alcohol and drugs, types of supports, resources, and treatments desired to attain this goal, and personal goals in the areas of social relationships, fun, recreational activities, hobbies, work and education, financial or legal circumstances, and spiritual, religious, or cultural practices.

The continuous development of these areas of inquiry over time will help the clinician focus on finding direction that is meaningful to the person with a coexisting disorder, on validating the person's unique experience, and on mutually discovering strengths that can be brought to bear on the situation at hand.

CASE MANAGEMENT TEAMS

Case management in the integrated treatment model does not mean that a professional expert or team of experts provides services to a "case." Case management in this approach is closer to the independent living model in disability and the consumer movement in mental health, where it is recognized that consumers have the strength and right to manage their own lives (Mackelprang and Salsgiver, 1999). Consequently, although individual team members may be expert in their respective fields, they have also become experts at collaboration with each other, and most importantly with the person they are trying to help. The purpose of the collaborative case management approach is to offer a menu of supports, services, and opportunities that are in tune with the person's direction rather than prescribing these services for the "case."

The Santa Barbara, California, Regional Health Authority (SBRHA) recently identified the typical needs of a woman with coexisting disorders on Temporary Assistance for Needy Families (TANF). These include mental health and substance abuse treatment, parenting education, child care, job-skills training, assistance in going back to school, legal aid, help with domestic violence, and transportation to appointments (Bearman, Claydon, Kincheloe, & Lodise, 1997). Although they don't mention it, housing is also a common need. When faced with a list of needs like this, many professionals have been trained to "fill up the hole" with referral after referral. Sometimes coercion is used to require the person to participate in what the case manager has decided is in their best interest, such as withholding income or other financial support. These practices reinforce the oppressive notion that a person with coexisting disorders cannot make decisions in his or her own best interest.

A staff member may have intense emotional reactions and disagreements about how to be an effective consultant to the person, particularly when there is a variety of unmet needs in the eyes of the professional. Clinicians who are used to working on an appointment schedule using a specific therapeutic process will find themselves needing to be more flexible in their ways of helping (Denning, 2000). For example, tackling a housing problem is more likely to come before therapy or insight or abstinence. Staff needs time to readjust and redefine their roles in an integrative treatment team. It takes about one year of training to solidify a team (Drake & Meuser, 2000), and it may take several years of work to make the necessary system changes (Evans & Sullivan, 1990). The good news is that it is demonstratively worth the effort. Persons with coexisting disorders can move from being "no one's clients" to becoming "everyone's clients" (Sciacca & Thompson, 1996) and hopefully move from being perceived as a "client" to being viewed as an individual, citizen, and/or consumer.

Creative Engagement Practices

According to the description of the new SBRHA program for dually diagnosed women on TANF, the designated intensive case manager will be the "single, human point of reference to coordinate care and assure participation" (Bearman et al., 1997, p. 364). In reality, "assuring participation" is a bit like ensuring abstinence—it's a good long-term goal. Because persons with coexisting disorders often present with disorganization, confusion, and a past history of unhelpful professional contacts and may live in an environment oppressed by poverty, violence, and ongoing substance misuse, it is understandably difficult for them to engage and remain active in a treatment process. Research on integrated treatment suggests it can be done. In fact, most persons with a dual diagnosis can be engaged in treatment for extended periods of time (beyond a year) (Meuser, Drake, & Noordsy, 1998). New ideas about stages of treatment and the role of the clinician in the engagement process have been critical in making this possible.

Many of the successful integrated treatment programs embrace a stages-of-treatment (or stage-wise treatment) model that involves matching a person's current motivational state to a particular stage (Brady et al., 1996; Mercer-McFadden et al., 1997). This concept builds on the model of five stages of change of Prochaska and DiClemente (1992), which includes precontemplation, contemplation, preparation, action, and maintenance (and sometimes a sixth stage, relapse) and suggests different intervention strategies for each stage (see chapter 3). For example, before a person can jump into active change or treatment there are usually some steps needed to enhance readiness to change. It is no longer necessary to label people "resistant" or "in denial" because they haven't done what we, the clinicians, want them to do when we want them to do it. Instead, the role of the clinician becomes one of understanding and respecting where people are in the cycle of change, and offering appropriate strategies for that stage.

The precontemplation stage (when a person doesn't even recognize the need to change) roughly translates to what is called the "engagement" phase of integrated treatment. The goal of engagement from a clinician's standpoint is to develop a therapeutic alliance with the person that is built on trust, not to attend to substance misuse. Without a trusting relationship, it is difficult to further any change in behavior other than temporary compliance. A key philosophy is to emphasize "respect for the person and empathy with their experience, and contrasts with a tendency of many treatment providers to blame them for a perceived failure to make progress" (Kavanagh et al., 1998, p. 142). Needless to say, it is a stretch for many traditionally trained substance abuse counselors to adopt this approach, but with training, team support, and the experience of more long-term success, substance abuse counselors are doing this all over the country.

Creative strategies for promoting engagement typically involve outreach, some kind of concrete practical assistance, crisis intervention services, support in building a wider arena of social networks, and efforts to stabilize the psychiatric symptoms (Meuser, Drake, & Noordsy, 1998). Outreach is especially important with persons who are homeless (see Case Study 2). Other examples of engagement strategies used in integrated programs include:

- Being available in an area populated by people who are homeless and meeting with them at a local diner, not a clinic; providing for basic needs such as clothes, showers, and food (Osher & Dixon, 1996)
- Helping people learn how to shop, clean apartments, and do laundry (Rosencheck et al., 1998)
- Assigning a substance abuse "consultation-liaison" person to a psychiatric inpatient unit in order to meet with designated patients with potential

coexisting AOD disorders and offer them education and options in a non-confrontational manner (Greenfield, Weiss, & Tohen, 1995)

- Providing nonverbal stress management training, such as basic yoga, progressive relaxation techniques, and gentle movement exercises (Brady et al., 1996)
- Addressing acute needs through crisis intervention for a housing, medical, or psychiatric emergency (Osher & Dixon, 1996)

If a person becomes acutely ill, actively suicidal, or dangerously psychotic, it may be absolutely necessary to use coercive interventions such as involuntary hospitalization in order to help the person stabilize. This kind of behavioral control can be seductive to professionals, especially when the clinician and/or the family really want the person to be abstinent. It's important to keep in mind that coercive interventions are only temporary and are designed to prevent immediate harm, not further the change process. Abstinence cannot be coerced in the long run. For the person to continue to move forward beyond a coercive intervention, it is still necessary to have a motivation to change.

STRENGTHS-BASED INTERVENTIONS

There are two important assumptions that set integrated treatment apart from historical mental health and substance abuse treatment in the United States. A major one is that persons with coexisting disorders are capable of making decisions and taking actions that will help them achieve their goals. A second premise is that "motivation for abstinence must reside *in the patient*, not in the clinician or family (Meuser, Drake, & Noordsy, 1998, p. 135). Together, these assumptions point the way to a variety of interventions that view persons with coexisting disorders through strengths perspective glasses.

Stage-wise treatment is a successful strategy that is built on the premise that people go through (and continue to recycle through) stages of change. The utility of stage-wise treatment was first demonstrated in the evaluation of the 13 Community Support Program federal demonstration projects between 1987 and 1991 (Mercer-McFadden et al., 1997). As discussed in the Creative Engagement Practices section, the menu of intervention strategies is respectfully offered and geared to whatever stage the person is in. Stages can be determined by finding out how much persons with coexisting disorders are aware of the negative consequences of the substance misuse to them, their motivation to change their substance use, and their goals for living and/or treatment. The model developed by Osher and Kofoed (1989), based on Prochaska and DiClemente's cycle of change (1992) and used in many integrated treatment models, divides the stages into four parts:

- *Engagement* (as described earlier), where there is little or no insight into the consequences of the substance misuse, no plan to change pattern of use, and no regular contact with treatment staff

- *Persuasion,* where there is still no motivation to change the substance use but where regular contact is occurring with a case manager or treatment staff, practical assistance and support is accepted, and psychiatric symptoms are stabilizing
- *Active treatment,* where the person has identified how substance misuse interferes with personal goals, is attempting to reduce or stop use, and is willing to pursue treatment strategies (such as self-help and psychoeducational groups, counseling, family therapy and education) to achieve goals
- *Relapse prevention,* where the person has been abstinent or has not experienced any negative consequences from substance use for at least 6 months and is willing to work on sustaining a meaningful recovery in all areas of life

Perhaps the most difficult stage for clinicians trained in traditional substance abuse or mental health practices is the persuasion stage. As described by Denning (2000), this is when dominant stereotypes, assumptions (such as that addicts routinely lie and deny their problems) and expectations about who is in control, may enter the potential therapeutic relationship. "The client expects to be controlled and does not want to be, and the therapist expects the client to want to be helped, to be willing to be controlled in some subtle way. When we view an addict as being a problem, or not motivated, or in denial, we are often speaking of this conflict of expectations" (p. 108). Clients are also likely to have their own expectations that they are mistrusted, even scary to the clinician, and feel protective about disclosing anything that might bring on negative consequences.

In order to break through these barriers, clinicians need to give up the illusion that they are in control. It is critical to rid ourselves of the idea that people with coexisting disorders will change their habits of drug or alcohol use just because it might be "good for them," *even if this is obvious to the clinician and the family.* When a clinician can embrace the fact that, like it or not, "motivation for abstinence must reside *in the patient,* not in the clinician or family" (Meuser, Drake, & Noordsy, p. 135), strategies for increasing motivation to formulate goals around substance use can begin. A practical suggestion from Denning (2000) for the beginning stages is to affirm clearly with clients that they have the right to live their own life and that your job as a therapist is to help them find their own goals and make decisions on how to reach them. Then expect to be tested on this assertion.

Motivational interviewing (MI, see chapter 3) is a particularly helpful strengths-based practice with persons who are in the "persuasion" stage; i.e., they haven't yet discovered a relationship between the misery they experience and their use of alcohol or drugs (Meuser, Drake, & Noordsy, 1998; Carey, 1996; Sciacca & Thompson, 1996). By helping clients to clarify goals and decide how their substance use interferes with their goals, it is possible to consistently address the important question that all of us ask at decision points, "What's in it for me?"

Goals that may be meaningful for persons with coexisting disorders include: getting or holding a job, finding housing, surviving or improving health, avoiding AIDS or death, getting admitted to detox for room and board when hungry or homeless, allowing medications to work, stopping the consequences of AOD use (such as increased anxiety, child protective service involvement), placating family or significant others. The fact that many of these goals result from the consequences to alcohol or drug use is not relevant in the beginning stages. The therapeutic goal is to establish an environment of trust and to provide concrete assistance, not judgment.

In a rare ethnographic study of substance abuse among people with severe mental illness, Alverson, Alverson, & Drake (2000) found that attaining four "positive quality-of-life factors" actually preceded and predicted sobriety among the people in the study. Furthermore, reduction of the factors preceded rather than followed a relapse into substance abuse. These important factors are similar to those for any persons recovering from substance abuse: a meaningful activity (job, hobby, social network), decent and stable housing, a meaningful relationship with someone who accepts them, and a positive, regular relationship with a mental health professional. The fact that, for the clients in this study, achieving these factors came before sobriety underscores the importance of focusing on the needs identified by the client, even when these needs do not include abstinence.

Motivational interviewing can also be used effectively in a brief session prior to psychiatric hospital discharge in order to enhance outpatient treatment entry into a dual diagnosis program. Daley and Zuckoff (1998) report using the MI principles of accepting the clients' ambivalence toward change as normal, avoiding confrontation, identifying current needs, wishes, and goals, exploring the risks associated with continued substance use and the probable impact on these goals of offering a menu of change options that may help clients, supporting clients' self-efficacy that positive change can occur, and inviting clients to consider the benefits of keeping their outpatient appointment as a first step. This process contrasts with the more usual directive to follow through with the outpatient appointment. As a result, the initial outpatient show rate almost doubled, from 35% to 67%, for the clients who received a brief MI session.

Harm reduction (see chapter 3) is another strengths-based practice used consistently in integrated treatment programs. Again, harm reduction does not mean "nonabstinence." In integrated treatment, it means that although abstinence may be assumed to be the safest goal for persons with coexisting disorders, any movement toward reducing use or reducing the consequences of use is encouraged. Using less often, using smaller amounts, experimenting with the "consequences" of abstinence for 24 hours, and using clean needles are all examples of attainable initial goals. Harm reduction has the additional advantage of being a "low-threshold" practice, in that persons are accepted as they are, with no "high-threshold" requirements, such as abstinence, that can provoke little or no participation in the program. In a harm reduction framework, changes, no matter how small, are examined with curiosity as to what effect the change had on the person's mood, psychiatric symptoms such as depression or anxiety, relationships with others, and identified goals in living. The role of the clinician is to support the person through these small changes by tuning into potential fears, by offering concrete help (such as medical or hospital admission assistance) when needed, and by raising hope that things can be better (Carey, 1996; Denning, 2000; Phillips & Labrow, 2000).

In the active treatment stage, when the person has identified how substance misuse interferes with his or her own personal goals and is attempting to reduce or stop use, psychoeducational and therapeutic groups may be helpful. A key ingredient found helpful in these groups is the maintenance of a highly supportive environment (Timko & Moos, 1998). This makes it possible to deal with all aspects of substance misuse, mental illness, the interaction of the two, relapse, or "slips" in a caring and nonconfrontational manner. Dealing with emotions and feelings is "very difficult" for the majority of persons with dual diagnoses according to a recent study (Laudet, Magura, Vogel, & Knight, 2000), so group support is critical in encouraging a person to be able to speak about these sensitive matters. Brady et al. (1996, p. 577) suggest the following practical guidelines from their experiences working with inner-city, chronically mentally ill persons with substance misuse problems:

- Use stress management techniques (relaxation and breathing exercises) to decrease distress.
- Emphasize links between alcohol and drugs and physical, psychological, and social problems.
- Teach group members an array of techniques to manage mental illness symptoms, including avoidance of alcohol and drugs.
- Maximize client participation.
- In later sessions, move into testimonials, role-playing, peer praise, and peer confrontation to enhance motivation for change.

Research on the effectiveness of specific types of treatment (individual, group, or family) is scarce. There is some evidence that attending a "dual-diagnosis group" correlates with a favorable outcome, especially when combined with intensive case management (Klein, Cnaan & Whitecraft, 1998), but no particular type of group appears to be more effective than another (Drake & Meuser, 2000). However, "more is better," according to the findings of Laudet et al. (2000), where higher levels of support from a greater number of people were linked to less substance use. One such group, called "The Good Chemistry Group," is a combination of therapy, psychoeducation, and peer support. Members are encouraged to have "natural highs" and "good chemistry" by getting involved in fun and healthy activities that don't require using alcohol or drugs (DiNitto & Webb, 1998).

Mutual-help groups such as Alcoholics Anonymous (see chapter 12) can provide much needed social support for some persons outside the professional arena. However, there is also research that suggests that many clients with major mental illness, especially schizophrenia, will have difficulties participating in these groups (Noordsy, Schwab, Fox, & Drake, 1996). Members may have trouble understanding severe mental illness and be uncomfortable with some of the behavioral manifestations of the illness. Historically, some AA members have refused to consider psychiatric medication as anything other than "drugs," and have urged people who very much need it to discontinue use. For these reasons, a referral to AA or NA should be accompanied by some help in linking them to a receptive group in the community.

Other suggestions for increasing the likelihood of a good experience in AA include: waiting to refer until the person is in the active treatment stage and wants abstinence; affirming that the person has the absolute right to choose whether to attend and participate; suggesting that he or she can be a "visitor" for a few meetings to observe and politely "pass" the invitation to read or talk during the meeting; giving them the AA-approved brochure "The AA Member—Medications and Other Drugs" that welcomes persons who are taking psychiatric medications (Alcoholics Anonymous [AA], 1984); introducing the person to an AA member who will take that person to his or her first meeting (Powell, Kurtz, Garvin, & Hill, 1996).

Special community support groups with limited professional involvement may also be very helpful. Double Trouble in Recovery (DTR) groups, which are adapted from AA for persons with coexisting mental disorders, have over 100 meetings in the United States. A recent study of 310 DTR members who had participated for at least one month revealed that 75% of them also attended either AA or NA; those who did not reported feeling judged, uncomfortable, or not accepted because of mental health issues or medication or felt that DTR met their needs. Participation in DTR was positively linked to recovery (Laudet et al., 2000).

Relapse prevention strategies for persons with coexisting disorders have a dual focus on substance abuse and mental health problems (Ziedonis & Trudeau, 1997; Nigam, Schottenfeld, & Kosten, 1992). For example, a social skills training group may be developed to emphasize problem solving, communication skills, management of psychiatric symptoms, medication compliance, and relapse prevention. Relapse and slips are generally handled in a nonjudgmental manner. Group members help bring out the circumstances and results of slips in order to help the person with a new plan (see Case Study 1). Group members learn to identify triggers and early warning signs of substance use and psychiatric symptoms and at the same time support hope and self-efficacy with each other. Depending on the membership, the group process may need to be adapted to fit the attention span and communication skills of the group.

Long-Term Consequences

A person with coexisting disorders is likely to experience problems that touch almost every aspect of life: basic needs such as housing, relationships, employment, medication stabilization, physical problems, and legal troubles. In addition to the many external problems, it takes a long time for the internal work needed to go from zero awareness that one even has a problem, to choosing and then maintaining successful solutions to the problem. It could be said that recovery involves building a whole new life, inside and outside. It is no wonder that stability takes months and years, not weeks. To learn about an innovative Seattle program that is based on harm reduction, see Box 8.1.

Research findings on treatment effectiveness indicate that the course of recovery involves gradual reductions in substance use for most persons with coexisting disorders (see Case Study 2 on Ms B.). Drake (1996) and other studies suggest that the proportion of clients attaining abstinence increases every six months, until at the end of three years almost half have attained abstinence.

Integrated Pharmacotherapy

The use of medications for both mental health and substance use disorders is a complex issue because of the interactions between some psychiatric medications and alcohol and drugs and because undermedication for psychiatric symptoms may cause a relapse in substance misuse. Ideally, a physician is part of the treatment team, and medication is integrated and closely monitored as part of the total integrated approach. Denning (2000) advises that the entire team have expertise in pharmacology and the potential drug interactions that may occur, be prepared to provide references to other clinicians, be willing to examine their own biases around medication for substance misusers, and engage in frequent discussions about these issues on behalf of each client. For example, it's important to distinguish "psychoactive" medications (such as opioids, stimulants, benzodiazepines, barbiturates, and other sedative-hypnotics), which can cause rapid changes in mood, thought, and behavior, from "nonpsychoactive" medications (such as lithium, antipsychotics, beta-blockers, antidepressants, monoamine oxidase inhibitors, antihistamines, anticonvulsants, and anticholoinergics) that normalize thinking processes.

Specific pharmacotherapies for persons with coexisting disorders are still in the beginning stage, and there is a lack of research, especially controlled studies, to guide clinicians. However, the Center for Substance Abuse Treatment (CSAT, 1994) offers these guidelines:

- Acute and severe symptoms that occur with such disorders as mania, psychotic depression, and schizophrenia require immediate medication.
- If symptoms are not acute, use a "stepwise" approach of (1) trying no medication for less severe problems, such as anxiety or mild depression, (2) adding nonpsychoactive medication if the symptoms do not lessen after detoxification and psychosocial approaches, and (3) adding psychoactive medications if the symptoms do not abate or if they get worse.

In summary, integrated treatment programs, as developed over the past 15 years, have begun to offer more hope to the person with coexisting disorders. Research affirms that when this type of treatment is provided over several years, clients attain higher rates of stable remission as well as improve their quality of life. The integrated approach embraces many strengths-based practices, such as

BOX 8.1

A DAY IN THE LIFE OF A MENTAL HEALTH CASE MANAGER
BY RUPERT VAN WORMER, MSW, SEATTLE, WASHINGTON

It is Monday morning, the busiest day of the week at the Downtown Emergency Service Center (DESC) Mental Health Program. After a half hour bus ride I arrive in downtown Seattle, more specifically to the Pioneer Square district, which is the old part of the downtown area. The agency itself is one block away from Yesler Way, famed for being the original Skid Road (later misnamed Skid Row). Hundreds of homeless people live in this area today. This area is reported as having the highest arrest rates in the entire city: Panhandling, public consumption of alcohol, drug dealing, and prostitution are common sights. The alleyway next to the building that houses the outpatient mental health program is commonly used by people as a place to smoke crack cocaine and inject heroin.

As I approach the front entrance to the clinic, where I work as a mental health case manager, I see a crowd of about 30 people, mostly our clients, waiting for the door to open at nine o'clock. I unlock the door to let myself in, and am greeted by four or five of my clients simultaneously; some just say hello, while others ask to meet with me immediately. I explain that I will see them after the clinic opens at nine. (In this job, it is important to set limits.) Entering the building, I lock the door behind me.

I have an interesting and unique caseload. Many of my clients are dually diagnosed. Several have either schizophrenia with coexisting chemical dependency or major depression with chemical dependency. Persons with schizophrenia generally are prescribed what are called "atypical antipsychotics," which include Clozaril, Risperdall, Seroquel, and Zyprexa. For depression, Paxil, Prozac, Zoloft, Effexor, and Wellbutrin are commonly prescribed. Drugs most commonly misused by my clients include: heroin, crack cocaine, methamphetamine, marijuana, and alcohol. Many of my clients also have physical health concerns as well, including hepatitis C, TB, HIV/AIDS, and diabetes.

At DESC, we endorse the harm reduction model. We would like to get our clients off of drugs; we settle for keeping them alive and helping them stay out of trouble. If someone has a bad liver, for example, I might advise him or her to smoke marijuana rather than taking drugs that would hurt the liver. For a man who is breaking antennae off of old cars (to use to smoke the crack), I might advise him to buy a glass pipe at the shop.

We run prerecovery treatment groups at the center; sometimes clients are nodding off in the group from heroin. Still, we'd rather have them come than to lose touch with them. We provide coffee and bagels and plenty of nurturance. The groups are unstructured, the focus on being open and honest about substance use. When our clients go off to AA or NA meetings or traditional treatment programs, though, they get confused. They are told to get off their antidepressants that the doctor here has urged them to take. Because of their emotional instability these clients can't handle the contradictions. Also, they often can't resist the temptation to use when they are off their antidepressants.

I pour myself a cup of coffee and walk back to my cubicle. I check my voice mail, taking notes of all the messages that require a response. Typically I have anywhere between 5 and 15 messages on a Monday morning. Often these messages are from clients or mental health workers reporting an incident, arrest, or hospitalization that occurred during after-hours. A few minutes after 9 A.M. the receptionist at the front desk pages me with a list of my clients who have requested to meet with me and are now waiting in the reception area. I try to be as fair as possible; however, clients with emergency situations are always bumped to the top of the list. I usually reserve the first hour or two of each day for this type of client, the "walk-ins." The rest of the day I meet with the more stable clients who have scheduled appointments.

Fourteen of my 28 clients are money management clients, which means that my agency is their representative payee. Their SSI (Supplemental Security Income) and SSDI (disability) checks are sent to my agency, and we assist these clients with their finances. For most of our payee clients this means we pay their bills and disperse cash to them between one and five times per week, depending on their level of need. At the end of each month, I sit down with these clients individually and help them plan the next month's budget. One client I work with comes in daily, Monday through Friday, to pick up $10 a day. He also picks up his daily medications during this time, at the nurse station. For many clients the money management program encourages treatment involvement. For example, a client I'll call Ben lived a life of instability until recently, when he became a payee client. Before this change his SSDI check was sent to his mother, who would then send a money order for the full amount ($688) at the beginning of each month. Ben would be flat broke in less than two weeks, have nothing to show for it, and would still live at the shelter to get room and board. During this time Ben had frequent drug binges, taking his psychiatric medications for schizophrenia inconsistently. This resulted in frequent psychiatric hospitalizations. While Ben was "decompensated" he would think he was a pedophile and would turn himself in at police stations. But after DESC became his representative payee, stability returned to his life one step at a time. Ben started coming in regularly for medications. I met with him twice a week, during which time I helped him fill out housing applications and encouraged him to continue taking his medications consistently. I also used our time together to discourage him from using alcohol and other drugs. After a few weeks of this I worked with him coaching him in role-playing for the interview with an apartment manager. He did well at the interview and was able to get "clean and sober" housing that provided daily medication monitoring.

The clients I see first thing in the morning are usually money management clients. Money is a good engagement tool. While I am giving them their money I have the opportunity to ask them how they are doing. I often ask questions relating to nutrition, housing, drug use, relationships, personal hygiene, medication compliance, and psychiatric stability. Some of these can be observed without needing to ask questions. A client who is "decompensated," for example, will often have worse-than-usual hygiene, may be responding to hallucinations, and may seem confused. A few things I always need to monitor for are suicidal ideation, homicidal ideation, and grave disability. Any of these could require immediate psychiatric hospitalization.

By the time 11:45 rolls around I will have met individually with nine clients for money management. Today their sessions range from 5 minutes to a half hour. Those clients who need additional time with me are given appointment times later in the week.

The afternoon is spent doing the progress notes for each of the client interactions I have had this morning and answering mail. Today there is a letter from the Social

continued

BOX 8.1   A DAY IN THE LIFE OF A MENTAL
           HEALTH CASE MANAGER
           (*Continued*)

Security Administration telling me that one of my clients is up for "disability review."
I fill out the multipage form and drop it in the outgoing mailbox.

Then it is off to the DESC Shelter, home to about 250 people each night, a
place to socialize or rest by day. The purpose of my visit is to look for a man in his
mid-40s diagnosed with schizophrenia who I have not seen in several weeks. (This
part of the job is referred to as "outreach and engagement.") As I walk through the
shelter hallway I am reminded of a 19th century insane asylum. It is dirty, there is a
foul odor, and there are dozens of disheveled-looking people lining the wall. Some
are standing or sitting, while others are stretched out asleep on the linoleum tile
floor. Scanning the faces, looking for my client, I notice one person talking to himself in "word salad." Then I see my client. He is leaning against a wall, staring
blankly. I say hello and try to interest him in reconnecting with mental health services
and suggest that we meet later to work on housing applications. We set a time and I
return to my office.

Back at the office, I check my voice mail: a few new messages but nothing urgent.
It is now 2:15 and my 2 o'clock appointment is still not here. I have in my office some
possessions that belong to a client who has recently moved into an assisted-living facility. Since this person's new residence is only about 10 blocks away, I decide now
would be a good time to bring them to her. Gathering her things, I put them in a bag
and start walking to her residence. After getting about a half block from my building, I notice one of my other clients, Joe, walking toward me. He stops in front of me
and says, "Guess what?" Since Joe has a big smile on his face, I expect that it will be
something positive. To my surprise, however, this is not a positive situation (a case
of inappropriate affect). Joe tells me that he has just swallowed all of his medications
and injected a gram of heroin, an obvious suicide attempt or suicidal gesture. I get

---

motivational interviewing, harm reduction, and stages of treatment interventions. Multidisciplinary teams with a variety of training and philosophical backgrounds have, over time, been able to put aside their differences and learn new
approaches to helping people in this vulnerable situation.

SUBSTANCE MISUSE AND DEVELOPMENTAL, PHYSICAL, AND COGNITIVE DISABILITIES

Substance misuse can stand in the way of a person's adequately dealing with an
adjustment to a disability as well as aggravate the disability itself. However,
until recently, substance misusers who have coexisting developmental, physical,
or cognitive disabilities have been largely ignored in treatment settings, research, professional training, and public awareness. The 1990 Americans with
Disabilities Act (ADA) helped changes begin by guaranteeing full participation
and access to community services and facilities for all people with disabilities.

him to come with me back to the clinic so we can get a "med list" from the nurse. After getting the list, we rush to the ER, pushing our way to the front of the line. I explain the situation to the intake nurse and give her the med list. While Joe is getting his stomach pumped, I talk to the hospital social worker and advocate for my client to be admitted into the inpatient psychiatric unit of the hospital after he is medically cleared. Feeling confident that the appropriate follow-up care will be provided, I leave.

It is now almost 5 P.M. A few blocks from the hospital is the assisted-living facility that was my original destination this afternoon. Fortunately I remembered to bring this other client's bag with me. I make this delivery and call it a day.

One of the toughest things about my job is the difficulty associated with trying to get clients into inpatient chemical dependency programs. Frequently clients will reach the point when they realize they are in need of inpatient chemical dependency treatment, and they are ready and willing to get the intensive treatment they need. The hard part for me at this moment comes when I have to tell them that I will try to get them on a list somewhere and it may be three months to a year before they will be admitted. This problem stems from the shortage of publicly funded inpatient chemical dependency centers. As a result, the centers that do exist have the option of being selective when it comes to choosing who gets in and who doesn't. Clients with a diagnosis of schizophrenia, bipolar mood disorder, or major depression as well as chemical dependency generally have a harder time getting into treatment than people who are not identified as having mental health issues in addition to chemical dependency issues. One client, a daily crack cocaine user, had his moment of clarity nearly six months ago. He completed an application to an appropriate treatment facility, and we are still waiting. Another client from our agency was awaiting an opening at another treatment center. But before she could get the help she needed, she was picked up by the police and was later sentenced to three years in prison for providing an undercover agent with crack cocaine.

Printed with the permission of Rupert van Wormer

Treatment programs and mental health centers were put on notice that they must adapt their programs to meet the needs of people with coexisting disabilities. However, findings from a national study suggest that at least 50% of all persons with a coexisting disability are still not being identified as such by the system that provides them services (Rehabilitation Research and Training Center on Drugs and Disability, 1995).

This section will focus on a wide range of disabilities, excluding the mental disorders already covered. Using the principle of the independent living movement that persons with disabilities share more commonality than differences in their experience of living, we will discuss common themes around traditional barriers to treatment, the development of new assessment tools, and new treatment practices relevant to persons with substance misuse and a coexisting disability. Because many people in the able culture still view people with disabilities in terms of what they cannot do or should not attempt to do and because helping agencies continue to reflect that bias, a strengths-based approach to practice is particularly important and will be emphasized. Space requirements limit detailed discussion of individual types of disability; we will attempt to compensate by using examples from a range of different disabilities.

Prevalence and Characteristics

Prevalence studies of substance misusers with coexisting disabilities are scarce. According to the Center for Substance Abuse Treatment (CSAT, 1998), one of the few states to keep comprehensive records on substance use disorder services for persons with disabilities is New York's Office of Alcoholism and Substance Abuse Services. In 1997, they reported that 22.4% of the total clients receiving substance use disorder services had a coexisting physical or mental disability. Of these, over half (58.9%) had a disability not related to mental illness, such as mobility impairment, visual impairment, or deafness. The CSAT suggests that because the reports were generated by treatment staff not trained in assessing specific disabilities, many disabilities may be underreported, such as traumatic brain injury, learning disability, and attention deficit–hyperactivity disorder (ADHD).

DiNitto and Webb's (1998) review of existing research on the prevalence of substance misusers with mental retardation suggests that this population is less likely to use or misuse alcohol and drugs than the general population. However, this finding may be the result of such factors as close supervision, reporting bias from institutional settings that prohibit alcohol or drug use, people's unwillingness to report use, or the fact that individuals with mental retardation are a protected class and securing informed consent to participate in research is difficult and time consuming. Findings from McGillicuddy and Blane's (1999) survey of substance use in persons with mental retardation ($n = 122$) living in the community suggest that the rate of alcohol misuse comes close to the rate in the general population. The percentage of use in the past month in this sample was alcohol 39%, nicotine 23%, and illicit drugs 4%. The majority of individuals (61%) did not use alcohol, while 21% were classified as users (no consequences), and 18% were classified as misusers (experienced consequences and met other misuse criteria, such as drinking to intoxication). Other studies report that persons with mental retardation experience the same kind of alcohol- or drug-related problems that persons with only substance misuse experience, such as troubles at work, problems with friends and family, and legal problems.

There are several studies indicating that persons with disabilities have a greater risk for alcohol and drug misuse than the general population. For example, spinal cord and head injuries are often related to accidents linked with the use of alcohol or drugs. In a review of the research, Heinemann and Hawkins (1995) found that between 17 and 68% of the persons with these injuries were intoxicated. Another study found heavy drinking in 55% of the sample six months before the spinal cord injury, which decreased to 20% one year following the injury (Heinemann, Schmidt, & Semik, 1994).

When compared to data from the National Household Survey on Drug Abuse (1994), women with disabilities appear to use illicit drugs at a higher rate than women in the general population. A study by Li and Ford (1998) on 900 women with a variety of disabilities found that marijuana was the substance most used in the last month (6.6%), followed by cocaine (0.7%), compared to women in the general population: use of marijuana (4.6%) and cocaine (0.5%). Risk factors associated with illicit drug use includes younger age, best friend who uses drugs, an entitlement attitude toward using drugs because of the disability, and being a self-reported victim of substance-abuse-related physical violence. Although chronic pain was reported by 43% of the women, a surprising finding was that chronic pain was not associated with the use of illicit drugs.

The Center for Substance Abuse Treatment (1998) estimates that, overall, coexisting disabilities (including psychiatric disorders) may affect up to 40% of all clients who enter substance use disorder treatment. New screening practices are needed to find these "hidden" conditions so that the program can be modified and adapted to meet the needs of such persons. The days of filling established treatment "slots" with a standard treatment program are over.

Assessing Treatment Barriers

In spite of the prevalence of substance misuse among people with disabilities, there is much evidence that they are less likely to enter or complete treatment. Likely reasons include physical, attitudinal, or communication barriers that make treatment unsatisfactory, irrelevant, or limited (CSAT, 1998). A Canadian survey of all the alcohol and drug treatment programs in Ontario found that few agencies offered services tailored especially for persons with disabilities (Tyas & Rush, 1993). Most of the programs (two-thirds of 219 programs) thought that persons with developmental or psychiatric disabilities should be served by programs designed especially for these groups; 82.4% thought clients with physical disabilities should be "mainstreamed" into existing programs. However, at the time of the survey, only 40% of the programs had wheelchair accessibility.

People with learning differences (mental retardation, borderline intelligence, learning disabilities, hyperactivity, and traumatic brain injury) can experience a number of barriers to effective treatment (Campbell, Essex, & Held, 1994). Insight-oriented approaches and the use of complex audiovisual aids and extensive writing assignments may be confusing. The popular modality of group treatment is likely to be too fast-paced or abstract or to demand behaviors that a person with a brain injury may not be able to sustain. Fellow group participants may have negative stereotypes of persons with learning differences. Programs may need to adapt by using picture books, "flash cards," and art therapy techniques.

Other barriers result from a lack of knowledge, experience, and understanding among treatment staff. Stereotypical beliefs that may be prevalent in the larger culture can also find a home in treatment staff. A list provided by CSAT (1998, p. 9) of commonly held beliefs that pose barriers to treatment includes:

- People with disabilities do not abuse substances.
- People with disabilities should receive exactly the same treatment protocol as everyone else so that they aren't singled out as different.
- A person is noncompliant when her disability prevents her from responding to treatment.
- A person with a disability will make other clients uncomfortable.
- People with disabilities will sue the program regardless of the services offered.
- People with disabilities deserve pity, so they should be allowed more latitude to indulge in substance use.

Communication barriers are particularly prevalent with deaf persons and persons with slow or impaired speech, significant respiratory problems, or delays in cognition. Accommodations need to be made by using sign language interpreters, telecommunication devices for the deaf (TDD), computer terminals and boards, and speech synthesizers.

It is a major premise of the independent living movement that "nonaccess in society resulted from architectural and attitudinal barriers rather than the dysfunction of the individual person with a disability" (Mackelprang & Salsgiver, 1999, p. 51). Architectural barriers include everything from no wheelchair access to a lack of transportation from the bus stop to the program entrance. The critical point is that when the physical, attitudinal, and communication barriers are removed, it becomes possible to establish a productive relationship that has a chance of being helpful to a person with coexisting disabilities.

Intake and Screening

As with any other person who might be seeking help, the most important task of the intake procedure is to begin to build trust and credibility with that person. This requires a nonconfrontational, supportive environment that will reduce anxiety, not increase it. If it is already known that the person has a particular disability, accommodations should already be made to eliminate functional barriers. For example, for persons in a wheelchair, the table should be at the right height; for deaf persons, a sign language interpreter must be available; for people with traumatic brain injury, questions should be concrete and checks for understanding should be made often. For a thorough discussion of potential accommodations needed, see CSAT (1998).

If a person is willing to seek help with stopping his or her substance misuse or in eliminating the consequences of such use, it is important to find out if there are any functional barriers that may get in the way. It is not necessary to diagnose a disability; that role is reserved for a disabilities expert (for example, specialized medical services or state vocational rehabilitation programs). It is necessary to find out if any functional adjustments are needed that could help the clinician be a more helpful consultant to this person.

An initial screening for disabilities is very practical: It helps identify potential programmatic barriers so that they can be modified. It is important to ask everyone involved in the intake process, "Do you need any accommodations to participate fully in this program?" Screening can also help identify areas where it may be beneficial for the person to link with other services. A basic screening instrument for identifying functional limitations that may pose barriers in treatment can be found in CSAT (1998, p. 21).

Treatment Practices

There are a number of therapeutic issues that need to be addressed in order to increase the likelihood of success of treatment. Treatment plans may feature different elements and concerns and may require more time, depending on the disability. A person with coexisting disabilities may have quite different reasons for wanting to abstain from alcohol or drugs. For example, the fact that alcohol can lower the seizure threshold for persons with traumatic brain injury (TBI) may be a motivation to quit drinking alcohol for such persons.

The CSAT 19 recommends that each task written on a treatment contract be accompanied by a list of specific accommodations needed for that task to be accomplished. For example, for persons with memory problems who are expected to attend group sessions, "Call and remind them that a session is occurring or assist them in creating memory books that include necessary information on group meetings" (CSAT, 1998, p. 49).

Modifications for counseling sessions could include being flexible with the time and length of the session, being sensitive to what matters may be more readily discussed in individual sessions, preparing for sessions by researching the disability, providing specific examples of behaviors and concepts to persons with cognitive disabilities, preparing accessible written materials, and finding alternative media. Behavioral therapy may be preferable to insight-oriented, psychodynamic approaches because it offers small, concrete steps to long-term goals (DiNitto & Webb, 1998).

Helwig and Holicky (1994, p. 229) suggest specific therapeutic issues that are common to many persons with physical disabilities and particularly trauma-induced disabilities:

> Learning to live in a world designed for able-bodied people who value normality and who shun difference, demands the ability to face and solve a never-ending string of problems . . . These problems include major changes in almost every aspect of life, including a loss of privacy in areas of self-care; devaluing, enabling, or patronizing social attitudes; loss of control or determination; and incredible stress on one's family and support system.

In addition, grief and loss issues around the disability and the addiction may be important therapeutic themes.

Motivational interviewing techniques have been found successful with adults with traumatic brain injury. By helping the person to assess his or her motivation to use alcohol and other drugs, identify and evaluate goals, resolve conflicts among interfering goals, and develop skills for reaching realistic goals, the person is engaged in immediately gratifying activities. Homework activities are designed to be positive, goal-oriented, and immediately measurable on a "goal ladder" that leads to a long-term goal. Results from an evaluation of using this approach with 60 persons with TBI during a 12-week treatment program suggest that motivational interviewing was effective in reducing substance use. At one-year follow-up, 40% maintained abstinence, 14% became abstinent, 38% continued using, and 8% began using (Heinemann, 1997).

Many authors discuss the need to practice from a strengths perspective when working with persons with a disability (Mackelprang & Salsgiver, 1999; CSAT, 1998). If a treatment goal is not met, it is important to look first at whether or not accommodations were sufficient to support the process, instead of immediately blaming the individual for resistance to treatment.

CONCLUSION

Twenty years ago, clinicians were still arguing about which disorder should be treated first: mental illness or substance dependence. Clients were falling through the categorical cracks. Since then, research has demonstrated that it works best when we treat both problems at once in an integrated team approach that coordinates the treatments of both systems. Strengths-based interventions, such as motivational interviewing, harm reduction, and stage-wise treatment, are successful strategies that help the clinician stay focused on the client's goals. Professionals who work with persons that have physical disabilities or cognitive impairments are recognizing that substance misuse problems can no longer be overlooked, and substance abuse treatment programs are making innovative accommodations to better serve these populations. The challenge now is for HMOs and state/federal funding sources to create reimbursement and policy practices that will enhance these developments.

CASE STUDIES

Case Study 1: Group Treatment Strengths
The following story is an example of how group members can support a person who has lapsed into drug use.

Sherry binged on IV cocaine nine months after entering the dual-diagnosis group. She reported this to the group at the next meeting and explained that one of her drug-abusing friends visited her and offered her cocaine. She told the group that she was feeling low on that day and was alone in her apartment without anything to do. She felt that she could not resist getting high, although she tried to resist at first. The group listened to her very carefully and sympathetically. They discussed and developed a relapse prevention strategy for this patient, as follows:

1. Don't allow your drug-using friends to visit you, and say "No" boldly.
2. Disconnect yourself completely from drug abusers.

3. Call one of the group therapists or any other member of the group when you are feeling low.

When she encountered the same situation the following week, she was able to say "No" and control herself. In the next session she happily told the group that this strategy worked for her.

From: Nigam, Schottenfeld, & Kosten, 1992.

Case Study 2: Long-Term Commitment

The following story illustrates the long-term commitment necessary to be helpful to a person with coexisting disorders.

Ms B is a 35-year-old Caucasian woman with a long history of frequent psychiatric hospitalization beginning at age 17. She has a diagnosis of schizophrenia (paranoid type) and at referral met criteria for binge-pattern alcohol dependence. Her drinking was associated with impulsive outbursts of violence, toward both herself and others. When not drinking, she was childlike and friendly, although persistently paranoid about the efforts of others to "poison her." She had been living in the streets and in the shelter system of a large urban city for 10 years prior to referral to an assertive community treatment (ACT) team that targeted homeless persons with severe mental illnesses.

After a six-month period of outreach and regular meetings at a local diner, she seemed increasingly comfortable with several members of the case management team and agreed to a low dose of antipsychotic medication that she took irregularly. She initially refused to discuss her alcohol use, stating "It's none of your business." Over the six months she acknowledged that she drank but vehemently denied that this alcohol use created any problems for her. At this point, she agreed to live in a transitional shelter that prohibited any substance use and provided on-site AA and NA group meetings. The ACT team was able to convince the shelter staff to waive their program requirement that all residents attend daily self-help meetings for Ms B because of her behavior in groups. The team assured the shelter staff that alcohol abuse would be addressed in individual meetings with Ms B.

She did not drink for almost three months while living at this shelter. During this time, the ACT team assisted her in obtaining Social Security disability benefits; the team was named as the representative payee for this income support. She was assisted in finding her own apartment, and being sober enabled her to gain access to housing subsidies. Although the team ensured that Ms B's rent and bills were paid, she would sometimes use the leftover funds to buy alcohol, which induced bizarre behavior. Whenever her landlord threatened eviction because of a behavioral disturbance, the ACT team would intervene by coming into the apartment to provide crisis counseling. These bingeing episodes became less frequent. Ms B slowly became willing to acknowledge that alcohol use was not in her best interest and agreed to try group educational meetings about alcohol. She became increasingly attached to her apartment and stated that she did not want to do anything that might lead to her becoming homeless again. The team used this information to gently persuade her to examine the likely consequences of ongoing alcohol abuse, and over time her drinking episodes disappeared entirely. Ms B's compliance with medication improved somewhat, but she remains suspicious and slightly paranoid.

From: Osher & Dixon, 1996.

Case Study 3: Diagnosis in a Team Setting

The following narrative, by an MSW working as a clinical social worker on an in-patient psychiatry unit at a large teaching hospital, expresses some of the challenges of diagnosis in a team setting:

> On several occasions, our team has had lengthy debates about the diagnosis of a particular client. Is he/she depressed because he/she can't get off drugs? Did the depression precede the drug use? If the depression preceded the drug use, at what point did they start to use drugs and how did that affect their depression? What is their diagnosis? Is it substance-induced mood disorder or is it a major depression with a coexisting substance dependence problem? Is the client's irritability due to: (1) a component of their mental illness, (2) the effects of withdrawing from their drug of choice (irritability is particularly common among people who are addicted to crack cocaine), (3) a component of a personality disorder, or (4) just a part of their personality style? Many times, each of the team members has a very different opinion about the diagnosis and the recommended course of treatment. It seems like a miracle when we can all agree. At other times, it is clear that we will not reach a consensus. When this happens, the attending psychiatrist ultimately makes the final call about the diagnosis and treatment that we will provide. Although I am surrounded by people with a clear medical model bias, I feel that my opinions and the bio-psycho-social-spiritual perspective I bring to the team are respected and valued by those I work with.

From: Crisp, 1999.

References

Alcoholics Anonymous (AA). (1984). *The AA member—medications and other drugs.* New York: AA World Services.

Alverson, H., Alverson, M., & Drake, R. E. (2000). *Community Mental Health Journal, 36*(6), 557–569.

American Psychiatric Association (APA). (2000). *Diagnostic and statistical manual of mental disorders, 4th edition, text revision (DSM-IV-R).* Washington, DC: Author.

Bearman, D., Claydon, K., Kincheloe, J., & Lodise, C. (1997). Breaking the cycle of dependency: Dual diagnosis and AFDC families. *Journal of Psychoactive Drugs, 29*(4), 359–367.

Blaszczynski, A. (1995, May). *Workshop of the assessment and treatment of pathological gambling.* Australian and New Zealand Association of Psychiatry, Psychology and the Law Conference, Melbourne, as reported in Coman, G., Evans, B., & Burrows, G. (1996).

Blume, S. B. (1997). Pathological gambling. In J. Lowinson, P. Ruiz, R. Millman, & J. Langrod (Eds.), *Substance abuse: A comprehensive textbook* (3rd ed.). Baltimore: Williams and Wilkins.

Brady, S., Hiam, C. M., Saemann, R., Humbert, L., Fleming, M., & Dawkins-Brickhouse, K. (1996). Dual Diagnosis: A treatment model for substance abuse and major mental illness. *Community Mental Health Journal, 32*(6), 573–579.

Breakey, W. R., Calabrese, L., Rosenblatt, A., & Crum, R. M. (1998). Detecting alcohol use disorder in the severely mentally ill. *Community Mental Health Journal, 34*(2), 165–174.

Campbell, J. A., Essex, E. L., & Held, G. (1994). Issues in chemical dependency treatment and aftercare for people with learning differences. *Health and Social Work, 19*(1), 63–70.

Carey, K. B. (1996). Substance use reduction in the context of outpatient psychiatric treatment: A collaborative motivational, harm reduction approach. *Community Mental Health Journal, 32,* 291–306.

Center for Substance Abuse Treatment (CSAT). (1994). *Assessment and treatment of patients with coexisting mental illness and alcohol and other drug abuse.* Treatment Improvement Protocol (TIP) Series 9. U.S. Department of Health and Human Services, Public Health Service. Rockville, MD: Author.

Center for Substance Abuse Treatment (CSAT). (1998). *Substance use disorder treatment for people with physical and cognitive disabilities.* Treatment Improvement Protocol (TIP) Series 29. U.S. Department of Health and Human Services, Public Health Service. Rockville, MD: Author.

Coman, G., Evans, B., & Burrows, G. (1996). Problem gambling: Treatment strategies and rationale for the use of hypnosis as a treatment adjunct. *Australian Journal of Clinical and Experimental Hypnosis, 24*(2), 73–91.

Crisp, C. L. (1999). Dual diagnosis: Substance abuse and mental health in an inpatient setting. In L. M. Greebman (Ed.), *Days in the lives of social workers: Forty-one professionals tell "real life" stories from social work practice* (2nd ed., pp. 171–174). Harrisburg: White Hat Community.

Daley, D. C., & Zuckoff, A. (1998). Improving compliance with the initial outpatient session among discharged inpatient dual diagnosis clients. *Social Work, 43*(5), 470–473.

Davis, D. R. (2002). The Queen of Hearts: Women and compulsive gambling. In S. L. Straussner & S. Brown (Eds.), *The handbook of women's addictions treatment: Theory and practice.* San Francisco: Jossey-Bass.

Dawe, S., Seinen, A., & Kavanagh, D. (2000). An examination of the utility of the AUDIT in people with schizophrenia. *Journal of Studies on Alcohol, 61,* 744–750.

Denning, P. (2000). *Practicing harm reduction psychotherapy: An alternative approach to addictions.* New York: Guilford Press.

DiNitto, D. M., & Webb, D. K. (1998). Compounding the problem: Substance abuse and other disabilities. In C. A. McNeece & D. M. DiNitto, *Chemical dependency: A systems approach* (2nd ed., pp. 347–390). Boston: Allyn & Bacon.

Drake, R. E. (1996). Substance use reduction among patients with severe mental illness. *Community Mental Health Journal, 32*(3), 311–314.

Drake, R. E., & Meuser, K. T. (2000). Psychosocial approaches to dual diagnosis. *Schizophrenia Bulletin, 26,*(1), 105–118.

Drake, R. E., & Wallach, M. A. (1993). Moderate drinking among people with severe mental illness. *Hospital and Community Psychiatry, 44,* 780–782.

Drake, R. E., Yovetich, N. A., Bebout, R. R., Harris, M., & McHugo, G. J. (1997). Integrated treatment for dually diagnosed homeless adults. *Journal of Nervous and Mental Disease, 185,* 298–305.

Evans, K., & Sullivan, J. M. (1990). *Dual diagnosis: Counseling the mentally ill substance abuser.* New York: Guilford Press.

Goff, D. C., Henderson, D. C., & Amico, E. (1992). Cigarette smoking in schizophrenia: Relationship to psychopathology and medication side effects. *American Journal of Psychiatry, 149,* 1189–1194.

Gold, M. S., Johnson, C. R., & Stennie, K. (1997). Eating disorders. In J. Lowinson, P. Ruiz, R. Millman, & J. Langrod (Eds.), *Substance abuse: A comprehensive textbook* (3rd ed., pp. 319–330). Baltimore: Williams & Wilkins.

Greenfield, S. F., Weiss, R. D., & Tohen, M. (1995). Substance abuse and the chronically mentally ill: A description of dual diagnosis treatment services in a psychiatric hospital. *Community Mental Health Journal, 31*(3), 265–277.

Heinemann, A. W. (1997). Persons with disabilities. In J. Lowinson, P. Ruiz, R. Millman, & J. Langrod (Eds.), *Substance abuse: A comprehensive textbook* (3rd ed., pp. 716–725). Baltimore: Williams & Wilkins.

Heinemann, A. W., & Hawkins, D. (1995). Substance abuse and medical complications following spinal cord injury. *Rehabilitation Psychology, 40*(2), 125–140.

Heinemann, A. W., Schmidt, M. F., & Semik, P. (1994). Drinking patterns, drinking expectancies and coping after spinal cord injury. *Rehabilitation Counseling Bulletin, 38*(2), 134–153.

Helwig, A., & Holicky, R. (1994). Substance abuse in persons with disabilities: Treatment considerations. *Journal of Counseling and Development, 72*, 227–233.

Is everybody crazy? (1998, January 26). *Newsweek*, 51–56.

Kavanagh, D. J., Young, R., Boyce, L., Clair, A., Sitharthan, R., Clark, D., & Thompson, K. (1998). Substance treatment option is psychosis (STOP): A new intervention for dual diagnosis. *Journal of Mental Health, 7*(2), 135–143.

Kessler, R. C., Nelson, C. B., & McGonagle, K. A. (1996). The epidemiology of co-occurring addictive and mental disorders: Implications for prevention and service utilization. *American Journal of Orthopsychiatry, 66*(1), pp. 17–31.

Klein, A., Cnaan, R., & Whitecraft, J. (1998). Significance of peer social support with dually diagnosed clients: Findings from a pilot study. *Research on Social Work Practice, 8*(5), 529–551.

Laudet, A. B., Magura, S., Vogel, H. S., & Knight, E. (2000). Addictions services: Support, mutual aid and recovery from dual diagnosis. *Community Mental Health Journal, 36*(5), 457–476.

Lehman, A. F., Myers, C. P., Dixon, L. B., & Johnson, J. L. (1996). Detection of substance use disorders among psychiatric inpatients. *Journal of Nervous and Mental Disease, 184*, 228–233.

Li, L., & Ford, J. (1998). Illicit drug use by women with disabilities. *American Journal of Drug and Alcohol Abuse, 24*(3), 405–418.

Mackelprang, R., & Salsgiver, R. (1999). *Disability: A diversity model approach in human service practice.* Pacific Grove, CA: Brooks/Cole.

McGillicuddy, N., & Blane, H. (1999). Substance use in individuals with mental retardation. *Addictive Behaviors, 24*(6), 869–878.

Mentally ill most likely to smoke. (2000, November 22). *USA Today*, 17A.

Mercer-McFadden, C., Drake, R. E., Brown, N. B., & Fox, R. S. (1997). The community support program demonstrations of services for young adults with severe mental illness and substance use. *Psychiatric Rehabilitation Journal, 20*(3), 13–24.

Meuser, K. T., Drake, R. E., & Noordsy, D. L. (1998). Integrated mental health and substance abuse disorders. *Journal of Practical Psychiatry and Behavioral Health, 4*, 129–139.

Meuser, K. T., Drake, R. E., & Wallach, M. A. (1998). A review of etiological theories. *Addictive Behaviors, 23*, 717–734.

Minkoff, K. (1996). Discussion of "Substance use reduction in the context of outpatient psychiatric treatment." *Community Mental Health Journal, 32*, 307–310.

Mowbray, C. T., Ribisl, K. M, Solomon, M., Luke, D. A., & Kewson, T. P. (1997). Characteristics of dual diagnosis patients admitted to an urban, public psychiatric hospital: An examination of individual, social, and community domains. *American Journal of Drug and Alcohol Abuse, 2,* 309–326.

National Gambling Impact Study Commission. (1999, June 18). *Report of the Commission.* Washington, DC: U.S. Government Printing Office. Available at www .ngisc.gov/reports/fullrpt.html

National Research Council. (1999). *Pathological gambling: A critical review.* Washington, DC: National Academy Press.

Nigam, R., Schottenfeld, R., & Kosten, T. (1992). Treatment of dual diagnosis patients: A relapse prevention group approach. *Journal of Substance Abuse Treatment, 9,* 305–309.

Noordsy, D. L., Schwab, B., Fox, L., & Drake, R. E. (1996). The role of self-help programs in the rehabilitation of persons with severe mental illness and substance use disorders. *Community Mental Health Journal, 32,* 71–81.

Osher, F. C., & Dixon, L. B. (1996). Housing for persons with co-occurring mental and addictive disorders. *New Directions for Mental Health Services, 70,* 53–54.

Osher, F. C., & Kofoed, L. (1989). Treatment of patients with psychiatric and psychoactive substance abuse disorders. *Hospital and Community Psychiatry, 40,* 1025–1030.

Quimby, E. (1995). Homeless clients' perspectives on recovery in the Washington, DC, Dual Diagnosis Project. *Contemporary Drug Problems, 22*(2), 265–289.

Phillips, P., & Labrow, J. (2000). Dual diagnosis—Does harm reduction have a role? *International Journal of Drug Policy, 11,* 279–283.

Powell, T. J., Kurtz, L. F., Garvin, C. D., & Hill, E. M. (1996). A model of AA utilization by persons with a dual diagnosis (the co-occurrence of alcoholism and severe mental illness). *Contemporary Drug Problems, 23,* 139–157.

Prochaska, J., & DiClemente, C. (1992). Stages of change in the modification of problem behaviors. In M. Hersen, R. M. Eisler, & P. M. Miller (Eds.), *Progress in behavior modification* (pp. 184–214). Sycamore, IL: Sycamore Press.

Regier, D. A., Farmer, M. E., Rae, D. S., Locke, B. Z., Keith, S. J., Judd, L. L., & Goodwin, E. K. (1990). Comorbidity of mental disorders with alcohol and other drug abuse. *Journal of the American Medical Association, 264,* 2511–2518.

Rehabilitation Research and Training Center on Drugs and Disability. (1995). *National Needs Assessment Survey results summary.* Dayton, OH: Author.

Rosenberg, S. D., Drake, R. E., Wolford, G. L., Meuser, K. T., Oxman, T. E., Vidaver, R. M., Carrieri, K. L., & Luckoor, R. (1998). Dartmouth assessment of lifestyle instrument (DALI): A substance use disorder screen for people with severe mental illness. *American Journal of Psychiatry, 155*(2), 232–238.

Rosencheck, R., Harkness, L., Johnson, B., Sweeney, C., et al. (1998). Intensive community-focused treatment of veterans with dual diagnoses. *The American Journal of Psychiatry, 155*(10), 1429–1433.

Saunders, J. B., Aasland, O. G., Babor, T. F., De La Fuente, J. R., & Grant, M. (1993). Development of the Alcohol Use Disorders Identification Test (AUDIT): WHO collaborative project on early detection of persons with harmful alcohol consumption: II. *Addiction, 88,* 791–804.

Sciacca, K., & Thompson, C. (1996). Program development and integrated treatment across systems for dual diagnosis: Mental illness, drug addiction, and alcoholism (MIDAA). *Journal of Mental Health Administration, 23*(3), 288–297.

Shulman, G. (1995). Reorienting CD treatment for dual diagnosis. *Behavioral Health Management,* September/October, pp. 30–33.

Smith, S. (1983). *Collected poems.* New York: New Directions.

Substance Abuse and Mental Health Services Administration (SAMHSA). (2001). New SAMHSA report shows value of integrating state mental health, substance abuse, and Medicaid data. Available online from www.samhsa.gov/news/

Timko, C., & Moos, R. H. (1998). Outcomes of the treatment climate in psychiatric and substance abuse program. *Journal of Clinical Psychology, 54*(8), 1137–1150.

Tyas, S., & Rush, B. (1993). The treatment of disabled persons with alcohol and drug problems: Results of a survey of addiction services. *Journal of Studies on Alcohol, 54,* 275–282.

Ziedonis, D. M., & Trudeau, K. (1997). Motivation to quit using substances among individuals with schizophrenia: Implications for a motivation-based treatment model. *Schizophrenia Bulletin, 23*(2), 229–238.

SOCIAL ASPECTS
OF ADDICTION

Addiction to substances and behaviors begins and ends in the context of social relationships and therefore must be treated in the larger context of the social network. Unlike traditional treatment, typically focused on the individual in a standardized format, strengths-based therapy looks to family and other support systems as a buffer against addiction and as an essential resource in recovery. Strengths-based therapy, moreover, starts where the client is and stays where the client is: in his or her role in the family and community life. The starting point in treatment should therefore be with the family, in terms of both risks and resiliencies. Accordingly, chapter 9, the first chapter in this part, describes family dynamics and strategies for engaging the family in treatment. Chapters 10 and 11 focus on race/ethnicity and gender, respectively. Gender is used in the broad sense here to encompass gender nonconformity as well as conformity in sex role behavior. Because they do not conform to society's definition of sexuality, gays, lesbians, bisexuals, and transgender persons are highly vulnerable to drug use and misuse.

The task for practitioners who work with these and all other populations is to help people tap into their individual and collective resources. Throughout this part of the book, therefore, attention is paid to family-centered (chapter 9), ethnic-sensitive (chapter 10), and gender-specific and gay-sensitive (chapter 11) interventions. Chapter 12, on mutual-help support groups, applies the strengths perspective to an appreciation for the role that mutual-help support groups play in recovery. Consistent with the model that is the guiding theme of this book, the focus is on the appreciation, rather than the depreciation, of strategies that work.

Chapter 13, the policy chapter, which stands apart from the others in Part 4, is linked to them by the common thread of a concern with the *social* side (as opposed to the biological or psychological aspects) of addiction. The chapters that comprise the final portion of this book, in short, relate to social (including cultural and political) factors because these factors relate to treatment. We start with the oldest and most fundamental and enduring of all social institutions—the family.

Mam asks him if he brought any money. He tells her times are hard, jobs are scarce, and she says, Is it coddin' me you are? There's a war on and there's nothing but jobs in England. You drank the money, didn't you? You drank the money, Dad. —FRANK MCCOURT (1996), *Angela's Ashes*, p. 270

FAMILY RISKS AND RESILIENCIES

CHAPTER **9**

INTRODUCTION

How we cope, how we see ourselves, how we love—these are the lessons learned at our mother's knee—and at our father's. Whether as ghosts or as active participants, our grandparents (often our nurturers) are there as well.

The family is a system composed of members in constant and dynamic interaction with one another. Patterns of interaction get established—who interacts with whom, who talks and who listens, who has the authority, and who is the controlling force behind the scenes. The family has a pattern, a rhythm that is more than the sum of its parts. Any change in the behavior of one of its members affects not only each of the others but the system as a whole. Addiction is often defined as an illness not just of the individual but of the whole family. Sometimes the misery is so intense that the system barely functions at all; such was the situation immortalized in *Angela's Ashes*. Children growing up in such families fail to get the nurturing and care they need. The anger in such a family is palpable. Because needs are not met, the webs of addiction and impaired parenting perpetuate themselves across generations.

For every alcoholic, compulsive gambler, and cocaine addict, the lives of at least four other people are consistently altered. These other individuals may be in as much pain as the addict; they also may require help in how to deal with the addict or with their own powerful feelings. Family therapy, even in only a few sessions, can be invaluable in reducing the significant others' feelings of guilt or confusion. Family therapy, moreover, can be invaluable in preparing the family for changes that are needed to enhance and maintain the addicted person's recovery. Sometimes the anger and resentment that significant others harbor needs to be addressed before a recovering family member is returned to the family setting. Sometimes, of course, the family environment itself is toxic, with all the participants having serious problems with drugs, for example. Here too, interventions must be directed toward the whole family. To treat the individual in isolation is to ignore the context in which much of that behavior takes place. To know the context, an understanding of the systemic intergenerational nature of addiction is essential.

That addiction is a family disease is a basic assumption of this book. The term *family disease* refers to the fact that the addicted family is malfunctioning. The chaos that the addict experienced in the abyss of his or her addiction is replicated in the chaos of the family. Even more than ordinary illness, addiction is a source of major stress that reverberates through the family system and affects the family's interactions with every other system in the community. The emotional and financial resources of the family may be almost entirely depleted by the stress of the addict's illness. Box 9.1 aptly depicts the havoc that methamphetamine addiction reaps on the parents, the children, and one Iowa community.

Because of the stigma of addiction, the family therapy field has devoted little effort to addictions-focused treatment and has tended to refer afflicted members to specialized services or self-help groups. And because of the difficulty that substance abuse treatment centers face in working with the whole family, combined with third-party reimbursement disincentives to do so, often little more than lip service is given to family members' needs by these treatment centers. Yet for children and partners in the family system, the need to sort out their feelings and to learn more about the nature of the problem that has so consumed them over the years is crucial for the long-term recovery of everyone involved. Too often, also, any family that doesn't match the traditional mold tends to be invisible while the importance of the extended family as a vital resource goes unrecognized.

Dedicated to the principle that addiction is a family illness, this chapter will start by reviewing the precepts of family systems theory, historical and modern, and then, through drawing on personal testimonials, show what addiction does to family rules, roles, and communication patterns and, above all, to love. As dramatically stated by Linda Leonard (1989): "All addictions are killers; each in its own way kills living in the moment, kills creativity, love, and the trusting faith of the inner child" (p. 196). In contrast to traditional family therapy, the family treatment interventions described in this chapter are designed to elicit resilience and healing in family members, rather than focusing on the family's presumed role in perpetuating addiction. We have adapted interventions to parallel the readiness of the family for change, a phase approach. The phase approach views treatment needs in terms of the five basic intervals, stretching from precontemplation through the maintenance period. The stages of family needs may or may not correspond directly to the addict's stage of recovery. This chapter concludes with a listing of exercises geared toward work with families in Family Week programming.

BOX 9.1	FAMILIES WRECKED BY METH EPIDEMIC LOSS

Parents neglect children when the craving for drugs control their lives

By now, Bill Newton's story, told from the Polk County Jail, is all too familiar among some Iowa families.

His girls, ages 2 and 6, will spend most of their childhood without their father.

His wife, if she chooses to stay with him through a 10-year prison sentence, will watch him turn gray from the confines of a prison visiting room.

And every night as the prison doors are locked shut, the former Des Moines salesman will stare at the walls of his cell and wonder at the devastation methamphetamine has wrought.

"I lost the best job in the world, my home, my family, and now my freedom—all of this in less than a year," he said. "Meth caused me to do things I cannot believe I did."

Experts say thousands of families like Newton's are paying dearly for Iowa's now raging methamphetamine epidemic. Since meth surfaced in earnest here in 1993, scores of formerly law-abiding Iowans—and occasionally entire families—have given themselves over to crime, violence, and financial ruin.

Family crises have not grabbed attention the same way some of the drug's more spectacular consequences have, but they are just as insidious, the experts say.

"We have to realize that people can't continue to do this drug and expect Iowa to be the same," said Polk County attorney John Sarcone, whose office prosecutes scores of offenses spurred by meth.

Kathryn Miller, executive director of Des Moines' Youth Law Center, said those who work closely with Iowa families have only recently begun to grasp the fallout.

"We're just now waking up to the gravity of the problem," said Miller, whose nonprofit law office represents abused and neglected children.

Hundreds of parents are losing custody of their children, a trend seen only in recent years as meth has secured its grip statewide, she said.

Newton, who was transferred recently to the state prison in Oakdale, said it took him just two months to become an addict. A former salesman for Radio Shack in Des Moines, the 29-year-old said he abandoned his family and his morals almost overnight to support a habit that quickly grew bigger than his $40,000-a-year-job.

Now, a year later, he is haunted by the tears shed by his mother, sister, and brother when they come to visit. Any hope he had of masking the shame of prison from his daughters have been dashed. Recently, he had to quit pretending he was in a hospital and give his 6-year-old what she most wanted for Christmas—a hug from her father in the Oakdale visiting room.

Source: *Des Moines Register*, January 4, 1999, p. 1A. Reprinted by permission of the *Des Moines Register*. Article by Lee Rood.

CLASSIC FAMILY SYSTEMS THERAPY

The leading proponents of family systems theory have tended to focus almost exclusively on interpersonal transactions (Johnson, 1986; van Wormer, 1995). From the classic systems perspective, a disorder such as mental illness, anorexia, or alcoholism is viewed as stemming from faulty family communication or functioning. In this tradition, the systems therapist does not do individual therapy, that is, try to fix "the identified patient." Rather, the patient is viewed solely within the context of the family, where the symptoms or problems presumably evolved (Keller, Galanter, & Weinberg, 1997; Hanson, 1996). Relationships and communication are stressed. The fact that the designated sick person in the family could truly be sick and be the source of the family's stress and malfunctioning is not considered.

Much of what we know as family mental illness patterns, systems theory, and therapy today was developed by Bowen in work with families of schizophrenic children (Lawson, Lawson, & Rivers, 2001). Key concepts concerning the intricacies of family communication, such as double-bind theory and the receiving of mixed messages, were seen as instrumental in the development of schizophrenia in the child. Following her work with Gregory Bateson, Virginia Satir helped popularize the notion of the role of family interaction in the "development of mental illness in a family member" (Chase-Marshall, 1976). Similarly, alcoholism was conceptualized by Bowen (1978) as a mere symptom of a problem in the larger family or social unit. Alcoholism, like schizophrenia, was not viewed as the problem but as the *solution* to the problem. Family therapy, divorced from alcoholism treatment, was the sole intervention required; once the family was working as a system, individual problems such as mental illness and alcoholism would evaporate.

The drug addict is viewed by classical family system theorists as "the symptom carrier" of the family dysfunction (Bradshaw, 1988). In his or her aberrant behavior, the addict helps maintain the family balance by deflecting attention away from the real problems (Kaufman & Kaufman, 1992). Common to all these systems thinkers is the belief that the key to changing the drinking behavior lies in strengthening interaction patterns among family members. The significance in addiction is in maintaining equilibrium in the family; remove the addict as scapegoat and another family member will start acting out, goes the thinking.

The literature on eating disorders, likewise, is rife with what we might term "systemic determinism." Minuchin (1974) and Nichols (1984) were only the first of thousands of theorists to place the source of anorexia in the tension within the family. A more recent offering, "The Impact of Family Dynamics on Anorexia," by Ellis-Ordway (1992), echoes the classic formulation. Feminist writers such as Rabinor (1994), however, decry what amounts to the "mother-blaming" that transcends the eating disorders literature. Fortunately, attention has shifted today to a recognition of the biochemical component in a number of disorders. The role of cultural factors, such as those involved in the development of anorexia and bulimia, is also recognized.

Consistent with the pathology focus, so engrained in the classical formulation, the need for the therapist to draw on the family as "a resource" has been overlooked. Moreover, family therapy too frequently has considered the systems in the interior of family life while neglecting the larger social systems in the community (Krestan, 2000). Only in the past few years, as Krestan indicates, has family therapy as a whole dealt with issues of cultural diversity at all. Credit is due to many families that, instead of being dysfunctional, have demonstrated remarkable survival skills while encountering multiple levels of oppression (for example, racism, heterosexism) in the larger social structure.

Missing from traditional theoretical models is a grounding in empirical research as well as a confusion of cause and effect. Communication patterns in a family containing a paranoid schizophrenic member might well appear bizarre. Sadly, there is some indication of harm done through this family-blaming orientation. Medical needs may have been overlooked; needed interventions may not have been provided; and the location of the problem in the family would have aroused feelings of guilt and anger in family members (Johnson, 1986). In an extensive ethnographic study of the families of the mentally ill, Hanson (1994) records the utter frustration of family members whose contributions were continually devalued in the process of family therapy.

Fortunately, thanks to the influence of the feminist movement and modern biological research concerning the etiology of mental disorders, family systems theory has reconceptualized much of its teachings. The addiction treatment field, to its credit, never did view the family as the source of pathology; addiction was seen as primary in its own right, as the cause rather than the symptom of family communication problems. In fact, with the disease model firmly entrenched and the focus on the *individual* alcoholic, the wonder is that the family was incorporated into treatment programming at all. That the family's needs do get addressed at all is probably a reflection of the increasingly interdisciplinary nature of the chemically dependent treatment field and the fact that so many practitioners in the field come from alcoholic family backgrounds. Professionals schooled in family counseling techniques, moreover, have brought to addictions work a modified and highly useful understanding of family pain and dynamics. In short, a gradual paradigm shift in thought from family-as-enemy to family-as-treatment-ally has occurred. Work with the whole family is now recognized, at least theoretically, as a vital component in addiction treatment (van Wormer, 1995). The introduction of *network therapy,* an approach that involves family members and peers in the client's relapse prevention efforts through the promotion of cohesion teamwork among network members, is a welcome addition to the chemical dependency field (Keller, Galanter, & Weinberg, 1997).

Focus on the Family

In addiction treatment, the focus has been on children of alcoholics, adult children of alcoholics, and rules and role-playing in the chemically dependent family. The family's stages of progression into the illness of alcoholism was first noted and graphically described by Joan Jackson (1954), who published an article on the subject in the *Quarterly Journal of Substance Abuse*. During the 1970s, when the family therapy movement began to gain momentum, the concept of viewing the family as a system led to the notion of alcoholism as a family disease (Brooks & Rice, 1997). Sharon Wegscheider's (1981) groundbreaking writing and films on "the family trap" marked a departure from the earlier, atomistic and individualistic approaches of addictions specialists. In her depiction of typical roles that members of the chemically dependent's family play, Wegscheider (now Wegscheider-Cruse) conceptualized alcoholism in terms of both its physical and its social dimensions. Her approach was highly practical in its implications and one with which family members could easily identify.

Popular author and public speaker Claudia Black was influenced by the writings of fellow social worker and systems theorist Virginia Satir. Black's (1981) thought-provoking book *It Will Never Happen to Me!* applied many of the fundamentals of systems theory concepts to family alcoholism treatment. Her "don't talk, don't trust, don't feel" formulation neatly summed up the dynamics in an alcoholic household. Dulfano, in her less widely known *Families, Alcoholism, and Recovery* (1982) offered a brief but dynamic ecological interpretation of the alcoholism syndrome.

In 1983, Lawson and Lawson published *Alcoholism and the Family,* which helped integrate family therapy concepts and substance abuse treatment. The view of the family as client was provided in this text. The second edition was published in 1998. Kaufman (1985) similarly provided helpful guidelines for family counseling in his *Substance Abuse and Family Therapy.* More recently, Wallen's (1993) *Addiction in Human Development* offered a developmental perspective to addiction treatment. Because alcoholic families often resist change, as Wallen noted, particular attention must be paid to their life cycle stages as the system adapts to the problem drinking of a family member. Families as well as individuals move through stages of recovery, recovery that affects the balance or equilibrium that has evolved through the underfunctioning of one family member. The final stage of recovery, according to Wallen, involves restoring the system to a balance, to maintain sobriety.

Al-Anon, founded in the 1950s to serve the families of AA members, today has groups in over 70 countries. In its early days, Al-Anon was only for wives, who often were seen as somehow responsible for their partners' drinking. Today, male partners of alcoholics, although a minority, are members of Al-Anon as well. The focus is on group support and establishing independence from the sick patterns associated with addiction.

The Twelve Steps used by Al-Anon were modified slightly to pertain to persons who are powerless not over alcohol but over another's use of alcohol. Individual work is directed toward independence and self-awareness. Learning that attempts to shield the alcoholic/addict from the consequences of his or her addiction are futile and counterproductive helps free the family members from the emotionally wearing attempt to control what cannot be controlled. Members are aided in achieving detachment from the active alcoholic/addict. Al-Anon members rave about the close personal bonds that develop from membership in this group. Recognition of one's powerlessness over another's addiction goes a long way toward reducing one's guilt feelings.

One of the most significant referrals the addictions counselor can make to family members of alcoholics is to a local Al-Anon group. Clients should be prepared for a kind of ritualistic openness and friendliness that may at first seem intrusive; they should be encouraged to visit several different meetings before deciding on whether or not to join. Self-help groups such as this are particularly appealing to clients who are outgoing and extraverted.

Alateen is the organization for children of alcoholic parents. Children are helped to achieve understanding of alcoholism and awareness of severe family problems. *Nar-Anon* is the comparable group for family members of narcotics users, and *Gam-Anon* that for the families of compulsive gamblers. Adult Children of Alcoholics (ACOA) is a rapidly growing group for those who grew up in alcoholic homes and who may have many unresolved feelings and issues pertaining to their family life. Members are encouraged to give full vent to their repressed feelings. Because emotions may be intense, newly sober alcoholics may be advised to achieve a lengthy sobriety first before joining such an endeavor.

FAMILY ADAPTATION TO ADDICTION

The concept of *adaptation* is a useful way to conceptualize the family's response to a member's addictive behavior. Adaptation is defined by Germain (1991) as an active process of self-change or environmental change or both, not a mere passive adjustment to circumstances. Adaptation flows from and helps alleviate stress caused in the family system by the drinking, gambling, compulsive sexual behavior, etc. Paralleling individual adaptation to stress by the addict is the awesome set of demands imposed on the family members. Each family will have its own peculiar style of adaptation—coping through hiding key resources (money), blaming, covering up for the addictive behavior, joining in the addiction, or becoming extremely touchy with outsiders. The stress of the addictive pattern (for example, gambling and winning, gambling and entering a losing streak) has a synergistic, or multiplying, effect throughout the family system and related social networks. The family, awkwardly, may come to serve in a mediating role between the addict and other systems—work, school, larger family. But gradually, as the illness progresses, the bridges between the alcoholic and his or her social world will be broken. The family may then adapt to the social isolation and continual stress of the progressing alcoholism, or members may regroup and form a reconstituted family without the addict. A third alternative, of course, is treatment for the addict both separately and within the context of the whole family. Treatment considerations would focus on the development of new, nondestructive communication patterns and adaptation to changes associated with recovery.

A teacher whose husband grew up in an alcoholic home comments (in personal correspondence of May 14, 2001) on Germain's concept of adaptation by the family to illness in an adult member:

> Perhaps my husband and his younger brother are good examples of Germain's premise. Bill was 16 and his brother, Eric, was 7 when their alcoholic father died. Eric was the younger child. Bill's perception had more years of exposure, while

Eric's remained that of a small child's view. Bill grew up to be a man who rarely drinks. Eric not only is an alcoholic, but his behavior when he was an active drinker landed him in prison. Bill basically hated his father because he saw more abuse and had to shoulder more responsibility because of the alcohol, while Eric did not. Their perceptions influenced the choices they made in living environments. Bill adapted by using the influence as a picture of how not to be. Eric saw that influence as a way to get people to do things for you so you can be "happy." His perception led him to choose similar environments to fill his need for a comfort zone. This environment influenced more abusive drinking and behavior, which ultimately led to his incarceration.

As Leo Tolstoy once wrote, "All happy families are alike, but every unhappy family is unhappy in its own way" (1917/1876, p. 1). Individuals within the same family, likewise, adapt differently to the same stress. Next we hear from one adult child of an alcoholic, a high school teacher:

> Communication in my family was much like Claudia Black's rules suggest. "Don't talk, don't trust, and don't feel." We were not allowed to talk about the problems of my dad's drinking and mental illness. If I attempted to talk about it, I was just told, "He's sick and can't help it." Communication was so poor that my mom participated in what I consider an unhealthy game to communicate with my dad. She would call one of my older sisters who lived outside the home and tell her something she wanted my dad to hear within his earshot. For instance, if she wanted to go to a baby shower, she would tell one of my sisters and hope my father would hear. Then he would ask her what she was talking about. Most of the time he didn't allow her to go anyway, but this was her method of trying. My father was guilty of unhealthy communication as well. He would stop talking to my mother for up to four days at a time if she said or did something he didn't like. He would then communicate sarcastically through me. If I would ask him why the television wasn't working right, he would say, "Ask your mother, she thinks she knows everything." He would tell me adult information while she was in the room. Although he was talking to me, he was really talking to her.
>
> I remember coming home and feeling like I was walking on eggshells every day because I never knew what the mood would be. I spent a lot of time being tense. We were not allowed to discuss our problems with outsiders or bring outsiders into the home. We were not allowed to have any feelings except laughter. If we were hurt, we could laugh but not cry. I was told exactly how to feel, so to this day I have a hard time describing how I actually feel. (from van Wormer's personal files)

As the addicted person learns to adapt to his or her lifestyle to accommodate to the tremendous demands of this illness, so the family unit adapts to the stress that has been imposed on its functioning. As various individuals come forward to fill the essential family *roles,* the integrity of the family is preserved; equilibrium is maintained, but at the expense of one or more of the individual members. If the addict later recovers, the operating family system will be "thrown out of whack," a crisis will occur, and individual and group adaptation will be required.

In summary, according to systems theory, the individual alcoholic is not viewed in isolation but as someone in dynamic interaction with the environment. Attention is paid to the complex ways in which individual persons, in terms of the roles they perform, are linked with other roles in the family.

WEGSCHEIDER'S ROLE THEORY

Wegscheider (1981) introduced a small, clanging mobile (the same device that hangs over a baby's crib) to represent the family interaction pattern; as one piece of the mobile is moved, the whole apparatus moves. Roles that individual family members play reinforce or clash with roles of other members.

Wegscheider, who, like Claudia Black, was inspired by Virginia Satir's role theory, labeled the following roles played in the chemically dependent family: the chemically dependent person, the "chief enabler," the hero, the scapegoat, the lost child, and the mascot. These types are based on her and others' observations; they should be regarded as ideal types only—their existence is not scientifically validated. Associated with upwardly mobile middle-class families, the following purported characteristics may or may not apply to other social classes and ethnic groups. (See Laurel Chaput's [2001] comparative analysis of styles of family functioning in the presence of substance misuse.) Van Wormer, in her practice in Norway, found that family members readily identified themselves and others in their families with these roles. Many identified with more than one role, saying, for example, "I was a little bit the hero and a little bit the clown growing up." The following descriptions are drawn from van Wormer's Family Week presentation in Norway (See van Wormer, 1995, for more details). Our purpose in presenting these roles is not because we believe they represent reality but because the concept of role-playing has been found helpful in engaging people in family systems work. The use of the children's labels is controversial; even the authors of this text disagree about their usefulness in family group programming. But we do agree that Wegscheider-Cruse's conceptualization has helped popularize the idea of family systems work and that this is a positive development. Please regard the descriptions that follow with appropriate skepticism.

The Chemically Dependent Person   This member of the family is gripped by contradictions. Sensitive to the point of touchiness, the chemically dependent person is selfishly preoccupied with the sources of addiction. Often charming and talented, this family member tends to see life events and personalities in terms of black and white, all or nothing. There is a tendency to escape the scene when very high expectations (of relationships, work, studies) are not realized. When a man occupies this role, he is often treated with great fondness by his children. The woman alcoholic/addict is inclined to be either divorced or married to a fellow alcoholic/addict. She is subject to strong criticism for her neglect of motherhood responsibilities.

The Family Manager   Because Wegscheider's term *chief enabler* has acquired pejorative connotations, in disregard of the survivorship nature of this role, we prefer the term *family manager*. The individual who occupies this position is often a sober partner of an alcoholic/addict. The role that the family manager assumes is to overfunction to compensate for the partner's underfunctioning. As the family sinks along with the alcoholic/addict into near ruin, this individual worries and nags and struggles to balance the checkbook. His or her denial in the early stages of the partner's addiction may be replaced by a frantic and bitter awareness later on. The person who occupies this position in the family structure suffers from a bad press that relates to the game he or she often ends up playing in conjunction with the games of the alcoholic. Counselors at treatment centers are quick to condemn the sober partner for some of the covering-up devices that make survival as a family possible. If not accorded a great deal of sensitivity, family managers are often plagued by feelings of shame and guilt.

The Hero   Often the firstborn child in the family, this high-achieving and very competent individual is constantly seeking approval. The family labels this child as the star—scholar, football hero, or performer. Inclined to suffer from low self-esteem, the child in this position tends to feel loved for what he or she *does* rather than who he or she *is*. Accustomed to babysitting and caring for younger siblings, this child often grows up to work in the helping professions. Perfectionism is a key risk. Marrying an alcoholic or addict is a risk, according to Wegscheider (1981) and Black (1981); such a marriage preserves the caretaking role from the family of origin.

The Scapegoat   This is the child, often the second born, whom everyone loves to blame. The negative label is applied and seems to stick. The irresponsible behavior that accompanies this role often lands the perpetrator in trouble. According to the typology, early pregnancy is a risk for girls and delinquency for boys; school performance is poor, and early experimentation with drugs and alcohol is common.

The Lost Child   This child lives in a fantasy world and is said to be little or no trouble. Although he or she may be lonely, this younger child can entertain him- or herself through endless playing with dolls or television or computer games. When family members fight, the lost child has an excellent escape mechanism. In order to grow into a responsible, mature adult, the boy or girl in this role requires a tremendous amount of help with self-expression and facing problems realistically.

The Mascot   Forever clowning, the occupier of this role helps provide comic relief for the family unit. Encouraged to be cute and to kid around, the mascot can attract much positive attention while distracting members from serious matters. Often hyperactive, this child has a short attention span, which may be linked in some way to the needs of the family. The means of escape is laughter.

But don't children in all families play roles? This is a commonly asked question when a counselor presents these role descriptions. The answer is yes. All of us play roles—in our families, at work, and in therapy groups. When stress is very high, the roles tend to become rigid and to be used as defense mechanisms, forms of escape. The children's roles, like that of the family manager, are best conceived of as normal responses to an abnormal situation.

The strengths inherent in the roles are rarely mentioned. And yet, the family manager typically has excellent organizational skills and flexibility. This person's capabilities and resourcefulness help the family survive. Angela, the mother described by Frank McCourt in *Angela's Ashes,* resorted to all sorts of compromising behavior in her struggle to keep her children from going hungry as the father squandered the family's money through drinking and lost jobs.

Children who grew up in addict/alcoholic homes often develop coping mechanisms that may be useful later. The hero, for example, learns to assume responsibility early, and often becomes a leader in adulthood. The scapegoat, who makes friends easily, may become a business success because of his or her willingness to take risks. The lost child has a great imagination and may write poetry or get involved in the arts. The mascot is often popular and, of course, knows how to use humor in creative and original ways.

The term *codependency,* originally used to describe the strain of being a partner to a chemically dependent person, has taken on a life far beyond the intent of the original uses of the term. Sometimes this phenomenon is described as a disease that precedes the relationship with an addict. Despite the lack of scientific evidence for such a conceptualization, the codependency movement has swept the country "in cultlike fashion" (Wetzel, 1991, p. 21). This movement and the associated self-help literature pathologize behaviors associated with female qualities, such as nurturance, as Sandra Anderson (1994) suggests.

Whereas early models blamed wives for their husbands' alcoholism, the most recent theoretical frameworks are more cautious in their formulations. The emphasis in family therapy, according to Simon, McNeil, Franklin, and Cooperman (1991), has shifted away from blaming the family for the *etiology* of the disease to blaming the family for the *perpetuation* of the disease. Taking a cross-cultural perspective, Cable (2000) points out the European American middle-class bias of the codependency movement, with its "one-size-fits-all" prescription for normality, including an emphasis on detachment, on taking care of oneself.

As early as 1987, the Hazelden Family Center disassociated themselves from use of this "diagnosis":

> The view we take at the Hazelden Family Center is rooted in health promotion, a systems approach to health problems. We believe that each member of the family has an innate power of self-healing, and we try to awaken that power within our clients. Our practices are based on a combination of Al-Anon principles and the family systems theories developed by Murray Bowen, Ph.D. Both de-emphasize the need for a diagnosable sickness, instead requiring a sincere desire to change.
>
> There are many ways to help families return to health, and we respect the philosophical differences that shape various practices in our growing field. *Codependency,* both as a clinical and popular term, brings some of these differences into focus. (Hazelden Publishing Co., 1987, p. 2)

Interestingly, the book *Codependent No More,* by Melody Beattie (1980), which has sold over 5 million copies, is published by Hazelden Publishing Company and sold in the treatment center's bookstore.

Instead of using the pejorative term *codependent,* our suggestion is that the more positive term *survivor* be applied to women (and men) who have done whatever is necessary to protect themselves and their families from the consequences of their partners' drinking and drug use. To describe the situation of a family member who is sinking into the abyss of illness along with the addict, the term *coaddict* might be used.

Despite the fact that the partners of alcoholics do not have a disease—only the symptoms of struggling against someone else's disease—individual and family therapy can be extremely beneficial in the healing process for these survivors. Work in the area of self-esteem can do much to help resolve powerful feelings accompanying years of abuse and unshared pain.

Family therapy interventions, to be effective, need to be geared toward the family's stage of recovery. This stage may or may not parallel the addict's motivation for change or actual changed behavior. The following scheme directs the therapist's attention to the needs of the family as they progress into wellness. Consistent with other chapters in this book, we are drawing on Prochaska and DiClemente's (1992) stages-of-change model.

STAGES OF CHANGE AND FAMILY TREATMENT

Research on the effectiveness of family counseling in enhancing recovery is sporadic. There is no Project MATCH utilizing family therapy techniques. Within Project MATCH, however, the success of treatment outcomes was shown to be related to the extent to which the client's social network was supportive of sobriety (U.S. Department of Health and Human Services, 1999). In their review of the literature, however, Waldron and Slesnick (1998) concluded that family therapy is an effective treatment for both adults and adolescents with problem substance use, that family intervention is associated with higher rates of treatment compliance and retention than is treatment without family involvement. Having a functioning support system is crucial in preventing a lapse into previous problematic behavior. And since family members often develop problems in response to someone else's drinking or other drug use, including early experimentation with psychoactive substances by children, getting the whole family together for counseling should be a standard of addiction prevention (Velleman, 2000). Family sessions offer an opportunity, moreover, to help children in the family understand some of the stresses their non-problem-drinking parent has been under, as Velleman suggests.

Precontemplation

At this stage it is unlikely the family unit will approach the treatment center for help. They might be encouraged to attend a Family Evening–type program, however, when a family member gets in trouble with the law, such as through a DWI (drinking while intoxicated) conviction and follow-up assessment or through a child welfare referral. In any case, rules of the family at this stage of recovery are likely to be of the "don't talk, don't trust, don't feel" variety (Black, 1981).

Contact with family members seen at this stage is apt to be short term and superficial. Sometimes families attend information-giving lectures. Generally,

FIGURE 9.1 | FAMILY FORMS

A. The enmeshed family: Spouses are estranged: one child is enmeshed with the father, one with the mother.

B. The isolated family: Lack of cohesion and social support. Each menber is protected by wall of defenses.

C. The healthy family: All are touching, but their boundaries are not overlapping.

Key: F = father, M = mother, C = child

Source: van Wormer (1995), p. 207.

counselors provide a description of family roles along with a discussion of characteristics of the so-called functional family. And what are the characteristics of a functional family? Open communication, respect for individual differences and boundaries, stable routines and rituals, and having fun and a sense of humor are among the qualities generally elicited (from the grouping of family members). Figure 9.1 depicts various family styles of interaction that can be shared with the group of family members. Participants will often volunteer to diagram their families of origin and current families in this manner. A discussion of healthy boundaries often ensues.

In working with a family in which there are addictive problems, the therapist might start by helping members to identify their family's goals. He or she asks open-ended questions, such as: "What brings you here?" "What would you like to happen in our work together?" "If you change some things, what would they be?" (U.S Department of Health and Human Services, 1999)

Typically, assessment of the individual with the addictive problems is done at this initial stage of treatment. As required by the court or insurance company, assessment most often is solely of the individual addict, with input from family members being provided, if at all, at a later stage. In so separating the addict from significant others, however, the opportunity is missed to engage family members in the process. The inclusion of family members from the start offers several advantages. Such inclusion provides a means of observing how family members relate as a unit, a means for discovering strengths in the addict's background, and an opportunity to provide education into the biological and psychosocial aspects of addiction. Besides, it is never too early to begin preparing the family for the changes members will need to make in conjunction with the addict's recovery. The first session may close with the assignment of tasks designed to get the family members to take some small steps in areas where change is feasible. One such step might be to attend a relevant support group, such as Al-Anon or Nar-Anon; involvement in such a group can be invaluable in helping members more toward change.

A Cautionary Note

Any time families are brought in for counseling, and especially when substance misuse is a factor, it is critical to screen for domestic violence. If there is violence against children or children are endangered, child welfare authorities must be notified. If the wife is being victimized, the husband or partner should be referred to a batterers' group. Collaboration between substance abuse treatment centers and women's shelters is crucial (see van Wormer, 2001). Couples in which there is battering should not be referred to conjoint counseling, because if the wife reveals secrets about the marriage—for example, some sort of inadequacy in her partner—she is at risk of being beaten when they return home. Even family counseling including the children with the mother is a high-risk proposition; an insecure and suspicious husband might question the children to find out what was said at the sessions. Down the line, after the batterer has been successfully treated, some family counseling may be attempted. Safety for all family members, however, must be the first consideration.

Contemplation

During the contemplation stage the family member acknowledges concerns and is considering the possibility of the need for change, for example, in recognizing that the loved one has a serious addiction problem. Psychologically the shift is from reluctance to acknowledge a problem to anger, anger caused by the suffering related to the drinking, gambling, etc.

The therapist often gets involved when a client requests counseling for help with a marital problem, domestic violence, or behavioral problems in the children. Then in assessing the client's needs and goals the role of addiction in the family life becomes apparent. Just as he or she does in working with addicts in early stage treatment, the therapist strives to elicit self-motivational statements of insight and ideas about solutions from the family clients. Reinforcement of clients' capabilities and survival skills are vital to help strengthen these persons to take action toward the desired solution. Possible actions that the family members might be willing to contemplate are: to meet with the therapist for several sessions of family counseling to communicate needs and expectations; to work toward getting the addict to receive help for the addictive behavior, perhaps through attending a self-help group such as AA; and work on plans for a trial separation. Whether or not the situation improves, family counseling of this sort can be a godsend for the partner and other family members; having a dispassionate but compassionate outsider to talk to can be immensely thera-peutic. In their interviews with parents who regained custody of their children after recovering from addiction, Akin and Gregoire (1997) found that parents attributed much credit to social workers who had faith that, despite their ad-diction and testing behavior, the parents had the capacity to change.

Although participation of significant others in treatment has been found to be one of the best predictors of cocaine abstinence, Laudet, Magura, Furst, Kumar, & Whitney (1999) found the male partners of cocaine-using women to be far more difficult to engage in family treatment than the female partners of users. The men's active drug use and their refusal to focus on this fact are among the reasons hypothesized for this finding.

Preparation

The theme for this stage of change can be summarized in the addict's partner or coaddict's attitude of "I can't take it any more. I am at the breaking point." Tasks for the counselor during this period are to help family members clarify their goals and strategies for effecting change, offer a list of options and advice if so desired, and steer the family toward social support networks. Boosting the partner's confidence at this stage is tremendously important.

A highly effective therapeutic technique that the family members of the ad-dict might want to consider is a formal intervention. Often associated with the Johnson Institute in Minneapolis, intervention is a process for providing feed-back to the person with addiction problems. Key persons in the addict's life are identified—these may include a doctor, a boss (if one's work is in jeopardy), a pastor, and close friends.

Action

At this point, let us assume the whole family is involved in counseling, all ex-cept for the addicted individual (see Loneck, 1995). All family participants are bent on seeing change happen. Family sessions at this stage are crucial in build-ing solidarity so that the addict will not be able to play one family member off against another. The sessions are crucial also in providing these individuals with the opportunity to ventilate their feelings—grief, rage, despair, etc.—and to learn about addiction as illness. In Box 9.2 Carroll Schuety, a counselor who

BOX 9.2	STEPS TO INTERVENE BY CARROLL SCHUETY, PATHWAYS TREATMENT CENTER, WAVERLY, IOWA

It's 2:30 Saturday morning. A car swerves and rolls up over the curb onto the lawn. The driver stumbles out of the car and staggers into the house. Suddenly, there is a shattering of glass as a lamp crashes to the floor and cursing echoes throughout the house. The spouse and children lie silently in their beds, not moving a muscle, fearful of provoking further anger in their spouse or parent. They listen for the sounds of heavy breathing as a sign that he or she is asleep so they can feel safe from verbal and/or physical abuse for a few more hours. Society assumes that alcoholism involves and destroys only the drinker and that the family suffers no devastating effects. Many people also believe that the spouse and children must remain passive and helpless as the drinker sinks deeper into the deadly disease of alcoholism. In fact, nothing is further from the truth. Family members can take constructive action to stop the destruction of the drinker and themselves through the process of an intervention.

What is an intervention? It is a method of confronting the drinker for the purpose of getting him or her into treatment. It is a confrontation that causes a family crisis that will bring the drinker to the painful realization that his drinking has caused problems and he cannot continue as he has been. This can be facilitated by a substance abuse counselor. Although, if a layperson understands the process, a counselor is not necessary.

The first step in organizing an intervention is to gather two or more persons together who have witnessed the destructive drinking behavior. The people could consist of family members, friends, clergy, coworkers, employers, or a physician. It has been my experience that children who have suffered from the behavior of the drinker are often most effective in forcing the drinker to see himself realistically.

In the second step, each person prepares a detailed written list of specific examples involving alcohol misuse that he or she has personally witnessed. These actual events force the drinker to admit that his or her concerns are legitimate. Another important

---

has herself conducted numerous successful interventions with Iowa farm families, describes the process.

Going from the point of view of counselor to family member, a young woman (in personal correspondence of January 28, 1999) provides this poignant account of her childhood memory of an intervention with her father:

> When I was around 13, we visited a counselor for a rehearsal. The next week my dad's brothers and sister, close friends who were recovering alcoholics, my mom, my sister, and I gathered at our house on the farm and dad came home. I think he was aware what was going on and became extremely emotional, crying with his head down at the table. I remember exactly where I was standing, at the end of the table against the wall with my sister, and when it came my turn to read my statement all I could say was "I want you to go because I love you" and began to sob. I remember going up to my mom and dad's room to get his suitcase and dad couldn't say a word; he just cried and hugged us and got in the car to go. It is one of the sad-

aspect of writing the lists and reading them to each other prior to the actual confrontation is that it unites the group. In preparing your list, you should avoid opinions and general statements such as:

> "You're always drinking."

> "You drink too much."

> "You might get fired."

> "Your drinking is getting worse."

You should point out instead:

> "Last month, I felt scared when you fell down the stairs and broke your foot after you had been drinking."

> "Last Thursday I saw you drinking on the job. I felt concerned because your job performance has been going down in the past few months."

> "I'm feeling scared because in the past year, you've been arrested twice for drunk driving offenses."

> "When you attended my school conferences, you were drunk and I felt embarrassed."

It is important to talk about your feelings when you share the situation that you are describing with "I feel" or "I felt" statements. Feeling statements will help reduce the defensiveness of the drinker.

You must, as an intervention team, agree on a "what if" clause in case the drinker rejects all your options by declaring, "I can do it myself, I'll just stop drinking." If this happens, you must persuade the drinker to make a commitment to enter treatment if his or her own attempt to quit is unsuccessful. It must also be understood that even one drink constitutes failure on his part. Another action that could be taken is to commit the person to treatment through a legal process. The local prosecutor's office or treatment center can usually provide the details.

Printed with permission of Carroll Schuety.

dest memories I experienced in childhood. He was gone for one month, and about three months after he returned we sold our farm and he relapsed, yet to return to treatment about a year later on his own will; he has been sober ever since. I can honestly say I am very proud of him.

Maintenance

More important than the role of family in assessment and treatment is the role of family in early recovery. As the addict's progress toward health and wholeness becomes more and more a reality, the family therapist may take on the role of facilitator to aid in the process of reconciliation. Members of the family may want to come to terms with lifelong feelings of rejection; there may or may not be a desire for forgiveness.

Brown and Lewis (1999) provide the most complete delineation in the literature of the therapeutic tasks and pitfalls involved in the process of recovery. *The Alcoholic Family in Recovery* draws on the experiences of members of four recovering families to describe the ways recovery has challenged and changed their relationships. Much of this process, as Brown and Lewis demonstrate, is painful.

Transition, as Brown and Lewis explain, is characterized by massive change that affects children and adults at every level. The environment feels unsafe; the family structure, after years of chaos, is not strong enough to handle change. In the counseling session, the therapist addresses the family concerns and recovery progress. Individual members may have issues from the past that they will want addressed at this time.

As behavioral changes are established in the family, the focus of sessions shifts toward maintenance of change independent of the therapist. Now that the problematic substance use has decreased and other family interactions have improved, other family problems (such as suppressed anger and an adolescent's substance misuse) may need to be addressed (Waldron & Slesnick, 1998). Family sessions at this point can help make the difference between sobriety and failure to change, and even between keeping the family together and divorce. The therapist can help the family anticipate stressors and support the addict in avoiding triggers and high-risk events.

A complete "what to do if" contingency plan needs to be set in motion in case of backtracking. Clients are given numbers to call and asked to come up with ideas for what to put in a step-by-step plan for getting the help they need. Harm reduction strategies and solutions to sustain the change in behavior should be explored in treatment aftercare counseling. The couple, moreover, often can benefit from receiving information concerning sexual problems that arise in the absence of alcohol and drug use; if the issue is sexual addiction, the posttreatment counseling needs are tremendous.

Together, the family members can benefit greatly with work in the areas of communication, decision making, and discussion of rules and how the rules will be enforced. Now that progress toward recovery is well under way, the stage is set for a shared groping for solutions to problems that may never have been identified without outside help. Ideally, the family therapist is a nonparticipant in the immediate, emotionally charged issues within the family (such as who takes responsibility over what and the division of labor). The focus of the therapist is not on the *content* of the interaction but on the *process* itself. Through skilled and friendly questioning, the therapist imparts awareness of the form of the interaction: "Have you noticed how whenever the two of you argue your son leans over backwards in his chair until you have to stop him?" "I notice when you cry, Mary, your daughter's eyes start watering up too. Does this suggest a strong closeness of feeling between the two of you?" "Who interrupts whom in this family?"

To handle the all-too-common situation of the newly sober father's bid to reestablish his role of authority in the family the therapist (T) might proceed as follows with the father, Bill (B):

T.: Bill, I'd like you to stop for a moment and check out what you're doing. You expressed concern that the children don't talk to you more openly. Right?

B.: Yes.

T.: Let's think about what just happened with Steve. He began to tell you how he felt about those reckless rides in the car and you cut him off with "Not now." Did you notice how he pulled back then? How did you feel, Steve, when your father cut you off in this way?

Instead of excessive emotionalism in family sessions, a calm, intellectual atmosphere should be encouraged. Members are helped to listen to each other. Heavy emotion can be defused. For example, if a mother becomes distraught, other members can be asked what they can do to provide support or how they feel about the outburst. In interviewing with the mother, the focus can be on the thoughts that accompany her feelings.

Emotions may need to be defused when couples shout at each other. A helpful intervention is to interrupt with a loud "Stop!" Each person is then requested to address the therapist individually and to take turns. To reinforce listening, the therapist can ask the nonspeaking partner to reiterate what he or she heard the speaker say.

Conversely, couples who are not connecting emotionally with each other can be asked to look at each other and speak directly to each other, not to the therapist. To encourage engagement in a mutual undertaking or to introduce new forms of communication, homework assignments can be given to strengthen the communication process.

Through the various intervention devices described in this section, the family systems therapist guides a family with a recovering member toward their own process of recovery. As the newly sober member regains responsibility within the family, other members have to adapt accordingly. Acting as a coach or guide, the therapist can help map the course of this adaptation. The entire family must be prepared to accept as a member a sober and somewhat changed person. Every person's role in the family alters in the process of one individual's change.

The following list of rules can be drawn up and passed out to family members. Members read the rules, practice them in sessions, and agree to abide by them at home:

- Attack the *behavior,* not the *person* or his or her background. Use a pleasant tone of voice; avoid yelling, hitting, cursing, or name-calling. Deal with one issue at a time—don't let your partner counter with "Well, if you think I'm bad you ought to see how you come across!" or "When you get a decent job, I'll think about it!"
- No mind reading. Don't say, "You are jealous" or "You're just angry because you . . . "
- Narrow the problem to a manageable size rather than focusing on vague wholes.
- No accusations and put-downs, such as "You're just like your father!"
- Don't rehash the past.

HEALING

In van Wormer (2000), the family chapter she wrote for a book on counseling gays, lesbians, and bisexuals, presented the "rename, reframe, and reclaim" model. This model, which is well adapted to the counseling needs of the family in recovery, is further developed here for family-of-addict counseling.

Rename

The particular choices of terminology are up to the family members and relate in part to the treatment model preferred. The addict, for example, may find that terms such as "recovering alcoholic," "recovering grateful alcoholic," and "recovered alcoholic" are positive attributions. The spouse or partner, hopefully, will not choose to call himself or herself a "codependent," but ultimately the choice belongs to the client. If the use of the label brings a good result, the therapist would do well not to argue over the nomenclature. Key questions for the therapist to consider are: Are the new truths and realizations derived from treatment having a positive effect on your life? Are these new concepts consistent with a positive self-concept? In the end, perception is what matters.

The challenge to practitioners in a field whose literature and other teachings are guided by a language of damage and defects is to adopt a language that corresponds to concepts of strengths and resilience. Helping the family members discover how well they have done under trying circumstances, their success in pulling together as a family unit, will go a long way toward reinforcing the strengths that otherwise would go unnoticed. Labels like "survivor" and "family manager" should be used whenever appropriate. Indeed, family members should be encouraged to take pride in their resourcefulness because they have survived (with or without the addict) the turmoil of addiction (*and* the stress of treatment), because they have not only endured but prevailed.

Adopting a language of strengths has important ramifications when the substance misuser in the family is an adolescent. Generally, the use of labels like "alcoholic" and "addict" should be avoided. At a stage of life when they haven't yet settled on an identity, the risk in having teens identify themselves as alcoholics and addicts is in creating a self-fulfilling prophecy, with negative consequences (Volpicelli & Szalavitz, 2000). Referring youths to AA and NA meetings also may present problems because of the customary use of forced labeling in these groups. Sometimes, on the other hand, the addict or alcoholic label is the more positive alternative, such as when delinquent or criminal behavior can be understood as a part of drug-related addictive behavior. Under these circumstances, a referral to a Twelve-Step program, such as NA, might pave the way toward a more positive self-image and reconciliation with one's family.

From a family systems standpoint, relabeling problem behavior such as compulsive shopping as an addiction as opposed to foolish behavior changes the meaning by casting it in a less malicious light. Renaming a relapse as a lapse similarly helps it to be seen as a mere setback, as something that is manageable. When dealing with events of the past, the explanation "That was a part of the

illness of addiction" helps family members get beyond individual blaming, reduces misunderstandings, and opens the door to more effective communication.
These healthier ways of viewing the problematic behavior based on the use of
more positive terminology is closely related to reframing.

Reframe

Positive reframing is a helpful, in fact an essential, technique used by the therapist to instill hope and pride in one's accomplishments. To the seasoned counselor, helping clients reframe their experiences is probably second nature. Take
relapse as an example; instead of treating this as a disaster, the counselor typically helps the client see this as a valuable learning experience. Clients can be
directed toward a more positive view of a situation through deliberate questioning. Looking over the whole addiction experience in retrospect, clients can be
asked, "Can you find anything positive that has come out of this experience?"
Somewhat amazingly, clients and family members typically say, for instance,
that it makes them understand one another better or that they want to help fellow addicts or families of addicts. Therapists and clients should refrain from
looking at children of alcoholics through a deficit framework, such as seems to
be the norm in addiction treatment circles. Instead, as Walker and Lee (1998)
rightfully tell us, the search should be for evidence of resilience in the families of
origin as well as in the current household. Children of alcoholics, as Walker and
Lee further indicate, do not necessarily become substance misusers; nor are
they doomed to marry addicted persons. The best insurance against such a happenstance is the development of a strong inner drive to achieve and a strong
support system for affirmation. Where other practitioners and theorists seek and
find defects in adult children of alcoholics ("guessing at what normal is"), for
example, the therapist of the strengths-based school will look for resilience—
and will probably find it.

   To Maria Carroll (1993), reframing one's reality is integral to the healing
process. For recovering persons, only when the bond to addiction is broken can
they move to higher things and embark on "a journey home." To Carroll, the
journey home entails constructing a personal reality, becoming disillusioned
with this reality, letting the ego-self disintegrate, surrendering, reframing the
old reality, and then allowing a new reality to develop as the transformed state.
Through surrendering to the reality of the present, the recovering addict moves
through a spiritual awakening toward wholeness and a sense of oneness with
humanity. The process is similar for family members, who are embarking on a
journey of their own, a journey from isolation to intimacy and from refusing to
reach out and seek help to a willingness to ask for help when they need it.

Reclaim

Healing is simply the inner change, the sense of peace that may result from
therapy work in labeling feelings and controlling them through cognitive techniques, reframing troubling events in one's life, and recognizing how past events

influence present feelings, thoughts, and behavior. Reclaiming lost and damaged childhood selves may occur through the joint effort embodied in the treatment relationship.

Healing often involves reclaiming what was lost either through drug addiction or in living in a family consumed with another's addiction. There is so much to reclaim: the fun in life; one's sense of peace and safety; one's spirituality; one's wholeness. Sometimes, to reclaim one's wholeness, the couple who were bonded by alcohol or other drug use find they have little else in common and can be enabled by the therapist to go their separate ways.

A prominent theme in the literature is that adult children of alcoholics find sources of strength and resilience in the nurturant parts of their cultural community and heritage (Cable, 2000). The emphasis on "we-ness," as Cable indicates, is integral to traditional Native American culture and can be reclaimed through collaboration with natural support systems in treatment.

A communitywide intervention, The Family Circles Program, helped American Indian families reclaim their cultural identity and pride. Described by van Stelle, Allen, and Moberg (1998), this program was designed to reduce alcohol and drug misuse among high-risk youths on a reservation in Wisconsin. The project reportedly was so successful that it had a ripple effect throughout the entire community.

CASE STUDY

The following case study recaptures van Wormer's yearlong, very up-and-down treatment relationship with "Kathy" and "Ed."

The challenge of treating this angry couple was such that, in order to treat them, I had to conjure up all my training as a sociologist as well as of a social worker. And as is typical with alcoholic clients in treatment, it was not the alcohol that was the focal point of the sessions. No, the focal point was violence—violence and money.

This couple is troubled. After seven stormy years of marriage they are literally and figuratively tearing each other apart. Ed has spent many nights in jail. "Because of racism," he says. "I never touched her." As I sit facing them both I notice the racial differences: he is black, she is white. Physical differences are pronounced also: he is large and muscular, she is small. But as we get into dialogue and emotions run wild, the personality and cultural differences, the seething hatred, are all that count.

Kathy speaks, complains bitterly, and words flow effortlessly while her husband, a laborer, quieter, struggles to get a word in. He is my client; I know and trust him. His wife he has described as a master manipulator, and today he has brought her in for me to see for myself.

If she hates him so much, how can she love him, I wonder. To help sort out this question, I have each client write out on a sheet of paper what is good and what is bad about their marriage. Kathy's negative list is three pages long; on the positive side she lists only one thing, "great sex." His list is sketchy, but he agrees on the physical attraction.

Money is their biggest source of conflict. I already know Ed is sneaking money from his family of origin. Kathy shouts, "I want every penny accounted for. We have two children to feed! Is he drinking away the money? Where does it go?"

Earlier, privately, after the last violent outburst, he told me she clawed herself on the chest with her own fingernails, then called the police. She claimed physical assault. Upon hearing this story I talked Ed into getting his own place. He did so, but then, according to him, she called up begging him to return. Because of the risk of violence between them I do not try to sort out the facts. My aim is to state the obvious: They can't live together and can't seem to stay apart. Yet they need to realize that for the children's sake they are better apart and sane than together and fighting.

After a request for them to work on communication, I bring out my Fighting Fair scheme, which lists the rules of communication. This conflict resolution scheme has rules such as: no name-calling, don't rehash the past, and practice exercises that go "I feel _____ when you _____." The purpose of this exercise is to help clients know their feelings and then to make requests of each other. Kathy, it turns out, is tormented with feelings of jealousy and possessiveness. She is putting all her energy into one failing relationship when her need is for other adult support. She is cut off from her family, who disapprove of her interracial marriage and biracial children. The best hope for connection to the wider community for her, therefore, is through active participation in self-help groups. I refer her to a private counselor to help her work on the source of her anger and to realize her need for close personal friends as a support system to help her as a single parent.

Ed, faithfully, sees me once a week for a year; he has had a year of sobriety and is making progress following through on goals. During this time I explain some of Kathy's behavior in terms of her ethnicity (white Anglo-Saxon Protestant), especially her beliefs about family boundaries and the nuclear family. I reinforce Ed in his strengths and help him arrange visitation with his children.

In the end, Kathy became a local leader in Women for Sobriety, and Ed grew to love his weekly AA support group. Once they developed support systems of their own, they went their separate ways, much healthier apart than they had ever been or would ever be together.

EXERCISES FOR FAMILY GROUPS

1. Family Sculpture
    Purpose: To portray roles in the family; to illustrate how the family works as a system. To help reveal feelings that accompany each role.

    The worker begins by explaining the technique to the family. This is a nonverbal technique that involves physical placement of persons in a sym-

bolic fashion. The "sculptor" moves various family members into particular positions. The exercise begins with everyone standing up. Talking is not
allowed. A family member volunteers to be the sculptor. The therapist in-
structs the sculptor to arrange the family members to show who is close to
whom and what people do together. The setting reproduced may be the
family at home in the evening or on an outing, such as a picnic. Following
the sculpture display, participants discuss the meaning of each sculpture
and how each felt about the role he or she played.

Family sculpture can be effectively used in a Family Week program.
Volunteers are asked to play the roles they play in their families or, in another variation, to play a very different role. Various roles, such as the addict, the family manager, the mother's helper, the rebel, and the athlete, are
given to participants. With the help of the therapist as sculptor, each
arranges him- or herself in a way that best represents the role. For instance,
the addict may be put high on the chair or seated stooped over the table.
The child who fantasizes when things get rough may stand in a corner or
watch television. The family manager may extend his or her arm around
the addict. All members freeze as for a portrait. Afterward, each person is
asked to recapture the feelings of being in the role. The audience and players discuss the meaning of what they saw.

2. Drawing Family Maps
    Purpose: To open discussion about family lines of communication and
    closeness and to help the family gain insight into where the boundaries are.

    The therapist draws a circle on a chalkboard or flip chart to represent
    a hypothetical family. For example, an alcoholic mother and daughter
    could be represented by two circles with boundaries that overlap. Typi-
    cally, if the mother cries, the daughter cries too. The sober father and the
    other daughter are also close, but these two, represented by two more
    circles, are apart from the others. Family members are asked to take turns
    drawing their families.

3. Family Relapse Prevention Plan
    Purpose: To help the addict and the family identify the warning signs of
    pending relapse.

    A list of warning signs is written by each participant. Signs must be
    clearly spelled out. Family members discuss these warning signs, such as
    extreme and obsessive devotion to work. They discuss what these symptoms
    meant in the past and reach agreement on what to do if they recur. An ac-
    tion plan is drawn up.

4. Genograms, or Family Tree
    Purpose: To provide information on patterns in families; to reveal possible
    hereditary and cultural themes that have been passed from generation to
    generation; to reveal similarities and differences across families joined by
    marriage.

    See Hartman and Laird (1983) for an illustration of how diagrams can
    be constructed through the use of symbols. A marital pair is indicated by a

line drawn from a square (male) to a circle (female). Divorce is indicated by two slash marks on the line. Words can be used for events, occupations, dates, and ethnic origins.

5. Have the family members arrive early to view a videotape portraying family roles. *Soft Is the Heart of a Child,* though somewhat dated, portrays the family roles memorably. Viewers can be asked to discuss the roles and relate the tape to their own lives.

Another option is to show one of Claudia Black's videotapes, for example, *Children of Denial,* in which she movingly describes the "don't talk, don't trust, don't feel" dynamic in alcoholic homes.

Movies can be custom-suited to the individual client. An African American survivor of family sex abuse might find a lot of meaning in watching the film adaptation of *I Know Why the Caged Bird Signs;* a southern white survivor might get in touch with her feelings in a viewing of *Bastard Out of Carolina.*

SUMMARY AND CONCLUSION

Family therapy is an exciting dimension of addiction treatment. Family work with alcoholics and other drug misusers is an area especially amenable to the biopsychosocial framework. Systems therapists can utilize a didactic focus to teach biological and physiological factors of substance misuse and the interlinkages among all the addictions. The psychological realm can be addressed through work on the thinking–feeling dyad. The social aspect relates to the systems component; this three-pronged focus can offer a shared assessment of the structure and interaction patterns in the family. Through this multidimensional approach the therapist can help prepare the family for accepting back a member who, in the words of the old Scottish hymn, "once was lost, but now is found." The therapist can help prepare the family to cope with setbacks and even eventual separation from the addict. Through the use of various communications exercises or of listening skills, workers can help family members deal with their own feelings of anger, shame, and guilt that have plagued them for a long, long time.

The family systems approach described in this chapter provides a view of the family as a system of interdependent parts. The commonly used metaphor of a mobile suspended from a ceiling was described: If one part moves, the other parts shift simultaneously. Counselors can use this metaphor as a starting point to educate clients about the boundary concept, the reciprocity of role-playing, and the development and enforcement of rules in the family.

Because addiction did not arise in a social vacuum, and the addicts did not suffer the consequences of addiction alone, attention needs to be directed toward the social environment. The growth process for the family often requires a period of chaos that precedes the old state's breaking down before the formation of a new state can occur. The family systems paradigm offers to addiction treatment a way of conceptualizing addiction as both an interpersonal and an intergenerational phenomenon. Even if the treatment agency lacks a full-fledged family program, individual counselors can usually invite clients to bring their significant others with them to sessions. The family should be regarded as a potential valuable resource. Unfortunately, the legacy of blaming the family still persists. This potential can be countered by using the "rename, reframe, re-claim" framework introduced in this chapter.

References

Akin, B., & Gregoire, T. (1997, July/August). Parents' views on child welfare's response to addiction. *Family in Society*, 393–404.

Anderson, S. C. (1994). A critical analysis of the concept of codependency. *Social Work*, 39(6), 677–685.

Beattie, M. (1980). *Codependent no more*. Center City, MN: Hazelden.

Black, C. (1981). *It will never happen to me!* New York: Ballantine.

Bowen, M. (1978). *Family therapy in clinical practice*. New York: Aronson.

Bradshaw, J. (1988). *Bradshaw on the family: A revolutionary way of self-discovery*. Pompano Beach, FL: Health Communications.

Brooks, C. S., & Rice, K. F. (1997). *Families in recovery: Coming full circle*. Baltimore: Paul H. Brookes.

Brown, S., & Lewis, V. (1999). *The alcoholic family in recovery: A developmental model*. New York: Guilford Press.

Cable, L. C. (2000). Kaleidoscope and epic tales: Diverse narratives of adult children of alcoholics. In J. Krestan (Ed.), *Bridges to recovery* (pp. 45–76). New York: Free Press.

Carroll, M. (1993). *Spiritual growth of recovery alcohol children of alcoholics*. Unpublished doctoral dissertation, University of Maryland, Baltimore.

Chaput, L. L. (2001). *Assessment of family functioning in a clinical population of ethnically diverse substance users: Implications for practice*. Unpublished doctoral dissertation, University of Texas, Arlington.

Chase-Marshall, J. (1976, September). Virginia Satir: Everybody's family therapist. *Human Behavior*, 25–31.

Dulfano, C. (1982). *Families, alcoholism, and recovery*. Center City, MN: Hazelden.

Ellis-Ordway, N. (1992). The impact of family dynamics on anorexia: A transactional view of treatment. In E. Freeman (Ed.), *The addiction process: Effective social work approaches* (pp. 180–191). New York: Longman.

Germain, C. (1991). *Human behavior in the social environment: An ecological view*. New York: Columbia University Press.

Hanson, J. (1996). Families' perspectives on the early years of mental illness. *Canadian Social Work Review*, 12(2). 236–247.

Hartman, A., & Laird, J. (1983). *Family-centered social work practice*. New York: Free Press.

Hazelden Publishing Company. (1987). Same thoughts on codependency. *Hazelden Professional Update*, 5(3), 2.

Jackson, J. (1954). The adjustment of the family to the crisis of alcoholism. *Quarterly Journal of Substance Abuse*, 15, 562–586.

Johnson, H. (1986). Emerging concerns in family therapy. *Social Work*, 31, 299–305.

Kaufman, E. (1985). *Substance abuse and family therapy*. Orlando, FL: Grune and Stratton.

Kaufman, E., & Kaufman, P. (1992). From psychodynamic to structural to integrated family treatment of chemical dependency. In E. Kaufman & P. Kaufman (Eds.), *Family therapy of drug and alcohol abuse*. Boston: Allyn & Bacon.

Keller, D., Galanter, M., & Weinberg, S. (1997). Validation of a scale for network therapy: A technique for systemic use of peer and family support. *American Journal of Drug and Alcohol Abuse, 23*(1), 115–128.

Krestan, J. (2000). Introduction. In J. Krestan (Ed.), *Bridges to recovery: Addiction, family therapy, and multicultural treatment* (pp. 1–12). New York: Free Press.

Laudet, A., Magura, S., Furst, R.T., Kumar, N., & Whitney, S. (1999). Male partners of substance-abusing women in treatment: An exploratory study. *America Journal of Drug and Alcohol Abuse, 25*(4), 607–618.

Lawson, A., & Lawson, G. (1998). *Alcoholism and the family: A guide to treatment and prevention* (2nd ed.). Gaithersburg, MD: Aspen.

Lawson, G., Lawson, A., & Rivers, R. C. (2001). *Essentials of chemical dependency counseling* (3rd ed.). Gaithersburg, MD: Aspen.

Leonard, L. (1989). *Witness to the fire: Creativity and the veil of addiction*. Boston: Shambhala.

Loneck, B. (1995). Getting persons with alcohol and other drug problems into treatment: Teaching the Johnson Intervention in the practice curriculum. *Journal of Teaching in Social Work, 2*(1/2), 31–48.

McCourt, F. (1996). *Angela's ashes: A memoir*. New York: Scribner.

Minuchin, S. (1974). *Families and family therapy*. Cambridge, MA: Harvard University Press.

Nichols, M. (1984). *Family therapy*. New York: Gardner Press.

Prochaska, J. O., & DiClemente, C. C. (1992). Stages of change in the modification of problem behaviors. In M. Hersen, R. M. Eisler, & P. M. Miller (Eds.), *Progress in behavioral modification* (pp. 184–214). Sycamore, IL: Sycamore Press.

Rabinor, J. R. (1994). Mothers, daughters, and eating disorders: Honoring the mother–daughter relationship. In P. Fallon, M. Katzman, & S. Wooley (Eds.), *Feminist perspectives on eating disorders* (pp. 272, 286). New York: Guilford Press.

Simon, C., McNeil, J., Franklin, C., & Cooperman, A. (1991). The family and schizophrenia: Toward a psychoeducational approach. *Families in Society, 72,* 323–334.

Tolstoy, L. (1917/1876). *Anna Karenina*. New York: Collier & Son.

U.S. Department of Health and Human Services. (1999). *Brief interventions and brief therapies for substance abuse: TIP series 34*. Rockville, MD: U.S. Government Printing Office.

van Stelle, K. R., Allen, G. A., & Moberg, D. P. (1998). Alcohol and drug prevention among American Indian families: The family circles program. *Drugs, 12*(1/2), 53–60.

van Wormer, K. (1995). *Alcoholism treatment: A social work perspective*. Belmont, CA: Wadsworth.

van Wormer, K. (2001). *Counseling female offenders and victims: A strengths-restorative approach*. New York: Springer.

van Wormer, K., Wells, J., & Boes, M. (2000). *Social work with lesbians, gays, and bisexuals: A strengths perspective*. Boston: Allyn & Bacon.

Velleman, R. (2000). The importance of family. In D. B. Cooper (Ed.), *Alcohol use* (pp. 63–74). Oxon, England: Radcliffe Medical Press.

Volpicelli, J., & Szalavitz, M. (2000). *Recovery options: The complete guide*. New York: Wiley.

Waldron, H. B., & Slesnick, N. (1998). Treating the family. In W. Miller & N. Heather (Eds.), *Treating addictive behaviors* (pp. 259–270). New York: Plenum Press.

Walker, J. P., & Lee, R. E. (1998). Uncovering strengths of children of alcoholic parents. *Contemporary Family Therapy, 20*(4), 521–538.

Wallen, J. (1993). *Addiction in human development: Developmental perspectives on addiction and recovery*. New York: Haworth.

Wegscheider, S. (1981). *Another chance: Hope and health for the alcoholic family*. Palo Alto, CA: Science and Behavior Books.

Wetzel, J. (1991). Universal mental health classification systems: Reclaiming women's experience. *Affilia, 6*(3), 8–31.

What sets the world in motion is the interplay of differences. —OCTAVIO PAZ

RACIAL, ETHNIC, AND CULTURAL ISSUES

CHAPTER 10

INTRODUCTION

In traditional substance abuse and addiction treatment, an alcoholic is an alcoholic, a compulsive gambler is a compulsive gambler, and nothing else really matters. Regardless of race, ethnicity, culture, age, class, or gender differences, everyone is predicted to go through the same inevitable progressive stages on the U-shaped "Jellinek curve," starting with occasional relief drinking (gambling, using drugs) and bottoming out with obsessive drinking (gambling, using drugs). Like the traditional medical paradigm in the United States, the disease is the focus (and the great equalizer)—not the holistic person. Research studies in addiction reflect this stance by historically focusing on white males as subjects and rarely reporting separate gender or racial/ethnic groups.

In contrast, a strengths perspective emphasizes a "not knowing" position; that is, it is the counselor's responsibility *not* to have preprogrammed answers but to find out what the best way is to match prevention and treatment strategies to diverse people from different ethnic communities. As noted by Gross (1995, p. 212), a scientific-positivist (medical model) stance from the clinician implies "knowing something 'permanent,' 'true,' 'universal,' and 'essential' about the other, when none of this is true." Rhodes and Johnson (1997) argue that the use of the medical model in addiction trivializes the life experiences of African American women because it ignores the sociopolitical context of racism, sexism, and poverty and instead focuses on individual pathology.

Posing as "expert" is particularly detrimental and prejudicial to establishing a working relationship with individuals and families from a culture/class/ethnicity different from your own. A strengths perspective calls for a more egalitarian balance, where both the clients and the clinician are learning as they go along. In addition, Straussner (2001, p. 20) notes that "helping them share positive information about their ethnic history, cultural values, traditions, and contributions enhances their self-worth and potential for recovery."

Since the 1970s, with pressure from women and a new consciousness raising regarding civil rights, the term *special population* began to be used in government publications and textbooks about substance misuse in order to highlight "groups" of people that are underserved by traditional treatment programs, are not included in research studies, or have unique characteristics (both strengths and needs), in other words, people who don't fit neatly into the substance use/treatment paradigm defined by the dominant culture. Treatment plans began to be "individualized," taking into consideration family, religious, ethnic, and community resources that are available to support recovery. Even so, most substance misusers receiving treatment in the United States still receive the same disease-concept AA facilitated treatment approach, regardless of their ethnic group. The national databases still lag behind by aggregating people into huge racial or ethnocultural categories (black, white, Hispanic, Asian, Native American) and ignoring the many subgroups within each major category (Straussner, 2001).

However, even with these problems, the substance abuse field is ahead of the compulsive gambling field in this effort. Mark and Lesieur (1992) focus on the dramatic exclusion of women and other populations (Asians, blacks, Hispanics, gays, lesbians) from the existing literature on pathological and problem gambling, concluding that "it is time for professionals in the field to rethink their conceptualization of problem gambling in terms of the various subgroups within the population at large, and *not* just the dominant culture" (p. 561). Although the authors stop short of contesting the addiction/disease model (which was first included in the DSM in 1980, based largely on the clinical experience of Dr. Robert Custer with white male gamblers), they do note that Custer's chart of the gambler's progression of disease (Custer, 1982) has never been tested on females or any other ethnocultural group. Furthermore, they point out, the classification scheme of gamblers in Custer and Milt's (1985) influential text *When Luck Runs Out* was based principally on the study of white male GA members and white male Veterans' Affairs patients.

Despite the uneven awareness that the use, progression, and recovery process is influenced by ethnocultural norms and values, most clinicians today would agree with Straussner (2001, p. 12) that "treatment must take into account the client's ethnocultural beliefs, customs, and values, particularly as they relate to AOD issues, as well as the social conditions that have an impact on the client's ethnocultural group." The crucial question then becomes "How can clinicians learn to be culturally competent and at the same time not stereotype a whole culture or race?" The practice of lumping people together by an obvious external trait such as race or ethnic practices is open to criticism because it doesn't take into account other important characteristics (such as social class) or the vast differences found within a particular group (Bradizza & Stasiewicz, 1999). Collins (1993) calls this practice "ethnic gloss."

To avoid stereotyping or "glossing" a particular ethnocultural group, factors other than race and ethnicity must be taken into consideration. Such factors include the individual's experience of oppression/discrimination, immigration status and experience, degree and effects of acculturation, language and communication skills and patterns, education/socioeconomic status, religion, age, gender, and family structure.

Many authors argue that the effects of being in a particular group cannot be separated from the effects of social class, and in fact many so-called "attributes" of ethnicity or culture are in reality effects of class. For example, close ties and reliance on extended family may be related to the bleak economic future of undereducated and poor individuals on their own. Class, or socioeconomic status, is related to a person's level of education and current employment/income status, but it clearly impacts every aspect of a person's life. As bell hooks (2000, p. 7) says,

> Class matters. Race and gender can be used as screens to deflect attention away from the harsh realities class politics exposes. Clearly, just when we should all be paying attention to class, using race and gender to understand and explain its new dimensions, society, even our government, says let's talk about race and racial injustice. It is impossible to talk meaningfully about ending racism without talking about class.

For example, in their ethnographic study on women and cocaine, Murphy and Rosenbaum (1997) note that race and economic class heavily influence geographic location, access to drugs, and a variety of other factors. In the example they use, Monique is poor and black; Becky is middle-class white. Their different status of race and class influences how potent the drugs are that are available (crack in poor inner cities vs. powdered cocaine in affluent suburbs), the relationship between sex and drugs in the particular social scene (Monique had to prostitute for money vs. Becky, who had a well-paying job), the ability of a person to maintain a "nondeviant" identity by being able to conceal drug use, the availability of resources to cushion the consequences of using illegal drugs, and the availability of options to leave the drug "scene" and move on to a different way of life (Monique went to a homeless shelter vs. Becky, who went to Hawaii with her dad). Thus, the combination of racial oppression *and* economic class profoundly influences the context of drug initiation, drug use patterns, and the consequences of drug misuse and addiction.

In the case of Native Americans and Alaska Natives, racial oppression has been taken to a level considered genocidal by some because of the warfare, disease, alcohol, and forcible removal of Native children to English-speaking boarding schools where they were not allowed to practice any aspect of their culture (Weaver, 2001). The subsequent cultural breakdown has been accompanied by years of poverty, unemployment, broken families, substandard living conditions, and meager educational opportunities for many Natives. Some writers explain Native alcohol and drug misuse as a psychological reaction to the loss of tradition and culture (Segal, 1998; Beauvais, 1998) or, in Lowery's (1998, p. 127) words, " a crisis of the spirit."

Other authors emphasize the effects of recent immigration by various racial/ethnic groups on substance use practices. Asian and Hispanic immigrants may face major stressors, such as crowded, inadequate housing, socioeconomic hardships, not speaking English, posttraumatic stress resulting from war and life in refugee camps, separation of families during the immigration process, and the inevitable rift between children brought up in the United States and their parents, who may cling to traditional ways. First-generation youth are vulnerable to substance misuse in an attempt to be accepted in the new culture. Many times, as acculturation increases, so do substance use problems. For example, among Hispanics, a higher level of alcohol consumption is linked to a higher level of acculturation, especially among women (Randolph, Stroup-Benham, Black, & Markides, 1998).

Makimoto (1998) points out that the consequences of immigration may be different even for the same ethnic group. For example, the Vietnamese and Cambodians who emigrated shortly after the war in 1975 were mostly well-educated people who had lived in urban areas; however, the second wave, in the 1980s, frequently included farmers and peasants who were illiterate in their own language, had been in refugee camps for a long period, and had experienced violence and starvation before coming to the United States. Although both groups are from Southeast Asia, their acculturation into and adjustment to the United States were markedly different.

Because of the "wildly heterogeneous" (Closser & Blow, 1993) nature of these various groups in terms of acculturation, economic class, and education, among other important variables, many writers pay lip service to the idea that it is not correct to generalize across cultures. Then they proceed to generalize (Gross, 1995). In the following discussion of Asian/Pacific Islanders, Alaskan/Native Americans, Hispanic Americans, and African Americans, we will avoid stereotyping by highlighting the complexity and diversity of each "group" and encouraging the reader to use this information as a launching pad for further investigation of subgroups. We will focus on strengths as well as traditional values of the most vulnerable in each group, that is, those who are recent immigrants, are poor, have a history of oppression, and may be undereducated, in an attempt to track influences on the path to drug initiation, drug use patterns, the consequences of drug misuse and addiction, and the resources available for recovery. Although the success of culturally specific treatment programs is a contested area that needs more research, we will describe several programs that have made progress in this area.

Given the great variability and number of factors that influence a person's cultural pattern within his or her group, we go back to the original question: How can counselors learn to be culturally sensitive and at the same time not stereotype a whole culture or race? Amodeo and Jones (1997) suggest a cultural framework for clinical practice that takes several variables into consideration when trying to understand an individual client from a culture different from their own. Elements of a cultural-specific assessment includes finding out the cultural attitudes, values, and behaviors of using alcohol and other drugs, how the problem is defined and identified, cultural ways of seeking help (where, when, and what type), the meaning and consequences of relapse, and the support available for recovery. All of these factors are in turn influenced by three other critical variables: the degree of acculturation, subgroup identity, and the context of migration (departure circumstances, trauma experience, and legal status).

For example, according to Bromley and Sip (2001), it is not unusual for traditional Cambodians to use herbs, drugs, and alcohol in moderation, when they were available, to treat suffering and stress in Cambodia. Cambodian immigrants suffered a great deal of stress from war, persecution, torture, refugee camps, and all of the problems of adjusting to a completely different culture and language when they finally got to the United States. Alcohol was suddenly much more available and affordable. The authors theorize (p. 329) that "many Cambodian refugees turned to alcohol to 'medicate' themselves from the impact of these horrifying experiences."

Each one of these variables can shed a whole new light on how to be helpful with a particular client or family and the particular strengths of the family experience. Unfortunately, because of time constraints on most clinical practices, this kind of careful, individualized, and culturally specific groundwork is likely to be put aside as something "nice" but impractical. However, we eventually pay the cost in terms of underutilized treatment programs and the failure to meet the needs of many vulnerable groups.

ASIAN AMERICANS AND PACIFIC ISLANDERS

The danger of lumping people into one group is obvious when you consider that this "group" consists of at least 30 Asian and 21 Pacific Islander ethnic groups with different languages, customs, and behaviors (Makimoto, 1998). In the United States Census (2000), "Asian" refers to people having origins in the Far East, Southeast Asia, or the Indian subcontinent. It includes people who identified themselves as "Asian Indian," "Chinese," "Filipino," "Korean," "Japanese," "Vietnamese," "Burmese," "Hmong," "Pakistani," or "Thai." The term "Native Hawaiian and Other Pacific Islander" refers to people having origins in the original peoples of Hawaii, Guam, Samoa, or other Pacific Islands, and includes people who identified themselves as "Native Hawaiian," "Guamanian or Chamorro," "Samoan," "Other Pacific Islander," "Tahitian," "Mariana Islander," or "Chuukese." Even with all this variety, there are numerous subgroups within each group that may form a distinct ethnic group with different ways of approaching substance use and addiction.

Prevalence Patterns

Since both education and economic class influence substance use patterns and the availability of resources to alleviate problems, the variability of these factors within the Asian and Pacific Islander group may help explain some of the variability of substance use patterns. In general, alcohol consumption is lower among Asian and Pacific Islanders than in non-Hispanic white populations. According to the Substance Abuse and Mental Health Services Administration (SAMHSA) (1998) analysis of the National Household Survey on Drug Abuse (1991–1993), the prevalence rate of illicit drug use, heavy cigarette use, alcohol dependence, and need for illicit drug use treatment was less among Asian/Pacific Islanders than Native Americans, Mexican Americans, Puerto Ricans, and African Americans. For example, the percentage of Asian/Pacific Islanders (age 12 and over) using any illicit drug in the last year is 6.5%, compared to 19.8% among Native Americans, 13% among Mexican Americans, Puerto Ricans, and African Americans, and 12% of the total population surveyed. The prevalence of persons needing drug abuse treatment was 1.7% for Asian/Pacific Islanders, compared to a high of 3.9% for African Americans and an estimate of 2.7% for the total U.S. population. Heavy alcohol use in the past month (age 12 and over) was estimated at 0.9% for Asian/Pacific Islanders, compared to a high of 6.9% for Mexican Americans and 5.1% for the total U.S. population. Treatment admissions for 1997 in the United States show that Asian/Pacific Islanders entered treatment at a lower rate (0.7%) than their incidence in the general population (2.4%) (SAMHSA, 1999).

The low rate of alcohol/drug misuse for the Asian/Pacific Islander group may be underreported and inaccurate because of several factors: (1) national database surveys have ignored this group and consistently put Asian/Pacific Islanders in the category of "other," (2) the low treatment rate may be the result of the lack of culturally relevant services, (3) methodological weaknesses in the research has resulted in an underestimation of the levels of substance misuse and dependency, and (4) there is a belief that alcoholism is rare in this group because of the absence of the enzyme aldehyde dehydrogenase in widely varying percentages of Asians and Pacific Islanders, which can cause "flushing" and discomfort when alcohol is ingested, although this has proven not to be true uniformly (Ja & Aoki, 1993; Closser & Blow, 1993).

There is a notable lack of information about alcohol consumption patterns and related problems of Indians, perhaps because they are a relatively small group and have the highest number of advanced education degrees (Makimoto, 1998). There are some comparisons available within the Asian group indicating that in California and Hawaii, Japanese Americans had the highest rate of lifetime and heavy drinkers and Chinese Americans had the lowest (Makimoto, 1998). Three-quarters of methamphetamine users in Hawaii are reported to be Asian/Pacific Islanders, and less than one-quarter are Caucasian (Freese, Obert, Dickow, Cohen, & Lord, 2000).

Sociocultural Factors

In addition to ethnic background, this group varies greatly in educational level and economic status. The median income figures for 1999 (United States Census, 2000) indicate that Asian and Pacific Islander households have the highest median income of any racial group, that is, $51,205. However, the poverty rate for this group is 10.7% (higher than the non-Hispanic white rate of 7.7%), suggesting that some groups have a higher-than-average economic status and other groups have a below-average economic status. Many Asian Pacific Islanders are marginalized and isolated because of language. Almost one-third (32.8%) of the people who spoke Asian/Pacific Islander languages in their families in 1990 were considered linguistically isolated, because no members over the age of 13 spoke English well enough to be integrated into mainstream life (Bureau of the Census, 1993).

There are also great differences in education status among this "group." Southeast Asians and Pacific Islanders, perhaps because of more recent immigration, tend to have lower educational status than Chinese Americans, Japanese Americans, and Indians (Makimoto, 1998). For example, one in every seven Asians and Pacific Islanders age 25 and over has an advanced degree beyond the bachelor's degree. Unfortunately, the high level of academic achievement for part of this group has led to the myth of Asians as the "model minority." This in turn has contributed to the erroneous belief that addiction is not problematic in this group (Ja & Aoki, 1993).

Although there is great variation because of economic class, education, and level of acculturation as to how traditional values are actualized in individual people, several authors have pointed out consistent traditional cultural themes that may pose barriers to getting help through mainstream treatment programs (Closser & Blow, 1993; Ja & Aoki, 1993; Makimoto, 1998; Mercado, 2000). On the other hand, these same values provide family support, family resources, and a family commitment to the best interests of the family member who may be suffering consequences from their addiction. Counselors will want to understand through a "not knowing" and respectful stance whether or not the following traditional immigrant Asian values and practices may apply.

- The theme of filial piety (devotion, obligation, duty) dominates traditional Asian culture. That is, the individual within the family is secondary to the interests of the family as a whole. Communications are indirect and based on roles within the family hierarchy. Emotions are not generally shared because that might emphasize the individual over the interdependent needs of the family.

- The initial response of the family to substance use or mental health problems may be to ignore it. It may not even be considered a problem as long as the individual continues to meet family responsibilities. Among many Southeast Asians, alcohol is viewed as a substance that has healing properties, and it is culturally acceptable for elderly persons to drink alcohol and smoke marijuana.

- If a problem gets identified and family functioning is threatened, the family risks deep shame and "losing face" in the community. To keep from "losing face," families may try to isolate the person with the problem from the community, shame or scold the person, and even reject the person. Extended family may be asked to intervene.

- Seeking outside help is equated to failure. When it does occur, families may have "quick-fix" expectations. The person with the problem is likely to be angry because of the family's "betrayal" and resistant when brought to treatment.

While traditional parents are practicing in ways that mirror their native countries, their sons and daughters may have acculturated to the point of relying more on their peers and popular culture. Consequently, attempts to rein them in using traditional methods of shaming and hierarchical processes may cause a great deal of family conflict.

Ja and Aoki (1993) suggest, from their experience at the Asian American Recovery Services in San Francisco, that it is helpful for counselors to take a structured approach to working with traditional families, using clear intake procedures and outlining rules and procedures. The authors recommend peer group processes that are provided within a framework of positive support. It is particularly helpful if the groups include other Asians. Because families are so critical to a person's well-being, family support should be offered using an educational rather than a confrontational approach.

Treatment Issues

Although dissatisfaction with standard treatment programs is common and treatment programs appear to be underutilized by this group, there is little outcome research that supports or doesn't support culturally specific treatment approaches (Closser & Blow, 1993). However, advocates of trying to meet the unique treatment needs of Asian/Pacific Islanders are not waiting for research results. In a survey of 294 drug treatment programs in ethnically diverse Los Angeles County, Polinsky, Hser, and Grella (1998) found that services were available in 36 languages, including Vietnamese and Cambodian, and clients speaking languages other than English or Spanish could be served by about one-fourth of the programs. The majority of the programs (68%) reported being able to meet the unique needs of Asian/Pacific Islanders.

Closser and Blow (1993, p. 205) state that "it is futile to search for a single treatment approach for all group members." This may be particularly true for the richly diverse group of Asian/Pacific Islanders. General strategies to become more user-friendly to this group involve hiring staff who come from and can speak the language of the primary target group, providing cultural training for all staff, incorporating the use of elders and native healers, using familiar healing strategies such as acupuncture, and incorporating culture-specific beliefs and spiritual practices about healing and recovery.

For example, a culturally based, women-centered residential treatment program in Hawaii uses Küpuna, elders of the Hawaiian Native community who carry wisdom and tradition in extended family, to develop parenting classes, facilitate traditional healing practices, provide child care, and act as counselors/listeners. Ethnographic interviewing of the women who participated in the program revealed positive perceptions about Küpuna involvement (Morelli & Fong, 2000). As one participant commented, "We'd sing and start talking about culture, about how the ancient Hawaiians used to live off the land, and spiritual things. If you had burdens or problems for the day or you weren't feeling right, they'd pray on you" (p. 42).

| BOX 10.1 | AN IMMIGRANT-RUN TREATMENT PROGRAM |

For years, Mohammed Arif denied he had a drinking problem. He saw himself as an immigrant success story: he had mastered a new language, earned enough to support relatives back in his native Pakistan, and fit right in when his fellow construction workers hit the bars at the end of the day.

"The thing about drinking was this false pride," Mr. Arif said, recalling the dark years when he failed to see how alcohol was corroding his new life. "There was all this finger-pointing in my family, and it would get me so mad. Why is everyone telling me I've got a drinking problem when it's me who's taking care of everybody?"

He eventually sought help, ricocheting from one detoxification program to another. It was not until he landed at Nav Nirmaan, the only New York City substance abuse treatment program run by and for immigrants from southern Asia, that he pulled himself and his family together.

"It made a big difference," said Mr. Arif, who now tells his story as a means of counseling other immigrants at the center, which is in Elmhurst, Queens. "When you're with people from your own background, your own culture, it's like there's no more curtain in front of your eyes."

Nav Nirmaan, which means "new beginning" in the Gujrathi language of western India, is at the vanguard of a growing trend in drug and alcohol treatment programs that not only provide counseling in the native language of immigrants, but also consider their particular cultural background and the traumas of the immigrant experience itself.

"In our cultural makeup, the cry for help is the last stage," said Roy V. Tellis, the Indian-born executive director of Nav Nirmaan. "There's a lot of shame involved, and there's the isolation. The typical Nav Nirmaan client, he said, is a man who lives in a cultural cocoon. He drinks as a form of socializing with other men from his home region, reads newspapers and watches television shows in his native language, and feels confusion and rage when his wife and Americanized children try to venture outside the tight circle of southern Asian culture. "It is a male-dominated patriarchal society," Mr. Tellis said. "And the father says: I work hard, I put food on the table. So what if I take a few drinks?"

From: "Tying Drug and Alcohol Programs," 1999.

The "challenge model," a strengths-based intervention developed by the Asian American Recovery Service in San Francisco and San Jose, California, is used as a culturally appropriate treatment model for adolescents. As described by Yuen and Nakano-Matsumoto (1998), features include acknowledgment and support of the strengths of resilient youth, nonconfrontational techniques to avoid "loss of face," home visits to engage families, community outreach and networking to other systems, affirmation of cultural identity and differences, and goal-oriented activities using a psychoeducational approach.

"Nav Nirmaan," the only New York City substance abuse treatment program run by and for immigrants from southern Asia, is an inspiring example of cultural specific programming (Box 10.1).

NATIVE AMERICANS AND ALASKAN NATIVES

While Asian Americans may be misrepresented by the myth of the "model minority" with few substance use problems, Native Americans and Alaska Natives have historically been stereotyped in opposite ways. On the one hand, the myth of the "drunken Indian" who is powerless over the white man's "spirits" still colors the popular culture; on the other hand, there is the "politically correct," romantic version of a uniform Indian culture that extols peacefulness, connectedness, and environmental soundness. These contrary beliefs are so widespread that Weaver (2001, p. 77) cautions that "few people have stopped to critically examine what is actually known and empirically supported."

Prevalence Patterns

In the United States, there are approximately 2.4 million (0.9% of the total population) American Indians and Alaska Natives, who comprise at least 300 different tribal or language groups (United States Census, 1999). In Alaska, Natives are 15.7% of the total population (Segal, 1998). In Canada, First Nations People comprise approximately 4% of the population (Graham, Swift, & Delaney, 2000). Many authors agree that it is difficult to make an accurate estimate of alcohol and drug misuse within this group because of the vast differences among Native populations being sampled and a historical distrust of researchers (Weaver, 2001). Differences in drinking patterns among various tribes are influenced by the same factors that influence variation among many ethnic or cultural groups; that is, they may be the result of differing cultural guidelines about tolerating deviant behavior, different socioeconomic conditions, different contexts of highly urban to remote rural areas, differing levels of acculturation to the dominant society, and/or the extent to which traditional values, language, and ways of life are practiced.

In a review of eight studies on drinking prevalence among American Indian adults, May (1996) found a wide variation among "current drinkers," ranging from 30% to 84%, compared to the 64% rate among the general population. The analysis of 1991–93 data from the National Household Survey on Drug Abuse (SAMHSA, 1998) reveals that American Indians and Alaska Natives had the highest rate of illicit drug use in the past year of all the 11 subgroups (19.8%) compared to the total population rate of 11.9%; the highest rate of marijuana use (15%) compared to the total population rate of 9.0%; the highest prevalence of those needing drug abuse treatment (7.8%) compared to the total population rate of 2.7%; the highest rate of cigarette use (52.7%) compared to the total population rate of 30.9%; and the highest rate of alcohol dependence (shared with Hispanic-Mexican) of 5.6% compared to the total population rate of 3.5%. Treatment admission data for 1997 in the United States show that American Indians/Alaskan Natives entered treatment at a higher rate (2.5%) than their incidence in the U.S. population (0.7%) (SAMHSA, 1999).

Among Indian youth as well as adolescents in general, drug and alcohol use go together. However, data from school surveys indicate that drug use is higher among Indian youth than among other adolescent groups, and marijuana use is significantly higher (Beauvais, 1998). One in five Canadian Native youth has used solvents, and more than half began to use solvents before they were 11 years old (Scott, 1997). Native American Indian youth also have high prevalence rates for use of inhalants, with estimated ranges between 17% and 22% (Herring, 1994). The concern is that inhalant use generally signals a serious level of drug involvement and suggests serious difficulties may lie ahead.

Drinking-related consequences are higher in Native populations as compared to other groups. According to the 1996 Indian Health Service report, the age-adjusted alcohol-related death rate was 5.6 times higher within the Indian population than in the general population; chronic liver disease and cirrhosis was 3.9 times as prevalent; alcohol-related fatal automobile accidents were 3 times as prevalent; alcohol-related suicide was 1.4 times as prevalent; and alcohol-related homicide was 2.4 times as prevalent. Native men are twice as likely as women to die from alcohol-related causes between the ages of 45 and 64 (Beauvais, 1998). One Native American woman working in substance abuse treatment in the Northwest described to one of the authors that her reservation was in a state of "perpetual mourning" because of the unremittingly high number of early deaths among people who know each other or are related through extended family.

Although there is disagreement about the prevalence of fetal alcohol syndrome (FAS) in the Native population, there is agreement that it is more prevalent among Native Americans than in the U.S. population as a whole. Prevalence rates vary from 6 to 30 times greater, and may reflect the variation among different Indian tribes. High rates have been found among some, such as the FAS rate of one in four children on the Pine Ridge and Rosebud Reservations in South Dakota (Weaver, 2001).

Sociocultural Factors

Social/economic and cultural factors are a potent force in the development of alcohol and drug misuse, the ability to get and receive help, and the availability of supports for a recovery process. According to Beauvais (1998, p. 257), "Many Indian people believe that the loss of their culture is the primary cause of many of their existing social problems, especially those associated with alcohol." The state has invariably been the colonizer of indigenous peoples, leaving a legacy of destruction and despair (Graham, Swift, & Delaney, 2000). A fundamental social problem in the Native community today is poverty. A three-year average poverty rate for American Indians/Alaska Natives (1997–1999) was 25.9%, compared to a national rate of 11.8% in 1999, with an estimated 700,000 living in poverty (United States Census, 2000). In addition, families have been broken for generations because of the boarding system imposed by the federal government, which had the intent of eliminating Indian culture and replacing it with white culture. Children were separated from their families by hundreds of miles for months, even years, at a time and were forbidden to talk in their native language or participate in any Native practices. Although government boarding schools were phased out in the 1970s, Native youth (about 20%) are still educated in some type of boarding school (Dick, Manson, & Beals, 1993, quoted in Weaver, 2001). War, poverty, disease, and displacement have taken a horrendous toll on Native families. For example, in 1900 an influenza epidemic spread throughout Alaska and killed 60% of the Eskimo and Athabascan people, often whole villages. As Lowery (1998, p. 131) states, "The sense of co-herence of an entire people was shattered at the turn of the century. There was no lawfulness, no cultural explanation, no magic, no predictability. The world truly went upside-down."

From this upside-down world, there are some indicators that a remarkable turnaround has begun to occur in some Native American communities, begin-ning with the civil rights and antipoverty programs of the 1960s and 1970s. By 1996, 134,000 non-Hispanic American Indians were enrolled in colleges and universities, up from 84,000 in 1980. The number of U.S. businesses owned by American Indians, Eskimos, and Aleuts increased 93% (to 102,271), compared to the 26% increase for all U.S. firms, and the receipts for these businesses in-creased 115% during the same period (United States Census, 1999). However, there are still many pockets of poverty, poor health, and "perpetual mourning" that exist in both reservation and urban areas.

In cultural areas, treatment and prevention programs have taken a lead in reinforcing, and in some cases teaching for the first time, traditional Native values by incorporating drumming, sweats, beading, medicine wheel philoso-phy, and other traditional practices into programming. The strong cultural and spiritual component is intended to help invigorate traditional practices as well as give the individual strength in the recovery process (Beauvais, 1998). Com-munity approaches to substance misuse and prevention are reinforcing tradi-tional values of caretaking and responsibility for those who come after them, as, for example, in fetal alcohol syndrome prevention programming. The Na-tive American Church, which uses peyote as a sacramental food and curative for substance misuse, had 250,000 members in the United States, Mexico, and Canada in 1996.

SPIRITUAL AND CULTURAL VALUES

It is presumptuous to speak of "Native American values" as if they were of one piece, given the differences among individuals and between tribes. However, there are some identifiable cultural beliefs prevalent among many Indian tribes that could impact the path to substance misuse and the path to recovery. Beau-vais (1998) points out that social factors, such as viewing drinking as a way of increasing bonding among family and friends and viewing sobriety as carrying a risk of being ostracized, may strongly influence the use of alcohol. Spiritual-ity is often mentioned as a dominant Indian value, manifested in the recogni-tion of the spirit and connectedness in all living things and in the responsibility the Creator gave to Indian people to preserve Mother Earth (Lowery, 1998). However, the idea that the responsibility for one's behavior lies in the hands of spiritual forces is contrary to the Western notion that change is a personal responsibility (Beauvais, 1998). The Indian idea calls for a ceremonial solution to problems and imbalances; the Western idea leads to more confrontational therapeutic practices. Because of the emphasis on spirituality in many Native cultures, addiction is seen as a "crisis of the spirit" and requires "a healing of the spirit, of the mind, and of the body within a larger framework of existence, the extended family network nested within community clan, tribe, and nation" (Lowery, 1998, p. 131).

For example, according to Garrett and Carroll (2000), the concept of the "medicine wheel" in Cherokee and many Plains Indian traditional cultures embraces a holistic framework by including four components of the inner circle: spirit, natural environment, body, and mind. The four directions in the circle represent the four winds: East (belonging), South (mastery), West (independence), and North (generosity). In this conception, disharmony, including substance misuse, results when a person is out of balance or out of harmony with the interaction of mind, body, spirit, and natural environment.

Treatment Issues

In the last 10 years, much of the substance abuse treatment provided by the Indian Health Service has shifted to local tribal control. In the process, there has been, as mentioned earlier, an increase in the use of traditional cultural and spiritual practices in treatment, including sweats, medicine wheels, drumming, beading, talking circles, and bringing in elders and medicine men to facilitate healing ceremonies However, there are no controlled studies that show whether these efforts work or not (Beauvais, 1998). Weaver (2001) points out that no single approach works for all Indian subgroups; some may benefit from traditional healing practices, others from mainstream treatment programs. A study by Support Services International (1996, as referenced in Daisy et al., 1998) on Indian Health Service adolescent regional treatment centers suggests that treatment success for this group involves family involvement, counselor skills in posttraumatic stress and abuse issues, long-term aftercare, and gender-specific groups for young Native women. Ethnographic studies and program evaluations have shown positive results of reconnecting people with substance use problems to their culture (Lowery, 1998). According to Kasee (1995, p. 84), "the availability of traditional religion is a major motivator for recovery for Indian clients, a process so frequent, it is colloquially referred to as 'going back to the blanket.'"

One such program is the Native American Counseling Center in the heart of Seattle, Washington (Shukovsky, 1996). Several counselors on staff are Native Americans, and other staff are trained to be sensitive to cultural differences. A typical day might find people with substance use and alcohol problems sitting in a traditional talking circle, passing an eagle feather around to signal each person's turn to tell their story. As one of the counselors, Ruben Peters, commented, "This feather is powerful medicine. Let this feather and their circle represent strength and recovery. This is the circle where the healing begins." In addition to standard mental health treatment, the center offers talking circles, the wisdom of elders, sweat lodges, powwows, feasts, and stories. "What we are about here is to help people reconnect with who they are," said Dr. Robin LaDue, the center's clinical supervisor and a member of the Cowlitz Tribe of western Washington. "The point is to empower them to define themselves— not be defined by external sources" (p. 81).

Harm reduction philosophy that incorporates the stages-of-change model of Prochaska and DiClemente (see chapter 3) is particularly respectful of the Native view that behavioral change is a circular process that occurs in gradual steps (Daisy, Thomas, & Worley, 1998). Harm reduction methods also support the involvement of the Native substance users and their community in the development of long-term plans that will benefit recovery. The authors point out that the traditional practice of the "talking circle" aligns well with harm reduction philosophy in that it provides an opportunity for community members to express their feelings and opinions on how alcohol/drugs/gambling has affected the community, how to manage it, and how the community can respond to problems. Such strategies that honor indigenous traditions of consensus building are needed to help heal the effect of colonialism on Native American or Canadian communities.

HISPANICS

Prevalence Patterns

The United States Census 2000 reports that Hispanics, who may be of any race, totaled 35.3 million persons, or about 13% of the total U.S. population. Of these people of Spanish/Hispanic/Latino origin 58.5% identified themselves as Mexican, 9.6% as Puerto Rican, 3.5% as Cuban, 2.2% as Dominican, 4.8% as Central American, 3.8% as South American, 0.3% as Spaniard, and 17.3% as "other Hispanic." Traditionally, Puerto Ricans identified themselves by class, not race (on a continuum of black to white), viewing skin color as unimportant. However, because of the racial dichotomy and prejudice experienced by Puerto Ricans who have moved to the United States, whiteness of skin has become more valued (Medina, 2001).

According to SAMHSA (1998), Hispanic subgroups vary significantly in the prevalence of alcohol and drug use and problems. The rate of illicit drug use (marijuana, cocaine, and other drugs), heavy alcohol use, alcohol dependence, and the need for drug treatment is higher for Mexican Americans and Puerto Rican Americans than for any other Hispanic subgroup and for the total population surveyed. The lowest rates in these categories are among Caribbean Americans, Central Americans, and Cuban Americans. For example, alcohol dependence varies greatly, from a high rate of 5.6% of Mexican Americans to 3.0% of Puerto Rican Americans, 2.8% of Central Americans, 2.1% of South Americans, and 0.9% of Cuban Americans compared to a total population rate of 3.5% (SAMSHA, 1999). Cigarette use shows a different pattern, with Hispanics from South America having the highest rate (31.3%), followed by Puerto

Rican Americans (32.7%), Mexican Americans (29.1%), Cuban Americans (27.3%), Caribbean Americans (21.2%), and Central American Hispanics (17.9%) as compared to the total population rate of 30.9%. Statistics for the United States in 1997 show that Hispanics entered treatment at a slightly higher rate (10.6%) than their incidence in the U.S. population (10.4%) (SAMHSA, 1999).

Overall, heavy drinking is significantly less prevalent among Latina women than among Latino men; however, the rate of cocaine use is similar to that for non-Hispanic whites, and crack use is higher than among non-Hispanic white women (Amaro, Nieves, Johannes, & Cabeza, 1998). The effect of acculturation on Latina women is more evident than among men regarding drinking patterns. Traditional sanctions against female drinking break down the more educated, employed, and middle class Mexican American women become. Hispanic youth have a higher rate of cocaine, marijuana, and crack use than any other group, and the concern is developing that Mexican American girls are becoming a high-risk group, with abstention rates only slightly higher than Mexican American boys (Alvarez & Ruiz, 2001).

One of the most devastating effects of substance misuse, including injecting drug use in this population, has been the transmission of HIV. AIDS was the second leading cause of death for Latinos in the age group of 25 to 44, and it was the leading cause of death for Hispanic women between 25 and 34 years of age (Centers for Disease Control and Prevention, 1995). Latina women account for 20% of all injection-related AIDS cases, yet they represent only 10% of the female population in the United States (Straussner, 2001). In addition, Mexican Americans are overrepresented among alcohol-related deaths; for example, Mexican American men have a 40% higher risk of death from cirrhosis than white males, even though the alcohol dependence rate is only somewhat higher (5.6% compared to 3.4%) (Alvarez & Ruiz, 2001).

Socioeconomic Factors

Education and economic status are improving slightly among Hispanics, but again there is wide variation among subgroups. Poverty is still a major risk factor. Hispanic families have a 25.6 % poverty rate, ranging from 31% for Puerto Ricans and Mexican Americans to 14% for Cuban Americans (United States Census, 2000). As in any culture of poverty, this condition provides few opportunities to buffer the hardships of life, few resources to avoid harmful social and health-related consequences of drinking and using drugs, and greater vulnerability to social sanctions such as jail, prison, and discrimination (Alvarez & Ruiz, 2001).

On the whole, Hispanics are the most undereducated of all ethnocultural groups in the United States, with high dropout rates (Puerto Ricans have the highest) and a high school graduation rate of only 56% in 1998 (Medina, 2001; Alvarez & Ruiz, 2001; United States Census, 2000). The proportion of Hispanics with a bachelor's degree in 1998 (11%) was not significantly different from the 10% of a decade earlier. Cuban Americans are the most educated subgroup, although slightly lower than non-Hispanic whites, and tend to be more achieve-ment oriented and politically conservative than other Hispanic subgroups (Rothe & Ruiz, 2001).

Cultural Factors

Traditional views of family and roles can be protective factors against using al-cohol and drugs; at the same time, they make it more difficult to seek help. Pro-tective factors identified in a study of 60 young, low-income, predominantly Mexican American women include a cohesive family of origin, adequate rule-setting by parents, and a strong social support system (Lindenberg et al., 1998). The authors suggest that early identification of both risk *and* resilience factors are important to prevention of substance misuse among high-risk populations.

Hispanic traditions sharply differentiate the roles of males and females (Alvarez & Ruiz, 2001; Rothe & Ruiz, 2001; Medina, 2001). Women are ex-pected to be the moral authority of the family and provide family connection and care for children, while men are expected to be the provider for the family as well as the disciplinarian and decision maker in financial matters. Women in traditional families are highly discouraged from using alcohol or drugs because of their critical role in child-rearing. Although there is great individual variance, many males relate strongly to the value of "machismo," that is, being brave, strong, a good provider, and dominant. Identification with these qualities may make it difficult to admit to problems with alcohol or drugs. Kinship (*familismo*) is highly valued, and extended family members commonly participate in child-rearing and other activities that support the family. Festive occasions, usually celebrated by the entire extended family, tend to promote excessive drinking among males (Hoffman, 1994).

Unfortunately, the stress of immigration, poverty, discrimination, isolation from extended family, and acculturation can cause dramatic effects and strain on the traditional Hispanic support system. These hardships may contribute to an attitude of fatalism, or the belief that life's problems are inevitable and must be accepted (Alvarez & Ruiz, 2001). There are indications that family ties may be weakening: Among Hispanic households, 28% are female headed with chil-dren under 18 years, compared to a 22% rate in the United States (Bureau of the Census, 1997). Higher levels of acculturation are generally associated with higher levels of drug and alcohol use, especially among women (Randolph et al., 1998). Cultural "gaps" between generations or between the person and the mainstream American culture may lead to acting-out behaviors for young people, which in America means alcohol and substance use.

Treatment Issues

The extent to which mainstream treatment is actually utilized by Hispanics is not clear. For example, data from a national Veterans' Administration study of hospitalized alcoholics indicates that Hispanic males were significantly less likely than Caucasian patients to complete treatment or attend detoxification and more likely to be hospitalized for other diagnoses (Booth, Blow, Cook, Bunn, & Fortney, 1992). On the other hand, in 1997 Hispanics were 10.6% of the treatment population, which is only slightly higher than their 10.4% prevalence in the U.S. population (SAMHSA, 1999). In their research on treatment utilization, Arroyo, Westerberg, and Tonigan (1998) found that even though Hispanic and non-Hispanic white clients used somewhat different treatment strategies (Hispanics attended less AA and more formal therapy), the post-treatment outcomes were very similar, and the range of treatment services was equally effective for both groups. This led the authors to conclude that "Hispanics do not need culturally specific treatment" (p. 291). One thing is clear in this contested area: There are no published results of clinical trials that might resolve the issue, so more research is needed.

Culturally appropriate treatment continues to be developed, concentrating on using the strong support system of Hispanic families (Seale & Muramoto, 1993). Language may be a significant barrier in accessing any mainstream treatment, and should be addressed by providing bicultural and bilingual staff as a minimum requirement (Rothe & Ruiz, 2001). The Alcohol Use Disorder and Associated Disabilities Schedule (AUDADIS), which is a structured diagnostic interview developed for the assessment of substance-related disorders and coexisting disorders, has been translated into Spanish and adapted for the Hispanic culture. A recent study found that Spanish AUDADIS demonstrates good to excellent levels of reliability and validity when tested with a sample of low-income Puerto Ricans (Canino et al., 1999). In general, confrontational approaches during assessment should be avoided in order not to offend the person's sense of honor and dignity. Rather, as Alvarez and Ruiz (2001) suggest, the clinician should thoroughly and respectfully review the assessment criteria (particularly quantity, frequency, and instances of "loss of control") to garner support for change.

"Machismo" barriers to admitting problems may be reframed by appealing to the Hispanic male's role and responsibility as the head of the family. For example, an Alcoholics Anonymous group in Los Angeles made up primarily of recent immigrants from Central America linked "machismo" with how AA makes it possible to be a head of family, how "overcoming is manly" and that one needs "to have balls" to stay sober each day (Hoffman, 1994). In a similar fashion, a clinician can reframe a fatalistic attitude toward the problem of substance misuse by commenting, "You are here for a reason. You were meant to be helped" (Alvarez & Ruiz, 2001).

Including key figures in the family or extended family in the treatment plan is recommended in order to bypass potential resistance and maximize the family support system. From a mainstream cultural perspective, a client's dependence on family members may be unusual, and even labeled "codependency." However, for many Hispanics, particularly women, a focus on individualism may be countertherapeutic and actually reduce the potential support available from family members. Medina (2001, p. 153) recommends working with the family to "support their strengths and needs and to clarify perceptions, feelings, and behaviors that would help them function as a family unit." An example of family involvement she offers is to develop a contract outlining the family goals and behaviors, which the family signs each week for six weeks, modifying as needed.

Hispanic women who enter substance abuse treatment, like women in general, may have additional needs beyond just addressing substance use. For example, Latina women entering substance abuse treatment in Massachusetts tend to be Puerto Rican, undereducated, single heads of household, living in unstable housing situations, with few employment skills and with language difficulties (Amaro et al., 1999). The most common coexisting disorder among this group was depression, and 80.3% reported a history of childhood abuse. The authors suggest that poor Latina mothers, like this group, demonstrate the needs to incorporate case management services in substance abuse treatment that will connect them to GED opportunities, English-language classes, and job skills training, as well as to address mental health problems like depression and the effects of abuse. In order to address these issues, several larger system funding categories and priorities will need to be changed, including the funding of an individualistic rather than a family-centered approach (see chapter 13).

AFRICAN AMERICANS

The United States Census (2000) reports that blacks or African Americans now comprise 12.3% of the population. Their ancestral home may be from many different parts of the world, including Africa, Central America, South America, and the Caribbean, or they may be recent immigrants. According to Harris-Hastick (2001), the term *African American* implies a common cultural identification with Africa and mainstream U.S. culture and some kind of response or adaptation to the racism, poverty, and oppression that exist within the United States. However, English-speaking immigrants from the Caribbean (West Indies, Jamaica, Bahamas, etc.) have a different history of slavery (one associated with their home country, not the United States), tend to maintain close ties to their home country and customs long after immigration, and come from countries where it is common for blacks to be middle-class, educated professionals in a position of power. Again, one size does not fit all.

Within the United States there is also much variation of custom and life circumstance, depending on which part of the country is home and whether home is in crowded inner cities, affluent suburbs, or remote rural areas. In spite of these many differences, most people of African ancestry in the United States share a common history of slavery, an ongoing fight for civil rights, and the stress of racial oppression that still exists.

Prevalence Patterns

According to the SAMHSA (1998) National Household Survey on Drug Abuse, 1991–1993, African Americans had a rate of alcohol use during the past year of 55.4%, compared to the total population rate of 66.4%; a rate of any illicit drug use of 13.1%, compared to the total population rate of 11.9%; a rate of marijuana use of 10.6%, compared to the total population rate of 9.0%; the highest rate of cocaine use of any subgroup (5.2%), compared to the total population rate of 2.5%; a rate of those needing drug abuse treatment of 3.9%, compared to the total population rate of 2.7%; a rate of alcohol dependence of 3.4%, compared to the total population rate of 3.5%; and a rate of cigarette use of 29.9%, compared to the total population rate of 30.9%. In general, African Americans were lower in these areas than Native Americans but higher than whites (non-Hispanic). In 1997, African Americans made up 24.5% of treatment admissions, about twice their incidence in the general population (12.2%).

African American women have a much higher abstention rate (51%) than African American males (35%) or white women (36%) and a slightly higher rate than Hispanic women (48%). The 5% that did drink heavily drank more alcohol than the white women on average (148 vs. 104 drinks a month) (Caetano & Kaskutas, 1995).

The consequences of heavy alcohol use are greater for African Americans, even though their alcohol dependence rate is the same as that of whites (3.4% for each, according to SAMHSA). African Americans are more likely to die of cirrhosis of the liver and alcohol-related car crashes (Jones-Webb, 1998). Since the mid-1980s, a major consequence of illicit drug use for African American men and women has been incarceration, in numbers far greater than their representation in the population. For example, 80% of imprisoned female crack cocaine offenders are reported to be African American women (Henriques & Manatu-Rupert, 2001). A pregnant African American woman who uses drugs or alcohol is much more likely to be reported to child abuse authorities than a white woman (Rhodes & Johnson, 1997). The specter of HIV/AIDS haunts the African American drug-using community. In 1997, the Centers for Disease Control and Prevention reported that African Americans were 52.1% of all new HIV cases, and African American intravenous drug users were the fastest-growing group (Wright, 2001).

Socioeconomic Factors

Although the African American poverty rate in 1999 was a high 23.6% compared to the nation's poverty rate of 11.8%, it did go down from an even higher 1998 rate of 26.1% (Bureau of the Census, 2000). In 1999, African Americans had the lowest median income ($27,910) compared to Hispanics ($30,735), American Indians/Alaska Natives ($30,784), non-Hispanic whites ($44,366), and Asian and Pacific Islanders ($51,205). However, almost half (48%) of African American married-couple families reported total money income in 1998 of $50,000 or more, which suggests a wide disparity of income within this group. Educational status was improving. In 1999 about 77% of African Americans 25 years old and over had completed high school. And the number of African Americans enrolled in colleges doubled from 1988 to 1998 (Bureau of the Census, 2000).

Higher social class appears to be a protective factor for African Americans; for example, frequent heavy drinking is associated with older age and low income in African Americans (while in whites it is associated with youth and high income) (Jones-Webb, 1998). However, too many African Americans live in poverty and are subjected to a number of socioenvironmental risk factors, including violence, racism, deteriorating housing, lack of resources, cutbacks in health care, and limited positive role models as more middle-class professionals move from inner cities to more affluent suburbs (Wright, 2001). African American women are victimized at an astounding rate: Homicide is a leading cause of death, and aggravated assault and rape rates are almost three times those reported for white women (Rhodes & Johnson, 1997). Illegal drug activity and the presence of crack houses within the community have had a devastating effect. This kind of unrelentingly negative environment contributes to alienation, powerlessness, and stress. In 1990, Taylor and Jackson found in a sample of African American women that stress had a direct and positive effect on alcohol consumption (the more stress, the more alcohol consumed).

In addition, African Americans have been unduly targeted by alcohol advertising in their communities. According to Woods (1998), 40% of the entire alcohol advertisement budget is targeted to African Americans. As she sees it, "We are victimized excessively by the day-to-day consequences of too much ethanol and not enough jobs, too much ethanol and no Head Start, too much ethanol and no affirmative action, and too much ethanol and too little compassion" (p. 310).

Cultural Factors

In spite of the risk factors, there are many strengths and protective factors in the culture of African American families. Traditions have survived from African heritage and been adapted to survive historical conditions like slavery and current conditions like racial oppression in the United States (Wright, 2001). Spirituality, the belief in a power greater than oneself and the importance of spiritual values over material things, is considered a key component of the Afri-centric worldview. It provides a central organizing framework for how African Americans see themselves and the importance of connections to others (Brome et al., 2000). Several studies have documented the importance of spirituality and religion in the everyday life of African Americans as a way of managing stress and negative events and supporting feelings of self-worth and personal control. Brome and her colleagues (2000) examined the relationship between spirituality and African American women in recovery from substance misuse and found that women who expressed a high level of spirituality had a more positive self-concept, a more active coping style, more positive attitudes toward parenting, more positive relationships with others, and an empowering coping stance. Spirituality appears to be "the cornerstone of hope" for many in the African American community, "enabling them to survive horrendous adversity" (Wright, 2001, p. 34).

Communal orientation and family support is also a protective factor in the African American community. Individual identity is often defined through relationship to family and extended family and through mutual aid. Family may include people who are not related by blood but are linked with the family through mutual-help arrangements such as child care. *Umoja*, the first of seven principles developed by Maulana Karenga (1977), states that an obligation of every African American is to maintain unity in the family and community. Children should be seen as a gift from God and provided with life-sustaining environments. Elders are to be respected and addressed by their titles to indicate respect, such as Mr., Mrs., Aunt, Reverend. Although many poverty-stricken inner-city environments are currently more hopeless than sustaining, African American Muslims are becoming active in developing community services in these environments (Wright, 2001).

Treatment Issues

Treatment barriers for African Americans can include culturally biased diagnostic tools, biased and even racist counselors, inadequate opportunities for treatment, program content not relevant to their life experiences, lack of consideration for keeping children in treatment, and, for pregnant women, the risk of prosecution or removal of their children by Child Protective Services (Wright, 2001; Bass & Jackson, 1997). The common use of group therapy in treatment programs can also be extremely difficult and confusing for many clients who emigrate from the Caribbean and place a high value on privacy (Harris-Hastick, 2001).

A study that conducted interviews with African American pregnant women who have used crack cocaine and other drugs during pregnancy revealed that all 83 women wanted a program that would not separate them from their children. The second major element in their ideal program would include some treatment program involvement with their significant other. Many had terminated from previous programs because they could not tolerate being away from their children and not being allowed to contact their significant others (Bass & Jackson, 1997).

Transference-countertransference issues related to gender and the reality of the dominance of white culture occur frequently. For example, a black male immigrant from the Caribbean who is used to having male authority in the family may be more likely to accept a white female counselor than a female counselor who is African American. Black Caribbean women may respond to a male counselor (authority figure) with passivity or anger, regardless of race (Harris-Hastick, 2001). In the course of treatment, African Americans may get in touch with repressed rage toward the racism and oppression they have experienced all their lives (Wright, 2001). Bell hooks (1993) connects the struggle of people to "recover" from the suffering and woundedness caused by political oppression/exploitation with the effort to break with addictive behavior. David Goodson, a youth shelter worker and himself an exconvict, speaking before a social work class, says it well in (cited in van Wormer, 2001, p. 79):

> I deal with a lot of cultural pain. The same issues come up again and again, and the issue of race always comes up, the issue of Who I am. Who am I as a black man? In a lecture I heard recently the speaker said the only thing that keeps people clean is the fear of dying of an overdose. But in my work we have to go beyond that and ac-

quire a love for life, a love for yourself, a love for your family, and so on. Sometimes we preach a message of *running from* rather than a message of salvation. My point is we have to go beyond fear to the positive. As African Americans we have to view this (drug use) as self-destructive behavior due to cultural self-hatred.

Because of the devastation from illegal drug activity, drug-related HIV, crack houses, and the co-occurring violence and family dislocation from incarceration, many African American communities are not at all in favor of harm reduction practices, such as needle exchange. As Imani Woods (1998, p. 301) notes, "People look at me like I'm crazy when I go to the black community to explain harm reduction. I am accused of supporting a policy that makes peace with genocide. How can one talk about 'reducing harm' to a people under siege? Harm reduction is seen as settling, giving up, accepting failure, and bargaining with the devil."

However, according to Woods, harm reduction practices are of value to this community because they encourage a more nonjudgmental attitude toward users, instead of vilification and stigmatization. The more that occurs, the better chance that the drug user has to build new attitudes that will help him or her diminish or stop drug use, such as looking squarely at his or her drug lifestyle and the consequences, developing a more positive feeling of worth as a black person, and finding alternative models of living. A change in attitudes and moderation of use can lead to a greater likelihood of employment and access to treatment. For harm reduction to succeed in the African American community, Woods advocates that it be presented, particularly to churchgoers, as a useful step toward eradication and that these efforts incorporate African American characteristics. These may include the use of oral communication, telling stories, a call-and-response type of presentation instead of the expert speaker/passive audience type of presentation, a working knowledge of African American culture and the complexities involved, and a respect for black priorities.

MODEL ETHNIC-CENTERED PROGRAMS

"Hi, I'm Michelle; I'm an addict. I always said I'm not grateful. I'm grateful for Mimi (counselor) and the new friends I've met. They clean." It is graduation day at Project Safe, a state-funded program in Rockford, Illinois. These words come from a segment of the unprecedented five-part PBS TV series produced by Bill Moyers (1998).

An outgrowth of a link between the child welfare department and an outpatient substance abuse treatment center, the Project Safe graduation speeches offer moving testimony to the impact on women's lives of a program designed for drug-using mothers. Although the program is more woman-centered than culturally specific, the clients are largely drug users from inner-city Rockford. As described by an external evaluator, "These women don't hit bottom; they *live* on the bottom. If we wait for them to hit bottom, they will die." The outreach worker, an African American, clean for seven years, is the chauffeur, counselor, and case manager; she brings women into the program and into the program's heart. "On a typical day, I drive about 100 miles a day, taking women to appointments," she says.

"We are two voices; we are singing; we are two voices; we are singing; we are not alone." This song, which extends to three voices, to four, to five, etc., expresses the program's philosophy in a stanza. "They step into community of recovery," the outreach worker explains. "Three mornings a week they have a refuge."

In a group session, the women's voices are heard:

> "I was here busted for crack cocaine, put on probation, which meant I was to do treatment (or 3–7 years state penitentiary). But once I entered the program I got to listening to others' problems."
>
> "The reason for my relapse is to show me I needed to do more work."
>
> "My babes is suffering. I don't know what to do." ("You're doing the best you can do," replies the worker.)

Moving westward to Waterloo, Iowa, we will discover a mixed-gender, African American–specific program at its outreach center. The religious flavor is strong. The perinatal program from the People's Clinic funnels high-risk women into Pathways' family-oriented program. Before managed care constraints allowed for flexibility, people in the community dropped in to get help as needed; paperwork requirements were minimal. Today, however, this kind of openness is history. Group sessions, nevertheless, instill pride in African American participants. Substance misuse is shown to be a legacy of the powerlessness of slavery.

Washington and Moxley (2001) used prayer to facilitate the recovery process in their work with African American women in inpatient treatment for substance misuse problems. Prayer and religious involvement were found to increase feelings of self-esteem, to enhance healing, and to meet the individuals' spirituality needs. Practitioners, as Washington and Moxley argue, who eliminate prayer from the helping process may only weaken their efforts to engage in culturally sensitive practice.

SUMMARY AND CONCLUSION

In this chapter we support the conclusion that all addicts are not alike by exploring differences among Asian/Pacific Islanders, African Americans, Native American/Alaska Natives, and Hispanics. Although there is great variation because of economic class, education, level of acculturation, and gender as to how traditional values are actualized in individual people, there is considerable agreement that taking into consideration and respecting racial and ethnic values is a critical part of engaging and maintaining people in the recovery process.

Strengths-based practices that focus on assessing what the person wants and the skills, resiliencies, and resources available within the person and the community are well suited to working with clients from different cultures. Instead of defining a medical diagnosis as the problem and a one-size-fits-all intervention as the solution, a strengths-based approach would gather information from the standpoint of the clients' view of their situation and help plan alternatives within the clients' cultural framework (Rapp, 1998). Harm reduction practices support helping an individual or a family develop an array of choices that fits their unique circumstances.

Developing cultural competence requires a commitment to learn much more about different cultures than could be presented in this chapter. There are numerous resources accessible on the Internet, but a good place to start is the *Substance Abuse Resource Guides* put out by SAMHSA (www.health .org/govpubs/) on Asian and Pacific Islanders, American Indians and Native Alaskans, Hispanic/Latino Americans, and African Americans. For example, the *Asian and Pacific Islander Americans Resource Guide* includes descriptions of videotapes available in English subtitled in various languages, such as Korean, Khmer, and Tagalog, and several that are in Chinese, Vietnamese, Cambodian, and other languages. In addition, the guide features abstracts from a variety of government publications and research journals that deal with cultural competence and ethnic differences; a list of groups, youth councils, and organizations around the United States that deal with specific ethnic groups; and a list of Internet access sites.

Putting cultural competence into practice requires a commitment to slow down and take time to ask a variety of questions from a "not knowing," non-expert position. It requires acknowledgment that, as counselors, we are just in the margins of the page that represents the richness and complexity of our clients' lives. We may visit, but we do not live there. In order even to visit, it will be necessary to become aware of our own "biases, racism, internalized oppression, power dynamics, and classism" so that we don't perpetrate these problems on others (Wright, 2001, p. 44).

References

Alvarez, L., & Ruiz, P. (2001). Substance abuse in the Mexican American population. In L. A. Straussner (Ed.), *Ethnocultural factors in substance abuse treatment* (pp. 111–136). New York: Guilford Press.

Amaro, H., Nieves, R., Johannes, S., & Cabeza, N. (1998). Substance abuse treatment: Critical issues and challenges in the treatment of Latina women. *Hispanic Journal of Behavioral Sciences, 21*(3), 266–282.

Amodeo, M., & Jones, L. (1997). Viewing alcohol and other drug use cross-culturally: A cultural framework for clinical practice. *Families in Society: The Journal of Contemporary Human* Services, 240–154.

Arroyo, J., Westerberg, V., & Tonigan, J. (1998). Comparison of treatment utilization and outcome for Hispanics and non-Hispanic whites. *Journal of Studies on Alcohol, 59*(3), 286–292.

Bass, L., & Jackson, M. (1997). A study of drug abusing African American pregnant women. *Journal of Drug Issues, 27*(3), 659–671.

Beauvais, F. (1998). American Indians and alcohol. *Alcohol Health and Research World,* 22(4), 253–260.

Booth, B., Blow, F., Cook, C., Bunn, J., & Fortney, J. (1992). Age and ethnicity among hospitalized alcoholics: A nationwide study. *Alcoholism, Clinical and Experimental Research,* 16(6), 1029–1034.

Bradizza, C., & Stasiewicz, P. (1999). Introduction to the special issue "Addictions in special populations." *Addictive Behaviors,* 24(6), 737–740.

Brome, D., Owens, M., Allen, K., & Vevaine, T. (2000). An examination of spirituality among African American women in recovery from substance abuse. *Journal of Black Psychology,* 26, 470–476.

Bromley, M., & Sip, S. (2001). *Substance abuse treatment issues with Cambodian Americans.* In S. L. A. Straussner (Ed.), Ethnocultural factors in substance abuse treatment (pp. 321–344). New York: Guilford Press.

Bureau of the Census. (1993). Current population survey. Washington, DC: U.S. Department of Commerce.

Bureau of the Census (1997). Resident population of the United States by race and Hispanic origin. Washington, DC: U.S. Department of Commerce.

Caetano, R., & Kaskutas, L. (1994). {full reference to come.}{full reference to come.}{full reference to come.}{full reference to come.}

Caetano, R., & Kaskutas, L. (1995). Changes in drinking patterns among whites, blacks and Hispanics, 1984–1992. *Journal of Studies on Alcohol,* 56, 558–565.

Canino, G., Bravo, M., Ramirez, R., Febo, V., Rubio-Stipec M., Fernandez, R., & Hasin, D. (1999). The Spanish Alcohol Use Disorder and Associated Disabilities Interview Schedule (AUDADIS): Reliability and concordance with clinical diagnoses in a Hispanic population. *Journal of Studies on Alcohol,* 60(6), 790–799.

Centers for Disease Control and Prevention. (1995). *HIV/AIDS Surveillance Report,* 7(2). Atlanta: U.S. Public Health Service.

Closser, M., & Blow, F. (1993). Special populations: Ethnic minorities, and the elderly. *Psychiatric Clinics of North America,* 16(1), 199–209.

Collins, L. (1993). Sociocultural aspect of alcohol use and abuse: Ethnicity and gender. *Drugs and Society,* 18(1), 89–116.

Custer, R. L. (1982). Gambling and addiction. In R. Craig & S. Baker (Eds.), *Drug dependent patients: Treatment and research* (pp. 367–381). Springfield, IL: Charles C. Thomas.

Custer, R. L., & Milt, H. (1985). *When luck runs out.* New York: Facts on File.

Daisy, F., Thomas, L., & Worley, C. (1998). Alcohol uses and harm reduction within the Native community. In G. Alan Marlatt (Ed.), *Harm reduction: Pragmatic strategies for managing high-risk behaviors* (pp. 327–350). New York: Guilford Press.

Dick, R., Manson, S., & Beals, J. (1993). Alcohol use among male and female Native American adolescents: Patterns and correlates of student drinking in a boarding school. *Journal of Studies on Alcohol,* 54(2), 172–177.

Freese, T., Obert, J., Dickow, A., Cohen, J., & Lord, R. (2000). Methamphetamine abuse: Issues for special populations. *Journal of Psychoactive Drugs,* 32(2), 177–182.

Garret, M., & Carroll, J. (2000). Mending the broken circle: Treatment of substance and dependence among Native Americans. *Journal of Counseling and Development,* 78(4), 379–388.

Graham, J. R., Swift, K. J., & Delaney, R. (2000). *Canadian social policy: An introduction.* Scarborough, Ontario: Prentice-Hall.

Gross, E. (1995). Deconstructing politically correct practice literature: The American Indian case. *Social Work, 40*(2), 206–213.

Harris-Hastick, E. (2001). Substance abuse issues among English-speaking Caribbean people of African ancestry. In L. A. Straussner (Ed.), *Ethnocultural factors in substance abuse treatment* (pp. 52–74). New York: Guilford Press.

Henriques, Z., & Manatu-Rupert, N. (2001). Living on the outside: African American women before, during, and after imprisonment. *The Prison Journal, 81*(1), 6–19.

Herring, R. (1994). Substance use among Native American Indian Youth: A selected review of causality. *Journal of Counseling and Development, 72*(6), 578–588.

Hoffman, F. (1994). Cultural adaptations of Alcoholics Anonymous to serve Hispanic populations. *International Journal of Addictions, 29*(4), 445–460.

hooks, b. (1993). *Sisters of the yam: Black women and self-recovery.* Boston: South End Press.

hooks, b. (2000). *Where we stand: Class matters.* New York: Routledge.

Ja, D., & Aoki, B. (1993). Substance abuse treatment: Cultural barriers in the Asian American Community. *Journal of Psychoactive Drugs, 25*(1), 61–71.

Jones-Webb, R. (1998). Drinking patterns and problems among African American: Recent findings. *Alcohol Health and Research World, 22*(4), 260–265.

Karenga, M. (1977). Kwanzaa: Origin, concepts, practice. Inglewood, CA: Kawaida. As referenced in Wright, E. (2001).

Kasee, C. (1995). Identity, recovery, and religious imperialism: Native American women and the New Age. *Women and Therapy, 16*(2–3), 83–91.

Lindenberg, C., Solorzano, R., Krantz, M., Galvis, C., Baroni, G., & Strickland, O. (1998). Risk and resilience: Building protective factors. An intervention for preventing substance abuse and sexual risk-taking and for promoting strength and protection among young, low-income Hispanic women. *American Journal of Maternal Child Nursing, 23*(2), 99–104.

Lowery, C. (1998). American Indian perspectives on addiction and recovery. *Health and Social Work, 23*(2), 127–135.

Makimoto, K. (1998). Drinking patterns and drinking problems among Asian Americans and Pacific Islanders. *Alcohol Health and Research World, 22*(4), 270–276.

Mark, M. E., & Lesieur, H. R. (1992). A feminist critique of problem gambling research. *British Journal of Addiction, 87,* 549–565.

May, P. (1996). Overview of alcohol abuse epidemiology for American Indian populations. In G. Sandefur, R. Rindfuss, & B. Cohen (Eds.), *Changing numbers, changing needs: American Indian demography and public health* (pp. 235–261). Washington, DC: National Academy Press.

Medina, C. (2001). Toward an understanding of Puerto Rican ethnicity and substance abuse. In L. A. Straussner (Ed.), *Ethnocultural factors in substance abuse treatment* (pp. 137–163). New York: Guilford Press.

Mercado, M. (2000). The invisible family: Counseling Asian American substance abusers and their families. *Family Journal,* 267–272.

Moyers, B. (1998, March 30). *Moyers on addiction: Close to home.* Part 2. Public Broadcasting System.

Morelli, P., & Fong, R. (2000). The role of Hawaiian elders in substance abuse treatment among Asian/Pacific Islander women. *Journal of Family Social Work, 4*(4), 33–44.

Murphy, S., & Rosenbaum, M. (1997). Two women who used cocaine too much. In C. Reinarman and H. Levine (Eds.), *Crack in America: Demon drugs and social justice.* Berkeley, CA: University of California Press.

Polinsky, M., Hser, Y., & Grella, C. (1998). Consideration of special populations in the drug treatment system of a large metropolitan area. *Journal of Behavioral Health Services and Research, 25*(1), 7–21.

Randolph, W., Stroup-Benham, C., Black, S., & Markides, K. (1998). Alcohol use among Cuban-Americans, Mexican-Americans, and Puerto Ricans. *Alcohol Health & Research World, 22*(4), 265–270.

Rapp, C. (1998). *The strengths model: Case management with people suffering from severe and persistent mental illness.* New York: Oxford University Press.

Rhodes, R., & Johnson, A. (1997). A feminist approach to treating alcohol and drug-addicted African American women. *Women and Therapy, 20*(3), 23–37.

Rothe, E., & Ruiz, P. (2001). Substance abuse among Cuban Americans. In L. A. Straussner (Ed.), *Ethnocultural factors in substance abuse treatment* (pp. 97–110). New York: Guilford Press.

Scott, K. (1997). Indigenous Canadians. Canadian Profile 1997. Available online at www.ccsa.ca/cp97nat.htm#indigenous

Seale, J., & Muramoto, M. (1993). Substance abuse among minority populations. *Primary Care, 20*(1), 167–180.

Segal, B. (1998). Drinking and drinking-related problems among Alaska natives. *Alcohol Health and Research World, 22*(4), 276–280.

Shukovsky, D. (1996, May 6). Healing circle returns Indian heritage: Mental health is attuned to cultural understanding. *Seattle Post-Intelligencer*, p. B1.

Straussner, S. L. (2001). Ethnocultural issues in substance abuse treatment: An overview. In L. A. Straussner (Ed.), *Ethnocultural factors in substance abuse treatment* (pp. 3–28). New York: Guilford Press.

Substance Abuse and Mental Health Services Administration (SAMHSA). (1998). Prevalence of substance use among racial/ethnic subgroups in the United States, 1991–1993. Online at www.health.org/govpubs/bkd262/index.htm

Substance Abuse and Mental Health Services Administration (SAMHSA). (1999). Treatment Episode Data Set (TEDS) 1992–1997. Drug and Alcohol Services Information System Series: S-7. Online at wwwdasis.samhsa.gov/teds97_m.htm

Support Services International. (1996). Evaluation of the Indian Health Service adolescent regional treatment centers. Silver Spring, MD: Indian Health Service. (As referenced in Daisy et al., 1998.)

Taylor, J., & Jackson, B. (1990). Factors affecting alcohol consumption in black women: Part II. *International Journal of the Addictions, 25*(12), 1415–1427.

Tying drug and alcohol programs to immigrants' backgrounds. (1999, June 16). *New York Times*, late edition (East Coast), 1–2.

United States Census. (1999). *American Indian heritage month.* U.S. Census Bureau's Public Information Office. Online at www.census.gov/Press-Release/www/1999/cb99ff14.html

United States Census. (2000). *Overview of race and Hispanic origin.* U.S. Department of Commerce, Economics and Statistics Administration. Online at www.census.gov

van Wormer, K. (2001). *Counseling female offenders and victims: A strengths-perspective approach.* New York: Springer.

Washington, O. G., & Moxley, D. P. (2001). The use of prayer in group work with African American women recovering from chemical dependency. *Families in Society 82*(1), 49–60.

Weaver, H. (2001). Native Americans and substance abuse. In S. L. Straussner (Ed.), *Ethnocultural factors in substance abuse treatment.* New York: Guilford Press.

Woods, I. (1998). Bringing harm reduction to the Black community. In G. Alan Marlatt (Ed.), *Harm reduction: Pragmatic strategies for managing high-risk behaviors* (pp. 301–326). New York: Guilford Press.

Wright, E. (2001). Substance abuse in African American communities. In L. A. Straussner (Ed.), *Ethnocultural factors in substance abuse treatment* (pp. 31–51). New York: Guilford Press.

Yuen, F., & Nakano-Matsumoto, N. (1998). Effective substance abuse treatment for Asian American adolescents. *Early Child Development and Care, 147,* 43–54.

GENDER AND SEXUAL ORIENTATION DIFFERENCES

CHAPTER

INTRODUCTION

In the last 20 years, a great deal of energy, resources, and research, along with many women's voices, have changed the way we look at traditional drug/alcohol treatment programming. Beginning in 1984 with the federal requirement that 5% of each block grant to the states be set aside for new or expanded alcohol and drug abuse services for women, a wide array of special services began to appear. Within another four years, the "War on Drugs" and the national press obsession with "crack babies" helped inspire Congress to double the federal set-aside in order to target programs for pregnant women and women with dependent children (see chapter 13). Grants became available to fund demonstration programs for women-only groups and treatment programs, for more supportive and less confrontational approaches, for programs with enhanced services such as parenting, skill development, and prevocational training, and for programs that incorporated prenatal/postnatal care, or at least child care while the woman was in treatment sessions. In 1993, the National Institutes of Health (NIH) mandated that enough women had to be included in clinical trials that gender differences could be tested.

During this same time frame, the voices of gay men and lesbians also began to be heard. The connection between injected drugs, the gay population, and the AIDS epidemic added pressure for federal funders to pay attention to gay males as a special population. An indication of the change is the National Institute on Drug Abuse (NIDA) five-year epidemiological study launched in 1991, which surveyed 1,067 respondents, 53% gay men and 47% lesbians.

Although these legislative and research changes signal an enormous shift in what has been heterosexual male–dominated research and treatment programming, the actual changing of treatment options for women, gay men, and lesbian women is still an ongoing effort. Researchers and practitioners continue to identify gender differences in biology, genetics, paths to dependence, responses to various treatment options, relapse, and social contexts, which suggest different prevention and treatment approaches for men and women. However, these findings are not yet widely applied to practice settings; when they have been, the research findings on the outcomes of specialized programs for women have produced mixed results. Very few studies have addressed outcomes in male-only interventions. There is also no consensus as to whether gay men and lesbians should be treated separately from heterosexual clients, or separately from each other.

This chapter will focus first on gender differences and then on sexual orientation differences that may affect a person's ability to resist addiction, seek and find treatment, and maintain recovery. Programs that are designed to enhance the ability of women, gay men, and lesbians to succeed in their recovery will be described. Controversies that surround these developments will be discussed and research findings will be offered to practitioners.

GENDER DIFFERENCES

All Women Are Not Alike, and Neither Are All Men

Before we lump people into gender categories to illustrate their differences, it's important to remember that all women are not alike and, of course, neither are all men. Scientists and researchers who adhere to a "developmental" approach to addiction stress the interplay of sociocultural, psychological, and neurobiological processes that influence each individual a little bit differently, depending on the person's age, gender, and ethnic group and on the cultural influences on each person's age cohort (U.S. Secretary of Health and Human Services, 2000). A European American man in his 20s who grew up in an impoverished inner-city environment in the 1990s (such as rap artist Eminem) is likely to have a much different drinking or drug use "trajectory" (a changing pattern over time) than a middle-class triethnic young man who grew up in the affluent suburbs (such as Tiger Woods).

Murphy and Rosenbaum (1997) argue that gender, race, and class are more important in shaping how people develop drug problems with illicit drugs than the drug itself. Thus, as described in an earlier chapter, "Becky," a typical white, middle-class young woman interviewed in their NIDA-sponsored research project, had more options for controlling her cocaine use than "Monique," a young black woman living in a poor inner-city neighborhood. Becky used cocaine within the protected context that is afforded the middle class—she had a job and resources to buy her own powder cocaine and the privacy to use it without being hassled by police, and thus could maintain a "nondeviant" identity. When

FIGURE 11.1 | ILLICIT DRUG USE AMONG WOMEN, BY PREGNANCY STATUS AND AGE, 1999

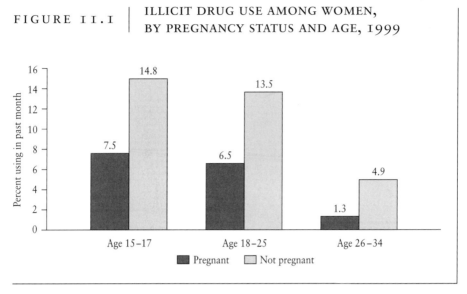

Source: National Household Survey on Drug Abuse, 1999, SAMHSA.

her period of heavy use became an unsatisfying experience that threatened other life goals that she had every opportunity to attain, she could rely on the resources of the middle class (school, family, job connections) to help her quit using. On the other hand, "Monique" was introduced to "crack," a more dangerous form of cocaine that was readily available in her neighborhood, quickly resorted to trading sexual favors for her drug as the only currency available, was frequently arrested on the streets, and became homeless and totally impoverished, with very few resources to deal with her predicament. Becky went to Hawaii with her father to make a break from cocaine use; Monique went to jail.

The protective power of race and class extends only to some women and men, and no one would claim it prevents addiction. However, it can condition and influence how a person uses drugs, alcohol, and gambling, and mediate the consequences of that use or misuse. Similarly, cultural differences around the world regarding the acceptance of alcohol for each gender and the extent to which sex roles are strictly defined appear to influence the wide variation of alcoholism. The Helzer et al. (1990) study of lifetime alcoholism prevalence rates shows a dramatic difference *between* genders in the same culture and *within* the same gender in different cultures. Edmonton, Canada, had a male-to-female ratio of 4:1, Taiwan a ratio of 18:1, South Korea a ratio of 16:1, St. Louis, Missouri, a ratio of 7:1, and Puerto Rico a ratio of 12:1. Thus a woman in South Korea may have a protective factor of cultural tradition about her role as a woman who doesn't drink alcohol that a woman in Edmonton does not have.

A final point to underscore the reality of within-gender differences can be seen in Figure 11.1, where we look at the female variations in drug use by age and pregnancy status in the United States. Young women between the ages of

15 and 17 using illicit drugs in the last month far outnumber their older sisters, and nonpregnant women outnumber pregnant women.

Gender Differences in Prevalence

The Substance Abuse and Mental Health Services Administration (SAMHSA) conducts a yearly survey, called the National Household Survey on Drug Abuse (NHSDA), to estimate the use of drugs, alcohol, and tobacco use, dependence, and treatment occurring within the United States (SAMHSA, 1999). Data from the 1999 survey indicate that, except for adolescents, males (54%) were more likely to report drinking alcohol in the past month than females (41.1%), more likely to report use of tobacco (36% for males, 24.3% for females), and more likely to report current illicit drug use (8.7% for males, 4.9% for females).

Among adolescents, the rate of current alcohol use was almost the same for girls (18.1%) and for boys (19.2%), the current use of illicit drugs was just slightly higher for boys (11.3%) than for girls (10.5%), and both were equally likely to report use of cigarettes in the last month (15%). Drug dependence rates in the last year are identical (see Figure 11.2). As has been noted, this may be "an equality women don't want" (Davis & DiNitto, 1998). Some would argue that women have always been drinking and using drugs more than shows up in research studies but that poor methodology, indifference, and sex role stereotyping have kept the numbers low (Babcock, 1996).

Compulsive gambling surveys consistently report that men are much more likely to be pathological or problem gamblers than are women. The National Research Council (1999) analysis of general population studies (not clinical or institutional) from 18 states conducted during the last 10 years reveals that the median proportion of men among pathological and problem gamblers ranged from 45% to 80%, with a median of 62%; the proportion of women among pathological and problem gamblers ranged from 20% to 55%, with a median of 38%.

Most of the state problem gambling helplines report that the percentage of women seeking help with gambling problems has been increasing. As early as 1993, an Alberta, Canada, study concluded that women are the gender group now most likely to experience gambling problems. In New Jersey, calls about women have doubled since 1990. In Texas, calls about women problem gamblers have increased from 34% in 1992 to 40% in 1999 (Texas Council on Problem and Compulsive Gambling, 2000). In Minnesota, 30% of the calls to the Minnesota Compulsive Gambling Hotline were about women in 1992, but by 1996 that percentage had risen to 42% ("Screening," 2000). In 1997, women made up 41.6% of the gambling treatment population in Minnesota and were more likely than men to receive a more serious score on the South Oaks Gambling Screen (Rhodes, Norman, Langenbahn, Harmon, & Deal, 1997).

Eating disorders are by far more prevalent in females, with studies reporting a male-to-female ratio of between 1:6 and 1:20 for anorexia nervosa/bulimia nervosa and a 1:2 ration for binge-eating disorders. According to Anderson (2000, p. 5), the diagnosis of eating disorders is gender-biased, because

FIGURE 11.2 | ILLICIT DRUG DEPENDENCE, BY AGE AND GENDER, 1999

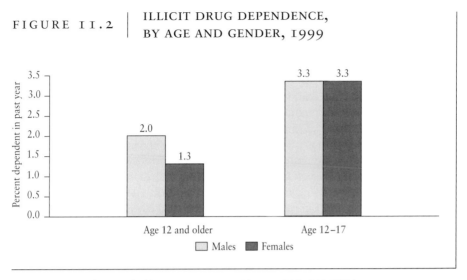

Source: National Household Survey on Drug Abuse, 1999, SAMHSA.

"most physicians and health care providers view the illness as a female or a homosexual disease." Males may also suffer from "reverse anorexia," a rarer form of eating disorder characterized by a fear of being too thin and a need to add muscle and weight.

Since 1965, men have been smoking less (a drop of 46%), while women have been smoking a little bit less (a drop of 35%). Consequently, the gender gap in smoking rates has narrowed. Adolescent girls and boys are now equally likely to smoke, and young women are gaining on this—sadly in an apparent attempt to lose weight. In response to the Virginia Slims advertisement, *MS Magazine* and others are asking "If we've come such a long way, why are we still smoking?" (Center on Addiction and Substance Abuse [CASA], 1996). (See chapter 6, the section on Teenage Drinking and Using, and chapter 7, the section on Eating Disorders).

Sociocultural Gender Differences

In the recent past (and even today), women who were identified as alcoholics, drug addicts, or compulsive gamblers were considered especially deviant and promiscuous. Kagle (1987) calls alcoholic women a "discredited social group" who suffer from a "double whammy" because they are both alcoholic and female. It seems reasonable to expect that women addicted to alcohol, drugs, or gambling would internalize these sociocultural forces. In interviews with women recovering from alcoholism, Davis (1997) found that the issue of shame was still alive, even in recovery, and, for some women, continued to be a slight barrier in their relationship to nonalcoholics because they felt their alcoholism (and all the behavior that went with it) would not be understood.

To what extent does the "shame factor" affect a woman's path to addiction or her ability to get help and to recover? It may be part of the larger environment of women's struggle for economic and political equality. Research into treatment effectiveness has shown that environmental factors may be the most significant variable in determining addiction treatment outcome (Fingarette, 1998). In other words, the stability of family ties, the economic and work situation, and the overarching cultural expectations of males and females in society are all vital correlates of recovery.

Women as a group are oppressed in many ways in the dominant culture of the United States. More women than men are poor, and women continue to be paid less than men. Indirect discrimination exists not just with treatment centers, but also with employment and educational organizations that don't provide a way for them to meet their child-rearing responsibilities. Cultural stereotypes cast women as illogical, emotionally unstable, and incapable of many tasks that require leadership, math skills, or mechanical skills and as dependent on men (Abramovitz, 1988). Women are far more likely to be subjected to violence and murder by men. These factors affect all women, but a woman who is trying to get help for an addiction may be particularly affected by her lack of money and resources, less tolerance and less support from partner and family, and the lack of treatment available for women with children. The findings of a study on vocational rehabilitation clients that compared substance users to nonusers suggest that women substance abusers are more seriously disadvantaged than the male substance abusers, because they share the psychosocial problems of both the women in the study *and* the substance users in the study, and (not surprisingly) the women had many more problems than the men (Davis & DiNitto, 1995). Studies of clients who enter treatment support these realities: Women are more dependent on welfare and/or disability payments, while men have more skilled jobs; women are more likely to lack employment skills; women are twice as likely to have children in their households and to report greater concerns about issues related to children, although both men and women were concerned about the effect of drug treatment on the custody of their children (Wechsberg, Craddock, & Hubbard, 1998).

Using a feminist methodology and analysis to look at environmental factors affecting women gamblers, Sarah Brown and Louise Coventry (1997) launched a community-based research project in Victoria, Australia, called "Queen of Hearts." The findings suggest that women compulsive gamblers may be the victims of social stereotypes and the economic and gender limitations imposed upon women. Even the definitions of gambling problems that focus on individual "pathology" instead of including a sociocultural framework "have serious stigmatizing effects, such as discouraging gamblers from seeking assistance, inviting moral and legalistic judgments, and invoking the label of 'deviant'"(p. 9).

Invisibility   Women are much less likely than men to be encouraged, cajoled, or browbeaten by partners into entering treatment for their addiction (Davis, 1997; Saunders, Wodak, & Williams, 1985). Other than the child welfare arena, women report feeling a sense of "invisibility" about their situation from their partners, their employers, and the professionals from whom they sought help. As a woman interviewed in the Davis study states (p. 156): "My parents didn't see that I had a drinking problem. Part of it was that they just didn't see a lot. They'd say, 'If your husband would give you some money, you'd be o.k.'"

Some of this invisibility may be because the partner or family member is drinking or using drugs so heavily him- or herself that recognition of a problem might be threatening. Having a male partner who is drinking or using drugs has consistently been found to be a predisposing factor (some would say the greatest factor) in a woman's addiction (Westermeyer, & Boedicker, 2000; Lex, 1995). In one study, 33% of female heroin addicts said a male (friend, spouse, or partner) influenced their decision to use narcotics; only 2% of male addicts said a woman was influential in their decision (Hser, Anglin, & McGlothlin, 1987).

Even when a woman finally gets to treatment, she is unlikely to get the family support available to men. Laudet, Magura, Furst, & Kumar (1999) found that men who were mostly active crack/cocaine users were able to give only passive and inconsistent support to their partners in treatment. Reasons included the men's own active use, their desire to maintain the relationship status quo where the man has the dominant role, their preoccupation working on their own recovery, their disagreement with abstinence as a necessity, and their desire to avoid the stigma attached to their female partner as an "addict." In contrast, men report that they are influenced positively by a spouse or partner to enter treatment or that they enter because of the criminal justice system (Grella & Joshi, 1999; Thom, 1987).

Being a Mom   In addition to the lack of familial support, women are less likely to enter treatment for many other reasons: (1) the obligation of child-rearing, (2) the unavailability of treatment slots for women with children or pregnant women, (3) barriers such as transportation and lack of child care, and (4) treatment programs not designed to meet these and other special needs of women clients. A recent study indicates the shocking unavailability of treatment to parents in the child welfare system in the United States. The Child Welfare League of America estimates that 67% of parents involved in the system need drug or alcohol treatment, yet services are available to only 31% (Young, Gardner, & Dennis, 1998). It is well recognized in the treatment field that many women do not participate in treatment because they are unable to obtain quality child care or because they fear being required to relinquish their children (Center for Substance Abuse Treatment [CSAT], 1994; Finkelstein, 1994).

Crime and Punishment   Addiction and the use of illicit drugs bring women into the criminal and civil justice system in a way unique to their gender. The criminalization of women who use illicit drugs during pregnancy and the termination of their parental rights have no male counterpart. Several states, such as South Carolina, have enacted laws requiring health officials to report women whose newborns test positive for drugs, even if the mother is already in treatment (van Wormer, 2001). Many women have lost custody of their children for the same reason. In Norway, the state may seize custody of the children, a right that may never be returned even though the mother may later achieve a good recovery.

Over the past decade, more than 240 women in 35 states have been criminally prosecuted for using substances during pregnancy thought to be harmful to their unborn (Rubin, 1998). *Whitner v. State,* a South Carolina Supreme Court decision that allowed a woman to be criminally prosecuted as a child abuser and sentenced to 10 years in jail for using an illicit drug during her pregnancy, is still on the books. Women reported being dragged to jail from the labor room, still bleeding from childbirth. The U.S. Supreme Court declined to hear an appeal of this ruling in 1998. Such groups as the National Association of Social Workers, the American College of Obstetricians and Gynecologists, and the National Association of Alcoholism and Drug Abuse Counselors supported the appeal. A milder approach is carried out in South Dakota, where new statutes force pregnant women with alcohol and drug problems into treatment for up to nine months (Aamot, 1998).

Consider the impact on pregnant and addicted women of the following ruling by Judge O. H. Eaton of the Seminole County Circuit Court (Florida). Judge Eaton found Jennifer Johnson guilty of delivering cocaine to her baby after the birth during the 60–90 seconds before the umbilical cord was clamped. His finding states:

> The fact that the defendant was addicted to cocaine at the time of these offenses is not a defense. The choice to use or not use cocaine is just that—a choice. . . . [P]regnant addicts have been on notice for years that taking cocaine may be harmful to their children. This verdict puts pregnant addicts on notice that they have a responsibility to seek treatment for their addiction prior to giving birth. Otherwise, the state may very well use criminal prosecution to force future compliance with the law or, in appropriate cases, to punish those who violate it. (*Florida v. Johnson,* Circuit Court, Seminole Co., July 13, 1989; in Siegal, 1997, p. 250)

Although illicit drug use is not limited to any class or race of women, black women and poor women are much more likely to be targeted for these policies. In one Florida study, pregnant black women were 10 times more likely to be reported for substance use than their white counterparts (Chasnoff, 1990). The result of such racist and oppressive policies has not been less drug use; rather, it has deterred especially at-risk poor women from sharing important information with their health providers and from seeking prenatal care at all (Siegal, 1997).

Good news came with the 2001 U.S. Supreme Court ruling that hospital workers cannot constitutionally test maternity patients for illegal drug use for litigation purposes without their consent. Whether any of the 10 plaintiffs who appealed in this case consented to the tests remains to be decided in the lower courts. This ruling is a victory for the individual's right to medical privacy (Greenhouse, 2001).

Jail and Prison   Largely because of the impact of the U.S. war on drugs and mandatory sentencing, the female prisoner population in the United States nearly doubled from 1990 to 1999 (Bureau of Justice Statistics, 1999). Worldwide, Canada is second only to the United States in the number of drug arrests per capita (Marron, 1996). Women offenders, especially in the younger age brackets, are arrested at increasingly high rates for drug offenses, and women

TABLE 11.1 | CORRECTIONAL FACILITIES PROVIDING SUBSTANCE ABUSE TREATMENT, BY FACILITY TYPE

Response Category	Total	Federal Prisons	State Prisons	Jails	Juvenile Facilities
Total correctional facilities responding to survey	7,243	129	1,069	3,067	2,978
Number of facilities providing treatment	2,731	121	602	1,000	1,008
Percentage of facilities providing treatment	37.7%	93.8%	56.3%	32.6%	33.8%

Source: Findings from Uniform Facility Data Set 1997 Survey of Correctional Facilities (SAMHSA, 2000).

of color have had the greatest overall increase in criminal justice supervision, including imprisonment. Illegal drugs were implicated more than alcohol in women's crimes; for men the pattern was reversed (Bureau of Justice Statistics, 1999). Many of the women are arrested when their spouses and partners are arrested for drug dealing; unfortunately, the law does not take into account the inequality in most of these male/female relationships (van Wormer, 2001).

Analysis of state-level data reveals that 45% of the women prisoners require treatment for chronic substance use compared to 22% of men requiring such treatment. Unfortunately, the treatment system is not sufficiently available to handle the need. In the California State system, for example, there is only one drug treatment program for female prisoners, and it has a waiting list of 70–90 (CASA, 1996). In 1997, federal prisons offered the highest percentage of substance abuse treatment, and local jails provided the least (see Table 11.1).

The good news is that jail or prison may be the first place anyone has offered treatment or talked to women about the abuse they've experienced. As told by women in recovery from drug addiction interviewed by Hirsch (1999, p. 2):

"I started using alcohol and pills when I was thirteen. I was raped when I was twelve, my father was an alcoholic, my mother was using pills. He used to beat her up all the time—it was pretty crazy. No, no one helped me. The (drug and alcohol treatment program in jail) is the first place anyone talked about it."

"(In jail) they had all different kind of classes—about being raped in the street, about being raped in your family. I needed both those classes."

"This is my first time in treatment. I couldn't get Medical Assistance, so I couldn't get treatment. Now I'm court-stipulated, so I can get treatment."

Violence   Violence against women is an area where the influence of sociocultural attitudes has been documented. Kantor and Straus (1989) discovered in an analysis of data from a national family violence survey that cultural approval of violence emerged as the strongest predictor of family violence, even more significant than the level of alcohol abuse. In the United States, we "approve" of violence through advertisements featuring malnourished women in stiletto heels and chains, films that show scenes of women being slapped around or raped, ineffective laws and law enforcement, and the lack of a viable well-resourced support system for women seeking help. A recent National Crime Victimization Survey reveals that more than 960,000 incidents of violence against a current or former intimate (spouse, boyfriend, or girlfriend) occur in America each year, and 85% of the victims are women (Greenfield et al., 1998). In 1996, there were 1800 murders committed by intimate partners, with three out of every four victims being female (Cooper & Eaves, 1996).

The use of alcohol and drugs has consistently been found to be a major factor in intimate-partner violence. In several studies, the significant correlation between the use of alcohol and intimate-partner violence against women holds after controlling for sociodemographic variables, hostility, and marital satisfaction. It holds across all ethnic groups and social classes (Kantor, 1993; Leonard, 1993). A descriptive study of the types of violence against women and the associated use of alcohol and illicit drugs by the perpetrator revealed that physical abuse was significantly higher for women with perpetrators who used drugs only as compared with perpetrators who used alcohol only (Willson et al., 2000). According to a large data analysis by the National Center on Addiction and Substance Abuse at Columbia University (CASA, 1996), 70% of drug-addicted, low-income pregnant women in methadone maintenance have been beaten—86% by their husbands or partners. Women who use cocaine become high risks for being murdered. In New York City, in the two-year period between 1990 and 1992, the number of fatal injuries following cocaine use was higher than the number of deaths from AIDS, cancer, or heart disease for young black and Hispanic women ages 15–24. Alcoholic women do not escape either; in one study of spousal abuse, alcoholic women were found to be nine times more likely to be slapped by their husband, five times more likely to be kicked or hit, five times more likely to be beaten, and four times more likely to have their lives threatened than were nonalcoholic women.

In the following illustration, we read the words of a North Carolina woman:

> I married an alcoholic. I married him because I thought he was the only guy who would ever show me any attention. In those seven years, I put up with mental abuse, physical abuse, and somewhat sexual abuse. The way that alcohol and marijuana played a role in my marriage—that was the only way of getting along with him. He was mean as a snake. He run me down onto the ground and start beating me. To relax, I drank, I smoked pot and go into my own little dream world. That's what the marijuana did, was put you in a dream state, where you would forget all the pain and all the anger and all the abuse and get high. Until the next morning, and then it started all over again. (Smith & Chescheir, 1995)

Substance-abusing women may be more at risk of victimization because they are violating gender-role expectations by the very fact of being intoxicated (Kantor, 1993). Miller, Downs, and Gondoli (1989) speculate that alcoholic women's stigmatization as being "sexually loose" may set them up for mistreatment. Moreover, if such women become verbally or physically aggressive, the violence in their partners may escalate. Studies of chemically dependent women in treatment suggest that they are more likely to initiate violence against partners than are battered women in shelters or women without alcohol problems. In any case, such alcoholic women experience more violence from their spouses than do women in a general household sample (Miller et al., 1989).

In addition to "domestic violence" (which some feminists prefer to call "household terrorism"), women are far more likely than men to be subjected to sexual violence (as children or adults). In the Drug Abuse Treatment Outcome Study (DATOS), one of the largest studies of clients entering substance abuse treatment ($N = 10,010$), women reported twice as much sexual abuse as did men. When physical and sexual abuse were combined, the women reported from three to six times more abuse (Wechsberg et al., 1998). In their study of 472 women aged 18 to 45, Miller, Downs, and Testa (1993) found that alcoholic women in treatment are more than five times (47%) likelier to experience forced penetration as a child than women in a general household sample (9%). There is a growing body of research that supports the relationship between childhood sexual abuse and subsequent substance abuse in women (Neumann, Houskamp, Pollock, & Briere, 1996; Wilsnack, Vogeltanz, Klassen, & Harris, 1997). In addition, the experience of childhood sexual and physical abuse is linked to a greater risk of sexually transmitted diseases (STDs) (El-Bassel et al., 1998), unintended pregnancy (Kenney, Reinholtz, & Angelini, 1997), and prostitution in women (Widom, Ireland, & Glynn, 1995). Men who experience sexual abuse are likelier than nonabused men to use drugs and engage in risky sexual behavior (Holmes & Slap, 1998; Pierre, Shrier, Emans, & DuRant, 1998).

The high rate of co-occurrence of substance use and violence (physical and sexual) has treatment implications. Traditional treatment for these problems is often ordered separately, in the case of domestic violence, to standard anger management treatments. Although there are treatment approaches developing that work with women dealing with child sexual abuse and addictions, the different models underlying the treatment approaches may not be in harmony (Hiebert-Murphy & Woytkiw, 2000). However, there is some evidence that addressing substance use and violence in an integrated way may have better results.

Psychological Differences by Gender

The field of modern psychology focuses primarily on the vulnerabilities and dysfunctions of normal mind processes and only lately is looking at resiliency factors and strengths of the mind. The question of precisely how environment and biology affect the mind and addictive processes is still being answered. Maybe men really are from Mars and women from Venus! It seems reasonable that sociocultural gender differences (in economics, victimization, support systems, etc.), as discussed earlier, would be reflected differently in the minds of men and women. For example, researchers on the effects of trauma propose that a lifetime of traumatic abuse, characteristic of many women who are addicted, causes low self-esteem and self-disgust that gravitates these women into situations of further abuse (Downs & Miller, 1997).

Besides low self-esteem, another indication of psychological distress, one that is more problematic for women, is a higher rate of co-occurring disorders. Among persons diagnosed with alcohol problems or dependence, 65% of women, compared with 46% of men, had a coexisting disorder, and women were more likely to be diagnosed with a third problem of physical and sexual abuse (V. Brown, Melchior, & Huba, 1999). A review of recent research indicates that women who are alcoholic have more major depressions, anxiety disorders, panic disorders, and phobias than alcoholic men, who are more frequently diagnosed with antisocial personality disorder. Similarly, women who are opiate and cocaine users have higher rates of affective disorders, anxiety disorders, and eating disorders than men. Antisocial personality disorder is more likely in men (Brady & Randall, 1999). The authors note that, in general, these differences are consistent with the differences in psychiatric disorders in the general population. However, there is a unique effect of depression on substance users; that is, depression is associated with relapse, especially in women (Schutte, Seable, & Moos, 1997).

Women with multiple problems, such as having childhood histories of trauma and diagnosis of substance abuse and a mental health disorder, have high rates of posttraumatic stress disorder (Teets, 1995). Such women have been characterized as carrying an overall problem "burden" because of the wide range of additional problems that also require help, such as housing instability, homelessness, physical health problems, risk for HIV/AIDS, and problems with child care. A recent study of 577 women in a residential substance abuse treatment program indicates the higher the "burden" level, the less likely such women will remain in treatment (V. Brown et al., 1999).

Men and women tend to smoke cigarettes to relieve different psychological states. "Males respond more to the nicotine's rewarding effects than do females, especially the dopamine-mediated euphoric effects," according to Dr. Neil Grunberg, professor of medical psychology, clinical psychology, and neuroscience at Uniformed Services University of the Health Sciences, Bethesda, Maryland ("New Study," 2000).

Men attempt to relieve boredom and fatigue or increase arousal and concentration by smoking; women attempt to control their weight and to decrease stress, anger, and other negative feelings. Although nicotine helps to decrease appetite and control weight in both genders, it has stronger effects on women. Women also have more difficulty in stopping smoking than men, and do not respond well to confrontational approaches in smoking cessation programs.

Gambling as psychological "pain medication" is a common theme in the stories of many women who are compulsive gamblers. In a pioneering study of women in Gamblers Anonymous, Lesieur (1987, p. 234) found that two major reasons for escape in over half the women interviewed ($n = 50$) were "escape from memories of parental upbringing and escape from troubled husbands and loneliness." In this sample, 40% of the women grew up in homes where one or both parents were addicted to alcohol or gambling. In addition, another 12%

had parents with other serious problems, such as bipolar illness and sexual abuse. Having "troubled husbands" was a reality for 60% of the women, who were married to alcoholics (35%), substance users (10%), or compulsive gamblers (15%).

The following story illustrates how using gambling as an escape from trouble worked for "Betty":

> When I first walked into a casino, my personal life was full of stress. Within a couple of months I was "zoning out," running from the stress of my life by feeding a slot machine. Six months after putting my first quarter into a machine I had progressed to losing a thousand dollars of plastic money a night. I can almost laugh now as I think of the stress I added to my life by going to the casino. Physically, I added the stress of no food or drink for hours on end, lack of sleep, and the anxiety of shuffling credit card limits. Emotionally, I left the casino crying all the way home, pounding the steering wheel and telling myself what a rotten, stupid person I was. Guilt consumed me. Spiritually, I was almost dead inside. ("Women Helping Women," 2000)

A common designation of many women like "Betty" is that they are "escape" gamblers, whereas men are more likely to be called "action" gamblers. Escape gamblers tend to become compulsive in their gambling in a span of 6 months to 3 years, play "luck" games such as bingo, slots, and video poker, and start playing as a recreation but quickly move into using gambling to "escape" from problems (Arizona Council on Compulsive Gambling, 2000; Lesieur & Blume, 1991). The lure of the "escape" is characterized by changing the feeling of stress or psychological discomfort into feeling "hypnotized," "in a trance," "having tunnel vision where nothing else mattered," or even "out of body."

In contrast, "action" gamblers tend to begin early in life, have a long-term problem (10–30 years), focus on "skill" games such as poker, horses, and sports, and seek "action" as well as escape. A gender comparison of a large treatment sample in Australia (Crisp et al., 2000) revealed from the assessment data ($n = 1292$, male $= 696$, female $= 583$) that women were 1.5 times more likely to gamble as a way of escaping from other problems than men. The women reported average debts that were less than half what was owed by the male gamblers. Women were far more likely to report using electronic gambling machines than males (91.1% vs. 61.4%) and more likely to play bingo (4.8% vs. 1.0%).

Although the descriptions of "action" and "escape" gamblers appear intuitively attractive, one may need to use caution in applying them. There could be a patronizing edge of the dominant culture in designating women as preferring "nonskill" gambling games and consequently not living up to the popular culture's idea of "real" gambling. Discounting out-of-control gambling behavior because it involves games like bingo only adds to the difficulties of these women in recognizing their own problems and getting help. In addition, there is growing evidence that men are participating more and more in what we have called the "escape gambler" profile. In 1999, 94% of the women and 49% of the men who called the Arizona Council on Compulsive Gambling Hotline identified themselves as an "escape gambler." The council makes an interesting point: "The accessibility of casino-type gambling is now affecting men who had no previous history of gambling or compulsive gambling in the same way it affects women. Perhaps the least previously identified and least understood compulsive gambler of all was the male 'escape gambler'" (Arizona Problem Council on Compulsive Gambling, 2000, p. 2).

Biological Differences by Gender

Earlier research on the pharmacology, genetics, and biological impact of alcohol and drugs were done primarily with males, with the assumption that the findings would apply equally to women. Not true. Beginning in the 1970s and 1980s, we began to realize that women and men differ in their biology and response to alcohol, tobacco, and other drugs in ways that have important treatment implications. A special report from the National Institute on Alcohol Abuse and Alcoholism (NIAAA, 1993) summarizes the collected data on women's physiological response to alcoholism. From this report we learn that, compared to men, women tend to:

1. Have a much shorter interval between onset of drinking-related problems and entry into treatment. In the past women started drinking heavily later than men, but today many high school girls drink to get drunk.
2. Experience a higher rate of physiological impairment earlier in their drinking careers. The consequences associated with heavy drinking may be accelerated or "telescoped" in women (problems of the liver, heart, reproductive organs).
3. Become intoxicated after drinking smaller quantities of alcohol. Women have more fat and lower body water content than men of comparable size, and because alcohol is diluted through body water, a woman drinking the same as a man of the same size will have a higher blood alcohol level. Also, women may have diminished activity of the primary enzyme involved in the metabolism of alcohol in the stomach, and a fluctuation in gonadal hormone levels during the menstrual cycle.
4. Have a much higher mortality rate from alcohol misuse, with increased risk of death stemming from organ damage, especially regarding the liver, brain, and heart.

According to the CASA (1996) report, women who have alcoholism are twice as likely to die as male alcoholics in the same age group, and their lives were an average of 15 years shorter than women who are not alcoholic. Suicide attempts are five times more likely in alcoholic than in nonalcoholic women of the same age and income.

Chronic heavy drinking is associated with negative effects on the sexual functions of both men and women. Men report loss of sexual interest, difficulty achieving erections, impotence, and premature ejaculation (NIAAA, 1993). Although many women and men attest to the disinhibiting qualities of alcohol, in reality alcohol acts as a depressant on physiological arousal. Women alcoholics persist in expecting greater sexual desire and enjoyment after drinking while at the same time reporting a variety of sexual dysfunctions, such as inhibition of ovulation, infertility, and depressed orgasm (Blume, 1997). In early sobriety, women have reported avoidance of sex, but another study of recovering alcoholic women who had a regular sexual partner showed significant improvement in sexual desire, arousal, and the ability to achieve orgasm as abstinence continued (Apter-Marsh, 1984).

Smoking affects the reproductive functions of women. Women who smoke are 1.3 to 3.4 times likelier than nonsmoking women to become infertile; cervical cancer is increased at least 50%; and middle-aged women who smoke are twice as likely to have early menopause. Unfortunately, a third of female smokers are overweight, which may make it harder for these women to quit smoking in our body-conscious culture (CASA, 1996).

The female propensity to weight obsession is also evident in eating disorders. *Feminist Perspectives on Eating Disorders,* edited by Fallon, Katzman, and Wooley (1994), is an invaluable resource for analyzing the role of gender in the etiology and treatment of eating disorders. Overeaters Anonymous (OA), the popular self-help group that has been immensely helpful to some women, is not spared from criticism in this biting and thought-provoking collection (see chapter 7 for a more positive view).

Some effects of illicit drugs vary with gender. In a review of current research, Millstein (2000), Deputy Director of NIDA, reports that women have decreased sensitivity to intranasal cocaine at certain times in their menstrual cycle. Marijuana is reported to enhance the sexual feelings of both men and women, but regular use in men may result in lower testosterone levels, affect sperm production and fertility, and cause erectile difficulties. In women, potential adverse affects include menstrual abnormalities, abnormal ova, and prolonged childbirth (Hubbard, Franco, & Onaivi, 1999; Bloodworth, 1987).

In the DATOS study of men and women entering drug treatment (including methadone treatment), women reported greater proportions of health-related issues (Wechsberg et al., 1998). For women, the rate of respiratory problems was the highest, followed by the rates of gynecological problems and then STDs. For men, respiratory problems also had the highest rate, followed by heart problems and then digestive problems. However, women have higher rates in all three problem areas.

Because of the strong connection to IV drug use, it's important to note that an HIV-infected woman with half the amount of virus in the bloodstream as an infected man will develop AIDS as quickly. Women are also diagnosed later in the course of AIDS and have poorer access to treatment (CASA, 1996).

Are there gender differences in the inheritance of alcoholism? Geneticists measure inheritability by looking at studies of adoptions, twins, and genetic markers (such as the D2 dopamine receptor). Examining all this evidence to date, McGue and Slutske (1996) conclude that an inherited component of alcoholism exists among males but that there is not unequivocal support for the existence of a heritable component to alcoholism among women. The primary reason there is no definitive answer about women's heritability is the small number of studies and limited sample sizes compared to the research on men. Estimates of the heritability (the proportion of variance attributable to genetic factors) among women have ranged from 0.00 to 0.56; among men there are consistent estimates ranging from 0.50 to 0.60. There is some evidence that women may be more susceptible to environmental factors. The authors conclude that there is some inherited contribution in women, but at this time the effect appears more modest than with men.

Treatment Implications

The gender differences in biology, genetics, paths to dependence, responses to various treatment options, relapse triggers, and social contexts suggest different prevention and treatment approaches for men and women. Women-only programs and special programs for pregnant and postpartum women have been developed to provide alternatives to traditional treatment, viewed as designed primarily for white males.

Typical components of such programs are to: (1) address some of the barriers to treatment that many women experience, such as lack of transportation, child care, and treatment availability, (2) change program goals and processes to accommodate "women's needs" for more support, less confrontation, job skill training, and parenting skills, and (3) embrace an "empowerment" model of change rather than the traditional abstinence-only Twelve-Step Minnesota Model, which is perceived as hierarchical, patriarchal, and ineffective. Many of these programs use female staff members so that women clients may feel more comfortable telling their stories. In a comparison of mixed-gender drug treatment programs and women's drug treatment programs in Los Angeles County ($N = 294$), Grella, Polinsky, Hser, and Perry (1999) found that women's drug treatment programs were significantly more likely to provide other services, such as children's activities, assistance in locating housing, transportation, life-skills services, practical and vocational skills, parenting skills, and anger management, client advocacy, and services specific to pregnancy (pediatric, prenatal, and postpartum services).

An example of a woman's program that has many of these attributes is "A Woman's Place," established in the mid-1980s to offer substance abuse treatment for women (LaFave & Echols, 1999). Although the program began by using the traditional Twelve-Step Minnesota Model with strict guidelines for compliance, homework, and attendance at AA, program staff became frustrated and disillusioned with the lack of success and the inconsistency between the values of "compliance" and "empowerment" for women. The authors note that "compliance" is not an attribute of the mutual-help program of Alcoholics Anonymous, which is based on voluntary participation and suggestions only; however, compliance is an element of "Twelve-Step-based" Minnesota Model programs (see chapter 12). In 1993, the program embraced different change models that emphasize choice, not compliance, such as solution-focused therapy (Berg & Miller, 1992) and motivational interviewing (Miller & Rollnick, 1991).

All aspects of the program were affected by this change. Women who are court ordered or come voluntarily to treatment are asked at the orientation session to choose which services they think they would like. If a woman is not concerned about her substance use, she is asked whether there are any other goals she would like to address and whether she is choosing to comply with the referral source. The menu of services includes day treatment, substance abuse groups once a week, a women's issues group, individual counseling, couples and family counseling, and case management services, including transportation. In contrast to a traditional Twelve-Step treatment model, the operating premise of this program is that, when offered choices, women will ultimately choose directions that help them function better.

Using the solution-focused approach, any period of sobriety or cutting down on alcohol or other drug use is celebrated, and the woman is questioned closely on how she was able to do this. For clients who are uncertain about the changes they want to make, motivational interviewing techniques are used to help them explore the meaning of the problem for them and make a decision about their motivation to change. According to the authors, preliminary quantitative and qualitative evaluations of the program suggest that using these approaches "has a favorable impact on participants' life functioning in a number of domains, and that participants feel that the program has benefited them in a variety of ways" (LaFave & Echols, 1999, p. 350).

As women experience personal growth and consciousness of their need for self-expression through group participation, however, they begin to reexamine their relationship patterns. As we hear from a 34-year-old African American woman, for example:

> He doesn't agree that I can be my own person, he's too controlling and possessive. . . . He didn't like the aftermath of it (drug treatment), he said I changed. He didn't like the way I changed. He said it was a side of me he never thought he'd see. Now I'm into my own independence. I'm not an agreeable person anymore because I'm standing up more for myself today. He doesn't like it. (Laudet et al., 1999, p. 623)

On the whole, outcome research on specialized women's programs has mixed results. Some studies suggest better treatment outcomes in specialized women's programs or women's groups within mixed-gender programs (Dahlgren & Willander, 1989) and others suggest no difference (Copeland, Hall, Didcott, & Biggs, 1993). Project MATCH, the NIAAA-funded major research study, found no gender-related differences in the outcomes of the three treatment approaches used in individual sessions with a large sample of male and female clients (Project MATCH Research Group, 1997). Studies that focus on matching patient/therapist gender have also found no difference in treatment retention (Sterling, Gottheil, Weinstein, & Serota, 1998) or outcome (Atkinson & Schein, 1996; Corrigan, 1995).

However, several qualitative studies (Kauffman, Dore, & Nelson-Zlupko, 1995; Nelson-Zlupko, Dore, Kauffman, & Kaltenback, 1996; Davis, 1997) that have interviewed recovering women participating in all-women's groups or programs tell a different story. Kauffman et al. (p. 361) conclude, from interviews with 34 women participating in two separate addictions programs, that "in order to treat chemically dependent women successfully, therapeutic interventions must attend to the full complexity of their lives, rather than focusing solely on addiction," and that these needs are better met in women-only treatment groups.

Consider this example of a woman who had participated in both coed and women's therapy groups in substance abuse treatment:

> Guilt puts you at risk of relapsing. You need to talk about it. Take me, for example. Giving up my twins for adoption . . . was the most painful, agonizing experience of my life. No one in either of the coed groups that I've been in knows that I put those babies up for adoption, only the women in this group. The reason being that I felt as if women—whether they agreed or not with my choice—would sympathize with what I had to do. Whereas men—well, I didn't expect a lot of sympathy. They make you feel guilty. . . . In the coed group I don't feel like I could have let it out or cried or that I would have gotten that good of a response. And that was an issue that, when I think about it now, if I wouldn't have been real careful, it could have pushed me over the edge. (Kauffman et al., 1995, p. 361)

In the Nelson-Zlupko et al. study (1996, p. 57), participants "overwhelmingly" felt that their needs were different from men, and that when they were in mixed-gender groups, these needs were either "silenced or minimized." All of the women in this study had attended at least two other treatment programs, with an average of four treatment experiences per person. These women affirmed previous research that being paired to a female counselor was not important; what they saw as critical to their success was respect from the counselor, no matter the gender.

Research that has focused on other outcomes, such as service provision and eliminating barriers to treatment, have found that specialized women's programs were more likely to provide services that meet typical women's needs, such as parenting training, empowerment, nutrition, child care, and transportation, and less likely to deny access to women with special needs such as pregnancy and mental problems (Prendergast, Wellisch, & Falkin, 1995; Grella et al., 1999). Through qualitative interviews of women in treatment, Nelson-Zlupko and her colleagues (1996) found another disturbing barrier to mixed-gender patient/therapist treatment: Sexual harassment of women clients by male counselors was spontaneously reported by over half of the study's participants, even though they were never asked about this in the interview.

The research findings to date have been criticized for flaws in design and methodology, a lack of comparison groups, and small sample sizes (Grella et al., 1999). The only experimental design has been the Dahlgren and Willander study (1989) that suggested that an all-woman's treatment approach offers more positive results. However, this study took place in Sweden, where improvement, not abstinence, is a legitimate treatment goal and positive-outcome measure.

Some critics would argue that traditional abstinence-only treatment for both genders produces discouraging results and that a different treatment model for both men and women is what's needed. Citing studies that indicate poor treatment outcome (for example, 52 to 75% of men and women in outpatient treatment drop out by the fourth session, Siegal, Rapp, Fisher, Cole, & Wagner, 1993; and between 40 and 60% that do complete treatment are not abstinent after one year, Hubbard, 1997), LaFave and Echols (1999) argue for increasing the flexibility of substance abuse treatment for all populations. Although their article argues for a choice-driven model for women as practiced in "A Woman's Place," they join Calamari, Cox, and Roth (1996) in advocating for a treatment model for men "that promotes hope, recognizes incremental changes, such as an increase in number of days of sobriety, and allows men to identify, express, and process their affective experiences" (p. 347). In her study on the outcome of treatment for Irish alcoholic women, Corrigan (1995) found that at one-year follow-up, the majority (71%) drank at some point since treatment; however, 43% had not been drinking for six or more months. She concludes that "the assumption that treatment programs should insist on total abstinence as the only acceptable treatment goal is particularly questionable in view of the fact that at follow-up only half of the women surveyed are in fact abstinent" (p. 52). At the very least, the research to date has not made clear whether providing specialized women's treatment is sufficient to better help women, or whether new approaches different from traditional abstinence-based treatment are needed (Grella et al., 1999).

SUBSTANCE ABUSE COUNSELING AND SEXUAL ORIENTATION

Heterosexism and *homophobia* are words used to describe the prejudice against lesbian, gay, bisexual and transgender people. *Homophobia* refers to fear of homosexuality, often of one's own tendencies in that direction; these tendencies may be displaced onto gays and lesbians. *Heterosexism*, the counterpart to racism and sexism, is prejudice against sexual minorities. Heterosexism includes stereotyping and a belief in myths. Among the myths pertaining to lesbians are: They hate men, and they turned lesbian after a bad experience with a man; lesbianism can be "corrected" with female hormonal treatment; lesbians would prefer to be heterosexual; in partnerships one woman plays the part of the man; and lesbians have a high rate of AIDS. In fact, lesbians, like heterosexuals, are a heterogeneous lot; their sex role behavior ranges from very feminine to very masculine. Some lesbians believe their identity is a preference or choice; others believe it is an innate tendency to be sexually and affectionally attracted to women. Among the categories of gay males, heterosexual males, heterosexual women, and lesbians, lesbians have the lowest rate of AIDS (*Journal of the American Medical Association* [JAMA], 1996).

Pervasive myths pertaining to gay males are: Homosexuality is a choice; gay males are attracted to children and at risk of molesting them; and gay males are effeminate. In fact, the overwhelming number of gay males believe their gayness is an innate characteristic, one often recognized in early to middle childhood (van Wormer, Wells, & Boes, 2000)—they prefer the term *sexual orientation* to *sexual preference,* accordingly (Cabaj, 1997). The vast majority of child molesters tend to be heterosexual (Cabaj, 1997; Tully, 2000). In sex role behavior and mannerisms, gay males range from effeminate to very masculine. Many gay men, however, have traits in common with women. In childhood, for example, their play was often less rough than that of other children, and they were often ridiculed in school for being "sissies" or "different" (CSAT, 2001).

Counselors need to be aware of the numerous myths our society generates so that they can establish rapport with gay and lesbian clients. The best way to build trust is to demonstrate openness about nonnormative living arrangements and sexuality. Use gay-friendly intake forms (including terms such as "partner" and "significant other"), display pamphlets that cater to a variety of ethnically and sexually diverse groups (for example, gay AA meeting listings), and use inclusive language in interviews and lectures (referring to "spouse or partner" rather than just "spouse").

Despite societal barriers to being gay, lesbian, bisexual, or (most of all) transgender in our society, there is no reason to assume that such clients need to work on any areas other than the services they came to receive. The focus of their treatment, therefore, should be no different than that of any other client.

Lesbians and Substance Misuse

For the past 15 years or so, there has been a growing awareness among gay men and lesbians that chemical dependency is a major problem in their respective communities, a problem that denies humans freedom and dignity (Kus, 1995). Because of a serious lack of empirically based national data, however, the exact incidence of substance use in lesbians is unknown. Studies focusing on women's alcohol and other drug use rarely consider sexual orientation as a variable, and studies on lesbian behavior rarely encompass addiction rates. The most commonly cited figure for alcohol-related problems in lesbian women is one out of three (Kus, 1990; JAMA, 1996). A survey of two metropolitan areas revealed that marijuana and tobacco use were approximately double among lesbians as compared to heterosexual women (Skinner, 1994). Many of the existing studies, however, are marred by obvious sample flaws, including the recruitment of respondents from gay bars (Hughes & Wilsnack, 1994). In the most comprehensive lesbian survey available, the National Lesbian Health Care Survey of 1987 (described by Bradford, Ryan, & Rothblum, 1994), 14% of the sample expressed worry about their use of alcohol, and, strikingly, in sharp contrast with heterosexual behavior, alcohol use increased with age. Recognition of the propensity for lesbians to use mood-altering substances, tobacco and alcohol companies have relentlessly targeted lesbians as a lucrative market (Goebel, 1994).

A massive research effort that pooled and analyzed data from seven health surveys of lesbian women and covered nearly 12,000 self-identified lesbians overall revealed a concentration of risk factors within this group (Raab, 2001). Relevant to addictive behavior, the collective data showed the following:

- About 55% of lesbians are current or former smokers, compared with 36% of women in general.
- Lesbians are slightly more likely to be heavy drinkers—averaging four drinks a day—than women overall.
- About 28% of lesbians are obese, compared to 19% of women in general.

There are several reasons why alcohol use among lesbians would be high. First is the role of the gay bar and women's bars as a key gathering place for coming-out and closeted lesbians. Second is the heavy drinking and active marijuana use among more mature members of this community, who function as role models. Third is the interactive relationship among stress attached to living what is regarded as a deviant lifestyle, relationship strain in the absence of public role models, and problems related to internalized homophobia, especially among lesbian youths. Finally, the fact that fewer lesbians than straight women are taking care of children gives them more freedom to party and indulge in substance use than persons tied down by parenting roles (van Wormer et al., 2000). People who feel good about themselves take care of themselves, as do most lesbians, but people who don't are inclined to jeopardize their health through the use of mood-altering substances.

Due to the unique needs of this special population and the need for lesbians, like other women, to deal with issues related to victimization and sexuality in a safe and understanding environment, a lesbian-affirming treatment atmosphere is essential. Unfortunately, substance abuse providers tend to hold traditional attitudes toward women's sex roles and to lack training in gay/lesbian dynamics (Underhill, 1991). A feminist, nonheterosexist model is appropriate in order to empower lesbians to make the personal adjustments (in thinking and behavior) necessary for recovery. For lesbian alcoholics in need of inpatient treatment, referral to a lesbian-friendly treatment center, such as the Pride Institute in Eden Prairie, Minnesota, or the Gables Recovery Home in Rochester, Minnesota, is appropriate. The expense, however, may be prohibitive for the client who lacks generous insurance coverage for inpatient treatment. A growing trend throughout the United States is the proliferation of health care clinics catering to lesbians ("Lesbian Clinics," 1999). This positive development has received its impetus from the awareness of the hostility that has been directed toward lesbians from medical professionals in traditional practice.

Gay/lesbian self-help groups such as Gay and Lesbian AA are widely available even in small cities across the United States. Since the 1980s, in fact, as VanGelder and Brandt (1996) indicate, heavy alcohol consumption lost ground within the lesbian community. Suddenly, according to these authors, there was a stronger AA crowd than a drinking crowd; lesbians attending the annual October Women's Weekend had a choice of seven Twelve-Step meetings per day.

Gay Males and Substance Misuse

Feminine men thrown into a jail cell, cross-dressers, adolescent gays at school: These are examples of males who are prone to be physically attacked and possibly even killed. The scapegoating of gay males, even more pronounced than that of lesbians, creates a major health risk, physically and mentally, for the survivors and victims of this terrifying kind of abuse.

Sometimes society's hatred is turned within. Remafedi, French, Story, Resnick, and Blum (1998), in their research on the relationship between suicide risk and sexual orientation, found evidence of a strong association between suicide risk and bisexuality or homosexuality in young males. A Canadian study conducted through the University of Calgary's center for the study of suicide interviewed young adult men who answered questions on portable computers (King, 1996). Results were startling, in that gay and bisexual subjects were found to have the highest rates of attempted suicide. Celibate males were found to have the highest rates of attempted suicide. The sample size for celibate males, however, was extremely small. The Canadian study is unique in that it is based on a cross section of young males, not on a sample of persons already known to be gay.

Religious fundamentalism was found to be associated with a risk of suicide in gay males, presumably because of their unresolved feelings of guilt. In their work in a psychiatric clinic in the early years of the AIDS epidemic, Flavin, Franklin, and Frances (1986) were disturbed to find that several suicidal gay patients had deliberately tried to contract AIDS as an indirect way of killing themselves. In helping gay men come to terms with their sexuality, a strengths approach is essential. Strategies of gay-positive counseling are described in van Wormer et al. (2000).

Heavy use of alcohol and other drugs has long been noted as a problem in the gay community. Although obtaining a random sample of gay men is extremely difficult, all the research that has been done confirms a high incidence of alcohol and other substance use; estimates range from 20% to 35% (van Wormer, 1995; Warn, 1997). Compared to lesbians, gay males are more likely to have multiple partners; sex and intimacy are more often split off in this group (Cabaj, 1997). Gay bars and clubs are central to the social fabric of gay life; cocaine, methamphetamines, and other dangerous drugs are readily available in after-hours clubs frequented by gay men (Warn, 1997). A glance at the ads in gay and lesbian magazines reveals a marketing blitz of hard liquor advertising that is far from subtle in its message.

Approximately 4 to 5% of heterosexual drug injectors are HIV positive. About 40% of men who have sex with men and shoot crystal meth are HIV positive, according to a study by Clay (1997). Clay discovered, in interviews with meth users in Washington State, that crystal meth is used as a powerful sexual facilitator, a means of overcoming sexual fears and reservations. When people are influenced by such strong chemicals, safe-sex practices, needless to say, are thrown to the wayside.

In a sample of 340 gay men from the Cleveland area, Ghindia and Kola (1996) found alcohol to be the drug of choice and cocaine use to be prevalent among those aged 25 through 39. Unique to this population, compared to heterosexual men, is that heavy alcohol consumption and associated problems continue across the life span rather than diminishing with age. One possible explanation is that gay men do not "settle down" as readily as heterosexual men and that they are freer to spend more time drinking. Another factor relating to their substance use is the tendency of sexual minorities to use mind-altering chemicals to break down their sexual inhibitions; such inhibitions or hang-ups are related to sexuality that is out of step with societal norms (Warn, 1997). In substance abuse treatment, one of the biggest challenges to sobriety for gays and lesbians entails learning how to initiate same-sex encounters without the aid of alcohol as a "social lubricant."

Transgender Individuals

The recent publication from the Center for Substance Abuse Treatment (2001), *A Provider's Introduction to Substance Abuse Treatment for Lesbian, Gay, Bisexual, and Transgender Individuals,* available free of charge from the Substance Abuse and Mental Health Services Administration (SAMHSA), offers a comprehensive discussion of multiple issues related to working with transgender individuals. As defined in this document: *Transgender* individuals are those who conform to the gender role expectations of the opposite sex or those who may clearly identify their gender as the opposite of their biological sex. In common usage, *transgender* usually refers to people in the transsexual group, which may include people contemplating or preparing for sexual reassignment surgery—called preoperative—or who have undergone sexual reassignment surgery—called postoperative. A transgender person may be sexually attracted to males, females, or both. *Transvestites* cross-dress, that is, wear clothes usually worn by people of the opposite biological sex. They do not, however, identify themselves as having a gender identity different from their biological sex or gender role (p. 5). See Table 11.2 for a list of do's and don'ts related to work with this population.

Bisexuality

Many studies indicate that women tend to be more bisexual by nature (flexible in terms of attraction to either gender) than men, who are more exclusively heterosexual or homosexual (CSAT, 2001; van Wormer et al., 2000). Major points for therapists to know is that a bisexual orientation is a separate identity in itself, one that is often refuted by both the heterosexual majority and by many gay men and lesbians. A complicating factor is that due to the strident heterosexism within the African American community, many people of color define themselves as bisexual even if they focus exclusively on people of the same sex (CSAT, 2001).

TABLE 11.2	DO'S AND DON'TS ABOUT WORKING WITH TRANSGENDER AND TRANSVESTITE CLIENTS

• Use the proper pronouns based on *their self-identity* when talking to/about transgender individuals.	• Don't call someone who identifies himself as a female *he* or *him* or call someone who identifies herself as male *she* or *her*.
• Get clinical supervision if you have issues or feelings about working with transgender individuals.	• Don't project your transphobia onto the transgender client or share transphobic comments with other staff or clients.
• Allow transgender clients to continue the use of hormones when they are prescribed. Advocate that the transgender client using "street" hormones get immediate medical care and legally prescribed hormones.	• Never make the transgender client choose between hormones and treatment and recovery.
• Require training on transgender issues for all staff.	• Don't make the transgender client educate the staff.
• Find out the sexual orientation of all clients.	• Don't assume transgender women or men are gay.
• Allow transgender clients to use bathrooms and showers based on their gender self-identity and gender role.	• Don't make transgender individuals living as females use male facilities or transgender individuals living as males use female facilities.
• Require all clients and staff to create and maintain a safe environment for all transgender clients. Post a nondiscrimination policy in the waiting room that explicitly includes sexual orientation and gender identity.	• Never allow staff or clients to make transphobic comments or put transgender clients at risk for physical or sexual abuse or harassment.

Source: CSAT (2001).

Treatment Issues

Gay and lesbian alcoholics and other substance users most often find themselves in predominantly heterosexual treatment centers. Because of the homophobia present in the typical treatment group, few gays and lesbians will want to take the risk of disclosing their sexual orientation. To encourage private sharing in individual sessions, the counselor will find it helpful to display literature about gay/lesbian AA meetings or a Safe Place symbol (placed on a pink triangle) on the office door. Counselors should not post the commonly seen slogan "I'm straight but not narrow," which many gays and lesbians construe as a subtle proclamation of the counselors' heterosexuality. To meet the needs of sexual diversity, every large agency should make a point of having one or more openly gay or lesbian counselors on the staff.

Pride Institute, a 36-bed facility in Eden Prairie, Minnesota, near Minneapolis, is a gay-specialized treatment center. Its unique program addresses issues such as internalized homophobia, low self-esteem, coming out to the family and friends, same-sex sexuality, early-childhood sexual abuse, and safe-sex practices, in addition to addictions education and treatment. Insurance payment plans, however, are reluctant to cover such intensive inpatient treatment due to cost-saving managed care restrictions. Most metropolitan communities today have gay-affirming outreach center programs. In even smaller cities, gay and lesbian Twelve-Step meetings provide gay and lesbian substance users with sober support networks and an opportunity for complete openness. Harm reduction treatment programs on the West Coast, for example, help clients reduce the harm to themselves sexually as well as in the area of substance use.

Treatment issues that concern all clients but that have special relevance to sexual minorities include: determining the client's comfort level with his or her sexual orientation; respecting gays and lesbians' heightened need for privacy and confidentiality; recognition of special health risks that pertain to sexual practices among intoxicated gay males; domestic violence issues (note that terms like "wife beating" are inadvertently heterosexist); dealing with child custody issues; and working with the family of origin regarding acceptance of their gay/lesbian children.

The organization Parents, Families, and Friends of Lesbians and Gays (PFLAG) is both a self-help and an advocacy group. Membership is open to gays and lesbians as well as to concerned members of the community. (For an in-depth description of the functioning of this remarkable group, see van Wormer et al., 2000). Substance abuse treatment centers can call on PFLAG at any time to present a panel, usually of the parents of gays and lesbians, who, in telling their personal stories, help to dispel the myths pertaining to homosexuality. Speakers from this group can also enlighten members of the treatment community about the significance of the coming-out process, a process that substance abuse practitioners might have the opportunity to assist clients in undergoing (Appleby & Anastas, 1998).

SUMMARY AND CONCLUSION

Vulnerability, victimization, substance misuse—these are the themes that emerged in this chapter on gender and sex orientation differences. Although there is considerable within-group variability, gender differences in biology, genetics, paths to dependence, responses to various treatment options, relapse triggers, and social contexts continue to be identified by research studies and practitioners. Women entering treatment have lower economic status, less support from their male counterparts, more needs for parenting and vocational skills, quicker and more severe physiological damage, more sexual and physical abuse in their backgrounds, and more needs for transportation and child care than men. Such differences suggest the desirability of gender-specific prevention and treatment approaches for women, and, indeed, many new programs have developed since the infusion of female-specific federal funding in the mid-1980s. At this date, however, research on the outcomes of women who receive treatment from women-only programs, from specialized women's groups within mixed-gender programs, or even from same-sex therapists have produced mixed results. Qualitative data from interviewing women who have experienced specialized women-only programming continues to support this approach.

Given the consistently poor results when measuring abstinence rates in abstinence-only traditional treatment approaches, some critics are calling for new models for both men and women that would incorporate more choice and less coercion. Several alternative approaches are discussed in this chapter; refer also to chapter 3 on Strengths-Based Helping Strategies.

Lesbians, gays, bisexuals, and transgender people have problems with discrimination and hate crimes that are horrendous. Their invisibility is one difficulty making problematic the pursuit of their rights, including the right to gay-affirmative or at least gay-sensitive treatment. Yet paramount is their need for whole-person counseling, for counseling that takes into account identities, relationships, and resiliencies. In recognition of this, specialized units are being set up nationwide, albeit only in the major cities.

References

Aamot, G. (1998, May 24). South Dakota laws designed to curb fetal alcohol syndrome. *Courier Journal*, A8.

Abramovitz, M. (1988). *Regulating the lives of women: Social welfare policy from colonial times to the present.* Boston: South End Press.

Anderson, A. (2000). Gender-related aspects of eating disorders: A guide to practice. *Journal of Gender-Specific Medicine.* Online at www.mmhc.com/jgsm/articles/JGSM9002

Appleby, G. A., & Anastas, J. W. (1998). *Not just a passing phase: Social work with gay, lesbian, and bisexual people.* New York: Columbia University Press.

Apter-Marsh, M. (1984). The sexual behavior of alcoholic women while drinking and during sobriety. *Alcoholism Treatment Quarterly, 1*(3), 35–48.

Arizona Council on Compulsive Gambling. (2000). *Escape vs. Action.* Online at www.azccg.org

Atkinson, D. R., & Schein, S. (1986). Similarity in counseling. *The Counseling Psychologist, 14,* 319–354.

Babcock, M. (1996). Does feminism drive women to drink? Conflicting themes. *International Journal of Drug Policy, 7*(3), 158–165.

Berg, I. K., & Miller, S. D. (1992). *Working with the problem drinker: A solution focused approach.* New York: Norton.

Bloodworth, R. C. (1987). Medical problems associated with marijuana abuse. *Psychiatric Medicine, 3*(3), 173–184.

Blume, S. (1997). Women: Clinical aspects. In J. Lowinson, P. Ruiz, R. B. Millman., & J. G. Langrod (Eds.), *Substance abuse: A comprehensive textbook.* Baltimore: Williams & Wilkins.

Bradford, J., Ryan, C., & Rothblum, E. (1994). National lesbian health care survey: Implications for mental health care. *Journal of Consulting and Clinical Psychology,* 62(2), 228–242.

Brady, K., & Randall, C. (1999). Gender differences in substance use disorders. *Addictive Disorders,* 22(2), 241–252.

Brown, S., & Coventry, L. (1997). *Queen of hearts.* Financial and Consumer Rights Council, Victoria, Australia. Online at home.vicnet.net.au/~fcrc/research/queen/part1.htm

Brown, V. B., Melchior, L. A., & Huba, G. J. (1999). Level of burden among women diagnosed with severe mental illness and substance abuse. *Journal of Psychoactive Drugs,* 31(1), 31–40.

Bureau of Justice Statistics. (1999). *Prisoners in 1998.* Washington, DC: U.S. Department of Justice.

Cabaj, R. (1997). Gays, lesbians, and bisexuals. In J. H. Lowinson, P. Ruiz, R. Millman, & J. Langrad (Eds.), *Substance Abuse: A comprehensive textbook* (3rd ed., pp. 725–732). Baltimore: Williams & Wilkins.

Calamari, J., Cox, W., & Roth, J. (1996). Group treatment for men with alcohol problems. In Michael Andronico (Ed.), *Men in groups: Insights, interventions, and psychoeducational work* (pp. 305–321). Washingon, DC: American Psychological Association.

Center on Addiction and Substance Abuse (CASA). (1996). Substance abuse and the American woman. Online at www.casacolumbia.org/usr_doc/5894.PDF

Center for Substance Abuse Treatment (CSAT). (1994). Practical approaches in the treatment of women who abuse alcohol and other drugs. Rockville, MD: DHHS/PHS.

Center for Substance Abuse Treatment (CSAT). (2001). *A provider's introduction to substance abuse treatment for lesbian, gay, bisexual, and transgender individuals.* Rockville, MD: SAMHSA.

Chasnoff, I. (1990). The prevalence of illicit drug or alcohol use during pregnancy and discrepancies in mandatory reporting in Pinellas County, Florida. *New England Journal of Medicine,* 322(1201).

Clay, C. (1997, Spring). Bisexual crystal injectors in Seattle. *Harm Reduction,* 18–19.

Cooper, M., & Eaves, D. (1996). Suicide following homicide in the family. *Violence and Victims,* 11(2), 99–112.

Copeland, J., Hall, W., Didcott, P., & Biggs, V. (1993). A comparison of a specialist women's alcohol and other drug treatment service with two traditional mixed-sex services: Client characteristics and treatment outcome. *Drug and Alcohol Dependence,* 32, 81–92.

Corrigan, E. (1995). *Outcome of treatment for Irish alcoholic women. Irish Journal of Psychological Medicine,* 12(2), 48–52.

Crisp, B., Thomas, S., Jackson, A., Thomason, N., Smith, S., Borrell, J., Ho, W., & Holt, T. (2000). Sex differences in the treatment needs and outcomes of problem gamblers. *Research on Social Work Practice,* 10(2), 229–242.

Dahlgren, L., & Willander, A. (1989). Are special treatment facilities for female alcoholics needed? A controlled 2-year follow-up study from a specialized female unit (EWA) versus a mixed male/female treatment facility. *Alcoholism: Clinical and Experimental Research,* 13(4), 499–504.

Davis, D. (1997). Women healing from alcoholism: A qualitative study. *Contemporary Drug Problems,* 24, 147–177.

Davis, D., & DiNitto, D. (1995). Gender differences in social and psychological problems of substance abusers: A comparison to nonsubstance abusers. *Journal of Psychoactive Drugs,* 28(2), 135–145.

Davis, D., & DiNitto, D. (1998). Gender and drugs: Fact, fiction, and unanswered questions. In C. A. McNeece & D. DiNitto, *Chemical dependency: A systems approach* (pp. 406–442). Boston: Allyn & Bacon.

Downs, W. R., & Miller, B. B. (1997). The longitudinal association between experiences of partner-to-woman abuse and alcohol problems of women. Unpublished manuscript.

El-Bassel, N., Gilbert, L., Krishnan, S., Schilling, R. F., Gaeta, T., Purpura, S., & Witte, S. S. (1998). Partner violence and sexual HIV-risk behaviors among women in an inner-city emergency department. *Violence and Victims, 13*(4), 1–17.

Fallon, P., Katzman, M. A., & Wooley, S. C. (Eds.). (1994). *Feminist perspectives on eating disorders.* New York: Guilford Press.

Fingarette, H. (1998). *Heavy drinking.* Berkeley: University of California Press.

Finkelstein, N. (1994). Treatment issues for alcohol and drug-dependent pregnant and parenting women. *Health and Social Work, 19,* 7–15.

Flavin, D., Franklin, J., & Frances, R. (1986). The acquired immune deficiency syndrome (AIDS) and suicidal behavior in alcohol-dependent men. *American Journal of Psychiatry, 143*(11), 1441–1442.

Ghindia, D., & Kola, L. (1996, November). Gay male substance abuse examined. *Issues of Substance, 8,* 11.

Goebel, K. (1994, November/December). Lesbians and gays face tobacco targeting. *Prevention Pipeline,* 105–107.

Greenfield , L. A., Rand, M. R., Craven, D., Flaus, P. A., Perkins, C. A., Ringel, C., Warchol, G., Mason, C., & Fox, J. A. (1998). *Violence by intimates: Analysis of data on crimes by current or former spouses, boyfriends, and girlfriends* (NCJ-167237). Washington, DC: U.S. Department of Justice, Bureau of Justice Statistics.

Greenhouse, L. (2001, March 22). Court curbs drug tests during pregnancy. *New York Times,* A1, A16.

Grella, C., & Joshi, V. (1999). Gender differences in drug treatment careers among clients in the National Drug Abuse Treatment Outcome Study. *American Journal of Drug and Alcohol Abuse, 25*(3), 385–406.

Grella, C. E., Polinsky, M. L., Hser, Y., & Perry, S. M. (1999). Characteristics of women-only and mixed-gender drug abuse treatment programs. *Journal of Substance Abuse Treatment, 17*(1–2), 37–44.

Helzer, J., Canino, G., Yeh, E., Bland, R., Lee, C., Hwu, H., & Newman, S. (1990). Alcoholism—North America and Asia. *Archives of General Psychiatry, 47,* 313–319.

Hiebert-Murphy, D., & Woytkiw, L. (2000). A model for working with women dealing with child sexual abuse and addictions: The Laurel Centre, Winnipeg, Manitoba, Canada. *Journal of Substance Abuse Treatment, 18,* 387–394.

Hirsch, A. (1999). Some days are harder than hard: Welfare reform and women with drug conviction in Pennsylvania. *Center for Law and Social Policy.* Online at www.clasp.org/pubs/TANFSTATE/SomeDays

Holmes, W. C., & Slap, G. B. (1998). Sexual abuse of boys: Definition, prevalence, correlates, sequelae, and management. *Journal of the American Medical Association, 280*(21), 1855–1862.

Hser, Y., Anglin, M., & Booth, M. (1987). Sex differences in addict careers. 3. Addiction. *American Journal of Drug and Alcohol Abuse, 13*(3), 231–251.

Hser, Y., Anglin, M., & McGlothlin, W. (1987). Sex differences in addict careers: Initiation of use. *American Journal of Drug and Alcohol Abuse, 13*(1), 33–57.

Hubbard, J. R., Franco, S. E., & Onaivi, E. (1999). Marijuana: Medical implications. *American Family Physician.* Online at www.findarticles.com/cf_0/m3225/9_60/58252718/print.jhtml

Hubbard, R. L. (1997). Evaluation and outcome of treatment. In J. H. Lowinson, P. Ruiz, R. B. Millman, & J. G. Langrod (Eds.), *Substance abuse: A comprehensive textbook* (pp. 499–512). Baltimore: Williams & Wilkins.

Hughes, T., & Wilsnack, S. (1994). Research on lesbian and alcohol: Gaps and implications. *Alcohol, Health and Research World, 18*(3), 202–205.

JAMA. (1996). Health care needs of gay men and lesbians in the United States. *Journal of the American Medical Association, 257*(17), 1354–1359.

Kagle, J. (1987). Women who drink: Changing images, changing realities. *Journal of Social Work Education, 23*(3), 21–28.

Kantor, G. K. (1993). Refining the brushstrokes in portraits of alcohol and wife assaults. In Susan E. Martin (Ed.), *Alcohol and interpersonal violence: Fostering multidisciplinary perspectives.* NIH Publication No. 93-3496, NIH Research Monograph 24 (pp. 281–290). Washington, DC: National Institutes of Health.

Kantor, G., & Strauss, M. (1989). Substance abuse as a precipitant of wife abuse victimizations. *American Journal of Drug and Alcohol Abuse, 15*(2), 173–189.

Kauffman, E., Dore, M. M., & Nelson-Zlupko, L. (1995). The role of women's therapy groups in the treatment of chemical dependence. *American Journal of Orthopsychiatry, 65*(3), 355–363.

Kenney, J. W., Reinholtz, C., & Angelini, P. J. (1997). Ethnic differences in childhood pregnancy and adolescent sexual abuse and teenage pregnancy. *Journal of Adolescent Health 21,* 3–10.

King, M. (1996, November 12). Suicide watch. *The Advocate,* 41–44.

Kus, R. (1990). Alcoholism in the gay and lesbian communities. In R. Kus (Ed.), *Keys to caring: Assisting your gay and lesbian clients* (pp. 66–81). Boston: Alyson.

Kus, R. (1995). Introduction. In R. Kus (Ed.), *Addiction and recovery in gay and lesbian persons* (pp. 1–3). Binghamton, NY: Haworth.

LaFave, L. M., & Echols, L. D. (1999). An argument for choice: An alternative women's treatment program. *Journal of Substance Abuse Treatment, 16*(4), 345–352.

Laudet, A., Magura, S., Furst, R., & Kumar, N. (1999). Male partners of substance-abusing women in treatment: An exploratory study. *American Journal of Drug and Alcohol Abuse, 25*(4), 607–627.

Leonard, K. E. (1993). Drinking patterns and intoxication in marital violence: Review, critique, and future directions for research. In Susan E. Martin (Ed.), *Alcohol and interpersonal violence: Fostering multidisciplinary perspectives.* NIH Publication No. 93-3496, NIH Research Monograph 24 (pp. 281–290). Washington, DC: National Institutes of Health.

Lesbian clinics tackle substance abuse, other problems. (1999, March 31). Available online at www.jointogether.org

Lesieur, H. (1987). The female pathological gambler. In W. R. Eadington (Ed.), *Gambling research: Proceedings of the seventh international conference on gambling and risk taking* (pp. 230–258). Bureau of Business and Economic Research, University of Nevada, Reno.

Lesieur, H., & Blume, S. (1991). When Lady Luck loses: Women and compulsive gambling. In N. Van Den Bergh (Ed.), *Feminist perspectives on addictions* (p. 181). New York: Springer.

Lex, B. (1995). Alcohol and other psychoactive substance dependence in women and men. In M. V. Seeman (Ed.), *Gender and psychopathology* (pp. 311–358). Washington, DC: American Psychiatric Press.

Marron, K. (1996). *The slammer: The crisis in Canada's prison system.* Toronto: Doubleday Canada.

McGue, M., & Slutske, W. (1996). The inheritance of alcoholism in women. In J. M. Howard, S. E. Martin, P. D. Mail, M. E. Hilton, & E. D. Taylor (Eds.), *Women and alcohol: Issues for prevention research,* Research Monograph No. 32 (pp. 65–92). Bethesda, MD: National Institutes of Health.

Miller, W. R., & Rollnick, S. (1991). *Motivational interviewing: Preparing people to change addictive behavior.* New York: Guilford Press.

Miller, B., Downs, W., and Gondoli, D. (1989). Spousal violence among alcoholic women as compared to a random household sample of women. *Journal of Studies on Alcohol, 50,* 533–540.

Miller, B. A., Downs, W. R., & Testa, M. (1993). Interrelationships between victimization experiences and women's alcohol use. *Journal of Studies on Alcohol,* Supplement no. 11, 109–117.

Millstein, R. (2000). Gender and drug abuse research. *Journal of Gender-Specific Medicine.* Online at www.mmhc.com/jgsm/articles/JGSM9812/specartdec.html

Murphy, S., & Rosenbaum, M. (1997). Two women who used cocaine too much. In C. Reinarman & H. Levine (Eds.), *Crack in America: Demon drugs and social justice* (pp. 98–112). Berkeley, CA: University of California Press.

National Institute on Alcohol Abuse and Alcoholism (NIAAA). (1993). *Eighth Special Report to the U.S. Congress on Alcohol and Health.* Rockville, MD: Author.

National Research Council. (1999, April 1). *Pathological gambling: A critical review.* Online at www.ngisc.gov/reports/fullrpt.html

Nelson-Zlupko, L., Dore, M. M., Kauffman, E., & Kaltenback, K. (1996). Women in recovery: Their perceptions of treatment effectiveness. *Journal of Substance Abuse Treatment, 13*(1), 51–59.

Neumann, D. A., Houskamp, B. M., Pollock, V. E., & Briere, J. (1996). The long-term sequelae of childhood sexual abuse in women: A meta-analytic review. *Child Maltreatment: Journal of the Professional Society on the Abuse of Children 1,* 6–16.

New study highlights gender's impact on addiction. (2000, February 21). *American Medical News* (Chicago).

Pierre, N., Shrier, L. A., Emans, S. J., & DuRant, R. H. (1998). Adolescent males involved in pregnancy: Association of forced sexual contact and risk behaviors. *Journal of Adolescent Health, 23*(6), 364–369.

Prendergast, M. L., Wellisch, J., & Falkin, G. P. (1995). Assessment of services for substance-abusing women offenders in community and correctional settings. *Prison Journal, 75,* 240–256.

Project MATCH Research Group. (1997). Matching alcoholism treatment to client heterogeneity: Project MATCH Posttreatment drinking outcomes. *Journal of Studies on Alcohol, 58,* 7–29.

Raab, B. (2001, April 27). Study: Lesbians have higher risk for some concerns. *Women's E News.* Available online at www.womensenews.org/article.cfm?aid=528

Remafedi, G., French, S., Story, M., Resnick, M., & Blum, R. (1998, January). The relationship between suicide risk and sexual orientation: Results of a population-based study. *American Journal of Public Health, 88,* 57–60.

Rhodes, W., Norman, J., Langenbahn, S., Harmon, P., & Deal, D. (1997). *Evaluation of the Minnesota State-Funded Compulsive Gambling Treatment Programs, Final Report, July 21, 1997.* Abt Associates, 55 Wheeler St., Cambridge, MA, 02138.

Rubin, R. (1998, August 12). Study: Hands-off pregnant drug users. *USA Today*, D1.

Saunders, J., Wodak, A., & Williams, R. (1985). Past experience of advice and treatment for drinking problems of patients with alcoholic liver disease. *British Journal of Addiction, 80,* 51–56.

Schutte, K. K., Seable, J. H., & Moos, R. H. (1997). Gender differences in the relations between depressive symptoms and drinking behavior among problem drinkers: A three-wave study. *Journal of Consulting Clinical Psychology, 65,* 392–404.

Screening for pathological gambling. (2000, June). *Beyond the Odds: A quarterly newsletter about problem gambling.* Online at www.miph.org/bto/jun00/screen.html

Siegal, H. A., Rapp, R. C., Fisher, J., Cole, C., & Wagner, J. H. (1993). Treatment dropouts and noncompliers: Two persistent problems and a programmatic remedy. In J. A. Inciardi, F. M. Tims, & B. W. Fletcher (Eds.), *Innovative approaches in the treatment of drug abuse: Program models and strategies* (pp. 109–122). Westport, CN: Greenwood Press.

Siegal, L. (1997). The pregnancy police. In C. Reinarman & H. Levine (Eds.), *Crack in America: Demon drugs and social justice.* Berkeley: University of California Press.

Skinner, W.F. (1994). The prevalence and demographic predictors of illicit and licit drug use among lesbians and gay men. *American Journal of Public Health, 84,* 1307–1310.

Smith, P. H., & Chescheir, N. (1995). *Battered substance-abusing women: A vulnerable and underserved population in North Carolina: Final report submitted to North Carolina Governor's Institute for Alcohol and Substance Abuse, Raleigh, NC.* North Carolina Governor's Institute for Alcohol and Substance Abuse, as quoted in CASA, 1996, p. 32.

Sterling, R. C., Gottheil, E., Weinstein, S. P., & Serota, R. (1998). Therapist/patient race and sex matching: Treatment retention and 9-month follow-up outcome. *Addiction, 93*(7), 1043–1050.

Substance Abuse and Mental Health Services Administration (SAMHSA). (1999). *National Household Survey on Drug Abuse.* Rockville, MD: Author.

Substance Abuse and Mental Health Services Administration (2000). *Substance abuse treatment in adult and juvenile correctional facilities: Findings from the Uniform Facility Data Set 1997 survey of correctional facilities.* Rockville, MD: Author.

Teets, J. (1995). Childhood sexual trauma of chemically dependent women. *Journal of Psychoactive Drugs, 27*(3), 231–238.

Texas Council on Problem and Compulsive Gambling. (2000, July 7). E-update on problem gambling news. *Women and problem gambling, 1*(23).

Thom. (1987). {full reference to come}.{full reference to come}.{full reference to come}.{full reference to come}.{full reference to come}.{full reference to come}.

Tully, C. T. (2000). *Lesbians, Gays, and the Empowerment Perspective.* New York: Columbia University Press.

Underhill, B. (1991). Recovery needs of lesbian alcoholics in treatment. In N. Van Den Bergh (Ed.), *Feminist perspectives on addictions* (pp. 73–86). New York: Springer.

U.S. Secretary of Health and Human Services. (2000). *Tenth special report to the U. S. Congress on alcohol and health.* Rockville, MD: National Institute on Alcohol Abuse and Alcoholism.

VanGelder, L., & Brandt, P. R. (1996). *The girl next door: Into the heart of lesbian America.* New York: Simon & Schuster.

van Wormer, K. (1995). *Alcoholism treatment: A social work perspective.* Belmont, CA: Wadsworth.

van Wormer, K. (2001). *Counseling female offenders and victims: A strengths-restorative approach.* New York: Springer.

van Wormer, K., Wells, J., & Boes, M. (2000). *Social work with lesbians, gays, and bisexuals: A strengths perspective.* Boston: Allyn & Bacon.

Warn, D. (1997). Recovering issues of substance-abusing gay men. In S. L. A. Straussner & E. Zelvin (Eds.), *Gender and addictions: Men and women in treatment* (pp. 387–410). Northvale, NJ: Jason Aronson.

Wechsberg, W., Craddock, S., & Hubbard, R. (1998). How are women who enter substance abuse treatment different than men? A gender comparison from the Drug Abuse Treatment Outcome Study. *Drugs and Society, 13*(1/2), 97–115.

Westermeyer, J., & Boedicker, A. (2000). Course, severity and treatment of substance abuse among women versus men. *American Journal of Drug and Alcohol Abuse, 26*(4), 523–535.

Widom, C., Ireland, T., & Glynn, P. (1995). Alcohol abuse in abused and neglected children follow-up: Are they at increased risk? *Journal of Studies on Alcohol, 56,* 207–217.

Willson, P., McFarlane, J., Malecha, A., Watson, K., Lemmey, D., Schultz, P., Gist, J., & Fredland, N. (2000). Severity of violence against women by intimate partners and associated use of alcohol and/or illicit drugs by the perpetrator. *Journal of Interpersonal Violence, 15*(9), 996–1008.

Wilsnack, S., Vogeltanz, N., Klassen, A., & Harris, R. (1997). Childhood sexual abuse and women's substance abuse: National survey findings. *Journal of Studies on Alcohol, 58,* 264–271.

Women Helping Women, Vol. II, No. 9. (2000, September 24). Online at www.female gamblers.org/wtow900.htm

Young, N., Gardner, S., & Dennis, K. (1998*). Responding to alcohol and other drug problems in Child Welfare: Weaving together practice and policy.* Washington, DC: Child Welfare Press.

From "The Twelve Promises for Beginners"

You will know your full name and address.
You will be able to find socks that match.
You will lose the fear of food.
You will be able to walk a straight line and pass the balloon test.
You will be able to answer the door without looking through the little hole.
You will realize what a mess you've been and thank God for your
Twelve-Step program. —ORIGIN UNKNOWN; FOUND ON
WWW.SOBERDYKES.ORG/JOKES.HTML

MUTUAL-HELP GROUPS: A STRENGTHS PERSPECTIVE

CHAPTER **12**

INTRODUCTION

Although mutual-help groups are typically organized around very serious problems, "The Twelve Promises for Beginners" is a good example of the "strengths" and humor that abound in such organizations. Newcomers and professionals who visit a Twelve-Step group for the first time are often shocked to hear laughter and fun-poking when dire situations are described by a fellow member. Later, they understand that the laughter comes from self-recognition and hope, and is a powerful part of the healing process for both listener and speaker. For example, in a recent all-women's meeting of Alcoholics Anonymous with over 50 women attending, a young woman named "Susan," three days out of detox at her first Alcoholics Anonymous (AA) meeting, had the following experience:

> SUSAN: (very softly) "I just got out of detox" . . .
> GROUP: (starts to get very quiet, side-conversations stop)
> SUSAN: "I don't know who I am . . . "
> GROUP: (very quiet now)
> SUSAN: (crying now) "I'm like a stranger in my own body . . . (puts her head down, sobbing) I just want to get fucked-up!"
> GROUP: (someone passes her the Kleenex box that has "Crying is healing" written on the outside with purple ink)

Many of the ideas expressed in this chapter appeared in the article "Making Meaning of Alcoholics Anonymous for Social Workers" by Diane Rae Davis and Golie Jansen, published in 1998 in *Social Work,* 43(2), 169–182. Permission granted from NASW Press for the reprinted portions.

SUSAN: "So . . . I guess I'll just take it slow . . . "
GROUP: (laughter all around, cheers, everyone starts clapping)
SUSAN: (smiles shyly)
GROUP: someone shouts, "Keep breathing!!!" and everybody laughs.

There are no easy cures or answers to many of the problems we experience as human beings. With solace, care, and support, we can, as social beings, help each other through difficult experiences that are sometimes excruciatingly painful and can lead to what Gamblers Anonymous members call "incomprehensible demoralization" when faced alone. In the last 50 years, divorce, job relocation, and changing family expectations have undermined the role extended families used to play in attempting to provide this kind of support. Mutual-help groups (an estimated half-million) have filled in the gap to deal with almost every human problem, including self-care groups for major diseases, recovery groups for addiction and other problems, and advocacy groups for certain circumstances (elderly, mentally ill, etc.). Today, approximately 10 million Americans participate in mutual-help groups each year, and 25 million have done so at some time during their life (Kessler, Mickelson & Zhao, 1997). Information on all these different types of groups is available through the American Self-Help Clearinghouse (White & Madara, 1995) and on the Internet.

In this chapter, we will describe the major mutual-help groups that have been helpful with persons who are oppressed by some addiction, including alcohol, drugs, food, gambling, and smoking. In order to understand the philosophy, purpose, and meeting behaviors of Twelve-Step programs, we will focus in depth on Alcoholics Anonymous, the model for Narcotics Anonymous, Overeaters Anonymous, Gamblers Anonymous, and Nicotine Anonymous. To the extent possible, recent research findings that indicate the effectiveness of these groups will be cited, although most research activity has been centered on Alcoholics Anonymous.

"Twelve-Step Facilitation" vs. Twelve-Step Mutual-Help Groups in the Community

Many "harm reductionists" and others aligned with strengths perspective practice see AA as the perpetrator of a monolithic disease model that requires abstinence and makes meeting attendance mandatory. This misconception may come from the confusion of "Twelve-Step facilitation" as practiced in professional treatment programs and the mutual-help Twelve-Step programs as they are practiced in the community.

The growth and spread of AA principles in professional treatment began in the United States in 1952 when a psychiatrist and a psychologist created a unique program at Wilmer State Hospital in Minnesota. As the program developed over the next three years, it featured the integration of professional staff with trained recovering alcoholics and embraced the disease model and the link to Twelve-Step groups, family involvement, abstinence from all addictive drugs, and client and family education on the effects of addiction, individualized treatment plans, and aftercare (Chappel & DuPont, 1999). This new model of treatment, subsequently, known as the Minnesota Model, was adopted by Hazelden in 1961 and spread so rapidly that by 1989, 95% of the treatment programs in the United States were basing their programs on the Twelve-Step AA program.

In actuality, the practice of AA in the community differs in fundamental ways from the "Twelve-Step facilitation" that is practiced in professional treatment centers. AA in the community is not "treatment." It is a spiritually based fellowship that supports the development and maintenance of abstinence for those who want it and offers "steps" for sobriety and lifelong character development. AA could hardly be more different in its structure than a typical public or private addiction treatment program. As noted by Chappel and DuPont (1999), AA groups in the community are self-supporting, led by fellow alcoholics, and free of charge. There is no federal or state funding, no licensing or monitoring by any regulatory agency, no records of attendance, no case records. In contrast, "Twelve Step facilitation" models implemented in treatment programs have paid professionals teach AA assumptions (powerlessness over alcohol, spirituality, Twelve Steps to recovery), require people to admit they are alcoholics, complete the work on the initial steps in a specific time frame, go to a certain number of AA meetings, charge money for the treatment program, and are monitored by state and federal regulators.

A fundamental difference between the writings of cofounder Bill Wilson, the philosophy of the Big Book of AA and professional treatment programs that practice "Twelve-Step facilitation" is around the issue of "compliance." As noted by LaFave and Echols (1999, p. 348), "Twelve-Step self-help programs stress the voluntary nature of attendance and offer their ideas as suggestions. . . . The highly directive nature of Twelve-Step treatment models is, therefore, a departure from the approach used in Twelve-Step self-help programs."

AA and other Twelve-Step groups do a delicate dance of keeping alive the voluntary nature of the mutual-help program, in spite of pressures from treatment centers and probation/parole officers on clients to bring back attendance slips signed by the chairperson of the particular group. As noted on the official AA Web site, "proof of attendance at meetings is *not* part of AA's procedure. Each group is autonomous and has the right to choose whether or not to sign court slips. In some areas the attendees report on themselves, at the request of the referring agency, and thus alleviate breaking AA members' anonymity."

Twelve-Step Programs and Harm Reduction

It may surprise some readers that the authors consider Twelve-Step mutual-help organizations such as Alcoholics Anonymous and Narcotics Anonymous to be consistent with a harm reduction philosophy. In addition to the voluntary nature of the program, there are other principles of Twelve-Step programs as practiced in the community that are consistent with harm reduction philosophy. A fundamental concept of the AA program is the need for self-assessment as to whether or not you "qualify" as a member, that is, "have a desire to stop drinking." This is based on the belief that alcoholics want to stop drinking because eventually their own experience and their failure at numerous experiments to control their drinking tell them they can no longer control it once they start. In other words, they have tried and failed at various harm reduction strategies, and consequently have reached the stage of actually having a desire to stop drinking (Zelvin & Davis, 2001). As noted in the *Big Book of Alcoholics Anonymous* (1976, p. 31):

> Here are some of the methods we have tried: Drinking beer only, limiting the number of drinks, never drinking alone, never drinking in the morning, drinking only at home, never having it in the house, never drinking during business hours, drinking only at parties, switching from scotch to brandy, drinking only natural wines, agreeing to resign if ever drunk on the job, taking a trip, not taking a trip, etc.

The critical issue is that people finally reach the decision to stop drinking *for themselves,* not because a professional person insisted on it. AA says (p. 31), "We do not like to pronounce any individual as alcoholic, but you can quickly diagnose yourself. Step over to the nearest barroom and try some controlled drinking."

Other concepts consistent with harm reduction philosophy practiced in Twelve-Step programs in the community are the ideas of limited control, that is, don't drink "one day at a time," rather than "never drink again," and the embracing of human fallibility (the only requirement for membership is "a desire to stop drinking," not "you have to have so much amount of abstinence to stay in this program). Michael White (2000, p. 32), codeveloper of the narrative therapy approach (see chapter 3), remarks that

> AA's responses to persons who turn back to the bottle are generally compassionate rather than judging. This is an antidote to the demoralizing sense of personal failure that is so often occasioned by such U-turns, and keeps the door open on options for persons to try again, and yet again. In response to these U-turns, the AA community just goes on reaching out. This is a reaching out by persons who have "been there," and who have a strong appreciation of the desperation that is experienced in this struggle.

ALCOHOLICS ANONYMOUS

Alcoholics Anonymous is the original prototype for other mutual-help groups that have adopted the Twelve Steps and traditions. As we explore this organization, it should be understood that the authors do not and cannot speak for Alcoholics Anonymous. (Official AA literature on various topics can be obtained by writing to Alcoholics Anonymous, Box 459, Grand Central Station, New York, NY 10163, or by accessing the Web site at www.alcoholics anonymous.org)

The meaning of "Alcoholics Anonymous" (AA) varies, depending on how we see ourselves in relation to this increasingly popular mutual-help program for alcoholics. Social workers have variously described AA as a set of principles developed by alcohol-dependent men (Nelson-Zlupko, Kauffman, & Dore, 1995), "a very successful model for self-help groups" (Borkman, 1989, p. 63), and disempowering to women (Rhodes & Johnson, 1994). Some feminists (Kasl, 1992) dismiss it as another white, middle-class male organization that enjoins women to depend on "having a Higher Power, which is usually described as an all-powerful male God" (p. 150) and to follow one journey to recovery "as defined by privileged males" (p. 147). For other feminists, the meaning of AA is quite different; Covington (1994) sees it as a "model for mutual-help programs" within which "women can find the most powerful resources for healing" (p. 4). Some researchers have concluded that "without question AA involvement has been associated with vast numbers of alcohol-dependent individuals becoming abstinent for long periods of time" (Emrick, 1987, p. 421), while others question whether it is even possible to assess the effectiveness of this organization in any kind of scientific manner (Harvard Mental Health Letter, 1996). Perhaps the greatest meaning of Alcoholics Anonymous, from the vantage point of the individual sober member of AA, is that "through its program he (she) attained sobriety" (Kurtz, 1979, p. 157).

In this section, we will address issues about women and other common criticisms regarding AA by reframing the meaning of AA from an alternative treatment or service delivery model to an understanding based on metaphor, using Rappaport's (1993) concept of "normative narrative communities" (p. 239). Viewing AA in this framework allows us to suggest meanings of key metaphors, or narratives, of the AA program. We will describe areas of program strength and potential barriers for clinicians (and, consequently, for those persons who consult with us) and review the research findings concerning the efficacy of this program.

A Thumbnail Sketch of Alcoholics Anonymous

Alcoholics Anonymous is an approach to recovery from alcoholism developed by and for alcoholics around 1935, a time when alcoholism was considered hopeless by the medical profession and a moral failing by most everyone. Bill Wilson and Dr. Bob Smith, both late-stage alcoholics and desperate for an alternative, joined together in the creation of anonymous support meetings that borrowed principles from the Oxford Group (a nondenominational Christian movement) and created other principles important to the recovery from alcoholism as they experienced it. Their ideas were eventually written in a book on paper so thick and bulky that the original volume of *Alcoholics Anonymous* (1939) was called "The Big Book," a title affectionately, and perhaps metaphorically, continued by AA members ever since, even though it is now a regular-sized book (Kurtz, 1979).

At the heart of the AA program is a group of principles "suggested" for recovery called the Twelve Steps (see the nearby box). These are specific individual actions, spiritual in nature, and "guides to progress, not perfection" (Alcoholics Anonymous, 1976, p. 60). They were painstakingly designed by fellow alcoholics to help a person obtain sobriety and make the spiritual transformation necessary to create a sober life that is worth living. In order for the developing AA groups to survive and function effectively, a set of principles called the

THE TWELVE STEPS
OF ALCOHOLICS ANONYMOUS

1. We admitted we were powerless over alcohol—that our lives had become unmanageable.
2. Came to believe that a Power greater than ourselves could restore us to sanity.
3. Made a decision to turn our will and our lives over to the care of God as we understood Him.
4. Made a searching and fearless moral inventory of ourselves.
5. Admitted to God, to ourselves and to another human being the exact nature of our wrongs.
6. Were entirely ready to have God remove all these defects of character.
7. Humbly asked Him to remove our shortcomings.
8. Made a list of all persons we had harmed, and became willing to make amends to them all.
9. Made direct amends to such people wherever possible, except when to do so would injure them or others.
10. Continued to take personal inventory and, when we were wrong, promptly admitted it.
11. Sought through prayer and meditation to improve our conscious contact with God, as we understood Him, praying only for knowledge of His will for us and the power to carry that out.
12. Having had a spiritual awakening as the result of these steps, we tried to carry this message to alcoholics, and to practice these principles in all our affairs.

Source: *Alcoholics Anonymous* (1976).

Twelve Traditions evolved to set forth a working philosophy for this mutual-help community. The foreword to the Second Edition of *Alcoholics Anonymous* (1955) explains the Twelve Traditions as they apply to community:

> No alcoholic man or woman could be excluded from our Society. . . . Our leaders might serve but never govern. . . . Each group was to be autonomous and there was to be no professional class of therapy. . . . There were to be no fees or dues. . . . There was to be the least possible organization, even in our service centers. . . . Our public relations were to be based upon attraction rather than promotion. . . . All members ought to be anonymous at the level of press, radio, TV, and films, and in no circumstances should we give endorsements, make alliances, or enter public controversies. (p. vii)

These twelve guidelines for a "nonorganization," although not as familiar as the Twelve Steps, have facilitated the creation and stability of more than 100,000 groups of Alcoholics Anonymous meetings in 150 countries, with more than 2 million members throughout the world at last count (Alcoholics Anonymous Web site, 2001). According to the Harvard Mental Health Letter (2000, p. 3), "by 1990, 9% of the entire American population (and 70% of those ever treated for alcoholism) had attended at least one AA meeting."

The program is recognized by many professionals as one of the most effective, user-friendly resources for helping alcoholics (Riordan & Walsh, 1994). Attributes of the program important to many counselors include a policy of no dues or fees, its availability in small towns, and, in medium to large cities, its usually offering an array of culturally diverse options for a variety of groups (such as women, veterans, elders, Native American, Hispanic, gay men, lesbians, newcomers, and even a group for Grateful "Deadheads" called the "Wharf Rats" (Epstein & Sardiello, 1990). Also, transportation for housebound persons or out-of-town visitors is frequently arranged through voluntary help from members who are "on-call" for such circumstances.

Research on Effectiveness

Although beset by methodological problems aggravated by the anonymous, voluntary, self-selection of AA membership, there is evidence to indicate that AA is an extremely useful approach for alcoholics trying to stop drinking. Emrick's (1987) review of surveys and outcome evaluations of AA alone or AA as an adjunct to professional treatment indicates that about 40 to 50% of those alcoholics who maintain long-term, active membership in AA will have several years of total abstinence while involved; and 60 to 68% will improve, drinking less or not at all during AA participation. A later meta-analysis by Emrick, Tonigan, Montgomery, & Little (1993) of 107 previously published studies found that greater AA involvement could modestly predict reduced alcohol consumption. Involvement or active participation in AA practices (such as "working the Twelve Steps"), rather than just attendance at AA meetings, was related to positive outcome in these findings and supported in other studies (Montgomery, Miller, & Tonigan, 1995; Snow, Prochaska, & Rossi, 1994). Project MATCH findings confirm that increased engagement in AA-related practices and having subjective spiritual experiences predict positive outcome (Tonigan, Miller, & Connors, 2000).

Other findings suggest that the length of AA attendance is correlated with months of abstinence (McBride, 1991). Combined with formal treatment programs, attendance at AA was found to be the only significant predictor of length of sobriety in a 10-year follow-up study of male and female patients, suggesting successful outcomes for persons who are involved with both (Cross, Morgan, Mooney, Martin, & Rafter, 1990). Other studies support the idea that AA is beneficial as an adjunct to formal treatment and when used as a form of aftercare (Walsh et al., 1991; Alford, Koehler, & Leonard, 1991).

These positive findings are not without their skeptics. Major criticisms include the large percentage of alcoholics that drop out of AA (according to AA's own survey, 50% after three months) (Galaif & Sussman, 1995; Chappel, 1993), contradictory studies that indicate AA works no better than other approaches, including no treatment (Miller & Hester, 1986; Peele, 1992), and findings that indicate no significant relationship between AA attendance and outcomes (Miller, Leckman, Delaney, & Tinkcorn, 1992; McLatchie & Lomp,

1988). In addition, methodological problems endemic to research on AA lead some researchers to dismiss such attempts as mere exercises in speculation (Harvard Mental Health Letter, 1996). For example, despite years of research, a definitive picture of a person's characteristics that can predict a positive or negative outcome with AA has not emerged (Tonigan & Hiller-Sturmhofel, 1994).

In the meantime, there is adequate (although not perfect) evidence to suggest that many alcoholics who become involved in AA will find something they can use to improve their lives on a long-term basis (Chappel, 1993) and, consequently, that social work professionals will benefit from more knowledge of this potentially valuable resource. Emrick (1987), after his extensive review of findings from the empirical literature, concludes that although AA is not for everyone (particularly those who just want to reduce their drinking), "nevertheless, AA has been demonstrated to be associated with abstinence for many alcohol-dependent individuals and thus the professional who comes in contact with alcoholics should become familiar with AA and utilize this self-help resource whenever possible" (p. 421).

Myths and Metaphors About Alcoholics Anonymous

Alcoholics Anonymous describes itself as a "simple program" that has only one requirement for membership, "a desire to stop drinking," and one primary purpose, "to carry its message to the alcoholic who still suffers" (Alcoholics Anonymous, 1976, pp. 58, 564). The apparent single-mindedness of this nonpolitical, self-supporting program masks a remarkably subtle and, in some ways, counterestablishment worldview that challenges dominant cultural expectations regarding hierarchy, power, and models of helping. Because AA is the language of narrative and metaphor, it is easily misunderstood without the context of lived experience and meaning-making of the membership as a whole. It is not surprising that AA is miscomprehended and misinterpreted. Flores (1988) notes that many of the critics of AA "fail to understand the subtleties of the AA program and often erroneously attribute qualities and characteristics to the organization that are one-dimensional, misleading, and even border on slanderous" (p. 203). AA has been called everything from a cult, to unscientific, totalitarian, and coercive (Flores, 1988). Common criticisms include: AA takes away power from groups that are already disenfranchised (such as women); AA adheres to the medical model of disease, not a strength perspective of wellness; the program is just another substitute addiction; AA requires total abstinence; AA is a religion/cult with a suspiciously white, male, dominant-culture, Christian God; AA forces people to constantly degrade themselves by introducing themselves as alcoholic; and AA meetings are undependable because they are run by nonprofessionals.

Because a lack of information and understanding is the most important factor in low referrals to self-help groups (Kurtz & Chambon, 1987), these criticisms require examination. What follows is an attempt to increase understanding of the AA program, with an aim of avoiding the pitfalls of what John

Wallace (1983) calls the unwary translator of AA, who "may find himself banging away at the concrete rather than flowing with the analogy" (p. 301).

Framing AA as a Narrative Community

Professional service providers, who live with concepts of treatment, clients, and service models, often understand AA as an alternative treatment model. This understanding, according to Rappaport (1993), is limited for gaining insight into what AA means to those who join. For a different understanding, he proposes to reframe the meaning of AA (and other mutual-help groups) in terms of a narrative perspective:

> In its simplest form, the narrative approach means understanding life to be experienced as a constructed story. The stories that people tell and are told are powerful forms of communication to both others and one's self. Stories order experience, give coherence and meaning to events, and provide a sense of history and of the future. (p. 240)

The stories are told in community, and these communities have powerful narratives about change, about themselves and their members. In this sense, AA can be seen as a "normative structure in social experience" (Rappaport, 1993, p. 246). It is a "normative structure" because it is more comparable to other voluntary associations of people "living lives," such as religious organizations, professional organizations, political parties, even families, than it is to a social service agency setting where clients come to receive services from professional helpers. In the narrative framework, people joining AA are not help-seekers, in search of treatment, but storytellers, who through telling and listening transform their lives. Personal stories become the narratives that define a "caring and sharing community of givers as well as receivers, with hope, and with a sense of their own capacity for positive change" (p. 245).

Consistent with postmodern thought, the narrative perspective embraces the idea that personal reality is itself constructed, as in a life story, and therefore has the capacity to be reconstructed throughout a person's life. In other words, as narrative therapists would say, "people make meaning, meaning is not made for us" (Monk, Winslade, Crocket, & Epston, 1997, p. 33). The AA community provides a safe harbor and a rich tradition of stories useful to reconstruct one's life story from that of a "hopeless alcoholic" to a person with "experience, strength, and hope." Hearing things in the stories of others can offer hope that your own life can be changed. For example, Smith (1993) cites this woman's experience in her early days in AA:

> A man I met told me that if I didn't think I belonged, I should hang around and I'd hear my story. Then a few weeks later, this girl got up and as she spoke, it started to dawn on me. I was so engrossed . . . every word she said I could relate to where I had come from. Here was this woman with seven or eight years in the program telling my story! (p. 696)

Smith (1993) elaborates on the process of individual integration into the "social world" of AA by describing how each step in the process of affiliation (attending meetings, sharing "experience, strength, and hope" in meetings, getting a sponsor, working the Twelve Steps of recovery, doing service work to help other alcoholics) enhances the person's comfort level in forming new relationships with others. It makes it possible for the individual to take some risks and experience small successes, it enhances self-esteem, and it leads to further commitment to the community. Understanding AA in a narrative framework where people tell stories about their lives within a community implies a conceptual shift from a rational (service delivery) model to a metaphorical (spiritual) understanding.

Michael White (2000, p. 31), codeveloper of narrative therapy, sees the principal metaphor in AA as a "right of passage," and believes that "the originators of Alcoholics Anonymous had great vision, and a profound understanding of the significance of rites of passage." According to White, "The center of AA is a ritual event that provides for a formalization of the stages of separation and reincorporation and for a marking of the turning points of persons' lives. This is accompanied by the convening of forums that provide the opportunity for persons to give testimony to the decisions they have made to break from excessive alcohol consumption, to the desires and purposes that motivate these decisions, and to tell and retell the stories of their lives before a group of witnesses, many of whom are veterans of such journeys."

The metaphorical level is the framework for the following interpretations of the meanings of AA.

The Metaphor of Powerlessness: "Giving in is the greatest form of control"
This koan (a mental puzzle used by practicing Buddhists as meditation material to further enlightenment) was created by "solution-focused" therapists to assist a practicing Buddhist client translate the first step of AA to something that utilized her Buddhist beliefs (Berg & Miller, 1992, p. 5). It is also a good example of how the language of AA can be understood as metaphorical. A parallel metaphor more familiar to Christians might be "in order to gain your life you must first lose it."

Step One of the Twelve Steps of Alcoholics Anonymous, "We admitted we were powerless over alcohol—that our lives had become unmanageable," is the cornerstone of recovery for alcoholics trying to get well through the AA program (Covington, 1994; Chappel, 1992; Kurtz, 1979; Alcoholics Anonymous, 1976). However, from a rational purview, it is also the stumbling block for many professionals who are concerned that AA pushes "powerlessness" on persons who are already powerless in the dominant culture. Wetzel (1991) voices these concerns regarding women: "The Twelve-Step program reinforces one's belief in one's powerlessness and the necessity to relinquish the self to a 'higher power' (something most women have been doing all their lives in a secular sense)" (p. 23).

In order for the nonaddicted to make sense of Step One, it is helpful to try and stand inside the circle of addiction and look around at the miserable state of affairs most women and men face when they first begin the road to recovery. The lived experience of the alcoholic is like the woman who said, "I was on an endless cycle of 'I'll do better tomorrow' and of course I was always drunk again by 9 o'clock that night"(Davis, 1996). A study of recovering alcoholics attending AA (DeSoto, O'Donnell, & DeSoto, 1989) revealed an extremely high rate of psychological distress (measured by the SCL-90) in the first three months of recovery, comparable to psychiatric inpatients. The authors comment: "With a life situation in disarray, suffering a protracted withdrawal syndrome, and experiencing cognitive deficits, it is a challenge indeed for an alcoholic to abstain from the drug that promises at least temporary relief" (p. 697).

The hard fact of being out of control with the addiction, no matter what you try to do, and having your life in shambles all around you, roughly translates to the understanding of "powerlessness" that is the starting point in the AA program. AA invites people who declare themselves eligible, to survey their world and to embrace the idea of Step One: "I am powerless *over alcohol,* and my life has become unmanageable" (Alcoholics Anonymous, 1976, p. 59). In other words, Step One says: Face the reality, and give up the illusion that you are in control of your use of alcohol. If people have doubts about their status, the Big Book suggests that they figure it out for themselves, experientially:

> Step over to the nearest barroom and try some controlled drinking. Try to drink and stop abruptly. Try it more than once. It will not take long for you to decide, if you are honest about it. It may be worth a bad case of the jitters if you get a full knowledge of your condition. (p. 31)

The organization invites those who have "lost the power of choice in drink" and have "a desire to stop drinking" to join the fellowship (Alcoholics Anonymous, 1976, pp. 24, 58). Accepting the metaphor of powerlessness, thereby accepting individual limitations, goes against the dominant Western cultural message of "pulling yourself up by the bootstraps," independence, competition, and will power. Bateson (1972) suggests that AA provides a paradoxical metaphor much like the title koan at the beginning of this section, in that "the experience of defeat not only serves to convince the alcoholic that change is necessary; it *is* the first step in that change . . . to be defeated by the bottle and to know it is the first 'spiritual' experience" (p. 313). Kurtz (1982) interprets this as a necessary step for alcoholics to alter their views of themselves from omniscient to "not God":

> Every alcoholic's problem has been, first, the claim of Godlike powers, especially "control." But the message insists the alcoholic is not in control, not even of self . . . and the first step toward recovery from alcoholism must be the acceptance and admission of this fact, obvious to others but tenaciously denied by every alcoholic. (p. 174)

The AA notion of powerlessness in the context of such group narratives transforms the competitive stance with others (who have tried to force them to stop drinking) into a complementary relationship with other alcoholics who are in the same boat, in the same meeting, and weaving and sharing similar stories of "experience, strength, and hope." Therefore, powerlessness in this context is a metaphor of connectedness, not isolation. It is a good example of the power of the "narrative community" to transform lives by reauthoring one's alcoholic experience. Stephanie Brown (1994) calls this a "power from within model" instead of a "power over" model (p. 26). An alternative understanding is what Riessman (1985) calls "self-help induced empowerment." He states that "when people join together with others who have similar problems to deal with those problems . . . they feel empowered; they are able to control some aspect of their lives. The help is not given to them from the outside, from an expert, a professional, a politician" (Riessman, 1985, p. 2). This is very different from the meanings of powerlessness associated with contemporary social and behavioral sciences, such as alienation, anomie, victimization, oppression, discrimination, and poverty (Borkman, 1989). Understanding this alternative meaning of powerlessness is helpful in resisting the temptation to oversimplify and interpret AA language in terms of social science terminology instead of the language of transformation.

The Metaphor of Disease: "Alcoholism is a threefold disease—mental, physical, and spiritual"   AA is often criticized for its support and promulgation of the "disease concept" of alcoholism (Riordan & Walch, 1994; Rhodes & Johnson, 1994), especially by some clinicians who adhere to the "strengths perspective." These two concepts have been presented as competing metaphors wherein the "disease concept" is negatively described as emphasizing the pathological not the healthy, where physicians and clinicians assume the expert role, clients are passive and not responsible for their predicament, and recovery goals are designed and directed by treatment staff. On the other side, the "strengths perspective" is optimistically portrayed as emphasizing wellness and nonhierarchical and collaborative helping relationships, and recovery goals are co-constructed by facilitators and clients (Saleebey, 1995; Evans & Sullivan, 1990).

Although these comparisons may not do justice to either metaphor, the discourse continues to be fueled by current interest in collaborative models of helping (feminist, narrative, solution-focused, motivational interviewing) and perhaps a desire to set these models apart as different from the medical model of helping. Further complications that obscure the issue of alcoholism as disease include a general inability to agree on just what "alcoholism" is, to have consensus on just what constitutes "disease," or to agree on a single theory that adequately describes the etiology of alcoholism (McNeece & DiNitto, 1994). The "disease concept," although still controversial among researchers and treatment professionals, has provided a means of diagnosing and expanding the treatment (and funding of treatment and research) of alcoholism, and done a great service in relieving the burden of guilt from both alcoholics and their family members (Burman, 1994).

In theory, the AA program leaves the debate to the professionals; it simply treats the controversy of alcoholism as disease as an "outside issue," following the principle of the Tenth Tradition of AA, which states, "Alcoholics Anonymous has no opinions on outside issues; hence the AA name ought never to be drawn into public controversy" (Alcoholics Anonymous, 1976, p. 564). Although the "Big Book" of Alcoholics Anonymous, the suggested guide to the program, avoids the term "disease," it does use the terms "malady," "illness," and "allergy" to suggest the hopelessness of the condition of active alcoholism. Kurtz's (1979) historical analysis states that Bill Wilson (the cofounder of AA) "always remained wary of referring to alcoholism as a 'disease' because he wished to avoid the medical controversy over the existence or nonexistence of a specific 'disease-entity'" (p. 22). It is somewhat ironic that in many current versions of the controversy, AA is linked firmly to the promulgation of the "disease concept" (for example, Burman, 1994; Rhodes & Johnson, 1994).

However, as Kurtz (1979) suggests, "the Alcoholics Anonymous understanding of alcoholism begs for exploration within the insight that disease can also be metaphor" (p. 200). He reminds us that disease as metaphor has been prevalent throughout history, beginning in antiquity with leprosy as "sin," to the black plague of decaying Europe, to the "white death" of tuberculosis in the slums of the industrial cities, to the malignancy of cancer in the postmodern era of uncontrolled growth and greed. "Alcoholism," or any number of "addictions," is perhaps the metaphor for modern-day separation and despair.

Many individual members of AA look upon "alcoholism" as a threefold "disease," involving spiritual, mental, and physical factors. This implies a unity of life, a holistic frame familiar to adherents of Native American traditions, Christian creationist philosophy, and Buddhist meditations, among others. Modern isolation and disconnectedness can be understood as arising from a foolish and doomed attempt to separate these unified parts of the whole person. To be fully human (and, in the case of the alcoholic, to want to live sober), the physical, mental, and especially spiritual parts must be integrated. AA members attempt to live out this metaphor on a practical level by working on a spiritual program that attends to the physical, mental, and spiritual needs of the alcoholic who still suffers.

The Metaphors of Dependence, Independence, and Interdependence   Another major criticism of AA is that it promotes dependency in the alcoholic by providing a substitute addiction or a "crutch" (Wallant, 1995; Chappel & DuPont, 1999). This is assumed to be bad, because it goes against the modern idea that the cure for dependence is absolute and total independence (Kurtz, 1979). Inherent in the metaphor of the dominant culture is the notion of "do it yourself," or self-reliance. In contrast, the Alcoholics Anonymous approach to extreme dependence (alcoholism) is to embrace the metaphor of connectedness. That is, we, as humans, are limited and dependent on other humans. Connecting with others through the fellowship of meetings, sponsors, and AA-sponsored events is perceived as a way to help strengthen one's identity, not shrink it. As one woman expressed this feeling, "By the end of the meeting I knew I was at home. I belonged there. Someone told their story and more than anything I felt connected to people again that I hadn't done in so long" (Lundy, 1985, p. 137).

According to Van Den Bergh (1991), the possibility of human connection may explain some of the increase in participation in Twelve-Step groups today:

> Patriarchy engenders isolation and anomie; recovery groups provide an antidote to the pain and angst of believing one is alone. Individuals come together to share their "experience, strength, and hope"; through that process a feeling of personal empowerment as well as community affiliation is experienced. (p. 27)

It may be helpful to note that the same criticisms about "creating dependence" are also aimed at psychotherapy, welfare assistance, certain religious communities, mothers, or any other entity that may offer a port in the storm of life. In spite of the dominant cultural suspicion that there is "something undesirable about all dependence" (Riordin & Walsh, 1994, p. 352), levels of dependence usually shift naturally as a person becomes more stable. Chappel and DuPont (1999) suggest that in the early stages of recovery after detox, every alcoholic or drug addict needs a healthy "substitute dependence," and, left to him- or herself, may choose another high-risk behavior, such as gambling, spending, sex, or eating. AA offers a way to begin the development of more healthy patterns.

In AA, newcomers may spend entire days in meeting after meeting, and it is routinely suggested that they attend "90 meetings in 90 days." As the length of sobriety and stability increases, participation generally shifts to helping others (making coffee, chairing meetings, sponsoring others). Many "old-timers" with years of sobriety continue participation to provide sponsorship and support for newcomers and because they depend on AA meetings to help them maintain their spiritual program, not just their sobriety. Independence, in the American sense of "doing it alone," is not the goal; instead, the individual (isolated by alcoholism and an array of negative social consequences) is taught in small steps how to depend on others and how to allow others to depend on him or her.

The Realities of Abstinence: One Day at a Time   The basic text of *Alcoholics Anonymous* (1976) suggests that "for those who are unable to drink moderately the question is how to stop altogether. . . . We are assuming, of course, that the reader desires to stop" (p. 34). As discussed earlier, the need for self-assessment, and the belief that underneath it all alcoholics want to stop drinking precisely because their own experience and numerous experiments tell them they can no longer control it once they start, is a fundamental concept of the AA program.

However, abstinence (if it means "never drink again") was considered too unrealistic, too absolute, perhaps too frightening to the alcoholics who created the AA program. Instead they developed the idea of limited control, that is, not drinking "one day at a time" instead of forever. According to Kurtz (1979) this message serves both to "protect against grandiosity and to affirm the sense of individual worthwhileness so especially important to the drinking alcoholic mired in self-hatred over his failure to achieve absolute control over his drinking" (p. 105). The concept of limited control and the embracing of human fallibility is another example of how the AA program stands apart from our dominant culture's obsessive drive for perfection. Several AA slogans underscore the concept of limited control: "Progress not perfection," "Easy does it," and "One day at a time." Recovery is seen as an ongoing process, more in tune with the feminist principle of emphasizing "process not product" (Van Den Bergh, 1991).

In the addiction field, programs or research that suggest an alcoholic can return to "controlled drinking" are seen as diametrically opposed to the AA premise of stopping drinking (Riordin & Walsh, 1994; McNeece & DiNitto, 1994). On one level of meaning, it is not surprising that the idea of teaching an alcoholic controlled drinking strikes the AA member as absurd, because in AA the alcoholic is *self-defined* as a person who cannot control her or his drinking. For those who can control it (through whatever means), the message is "Our hats are off to him" (Alcoholics Anonymous, 1976, p. 31). On another level of meaning, focusing on controlling drinking misses the point. In AA, the alcoholic that has lost control does not just have a bad habit and does not just need to stop drinking. That is only the first step in eliminating an "alcoholic" lifestyle based on self-centeredness, immaturity, and spiritual bankruptcy (Flores, 1988; Kurtz, 1979). As discussed earlier, the alcoholic is viewed as having a threefold problem, involving mental, spiritual, and physical suffering. In AA, eliminating drinking is only the first step, although it is both necessary and essential, to begin the process of recovery.

The Metaphor of Higher Power: "It's my soul-self"   Lamb of God, Ancient Thing, Buddha, Yahweh, Love, Truth, Oneness, the Light, Mother God, Mother Nature, God, the Thursday evening "Insanity to Serenity" AA meeting, the Friday at 7 A.M. "Eye-openers" meeting; all of these and many other versions may describe an AA member's Higher Power. The encouragement to choose the nature of this power is a freedom that underlies the spiritual nature of the AA program and distinguishes it from an organized religious program. The emphasis is not on what kind of "Higher Power" is embraced, but that the idea of human limitations and "a power greater than ourselves" is accepted. For atheists, Bill Wilson recommended that the "Higher Power" be the AA group they were attending—"When they come in, most of their AA group is sober, and they are drunk. Therefore, the group is a 'Higher Power.' That's a good enough start, and most of them do progress from there. I know how they feel because I was once that way myself" (Bill W., 1967, p. 226).

For some, the Higher Power is located *within* the self. For example, in Covington (1994), Maureen describes how important it was to let go of the "ego" on the outside and seek the "bigger self" inside:

> Developing a sense of self is critical to my well-being. . . . There is a power in me that's greater than the small self I've been accustomed to; it's larger than the way I've been trained to think about who I am. It's my soul-self. In cooperating with it, I surrender to a part of me that carries wisdom and truth. It brings me back into harmony and balance with myself—that's what spirituality is for me. (p. 35)

Step Two, "Came to believe that a power greater than ourselves would re-store us to sanity," and Step Three, "Made a decision to turn our will and our life over to the care of God, as we understand Him" (Alcoholics Anonymous, 1976, p. 59), are the spiritual cornerstones of the AA program. These two steps suggest that alcoholics connect with the healing energy (grace, Godness) of the world and/or within themselves and become receptive to spiritual guidance, whether that source be the wisdom of their AA group on staying sober or some other version of a "power greater than themselves."

A literal reading of the first three steps has been interpreted by some femi-nists (Kasl, 1992) as sacrificing and martyring oneself for the sake of others, no-tably males. However, as Clemmons (1991) notes, the Third Step "does not promote this kind of detrimental repression, but it does suggest that we must be willing to let go of people and situations outside of our control. . . . 'Letting go' halts the alcoholic/addict's efforts to control the uncontrollable and focuses on developing and listening to the true self" (p. 104). In other words, power is seen not in relational terms with other people, but vis-à-vis the addiction. The power of the alcohol, or the "small self" as Maureen put it, is "let go" through the shift of accepting a Higher Power.

AA is fundamentally a spiritual program (Kurtz, 1979; Galanter, 1999). Many clinicians have difficulty with this position; as a counseling profession, we have historically focused rationally on the temporal conditions of our clients and their environment, excluding the spiritual. In addition, Galanter (1999) points out that most psychiatrists (56%) don't believe in God or a higher power themselves, in contrast to the 94% of Americans who do. He cites an interest-ing study on medical students who were treating indigent, hospitalized addicts. The addicts ranked spirituality and belief in God as the most important com-ponent of their recovery; the medical students considered these factors to be the least important. In that mindset it is easy to construe AA's concept of Higher Power as religion, and the metaphor of "letting go" of "those things we cannot change" as passive dependency.

Storytelling as Metaphor: "Hi, my name is Joe and I'm an alcoholic"   Many observers of AA fail to grasp the complex and metaphorical meanings of com-mon terms and practices as they are used by AA members. Wallace (1983) notes that "the extended meanings that characterize the AA language system will continue to elude external observers who remain at literal, concrete levels of analysis and fail to consider the nature of symbolic communication and the purposes it serves in complex social contexts and transactions" (p. 302). For example, it is common practice (but not required) to introduce oneself in AA meetings with your name, followed by "and I'm an alcoholic." This greeting has been interpreted by some critics to be a countertherapeutic reinforcement of a negative label, but as Smith (1993) points out, "It is understood by AA members that the word takes on a different and positive meaning in the context of AA" (p. 702). Using Wallace's (1983) idea of illustrating how a common AA slogan can have various meanings depending on the context, the meaning of the

"I'm Joe and I'm an alcoholic" greeting in the context of an AA meeting could be any or all or none of the following:

1. I have faced the reality that I am alcohol dependent and I want to quit drinking. Harm reduction strategies have not worked for me and I cannot control my drinking.
2. I have suffered and caused others to suffer, just like you.
3. I don't buy in to the shame attached to this label by the outside world.
4. Even though I am an alcoholic and my natural state would be to be drinking, I'm sober today and participating in this meeting to help my mental, spiritual, and physical recovery.
5. Even though I'm not drinking today, there is a part of me that is immature and self-centered, spiritually bankrupt, egotistical, superficial, i.e., an "alcoholic personality" that sometimes operates in the world in a "drunk mode," or "dry drunk." I claim this part, instead of trying to hide my problems in living under a superficial sheen of perfection.
6. I'm grateful to be an alcoholic because having this condition put me on a spiritual path that I never would have found otherwise.
7. I'm not unique, better than, worse off, or any different than any of the rest of you in this meeting. We are here to confront a common problem and to help each other.

These possibilities are extended meanings that can occur within the context of a particular meeting and that are dependent on the circumstances and histories of individuals who are introducing themselves. Central to the meanings of AA phrases and language is a redefinition of the experience of being an alcoholic. A "practicing alcoholic" (one that is currently drinking) may be better understood in AA as practicing a flawed way of life, dominated by self-centeredness, superficiality with others, and spiritual bankruptcy. The personal stories told in AA, "what we used to be like, what happened, and what we are like now" (Alcoholics Anonymous, 1976, p. 58), are vehicles for making sense of the chaos of the typical alcoholic's life by redefining it within this logic. As Marion describes the process in Maracle (1989):

> The more I went to meetings, the more I heard what other people said, I'd come home and think about it. I'd reflect on my own life, far back, up close, when I started drinking, what happened, how much of my life was related to alcohol, drinking. That's how I began to connect the depression and the drinking. I began to connect information, to put pieces together. I'd really *listen* at meetings. *Hear* what people said. And think about it all. And about me. I got real serious about trying to understand. (p. 154)

Thune's (1977) analysis of AA from a phenomenological perspective argues that it is precisely *because* AA members are taught to reinterpret their alcoholic life story as spiritually bankrupt that they can give meaning to a past filled with degradation and chaos and can have hope for the creation of a different future. Thus the AA approach to recovery, which aims for a transformed life based on spiritual principles instead of "alcoholic" strategies, is quite different from approaching alcoholism as merely a disease or a bad habit to be reformed. The deeply individual piece of transformation, within the context of the narrative community, transcends the dichotomies of self/other, exemplifying the embedded interdependence of these communities.

Who Does AA Benefit?

Researchers and clinicians would like to know more about who exactly would benefit the most from a Twelve-Step group like AA and who would be least likely to benefit. Unfortunately, there is no definitive answer to this important question. A major goal of Project MATCH was to be able to predict which treatment approach would be more effective given client characteristics. However, only four out of 21 possible matches were detected, and one of these matches disappeared after one year (Fuller & Hiller-Sturmhofel, 1999). An earlier study by Montgomery, Miller, and Tonigan (1995) found that AA attendees, when compared with nonattendees, could not be distinguished by pretreatment patient characteristics and that there was no evidence of an "AA personality." However, there continue to be concerns about whether AA is too "culture bound" with American, white, heterosexual, male dominance to be of any help to other groups, such as women, homosexuals, and people from different races and cultures. As one of the authors heard from a woman in an open AA meeting in Scotland, "I never thought I could identify with an American male stockbroker! (i.e., Bill W.)."

Women comprise a steadily increasing membership in Alcoholics Anonymous. In 1992, women under 30 made up an estimated 43% of AA members; women of all ages made up an estimated 35% of members, compared with 30% in 1983 and 22% in 1968 (Alcoholics Anonymous, 1992). However, many women in AA continue to react to the predominance of sexist language in the AA Big Book, which remains unchanged since the original edition (1939), "13th stepping" (soliciting more than friendship from vulnerable, new members), and the tendency in some groups to be dominated by male chairpersons who call primarily on male members to share their stories. Consequently, in many medium-sized towns and certainly in larger cities, "women-only" groups have developed to alleviate some of this tension. Other women take a more direct approach:

> In my early days, I got white-out and took out all the "Gods" and "he's" in the Big Book. I wrote in the word "hope" for higher power and God. That was an essential change for me. I have told newcomers, if you object to the literature, don't read it. Or fix it. I wish they—AA—would fix it. (Hall, 1996, p. 127)

In order to meet many of the objections to the wording of the Twelve Steps while preserving their aesthetic quality and succinctness, van Wormer (2001) introduced a modified version, "The Nine Steps to Recovery." In this version, the language is more consistent with the strengths perspective, more inclusive of various cultural and religious traditions, and gender neutral. For example,

Step three is reworded to "Made a decision to turn our will and our lives to the care of a Higher Power as we understand him, her, or it" (p. 316).

There are also specialized meetings for a variety of groups, such as veterans, Hispanics, gay, lesbian, elders, and Native Americans. However, not all problems can be solved by specialized groups, as demonstrated by the different responses from lesbian women interviewed by Joanne Hall (1996, pp. 122–124). Some lesbian women felt perfectly comfortable in mainstream AA:

> "It's comforting for me to see people from all walks of life who have the same disease as me. It's not just a bunch of dykes, you know? I just need to see that sometimes." (p. 122)

> "AA is really great. All these people who are not like you are interested in keeping you sober. They call you—and you don't know why they wanna be around you, but they do anyway. I thought it was beautiful that these strangers that I had nothing in common with would call me and cared about me and would sit with me." (p. 123)

Others felt that the inclusion of culturally distinct persons in AA is superficial and that lesbian groups were important for identification:

> "The lesbian AA groups are so much more open-minded. . . . The straight AA groups I find are real traditionally AA. In lesbian meetings other things can come out, like talking about incest, or just about living the life of a lesbian." (p. 123)

Still others rejected lesbian meetings because AA mainstream values lacked prominence in the specialized meetings and because they feared being "engulfed, sexualized, or rejected by women who were 'just like me' when they attended these lesbian meetings" (p. 124).

Some commentators raise concerns that African Americans are less likely to associate with AA because it is culturally bound by middle-class white Americans. A recent cross-sectional study by Kaskutas, Weisner, Lee, and Humphries (1999) found that African Americans are about twice as likely as whites to report having attended AA as part of treatment but that whites are more likely to go to AA on their own. Although both groups are equally likely to actively engage in the program, they participate differently: African Americans were more likely to say they felt like a member of AA (64% vs. 54% of whites) and had a spiritual awakening as a result of AA (38% vs. 37%), whereas whites were more likely to have had a sponsor (23% vs. 14%) and to have read program literature (77% vs. 67%).

Project MATCH found no significant differences in the rates of AA attendance among African American, Hispanic, and white clients. Hispanic clients reported a higher level of AA involvement (such as working the Steps, having a sponsor, celebrating sobriety birthdays) than white clients (Tonigan, Connors, & Miller, 1998).

The spread of AA to 150 diverse countries and the publication of AA literature in at least eight languages would argue that AA's philosophy is flexible and broad enough that many different kinds of people can find a way to benefit. Because of Tradition Ten, "Alcoholics Anonymous has no opinion on outside issues; hence the AA name ought never be drawn into public controversy" (Alcoholics Anonymous, 1976, p. 564), AA is not involved with any political organizations or social movements that might taint the single purpose of this organization, which is to "carry its message to the alcoholic who still suffers."

GAMBLERS ANONYMOUS

Gamblers Anonymous (GA) is a Twelve-Step mutual-help program of men and women "who share their experience, strength, and hope with each other that they may solve their common problem and help others to recover from a gambling problem" (Gamblers Anonymous, 2000, p. 2). The GA program acknowledges Alcoholics Anonymous (AA) as a guide and foundation and utilizes the same Twelve Steps of recovery and the same organizational principles. The only requirement for membership is "a desire to stop gambling" (p. 2); consequently, abstinence from gambling is a goal.

Like AA, GA is run entirely by recovering individuals, in this case compulsive gamblers, who volunteer their time to be sponsors, chair meetings, arrange for meeting places, secure GA literature, and respond to requests for help day and night. GA meetings are available in all 50 states and are accessible online. GA meetings can be found by calling your state problem gambling 1-800-Helpline, looking in the yellow pages of the phone book for a local contact number, or accessing the Gamblers Anonymous International Service Office online site (gamblersanonymous.org). The number of GA chapters has increased from 650 in 1990 to 1328 in October of 1998, which may indicate some impact from the rapid expansion of legalized gambling (National Gambling Impact Study Commission, 1999).

Although GA is "probably the most popular intervention for pathological gambling" (Blanco, Ibanez, Saiz-Ruiz, Blanco-Jerez, & Nunes, 2000, p. 402), like its counterpart AA, it is not without critics. GA is also perceived by many as a white, male, middle-class organization that is not user-friendly to women. This may still be the case in some areas, but it appears the landscape is changing rapidly as more women seek help for gambling problems. For example, according to the Arizona Council on Compulsive Gambling (2000), even though GA started in that state in 1973,

> for the first 18 years, a few women walked through the doors . . . and left. By their own admission, the men didn't quite know what to do with them. The women were told they hadn't gambled long enough; they hadn't lost enough to be real gamblers. They didn't play real games. Their tears and their stories were ridiculed. They were "hit" on, "Let's go for coffee . . . at my place, baby." They didn't stay. The men said, "Women just don't seem to have what it takes to stay in recovery." (Arizona Council on Compulsive Gambling, 2000)

The year 1992 marked a change in Arizona, when one woman (Marilyn L.) started a "women preferred" GA meeting in her home. Although the meeting struggled in the beginning, by 1999 there were three "women preferred" meetings out of the 19 GA meetings in the Phoenix area. The Arizona Council estimates that women now make up about 40% of the GA meeting attendance.

Preliminary responses to an online survey of recovering women (Davis, 2002) support the idea that "times are changing," but a gender barrier can still exist. Some women noted barriers: "When I came into GA in 1991, the men didn't think slot players were real gamblers," and "I'm a woman, so they ignored me the first three months." On the other hand, many of the women responding to the survey felt welcomed: "Although I was the only woman, I felt welcomed," "I did not feel alone," "They understood my problem as no one who is not a compulsive gambler ever will," "When I finally began attending regularly, I felt welcomed in every way . . . mostly, I felt that I belonged somewhere."

How well does GA work? Members of GA will readily admit that "attending GA ruins your gambling," but whether participating in meetings makes a significant impact on long-term abstinence is not known from the small number of research studies available (National Research Council, 1999). Like studies of AA, serious methodological problems arise from the voluntary, anonymous, self-selection of GA membership. One study (Stewart & Brown, 1988) indicates that total abstinence from gambling was reported by only 8% of the GA members studied one year after their first attendance, and by only 7% after two years. On the other hand, Taber, McCormick, Russo, Adkins, & Ramirez (1987) found that attending GA was helpful in maintaining abstinence: 74% of the abstinent gamblers in their sample attended at least three GA meetings in the prior month, compared with only 42% of those who continued to gamble. There is some evidence that attending GA combined with professional help may improve outcomes (Lesieur & Blume, 1991; Blackman, Simone, & Thoms, 1989). Clearly, more research, and research that is gender-specific, is needed in this area.

OTHER TWELVE-STEP GROUPS

As already mentioned, there are numerous other Twelve-Step groups available to help with every possible addiction. Space requirements preclude describing every one of them. The Twelve Steps and Twelve Traditions of Alcoholics Anonymous have been translated to deal with many addictive problems. For example, in Narcotics Anonymous (NA) drug terminology is substituted for alcohol, in Cocaine Anonymous (CA) cocaine is substituted for alcohol, in Nicotine Anonymous (NA) nicotine is substituted for alcohol, and so on.

NA was started in the 1950s when polyaddiction became more common and some "pure alcoholics" in AA were uncomfortable when discussion often included more than just alcohol. Similarly, Cocaine Anonymous emerged with the increased use of this drug and the differences in lifestyle, drug-seeking behaviors, and consequences of this drug. For more information on various Twelve-Step groups that deal with specific types of addiction, the Internet is a bountiful resource.

OTHER MUTUAL-SUPPORT GROUPS

There are also a variety of other types of mutual-help groups that offer support for addictive behavior that are fundamentally different in philosophy and purpose from Twelve-Step groups. For example, the three groups we will briefly describe as examples do not emphasize reliance on a "higher power" for recovery, do not offer sponsorship for new members, and do not expect members to attend for life. However, like AA, substantial empirical support for their effectiveness is lacking, they are self-supporting, and they offer meetings at no charge.

Women for Sobriety (WFS)

Women for Sobriety (2000; see Web site: www.womenforsobriety.org) was founded by Jean Kirkpatrick, Ph.D., in 1976 in order to address the unique issues for women that might be barriers to their recovery, such as lack of self-esteem, depression, and overwhelming feelings of guilt. WFS sees alcoholism as a physical disorder, like diabetes. Kirkpatrick sees spirituality as a goal for recovery but stresses that WFS is not a "God-oriented program." She asks, "Do diabetics go to God-oriented meetings for their diabetes?"(Kirkpatrick, 2001). Instead, the WFS meetings stress the "New Life" Program of Acceptance, which is based on Thirteen Statements. These include positive self-statements such as "Negative thoughts destroy only myself" and "The past is gone forever." (For a complete list see www.womenforsobriety.org) WFS recommends that women review these statements each morning, use one of them consciously all day, and review its effects at the end of the day.

Meetings are led by a Certified Moderator, a person with at least one year of sobriety and certified knowledge about WFS principles. Meetings are open to all women alcoholics and to those with prescription drug problems. According to Horvath (1997), in 1996 WFS had at least 300 meeting in 40 states and 50 meetings in other countries (primarily Canada, Australia, New Zealand, Ireland, and Finland). He cites two studies by Kaskutas (1994, 1995) that support the idea that women attending WFS find support, nurturance, and a safe environment for discussion about women's issues. However, another study of 115 women in AA or WFS (Talan, 1982) found no differences between groups on reaction to the groups, length of time attending, or treatment outcome.

SMART Recovery

SMART, which stands for Self Management and Recovery Training, is another alternative mutual-help group, started in 1992 as an offshoot of Rational Recovery (see Web site at www.smartrecovery.org). This approach is drawn from the principles of cognitive-behavioral therapy and particularly from rational emotive behavior therapy, as developed by Albert Ellis, Ph.D. Addiction is viewed more as a maladaptive behavior than a disease, and could arise from both substance use (i.e., alcohol, nicotine, caffeine, food, illicit drugs, and prescribed medications) and involvement in activities (such as gambling, sexual behavior, eating, spending, relationships, and exercise). As stated on their Web site "Purposes and Methods," "We assume that there are degrees of addictive behavior, and that all individuals to some degree experience it."

SMART Recovery attempts to fill in the gap posed by the following questions, raised by Nick Rajacic, coordinator of the Keweenaw Area SMART Recovery Program (www.smartrecovery.org):

> Why can't people be encouraged and motivated to creatively seek their own solutions instead of looking for answers outside of themselves in the form of groups and Higher Powers? Why can't people just be taught effective skills to cope with the problems of living sober in a drug-using culture? Why can't they just be taught the cognitive-behavioral skills of emotional self-management? Why can't they develop new and rewarding lifestyles around interests other than recovery alone?

There are two primary goals of the program: (1) to help individuals gain independence from addictive behavior (through abstinence), and (2) to teach people how to enhance and maintain motivation to abstain, cope with urges, manage thoughts, feelings, and behavior, and balance momentary and enduring satisfactions (www.smartrecovery.org). To accomplish this, cognitive-behavioral techniques, communication skills, anger management skills, and stress management techniques are incorporated into the meetings.

Meetings typically include discussions of the primary goals, activating events (urges, life happenings, or any other experiences that might lead to negative consequences), and analysis of the events using a cognitive approach. Personal homework projects are usually assigned to put ideas from the meetings into practice. Current meeting locations are listed, by states and contacts, on their Web site. There are approximately 260 different meetings in the United States and meetings in Canada, Australia, Scotland, and Sweden.

SMART meeting coordinators are volunteers, trained from literature available through the Web site and recommended readings and the regular consultation of a volunteer professional advisor, typically a licensed professional with addiction training and experience. To date, no research studies of SMART are published, but there is a clinical trial in progress.

Moderation Management (MM)

Moderation Management, as the name implies, is a mutual-help group dedicated to supporting individuals who have a desire to drink alcohol moderately. Drinking problems are viewed as bad habits, rather than a disease. MM is not intended for "those who experience significant withdrawal symptoms when they stop drinking, or those with any physical or mental condition, including pregnancy, that could be adversely affected by alcohol, even in moderate amounts. Also not intended for former dependent drinkers who are now abstaining" (www.moderation.org). Rather, MM may be viewed as a prevention measure or a harm reduction strategy for persons who wish to drink moderately. Moderation is defined for males as no more than four drinks per day, no more than four drinking days per week, and no more than 14 standard drinks per week; for females moderation is considered to be no more than three standard drinks per day, no more than four drinking days per week, and no more than nine drinks per week.

MM strategies include a voluntary abstention from alcohol for 30 days, during which the person is asked to examine how drinking has affected his or her life, write down priorities, and take a look at how much, how often, and under what circumstances drinking occurs. Moderate drinking levels are set using the MM guidelines, and the person is encouraged to try cognitive-behavioral techniques found in several recommended texts. MM recommends 6–18 months of weekly meetings, which is devoted to discussion of MM goals and activities since the last meeting.

MM has recently been under fire in the press and from the National Council on Alcoholism and Drug Dependence (NCADD) because of the tragic experience of MM founder Audrey Kishline (Verhovek, 2000). Mrs. Kishline pleaded guilty to two counts of vehicular homicide after a binge-drinking episode in March 2000 in which she drove in the wrong lane and caused a collision that killed two people.

Although Mrs. Kishline had resigned from MM the previous January, stating she had shifted her drinking goal to abstinence and attending AA, many who are abstinence-only proponents took the opportunity to hold up her experience as an example of "denial in action" and "the delusion behind the idea that alcoholics can be taught to drink without harm" (Verhovek, 2000). The Board of Directors of MM counter this by reminding people that Mrs. Kishline adhered to the basic tenets of MM by shifting her goal to abstinence when she couldn't maintain moderate drinking. Like many members of AA and other support groups, she relapsed, which should not be blamed on AA or MM but should be seen as a personal tragedy (Moderation Management, 2000).

Current face-to-face meetings and chat rooms can be found on the MM Web site. Currently no studies of MM have been published.

HOW TO SUPPORT CLIENT INVOLVEMENT IN MUTUAL-HELP GROUPS

With the empirical support from Project MATCH that showed Twelve-Step facilitation groups were as effective as cognitive-behavioral groups and motivation enhancement groups (Galanter, 1999), there is increased attention in the literature on how to facilitate Twelve-Step participation. Caldwell (1999) recommends a strengths-based approach, in which clinicians focus on areas where clients feel comfortable with AA or have needs or interests that could be satisfied by AA attendance. In order to do that, clinicians need to find their own areas of comfort with mutual-help approaches.

However, as noted in Davis and Jansen (1998), the habits, practices, and context of professional counselors are likely to be very different from those in the mutual-help community. Getting comfortable with mutual-help groups may be more difficult because of professional adherence to a practice model of "regarding people as recipients of services" and the thought that "the alternatives available to them are viewed as treatments or programs" (Rappaport, 1993, p. 241). Further complications include the reality ("always there and typically ignored," according to Riessman, 1985, p. 2) that the help given by our professional practice is embedded in the context of paid services, while the help provided by mutual-aid groups such as AA is free of charge.

However, there appears to be some common ground on a metaphorical level. Both systems embrace empowerment, connectedness, interdependence, and, most importantly, the principle that people can change, regardless of how oppressed they may find themselves in their circumstances. Readers are encouraged to discover their own meanings of the similarities and differences between their professional social work practice and the help offered by mutual-help groups by putting themselves in a position to experience firsthand the mutual-help community and the hope that is offered there to many persons.

For many clinicians it is helpful to attend at least one meeting of the mutual-help groups in your area. However, attending one "open" AA meeting may not be sufficient. Montgomery and colleagues (1995) found a wide variation in AA groups in terms of their social structure and characteristics, such as cohesiveness, aggressiveness, and expressiveness. If you are in a medium-size or large city, you may find an array of options or types of meetings that appeal to groups such as men, women, gay men, lesbians, veterans, elders, smokers, and nonsmokers. As a visitor, you are invited to attend any meeting identified as "open." "Closed" meetings are reserved for those who have a desire to stop drinking.

For information regarding meeting times and schedules (which change frequently), consult the yellow pages of the phone book under "Alcoholism," the classified ads in the local newspaper, or the Internet addresses listed in this section. In larger towns, call the AA central office in your area (run by volunteers, not paid staff) to get the meeting schedule. In Twelve-Step groups, visitors and newcomers may be asked to identify themselves by their first names only when they attend an open meeting. As members talk, they identify themselves by their first name only, not their profession, not their family name, not where they live. The practice of anonymity is considered by many Twelve-Step members to be a spiritual foundation of recovery (Chappel, 1992). As a respectful visitor, it is critical to honor this tradition (for further descriptions of AA steps, traditions, and meetings, see Riordan & Walsh, 1994; Chappel, 1992; N. Miller & Mahler, 1991; and Caldwell, 1999).

Suggestions from Chappel and DuPont (1999) for how psychiatrists can support clients in mutual-help programs include facilitating a meeting between the client and a temporary contact from the mutual-help group, working with the natural resistance and ambivalence that clients may have about attending meetings, helping dual-diagnosis clients understand AA's and NA's singleness of purpose, and getting comfortable with the spiritual dimensions of healing.

SUMMARY AND CONCLUSION

Much more could be said to describe the various methods and purposes of mutual help, but the purpose of this chapter was limited to introducing counselors to a way of understanding some of the primary features of several main mutual-help organizations. Alcoholics Anonymous, as practiced in the community, is the original prototype of Twelve-Step mutual-help organizations, such as Narcotics Anonymous, Nicotine Anonymous, and Gamblers Anonymous. This organization is seen as a narrative community where identity transformation takes place through the telling of stories and the identification of personal meanings of metaphors. Spirituality is central to the healing process in Twelve-Step communities.

In contrast, Women for Sobriety, SMART Recovery, and Moderation Management do not require a spiritual orientation. WFS and SMART are both abstinence-based programs; MM is designed to help problem drinkers drink moderately. All of these programs and many more can be accessed through the Internet, and most have online meetings and chat rooms.

At a minimum, the members of these mutual-help programs can offer acceptance on a deep level to persons who have been isolated and shamed by their circumstances, and can affirm the hope that one can recover. For these reasons alone, a referral, with some preparation as to how the meetings are conducted, how to find the meetings, and a brief summary of the meeting format, should be considered.

References

Alcoholics Anonymous. (1939, 1955, 1976). *Alcoholics Anonymous: The story of how many thousands of men and women have recovered from alcoholism.* New York: Alcoholics Anonymous World Services.

Alcoholics Anonymous. (1992). *Alcoholics Anonymous membership survey.* New York: Alcoholics Anonymous World Services.

Alcoholics Anonymous Web site. (2001). Online at www.alcoholics-anonymous.org

Alford, G .S., Koehler, R. A., & Leonard, J. (1991). Alcoholics Anonymous–Narcotics Anonymous model in patient treatment of chemically dependent adolescents: A 2-year outcome study. *Journal of Studies on Alcohol, 52*(2), 118–126.

Arizona Council on Compulsive Gambling. (2000). Women and recovery in Arizona: A brief history. Online at www.azccg.org

Bateson, G. (1972). *Steps to an ecology of mind.* New York: Ballantine.

Berg, I., & Miller, S. (1992). *Working with the problem drinker: A solution-focused approach.* New York: Norton.

Bill W. (1967). *As Bill sees it.* New York: Alcoholics Anonymous World Services.

Blackman, S., Simone, R., & Thoms, D. (1989). The Gamblers Treatment Clinic of St. Vincent's North Richmond Community Mental Health Center: Characteristics of the clients and outcome of treatment. *International Journal of Addictions, 24,* 29–37.

Blanco, C., Ibanez, A., Saiz-Ruiz, J., Blanco-Jerez, C., & Nunes, E. (2000). Epidemiology, pathophysiology and treatment of pathological gambling. *CNS Drugs, 13*(6), 397–407.

Borkman, T. (1989, Spring). Alcoholics Anonymous: The stories. *Social Policy, 58–63.*

Brown, S. (1994). Alcoholics Anonymous: An interpretation of its spiritual foundation. *Behavioral Health Management, 14*(1), 25–27.

Burman, S. (1994). The disease concept of alcoholism: Its impact on women's treatment. *Journal of Substance Abuse Treatment, 11*(2), 121–126.

Caldwell, P. (1999). Assessing the connection to Alcoholics Anonymous in early recovery: Recommendations for an "Affiliation Index." *Alcoholism Treatment Quarterly, 17*(4), 1–14.

Chappel, J. N. (1992). Effective use of Alcoholics Anonymous and Narcotics Anonymous in treating patients. *Psychiatric Annals, 22*(8), 409–418.

Chappel, J. N. (1993). Long-term recovery from alcoholism. *Recent Advances in Addictive Disorders, 16*(1), 177–187.

Chappel, J. N., & DuPont, R. L. (1999). Twelve-step and mutual-help programs for addictive disorders. *Addictive Disorders, 22*(2), 425–447.

Clemmons, P. (1991). Feminists, spirituality, and the Twelve Steps of Alcoholics Anonymous. *Women and Therapy, 11*(2), 97–109.

Covington, S. S. (1994). *A woman's way through the Twelve Steps.* Center City, MN: Hazelden.

Cross, G. M., Morgan, C. W., Mooney, A. J., Martin, C. A., & Rafter, J. A. (1990). Alcoholism treatment: A ten-year follow-up study. *Alcoholism: Clinical and Experimental Research, 14*(2), 169–173.

Davis, D. (1996). Women healing from alcoholism: A qualitative study. *Contemporary Drug Problems, 24,* 147–177.

Davis, D. (2002). *Women who are taking their lives back from compulsive gambling.* Online survey at sswhs.ewu.edu/gambling

Davis, D., & Jansen, G. (1998). Making meaning of Alcoholics Anonymous for social workers: Myths, metaphors and realities. *Social Work, 43*(2), 169–182.

DeSoto, C. B., O'Donnel, W. E., & DeSoto, J. L. (1989). Long-term recovery in alcoholics. *Alcoholism: Clinical and Experimental Research, 13*(5), 693–697.

Emrick, C. D. (1987). Alcoholics Anonymous: Affiliation processes and effectiveness as treatment. *Alcoholism, Clinical and Experimental Research, 11* (5), 416–423.

Emrick, C. D., Tonigan, J. S., Montgomery, H. A, & Little, L. (1993). Alcoholics Anonymous: What is currently known? In B. S. McCrady & W. R. Miller (Eds.), *Research on Alcoholics Anonymous: Opportunities and alternatives.* Piscataway, NJ: Rutgers Center of Alcohol Studies.

Epstein, J., & Sardiello, R. (1990). The Wharf Rats: A preliminary examination of Alcoholics Anonymous and the Grateful Deadhead phenomena. *Deviant Behavior, 11,* 245–257.

Evans, K., & Sullivan, J. (1990). *Dual diagnosis: Counseling the mentally ill substance abuser.* New York: Guilford Press.

Flores, F. J. (1988). *Group therapy with addicted populations.* New York: Haworth.

Fuller, R., & Hiller-Sturmhofel, S. (1999). Alcoholism treatment in the United States: An overview. *Alcohol, Research, and Health, 23*(2), 69–77.

Galaif, E. R., & Sussman, S. (1995). For whom does Alcoholics Anonymous work? *International Journal of the Addictions, 30*(2), 161–184.

Galanter, M. (1999). Research on spirituality and Alcoholics Anonymous. *Alcoholism: Clinical and Experimental Research, 23,* 716–719.

Gamblers Anonymous. (2000). *Gamblers Anonymous: A New Beginning* (4th ed.). Los Angeles: Author.

Hall, J. (1996). Lesbians' participation in Alcoholics Anonymous: Experiences of social, personal, and political tensions. *Contemporary Drug Problems, 23,* 113–139.

Harvard Mental Health Letter. (1996). *Treatment of Alcoholism, Part II, 13*(3), 1–5.

Horvath, A. (1997). Alternative support groups. In J. Lowinson, P. Ruiz, R. Millman, & J. Langrod (Eds.), *Substance abuse: A comprehensive textbook* (pp. 390–396). Baltimore: Williams and Wilkins.

Kaskutas, L. (1994). What do women get out of self-help? Their reasons for attending Women for Sobriety and Alcoholics Anonymous. *Journal Substance Abuse Treatment, 11,* 185–195.

Kaskutas, L. (1995). *An analysis of "Women for Sobriety."* Unpublished, doctoral dissertation, University of California, Berkeley.

Kaskutas, L., Weisner, C., Lee, M., & Humphries, K. (1999). Alcoholics Anonymous affiliation at treatment intake among white and black Americans. *Journal of Studies on Alcohol, 60*(6), 810–817.

Kasl, C. D. (1992). *Many roads, one journey: Moving beyond the Twelve Steps.* New York: Harper Perennial.

Kessler, R., Mickelson, K., & Zhao, S. (1997). Patterns and correlates of self-help group membership in the United States. *Social Policy, 27,* 27–46.

Kirkpatrick, J. (2001). *Spirituality.* Online at www.womenforsobriety.org/articles

Kurtz, E. (1979). *Not-God: A history of Alcoholic Anonymous.* Center City, MN: Hazelden.

Kurtz, E. (1982). Why AA works. The intellectual significance of Alcoholics Anonymous. *Journal of Studies on Alcohol, 43,* 38–80.

Kurtz, L. F., & Chambon, A. (1987). Comparison of self-help groups for mental health. *Health and Social Work, 12,* 275–283.

LaFave, L., & Echols, L. (1999). An argument for choice: Meeting the needs of chemically dependent women. *Journal of Substance Abuse Treatment, 16*(4), 345–352.

Lesieur, H., & Blume, S. (1991). Evaluation of patients treated for pathological gambling in a combined alcohol, substance abuse and pathological gambling treatment unit using the Addiction Severity Index. *British Journal of Addiction, 86,* 1017–1028.

Lundy, C. (1985). *Social role enactment and the onset, maintenance and cessation of alcohol dependence in women.* Unpublished doctoral dissertation, Florida State University, Tallahassee.

Maracle, M. F. (1989). *Beyond abstinence: A study of recovery among women in Alcoholics Anonymous.* Unpublished doctoral dissertation, Washington University, St. Louis.

McBride, J. L. (1991). Abstinence among members of Alcoholics Anonymous. *Alcoholism Treatment Quarterly, 8*(1), 113–121.

McLatchie, B. H., & Lomp, K. G. E. (1988). Alcoholics Anonymous affiliation and treatment outcome among a clinical sample of problem drinkers. *American Journal of Drug and Alcohol Abuse, 14,* 309–324.

McNeece, C., & DiNitto, D. (1994). *Chemical dependency: A systems approach.* Englewood Cliffs, NJ: Prentice Hall.

Miller, N., & Mahler, J. (1991). Alcoholics Anonymous and the AA model for treatment. *Alcoholism Treatment Quarterly, 8*(1), 39–51.

Miller, W. R., & Hester, R. K. (1986). Matching problem drinkers with optimal treatments. In W. R. Miller & N. Heather (Eds.), *Treating addictive behaviors: Processes of change* (pp. 175–203). New York: Plenum Press.

Miller, W. R., Leckman, A. L., Delaney, H. D., & Tinkcorn, M. (1992). Long-term follow-up of behavioral self-control training. *Journal of Studies on Alcohol, 53,* 249–261.

Moderation Management (MM). (2000). Online at www.moderation.org

Monk, G., Winslade, J., Crocket, K., & Epston, D. (1997). *Narrative therapy in practice: The archaeology of hope.* San Francisco: Jossey-Bass.

Montgomery, H. A., Miller, W. R., & Tonigan, J. S. (1995). Does Alcoholics Anonymous involvement predict treatment outcome? *Journal of Substance Abuse Treatment, 12*(4), 241–246.

National Gambling Impact Study Commission. (1999, June 18). *Report of the Commission.* Washington, DC: Government Printing Office. Online at www.ngisc.gov/reports/fullrpt.html

National Research Council. (1999, April 1). *Pathological gambling: A critical review.* Online at books.nap. edu/books/0309065712

Nelson-Zlupko, L., Kauffman, E., & Dore, M. (1995). Gender differences in drug addiction and treatment: Implications for social work intervention with substance-abusing women. *Social Work, 40*(1), 45–54.

Peele, S. (1992). Alcoholism, politics, and bureaucracy: The consensus against controlled-drinking therapy in America. *Addictive Behaviors, 17,* 49–62.

Rappaport, J. (1993). Narrative studies, personal stories, and identity transformation in the mutual-help context. *Journal of Applied Behavioral Science, 29*(2), 239–256.

Rhodes, R., & Johnson, A. (1994). Women and alcoholism: A psychosocial approach. *Affilia, 9,* 145–156.

Riessman, F. (1985, Winter). New dimensions in self-help. *Social Policy,* 2–4.

Riordan, R., & Walsh, L. (1994). Guidelines for professional referral to Alcoholics Anonymous and other Twelve Step Groups. *Journal of Counseling and Development, 72,* 351–355.

Smith, A. R. (1986). Alcoholism and gender: Patterns of diagnosis and response. *Journal of Drug Issues, 16*(3), 407–419.

Smith, A. R. (1993). The social construction of group dependency in Alcoholics Anonymous. *Journal of Drug Issues, 23*(4), 689–704.

Snow, M. G., Prochaska, Jo. O., & Rossi, J. S. (1994). Processes of change in Alcoholics Anonymous: Maintenance factors in long-term sobriety. *Journal of Studies on Alcohol, 55,* 362–371.

Stewart, R., & Brown, R. (1988). An outcome study of Gamblers Anonymous. *British Journal of Psychiatry, 152,* 284–288.

Taber, J., McCormick, R., Russo, A., Adkins, B., & Ramirez, L. (1987). Follow-up of pathological gamblers after treatment. *American Journal of Psychiatry, 144,* 757–761.

Talan, B. (1982). *Power and control: Predictors for the alcoholic woman's choice and effectiveness of treatment.* Unpublished doctoral dissertation, University of Detroit, Detroit, MI.

Thune, C. (1977). Alcoholism and the archetypal past: A phenomenological perspective on Alcoholics Anonymous. *Journal of Studies on Alcohol, 38,* 75–88.

Tonigan, J. S., Connors, G., & Miller, W. (1998). Special populations in Alcoholics Anonymous. *Alcohol, Health, and Research World, 22*(4), 281–285.

Tonigan, J. S., & Hiller-Sturmhofel, S. (1994). Alcoholics Anonymous: Who benefits? *Alcohol Health & Research World, 18*(4), 308–310.

Tonigan, J. S., Miller, W., & Connors, G. (2000). Project MATCH client impressions about Alcoholics Anonymous: Measurement issues and relationship to treatment outcome. *Alcoholism Treatment Quarterly, 18*(1), 25–41.

Van Den Bergh, N. (1991). *Feminist perspectives on addictions.* New York: Springer.

van Wormer, K. (2001). *Counseling female offenders and victims: A strengths-restorative approach.* New York: Springer.

Verhovek, S. (2000, July 9). Advocate of moderation for heavy drinkers learns sobering lesson. *New York Times* (Late Edition), 1, 10.

Wallace, J. (1983). Ideology, belief and behavior: Alcoholics Anonymous as a social movement. In E. Gottheil, K. Draley, T. Skolada, & H. Waxman (Eds.), *Etiologic aspects of alcohol and drug abuse* (pp. 285–305). Springfield, IL: Charles C. Thomas.

Wallant, K. B. (1995). *Creating the capacity for attachment: Treating addictions and the alienated self.* Northvale, NJ: Jason Aronson.

Walsh, D. C., Hingson, R. W., Merrigan, D. M., Levenson, S. M., Cupples, L. A., Herren, T., Coffman, G., Becker, C. A., Barker, T. A., Hamilton, S. K, McGuire, T. G., & Kelly, C. A. (1991). A randomized trial of treatment options for alcohol-abusing workers. *New England Journal of Medicine, 325*(11), 775–782.

Wetzel, J. W. (1991). Universal mental health classification systems: Reclaiming women's experience. *Affilia, 6*(3), 8–31.

White, B., & Madara, E. (1995). *The self-help source book: Finding and forming mutual-aid self-help groups* (5th ed.) Denville, NJ: American Self-Help Clearinghouse.

White, M. (2000). *Reflections on narrative practice: Essays and interviews.* Adelaide, South Australia: Dulwich Centre Publications.

Women for Sobriety. (2002). Online at www.womenforsobriety.org

Zelvin, E., & Davis, D. (2001). Harm reduction and abstinence-based recovery: A dialogue. *Journal of Social Work Practice in the Addictions, 1*(1), 121–135.

For over a hundred years, U.S. drug policy has been forged by symbolic politics and special interests, by moral entrepreneurs and media magnification, and by efforts of dominant groups to control "threatening" others from different races and lower classes. —CRAIG REINARMAN & HARRY G. LEVINE, 1997

PUBLIC POLICY

CHAPTER **13**

INTRODUCTION

The impact of public policies on the availability of resources, treatment methods, the extent to which addicts are penalized, jailed, and punished, and the shaping of public opinion has been emphasized throughout this text. In this chapter, we will highlight several current social policies that affect one of the most important public health and social issues facing the United States, that is, how to deal effectively and compassionately with persons who are struggling with addiction and the consequences of addiction.

The authors take the position that the social context of drug use has helped create our drug problems. Instead of practicing harm reduction, many U.S. policies have created a context of "harm maximization" that only makes things worse, never better. This may partly be the result of what Reinarman and Levine (1997) call "pharmacological determinism," that is, the practice in U.S. culture of treating illicit drugs like contagious diseases that are inherently and uniformly dangerous. In contrast, we endorse the more complicated idea that the social/legal setting and cultural context within which it is used condition the use of alcohol, drugs, gambling, over-/under-eating, or any addictive behavior. For example, in Britain many heroin addicts have been found to function successfully in their work and lead normal lives, whereas in the United States they would be incarcerated for possession of an illegal substance, would probably not have access to clean needles, and would be reduced to criminal behaviors to support their addiction. Drug policies, the social context of "zero tolerance," and exaggerated public fears have all shaped this outcome. There are many alternatives to current policies that would be more compassionate, have more support from scientific evidence, and actually address the problems related to addiction. We will discuss the need to disengage from the polarized debate of "legalization vs. criminalization" and find a middle way to move forward. In addition, we will review recent welfare reforms that impact people with alcohol or drug problems and briefly address the current lack of social policy and research funding in the area of compulsive gambling.

WELFARE REFORM

Recent welfare reforms are having direct and indirect effects on people who are poor and have alcohol or drug problems. Federal guidelines for Temporary Assistance for Needy Families (TANF) encourage states to deny cash assistance or Food Stamps to women with recent drug felony convictions, and only 27 states have sought an exemption from this requirement (Hirsch, 1999). This legislation applies to males and females, but single mothers and women in public assistance prenatal clinics, who predominate in the welfare system, carry the brunt. Bureau of Justice Statistics estimate that approximately 61,000 women were convicted of felony drug offenses in state and federal courts in the United States during 1996 alone. Of those women, 43% were convicted of possession of drugs, not sales. Hirsch's study (1999) in Pennsylvania of women with drug convictions who are affected by this provision found that the overwhelming majority of the women had no prior drug convictions and that their felony convictions are for very small quantities of drugs (often only $5 or $10 worth).

Other TANF regulations promote routine drug testing, and some states require abstinence contracts. This has resulted in a dramatic change from the old AFDC system, where only 14% of the states even routinely asked applicants about their drug or alcohol use. Now welfare departments are forging stronger links to substance abuse treatment as a strategy to move recipients into the workforce (Schmidt & McCarty, 2000). Changes in other welfare programs that affect women and men equally include the 1997 removal of all disabilities that were due exclusively to alcohol or drug addiction from eligibility for federal Supplemental Security Income (SSI). General Assistance (GA) programs, which are considered by many the "last resort" for single men and women, have closed down on the local level across the United States, and nearly half of the recipients were single women (Schmidt & McCarty, 2000). Clearly, access to treatment services will be even less because of these new economic barriers.

New policies are needed to counteract the effects of diminished coverage for general health and treatment. Gresenz, Watkins, & Podus (1998) suggest that extending Medicaid eligibility to former SSI recipients would improve treatment access. They also encourage state and local governments to make public treatment available without extensive waiting periods and to assist dually diagnosed individuals in making new applications to SSI on the basis of their mental impairment.

POLICIES PERTAINING TO THE
TREATMENT PROFESSION

Managed Care

The substance abuse counseling profession, like any of the helping professions, is largely defined in terms of national laws, local and national fiscal reimbursement policies, and the availability of adequate health care resources. Specific laws protecting consumers' rights, for example, the right to privacy, also have a bearing upon how a profession operates. For addictions providers, legislative mandates provide treatment for certain populations (such as offenders on suspended prison sentences) but not for others. Such mandates shape the nature of addictions work in terms of the clientele served as well as the types of services rendered (for example, total abstinence from alcohol and other drugs may be required for probationers).

Historically, addiction treatment has been marginalized rather than integrated with the rest of the health care system. Today, due to rapidly rising costs of general health care in the United States—costs related to the demand for expensive new technologies and the aging of the population—there is a strong impetus to cut costs in other directions. Working Americans who typically get their health care coverage from their place of work are being moved over from traditional health insurance to managed care plans. The purpose of managed care is not to manage care but to manage costs. Severe limits have been placed on mental health services and substance abuse treatment under these plans.

In its emphasis on cost-containment, managed care has tended to place increasingly restrictive policies on inpatient detoxification treatment, limiting financial coverage for psychotherapeutic addiction treatment to only brief outpatient visits, and an emphasis on psychiatric medication, instead of, rather than in addiction to, individual therapy ("Managed Care Takes Toll," 1999). Managed care is not only a phenomenon in the private sector but a major force in Medicaid health reform proposals as well. Yet as data from national statewide studies show, every dollar of treatment saves at least seven dollars in other medical and social costs (Center on Addiction and Substance Abuse [CASA], 2001).

While many private, for-profit treatment centers, especially residential units, are closing their doors, there is a tremendous demand for services for the polydrug-addicted, often mentally ill clients for whom treatment is mandated by the courts. New treatment programming models emphasize case management as well as networking with vocational rehabilitation services, family services, and probation and parole departments. One promising development, similar to the drug court movement, is the mental health court movement. This approach is designed to help mentally ill persons in trouble with the law stay out of jail by diverting them into treatment. The mental health court in Seattle is helping mentally ill clients (the term *defendant* is avoided) receive treatment for substance misuse problems as well as their mental disorders. Preliminary results are excellent (Parker, 2001).

The days of independent alcoholism treatment centers staffed by licensed alcoholism counselors are over. The "new" addictions therapist must be highly versatile and knowledgeable concerning the major mental disorders as well as the currently popular drugs of misuse and the treatment of persons with dual diagnoses. A strong background in psychology, mental health counseling, or clinical social work is recommended.

Federal funding for addiction treatment has fallen well below the need; the bulk of the money is diverted into the war on drugs, with billions put into military operations in Latin America alone. Across the states, however, the trends are more rational and cost saving; state after state is moving to fund community-based programs for youths and other prevention services. California has passed legislation sending all first-time drug offenders into intensive treatment. Some of the money, as in Iowa and Nebraska, comes from the national tobacco settlement funds and is appropriately being funneled into treatment.

The Law and Ethical Codes

Respect for client confidence is not only an important aspect of the practitioners' code of ethics but also strictly regulated under federal law pertaining specifically to "alcohol and drug abuse patient records." The law pertaining to alcohol and drug abuse treatment is unique. Rules set forth in federal regulations, entitled "Confidentiality of Alcohol and Drug Abuse Patient Records," apply to all agencies that provide alcoholism and drug abuse treatment or prevention. The rules are far more stringent than for any other category of treatment. The general rule is: No disclosure without the patient's consent. Even with consent, information may not be released that is harmful to the patient. Exceptions to confidentiality restrictions are: suspected child abuse or neglect, medical emergencies, and life-threatening situations.

Involuntary commitment proceedings are fraught with ethical and legal dilemmas. The purpose of the proceedings is to send an individual, for his or her "own good," to a jail-like facility for "treatment." This is usually a life-and-death situation, the individual in question being at risk of harm to himself/herself or others. The first step for the counselor involved in such proceedings is to obtain the facts. Providing information to those outside the treatment program or requests for information from other sources generally requires the client's written permission (McNeece & DiNitto, 1998). Such an authorization states the name of the agency, type of information requested, how the information will be used, the agency requesting the information, the date of the request, and the date on which the release expires (usually six months later). Requests should be obtained, ordinarily, from lawyers, all family members who may be involved with the client, and relevant agencies with which the client is in communication. Legal complications occur when the client, under proper legal advice, refuses to sign the Consent-for-Release-of-Information form. It becomes impossible under these circumstances to contact family members as witnesses or for input. Should the patient be committed, based on medical evidence alone, further restrictions apply regarding communication with the state treatment facility. Treatment and hospital records may not be released to the treatment center, nor may the name of the patient be revealed before his or her arrival (van Wormer, 1995).

Related to the legal constraints on a profession are ethical considerations. Most professions have a code of ethics to protect clients' rights and to discipline members of the profession if they violate those rights. For substance abuse counselors, each state has its own code of ethics. Typical provisions are: nondiscriminatory behavior with clients on the basis of race, color, gender, sexual orientation, age, disability, etc; continuing professional and educational growth; not exploiting clients sexually or financially; agreement to report professional misconduct of colleagues such as violations of client confidentiality.

One legal issue of particular concern to addictions practitioners working with offenders was the ruling in the Seventh Circuit Court of Appeals in Wisconsin (*Kerr v. Farrey*, 1996). A prisoner's (Kerr's) First Amendment rights were violated, according to this ruling, because he was coerced into attending an NA program. Had Kerr not attended, he would have been transferred to a medium-security prison. Because the NA program was ruled to be religious, not secular, Kerr had a right to refuse treatment. Other court rulings—these were at the U.S. District Court level—have enforced the same principle of separation of church and state. Significantly, as Alexander (2000) indicates, it is the lack of availability of treatment options that is the key factor. If a prison offers options such as SMART recovery and Women for Sobriety, in addition to AA or NA attendance, the prisoners' rights are not violated.

THE WAR ON DRUGS

The "war on drugs" and the policies that enforce it cost the American taxpayer more than $40 billion a year and have resulted in the incarceration of 2 million men and women in the United States (Thevenot, 1999). In 1999, the then "drug czar" General Barry McCaffrey admitted, "We have a failed social policy and it has to be reevaluated" (Egan, 1999). In a recent nationwide telephone poll conducted by Princeton Survey Research Associates, three out of four Americans said we are losing the drug war (Pew Research Center, 2001). The failures of this policy include social and legal injustice on a wide scale, racial oppression, wasted resources spent in a futile attempt to reduce the availability of drugs, and the relentless spread of misinformation and propaganda to the American public.

Unfortunately, the "war" goes on, led by our current "drug czar," John P. Walters, who supports international control efforts at the expense of treatment, and Attorney General John Ashcroft, who said, "I want to escalate the war on drugs. . . . I want to renew it. . . . I want to refresh it, relaunch it, if you will" (Nadelman, 2001). There is hope for some middle ground here, between the side that pushes for legalization and the side that pushes for continuation and even escalation of the war on drugs. For example, in spite of his appointments of Walters and Ashcroft, President George W. Bush said in January of 2001 that "I think a lot of people are coming to the realization that maybe long minimum sentences for first-time users may not be the best way to occupy jail space and/ or heal people from their disease" (Nadelman, 2001). At the 2000 Republican National Convention Colin Powell, now Secretary of State, condemned the incarceration of "2 million Americans who, while paying for their crimes, are not paying taxes, are not there for their children, and are not raising families" (Nadelman, 2001). The middle ground that is being developed and proposed by several groups will be presented in more detail at the end of this chapter.

What is the "war on drugs"? The essential features of the "war" were developed over a decade ago under the leadership of President Bush (Sr.), and have changed very little to date, in spite of growing pressure from numerous constituencies (especially judges who have to carry out the mandatory minimum sentences required by Congress and state legislatures). These features include (1) mandatory minimum sentences and the criminalization of everything that has to do with marijuana, cocaine, heroin, methamphetamines, or other drugs that have been designated illegal, (2) the presumption that abstinence is the only right relationship to those drugs, (3) support for the strategy of international interdiction practices, such as eradicating poppy fields in South America and increasing border surveillance, in order to diminish the supply of drugs in the United States, and (4) using various practices of enforcement such as drug testing, wiretapping, and forfeiture of property.

MANDATORY SENTENCING

Mandatory minimum sentence laws require judges to sentence drug offenders to a certain number of years in prison without parole, often a minimum of five years and up to life imprisonment. They are usually triggered by the total amount of drugs with which the defendant is alleged to have been involved; however, they also apply to anyone involved in a "drug conspiracy." Congress passed mandatory minimum sentence laws for drug offenses in 1986 and 1988 to ensure that "the federal government's most intense focus ought to be on major traffickers, . . . the heads of organizations who are responsible for creating and delivering very large quantities of drugs" (Thevenot, 1999, p. 2). State legislatures added their own versions of mandatory minimums (in Washington State it's called "Three Strikes and You're Out!") during the 1970s and 1980s.

In order to get the big picture of the effect of mandatory minimum sentences, it is helpful to review current figures. According to the U.S. Sentencing Commission (1999), drug convictions were the largest single category of federal convictions in 1999 (41.7% of all convictions). Half involved cocaine trafficking (22.1% powder, 22.9% crack), 31.5% involved marijuana, 12.8% involved methamphetamine, and 8.0% involved heroin. Of the 22,787 persons sentenced in that year, 42% were Hispanic, 31.2% black, and 25% white. A

| BOX 13.1 | SUZAN'S STORY |

Suzan Penkwitz, the San Diego mother of a two-year-old son, had never even seen heroin until she was arrested when returning to the United States from Mexico. Her friend Jenny had asked her to go along on a drive south of the border, avowedly to help Jenny get her mind off a recent break-up with her boyfriend. Suzan did what she thought a good friend should do. She had no idea that Jenny was really going to Mexico to pick up 43 pounds of heroin. "I never imagined myself going to prison. Never ever!" says Suzan, who is serving a six-and-a-half-year sentence at the Federal Prison Camp for women in Dublin, California. Because of the way the system works, Jenny, who admitted her involvement and agreed to testify against Suzan, got out after serving only six months.

"Out of the 300 women here, I'd say 80% have stories similar to mine." Suzan says. "First-time, nonviolent, low-level drug offenders. I've met women who got five years for what the feds call 'improper use of the telephone': answering the phone for what later turned out to be a drug sale. Not being involved, mind you, but just answering [their own] phone. And of course, the snitches that helped put them here all get off with little or no time. I don't think I've met any high-level drug dealers here. All these women had boyfriends, or husbands, or acquaintances that used them and then let them hang. It's amazing. My roommates are 48, 50, and 58 years old. Sweet, talented ladies, grandmas, doing 14 years for 'drug conspiracy.' It all seems so pointless and tragic."

Source: Szalavitz (1998).

10-year mandatory minimum sentence was applicable in 54.9% of the crack cocaine cases and 49.9% of the methamphetamine cases. The average sentence ranged from 10 years for crack cases to 2.8 years for marijuana cases.

The growth of the prison industry since the federal mandatory guidelines have been in effect has been explosive and dramatic. In 1986, when federal mandatory minimum sentences were enacted, the Bureau of Prisons budget was $0.7 billion. President Bush's fiscal year budget announced for 2002 is $4.7 billion, with another $1 billion for more prison construction.

Since 1987, the number of women in federal prison on drug charges has quadrupled. More than half of all women offenders are caring for minor children, and many are pregnant when they enter prison, but judges are not allowed to take this into consideration when sentencing. "Absolute gender equity in sentencing has turned out to be a war on children," said Minneapolis Judge James Rosenbaum (Thevenot, 1999, p. 4).

To put a human face on these statistics we turn to what happened to Suzan Penkwitz, the San Diego mother of a two-year-old son, who is presently incarcerated at the Federal Prison Camp for women in Dublin, California. Maia Szalavitz (1998), who recently served as series researcher for the Bill Moyers special *On Addiction: Close to Home*, a five-part PBS TV series, wrote the portion of Suzan's story shown in Box 13.1.

The case of Suzan Penkwitz illustrates another feature of the mandatory minimum sentence laws that has caused the incarceration of low-level, first-time, and even innocent people. The only way a federal drug defendant can avoid a mandatory minimum sentence is to provide "substantial assistance" to prosecutors by testifying against other drug defendants. Unfortunately, providing "substantial assistance" may allow major drug traffickers who have more information to "buy" their way into substantially reduced sentences by testifying against the people who work under them or against people who are merely accidentally involved, like Suzan. The November Coalition, a national coalition of families and people whose lives have been seriously affected by the government's present drug policy, is one organization that has taken on the mission of bringing these stories to the public and lobbying for changes in the mandatory minimum sentence laws (see Web site www.november.org).

A further serious problem of current sentencing policies is the disproportionate effect on African Americans and Hispanics. Because of the Sentencing Project report in 1995, it became well known throughout the country that one in three black men between the ages of 20 and 29 were under correctional supervision or control (Mauer & Huling, 1995). While African Americans make up approximately 12% of the population and had a 7.7% rate of current illicit drug use (Substance Abuse and Mental Health Administration [SAMHSA], 2000), black males accounted for 52% of the federal prison population that was committed for drug offenses in 1999 and represented 35% of the persons arrested for drug offenses (*Sourcebook of Criminal Justice Statistics*, 1999).

CIVIL ASSET FORFEITURES

A little-known feature of the war on drugs is the practice of law enforcement's taking the money and property of persons "involved" in a drug crime without the owners' being convicted, indicted, or even arrested for a particular crime. According to Blumenson and Nilsen, in the *University of Chicago Law Review* (1998), 80% of people who have property forfeited are not charged with a crime. Even when the charges are dismissed, the results can be devastating. Judith Roderick's story is an example of what can happen to anyone (Box 13.2).

Although it seems incredible in America that a person's money and property can be seized on the presumption of guilt instead of innocence, federal and state law enforcement agencies are doing just that, and keeping most of the proceeds. In Washington State, police have seized a total of nearly $43 million in suspected drug property over the past six years. Because of the abuses that have occurred with this kind of police power, several states have initiated reforms that toughen legal standards for forfeiture, require a criminal conviction before seizure, and send the forfeited property to other budget categories, such as education, rather than law enforcement. On the national level, efforts to reform civil asset forfeiture have been led by U.S. Representatives Henry Hyde (R-IL) and John Conyers (D-MI) but have been resisted by the U.S. Justice Department.

| BOX 13.2 | JUDITH'S STORY |

When 55-year-old tax consultant Judith Roderick returned from a long-awaited birth-day cruise four years ago, police were waiting. She was searched, questioned, arrested, and led in handcuffs to a waiting van, which took her on an hour-long ride to jail.

Sheriff's deputies seized the Lacey, WA, grandmother's computers, tax software, client records, and two motorcycles. They cleaned out four bank accounts, leaving a slew of checks to bounce. The reason: Roderick had done $500 worth of routine work on a land trust for a tax client whom police suspected of drug dealing. Thurston County sheriff's investigators, who made the arrest, suspected her of laundering the man's money.

Her business was devastated. Her scared employees quit. Roderick had to buy a new computer and software. She borrowed the money. Roderick was never convicted of a crime. All charges were dismissed. Yet it still took two years to win back the seized property. The raids left her reputation and business with a black eye.

"I'm in debt up to my ears," she said.

Source: Roesler (2001).

PUNISHING THE PREGNANT AND ADDICTED

The prosecution of women who are pregnant and addicted and the removal of their children from their care and custody is another repressive side effect of the war on drugs. As discussed in chapter 11, over the past decade more than 240 women in 35 states have been criminally prosecuted for using substances thought to be harmful to their unborn during pregnancy (Rubin, 1998). Many more have lost custody of their children, because several states now consider "child neglect" to include prenatal exposure to controlled substances (Siegel, 1997). Women continue to be singled out for blame for using drugs during pregnancy, as they were in the late 19th and early 20th centuries. It appears easier to blame individual women than to acknowledge that the problem of substance use for women has been aggravated by the increase in poverty, homelessness, substandard education, and lack of health care and treatment options since the 1980s (Rosenbaum & Irwin, 1998). In spite of the NIDA research and demonstration studies on drug use among pregnant women, drug treatment for poor, pregnant women is harder to find than prenatal care (Siegel, 1997).

The public has become even more judgmental when the media publicized "crack houses," the degradation of women who resorted to sex in exchange for crack, and the so-called "crack babies" who were the result of such activities (Kandall, 1998). Women described as "junkie broads," "junkie chicks," or "bag brides" led to the public perception that the only way to deal with the problem was to lock the mothers away. The well-publicized 1985 study by Chasnoff, Burns, Schnoll, and Burns of cocaine-exposed infants made dire predictions about long-term negative effects on the children's developmental progress.

Several years later, in a not-so-well-publicized study, Chasnoff, Griffith, Freier, and Murray (1992) found that most of the cocaine-exposed babies appear normal by age two, with no detectable behavioral or learning difficulties. A recent review of 36 research studies with comparison groups (Frank, Augustyn, Knight, Pell, & Zuckerman, 2001, p. 1614) concludes that "there is no convincing evidence that prenatal cocaine exposure is associated with developmental toxic effects that are different in severity, scope, or kind from the sequelae of multiple other risk factors." "Crack babies" are more accurately described as "poverty babies," who suffer from the mother's risk factors of substandard environmental conditions and poor health care as well as other factors, including prenatal exposure to tobacco, marijuana, or alcohol.

The unfortunate consequence of legal threats to pregnant women has been to deter women from seeking prenatal care at all. In addition, policies intended to respond to the concerns about drug use during pregnancy have been slow to make a positive difference (Kandall, 1998). In 1992, the Department of Health and Human Services committed to a strong emphasis on prevention, intervention, and treatment, with monies to states for prevention and treatment services for pregnant and parenting drug-using women. However, long waiting lists, lack of specific treatment services, lack of money, and the fear of health professionals and legal threats still dominate the health care system for pregnant drug-using women (Kandall, 1998). Perhaps the key issue here is not about punishing drug use in pregnant women, but about addressing women's basic social and health needs, which exist with or without pregnancy and will not end with delivery.

Systems of Payment and Insurance Coverage

As noted in chapter 11, on gender differences, women entering treatment, especially women from cultures that are highly family oriented, do better with treatment that is comprehensive, involves children, is family focused, and lasts long enough to engage the participant in skills or language training when appropriate. The system of payment and reimbursement from state and federal funding sources does not support any of these goals. Amaro, Nieves, Johannes, and Cabeza (1999) found that funding obstacles include reimbursement rates that do not cover costs of care, categorical funding that impedes coordination of funding streams, especially between mental health and substance abuse services, and a reimbursement schedule geared to individuals, not families.

HARM REDUCTION

Needle exchange programs to prevent the spread of HIV/AIDS infection and methadone maintenance are the best-known and relatively accepted harm reduction programs in the United States. In 1994, three-quarters of all new people with HIV infections in the United States contracted the virus via illegal injection drug use. A 1997 report from the National Institutes of Health concluded that needle exchange programs "show a reduction in risk behaviors as high as 80% in injecting drug users, with estimates of a 30% or greater reduction of HIV" (Health and Human Services fact sheet, 1998). Yet needle exchange programs serve only about 15% of the people who inject illegal drugs (Nadelman, 1997, quoting the results of an epidemiological study from the Centers for Disease Control). Congress has prohibited the use of federal funds for needle exchange programs since 1989, even though the Secretary of Health and Human Services (Donna Shalala in 1997) made the necessary determination—for releasing federal funding—that such programs reduce the transmission of HIV and do not encourage the use of illegal drugs. Needle exchange programs remain illegal in many jurisdictions throughout the country. The situation is so dire that there are reports that some drug dealers have started providing clean syringes to their customers (Nadelman, 1997).

In contrast, other countries, such as Switzerland, Australia, England, the Netherlands, Scotland, and Thailand, have responded to the spread of HIV by removing restrictions on purchasing syringes and have developed free, accessible syringe exchange programs. Some, such as England and Switzerland, have established heroin prescription programs where users can stabilize or decrease the use of heroin, hold legitimate employment, and live normal lives without the threat of AIDS.

METHADONE MAINTENANCE

Methadone maintenance programs represent the other major harm reduction strategy that has been used successfully in the United States for the past 30 years. Methadone, administered in a daily dose, blocks heroin's narcotic effects while preventing withdrawal symptoms. However, in spite of their success, programs in the United States are so tightly regulated that they serve less than 15% of those who might be helped (Rounsaville & Kosten, 2000). The most restrictive requirement is that methadone can be prescribed only by "comprehensive treatment programs," which leaves out physicians in private offices, hospital clinics, community health centers, etc. Efforts to change this restriction have been resisted by the American Methadone Treatment Association, which insists that strict criteria (such as three years of complete abstinence and three years of employment) be applied to eligibility for such a program. A pilot program in Seattle now treats 10 patients, but they require evidence of no drug use for at least eight years (Newman, 2000).

Another issue in the United States is the low dosage level of methadone that is administered in many clinics as a matter of policy. According to a recent study, the majority of methadone clients receive a suboptimal dose (D'Aunno, Folz-Murphy, & Lin, 1999). Many clinics do not adjust dosages according to the needs of the clients, but rely on fixed dosages. These dosages can vary widely, from 25 mg per day for all clients to 60 mg. In an investigation of the effectiveness of a higher dose, Strain, Bigelow, Liebson, and Stitzer (1999) found that a higher dose of 80–100 mg per day to be more effective in reducing heroin use than a lesser dose of 40–50 mg. Given the current increase in heroin use in many cities and the HIV/AIDS epidemic among IV drug users, it simply seems reasonable to remove the restrictions on access and dosage to maximize the benefit of this program to all who can use it.

THE MIDDLE ROAD

There are those who would describe the controversies of the war on drugs as an argument between legalization and criminalization. Legalization proponents see the "zero-tolerance" policies of the United States as incredibly harsh and punitive. As Robin Ellins, a proprietor of a hemp products store in Toronto, Canada, said, "Thank God, I'm in Canada. I just can't believe what's going on down there. . . . That's a war against people" ("Canada Continues Moving," 2001). Canada's movement toward the decriminalization of small amounts of marijuana and expanding the medicinal use of marijuana is supported by the *Canadian Medical Association Journal* and is being considered by a new Parliament committee on drug matters ("Canada Continues Moving," 2001).

However, even though Canadian policies are conservative compared to those of the Dutch, where "coffee shops" also sell joints of marijuana, they are unlikely to receive a warm reception anytime soon in the United States. In spite of the unpopularity of the war on drugs and the public's sense of futility that we are "losing it," 66% of Americans in a recent poll still supported interdiction strategies (Pew Research Center, 2001). About as many people (47%) supported mandatory minimum sentences as opposed them (45%). Both white and black women had a more punitive approach than white or black males. For example, 53% of men of both races felt that too many people are in jail for drug possession, while only 41% of their female counterparts agreed with that.

At the same time, a majority of Americans (52%) believed that drug use should be treated as a disease, compared to 35% who favored treating it as a crime. The results also indicate that public concern over the problem of illegal drug use has receded since the massive media onslaught of the late 1980s. In 1990, 37% of the public cited alcohol/drugs as the most important national problem; in 2001, only 6% felt that way.

Given both a compassionate and still get-tough American public, it may be an ideal time to act on some middle-ground social policies that could be more appealing to the majority than legalization or criminalization. For example, The Federation of American Scientists (1997, p. 2), a privately funded nonprofit policy organization whose Board of Sponsors includes 58 of America's Nobel laureates in the sciences, calls for "a third way" that is based on science and evaluated by the results of the policies, not their symbolic value. Robert MacCoun, Associate Professor of Public Policy at the University of California at Berkeley, who spoke at the press conference outlining the group's objectives, used the example of harm reduction programs. "You have to do the evaluation program-by-program. . . . Unfortunately, serious discussion of how best to reduce damage has been made difficult by the suspicion that harm reduction is a 'Trojan horse' or 'slippery slope' towards legalization." Another participant, Dr. Charles Schuster, former director of NIDA, stated, "It's time to start passing laws and running programs based on what research has shown us about the problems, not on what public opinion polls say. There is excellent evidence that appropriate treatment reduces drug use. There is no evidence that stiffer prison terms for dealers reduce drug use. At some point our policies ought to start to reflect that."

The Federation of American Scientists published 14 "Principles for Practical Drug Policies" in September, 1997 (see the full document at fas.org/drugs/Principles.htm). Among the highlights are a recognition that social concern about diminishing self-control through drugs should extend to licit and illicit substances alike; that damage can be reduced by "shrinking the extent of drug abuse as well as by reducing the harm incident to any give level of drug consumption"; that legalizing drugs will not solve the current problems; that the use of "disproportionate punishments to express social norms is neither just nor a prudent use of public funds and scarce prison capacity"; and that treatment that reduces damage but does not produce immediate abstinence should be regarded as "incomplete successes rather than as unredeemed failures."

Joseph Califano (2001a, p. 2), Director of the National Center on Addiction and Substance Abuse at Columbia University (CASA) and another voice of the middle road, notes that President Bush's proposed budget increases of 16% for NIDA and 11% for NIAAA are "steps in the right direction" but still fall short of the commitment needed to turn around the disproportionate use of funds on interdiction efforts. An extensive CASA survey (Califano, 2001b, p. 2) of state budgets that considered all the costs of substance use and addiction in 16 budget categories revealed that of every dollar the states spent on dealing with substance use and addiction, 96 cents went to "shoveling up the wreckage" and only four cents was used to prevent and treat it. These results add more reason to support the currently proposed Drug Education, Prevention and Treatment Act, which will fund treatment in prisons, drug courts, and diversion programs, provide more treatment in rural areas, provide funds for drug-free school models and research and evaluation of the effectiveness of treatment and prevention programs (Califano, 2001c).

While social policy change in a progressive direction has been tediously slow at the federal level, there are many exciting initiatives at the state and local levels, most of them geared to the provision of treatment in lieu of incarceration for drug misusers. The introduction of the drug court system is the most conspicuous of these initiatives. It is crucial for practitioners in this field and social workers in this and related fields to engage in policy analysis in order to influence legislation through lobbying at the state and local levels. For up-to-date facts that should be of interest to policymakers seeking cost-effective alternatives to incarceration, see "Making Drug Policy at the State Level" at www.drugstrategies.org/criticalchoices.

POLICIES RELATED TO GAMBLING

Between 1976 and 1997, revenues from legal gambling in the United States grew nearly 1,600%, reaching more than $50 billion. Thirty-seven states and the District of Columbia have lotteries; 28 states authorized casino gambling (including Indian casinos). Because of the explosive growth of the gambling industry (renamed "gaming" by the industry), Congress created the National Gambling Impact Study Commission (NGISC) in 1996 to study the impact of gambling in the United States and recommend ways to regulate it. According to Common Cause (2000), the gambling industry so feared supervision, regulation, and potential new taxes that it more than doubled its campaign contributions to $5.4 million in PAC and soft money contributions to both parties in 1995–96, and was successful in watering down the powers of the commission and stacking it with the appointment of several pro-gambling people. Nevertheless, the NGISC Report (1999) has been instrumental in alerting many to the lack of policies and regulation, which has impact on those people who may become or already are addicted to gambling.

In the United States, there is very little funding from state and private revenues that go to treating addicted gamblers. As reported by the National Research Council, Committee on the Social and Economic Impact of Gambling (1999, ch. 6, p. 12), "The need to provide treatment for pathological gambling has not been widely recognized." Most health insurers and managed care providers do not reimburse for pathological gambling treatment. State helplines are now operating in only 35 of the 47 states that have some type of legalized gambling. About half of these states support some type of treatment with public funding, but the level of funding is miniscule compared to income the state receives from gambling enterprises. For example, in Minnesota in 1997, treatment allocations for gambling made up 0.5% of the state's income from gambling; in New York in 1998, treatment allocations were 0.1% of the state's income from gambling (National Research Council, 1999). The majority of states do not even receive this paltry level of funding for treatment. It is no wonder that Lesieur (1998, p. 165) concludes that "legislatures and the gaming industry are paying lip service to the problem."

A policy recommendation of NGISC (1999, p. 34) is that states mandate private and public insurers and managed care providers to "identify successful treatment programs, educate participants about pathological gambling and treatment options, and cover the appropriate programs under their plans." In addition, the commission urges that state and tribal government use a proportion of their gambling revenue to fund problem gambling–specific research, prevention, education, and treatment programs.

Other important recommendations by NGISC include restricting all gambling to those who are at least 21 years of age (many states allow lottery tickets to be sold to 18-year-olds), rolling back slot machines in neighborhood outlets, banning betting on collegiate and amateur athletic events, banning aggressive advertising that targets impoverished neighborhoods and youth, prohibiting Internet gambling and passing legislation stating that any credit card debts incurred while gambling on the Internet are unrecoverable, and banning credit card cash advance machines from the immediate area where gambling takes place.

To date, there has been very little research on problem/pathological gambling; of the little that does exist, only a small portion includes women. Three changes in national policy recommended by the NGISC could have an enormous impact on this dismal state of affairs: (1) Add gambling to the National Household Survey on Drug Abuse and any other appropriate national surveys on mental health; (2) initiate and fund research by the National Institutes of Health, SAMHSA, or any other appropriate federal agency; and (3) require all state and tribal governments to cooperate fully in any research undertaken by the state in order to fulfill these recommended policies.

The "Queen of Hearts" Australian project (Brown & Coventry, 1997) elicited suggestions from women for larger system interventions and policies that would be helpful to women who are problem gamblers. These include: (1) timely access to other supporting services, such as mental health and especially financial counseling, (2) access to female counselors because of the need to disclose problems such as physical, sexual, and emotional abuse, (3) easily accessible services in downtown areas as well as rural environments where services are colocated with other supportive services to lessen stigmatization and promote referrals, (4) involvement of all the groups associated with gambling (including financial institutions, gaming operators, and government) to work on solutions, instead of leaving it up to the "victims" to cope, (5) establishing alternative recreations for women in neighborhoods, and (6) decreasing the accessibility of gaming venues by removing them from shopping centers, strip malls, clubs, and hotels throughout the state.

SUMMARY AND CONCLUSION

At the public policy level, we have looked beyond the problems of the individual person to the bigger picture of how our society cares for its members who may be vulnerable with the consequences of addiction at one time or another in their lives. We ask the questions "What do we do as a society for the poor and addicted? How do we care for women and other minorities who may be quadruple-oppressed by also being poor, addicted, and HIV-positive?

Positive policies, such as funding drug courts, spending public money on prevention and treatment, building safety nets of health care, job, and education opportunities, and supporting harm reduction policies like methadone maintenance and needle exchanges, are under way. However, the impact of criminalization, mandated minimum sentences, civil forfeiture, punishing pregnant and addicted women, and restricting access to harm reduction programs such as methadone maintenance and needle exchanges far outweighs these benefits.

We are at a crossroads in this country in terms of public policy. We can go forward with a reasoned compassionate approach that is "user friendly" to those who want to change their relationship to an addiction, or we can continue to punish and shame them in an effort to make them give it up. We can make accurate information available to the public that may prevent addiction to gambling, or we can pretend that gambling has no addictive qualities and merely provides needed money to states in lieu of taxes. In each area of public policy we have discussed, there is a choice to be made. We agree with Kleiman (1998) that a quick fix for better policies is not an option in the near future. We also hope with him that some elected officials and nationally appointed decision makers will risk being called "soft on drugs" and pursue a "slow fix" that will begin the shift to more realistic policies that will reduce the social damage of addiction. As Kleiman (1998, p. 8) states, "Even when optimism is unjustified, hope remains a virtue."

References

Alexander, R. (2000). *Counseling, treatment and intervention: Methods with juvenile and adult offenders.* Belmont, CA: Wadsworth.

Amaro, H., Nieves, R., Johannes, S., & Cabeza, N. (1999). Substance abuse treatment: Critical issues and challenges in the treatment of Latina women. *Hispanic Journal of Behavioral Sciences, 21*(3), 266–282.

Blumenson, E., & Nilsen, E. (1998). Policing for profit: The Drug War's hidden economic agenda. *University of Chicago Law Review, 65,* 35–114.

Brown, S., & Coventry, L. (1997). *Queen of Hearts.* Financial & Consumer Rights Council, Victoria, Australia. Online at home.vicnet.net.au/~fcrc/research/queen/part1.htm

Califano, J. (2001a, January 29). *Shoveling up: The impact of substance abuse on state budgets.* National Center on Addiction and Substance Abuse at Columbia University. Newsletter. Online at www.casacolumbia.org

Califano, J. (2001b, February 13). *Drug Education, Prevention and Treatment Act of 2001.* National Center on Addiction and Substance Abuse at Columbia University. Newsletter. Online at www.casacolumbia.org

Califano, J. (2001c, May 8). *Learning from Robert Downey, Jr.* National Center on Addiction and Substance Abuse at Columbia University. Newsletter. Online at www.casacolumbia.org

Canada continues moving toward legalized marijuana. (2001, May 29). *Spokesman Review,* 2.

Center on Addiction and Substance Abuse (CASA). (2001). *Shoveling up: The impact of substance abuse on state budgets.* Columbia University. Available online at www.casacolumbia.org

Chasnoff, I., Burns, W., Schnoll, S., & Burns, K. (1985). Cocaine use in pregnancy. *New England Journal of Medicine, 313,* 666–669.

Chasnoff, I., Griffith, D., Freier, C., & Murray, J. (1992). Cocaine/polydrug use in pregnancy. Two-year follow-up. *Pediatrics, 89,* 284–289.

Common Cause. (2000). *Paying the price: How tobacco, gun, gambling, and alcohol interests block common sense solutions to some of the nation's most urgent problems.* Online at www.commoncause.org/publications/campaign_finance.htm

D'Aunno, T., Folz-Murphy, N., & Lin, X. (1999). Changes in methadone treatment practices: Results from a panel study, 1988–95. *American Journal of Drug Alcohol Abuse, 25*(4), 681–699.

Egan, T. (1999, February 28). War on crack retreats, still taking prisoners. *New York Times*, 1.1.

Federation of American Scientists. (1997, September 2). *Press conference: Drug experts call for "Third Way"—neither drug war nor legalization.* National Press Club, Washington, DC. Online at fas.org/drugs/drugspr.htm

Frank, D., Augustyn, M., Knight, W., Pell, T., & Zuckerman, B. (2001). Growth, development, and behavior in early childhood following prenatal cocaine exposure. *Journal of the American Medical Association, 285*, 1613–1625.

Gresenz, C., Watkins, K., & Podus, D. (1998). Supplemental Security Income (SSI), Disability Insurance (DI), and substance abusers. *Community Mental Health Journal, 34*(4), 337–350.

Health and Human Services fact sheet. (1998). *Needle exchange programs: Part of a comprehensive HIV prevention plan.* Online at www.hhs.gov/news/press/1998pres/980420b.html

Hirsch, A. (1999). *"Some days are harder than hard": Welfare reform and women with drug convictions in Pennsylvania.* Center for Law and Social Policy. Online at www.clasp.org/pubs/TANFSTATE/SomeDays/SomeDaystableofcontents.htm

Kandall, S. (1998). Women and addiction in the United States—1920 to the present. In C. L. Wetherington & A. B. Roman (Eds.), *Drug addiction research and the health of women* (pp. 53–80). National Institutes of Drug Abuse, NIH Publication No. 98-4290. Online at www.nida.nih.gov/WHGD/DARHW-Download2.html

Kerr v. Farrey. 95 F. 3rd 472 (7th Circuit Court, 1996).

Kleiman, M. (1998). Drugs and drug policy: The case for a slow fix. *Issues in Science and Technologies, XV*(1). Online at fas.org/drugs/slowfix.htm

Lesieur, H. (1998). Costs and treatment of pathological gambling. *Annals of the American Academy of Political and Social Science, 556*, 153–172.

Managed care takes a toll on substance-abuse treatment. (1999, July 15). Available online at www.jointogether.org

Mauer, M., & Huling, T. (1995). Young black Americans and the criminal justice system: Five years later. Washington, DC: The Sentencing Project.

McNeece, C. A., & DiNitto, D. M. (1998). *Chemical dependency: A systems approach.* Boston: Allyn & Bacon.

Nadelman, E. (1997). Drug prohibition in the U.S.: Costs, consequences, and alternatives. In C. Reinarman & H. Levine (Eds.), *Crack in America: Demon drugs and social justice* (pp. 288–316). Berkeley: University of California Press.

Nadelman, E. (2001, May 18). Change of tune on drug policy? *Los Angeles Times.* Online at www.drugpolicy.org

National Gambling Impact Study Commission. (1999, June 18). *Report of the Commission.* Washington, DC: Government Printing Office. Online at www.ngisc.gov/reports/fullrpt.html

National Research Council. (1999, April 1). *Pathological gambling: A critical review.* Online at books.nap.edu/books/0309065712

Newman, R. (2000, May 3–5). *Heroin addiction and related clinical problems.* Paper presented at 4th European Opiate Addiction Treatment Association Conference, Arezzo, Italy. Online at www.drugpolicy.org

Parker, L. (2001, June 26). Court offers mentally ill an alternative to jail. *USA Today,* 1A.

Pew Research Center. (2001). Princeton Survey Research Associates Survey. Online at www.people-press.org/drugs01rpt.htm

Reinarman, C., & Levine, H. (1997). Crack in context: America's latest demon drug. In

C. Reinarman & H. Levine (Eds.), *Crack in America: Demon drugs and social justice* (pp. 1–17). Berkeley: University of California Press.

Roesler, R. (2001, May 24). Forfeiture standards questioned. *Spokesman-Review,* B1–B4.

Rosenbaum, M., & Irwin, K. (1998). Pregnancy, drugs, and harm reduction. In C. L. Wetherington & A. B. Roman (Eds.), *Drug addiction research and the health of women* (pp. 309–318). National Institute of Drug Abuse, NIH Publication No. 98-4290. Online at www.nida.nih.gov/WHGD/DARHW-Download2.html

Rounsaville, B., & Kosten, T. (2000). Treatment for opioid dependence. *Journal of the American Medical Association, 283,* 1337–1338.

Rubin, R. (1998, August 12). Study: Hands off pregnant drug users. *USA Today,* D1.

Schmidt, L., & McCarty, D. (2000). Welfare reform and the changing landscape of substance abuse services for low-income women. *Alcoholism: Clinical and Experimental Research, 24*(8), 1298–1311.

Siegal, L. (1997). The pregnancy police fight the War on Drugs. In C. Reinarman & H. Levine (Eds.), *Crack in America: Demon drugs and social justice* (pp. 249–259). Berkeley: University of California Press.

Sourcebook of criminal justice statistics. (1999). Online at www.albany.edu/sourcebook

Strain, E., Bigelow, G., Liebson, I., & Stitzer, M. (1999). Moderate- vs. high-dose methadone in the treatment of opioid dependence: A randomized trial. *Journal of the American Medical Association, 281,* 1000–1005.

Substance Abuse and Mental Health Administration (SAMHSA). (2000). *Expanded National Household Survey.* Online at www.samhsa.gov/hhsurvey

Szalavitz, M. (1998, Winter). U.S. war on drugs, war on women. *On The Issues Magazine.* Online at www.mapinc.org/drugnews/v99.n001.a06.html

Thevenot, C. (1999). Crises of the antidrug effort, 1999. The Criminal Justice Policy Foundation. Online at www.cjpf.org/pubs/crises

U.S. Sentencing Commission. (1999). *1999 Annual Report.* Online at www.ussc.gov

van Wormer, K. (1995). *Alcoholism treatment: A social work perspective.* Belmont, CA: Wadsworth.

EPILOGUE:
PROVIDING OPTIONS

Writing a book is a journey; there are the things one expects to find all mapped out and researched, and there are the unexpected discoveries along the way. In scholarly terms, there are the truths one plans to include and the truths that seem to emerge of their own accord from the process.

The major task in writing this book was to present an understanding of addiction, one of the most fascinating and baffling of human conditions, an understanding that would encompass truths from biology, psychology, and sociology. The major challenge, one that never left us, was somehow to make sense of addiction. Addictive behavior (that insatiable thirst for something), by its very nature, of course makes no sense: What sense is there in a woman so hooked on winning at video poker that she won't take a break to use the toilet? What sense does it make when a father in Thailand sells his daughter into prostitution to get money for another fix of heroin or the leader of our country risks the presidency for a moment's gratification?

REVELATIONS

A major theme that emerged in this writing was the importance of motivation. How do you get people who have problems caused by chemicals they have learned to use to get a high (or to escape a low) to come in the door and say, "I'd like to talk about my drug use" or more generally, "I need someone to talk to." Programs built on abstinence-only models, the use of forced self-labeling, and urinalysis monitoring have their place, but such forms of treatment are hardly inviting. So the question becomes, not which of the treatments available (forget for the moment that only one may be available) is best, but how far and how fast will people go toward recovery? And how long will they maintain their progress when treatment is done?

Offering a warm, hospitable environment for treatment is critical. Being able to move to the rhythm set by the client/consumer, not by some faraway bureaucrat (from the insurance company or court) is critical as well. Here is where the theory known as motivational enhancement comes in. For each of the populations studied in this book—alcoholics; drug addicts; persons with eating disorders; compulsive gamblers, shoppers, and the like; addicts with mental disorders; the young and the old; African/Latino Americans and European Americans; straight and gay; and even families in need of help—we presented interventions geared toward the group's stages of change. Such interventions were timed, a sort of phase approach, to meet clients where they were rather than where we'd like them to be.

Central to motivationally based treatment, and to the strengths perspective of which it can be considered a part, is the element of choice. In this tradition, practitioners do not encourage clients to rely on their expertise. Instead, through dialogue, they help clients discern the pros and cons (for their families and themselves) of any particular course of action. In addiction treatment, choice entails presenting options, for example, trying to find a compatible self-help group such as AA or Al-Anon (GA or OA), or giving a Twelve-Step group a chance, or linking up with a faith-based group if the client is inclined in a religious direction, or attending a moderation management group to control the impulse to binge, or, alternatively, attending no group at all, perhaps choosing individual counseling periodically to work on reducing the harm. Several U.S. District Courts, as mentioned in chapter 13, have confirmed the legal right of criminal justice offenders to have an option to participate in a Twelve-Step group. Other clients should have this privilege as well. There is no "one size fits all" in treatment.

In summary, the imperative of providing options for enhancing client motivation was one of the truths that emerged in the writing of this book. Other truths emerged as well, some from research (such as that of the impact of craving as seen in brain imaging) and some through the creative process itself, the blending of science and art.

Delving into history, we gained a perspective on the present-day U.S. war on drugs, a "war" so clearly rooted in our puritanical past. We learned from a historical perspective how much the support for the legal prohibition of drugs has been associated with the fear of a given drug's effect on a specific minority group, whether of opium on the Chinese or marijuana on the Chicanos or crack cocaine on African Americans. The combination of wild media reports and politics has resulted in highly punitive legislation in each case. The projection of blame on foreign nations as a source of supply was (is) another political trend with historical roots.

A further revelation that emerged from our study of the history of treatment was just how formidable an advance was the introduction of the disease model. Within the context of American moralism and the work ethic, the spread of respect for the work of AA ensued, coupled with a belief that alco-holism was a disease. The shift from a label of the "bad" to the "mad," which has so often been belittled, was, on the whole, a positive development. Now treatment replaced punishment as the standard response. (Today, in many cases, the treatment *is* the punishment.) Respect for alcoholics and other drug addicts in recovery, for men and women who so often have assumed leadership roles in their communities, was an outgrowth of the alcoholism-as-a-disease movement. Economic aspects of the movement did not go unnoticed; critics rightly ridiculed the hypocrisy of a society marketing harmful drugs such as to-bacco and hard liquor and then marketing the treatment for those who suc-cumbed to the grip of addiction. The *diseasing* of society—women who love too much, men who love too little, the credo that abstinence is the only cure for indulgence—was countered by a resurgence of a new form of *moralism*. The factor behind substance misuse is irresponsibility—so goes the explanation popularized in the 1990s.

Arguably, this opposing dogma reflects the maelstrom within North Amer-ican society itself concerning the use of alcohol and other drugs. Alcohol con-sumption, promoted vigorously by advertisers on the one hand, is on the other hand simultaneously restricted through harsh legislation, especially concerning persons under the age of 21. Lacking is a focus on health and moderation. The criminalization of other drug use has led to a war on drugs, fought both mili-tarily, to wipe out the supply side of drugs, and on the home front, through mass incarcerations. Each of the two battling ideologies, both influential today, though with different audiences, describes a small part of the whole. Their sole common ground is in their narrowness and in their contempt for proponents of the opposite camp. Both extreme positions promote doctrine to the neglect of the *individual,* the human being described eloquently by Dennis Wrong (1976, p. 112) as "that plausible creature whose wagging tongue so often hides the despair in his heart." In this case, the forgotten individual is the alcoholic or addict. Somewhere between overdiseasing the society and blaming addicts for their addictive behavior lies a middle way. Somewhere between criminalization and legalization of harmful drug use there is a middle way (as described in chapter 13) as well.

COMMENT

Increasingly, at the start of our new century, there is a realization that a single model of addiction and treatment does not fit all, even for offenders within the criminal justice system. There are varieties in treatment needs among males, de-pending on their personality characteristics and the character of their addic-tion, and there are the special needs of women of childbearing age, of older men and women, and of gays and lesbians. Culturally specific programs for treat-ment effectiveness with various racial, religious, and ethnic populations are es-sential. Common to all these approaches is the realization that instead of try-ing to eliminate illegal drugs through fighting a war on drugs that is played out as a war on drug users, we can focus on limiting the damage that some people do to themselves and to society through this drug misuse.

Harm reduction services provide individualized treatment and strengthen community action. Harm reduction initiatives, in contrast to the "zero tolerance" approach, include policies such as needle exchange (which has been shown to reduce the spread of AIDS), methadone maintenance to enable addicts to live fairly normal lives, and therapy grounded in motivational enhancement principles to help clients move at their own pace from levels of heavy alcohol and other drug consumption to ever-decreasing levels of drug use. Harm reduction concentrates on achievable goals based on client self-determination; interventions are timed to relate to where the client is in his or her readiness to change. Interventions ideally are timed also to relate to the stages of recovery— biological, psychological, social, and spiritual.

OVERVIEW OF THE BOOK

The three opening chapters of the book were conceived as a prologue to the more detailed discussion that followed. Chapter 1, The Nature of Addiction, took us right into the pain and sorrow associated with substance misuse and dependence, contrasted with the miracle that is recovery. Chapter 2, Historical Perspectives, could have been subtitled, "When Will We Ever Learn?" Here society's futile attempts to control the flow of drugs and people's bad habits were chronicled. The presentation of the strengths perspective (chapter 3), a conceptualization borrowed from social work, showed how a focus on people's strengths is a viable, indeed essential, element in addiction treatment.

Consistent with the biopsychosocial framework of addiction treatment, the core material of this text is organized into three major sections; each section corresponds to one key component in addiction, with ramifications for treatment. The *biological* component (part 2) focused on exciting new research uncovering the biochemical basis of tolerance, withdrawal, craving, and the memory factor in addiction. As science learns more and more about the key role of the brain in addiction and can demonstrate through magnetic resonance imaging how the addicted brain is different from the nonaddicted brain, there is fresh hope for new treatments. A description of such pharmaceutical remedies was the subject of chapter 5, Interventions Related to Biology. Strategies for group therapy, along with recommended exercises directed toward early-stage recovery, were provided in this chapter.

The *psychology* of addiction is the second major division of this text. Under the rubric of psychology—part 3 of the book—first addiction and its treatment across the life span were viewed (chapter 6). Special attention was paid in this chapter to gender-specific treatment, assessment, spiritual healing, and relapse prevention strategies. Cognitive work was the theme of chapter 7, on behavioral addictions; group strategies geared toward the thinking/feeling configuration were described. For work with the dually diagnosed, the case was made in chapter 8 for integrated treatment (as opposed to separate treatment for mental disability and for addiction).

The *social aspects* of addiction made up the concluding portion of this book, Part 4. Chapter 9 explored family risks and resiliencies. The focus was on how addiction affects the lives of the addict's loved ones (sometimes to the point that the love flies out the window). Innovations of this chapter, and of this book, were the adaptation of the stages-of-change model to family recovery and the "rename, reframe, reclaim" framework for strengths-based treatment.

Strengths-based approaches were also directed toward the ethnicity-sensitive interventions described in chapter 10 and the gender-specific topics covered in chapter 11. Half of the latter chapter dealt with sexual orientation and substance misuse issues. Chapter 12 examined mutual-help groups, especially Twelve-Step groups, from the strengths approach that is usually directed toward people as individuals. Here the questions considered were: What are the strengths of Twelve-Step treatment? How have Twelve-Step groups helped people? What are their strong points? What are some alternative mutual-help groups?

Addiction Treatment: A Strengths Perspective concluded with a survey of public policy. This time, harm reduction was viewed in policy terms rather than practice terms. Chapter 13 described governmental policies affecting treatment provision and funding as well. Far from a narrow or radical ideology, harm reduction is simply realistic, about saving lives. Broad in focus, harm reduction, as we saw in earlier chapters, helps clients make healthy choices; joining a Twelve-Step, total-abstinence group is one such option.

The most unique feature of this book, we think, is not the presentation of content in neat bio/psycho/social divisions (a challenge in itself) or the inclusion of eating disorders and compulsive gambling and Internet use along with the chemical addictions. No, the uniqueness is that our application of the principles of the strengths perspective was directed first to treatment modalities at all, then that we looked for the strong points in various treatments that are often viewed as in opposition to one another. Consistent with this perspective, we extend our appreciation to the vibrant field of addictions and to the many dedicated workers who have passed this way. The large number of recovering alcoholics and other addicts in society, some of whom are professionals in the field themselves, is testimony to the quality of that work. The field is changing rapidly: But what now is, is not necessarily better than what was.

Reference

Wrong, D. (1976). The oversocialized conception of man in modern sociology. In L. Coser & B. Rosenberg (Eds.), *Sociology theory* (pp. 104–113). New York: Macmillan.

APPENDIX: RESOURCES

Associations/Coalitions

Coalition Against Present Drug Policy: www.november.org
Harm Reduction Coalition: www.harmreduction.org
National Association of Alcoholism and Drug Abuse Counselors: www.naadac.org
National Association of Social Work, ATOD section: www.naswdc.orgsections/
    ATOD/resources.html
Restorative Justice: www.restorativejustice.org
Social Workers Helping Social Workers, confidential voice mail: 641-422-7485

Centers/Institutes/Councils

American Council for Drug Education: www.acde.org
Center for Alcohol and Addiction Studies: center.butler.brown.edu
Center for Drug Abuse Research: www.pitt.edu~cedar/navigat.htm
Child Welfare League of America: www.cwla.org
Drug Abuse Research Center at UCLA: www.medsch.ucla.edusom/npi/DARC
Drug Strategies, "Making Drug Policy at the State Level": www.drugstrategies
    .orgcriticalchoices
Hazelden: www.hazelden.org
Johnson Institute Foundations: www.jifoundation.org
Moderation Management: www.moderation.org
National Alcohol Research Centers: silk.nih.gov/silk/niaaa1/grants/resctrs1198.htm
National Center on Addiction and Substance Abuse at Columbia University: www
    .casacolumbia.org
Pride Institute (treatment for gays and lesbians): www.pride-institute.com

National Council on Alcoholism and Drug Dependence: www.ncadd.org
Rational Recovery: www.rational.org
Self management and recovery training: www.smartrecovery.org

Federal Government

National Clearinghouse for Alcohol and Drug Information: www.health.org
National Institute on Alcohol Abuse and Alcoholism: www.niaaa.nih.gov
National Institute on Drug Abuse: www.nida.nih.gov
National Institute of Justice: www.ojp.usdoj.gov/nij
National Institute of Mental Health: www.nimh.nih.gov
National Women's Resource Center: www.nwrc.orgdefault.htm
Office of National Drug Control Policy: www.whitehousedrugpolicy.gov
Substance Abuse and Mental Health Services Administration: www.samhsa.gov

International

Substance Abuse Network of Ontario: www.sano.camh.net
World Health Organization: www.who.org

Prevention

Drug and Alcohol Treatment and Prevention Global Network: www.drugnet.net
Help for smokers: www.quitnet.org
National Inhalant Prevention Coalition: 800-269-4237

Research

Addiction Treatment Forum: www.atforum.com
For gays and lesbians: www.health.orgfeatures/lgbt/substance.htm
Latino web: www.latinolink.com
Information on eating disorders, teen substance abuse, and gambling: addictions.net
Substance abuse and gun violence resource: www.jointogether.org/*home*
Web of Addictions: www.well.com/user/woa

Self-Help

Adult Children of Alcoholics World Service Organization: www.adultchildren.org
Alcoholics Anonymous: www.alcoholics-anonymous.org
Al-Anon/Alateen: www.alanon.org
Children of Alcoholics Foundation: www.coaf.org
Cocaine Anonymous: www.ca.org or www.cocaineanonymous.com
Families of compulsive gamblers: www.gam-anon.org
Families of drug addicts: www.narcanon.org
Gamblers Anonymous: www.gamblersanonymous.org
Gay AA meetings: www.geocities.com
Narcotics Anonymous: www.na.org
National Association for Children of Alcoholics: www.health.orgnacoa

National Association for Native American Children of Alcoholics: www.ael.orgeric/ned/ned019.html

National Organization on Fetal Alcohol Syndrome: www.nofas.org

Students against Destructive Decisions (also Students against Drunk Driving): www.saddonline.com

Women for Sobriety: www.womenforsobriety.org

INDEX

AA. *See* Alcoholics Anonymous

Abadinsky, H., 45, 49, 59, 107, 114

Abramovitz, M., 344,

abstinence, xv, 26, 27, 28, 70, 72, 74, 75, 85, 419

acupuncture, 160–161

addiction: and biology, 97–145; definition of, 4, 9, 60; diagnosis of, 5; field of, xiv–xv, xviii; grip of, 15–17, 125; nature of, 1–33, 97

adolescents, 176–195, 215, 219, 302, 342; and brain, 176; and prevention, 189–194; statistics, 177–179, 185

advertising, 179

African Americans, 195, 207, 311, 328–332, 389, 408; drug use, 178, 329; slavery, 43; women, 329

aftercare, 89

AIDS, 27, 59, 114, 325, 329, 353, 360; prevention, 74, 75, 191

Akers, R., 148

Akin, B., 297

Al-Anon, 191, 288–289

Al-Ateen, 191

alcohol: controlled drinking of, 76; distilled, 41, 43; history of, 37–49; misuse, 76, 121, 125, 132, 134–135, 177–78, 179; properties of, 98–106, 132; toll of, 99–100, 178

Alcoholics Anonymous (AA): criticism of, xv, 21–22, 374–375; history of, 51–53, 148, 375–376; and referral, 264, 327, 420; and spirituality, 19, 20, 205

alcoholism, 9, 10, 53–57, 135, 200, 271; counselors, 83; and medical treatment, 152–153; treatment, 88–90. *See also* prevention

Alexander, R., 194–195

Alvarez, L., 325

American Medical Association, 10, 11, 56, 233

American Psychiatric Association, 4–6

Amodeo, M., 20, 314

Anderson, S., 195, 293

anger management, 237–238, 239

anorexia, 40, 215–218; and harm reduction, 84, 86; in men, 221